Lecture Notes in Computer Science

Edited by G. Goos, J. Hartmanis and

T0230321

Springer
Berlin
Heidelberg
New York
Barcelona
Hong Kong
London
Milan
Paris
Tokyo

Richard J. Boulton   Paul B. Jackson (Eds.)

Theorem Proving
in Higher Order Logics

14th International Conference, TPHOLs 2001
Edinburgh, Scotland, UK, September 3-6, 2001
Proceedings

 Springer

Series Editors

Gerhard Goos, Karlsruhe University, Germany
Juris Hartmanis, Cornell University, NY, USA
Jan van Leeuwen, Utrecht University, The Netherlands

Volume Editors

Richard J. Boulton
University of Glasgow, Department of Computing Science
17 Lilybank Gardens, Glasgow G12 8QQ, Scotland, UK
E-mail: boulton@dcs.gla.ac.uk

Paul B. Jackson
University of Edinburgh, Division of Informatics
James Clerk Maxwell Building, King's Buildings
Edinburgh EH9 3JZ, Scotland, UK
E-mail: pbj@dcs.ed.ac.uk

Cataloging-in-Publication Data applied for

Die Deutsche Bibliothek - CIP-Einheitsaufnahme

Theorem proving in higher order logics : 14th international conference ;
proceedings / TPHOLs 2001, Edinburgh, Scotland UK, September 3 - 6, 2001.
Richard J. Boulton ; Paul B. Jackson (ed.). - Berlin ; Heidelberg ; New York ;
Barcelona ; Hong Kong ; London ; Milan ; Paris ; Tokyo : Springer, 2001
   (Lecture notes in computer science ; Vol. 2152)
   ISBN 3-540-42525-X

CR Subject Classification (1998): F.4.1, I.2.3, F.3.1, D.2.4, B.6.3

ISSN 0302-9743
ISBN 3-540-42525-X Springer-Verlag Berlin Heidelberg New York

Springer-Verlag Berlin Heidelberg New York
a member of BertelsmannSpringer Science+Business Media GmbH

http://www.springer.de

© Springer-Verlag Berlin Heidelberg 2001
Printed in Germany

Typesetting: Camera-ready by author, data conversion by Christian Grosche, Hamburg
Printed on acid-free paper   SPIN 10845517   06/3142   5 4 3 2 1 0

Preface

This volume constitutes the proceedings of the *14th International Conference on Theorem Proving in Higher Order Logics* (TPHOLs 2001) held 3–6 September 2001 in Edinburgh, Scotland. TPHOLs covers all aspects of theorem proving in higher order logics, as well as related topics in theorem proving and verification.

TPHOLs 2001 was collocated with the *11th Advanced Research Working Conference on Correct Hardware Design and Verification Methods* (CHARME 2001). This was held 4–7 September 2001 in nearby Livingston, Scotland at the Institute for System Level Integration, and a joint half-day session of talks was arranged for the 5th September in Edinburgh. An excursion to Traquair House and a banquet in the Playfair Library of Old College, University of Edinburgh were also jointly organized. The proceedings of CHARME 2001 have been published as volume 2144 of Springer-Verlag's *Lecture Notes in Computer Science* series, with Tiziana Margaria and Tom Melham as editors.

Each of the 47 papers submitted in the full research category was refereed by at least 3 reviewers who were selected by the Program Committee. Of these submissions, 23 were accepted for presentation at the conference and publication in this volume. In keeping with tradition, TPHOLs 2001 also offered a venue for the presentation of work in progress, where researchers invite discussion by means of a brief preliminary talk and then discuss their work at a poster session. A supplementary proceedings containing associated papers for work in progress was published by the Division of Informatics at the University of Edinburgh.

The organizers are grateful to Bart Jacobs and N. Shankar for agreeing to give invited talks at TPHOLs 2001, and to Steven D. Johnson for agreeing to give an invited talk at the joint session with CHARME 2001. Much of Bart Jacobs's research is on formal methods for object-oriented languages, and he is currently coordinator of a multi-site project funded by the European Union on tool-assisted specification and verification of JavaCard programs. His talk covered his own research and research of this project. A three page abstract on the background to his talk is included in this volume. N. Shankar is one of the principal architects of the popular PVS theorem prover, and has published widely on many theorem-proving related topics. He talked about the kinds of decision procedures that can be deployed in a higher-order-logic setting and the opportunities for interaction between them. We are very pleased to include an accompanying paper in these proceedings. Steven D. Johnson is a prominent figure in the formal methods community. His talk surveyed formalized system design from the perspective of research in interactive reasoning. He contrasted two interactive formalisms: one based on logic and proof, the other based on transformations and equivalence. The latter has been the subject of Johnson's research since the early 1980s. An abstract for this talk is included in these proceedings, and a full accompanying paper can be found in the CHARME 2001 proceedings.

The TPHOLs conference traditionally changes continent each year in order to maximize the chances that researchers all over the world can attend. Starting in 1993, the proceedings of TPHOLs and its predecessor workshops have been published in the following volumes of the Springer-Verlag *Lecture Notes in Computer Science* series:

1993 (Canada)	780		1997 (USA)	1275
1994 (Malta)	859		1998 (Australia)	1479
1995 (USA)	971		1999 (France)	1690
1996 (Finland)	1125		2000 (USA)	1869

The 2001 conference was organized by a team from the Division of Informatics at the University of Edinburgh and the Department of Computing Science at the University of Glasgow.

Financial support came from Intel and Microsoft Research. The University of Glasgow funded publicity and the University of Edinburgh loaned computing equipment. This support is gratefully acknowledged.

June 2001   *Richard J. Boulton, Paul Jackson*

Conference Organization

Richard Boulton	(Conference Chair)
Paul Jackson	(Program Chair)
Louise Dennis	(Local Arrangements Co-chair)
Jacques Fleuriot	(Local Arrangements Co-chair)
Ken Baird	(Local Arrangements & Finances)
Deirdre Burke	(Local Arrangements)
Jennie Douglas	(Local Arrangements)
Gordon Reid	(Computing Support)
Simon Gay	(Publicity Chair)
Tom Melham	(TPHOLs/CHARME Coordinating General Chair)

Program Committee

Mark Aagaard (Waterloo)
David Basin (Freiburg)
Richard Boulton (Glasgow)
Albert Camilleri (Netro)
Victor Carreño (NASA Langley)
Gilles Dowek (INRIA Rocquencourt)
Harald Ganzinger (MPI Saarbrücken)
Ganesh Gopalakrishnan (Utah)
Jim Grundy (Intel)
Elsa Gunter (NJIT)
John Harrison (Intel)
Doug Howe (Carleton)
Bart Jacobs (Nijmegen)

Paul Jackson (Edinburgh)
Sara Kalvala (Warwick)
Michael Kohlhase (CMU & Saarbrücken)
J Moore (Texas, Austin)
Sam Owre (SRI)
Christine Paulin-Mohring (Paris Sud)
Lawrence Paulson (Cambridge)
Frank Pfenning (CMU)
Klaus Schneider (Karlsruhe)
Henny Sipma (Stanford)
Konrad Slind (Cambridge)
Don Syme (Microsoft)
Sofiène Tahar (Concordia)

Invited Speakers

Bart Jacobs (Nijmegen)
Steven D. Johnson (Indiana) (*joint with CHARME 2001*)
N. Shankar (SRI)

Additional Reviewers

Andrew A. Adams
John Cowles
Paul Curzon
Abdelkader Dekdouk
Leonardo Demoura
Ewen Denney
Jonathan Mark Ford
Ruben Gamboa

John Gunnels
Martin Hofmann
Matt Kaufmann
Robert Krug
John Longley
Helen Lowe
Tobias Nipkow
Randy Pollack

Christine Röckl
Harald Ruess
N. Shankar
Jun Sawada
Alan Smaill
Luca Vigano
Burkhart Wolff

CHARME 2001 Organization

Tom Melham   (Conference Chair)
Tiziana Margaria   (Program Chair)
Andrew Ireland   (Local Arrangements Chair)
Steve Beaumont   (Local Arrangements)
Lorraine Fraser   (Local Arrangements)
Simon Gay   (Publicity Chair)

Table of Contents

JavaCard Program Verification

Bart Jacobs

Computing Science Institute, University of Nijmegen
Toernooiveld 1, 6525 ED Nijmegen
bart@cs.kun.nl
http://www.cs.kun.nl/~bart

Abstract. This abstract provides some background information on smart cards, and explains the challenges these cards represent for formal verification of software.

Smart Card Trends

Increasingly, physical keys are being replaced by cryptographic keys, which are typically a thousand bits in size. Modern smart cards are the ideal carriers for such keys, because they have enough computing power to do the necessary en- or de-cryption on-card, so that the secret key never has to leave the card. Smart cards are meant to be tamper-resistant secure tokens, typically bound to individuals via a PIN, possibly in combination with biometric identification.

Modern smart cards contain a standard interface (API) for a mini-operating system which is capable of executing application programs (called *applets*) written in high-level languages. The standard language in this area is JavaCard [Che00], which is a "superset of a subset" of Java: it is a simplified version of Java (no threads, multi-dimensional arrays, floats or doubles) with some special features, like persistent objects and a transaction-commit mechanism. Two further characteristics of modern smart cards are:

- **Multi-application.** One card can hold multiple applets for different applications. These are typically centered around the basic cryptographic functions, in for example banking, telecommunication (GSM or UMTS SIMs), access to buildings or networks, identification, voting, *etc.*) Limited communication can be allowed between applets, *e.g.* for automatically adding loyalty points after certain commercial transactions.
- **Post-issuance Downloading.** In principle, it is possible to add applets to a card after it has been issued. This option gives enormous flexibility, but is disabled for security reasons in all currently operational cards.

Security evaluation and certification are very important in the smart card area, because cards are distributed in large numbers for security critical applications. Correctness should be established both for the card platform, and for applets.

R.J. Boulton and P.B. Jackson (Eds.): TPHOLs 2001, LNCS 2152, pp. 1–3, 2001.
© Springer-Verlag Berlin Heidelberg 2001

Challenges for Formal Methods

The so-called Common Criteria[1] form a standard for the evaluation of IT security. They are much used for smart cards. The Common Criteria involve seven different levels of evaluation, where the two highest levels (6 and 7) require the explicit use of formal methods. Currently available smart cards are evaluated at levels 4 and 5, but there is a clear pressure to move to higher levels. Therefore the smart card industry is open to the use of formal methods. For the formal verification community smart cards form an ideal target since they are within reach of existing verification tools, because of their limited size.

VerifiCard: Aims

In 2000 a European research consortium called VerifiCard[2] was set up, with support from the European Union's IST programme. Its aim is to apply the existing verification tools (mostly theorem provers, but also model checkers) to establish the correctness of JavaCard-based smart cards. The approach is pragmatic: no new development of semantics of Java(Card) from scratch, but application of available expertise and experience in Europe in tool-assisted formal methods, to see what can be achieved in a concentrated effort in a small, well-defined area. This is a potential killer application for formal methods in software verification, which can cut in two directions: if this succeeds, the success may spread to other areas. But if this fails there may be a serious setback for formal methods in software: it is bad news if these methods cannot deliver for such relatively small systems as smart cards.

VerifiCard: Work

The VerifiCard consortium consists of five academic partners, some of which are well-known in the TPHOLs community: Nijmegen (coordinator; Jacobs, Poll), INRIA (Barthe, Bertot, Jensen, Paulin-Mohring), Munich (Nipkow, Strecker), Hagen (Poetzsch-Heffter), SICS (Dam). Also, the consortium involves two smart card manufacturers: Gemplus and SchlumbergerSema (formerly Bull CP8). The planned work is roughly divided along two lines: source code / byte code, and platform / applets. The work involves for instance formalization of the JavaCard virtual machine and byte code verifier, non-interference properties, and specification and verification of the API and of individual applets. Towards the end of the project the industrial partners will carry out a tool-evaluation, to see which approaches can contribute most to their evaluation needs.

Scientific Work of Nijmegen

The talk will elaborate on the work done at Nijmegen, as part of VerifiCard. This involves verification of JavaCard programs, that are part of the API and applets.

---

[1] See http://www.commoncriteria.org.
[2] See http://www.verificard.org.

The correctness properties are specified using the interface specification language JML [LBR99], developed by Gary Leavens *et al.* in Iowa, see *e.g.* [PBJ01]. A Java(Card) program with JML annotation is translated to PVS using the LOOP tool [BJ01]. Actual verification in PVS proceeds via a tailor-made Hoare logic for JML [JP01]. See [BJP01] for a small case study, involving the AID class from the JavaCard API. Basically, the verification technology for Java is there, but scaling it up to larger programs is still a real challenge.

References

BJ01.   J. van den Berg and B. Jacobs. The LOOP compiler for Java and JML. In T. Margaria and W. Yi, editors, *Tools and Algorithms for the Construction and Analysis of Software (TACAS)*, number 2031 in Lect. Notes Comp. Sci., pages 299–312. Springer, Berlin, 2001.

BJP01.   J. van den Berg, B. Jacobs, and E. Poll. Formal specification and verification of JavaCard's Application Identifier Class. In I. Attali and Th. Jensen, editors, *Proceedings of the Java Card 2000 Workshop*, Lect. Notes Comp. Sci. Springer, Berlin, 2001.

Che00.   Z. Chen. *Java Card Technology for Smart Cards*. The Java Series. Addison-Wesley, 2000.

JP01.   B. Jacobs and E. Poll. A logic for the Java Modeling Language JML. In H. Hussmann, editor, *Fundamental Approaches to Software Engineering (FASE)*, number 2029 in Lect. Notes Comp. Sci., pages 284–299. Springer, Berlin, 2001.

LBR99.   G.T. Leavens, A.L. Baker, and C. Ruby. JML: A notation for detailed design. In H. Kilov and B. Rumpe, editors, *Behavioral Specifications of Business and Systems*, pages 175–188. Kluwer, 1999.

PBJ01.   E. Poll, J. van den Berg, and B. Jacobs. Formal specification of the JavaCard API in JML: The APDU class. *Comp. Networks Mag.*, 2001. To appear.

View from the Fringe of the Fringe
(Joint with CHARME 2001)

Steven D. Johnson

Computer Science Department
Indiana University, Lindley Hall, Room 215
150 S. Woodlawn, Bloomington, IN 47405-7104, USA

Abstract. Formal analysis remains outside the mainstream of system design practice. Theorem proving is regarded by many to be on the margin of exploratory and applied research activity in this formalized system design. Although it may seem relatively academic, it is vital that this avenue continue to be as vigorously explored as approaches favoring highly automated reasoning. Design derivation, a term for design formalisms based on transformations and equivalence, represents just a small twig on the theorem-proving branch of formal system analysis. A perspective on current trends in is presented from this remote outpost, including a review of the author's work since the early 1980s.

A full accompanying paper can be found in the CHARME 2001 proceedings [1].

References

[1] Steven D. Johnson. View from the fringe of the fringe. In Tiziana Margaria and Tom Melham, editors, *Proceedings of 11th Advanced Research Workshop on Correct Hardware Design and Verification Methods (CHARME 2001)*, volume 2144 of *Lecture Notes in Computer Science*. Springer Verlag, 2001.

R.J. Boulton and P.B. Jackson (Eds.): TPHOLs 2001, LNCS 2152, pp. 4–4, 2001.
© Springer-Verlag Berlin Heidelberg 2001

Using Decision Procedures
with a Higher-Order Logic*

Natarajan Shankar

Computer Science Laboratory
SRI International, Menlo Park CA 94025 USA
shankar@csl.sri.com
http://www.csl.sri.com/~shankar/
Phone: +1 (650) 859-5272 Fax: +1 (650) 859-2844

Abstract. In automated reasoning, there is a perceived trade-off between expressiveness and automation. Higher-order logic is typically viewed as expressive but resistant to automation, in contrast with first-order logic and its fragments. We argue that higher-order logic and its variants actually achieve a happy medium between expressiveness and automation, particularly when used as a front-end to a wide range of decision procedures and deductive procedures. We illustrate the discussion with examples from PVS, but some of the observations apply to other variants of higher-order logic as well.

It does not matter if a cat is black or white so long as it catches mice.

Deng Xiaoping

Expressiveness and automation are the two basic concerns for formalized mathematics. In theoretical terms, expressiveness is characterized by the range of concepts that can be captured within a given logic. For practical application of logic, the directness with which concepts can be captured and manipulated in the logic is also important. The theoretical idea of automation for a given logic is usually in terms of the degree of solvability or unsolvability of its decision problem. We argue that such characterizations are theoretically interesting but irrelevant in practice. A more important quality for a logic is the degree to which useful fragments of the logic can be supported by means of automation. We have used the higher-order logic of PVS (SRI's Prototype Verification System) [ORS92,ORSvH95] as an interface to various automated procedures. We assess the effectiveness of the PVS logic, and higher-order logic in general, as a logical front end.

Logics based on higher-order types have a long and distinguished history in the foundations of mathematics. Paradoxes such as that of Russell (the set of

---

* This work was funded by NSF Grant CCR-0082560, DARPA/AFRL Contract F33615-00-C-3043, and NASA Contract NAS1-00079.

R.J. Boulton and P.B. Jackson (Eds.): TPHOLs 2001, LNCS 2152, pp. 5–26, 2001.

all those sets that do not contain themselves as elements) led to various restrictions on hitherto unquestioned logical principles such as unrestricted comprehension. Whitehead and Russell's system Principia Mathematica (PM) [WR27] introduced a type system consisting of the types of individuals, sets of individuals, sets of sets of individuals, and so on. Overlaid on this type hierarchy was a notion of order so that a term of order k could only contain quantification over variables of lower order to ensure predicativity. However, as Chwistek (see Hatcher [Hat68]) showed, the axiom of reducibility (comprehension) renders the system equivalent to a simple type theory with impredicative comprehension. Ramsey [Ram90] showed that the basic type system was sufficient to avoid the logical paradoxes (such as Russell's). Predicativity did not actually address the epistemological paradoxes (such as the Liar's paradox) since these had to do with the interpretation of concepts expressed in the logic and not with the means of definition. Church [Chu40] presented a system based on a simple type theory with types for individuals and propositions, and a type $[A{\to}B]$ for any types A and B. Church's system is based on the simply typed lambda-calculus with Church numerals, an axiom of infinity, and operators for universal quantification and choice. Church's system is equivalent in power to Zermelo's set theory. Most modern higher-order logics are based on Church's system.[1]

Many automated reasoning systems have been based on higher-order logics. Perhaps the earliest of these is de Bruijn's Automath proof checker [dB80] which employs a dependently typed metalogic to represent judgments and derivations. The TPS system [AINP88] is one of the earliest automated theorem provers based on a higher-order logic. TPS has been used to automatically find succinct higher-order proofs for several interesting theorems. Many of the systems developed during the 1980s such as HOL [GM93], Veritas [HD92], and EHDM [vHCL+88,RvHO91] are based on higher-order logic. The Nuprl system [CAB+86] is based on a constructive system of higher types and universes inspired by the type theories of Martin-Löf. The Coq system [CH85,DFH+91] also features a similar constructive type theory with impredicative type quantification and abstraction. Isabelle [Pau94] is a metalogical framework that uses higher-order Horn clauses to represent inference rules. λ-Prolog [NM90] is a similar metalogical framework based on the hereditary-Harrop fragment of higher-order logic.

There is a general impression that higher-order logics are not easily automated. We get a different picture if we view higher-order logic as a framework for embedding small and useful sublogics that are more readily amenable to automation [Gor88]. The convenience of higher-order logic is that other formalisms including program logics, modal and temporal logics, can be embedded directly and elegantly within it. Given such embeddings, it is easy to recognize those fragments that are well-supported by automation. The decision as to whether a

---

[1] Excellent surveys of the logical aspects of higher-order logic have been given by Feferman [Fef78], Andrews [And86], van Bentham and Doets [vBD83], and Leivant [Lei94].

problem is in a decidable fragment can itself be undecidable. By allowing other logics to be embedded within it, higher-order logic makes it easy to recognize when an assertion falls within a decidable fragment. The dialogue between the proof designer and the theorem prover is guided by the goal of reducing a given problem into a form that has been effectively automated. The sharing of results between different automated deductive procedures is straightforward because the higher-order logic serves as a common semantic medium. The term *glue logic* has been applied to this function, but higher-order logic is not merely an interlingua. It supports both the direct expression and effective manipulation of formalized mathematics.

Boyer and Moore [BM86] have already argued that the integration of decision procedures into an automatic theorem prover can be a delicate matter. This is even more acutely the case with an interactive prover. Decision procedures must ensure that the interaction is conducted at a reasonably high-level by eliminating trivial inferences. At the same time, the internal details of the decision procedures must, to the extent possible, be concealed from the human user. On the other hand, decision procedures can be used with greater resilience in an interactive context through the use of contextual knowledge and the "productive use of failure" [Bun83].

Highly automated deduction procedures are crucial for achieving useful results within specific domains. The primary challenge for interactive theorem proving is that of integrating these procedures within a unifying logic so that they can be combined into a proof development in a coherent manner. In contrast, the Automath [dB80] and LCF [GMW79] systems emphasize formality, foundational reductions, and fully expansive formal proof construction over automation. In the LCF approach, ML is used as a metalanguage in which theorems are an inductively defined datatype, *tactics* are defined as a way of introducing derived inference rules in a sound manner, and *tacticals* are used for combining tactics.

Soundness is an obviously critical property of a deductive procedure, but *manifest soundness* as ensured by *fully expansive* proofs must be balanced against the efficiency of the procedure, its transparency, usability, and interoperability with other procedures. Fully expansive proof construction [Bou93,Har96] is a powerful organizing principle and an effective technique for achieving soundness, but at the algorithmic level, it requires a serious investment of time and effort that can be justified only after a great deal of experimentation. Eventually, it will be both prudent and feasible to verify the soundness of these deductive procedures (as demonstrated by Théry's verification [Thé98] of Buchberger's algorithm), but expanded proofs might still be useful for applications such as proof-carrying code [NL00].

The initial goal in the development of PVS was not dissimilar to that of the LCF family of systems with a fixed set of inference rules and a tactic-like mechanism for combining useful patterns of inference. More recently, we have come to view PVS as a semantic framework for integrating powerful deductive procedures. This viewpoint is similar to that of the PROSPER project [DCN+00] though PVS employs a tighter and more fine-grained coupling of deductive procedures. Other ways of combining PVS with other existing automation have been studied by Martin and her colleagues [DKML99] for adding soundness checks to computer algebra systems, Buth [But97] for discharging proof obligations generated by PAMELA from VDM-style specifications, and the LOOP system of Jacobs and his colleagues [JvdBH+98] for verifying object-oriented systems described in Java, among others.

We outline the PVS logic (Section 1) and present a few examples of deductive procedures that have been used to automate proof development in its higher-order logic. The deductive procedures include extended typechecking (Section 2), evaluation (Section 3), ground decision procedures for equality (Section 4), and symbolic model checking (Section 5). Most of these procedures can be employed within modest extensions to first-order logic, but the use of higher-order logic extends the range of applicability without compromising the automation. Many of the methods have been described in detail elsewhere and not all of these are original with PVS. The PVS system is a work in progress toward a vision of interactive proof checking based on exploiting the synergy between expressiveness and automation. The present paper is a progress report on some of the experiments on this front and an attempt to connect the dots.

1   The PVS Higher-Order Logic

The core of the PVS higher-order logic is described in the formal semantics of PVS [OS97]. The types consist of the base types `bool` and `real`. Compound types are constructed from these as tuples $[T_1, \ldots, T_n]$, records $[\#l_1 : T_1, \ldots, l_n : T_n\#]$, or function types $[S{\to}T]$. Predicates over a type T are of type $[T{\to}\text{bool}]$. Predicate subtypes are a distinctive feature of the PVS higher-order logic. Given a predicate p over T, $\{x : T \mid p(x)\}$ is a predicate subtype of T consisting of those elements of T satisfying p. Dependent versions of tuple, record, and function types can be constructed by introducing dependencies between different components of a type through predicates. Let $T(x_1, \ldots, x_n)$ range over a type expression that contains free variables from the set $\{x_1, \ldots, x_n\}$. A dependent tuple has the form $[x_1 : T_1, x_2 : T_2(x_1), \ldots, T_n(x_1, \ldots, x_{n-1})]$, a dependent record has the form $[\#x_1 : T_1, x_2 : T_2(x_1), \ldots, x_n : T_n(x_1, \ldots, x_{n-1})\#]$, and a dependent function type has the form $[x : S{\to}T(x)]$.

Predicate subtyping can be used to type partial operations but it can also be used to declare more refined type information than is possible with simple types [ROS98]. As examples, the division operation is declared to range over non-zero denominators, and the square-root operation is declared to take a non-negative argument. The range of an operation can also be constrained by subtyping so that the absolute-value function can be asserted to return a non-negative result. At the first-order level, types such as the natural numbers, even numbers, prime numbers, subranges, nonempty lists, ordered binary trees, and balanced binary trees, can be defined through predicate subtyping. An empty subtype of any given type can be easily defined. At higher types, predicate subtyping can be used to define types such as injective, surjective, bijective, and order-preserving maps, and monotone predicate transformers. Arrays can be typed as functions with subranges as domains. Dependent typing at higher types admits, for example, the definition of a finite sequence (of arbitrary length) as a pair consisting of a length and an array of the given length. Length or size preserving maps can be captured by dependent types. A sorting operation can be typed to return an ordered permutation of its argument. A choice operation that picks an arbitrary element from a nonempty set (predicate) can be captured by dependent typing.

Predicate subtypes and dependent types are conservative extensions to the simply typed higher-order logic. Any concept that can be defined with the use of subtypes and dependent types, can be captured within the simple type system. As examples, division by zero can be defined to return a chosen arbitrary value, and finite sequences can be defined from infinite sequences by ignoring the irrelevant values. However, this embedding has the disadvantage that the equality operation on finite sequences has to be defined to ignore these irrelevant elements or they have to be coerced to a fixed element. Either option adds some overhead to the formal manipulations involving such types.

In addition to variables x, constants c, applications $f(a)$, and abstractions $\lambda(x : T) : a$, PVS expressions include conditionals IF a_1 THEN a_2 ELSE a_3ENDIF, and updates $e[a := v]$ where e is of tuple, record, or function type and a is respectively, a tuple component number, a record field name, or a function argument.[2] The update construct is an interesting extension. Although, for a given type, the update operation can be defined by means of copying, there are some important differences. In executing higher-order specifications as programs, it is possible to identify update operations that can be executed by a destructive or in-place udpate. Such destructive updates yield substantial efficiencies over copying. The update operation has the property of being polymorphic with respect to structural subtyping.[3]

2 Typechecking in PVS

Typechecking of PVS terms is undecidable in general because it can yield arbitrary formulas as proof obligations. For example, the singleton subtype of the

---

[2] The actual update construct also admits simultaneous and nested updates.

[3] Structural subtyping is different from predicate subtyping. For example, a record type r that has fields l_1, l_2, and l_3, of types T_1, T_2, and T_3, is a structure subtype of a record s with field l_1 and l_2 with types T_1 and T_2. Updates are structural subtype polymorphic in the sense that any update operation that maps s to s is also a valid update from r to r. Structural subtyping is not yet part of the PVS logic but it nevertheless illustrates the nontriviality of the update operation.

booleans consisting of the element TRUE is a valid type for any valid sentence in the logic. Other judgments such as equalities between types, the subtyping relation between types, and the compatibility between types are also similarly undecidable.

Typechecking of a PVS expression a with respect to a context Γ which is a list of declarations for type names, constants, and variable names, is given by means of an operation $\tau(\Gamma)(a)$ that either signals an error, or computes the canonical type of a with respect to Γ and a collection of proof obligations ψ. Typechecking is usually specified by type inference rules, but we have opted for a functional presentation because it gives a deterministic algorithm that constructs a canonical type for a given term. Proof obligations are generated with respect to this canonical type. The semantic mapping for a well-formed term is also given by a recursion similar to that of τ, and the soundness proofs follow the same structure. Type correctness of a with respect to Γ holds when all the proof obligations have been discharged.

The typechecking of application expressions is worth examining in some detail since it captures the key ideas. The context Γ includes formulas corresponding to any governing conditions, in addition to declarations. The corresponding case in the definition of τ is given below.

$$\tau(\Gamma)(f\ a) = B', \text{ where } \mu_0(\tau(\Gamma)(f)) = [x : A{\to}B],$$
$$\tau(\Gamma)(a) = A',$$
$$(A \overset{a}{\sim} A')_\Gamma,$$
$$B' \text{ is } B[a/x],$$
$$\vdash_\Gamma \pi(A)(a)$$

The body of the definition for $\tau(\Gamma)(f\ a)$ first computes the canonical type $\tau(\Gamma)(f)$ for f and the canonical type $\tau(\Gamma)(a)$ as A'. The direct maximal supertype of $\tau(\Gamma)(f)$ must be a possibly dependent type of the form $[x : A{\to}B]$ for some types A and B, or typechecking fails. The expected type A and actual type A' must be compatible, i.e., $(A \overset{a}{\sim} A')_\Gamma$, and this compatibility test generates proof obligations that must be discharged. The types int of integers, and nat of natural numbers, are compatible since they have a common supertype. The types [nznat→int] and [posnat→nat], where nznat is $\{x : \mathtt{nat} \mid x \neq 0\}$ and posnat is $\{x : \mathtt{nat} \mid x > 0\}$, are also compatible since the domain types are equal (modulo the verification of the proof obligation $\forall(x : \mathtt{nat}) : x \neq 0 \iff x > 0$), and the range types are compatible. Finally, any proof obligations corresponding to constraints on a with respect to the expected type A, namely $\pi(A)(a)$ must also be discharged.

Typical proof obligations involve little more than subranges and interval constraints. For example, arrays in PVS are just functions on subrange types and array bounds checking ensures that for any array access $a(i)$, i occurs within the subrange corresponding to the index type of a. Proof obligations corresponding to subtype constraints in the range are generated, for example, to demonstrate that the absolution-value operation returns a non-negative result. Range subtype constraints are interesting because they can be used to verify properties that might otherwise require inductive reasoning. For example, a function which halves an even integer can be defined as

$$half(x : \textbf{even}) : \{y : \textbf{int} \mid 2 * y = x\}$$
$$
\begin{aligned}
= \ &\texttt{IF} && x = 0 \\
&\texttt{THEN} && 0 \\
&\texttt{ELSIF} && x > 0 \\
&\texttt{THEN} && half(x - 2) + 1 \\
&\texttt{ELSE} && half(x + 2) - 1 \\
&\texttt{ENDIF.}
\end{aligned}
$$

The type **even** is defined as $\{x : \textbf{int} \mid even?(x)\}$. The range type captures the constraint that $2 * half(x) = x$. The subtype proof obligations generated are

1. $\forall(x : \textbf{even}) : x = 0 \supset 2 * 0 = 0$. The return value 0 when $x = 0$ must satisfy the subtype $\{y : \textbf{int} \mid 2 * y = x\}$.
2. $\forall(x : \textbf{even}) : x \neq 0 \wedge x > 0 \supset even?(x - 2)$. The argument $x - 2$ in the recursive call $half(x - 2)$ must satisfy the constraint given by the subtype **even**.
3. $\forall(x : \textbf{even}, z : \{y : \textbf{int} \mid 2 * y = x - 2\}) : x \neq 0 \wedge x > 0 \supset 2 * (z + 1) = x$. The return value $half(x - 2) + 1$ satisfies the constraint given by the range type $\{y : \textbf{int} \mid 2 * y = x\}$.
4. $\forall(x : \textbf{even}) : x \neq 0 \wedge \neg x > 0 \supset even?(x + 2)$. The recursive call argument $x + 2$ satisfies the constraint given by **even**.
5. $\forall(x : \textbf{even}, z : \{y : \textbf{int} \mid 2 * y = x + 2\}) : x \neq 0 \wedge \neg x > 0 \supset 2 * (z - 1) = x$. The return value $half(x + 2) - 1$ satisfies the constraint given by the range type $\{y : \textbf{int} \mid 2 * y = x\}$.

Proof obligations are also generated to ensure the termination of recursive definitions. For example, the above definition of *half* can be shown to be well-formed with respect to termination by supplying the termination measure $\lambda(x : \textbf{even}) : abs(x)$ and the well-founded ordering relation $<$ on natural numbers. The termination proof obligations generated are

1. $\forall(x : \textbf{even}) : x \neq 0 \wedge x > 0 \supset abs(x - 2) < abs(x)$.
2. $\forall(x : \textbf{even}) : x \neq 0 \wedge \neg x > 0 \supset abs(x + 2) < abs(x)$.

All these proof obligations can be trivially discharged using decision procedures such as those outlined in Section 4. Conversely, the subtype constraints are exploited by the ground decision procedures. Since it is possible to build in arbitrarily complex subtype constraints, some proof obligations might require interactive proof. The handling of predicate subtypes requires a fair bit of infrastructure. Subtyping *judgments* can be used to cache subtype information. One kind of subtyping judgment merely introduces more refined typing on an existing constant. For example, the numeral constant 2 can be introduced as an natural number, but judgments can be introduced to assert that 2 is also an even number and a prime number. The subtyping judgments generate proof obligations that must be discharged for type correctness. Subtyping judgments are invoked by the type checker for annotating terms and propagating type information that is more refined than the canonical type so that the corresponding type correctness proof obligations are not generated. For the absolute-value operation *abs* of type [real→real], a judgment can be used to assert that $abs(x)$ has type int if x has type int. This way, when the term $abs(a)$ is typechecked where a has type int, the typechecker deduces that $abs(a)$ also has type int.

Another form of judgment is used to record a subtyping relation between two types. For example, a judgment can be used to note that a subrange from a positive natural number up to another natural number is a subtype of the positive natural numbers. Judgments are similar to the intersection type discipline [CDC80] for Curry-style type inference systems. PVS uses a Church-style type discipline and judgments are used for type propagation rather than inference.

3   Executing PVS Specifications

Evaluation is the simplest of all decision procedures. It has many uses within a proof checker. First, specifications can be validated by executing them on known test suites. This is a useful way of ensuring that the specifications capture the specifier's intent. Second, evaluation can be used to obtain executable code from a specification so that the program that is executed is essentially identical to the program that has been verified. Third, evaluation can be used to efficiently simplify executable expressions. Fourth, evaluation can be used to add a reflective capability so that metatheorems involving deductive procedures for a logic can be verified in the logic itself, and the resulting procedures can be efficiently executed.[4] An evaluation capability was added to PVS in response to a practical need identified by researchers at Rockwell Collins [HWG98] for validating hardware descriptions used in processor verification.

There are several options in designing an execution capability for PVS. One option is to build an interpreter for the language, but its efficiency would be a serious bottleneck. A second option is to write a compiler for the language to compile source code down to the machine code, but this would involve redoing work that has already been done for more widely used programming languages. The option we have taken has been to write code generators from PVS to other high-level languages. The compilers for these language can be used to perform low-level optimizations while high-level transformations can be carried out within the logic. The generated code can also be integrated with other, possibly non-critical, code.

---

[4] Boyer and Moore [BM81] were the first to emphasize executability in the context of theorem provers.

A surprisingly large fraction of higher-order logic turns out to be executable. The executable PVS expressions are those that do not contain any free variables, uninterpreted constants, or equalities between unbounded higher-order types.[5] Any high-level language can serve as the target for code generation from PVS. We have used Common Lisp as the target language since it is also the implementation language for PVS, but several other languages would be equally suitable. Since PVS functions are total, both lazy and eager evaluation would return the same result. Currently, code generation is with respect to an eager order of evaluation. The result of evaluation following code generation from PVS might contain closures, and hence may not be translatable back into PVS. A PVS expression of *non-functional* type, i.e., one that does not contain type components that are of function type, can be evaluated to return a value that is a PVS expression. Executable equality comparisons are those between terms of non-functional type.

Let $[\![e]\!]_\rho$ represent the Common Lisp code generated corresponding to the PVS expression e where ρ binds PVS variables to the corresponding Common Lisp identifiers. A PVS definition of a constant c of type T has the form $c : T = e$. It is translated to (DEFUN C () E), where E is $[\![e]\!]_\emptyset$. The primitive PVS arithmetic and logical operations are mapped to the corresponding Lisp operations. The boolean constants TRUE and FALSE are mapped to T and NIL, respectively. The integer numerals are mapped to the corresponding Common Lisp numerals. Tuples and records are mapped Common Lisp vectors so that the corresponding projection operations are mapped to vector accesses. Equality on non-functional types is mapped to the equalp operation. A lambda-abstraction $\lambda(x : T) : e$ in PVS is mapped to (FUNCTION (LAMBDA (X) E)), where E is $[\![e]\!]_{\rho\{x\leftarrow X\}}$, and $[\![e]\!]_{\rho\{x\leftarrow X\}}$ is the result of translating the PVS expression e in the context of the free variable x being associated with the Common Lisp variable X. PVS conditional expressions are directly mapped to Common Lisp conditional forms.

$$[\![n]\!]_\rho = n \qquad\qquad \text{for numeral } n$$
$$[\![\text{TRUE}]\!]_\rho = \text{T}$$
$$[\![\text{FALSE}]\!]_\rho = \text{NIL}$$
$$[\![(a_1,\ldots,a_n)]\!]_\rho = (\text{vector } [\![a_1]\!]_\rho \ \ldots \ [\![a_n]\!]_\rho)$$
$$[\![\text{p}_i\ a]\!]_\rho = (\text{svref } [\![a]\!]_\rho \ j), \qquad\qquad \text{where } j = i - 1$$
$$[\![f\ a]\!]_\rho = (\text{FUNCALL } [\![f]\!]_\rho \ [\![A]\!]_\rho)$$
$$[\![(\text{IF}(a,b,c))]\!]_\rho = (\text{IF } [\![a]\!]_\rho \ [\![b]\!]_\rho \ [\![c]\!]_\rho)$$
$$[\![(\lambda(x : T) : e)]\!]_\rho = (\text{FUNCTION (LAMBDA (X) E)), where E} = [\![e]\!]_{\rho\{x\leftarrow X\}}$$

PVS update expressions are first eliminated prior to translation through the transformations so that the above translation to Common Lisp can be applied to the expression without updates.

$$f[(a) := e] = (\lambda j : \text{IF}(j = a, e, f(j))), f \text{ has function type}$$

---

[5] PVS 2.3 does not evaluate the full executable subset. It ignores all equalities between higher-order types, and evaluates quantification only over a limited class of types of finite size.

$$r[(a) := e] = (\#l_1 := l_1(r), \ldots, l_i := e, \ldots \#), r \text{ has record type}, a \equiv l_i$$
$$t[(a) := e] = (\mathtt{p_1} \ t, \ldots, e, \ldots), t \text{ has tuple type}, a \equiv i$$

The naïve translation above generates code that is inefficient in a number of ways. Most significantly, the translation of updates through copying causes computations to be grossly inefficient in time and space. Static analysis can be used to identify occurrences of update expressions that can be safely executed in a destructive manner. For simplicity, we restrict attention to one-dimensional array updates of the form $a[i := v]$ occurring in the context of an expression $e[]$. Some examples illustrate the subtleties of destructive update optimizations. We write $f(x_1, \ldots, x_n) = e$ as an alternative form for the definition $f = \lambda(x_1, \ldots, x_n) : e$. Let $\mathtt{Arr}$ be an array type from the subrange $[0..9]$ to the integers, i.e., the function type $[[0..9] \rightarrow \mathtt{int}]$. Let A and B be variables of type $\mathtt{Arr}$. An array lookup is then written as $A(i)$ and a (nondestructive) array update has the form $A[(c) := d]$. Pointwise addition on arrays $A + B$ is defined to return (a reference to) an array C such that $C(i) = A(i) + B(i)$ for $0 \le i < 10$. Consider the definitions

$$f_1(A) = A + A[(3) := 4]$$
$$f_2(A, i) = A(i) + A[(3) := 4](i)$$
$$f_3(A) = A[(3) := f_2(A, 3)]$$
$$f_4(A, B) = A + B[(3) := 4]$$
$$f_5(C) = f_4(C, C)$$

When executing $f_1(A)$, the update to A cannot be carried out destructively since the original array is an argument to the $+$ operation. The evaluation of $A[(3) := 4]$ must return a reference to a new array that is a suitably modified copy of the array A. However, in the evaluation $f_2(A)$, given an eager, left-to-right evaluation order, the expression $A(i)$ will be evaluated prior to the update $A[(3) := 4]$. Since the original value of A is no longer used in the computation, the array can be updated destructively.[6] This optimization assumes that array A is not referenced in the context where $f_2(A, i)$ is evaluated. For example, in evaluating $f_3(A)$, it would be incorrect to execute f_2 so that A is updated destructively since there is a reference to the original A in the context when $f_2(A, 3)$ is evaluated. The update to array B in $f_4(A, B)$ can be executed destructively provided A and B are not aliased to the same array reference. Such aliasing happens, for instance, in the evaluation of $f_5(C)$.

The task is that of statically analyzing the definitions of programs involving function definitions such as those of f_1, f_2, f_3, f_4, and f_5, in order to identify those updates that can be executed destructively. Our analysis processes the definition $f(x_1, \ldots, x_n) = e$ of a function f and produces a definition

---

[6] If a lazy order of evaluation was being employed, this optimization would depend on the order in which the arguments of $+$ were evaluated.

of the form $f^D(x_1, \ldots, x_n) = e^D$, where some occurrences of updates of the form $e_1[(e_2) := e_3]$ in e have been replaced by destructive updates of the form $e_1[(e_2) \leftarrow e_3]$. It also returns a *safety condition* $Sc(f)$ under which it is safe to use f^D instead of f. The safety condition is a partial map from the set of variables $\{x_1, \ldots, x_n\}$ to its power set. If x_i is in the domain of $Sc(f)$, then x_i is possibly destructively updated in f^D, and the variables $Sc(f)(x_i)$ are live in the context of the destructive update. For the examples above, the analysis yields

$$
\begin{array}{ll}
f_1^D(A) = A + A[(3) := 4] & Sc(f_1) = \emptyset \\
f_2^D(A, i) = A(i) + A[(3) \leftarrow 4](i) & Sc(f_2) = \{A \mapsto \emptyset\} \\
f_3^D(A) = A[(3) \leftarrow f_2(A, 3)] & Sc(f_3) = \{A \mapsto \emptyset\} \\
f_4^D(A, B) = A + B[(3) \leftarrow 4] & Sc(f_4) = \{B \mapsto \{A\}\} \\
f_5^D(C) = f_4(C, C) & Sc(f_5) = \emptyset
\end{array}
$$

The update analysis is described in greater detail in unpublished manuscripts [Sha99].[7] We informally describe the analysis for checking when destructive updates are safe in an definition, but do not give the full details on how such updates are identified. The analysis uses three sets of variables that are subsets of a free variable in an expression. The set of *output variables* $O(a)$ consists of the mutable free variables in a that can potentially share structure with the value of a. The set of *active variables* $Ac(a)$ contains $O(a)$ but also includes those mutable variables that may occur in a closure within the value of a. The set of *live variables* $L(e[])$ contain the variables that are potentially live at the point where the hole $[]$ is evaluated. We skip the definitions of these operations and instead illustrate them on the above examples.

1. $f_1(A) = A + A[(3) := 4]$: $Ac(A) = \{A\}$, $O(A) = \{A\}$, and $L(A + []) = \{A\}$. Since the variable A is live in the context $A + []$ and possibly updated in the update expression $A[(3) := 4]$ that fills the hole, it is not safe to translate this update into a destructive one.

2. $f_2(A, i) = A(i) + A[(3) := 4](i)$: $Ac(A(i))$ is $\emptyset$, and hence, $L(A(i) + [](i)$ is also $\emptyset$. Since A, the only variable that is possibly updated in the update expression $A[(3) := 4](i)$, is not live in the context $A(i) + [](i)$, it is safe to transform this update into a destructive one. Since $L(A(i) + [])$ is $\emptyset$, $S(f_2)$ maps A to $\emptyset$.

3. $f_3(A) = A[(3) := f_2(A, 3)]$: $L(A[(3) := []])$ is $\{A\}$, and since f_2^D possibly updates A, the nondestructive version of f_2 must be used. The outer update can be executed destructively since $L([])$ is $\emptyset$, and $Sc(f_3)$ maps A to $\emptyset$.

4. $f_4(A, B) = A + B[(3) := 4]$: $L(A + [])$ is $\{A\}$, and $O(B)$ is $\{B\}$. Since the intersection of $L(A + [])$ and $O(B)$ is empty, the update can be carried out destructively while noting that $Sc(f_4)$ maps B to $\{A\}$.

5. $f_5(C) = f_4(C, C)$: we observe that $Sc(f_4)(B)$ is $\{A\}$, and since C is the actual expression for the formal parameter B, we have that $O(C)$ is $\{C\}$, and

---

[7] The analysis given here is for the first-order setting with flat arrays. The actual implementation is different in that it deals with a richer language and employs aggressive approximations.

the actual expression for A is C, and $Ac(C)$ is $\{C\}$. Since the intersection is nonempty, it is not safe to invoke the destructive version of f^4 in this definition.

Code generation with the destructive update optimization yields dramatic time and space efficiencies provided the specifier ensures that definitions are written with singly threaded updates. With destructive updates and other high-level optimizations, a functional language can be competitive in performance with the corresponding C program. Currently, the Common Lisp code generated from PVS specifications are around four times slower than the best possible implementations we could carry out of the corresponding C programs, but this gap can easily be narrowed further. If the PVS specifications have been type-checked and all the proof obligations have been discharged, then the only way the generated code can crash during execution is by exceeding a resource bound such as stack space. The PVS type system thus ensures the maximal level of safe execution that can be extracted from any type system for a language that admits unbounded computations.

Draghicescu and Purushothaman [DP93] were the first to use an abstract interpretation in terms of sets of mutable variables but their analysis algorithm is very complex. The destructive update optimization above is similar to one given independently and earlier by Wand and Clinger [WC98].

4   Ground Decision Procedures

We have already seen that higher-order logic with predicate subtypes yields a refined system for typing well-formed expressions including those that generate well-formed computations. Typechecking with predicate subtypes requires the discharging of type-correctness proof obligations. Many typical proof obligations can be discharged automatically through the use of ground decision procedures for equality and arithmetic inequality. Ground decision procedures decide quantifier-free statements, namely those that contain free variables that are implicitly universally quantified at the outermost level. Congruence closure [Koz77,NO80,Sho78,DST80] can be used as a decision procedure for equality for terms built from variables and uninterpreted functions. Most proof obligations contain a combination of uninterpreted function symbols and function symbols that are interpreted within a theory such as linear arithmetic. Nelson and Oppen [NO79] gave a method for combining decision procedures for disjoint theories. Shostak [Sho84] gave a procedure for constructing decision procedures for the combination of solvable and canonizable theories. The PVS decision procedures are based on those of Shostak. In a recently analysis [RS01], we found these procedures to be nonterminating and incomplete, and constructed a sound, complete, and terminating combination algorithm. The corrected decision procedure is described below. It forms the basis of the ICS decision procedures [FORS01] implemented at SRI.

Ground equality decision procedures must verify sequents of the form $T \vdash a = b$ where T is a list of equalities and the free variables in $a = b$ are a subset of those in T. If the function symbols in T, a, and b are uninterpreted, then congruence closure yields a decision procedure. Let $f^3(x)$ abbreviate $f(f(f(x)))$ and $f^5(x)$ abbreviate $f(f(f(f(f(x)))))$. If f is uninterpreted in $f^3(x) = f(x) \vdash f^5(x) = f(x)$, then the equivalence classes over the term universe of sequent generated by the antecedent equality are $\{x\}$, $\{f(x), f^3(x), f^5(x)\}$, and $\{f^2(x), f^4(x)\}$. This partition clearly validates the conclusion $f^5(x) = f(x)$.

Congruence closure alone will not work with a mix of interpreted and uninterpreted functions, since it will be unable to verify $x + y = z \vdash x = z - y$, for example. Let FALSE be an abbreviation for $0 = 1$, then the example

$$f(x - 1) - 1 = x + 1, \ f(y) + 1 = y - 1, \ y + 1 = x \vdash \text{FALSE},$$

contains the uninterpreted function f and interpreted operations $+$, $-$, and 1. Shostak's procedure can be used to decide the combination of a canonizable and solvable theory τ with that of equality over uninterpreted function symbols. The conditions of solvability and canonizability are quite technical and a detailed exposition appears elsewhere [RS01]. Roughly, a *canonizable* theory τ is one where there is a canonizer σ so that $\vdash_\tau a = b$ iff $\sigma(a) \equiv \sigma(b)$ for τ-terms a and b. A term a is in canonical form if $\sigma(a) = a$. The term $\sigma(a)$ must always be canonical as must all its subterms, and it must contain no variables that are not already in a. A σ-model is a model M where $M \models a = \sigma(a)$ for any τ-term a, and $M \not\models a = b$ for distinct, canonical, variable-free τ-terms a and b.

The theory τ is *solvable* if there is an operation *solve* such that for any equality $a = b$ between τ-terms, $solve(a = b)$ returns $\bot$ if $a = b$ is unsatisfiable in any σ-model, and otherwise, it returns a *solution* set of equalities S of the form $\{x_1 = t_1, \dots, x_n = t_n\}$ where each x_i must appear in $a = b$ and not in t_i nor in any other equality $x_j = t_j$ for $i \neq j$. The terms t_j must be canonical. The equality $a = b$ and the set S must be σ-equivalent in the sense that for any assignment ρ, ρ σ-satisfies $a = b$ iff it has some extension ρ' that σ-satisfies S. Note that S might contain variables that are not in $a = b$. Solution sets are essentially idempotent substitutions and can be applied to a term a as $S[a]$ and the composition of substitutions is represented as $S \circ S'$ while noting that the right-hand sides must be kept in σ-normal form.

For a sequent $T \vdash a = b$ containing only τ-terms from a canonizable and solvable theory τ, a decision procedure can be given as follows. Let T be of the form $c_1 = d_1, \dots, c_n = d_n$. A solution set is computed by the iteration given by

$$S_0 = \emptyset$$
$$S_{i+1} = S_i \circ solve(S_i[c_{i+1}] = S_i[d_{i+1}]),$$

where $S \circ S' = \bot$ if either $S = \bot$ or $S' = \bot$. The sequent is valid if either $S_n = \bot$ or $\sigma(S_n[a]) \equiv \sigma(S_n[b])$. Thus, an assignment ρ σ-satisfies $\bigwedge_{i=1}^{n} c_i = d_i$ iff it can be extended to a ρ' that σ-satisfies S_n. If $\sigma(S_n[a]) \equiv \sigma(S_n[b])$, then ρ' σ-satisfies

$a = S_n[a] = \sigma(S_n[a]) = \sigma(S_n[b]) = S_n[b] = b$. Otherwise, ρ σ-satisfies T but not $a = b$ and hence $T \vdash a = b$ is not valid.

The basic algorithm gets quite complicated when uninterpreted functions are introduced. A term $f(a_1, \ldots, a_n)$ is said to be uninterpreted if f is uninterpreted. The combined decision procedure must regard uninterpreted terms as variables when solving and canonizing, while identifying congruent uninterpreted terms using congruence closure. Given a solution set S, we define some basic operations. The operation $S\{a\} = \sigma(S[a])$, and $S\langle a\rangle$ returns $S(a)$ if a is a variable, $\sigma(f(S\langle a_1\rangle, \ldots S\langle a_n\rangle))$ if $a \equiv f(a_1, \ldots a_n)$ and f is interpreted, and $S(f(b_1, \ldots, b_n))$ if $a \equiv f(a_1, \ldots, a_n)$, $S(b_i) \equiv S\langle a_i\rangle$ for $0 < i \le n$, and $f(b_1, \ldots, b_n) \in dom(S)$. The set of subterms of an equality $a = b$ is written as $\lceil a = b \rceil$.

$$S_0 = \emptyset$$
$$S_{i+1} = cc(S'_i \circ R), \text{ where}$$
$$S'_i = S \cup \{e = e | e \in \lceil \hat{a}_{i+1} = \hat{b}_{i+1} \rceil - dom(S)\}$$
$$\hat{a}_{i+1} = S\langle a_{i+1}\rangle$$
$$\hat{b}_{i+1} = S\langle b_{i+1}\rangle$$
$$R = solve(\hat{a}_{i+1} = \hat{b}_{i+1})$$

The operation $cc(S)$ performs the congruence closure of S. In each iteration, it picks out a pair of left-hand sides $f(a_1, \ldots, a_n)$ and $f(b_1, \ldots, b_n)$ in S that are congruent with respect to S (f is uninterpreted and $S(a_i) \equiv S(b_i)$ for $0 < i \le n$), and merges the right-hand sides (when these are distinct) by solving and composing the solution. The *solve* and composition operations treat uninterpreted terms as variables. The soundness, completeness, termination, and complexity of the above procedure are discussed elsewhere [RS01].

Example 1. Consider $f(x - 1) - 1 = x + 1$, $f(y) + 1 = y - 1$, $y + 1 = x \vdash$ **FALSE** *from above. Starting with $S \equiv \emptyset$ in the base case, the preprocessing of $f(x - 1) - 1 = x + 1$ causes the equation to be placed into canonical form as $-1 + f(-1 + x) = 1 + x$ and S is set to*

$$\{1 = 1, -1 = -1, x = x, -1 + x = -1 + x,$$
$$f(-1 + x) = f(-1 + x), 1 + x = 1 + x\}.$$

Solving $-1 + f(-1 + x) = 1 + x$ yields $f(-1 + x) = 2 + x$, and S is set to

$$\{1 = 1, -1 = -1, x = x, -1 + x = -1 + x,$$
$$f(-1 + x) = 2 + x, 1 + x = 1 + x\}.$$

No unmerged congruences are detected. Next, $f(y) + 1 = y - 1$ is asserted. Its canonical form is $1 + f(y) = -1 + y$, and once this equality is asserted, the value of S is

$$\{1 = 1, -1 = -1, x = x, -1 + x = -1 + x,$$
$$f(-1 + x) = 2 + x, 1 + x = 1 + x, y = y,$$
$$f(y) = -2 + y, -1 + y = -1 + y, 1 + f(y) = -1 + y\}.$$

Next $y + 1 = x$ is processed. Its canonical form is $1 + y = x$ and the equality $1 + y = 1 + y$ is added to S. Solving $y + 1 = x$ yields $x = 1 + y$, and S is reset to

$$\{ 1 = 1, -1 = -1, x = 1 + y, -1 + x = y,$$
$$f(-1 + x) = 3 + y, 1 + x = 2 + y, y = y,$$
$$f(y) = -2 + y, -1 + y = -1 + y,$$
$$1 + f(y) = -1 + y, 1 + y = 1 + y \}.$$

The congruence close operation cc detects the congruence $f(1 - y) \overset{S}{\sim} f(x)$ and invokes merge on $3 + y$ and $-2 + y$. Solving this equality $3 + y = -2 + y$ yields $\perp$ returning the desired contradiction.

The ground decision procedures can be used in an incremental manner. Assertions can be added to update the context given by the state of the data structures used by decision procedures. Assertions can be tested for truth or falsity with respect to a given context. In PVS, ground decision procedures are used to build up a context associated with each sequent in a proof consisting of type information and the atomic formulas in the sequent. Many of the leaf nodes of a proof consist of sequents that have been verified by the ground decision procedures. These procedures are also used to simplify expressions using the contextual information given by the governing conditionals and type information from bound variables. The simplifier based on the decision procedures is used to automatically discharge proof obligations that arise in rewriting either through conditions of conditional rewrite rules or through subtype conditions on a matching substitution.

5   Finite-State Methods

Temporal properties of finite-state transition systems form an important decidable class that can be captured elegantly within higher-order logic. A transition system consists of a state type Σ, an initialization predicate I over Σ, and a transition relation N over $[\Sigma, \Sigma]$. Various predicate transformers can be defined as below.

- Pre-image: $pre(N)(p)(s_1) \equiv (\exists s_2 : N(s_1, s_2) \wedge p(s_2))$.
- Pre-condition: $\widetilde{pre}(N)(p)(s_1) \equiv (\forall s_2 : N(s_1, s_2) \supset p(s_2))$.
- Post-condition: $post(N)(p)(s_2) \equiv (\exists s_1 : N(s_1, s_2) \wedge p(s_1))$.

Operators like $pre(N)$, $\widetilde{pre}(N)$, and $post(N)$ are examples of *monotone* predicate transformers, i.e., maps T on $[\Sigma \rightarrow \mathbf{bool}]$ such that

$$p_1 \sqsubseteq p_2 \supset T[p_1] \sqsubseteq T[p_2],$$

where $p_1 \sqsubseteq p_2 \equiv (\forall s : p_1(s) \supset p_2(s))$.

A fixed point of a predicate transformer T is a predicate p such that $p = T[p]$. When T is a monotone predicate transformer, the Tarski-Knaster theorem [Tar55] guarantees the existence of least and greatest fixed points. The least fixed point of a monotone predicate T is written as $\mu X : T[X]$ and can be defined as the greatest lower bound of the predicates X such that $T[X] \sqsubseteq X$, i.e., $\bigcap\{X | T[X] \sqsubseteq X\}$. The greatest fixed point of T is written as $\nu X : T[X]$ and can be defined as the least upper bound of the predicates X such that $X \sqsubseteq T[X]$, i.e., $\bigcup\{X | X \sqsubseteq T[X]\}$.

The temporal connectives of CTL can be defined using the fixed point operators over suitable predicate transformers. For example, the equality

$$[\![\mathbf{A}(B \ \mathbf{U} \ C)]\!](s) = (\mu X : C \vee (B \wedge \widetilde{pre}(N)(X)))(s)$$

holds because the right-hand side is satisfied by exactly those states s that can always reach a state satisfying C along a finite computation path of states satisfying B. The predicate characterizing the reachable states of a transition system K of the form $\langle \Sigma, I, N \rangle$ can be defined as

$$\mu X : I \vee post(N)(X).$$

It is possible to develop the fixed point characterization of the temporal operators in two directions. In one direction, the proof theory of these operators can be derived from the fixed point definitions. In the second direction, automated procedures called model checkers can be developed for verifying temporal properties of transition systems over finite types Σ. The higher-order logic characterization above can be used for both purposes without any change. Thus, model checking and deductive methods are merely different but compatible verification techniques.

The higher-order logic formalization of transition systems and their properties can be used in two ways in model checking. In the symbolic model checking approach, the fixed point iteration is carried out by binary-coding the state so that a truth-value assignment represents a state. The initialization predicate, the transition relation, and temporal properties then become boolean functions. The fixed point iterations can be carried out over some boolean function representation such as reduced, ordered, binary decision diagrams (ROBDD). Another approach, that of bounded model checking, is carried out by encoding the search for a bounded length counterexample to a property as a boolean satisfiability problem. PVS employs an ROBDD-based symbolic model checker [BRB90,BCM+92,Jan93] as a decision procedure for the finite mu-calculus.

The integration of model checking and deductive methods is not all that straightforward. The decision procedures from Section 4 can often be used to automatically discharge the subgoals that arise in an interactive proof, but few of the subgoals in a deductive verification would directly succumb to model checking. Transition system properties can sometimes be verified by building finite-state abstractions that are amenable to model checking. Even when such a finite-state abstraction is not immediately verified by model checking, it is possible to extract useful intermediate properties.

Deductive methods have difficulties with control-intensive systems where abstraction and model checking are quite successful. Invariants are properties of transition systems that are satisfied in all reachable states. Deduction requires an inductive invariant that is preserved by each transition. Finding inductive invariants is not easy. Model checking can restrict its exploration to the reachable states and thus avoids constructing inductive invariants. Abstraction is a useful way of decomposing the verification task between deductive and explorative methods. An abstraction mapping indicates how the concrete state is mapped to a finite state. In the case of predicate abstraction, the abstract state contains booleans that capture predicates on the concrete state. An abstract model approximating the behavior of the concrete transition system can be constructed by using a theorem prover to eliminate abstract transitions that have no concrete counterpart. Then the reachable states of the resulting abstract transition system can be used to construct a valid invariant for the concrete transition system.

Ground decision procedures play a crucial role in the construction of an abstract transition system from a concrete one based on a given abstraction map. This construction involves a large number of small-sized proof obligations that are mostly dischargeable using decision procedures.

Predicate abstraction was first used by Graf and Saïdi [SG97] to construct the abstract reachability graph of a transition system with respect to an abstraction map. The InVest system [BLO98] uses the elimination method mentioned above to construct abstractions of transition systems described in a fragment of PVS. An abstraction capability for the mu-calculus has been added to PVS in order to abstract transition systems along with their temporal properties [SS99,Sha01].

6 Discussion

We have barely scratched the surface of the kinds of problems that can be naturally expressed and effectively automated using higher-order logics. As a pragmatic point, we have argued that higher-order logic provides a good balance between expressiveness and automation by embedding useful formalisms for which there is good automation support. Most of these problems can already be expressed in second-order or third-order logic, but the full range of finite-order types adds very little complexity. The directness with which these logics can be embedded in higher-order logic allows the decision procedures to be used without having to span the semantic gap between diverse logics.

We have shown a few ways in which decision procedures interact synergistically with higher-order logic. They can be used to add expressivity to the type system through predicate subtypes and dependent types. Static analysis can be applied to higher-order programs to infer safe destructive array updates. The resulting optimized programs can be executed with efficiencies that are comparable with implementations in low-level imperative programming languages. Fixed point calculi can be embedded in higher-order logic. A number of temporal logics can be defined using the fixed point operators. The finite-state version of the fixed point calculus can be decided using a BDD-based symbolic model checker. Ground decision procedures can be used to construct finite-state abstractions from large or infinite-state transition systems. Decidable fragments of higher-order logic can be used to verify properties of parametric systems.

The synergy between expressiveness and automation can be further explored along a number of lines. We have examined evaluation in a functional sublanguage of higher-order logic. A number of high-level optimizations can be explored in the context of a theorem proving environment. It is also possible to embed programming vernaculars such as logic programming [Sym98] and imperative programming. Higher-order logic programming with the use of higher-order syntactic encoding has emerged as an important medium for metaprogramming [NM90]. A number of useful decision procedures from computer algebra, operations research, and engineering, can also be usefully incorporated into a theorem proving environment. Drawing inspiration from the work of Boyer and Moore [BM81], a metaprogramming capability can be used to reflectively develop a theorem proving system within itself in a bootstrapped manner.

Proof search is an area where PVS is currently inadequate. First-order proof search methods have been successfully used in Isabelle [Pau98]. Proof search methods within the full higher-order logic have had some selective successes [AINP88,BK98], but quantifier-elimination methods and proof search methods for limited fragments are more likely to yield profitable results in the short run.

The entire enterprise of theorem proving in higher-order logics is poised at an interesting confluence between expressiveness and automation, principle and pragmatism, and theory and practice. Significant breakthroughs can be anticipated if we see synergies rather than conflict in this confluence.

Acknowledgments

I thank the TPHOLS'01 conference chair Richard Boulton, the programme chair Paul Jackson, and the programme committee, for their kind invitation. I am also grateful to the TPHOLS community for stimulus and inspiration. Michael Kohlhase was generous with his insights on higher-order proof search. Paul Jackson gave me detailed and helpful comments on an earlier draft, as did Sam Owre and John Rushby. The ideas and results presented here are the fruits of collaborations with several people including Sam Owre, John Rushby, Sree Rajan, Harald Rueß, Hassen Saïdi, and Mandayam Srivas.

References

AINP88.   Peter B. Andrews, Sunil Issar, Daniel Nesmith, and Frank Pfenning. The TPS theorem proving system. In E. Lusk and R. Overbeek, editors, *9th International Conference on Automated Deduction (CADE)*, volume 310 of *Lecture Notes in Computer Science*, pages 760–761, Argonne, IL, May 1988. Springer-Verlag.

And86.   Peter B. Andrews. *An Introduction to Logic and Type Theory: To Truth through Proof.* Academic Press, New York, NY, 1986.

BCM$^+$92.   J. R. Burch, E. M. Clarke, K. L. McMillan, D. L. Dill, and L. J. Hwang. Symbolic model checking: 10^{20} states and beyond. *Information and Computation*, 98(2):142–170, June 1992.

BK98.   Christoph Benzmüller and Michael Kohlhase. Extensional higher-order resolution. In H. Kirchner and C. Kirchner, editors, *Proceedings of CADE-15*, number 1421 in Lecture Notes in Artificial Intelligence, pages 56–71, Berlin, Germany, July 1998. Springer-Verlag.

BLO98.   Saddek Bensalem, Yassine Lakhnech, and Sam Owre. Computing abstractions of infinite state systems compositionally and automatically. In Hu and Vardi [HV98], pages 319–331.

BM81.   R. S. Boyer and J S. Moore. Metafunctions: Proving them correct and using them efficiently as new proof procedures. In R. S. Boyer and J S. Moore, editors, *The Correctness Problem in Computer Science*. Academic Press, London, 1981.

BM86.   R. S. Boyer and J S. Moore. Integrating decision procedures into heuristic theorem provers: A case study with linear arithmetic. In *Machine Intelligence*, volume 11. Oxford University Press, 1986.

Bou93.   R. J. Boulton. Lazy techniques for fully expansive theorem proving. *Formal Methods in System Design*, 3(1/2):25–47, August 1993.

BRB90.   K. S. Brace, R. L. Rudell, and R. E. Bryant. Efficient implementation of a BDD package. In *Proc. of the 27th ACM/IEEE Design Automation Conference*, pages 40–45, 1990.

Bun83.   Alan Bundy. *The Computer Modelling of Mathematical Reasoning.* Academic Press, London, UK, 1983.

But97.   Bettina Buth. PAMELA + PVS. In Michael Johnson, editor, *Algebraic Methodology and Software Technology, AMAST'97*, volume 1349 of *Lecture Notes in Computer Science*, pages 560–562, Sydney, Australia, December 1997. Springer-Verlag.

CAB$^+$86.   R. L. Constable, S. F. Allen, H. M. Bromley, W. R. Cleaveland, J. F. Cremer, R. W. Harper, D. J. Howe, T. B. Knoblock, N. P. Mendler, P. Panangaden, J. T. Sasaki, and S. F. Smith. *Implementing Mathematics with the Nuprl Proof Development System.* Prentice Hall, Englewood Cliffs, NJ, 1986.

CDC80.   Mario Coppo and Mariangiola Dezani-Ciancaglini. An extension of the basic functionality theory for the lambda-calculus. *Notre Dame J. Formal Logic*, 21(4):685–693, 1980.

CH85.   T. Coquand and G. P. Huet. Constructions: A higher order proof system for mechanizing mathematics. In *Proceedings of EUROCAL 85, Linz (Austria)*, Berlin, 1985. Springer-Verlag.

Chu40.   A. Church. A formulation of the simple theory of types. *Journal of Symbolic Logic*, 5:56–68, 1940.

dB80.   N. G. de Bruijn. A survey of the project Automath. In *To H. B. Curry: Essays on Combinatory Logic, Lambda Calculus and Formalism*, pages 589–606. Academic Press, 1980.

DCN⁺00.   Louise A. Dennis, Graham Collins, Michael Norrish, Richard Boulton, Konrad Slind, Graham Robinson, Mike Gordon, and Tom Melham. The PROSPER toolkit. In Susanne Graf and Michael Schwartzbach, editors, *Tools and Algorithms for the Construction and Analysis of Systems (TACAS 2000)*, number 1785 in Lecture Notes in Computer Science, pages 78–92, Berlin, Germany, March 2000. Springer-Verlag.

DFH⁺91.   Gilles Dowek, Amy Felty, Hugo Herbelin, Gérard Huet, Christine Paulin-Mohring, and Benjamin Werner. The COQ proof assistant user's guide: Version 5.6. Rapports Techniques 134, INRIA, Rocquencourt, France, December 1991.

DKML99.   Martin Dunstan, Tom Kelsey, Ursula Martin, and Steve Linton. Formal methods for extensions to CAS. In Jeannette Wing and Jim Woodcock, editors, *FM99: The World Congress in Formal Methods*, volume 1708 and 1709 of *Lecture Notes in Computer Science*, pages 1758–1777, Toulouse, France, September 1999. Springer-Verlag. Pages 1–938 are in the first volume, 939–1872 in the second.

DP93.   M. Draghicescu and S. Purushothaman. A uniform treatment of order of evaluation and aggregate update. *Theoretical Computer Science*, 118(2):231–262, September 1993.

DST80.   P.J. Downey, R. Sethi, and R.E. Tarjan. Variations on the common subexpressions problem. *Journal of the ACM*, 27(4):758–771, 1980.

Fef78.   Solomon Feferman. Theories of finite type related to mathematical practice. In Jon Barwise, editor, *Handbook of Mathematical Logic*, volume 90 of *Studies in Logic and the Foundations of Mathematics*, chapter D4, pages 913–972. North-Holland, Amsterdam, Holland, 1978.

FORS01.   J-C. Filliâtre, S. Owre, H. Rueß, and N. Shankar. ICS: Integrated canonizer and solver. In *CAV 01: Computer-Aided Verification*. Springer-Verlag, 2001. To appear.

GM93.   M. J. C. Gordon and T. F. Melham, editors. *Introduction to HOL: A Theorem Proving Environment for Higher-Order Logic*. Cambridge University Press, Cambridge, UK, 1993.

GMW79.   M. Gordon, R. Milner, and C. Wadsworth. *Edinburgh LCF: A Mechanized Logic of Computation*, volume 78 of *Lecture Notes in Computer Science*. Springer-Verlag, 1979.

Gor88.   M. J. C. Gordon. Mechanizing programming logics in higher order logic. Technical Report CCSRC-006, Cambridge Computer Science Research Center, SRI International, Cambridge, England, September 1988.

Har96.   John Harrison. Stålmarck's algorithm as a HOL derived rule. In J. von Wright, J. Grundy, and J. Harrison, editors, *Proceedings of the 9th TPHOLS*, number 1125 in Lecture Notes in Computer Science, pages 251–266, Berlin, Germany, 1996. Springer-Verlag.

Hat68.   William S. Hatcher. *Foundations of Mathematics*. W. B. Saunders Company, Philadelphia, PA, 1968.

HD92.   F. K. Hanna and N. Daeche. Dependent types and formal synthesis. In C. A. R. Hoare and M. J. C. Gordon, editors, *Mechanized Reasoning and Hardware Design*, pages 121–135, Hemel Hempstead, UK, 1992. Prentice Hall International Series in Computer Science.

HV98.   Alan J. Hu and Moshe Y. Vardi, editors. *Computer-Aided Verification, CAV '98*, volume 1427 of *Lecture Notes in Computer Science*, Vancouver, Canada, June 1998. Springer-Verlag.

HWG98.   David Hardin, Matthew Wilding, and David Greve. Transforming the theorem prover into a digital design tool: From concept car to off-road vehicle. In Hu and Vardi [HV98], pages 39–44.

Jan93.   G. L. J. M. Janssen. *ROBDD Software*. Department of Electrical Engineering, Eindhoven University of Technology, October 1993.

JvdBH+98.   Bart Jacobs, Joachim van den Berg, Marieke Huisman, Martijn van Berkum, Ulrich Hensel, and Hendrick Tews. Reasoning about Java classes. In *Proceedings, Object-Oriented Programming Systems, Languages and Applications (OOPSLA'98)*, pages 329–340, Vancouver, Canada, October 1998. Association for Computing Machinery. Proceedings issued as ACM SIGPLAN Notices Vol. 33, No. 10, October 1998.

Koz77.   D. Kozen. Complexity of finitely represented algebras. In *Proc. 9th ACM STOC*, pages 164–177, 1977.

Lei94.   Daniel Leivant. Higher order logic. In D. M. Gabbay, C. J. Hogger, and J. A. Robinson, editors, *Handbook of Logic in Artificial Intelligence and Logic Programming, Volume 2: Deduction Methodologies*, pages 229–321. Clarendon Press, Oxford, 1994.

NL00.   George C. Necula and Peter Lee. Proof generation in the touchstone theorem prover. In David McAllester, editor, *Automated Deduction—CADE-17*, volume 1831 of *Lecture Notes in Artificial Intelligence*, pages 25–44, Pittsburgh, PA, June 2000. Springer-Verlag.

NM90.   G. Nadathur and D. Miller. Higher-order Horn clauses. *Journal of the ACM*, 37(4):777–814, 1990.

NO79.   G. Nelson and D. C. Oppen. Simplification by cooperating decision procedures. *ACM Transactions on Programming Languages and Systems*, 1(2):245–257, 1979.

NO80.   G. Nelson and D. C. Oppen. Fast decision procedures based on congruence closure. *Journal of the ACM*, 27(2):356–364, 1980.

ORS92.   S. Owre, J. M. Rushby, and N. Shankar. PVS: A prototype verification system. In Deepak Kapur, editor, *11th International Conference on Automated Deduction (CADE)*, volume 607 of *Lecture Notes in Artificial Intelligence*, pages 748–752, Saratoga, NY, June 1992. Springer-Verlag.

ORSvH95.   Sam Owre, John Rushby, Natarajan Shankar, and Friedrich von Henke. Formal verification for fault-tolerant architectures: Prolegomena to the design of PVS. *IEEE Transactions on Software Engineering*, 21(2):107–125, February 1995.

OS97.   Sam Owre and Natarajan Shankar. The formal semantics of PVS. Technical Report SRI-CSL-97-2, Computer Science Laboratory, SRI International, Menlo Park, CA, August 1997.

Pau94.   Lawrence C. Paulson. *Isabelle: A Generic Theorem Prover*, volume 828 of *Lecture Notes in Computer Science*. Springer-Verlag, 1994.

Pau98.   L. Paulson. The inductive approach to verifying cryptographic protocols. *Journal of Computer Security*, 6(1):85–128, 1998.

Ram90.   F. P. Ramsey. The foundations of mathematics. In D. H. Mellor, editor, *Philosophical Papers of F. P. Ramsey*, chapter 8, pages 164–224. Cambridge University Press, Cambridge, UK, 1990. Originally published in *Proceedings of the London Mathematical Society*, 25, pp. 338–384, 1925.

ROS98.   John Rushby, Sam Owre, and N. Shankar. Subtypes for specifications: Predicate subtyping in PVS. *IEEE Transactions on Software Engineering*, 24(9):709–720, September 1998.

RS01.   Harald Rueß and Natarajan Shankar. Deconstructing Shostak. In *Proceedings 16th Annual IEEE Symp. on Logic in Computer Science*, pages 19–28. IEEE Computer Society Press, 2001.

RvHO91.   John Rushby, Friedrich von Henke, and Sam Owre. An introduction to formal specification and verification using EHDM. Technical Report SRI-CSL-91-2, Computer Science Laboratory, SRI International, Menlo Park, CA, February 1991.

SG97.   Hassen Saïdi and Susanne Graf. Construction of abstract state graphs with PVS. In Orna Grumberg, editor, *Computer-Aided Verification, CAV '97*, volume 1254 of *Lecture Notes in Computer Science*, pages 72–83, Haifa, Israel, June 1997. Springer-Verlag.

Sha99.   N. Shankar. Efficiently executing PVS. Project report, Computer Science Laboratory, SRI International, Menlo Park, CA, November 1999. Available at http://www.csl.sri.com/shankar/PVSeval.ps.gz.

Sha01.   Natarajan Shankar. Automated verification using deduction, exploration, and abstraction. In *Essays on Programming Methodology*. Springer-Verlag, 2001. To appear.

Sho78.   R. Shostak. An algorithm for reasoning about equality. *Comm. ACM*, 21:583–585, July 1978.

Sho84.   R. E. Shostak. Deciding combinations of theories. *Journal of the ACM*, 31(1):1–12, 1984.

SS99.   Hassen Saïdi and N. Shankar. Abstract and model check while you prove. In Nicolas Halbwachs and Doron Peled, editors, *Computer-Aided Verification, CAV '99*, volume 1633 of *Lecture Notes in Computer Science*, pages 443–454, Trento, Italy, July 1999. Springer-Verlag.

Sym98.   D. Syme. *Declarative Theorem Proving for Operational Semantics*. PhD thesis, University of Cambridge, 1998.

Tar55.   A. Tarski. A lattice-theoretical fixpoint theorem and its applications. *Pacific J. of Math.*, 5:285–309, 1955.

Thé98.   Laurent Théry. A certified version of Buchberger's algorithm. In H. Kirchner and C. Kirchner, editors, *Proceedings of CADE-15*, number 1421 in Lecture Notes in Artificial Intelligence, pages 349–364, Berlin, Germany, July 1998. Springer-Verlag.

vBD83.   Johan van Benthem and Kees Doets. Higher-order logic. In Dov M. Gabbay and Franz Guenthner, editors, *Handbook of Philosophical Logic-Volume I: Elements of Classical Logic*, volume 164 of *Synthese Library*, chapter I.4, pages 275–329. D. Reidel Publishing Company, Dordrecht, Holland, 1983.

vHCL⁺88.   F. W. von Henke, J. S. Crow, R. Lee, J. M. Rushby, and R. A. Whitehurst. The EHDM verification environment: An overview. In *Proceedings 11th National Computer Security Conference*, pages 147–155, Baltimore, MD, October 1988. NBS/NCSC.

WC98.   Mitchell Wand and William D. Clinger. Set constraints for destructive array update optimization. In *Proc. IEEE Conf. on Computer Languages '98*, pages 184–193. IEEE, April 1998.

WR27.   A. N. Whitehead and B. Russell. *Principia Mathematica*. Cambridge University Press, Cambridge, revised edition, 1925–1927. Three volumes. The first edition was published 1910–1913.

Computer Algebra Meets Automated Theorem Proving: Integrating Maple and PVS

Andrew Adams[1], Martin Dunstan[2], Hanne Gottliebsen[3], Tom Kelsey[3],
Ursula Martin[3], and Sam Owre[4]

[1] School of CS, Cyb and EE, University of Reading
Reading RG6 6AY, UK
[2] NAG LTD, Wilkinson House, Jordan Hill Road
Oxford OX2 8DR, UK
[3] School of Computer Science, University of St. Andrews
St Andrews KY16 9SS, UK
[4] Computer Science Laboratory, SRI International
333 Ravenswood Avenue, Menlo Park CA 94025, USA

Abstract. We describe an interface between version 6 of the Maple computer algebra system with the PVS automated theorem prover. The interface is designed to allow Maple users access to the robust and checkable proof environment of PVS. We also extend this environment by the provision of a library of proof strategies for use in real analysis. We demonstrate examples using the interface and the real analysis library. These examples provide proofs which are both illustrative and applicable to genuine symbolic computation problems.

1 Introduction

In this paper we describe an interface between version 6 of the Maple computer algebra system, henceforth CAS, and the PVS automated theorem prover, ATP. CAS like Maple (which has 1 million users, mostly in the educational sector) incorporate a wide variety of symbolic techniques, for example for factoring polynomials or computing Gröbner bases, and increasingly some numerical elements also. They provide a mathematical programming environment and facilities such as graphics and document generation. They have enjoyed some outstanding successes: for example 't Hooft and Veltman received the 1999 Nobel Prize in Physics, Veltman for using computer algebra to verify 't Hooft's results on quantum field theory. The advantages of combining symbolic/numeric computation with logical reasoning are evident: improved inference capability and increased expressivity. A human performing symbolic mathematics by hand will make automatic use of the logical framework upon which the mathematics is based. A human performing similar calculations using a CAS has to supply the same logical framework; there is, in general, no sound reasoning system built in to the CAS. Our objective is to provide the CAS user with an interface to an ATP, so that certain side conditions which are implicit in many analytic symbolic computations can be highlighted, checked, and either verified or flagged as an error. The user interacts with the CAS, making calls to the ATP system which acts as a black box for the provision of formal proofs.

R.J. Boulton and P.B. Jackson (Eds.): TPHOLs 2001, LNCS 2152, pp. 27–42, 2001.
© Springer-Verlag Berlin Heidelberg 2001

While there have been many projects aimed at combining the calculation power of CAS with the logical power of ATP systems, the basic approach is always from the point of view of a user interested in completely correct developments. That is, the point of view of a theorem proving user who wishes to have powerful calculation available to generate existential witnesses or factorisations. Our approach takes the view point of a user of a CAS who simply wishes it to be more robust. Current users of CAS, while not pleased when incorrect results are generated, are nevertheless willing to accept a certain level of deficiency as a trade-off for the utility of the system. We aim to improve the existing support for users of CAS by adding to the correctness in an incremental way, with a black box ATP system supporting better computer algebra calculation. The work described in this paper is another step toward this goal, though much remains to be done, both in terms of developing the formalisations needed in ATP systems and in re-engineering the algorithms implemented in CAS to take advantage of the black box without losing the speed and power of existing CAS implementations.

The aims of this paper are (i) to describe the design and implementation of the interface (Section 3), and (ii) to illustrate its power by describing the automated verification of properties needed to ensure correctness of routines for differential equations in Maple (Section 4). The remainder of this introduction provides motivating examples, and briefly describe the systems involved and the background to the project. In Section 2 we discuss the extension to PVS which allows automated proofs of side conditions, continuity and convergence for elementary functions with parameters. One use of the interface is the checking of the validity of input to certain Maple procedures. For example, when solving a differential equation, one must ensure that the input function $f(x, y)$ is continuous (and thus defined) on the required region. This is not done by Maple, and so Maple might return an answer that looks like a plausible solution even if the input is not of the right form. However, using the interface one can verify the continuity of $f(x, y)$. Although our current PVS implementation of continuity checking relies on a fairly simple method for verifying continuity, it does handle a large class of functions well.

1.1 Motivating Examples

In this section we show that CAS output can be misleading or incorrect. A typical CAS will have no general mechanism for checking that results are mathematically correct. Hence errors can arise in the determination of equality of two expressions, or in the definedness of expressions with respect to symbolic parameters. By not formally checking each result, CAS output can propagate errors throughout a complicated symbolic calculation, and hence produce invalid results. The following examples illustrate typical problems which can occur.

Simplification. The expression $\sqrt{x^2}$ will not automatically simplify to x in a CAS, since this is incorrect for negative x. Maple provides a mechanism for assuming that variables (and functions) have properties such as negativity (or differentiability), but the system can still fail to simplify expressions containing square roots correctly. To see this, consider the expressions $a = |x - y|$ and

$b = |\sqrt{x} + \sqrt{y}||\sqrt{x} - \sqrt{y}|$, where x and y are positive reals. Suppose a Maple user wishes to verify that $a = b$. The commands available are

```
> a := abs(x-y);
```

$$a := |x - y|$$

```
> b := abs(sqrt(x)+sqrt(y))*abs(sqrt(x)-sqrt(y));
```

$$b := |\sqrt{x} + \sqrt{y}| \, |\sqrt{x} - \sqrt{y}|$$

```
> assume(x > 0): assume(y > 0):
> verify(a,b);
```

$$false$$

```
> verify(a,b,equal);
```

$$FAIL$$

Note that issuing a command `assume (y > 0)` binds all future occurrences in this Maple session of the parameter y to be positive unless a new assumption about y is issued. However, not all algorithms will check the assumption database for information about the parameters included in their arguments. It is evident that there is a problem with the robustness of the Maple `verify` command: `verify(a,b)` returns `false` for this example; the heuristic simplification techniques used to reduce $a - b$ to zero are inadequate. `verify(a,b,equal)` uses a more sophisticated set of heuristic techniques, but still fails to provide the expected result, namely `true`. Hence, for this example, the output from Maple is either an admission of failure or misleading to the user.

Definedness and Parameters. Consider the definite integral

$$\int_0^b \frac{1}{x - a} dx \tag{1}$$

where a and b are positive real parameters. Maple returns the solution $\log(b - a) - \log(a) - i\pi$, which, when $a = 1$ and $b = 2$, reduces to $-i\pi$ which is a complex number, and hence incorrect. Maple does not check that the function is defined everywhere in the interval of integration; in this case that a is not in $(0, b)$.

Continuity Checking. Maple has an inbuilt procedure for checking properties of functions and expressions. This procedure does not always return correct results:

```
> is(x -> (1/x)+1-(1/x),continuous);
```

$$false$$

Even the assumption of positive arguments does not solve the problem:

```
> assume(y > 0):
> is(y -> (1/y)+1-(1/y),continuous);
```

$$false$$

The Maple/PVS interface described in this paper is designed to address the problem of the lack of verification of CAS results. The Maple user works in the usual Maple environment, and has access to a formal, checkable proof mechanism which has been extended to deal with properties of real valued expressions involving parameters, such as those given in the above examples. In Section 4.1 we use the Maple/PVS interface to prove that

$$|x - y| = |\sqrt{x} + \sqrt{y}||\sqrt{x} - \sqrt{y}| \quad \text{for} \quad x, y > 0 \tag{2}$$

and that

$$b > a > 0 \implies \exists x \in (0, b) \quad \text{such that} \quad x \notin \mathbb{R} \setminus \{a\} . \tag{3}$$

These proofs allow the user to correct, modify or disregard the incorrect results from Maple.

1.2 Background

Previous approaches to the combination of CAS and ATP are discussed and classified in [8]. We mention selected examples which are direct or indirect predecessors to this work. All approaches share the common problem of communicating mathematical information between the CAS and ATP systems. One solution is to define a standard for mathematical information that can, in principle, be understood by any mathematical computation system. Examples of this common knowledge approach include the OpenMath project [1,11], and protocols for the exchange of information between generic CAS and ATP systems [5,15]. Another solution is the sub-package approach, in which communication issues are side-stepped by building an ATP within a CAS. Examples include Analytica [4], REDLOG [12], the Theorema project [6,7], and a logical extension to the type system of the AXIOM CAS [18,25]. The third common approach involves the choice of preferred CAS and ATP environments, and the construction of a specific interface for communication between them. Examples include Maple-HOL [16], Maple-Isabelle [3], and Weyl-NuPrl [17].

The common-knowledge approach depends on wholesale acceptance of the protocols by both the CAS and ATP communities. Since this has not yet happened, we concentrate on the remaining two approaches. The sub-package approach has the advantage that communication is easy, and the disadvantage that implementation of an ATP in a language designed for symbolic/numeric computation can be hard. In particular, there may be problems with misleading or incorrect output from CAS routines, which adversely affect the soundness of the proof system. For example, the simplification error described in Section 1.1 could lead to an undetected division by zero, which could propagate logical errors.

The specific interface approach has the advantage that the target CAS and ATP are implemented and developed by experts in the respective technologies, and the disadvantage that communication problems remain. Another issue is the relationship between the systems. In the examples mentioned above, the primary system in use was the ATP, and the CAS was used as an oracle to provide calculation steps. By contrast the motivation for our work is to support the users of computer algebra systems in their work by giving them the opportunity to use the rigour of theorem prover when they wish, completely automatically in some cases. This has the advantage that users can use all the facilities of the

CAS, but the theorem prover implementation can be restricted. Since Maple is a programming language calls to a prover can be embedded in procedures and made invisible to the user.

The objective of this project is to develop a specific interface which links the major commercial CAS Maple [19] to the widely used ATP PVS [21] in a way which minimises the inherent problems of linking two unrelated systems. We also utilise recent extensions to PVS [14,2] which allow reasoning in the theory of real analysis, so that properties of symbolic expressions can be described and checked. The project is in approach similar to the PROSPER toolkit [10], which allows systems designers using CAD and CASE tools access to mechanised verification. The PROSPER paradigm involves the CAD/CASE system as the master, with a slave proof engine running in the background. We have also adopted the PROSPER architectural format: a core proof engine which is integrated with a non-formal system via a script interface. Our target, however, is the engineering/scientific/mathematical community of CAS users.

1.3   Maple

Maple [9] is a commercial CAS, consisting of a kernel library of numeric, symbolic and graphics routines, together with packages aimed at specific areas such as linear algebra and differential equations.

The key feature of version 6 of Maple is that it was designed to run a subset of the NAG numerics library. We utilise this ability to extend Maple by running PVS as a subprocess.

1.4   PVS

PVS [23] supports formal specification and verification and consists of a specification language, various predefined theories and a theorem prover which supports a high level of automation. The specification language is based on classical, typed higher-order logic and supports predicate and dependent sub-typing.

PVS is normally run using Gnu or X emacs for its interface, but can also be run in batch mode or from a terminal interface. However, running PVS via emacs provides many useful features such as abbreviations for prover commands and graphical representations of proofs and library structures. The core of PVS is implemented in Allegro Common Lisp.

1.5   Design Issues

The overall view of our system is one in which the user interacts with the CAS, posing questions and performing computations. Some of these computations may require ATP technology, either to obtain a solution or to validate answers obtained by existing computer algebra algorithms. In such cases the CAS will present the theorem prover with a number of lemmas and request it to make some proof attempts. The results of these attempts, whether successful or otherwise, will guide the rest of the computation within the CAS: the theorem prover acts as a slave to the CAS.

The system has a tightly coupled architecture. In such a system, the theorem prover shares the same resources as the computer algebra system and is directly controlled by it.

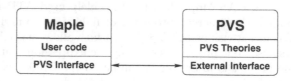

Fig. 1. Tightly Coupled System.

2   The PVS Real Analysis Library

Our goal is to provide automatic support for reasoning about real valued CAS expressions. The basic PVS libraries are insufficient for proving properties such as continuity or convergence of functions. It was therefore necessary to extend PVS with (i) libraries of real analysis definitions and lemmas, and (ii) specialist proof strategies.

A description of a PVS library of transcendental functions was provided in [14]. The library can be used to check continuity of functions such as

$$e^{x^2+|1-x|} \ . \tag{4}$$

The library is based on Dutertre's real analysis library [13] and contains a development of power series, which is used to describe and reason about functions such as *exp*, *cos*, *sin* and *tan* and their inverses. The library also contains a large set of lemmas about properties of these functions as provided by mathematics textbooks.

A particular focus of this library is supporting automation. There are two ways of automating proofs in theorem provers: writing purpose-built strategies; or using pre-defined widely applicable strategies. The latter method (such as `blast-tac` in Isabelle [24] or `grind` in PVS) is the one we have primarily used, although we have also written some special purpose strategies. Application of the PVS generic tactic `grind` can be quite difficult. In order to improve the performance of `grind` (both in terms of speed of proof and in the number of conjectures it will prove automatically) we have introduced various type judgements [22] into our development. These judgements allow grind to apply generic theorems to our specific tasks, effectively by giving hints to the matching algorithm searching for appropriate theorems in the development.

The method used for *continuity checking* is what one might call the High School method. It is based on the theorems that the constant functions and the identity function are continuous everywhere, and that well-founded combinations using the following operators are also continuous: addition, subtraction, multiplication, division, absolute value and function composition. Also, the functions *exp*, *cos*, *sin* and *tan* are continuous everywhere in their domains,[1] which means that we can prove that functions such as (4) are continuous on the whole of their domain. The continuity checker is invoked by using the strategy `cts`, which performs all the necessary theory instantiations.

Since [14] some changes have been made to the basic analysis library as some definitions were discovered to be unsuitable. This particularly concerns the definition of convergence of functions. Dutertre's definition of convergence was unusual in that it coincided with the definition of continuity. This is seen by the "theorem" in Dutetre's development:

```
continuity_def2 : THEOREM
    continuous(f, x0) IFF convergent(f, x0) .
```

We changed the definition of convergence of functions to the more usual one, so that the above is no longer a theorem, and also made other necessary changes to the rest of the theory.

As well as changes to the underlying theories we have extended the implementation of the continuity checker. In particular, it is now possible to check functions such as $1/(cos(x)+2)$ for continuity. This has been implemented using judgements to assert that *cos* and *sin* are always within $[-1; 1]$ and that adding (or subtracting) something strictly greater that 1 will return a non-zero real value.

As well as a continuity checker we now have a convergence checker; this will check if a certain function has a limit at some point (or indeed everywhere in its domain). We can prove, for example, that the function

$$-\pi - 1 + \pi * e^{1-cos(x)} \tag{5}$$

has a limit at the point

$$arccos(1 - log(\frac{1+\pi}{\pi})) . \tag{6}$$

The convergence checker is implemented in the strategy `conv-check`, and it works in the same syntax directed way as the continuity checker, and so has similar capabilities and limitations.

3 Implementation

In this section we describe the work undertaken to develop our Maple/PVS system. We have created a tightly coupled system under UNIX with PVS being controlled by Maple as if it was a "normal" user. That is, PVS believes that it is interacting with someone entering commands from a terminal rather than, for example, a pipe to another program.

---

[1] Note that the domain of tan excludes all points with value of the form $(2n + 1)\pi/2$ and that it is continuous everywhere else.

3.1   Extending Maple

Although Maple provides its own programming language, it was necessary to make use of the Maple interface to external functions written in C. By writing a small amount of "glue" in C to handle the creation and management of new processes, low-level PVS interactions and other support facilities, we are able to present a simplified PVS interface to users of the Maple language.

An example of the Maple code that we use to import C functions is:

```
PvsSend:= define_external(
    'pvsSend',
        handle :: integer[4],
        message :: string[],
        RETURN :: boolean[4],
        LIB = "maple_pvslib.so"
);
```

Here the C function `long pvsSend(long handle, char *message)` is imported into Maple as an external procedure called `PvsSend`. The compiled C for `pvsSend` is stored in the shared object called `maple_pvslib.so`.

Only seven of our C functions are imported into Maple in this way and provide a basic low-level interface to PVS. Built on top of these are a number of higher-level functions written in the Maple language. For example, the Maple function used to start a PVS session with a particular context is:

```
PvsStart := proc(dir::string)
    # Start PVS using imported C function
    pvs := PvsBegin();

    # Send data to PVS via imported C function
    PvsSend("(change-context \"" || dir || "\")");

    # Wait for prompt using another imported C function
    PvsWaitForPrompt(pvs);

    pvs;
end proc
```

These Maple procedures are supplied as a module, which allows users to import them as a library package. The library must be added to Maple by each user before the interface can be used. The library can then be accessed at each session by the command:

> `with(PVS);`

[*PvsLineFind*, *PvsPrintLines*, *PvsProve*, *PvsQEDfind*, *PvsReadLines*, *PvsSendAndWait*, *PvsStart*]

which loads the listed commands from the Maple module PVS.

3.2   Maple/PVS Communication

Maple/PVS communication has been implemented in two parts. Firstly, a simple lexical analyser (**pvs-filter**) recognises PVS output and translates it into a format that is easier to parse by other tools (such as the Maple interface). Secondly, a small Tcl/Tk application (**pvs-ctl**) acts as a broker between Maple, PVS and the Maple/PVS user. This broker application is launched from Maple as the child process instead of the PVS-Allegro LISP image and uses **pvs-filter** to simplify the processing of PVS-Allegro output:

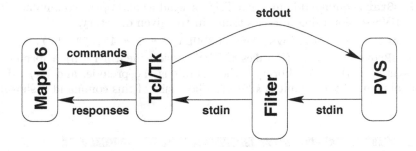

Fig. 2. Maple/PVS System.

Under normal use, Maple sends PVS commands to **pvs-ctl** which passes them directly to PVS-Allegro. Responses are translated by **pvs-filter** and examined by **pvs-ctl**. Anything that needs the user's attention is handled interactively by **pvs-ctl** allowing the user to respond directly to PVS-Allegro without Maple being aware of it. Status messages from PVS-Allegro are displayed graphically by **pvs-ctl** along with other output describing how proof attempts are progressing. Again, none of this reaches Maple—only the information that Maple actually needs. At present, Maple only needs to know about PVS prompts (so that it can send the next command), and Q.E.D. messages indicating that a proof attempt was successful.

The benefits of this system are significant: for the Maple programmer PVS appears as a black-box which is controlled via a trivial protocol. Maple sends a command to the black-box and reads response lines until a prompt is found. If any of these lines contains a Q.E.D. line then the command was successful, otherwise it was not. Simplicity is important because Maple is designed for solving computer algebra problems, and not for text processing.

For the Maple/PVS user the **pvs-ctl** application provides a graphical display of the current state of the system. Not only can progress be monitored, but interaction with PVS-Allegro is available when needed. If PVS stops in the middle of a proof attempt and asks for a new rule to apply, the novice user can respond with (**quit**) while the expert user might be able to guide the proof further.

3.3 Simple Examples

We now provide straightforward examples of the use of the interface. Neither of the examples involves our PVS real analysis library; they demonstrate only the mechanics of the interface, and illustrate the master/slave relationship between Maple and PVS.

We assume that the Maple user has installed locally the C code, shell scripts and Maple library described in Section 3, and PVS. The first task is to initialise the interface, and check that we can prove that $2 + 2 = 4$:

```
>  pvs := PvsStart("../pvslib"):
```

The `PvsStart` command launches a Tcl/Tk window and opens communications with a PVS session using libraries found in the given directory.

```
>  ex1 := PvsProve(pvs, "g: FORMULA 2 + 2 = 4", "", ""):
```

The `PvsProve` command (i) takes a PVS session identifier, (ii) a formula in PVS syntax, (iii) a PVS library - the default is the prelude, and (iv) a PVS proof command - the default is `ASSERT`. The result of this command is shown in Figure 3.

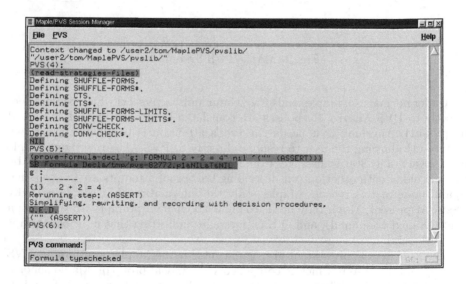

Fig. 3. Tcl/Tk Window for the Maple/PVS Interface.

We confirm in Maple that the proof was successful using the `PvsQEDfind` command:

```
>  PvsQEDfind(ex1);
```

$$true$$

The second elementary example is a proof that the definite integral given in Section 1.1 is undefined for certain values of its parameters. We prove property (3) via the command:

```
>   PvsProve(pvs, "def: LEMMA FORALL (a,b:posreal) :
>   b > a IMPLIES EXISTS (x:real) : 0 <= x AND x <= b AND
>   not(member[real](x,({z:real|z /=a})))",
>   "", "then (skosimp*)(then (inst 1 \"a!1\")(grind))");
```

For this example the proof argument to **PvsProve** is rather more complicated, and represents a single statement of the sequential PVS proof by repeated Skolemisation and flattening, explicit instantiation, and use of the **grind** tactic.

The above examples show that the Maple user controls the interface using Maple commands in a Maple session. The user can check that proof attempts have succeeded without needing to interact with (or even view) the Tcl/Tk window. This is present only as a gateway to PVS, used when proof attempts fail, or when a record of the logical steps used in a proof is needed.

4   Applications

In this section we demonstrate the use of the Maple/PVS interface to obtain proofs which use lemmas from the real analysis library discussed in Section 2. We motivate the use of the proof strategies contained in the library by first proving results without them.

4.1   Continuity of $\sqrt{x}$ for $x > 0$

Consider the following proof that $\sqrt{x}$ can be shown to be continuous for $x > 0$ by choosing $\delta = \epsilon\sqrt{x_0}$ in the definition of continuity:

$$
\begin{aligned}
\delta &= \epsilon\sqrt{x_0} & \Longrightarrow \\
\delta &\leq \epsilon(\sqrt{x} + \sqrt{x_0}) & \Longrightarrow \\
|\sqrt{x} - \sqrt{x_0}| < \frac{\delta}{\sqrt{x} + \sqrt{x_0}} &\Longrightarrow |\sqrt{x} - \sqrt{x_0}| < \epsilon & \Longrightarrow \\
|\sqrt{x} + \sqrt{x_0}||\sqrt{x} - \sqrt{x_0}| < \delta &\Longrightarrow |\sqrt{x} - \sqrt{x_0}| < \epsilon & \Longrightarrow \\
|x - x_0| < \delta &\Longrightarrow |\sqrt{x} - \sqrt{x_0}| < \epsilon
\end{aligned}
$$

$$(7)$$

The equality used is the example given in Section 1.1. The proof using the Maple/PVS interface is obtained with the command:

```
>   ex3 := PvsProve(pvs, "sqrt_eq: LEMMA FORALL (x,y:posreal) :
>   abs(root(x,2)-root(y,2))*abs(root(x,2)+root(y,2)) =
>   abs(x-y)", "roots", "then (skolem!)(then (use
>   \"sqrt_difference\")(then (use \"abs_mult\")(assert)))");
```

Here we are using the PVS **roots** theory. We use this theory again to prove that

$$
|\sqrt{x} + \sqrt{x_0}||\sqrt{x} - \sqrt{x_0}| < \sqrt{x_0}\delta \implies |\sqrt{x} - \sqrt{x_0}| < \epsilon \tag{8}
$$

```
>   ex4 := PvsProve(pvs, "sqroot_ineq: LEMMA
>   FORALL (eps,x,y:posreal) :
>   abs(root(x,2)-root(y,2))*abs(root(x,2)+root(y,2))
>   < eps*root(y,2) IMPLIES abs(root(x,2)-root(y,2)) < eps",
>   "roots", "then (skosimp)(then (lemma
>   \"both_sides_times_pos_lt1\" (\"x\"
>   \"abs(root(x!1,2)-root(y!1,2))\"
>   \"pz\" \"abs(root(x!1,2)+root(y!1,2))\" \"y\"
>   \"eps!1\"))(grind))");
```

This example demonstrates the greater proof power of the interface. Maple alone fails to obtain the identities needed in the above proof. Unfortunately, we need several explicit commands to guide PVS in each proof. The next stage of the development of the interface is the provision of a suite of strategies for performing analysis proofs with much less user guidance.

4.2   Using the Real Analysis Library

The previous example involved the sequential proof of properties of a standard ϵ-δ real analysis definition. By using the real analysis library described in Section 2, we can prove continuity and convergence directly for a wide range of functions. To illustrate this we use the PvsProve command with top_analysis as the library, and with either cts or conv-check as the proof strategy. For example, consider the initial value problem (IVP)

$$y'(x) = f(x, y), \quad y(a) = \eta \tag{9}$$

where y' denotes denotes the derivative of $y(x)$ with respect to x. Let D denote the region $a \leq x \leq b$ and $-\infty < y < \infty$. Then Equation 9 has a unique differentiable solution, $y(x)$, if $f(x, y)$ is defined and continuous for all $(x, y) \in D$, and there exists a positive constant L such that

$$|f(x, y_0) - f(x, y_1)| \leq L|y_0 - y_1| \tag{10}$$

holds for every (x, y_0) and $(x, y_1) \in D$.

Our intention is to use the interface and the real analysis library to verify conditions on the input function, $f(x, y)$, and the Maple solution, $y(x)$, of the IVP. For example, we prove that

$$f(x, y) = \frac{1}{e^{\pi - |6cos(x)|}} \tag{11}$$

is defined and continuous on the real number line using the cts strategy:

```
>   ex5 := PvsProve(pvs, "g: LEMMA FORALL (y:real) :
>   continuous(lambda (x:real) : 1/exp(pi - abs(6*cos(x))),y)",
>   "top_analysis", "cts");
```

For an example of the verification of properties of a Maple solution, we consider the IVP

$$y'(x) = sin(x)y(x) + sin(x)y(x)^2, \quad y(0) = \pi . \tag{12}$$

We can obtain a closed form solution using a Maple procedure:

$$y(x) = \frac{-\pi\, e^{(-\cos(x)+1)}}{-1 - \pi + \pi\, e^{(-\cos(x)+1)}} \tag{13}$$

Since the IVP is of generalised Riccati type [20], we can check that the solution has only removable poles, i.e. that the solution has a limit at those points at which it is undefined. In other words, we prove that

$$\pi e^{1-\cos(x)} - \pi - 1 \tag{14}$$

is convergent (i.e. has a limit) at

$$x = arccos(1 + \log(\frac{1+\pi}{\pi})) \tag{15}$$

via the `conv-check` strategy:
```
>   ex6 := PvsProve(pvs, "g: LEMMA convergent(LAMBDA (x:real) :
>   -pi-1+pi*exp(1-cos(x)),acs(1+ln((1+pi)/pi)))",
>   "top_analysis", "conv-check");
```
We can also verify the the solution in (13) can never be zero, using the `grind` strategy:
```
>   ex1 := PvsProve(pvs, "g: FORMULA FORALL (x:real) :
>   -pi*exp(-cos(x)+1)/= 0", "top_analysis", "grind :defs NIL");
```
These examples demonstrate the inference capability and expressivity of the interface augmented with a library of analytic proof strategies. The results can not be proved within Maple, and are not easy to prove by hand.

4.3   A Generic Application to IVPs

We now describe a methodology for validating and improving Maple procedures for solving IVPs of the form

$$y'(x) = r(x) - q(x)y(x), \quad y(a) = \eta, \quad x \in [a, b] \tag{16}$$

We can use the interface to check the following requirements on inputs (bearing in mind that each input can be a complicated symbolic expression involving parameters):

1. $r(x)$ and $q(x)$ are continuous over $[a, b]$;
2. $r(x) - q(x)y(x)$ is continuous, Lipschitz, and/or differentiable over $[a, b]$.

Answers to these questions provide a formal check on the existence and uniqueness of solutions for the given finite range. For example, we proved the continuity of $\sqrt{x}$ for all positive x in Section 4.1. We can prove that $\sqrt{x}$ is not Lipschitz for $x \in (0, 1)$ using the interface. Information regarding existence and uniqueness can be used to fine tune the procedure used to obtain a solution, by using relevant `assumes` clauses in Maple (e.g. `assume(r(x) - q(x)y(x), continuous)`) so that specialised solution techniques can be safely used.

Once a solution, $y(x)$, has been obtained, we can use the interface to check properties such as

1. $y'(x) - f(x, y) = 0$;
2. $y(a) = \eta$;
3. $y(x)$ has removable poles, non-removable branch points and/or is itself continuous.

The following prototype Maple procedure takes $r(x)$, $q(x)$, a, η and b, and supplies answers to some of the above questions using the inbuilt Maple dsolve procedure for obtaining $y(x)$.

> *qsolve* := **proc**(*r, q, a, η, b*)
> **local** *pvs, z1, z2, z3, z4, z5, z6, sol, diffsol*;
> *pvs* := PvsStart("../pvslib");
> *z1* := PvsProve(*pvs*,
>   "g: FORMULA FORALL (v:I[a,b]) : continuous(lambda (x:I[a,b]) : r(x), v)",
>   "top_analysis", "cts");
> *z2* := PvsProve(*pvs*,
>   "g: FORMULA FORALL (v:I[a,b]) : continuous(lambda (x:I[a,b]) : q(x), v)",
>   "top_analysis", "cts");
> **if not** (PvsQEDfind(*z1*) **and** PvsQEDfind(*z2*)) **then** ERROR('*invalid input*')
> **else**
>   *sol* := dsolve({diff(y(x), x) = r(x) − q(x)y(x), y(a) = η}, y(x));
>   *diffsol* := diff(*sol*, x);
>   *z4* := PvsProve(*pvs*,
>   "g: FORMULA FORALL (v:I[a,b]) : diffsol(v) = r(v) - q(v)*sol(v)",
>   "top_analysis", "grind");
>   *z5* :=
>   PvsProve(*pvs*, "g: FORMULA sol(a) = eta", "top_analysis", "grind");
>   *z2* := PvsProve(*pvs*,
>   "g: FORMULA FORALL (v:I[a,b]) : continuous(lambda (x:I[a,b]) : sol(x),v)",
>   "top_analysis", "cts")
> **fi**;
> **if not** (PvsQEDfind(*z4*) **and** PvsQEDfind(*z5*) **and** PvsQEDfind(*z6*)) **then**
>   ERROR('*invalid solution*')
> **else** *sol*
> **fi**
> **end**

Maple does have built in procedures for answering many of these questions, but, as shown in Section 1.1, can fail to detect the equality of two straightforward expressions and the continuity of a simple function. Using the interface helps the user to validate both the input and output of problems, and hence leads to improved use and understanding of the CAS.

5 Conclusions

We have presented an interface between Maple and PVS. The interface gives Maple users access to the proof capabilities of PVS, thus providing a means to gain more formal knowledge of Maple results.

We have created a tightly coupled interface between Maple and PVS, under which PVS is controlled by Maple. A small Tcl/Tk application sits between Maple and PVS, so that PVS looks like a black box to the Maple user. However, it also allows a more experienced user to interact directly with PVS.

In Section 1.1 we saw that Maple can fail to recognise a seemingly obvious equality, which could lead to an undetected division by zero, and also that Maple might apply standard procedures without checking validity of the input. In Section 4 we showed how the interface can be used to correct these errors.

Our aim is to extend the applicability of the interface in two ways. Firstly the extension of the real analysis library discussed in Section 2 by adding new strategies, and secondly by providing Maple procedures which automate the checking of validity of input and output, as described in Section 4.3. These extensions will require an improvement in the communication between the two systems, both in terms of syntax of expressions, and in decision procedures based on failed proof attempts.

References

1. ABBOTT, J., VAN LEEUWEN, A., AND STROTMAN, A. Objectives of OpenMath. Available from, Jan. 1995,
   http://www.rrz.uni-koeln.de/themen/Computeralgebra/OpenMath/.
2. ADAMS, A., GOTTLIEBSEN, H., LINTON, S., AND MARTIN, U. Automated theorem proving in support of computer algebra: symbolic definite integration as a case study. In *Proceedings of the 1999 International Symposium on Symbolic and Algebraic Computation, Vancouver, Canada* (1999), ACM Press.
3. BALLARIN, C., HOMANN, K., AND CALMET, J. Theorems and algorithms: An interface between Isabelle and Maple. In *Proceedings of the International Symposium on Symbolic and Algebraic Computation* (1995), A. Levelt, Ed., ACM Press, pp. 150–157.
4. BAUER, A., CLARKE, E., AND ZHAO, X. Analytica - an experiment in combining theorem proving and symbolic computation. *Journal of Automated Reasoning 21* (1998), 295–325.
5. BERTOLI, P., CALMET, J., GUINCHIGLIA, F., AND HOMANN, K. Specification and integration of theorem provers and computer algebra systems. In *Artificial intelligence and symbolic computation (Plattsburgh, NY, 1998)*, no. 1476 in Lecture Notes in Computer Science. Springer-Verlag, 1998.
6. BUCHBERGER, B. Symbolic computation: Computer algebra and logic. In *Frontiers of Combining Systems* (1996), F. Baader and K. Schultz, Eds., Applied Logic Series, Kluwer Academic Publishers, pp. 193–220.
7. BUCHBERGER, B., JEBELEAN, T., KRIFTNER, F., MARIN, M., TOMUTA, E., AND VASARU, D. A survey of the theorema project. In *Proceedings of the 1997 International Symposium on Symbolic and Algebraic Computation* (1997), W. Kuechlin, Ed., ACM Press, pp. 384–391.

8. CALMET, J., AND HOMANN, K. Classification of communication and cooperation mechanisms for logical and symbolic computation systems. In *Frontiers of Combining Systems: Proceedings of the 1st International Workshop, Munich (Germany)* (1996), F. Baader and K. U. Schulz, Eds., Applied Logic, Kluwer, pp. 221–234.

9. CHAR, B. W. *Maple V language Reference Manual*. Springer-Verlag, 1991.

10. DENNIS, L. A., COLLINS, G., NORRISH, M., BOULTON, R., SLIND, K., ROBINSON, G., GORDON, M., AND MELHAM, T. The PROSPER Toolkit. In *Proceedings of the 6th International Conference on Tools and Algorithms for the Construction and Analysis of Systems* (2000), vol. 1785 of *Lecture Notes in Computer Science*, Springer-Verlag.

11. DEWAR, M. Special Issue on OPENMATH. *ACM SIGSAM Bulletin 34*, 2 (June 2000).

12. DOLZMANN, A., AND STURM, T. REDLOG: Computer algebra meets computer logic. *ACM SIGSAM Bulletin 31*, 2 (June 1997), 2–9.

13. DUTERTRE, B. Elements of mathematical analysis in PVS. In *Theorem Proving in Higher Order Logics: 9th International Conference, TPHOLs '96* (Turku, Finland, Aug. 1996), J. von Wright, J. Grundy, and J. Harrison, Eds., vol. 1125 of *Lecture Notes in Computer Science*, Springer-Verlag, pp. 141–156.

14. GOTTLIEBSEN, H. Transcendental Functions and Continuity Checking in PVS. In *Theorem Proving in Higher Order Logics: 13th International Conference, TPHOLs 2000* (2000), J. Harrison and M. Aagaard, Eds., vol. 1869 of *Lecture Notes in Computer Science*, Springer-Verlag, pp. 198–215.

15. GRAY, S., KAJLER, N., AND WANG, P. S. MP: A Protocol for Efficient Exchange of Mathematical Expressions. In *Proc. of the International Symposium on Symbolic and Algebraic Computation (ISSAC'94), Oxford, GB* (July 1994), M. Giesbrecht, Ed., ACM Press, pp. 330–335.

16. HARRISON, J., AND THÉRY, L. Reasoning about the reals: the marriage of HOL and Maple. In *Logic Programming and Automated Reasoning* (1993), A.Voronkov, Ed., no. 698 in Lecture Notes in Artificial Intelligence, LPAR'93, Springer-Verlag, pp. 351–359.

17. JACKSON, P. *Enhancing the NUPRL Proof Development System and Applying it to Computational Abstract Algebra*. PhD thesis, Department of Computer Science, Cornell University, Ithaca, New York, Apr. 1995.

18. JENKS, R. D., AND SUTOR, R. S. *AXIOM: the scientific computation system*. Numerical Algorithms Group Ltd., 1992.

19. MONAGAN, M., GEDDES, K., HEAL, K., LABAHN, G., VORKOETTER, S., AND MCCARRON, J. *Maple6 Programming Guide*. Waterloo Maple Inc., 2000.

20. MURPHY, G. M. *Ordinary differential equations and their solutions*. D. van Nostrand Company, Inc., 1960.

21. OWRE, S., SHANKAR, N., AND RUSHBY, J. M. *User Guide for the PVS Specification and Verification System*. Computer Science Laboratory, SRI International, Menlo Park, CA, February 1993.

22. OWRE, S., SHANKAR, N., RUSHBY, J. M., AND STRINGER-CALVERT, D. W. J. *PVS Language Reference*. Computer Science Laboratory, SRI International, Menlo Park, CA, Sept. 1999.

23. OWRE, S., SHANKAR, N., RUSHBY, J. M., AND STRINGER-CALVERT, D. W. J. *PVS System Guide*. Computer Science Laboratory, SRI International, Menlo Park, CA, Sept. 1999.

24. PAULSON, L. C. *The Isabelle Reference Manual*. Computer Laboratory, University of Cambridge, February 2001.

25. POLL, E., AND THOMPSON, S. Adding the axioms to AXIOM: Towards a system of automated reasoning in Aldor. Tech. Rep. 6-98, Computing Laboratory, University of Kent at Canterbury, May 1998.

An Irrational Construction of $\mathbb{R}$ from $\mathbb{Z}$

Rob D. Arthan

Lemma 1 Ltd., 2nd Floor, 31A Chain Street
Reading RG1 2HX, UK
rda@lemma-one.com

Abstract. This paper reports on a construction of the real numbers in the ProofPower implementation of the HOL logic. Since the original construction was implemented, some major improvements to the ideas have been discovered. The improvements involve some entertaining mathematics: it turns out that the Dedekind cuts provide many routes one can travel to get from the ring of integers, $\mathbb{Z}$, to the field of real numbers, $\mathbb{R}$. The traditional stop-over on the way is the field of rational numbers, $\mathbb{Q}$. This paper shows that going via certain rings of algebraic numbers can provide a pleasant alternative to the more well-trodden track.

1 Introduction

1.1 Automated Theorem Proving Background

ProofPower is a suite of tools supporting specification and proof in a range of formalisms. At the heart of the tools is the logical kernel for HOL, which is a re-engineering of the kernel of the Classic HOL system[7]. This re-engineering[1] was undertaken by ICL between 1988 and 1992 to meet requirements for a tool to reason about security properties expressed in Z[10]. Since 1993 ProofPower has been applied to research and development in methods for specification and verification of safety-critical systems. In 1994, a method for specifying and verifying Ada code called the Compliance Notation[12, 15] was implemented to form the Compliance Tool component of ProofPower. Research and development into the notation and the tool continues informed by a number of successful applications and case studies and the tool is currently being put to work on significant verification problems in the military avionics domain.

Early versions of the Compliance Tool had only vestigial support for the Ada data types that represent real numbers. However, investigation of actual code in the intended applications domain has shown that real programmers do use reals. During 1999 and 2000 it became clear that proper support for Ada real types was essential. In 2000, the Defence and Evaluation Research Agency, the designers and main users of the Compliance Notation, commissioned Lemma 1 Ltd., who now develop and market ProofPower, to provide this support.

Ada real types in the Compliance Tool use a formalisation of the real numbers in Z, which, in turn, is based on a theory of the real numbers in ProofPower-HOL.

R.J. Boulton and P.B. Jackson (Eds.): TPHOLs 2001, LNCS 2152, pp. 43–58, 2001.

The ProofPower-HOL theory was developed in November 2000 by the present author using some novel methods intended to make use of the fact that ProofPower-HOL already possessed reasonably well-supported theories for both natural number and integer arithmetic.

As is the norm in the HOL community, the theory of the reals in ProofPower-HOL is developed by conservative extension rather than by axiomatisation. Indeed, just to assert the axioms of the reals, characterised say, as a complete ordered field, would be a relatively trivial (albeit error-prone) exercise. The merits of conservative extension over axiomatisation by *fiat* have been widely discussed, see[8] for a survey.

I should remind the reader that HOL is a typed logic with well-defined principles of conservative extension for introducing new types and constants. The defining property for a new constant $c : \tau$ can be an arbitrary satisfiable predicate defined on the type τ, e.g., one might introduce a constant Sqrt $: \mathbb{N} \to \mathbb{N}$, with defining property: $\forall m \bullet (\text{Sqrt } m)^2 \leq m < (\text{Sqrt } m + 1)^2$. The HOL logical kernel imposes a proof obligation to ensure that the defining property is indeed satisfiable so that the introduction of the constant is conservative.

The defining property for a new type has a standard form asserting that the new type is in one-to-one correspondence with a non-empty subset of an existing type. Again a proof obligation is imposed to ensure that the subset is non-empty. As an example, one can introduce a type with a given finite number of elements by requiring it to be in one-to-one correspondence with an appropriate interval of natural numbers. This simple subtyping mechanism, combined with the power of the primitive type constructors, allows a wide variety of standard type constructions to be carried out. For example, given an equivalence relation on an existing type τ, the quotient type (with one element for each equivalence class) can be formed as a subtype of the power set type $(\tau)\text{SET}$.

John Harrison[8] has developed a very elegant refinement of the method of fundamental sequences which is well adapted to constructing a theory of reals using the natural numbers as a starting point. The present author would not hesitate to recommend Harrison's approach in a context where a good theory of integers is not to hand. If the integers are available, the approach of the present paper is offered as an alternative which has its attractions. In particular:

- There is no need to work with equivalence classes[1]
- the only subtype[1] that needs to be created is the type, $\mathbb{R}$, of the real numbers themselves;
- the theories of order, addition and multiplication are dealt with in succession, each one building on what has come before and providing reusable theory for use in later work.

---

[1] While automation can make dealing with equivalence classes and subtypes straightforward, these devices inevitably involve additional proof obligations.

1.2 Mathematical Background

The textbook journey from $\mathbb{Z}$ to $\mathbb{R}$ is the composite of two standard means of transport. First we take the ring $\mathbb{Z}$ and form its field of fractions, $\mathbb{Q}$ and note that the order structure on $\mathbb{Z}$ carries over to $\mathbb{Q}$. However, $\mathbb{Q}$ is incomplete — numbers such as $\sqrt{2}$ and π fail to show up at this stage of the trip. To remedy this, we appeal to something like the Dedekind completion by cuts, or Cantor's method of fundamental sequences (a.k.a. Cauchy sequences) to arrive at our goal $\mathbb{R}$. Excellent surveys of the terrain are given in [5, 8]. In the sequel, we will concentrate on the Dedekind cuts construction. In an elementary treatment, this construction is presented along something like the following lines.

i) The rational numbers $\mathbb{Q}$ are constructed (e.g., as equivalence classes of pairs $(m, n) : \mathbb{Z} \times \mathbb{N}_1$, with (m, n) representing the fraction m/n). The rational numbers are then shown to comprise an ordered field.

ii) A Dedekind *cut* is now defined to be any non-empty set, C, of rational numbers which is, *(a)*, downwards-closed (i.e., if $q \in C$, then any rational number $p < q$ is also in C), *(b)*, unbounded above in itself (i.e., for any $q \in C$, there is a $p \in C$ with $q < p$), and *(c)* bounded above in $\mathbb{Q}$ (i.e., for some $q \in \mathbb{Q}$, every $p \in C$ satisfies $p < q$). $\mathbb{R}$ is defined to be the set of all such cuts.

The rational numbers $\mathbb{Q}$ are identified with a subset of $\mathbb{R}$, the set of *rational cuts*, by associating $q \in \mathbb{Q}$ with the cut compromising all rational numbers less than q.

The set of cuts is shown to be linearly ordered by set-theoretic inclusion and this ordering is shown to agree with the usual ordering on $\mathbb{Q}$ when restricted to rational cuts. This ordering is seen to be complete (i.e., any non-empty subset of $\mathbb{R}$ that is bounded above has a supremum in $\mathbb{R}$). Indeed, the supremum of a bounded set of cuts turns out to be its set-theoretic union.

iii) Addition of cuts is now defined as follows: if C and D are cuts, the sum $C + D$ is defined to be the set of all sums $p + q$ where $p \in C$ and $q \in D$. This is shown to be a cut and so defines a binary operation $\mathbb{R} \to \mathbb{R} \to \mathbb{R}$, which is then shown to be associative and commutative and to have the rational cut corresponding to $0 \in \mathbb{Q}$ as an identity element.

iv) The additive inverse operator is now defined as follows: if C is a cut, $-C$ is defined to be the set of all $q \in \mathbb{Q}$ such that $p + q < 0$ for every $p \in C$. Again, this is shown to be a cut and so to define a unary operator $\mathbb{R} \to \mathbb{R}$, which is an inverse for the addition.

v) Multiplication and its inverse are defined in a similar fashion to addition and additive inverse, but with some complications due to signs. The interactions among the ordering relation, the additive structure and the multiplicative structure are investigated and we conclude that $\mathbb{R}$ is a complete ordered field.

An analysis of what is being assumed and what the arguments actually prove here reveals a number of useful facts:

– Step (ii) applies to any ordered set. This is the Dedekind-MacNeille completion theorem. For more on this, see, for example, [4]. The algebraic structure of $\mathbb{Q}$ is irrelevant here. Indeed, the completion of any countable, unbounded, densely ordered set is known by a theorem of Cantor to have the same order type as $\mathbb{R}$ (see, for example, [11]).

- Step (iii) makes no use of the multiplicative structure of $\mathbb{Q}$ — only its ordering and its additive structure are needed. However, it is not the case that just any ordered commutative group will do[2]. In fact, what is required is that $\mathbb{Q}$ contains arbitrarily small positive elements, or equivalently, it is densely ordered: for any $x < y$, there is a z with $x < z < y$. Density is required in verifying that the rational cut determined by 0 is indeed an identity for addition.

- Step (iv) also makes no use of the multiplicative structure except for the ability (which exists in any group) to "multiply" elements by natural numbers. However density is not sufficient to make the proof go through[3]. It turns out that we require the archimedean property on the additive group $\mathbb{Q}$: for any positive elements, x and y, there is an $n \in \mathbb{N}$ such that $y < nx$. Here nx denotes the n-fold sum $x + x + \ldots + x$.

- Finally, essentially by a theorem of Hölder [9], step (v) is an instance of a general construction that is independent of the details of the additive structure. Hölder's theorem is usually stated as saying that any archimedean ordered group is isomorphic to a subgroup of the real numbers under addition. Consequently, the completion of any ordered group that is both dense and archimedean must be isomorphic to the real numbers, and so must admit a multiplication. Moreover, the method of the proof of Hölder's theorem comes close to providing a definition for the multiplication.

1.3 A New Approach

The observations of the previous section suggest new approaches to constructing the real numbers. The rest of this paper is mainly concerned with presenting one such approach and is organised as follows:

Section 2 discusses the Dedekind-MacNeille completion theorem. This is well-known and so the discussion is very brief.

Section 3 discusses how the additive structure of the real numbers may be derived from the Dedekind-MacNeille completion of any dense, archimedean, ordered group. Again this is very brief — the classical proofs go through without change.

Section 4 is concerned with deriving the multiplicative structure of the real numbers from the additive structure. This seems to be one of those topics that is well-known but rarely written down, so we give a complete, albeit rather condensed, discussion.

Section 5 is the main contribution of this paper. It provides a source of dense, archimedean, ordered groups that are algebraically much simpler than the

---

[2] E.g., try using $\mathbb{Z}$ in place of $\mathbb{Q}$.

[3] E.g., try using the product group $\mathbb{Z} \times \mathbb{Q}$ with the lexicographic order in place of $\mathbb{Q}$.

rational numbers. The groups considered are the additive groups of the rings $\mathbb{Z}[\alpha]$ where α can be any one of a variety of irrational numbers. For definiteness, we concentrate on the case $\alpha = \sqrt{2}$.

Section 6 offers my confession that the construction outlined in the present paper is not what was actually done in November 2000 for the ProofPower product. The construction used algebraic structures weaker than ordered groups as its basis. The derivation of the additive structure of the reals from these weaker systems has to be more general than the construction described in this paper. In comparison, the approach proposed here provides some considerable economies in the proofs.

Section 7 gives some concluding remarks.

The present paper deliberately concentrates on the mathematics rather than the details of the particular formalisation in ProofPower. This is because some of the mathematics is not very accessible in the literature and some parts of it are believed to be new, whereas how to formalise the mathematics will depend on the system being used and should be fairly clear to a competent user of any adequately expressive system.

Demo versions of the ProofPower treatment of the material outlined in this document are available on the World-Wide Web[4]. The reader is referred to that material for further details of the formalisation.

The construction described in this document may seem at first sight to be rather exotic. However, from several points of view it can be seen as quite natural. One such point of view is this: let us take it as given that we wish to avoid the expense of constructing the rationals and tools to reason about them prior to constructing the reals, since $\mathbb{Q}$ will appear as a subfield of $\mathbb{R}$ in any case. As a substitute for $\mathbb{Q}$, we look for a dense subgroup of $\mathbb{R}$ which is simple enough to be directly amenable to existing tools for reasoning about the integers. A subgroup such as $\mathbb{Z}[\sqrt{2}]$, which is isomorphic as an additive group to the cartesian product $\mathbb{Z} \times \mathbb{Z}$, would do nicely. However we will need an easy way of working with the ordering that $\mathbb{Z}[\sqrt{2}]$ receives as a subgroup of $\mathbb{R}$. As we will see in section 5.2 of this paper, it turns out that there is a very tractable description of this ordering and the properties needed of $\mathbb{Z}[\sqrt{2}]$ are very easy to prove.

2   Dedekind-MacNeille Completion

The Dedekind-MacNeille completion theorem proves to be simplicity itself. In the ProofPower treatment, MacNeille's generalisation of the Dedekind construction to partially ordered sets was not needed, so the theory was developed for linearly ordered sets only.

The result we have to prove is that any unbounded, dense, linearly ordered may be embedded as an unbounded dense subset of a complete ordered set. The actual statement of the theorem gives an explicit witness for the complete

---

[4] Follow the link from http://www.lemma-one.com/papers/papers.html.

ordered set. This is very simple first-order set theory and the main proofs were found in the course of one day.

Once one has a suitable densely ordered set, S say, the theory of Dedekind-MacNeille immediately enables one to define the type $\mathbb{R}$. The defining property for the new type is entirely order-theoretic and just states that there $\mathbb{R}$ admits a linear order which is dense and complete and admits an embedding of S as an unbounded, dense subset. On the basis of this type definition, it involves a trivial proof to define the constant $<: \mathbb{R} \to \mathbb{R} \to \mathbb{B}$ that gives the ordering on the real numbers. One can then define the supremum operator[5] $\mathsf{Sup} : (\mathbb{R})\mathsf{SET} \to \mathbb{R}$. $\leq, >$ and $\geq$ can also conveniently be defined at this stage.

At this point, one can start to develop useful, reusable, theory about the ordering and the supremum operator. E.g., one can show that for non-empty, bounded above, sets A and B, a sufficient condition for $\mathsf{Sup}(A) \leq \mathsf{Sup}(B)$ is that $A \subseteq B$. This theory is useful both in the rest of the construction and in ordinary use of the theory of reals once the construction is complete.

3   Defining the Additive Structure

Defining the additive structure of the reals given a dense, archimedean, ordered group is essentially what is achieved in steps (iii) and (iv) of the classical Dedekind cuts construction as described in section 1.2 above. The reader is referred to any good calculus textbook for the details, e.g., [14]. However, some descriptions, e.g., that in [5], skate over the role of the archimedean property.

As with the order structure, new constants $+ : \mathbb{R} \to \mathbb{R} \to \mathbb{R}$, $0_\mathbb{R} : \mathbb{R}$ and $- : \mathbb{R} \to \mathbb{R}$ are introduced and their elementary properties derived. Particularly useful are theorems about cancellation of like terms on either side of an equality or inequality.

4   Defining the Multiplicative Structure

The author has been unable to find an accessible modern treatment of the derivation of the multiplicative structure in the literature. This is probably because results like Hölder's theorem are generally given in a context where the real numbers are already available.

The arguments needed are, in essence, all given in a paper by Behrend[2]. However, Behrend's arguments are set in a context which is rather different from ours. The ProofPower treatment uses a recasting of the core arguments from Behrend in modern dress. It also delivers theorems which may be of general use in further development of the theory.

So let us assume that R is a non-trivial complete ordered commutative group. We want to show that R can be equipped with a multiplication turning it into

---

[5] Sup is conceptually a partial function. It is formalised in ProofPower as a total function whose defining property reveals no information about values of the function which are conceptually undefined.

an ordered field. To this end, let us fix some positive element $1_R : R$ which we will make into the multiplicative identity element of the field.

The basic idea is that, if R can be turned into an ordered field, then, for any $x : R$, multiplication by x determines an additive group homomorphism $R \rightarrow R$. Moreover, if x is positive, multiplication by x is (strictly) order-preserving (i.e., $xy < xz$ whenever $y < z$). Thus we can hope to derive the multiplicative structure by investigating the order-preserving additive homomorphisms $R \rightarrow R$. Let us call these OPAHs.

It is not hard to see that OPAHs are necessarily injective functions[6]. What is true, but somewhat harder to prove is that OPAHs are also surjective. To prove this we first observe that any subgroup of R containing arbitrarily small positive elements is dense in R. Now the image of an OPAH, f, is a subgroup of R and it is not hard to see that it contains arbitrarily small positive elements[7]. Thus the image of f is a dense subgroup of R. So any OPAH, f, is an order-preserving injective function from R to a dense subset of itself; but viewed as a subset of R ordered as a subset of R, the image of f must be complete because R is complete, and f is order-preserving. It is now not hard to see that the image must be equal to R and so f is indeed surjective[8].

A homomorphism $f : R \rightarrow R$ is said to be *central* if it commutes with every homomorphism $g : R \rightarrow R$, i.e., if $f(g(x)) = g(f(x))$ for every $x \in R$. Central OPAHs (COPAHs) will serve for us as a substitute for the multiplication by natural numbers used in [2] and other treatments such as [9].

What we now want to show is that COPAHs abound. To see this, let $\delta \in R$ be any positive element. Consider the set $A = A_\delta$ of elements, $x \in R$ such that either $x = 0$ or for some COPAH g, we have $g(\delta) = x$ or $g(\delta) = -x$. Then it is not very hard to see that A is a dense subgroup of R. Density is the only tricky part. For density, one verifies that the function $t : R \rightarrow R$ defined by $t(x) = x + x$ is a COPAH. Since COPAHs are OPAHs, and OPAHs are surjective, t has an inverse $h : R \rightarrow R$, and h is then itself a COPAH with the property that, for any $x \in R$, we have $x = h(x) + h(x)$. I.e., h is "division by 2". It follows that A has no least positive element[9], i.e. A is dense.

In fact, the dense subgroups A_δ defined in the previous paragraph are complete and so $A_\delta = R$ for every positive δ. I.e., for any $x \in R$ with $x \neq 0$, there is a COPAH g, such that either $x = g(\delta)$ or $x = -g(\delta)$. The proof of this requires us to show, in effect, that the (pointwise) supremum of a bounded family of COPAHs is itself a COPAH. We omit the details, just noting that the key is to show that if f and g are two OPAHs, then if $f(x) < g(x)$ for some positive x, then $f(x) < g(x)$ for every positive x. This is proved essentially by the argument

---

[6] If $f(x) = f(y)$, then $x < y$ and $y < x$ are both impossible, so we must have $x = y$.

[7] It contains some positive elements, e.g., $f(1_R)$; if it contained a least positive element, $f(\epsilon)$, say, then by density of R there would be a δ with $0 < \delta < \epsilon$, but then $f(\delta)$ is positive and smaller than $f(\epsilon)$.

[8] Consider a least positive element that is not in the image.

[9] If $x = f(\delta)$ were such an element, with f the COPAH that testifies to $x \in A$, then $g = h \circ f$ is also a COPAH and $g(\delta) < f(\delta)$.

of the uniqueness half of the main theorem in [2], using COPAHs rather than multiplication by natural numbers to show that it is not possible for $f(y) \geq g(y)$ for any y.

What we have just proved is that for any positive $\delta \in R$ and any non-zero $x \in R$, there is a COPAH, g, with $g(\delta) = x$ or $g(\delta) = -x$, and this may be shown to be unique. Fixing $\delta = 1_R$, this says that for every positive x, there is a unique $g = g_x$ such that $g(1_R) = x$. We now define multiplication by x by $xy = g_x(y)$. This definition may be extended to cover the case when $x \leq 0$ in the obvious way, and making heavy use of the uniqueness of g_x, one shows that this turns R into ring with unit 1_R. Since COPAHs are bijections, this ring is actually a field and all the properties of an ordered field follow. For the details, we refer to [2] yet again — this part of the argument translates easily into the present context.

In ProofPower this part of the construction was not difficult, but was a little time-consuming. It took perhaps 5 days to discover and formalise the arguments, which provide the consistency proofs for the definitions of the constants $* : \mathbb{R} \to \mathbb{R} \to \mathbb{R}$ and $^{-1} : \mathbb{R} \to \mathbb{R}$ giving multiplication and multiplicative inverse for the real numbers.

5   An Alternative to $\mathbb{Q}$

In this section, we construct a dense, archimedean ordered commutative group. Given the arguments of sections 2, 3 and 4 above, this is all that is needed to complete our construction of the reals. The group we use is called $\mathbb{Z}[\sqrt{2}]$. It is introduced in section 5.1 below. In fact, since it involves little extra work, we will show that $\mathbb{Z}[\sqrt{2}]$ is actually an ordered ring.

5.1   Calculating in $\mathbb{Z}[\sqrt{2}]$

Imagine using a square with 1-inch sides to mark off points along the real number line starting at the fixed base point 0. Using a side of the square you can mark off any whole number of inches to the left or the right of the base point. However, you can use the diagonal of the square to mark off distances in either direction too. Pythagoras' theorem says that the diagonal is $\sqrt{2} = \sqrt{1^2 + 1^2}$ inches long. So, the points you can mark off are precisely the real numbers $a + b\sqrt{2}$ where a and b are integers. These are the numbers that make up the ring $\mathbb{Z}[\sqrt{2}]$.

Addition and additive inverse in $\mathbb{Z}[\sqrt{2}]$ is easy to describe purely in terms of integer arithmetic; describing multiplication is not much harder:

$$(a + b\sqrt{2}) + (c + d\sqrt{2}) = (a + c) + (b + d)\sqrt{2}$$
$$-(a + b\sqrt{2}) = (-a) + (-b)\sqrt{2}$$
$$(a + b\sqrt{2})(c + d\sqrt{2}) = (ac + 2bd) + (ad + bc)\sqrt{2}.$$

In the sequel we will often turn facts about the real numbers into definitions. Here, if we consider pairs (a, b) where a and b are integers, we can define addition, negation and multiplication as follows:

$$(a, b) + (c, d) = (a + c, b + d)$$
$$-(a, b) = (-a, -b)$$
$$(a, b)(c, d) = (ac + 2bd, ad + bc).$$

One may then check that the above definitions turn the set, $\mathbb{Z} \times \mathbb{Z}$, of all pairs of integers into a ring with zero element $\mathbf{0} = (0, 0)$ and unit element $\mathbf{1} = (1, 0)$.

The pairs $(a, b) \in \mathbb{Z} \times \mathbb{Z}$ thus give a model, defined solely in terms of integer arithmetic, for the arithmetic of all real numbers of the form $a + b\sqrt{2}$. From now on, we shall refer to this model as $\mathbb{Z}[\sqrt{2}]$. It is here that $\mathbb{Z}[\sqrt{2}]$ has its main advantage over $\mathbb{Q}$: the verifications of the ring laws reduce to equations over the integers that are easily solved by a linear arithmetic decision procedure. Stating and proving the laws took the author less than half an hour in ProofPower.

5.2   The Ordering of $\mathbb{Z}[\sqrt{2}]$

Given members $\mathbf{y} = (c, d)$ and $\mathbf{z} = (e, f)$ of $\mathbb{Z}[\sqrt{2}]$, how do we decide the relative order of the real numbers $y = c + d\sqrt{2}$ and $z = e + f\sqrt{2}$ that $\mathbf{y}$ and $\mathbf{z}$ represent?

To simplify the problem a little, I should explain that it is enough to decide, given any $\mathbf{x} = (a, b)$ in $\mathbb{Z}[\sqrt{2}]$, whether or not $x = a + b\sqrt{2}$ is positive (i.e., greater than 0). For, in $\mathbb{R}$, we know that $y < z$ precisely when $0 < z - y$. In general, to define an ordering on a (commutative) group, G, it is enough to identify a subset P of "positive elements". This subset must be closed under the group operation (addition), must not contain 0, and must be such that, for any non-zero element, g, of G, either g or $-g$ belongs to P. Given such a subset, P, defining $g < h$ to mean $h - g \in P$ gives a linear ordering of the elements of G compatible with the addition in G, in the sense that whenever $g < h$, then, also, $g + k < h + k$ for any k in G.

In the case of $\mathbb{Z}[\sqrt{2}]$, a first attempt at a rule for deciding whether $\mathbf{x} = (a, b)$ is positive would be to consider four cases as follows: *if*, (i), *a and b are both positive then* $\mathbf{x}$ *certainly represents a positive real number; if*, (ii), *neither of a and b is positive then* $\mathbf{x}$ *certainly does not represent a positive real number; otherwise, to ensure that* $\mathbf{x}$ *represents a positive real number, we must have either,* (iii), *that a is negative and b is positive and* $a^2 < 2b^2$ *or,* (iv), *that a is positive, b is negative and* $a^2 > 2b^2$.

Unfortunately the above rules for identifying the positive numbers is not at all convenient[10]. It involves four cases, and when we try to verify the properties we require of the set of positive elements, the cases multiply and we find ourselves having to do some not very nice algebra in each case. While there are some symmetries between the cases, to show that the set of positive elements is closed

---

[10] Nonetheless, proving that $\mathbb{Z}[\sqrt{2}]$ becomes an ordered group under this definition is set as an exercise in the well-known textbook on algebra by Birkhoff and MacLane[13]. They also set the case $\mathbb{Z}[\sqrt{3}]$ as an asterisked, i.e., hard, exercise.

under addition requires verification of several different kinds of quadratic diophantine inequality whose proofs require some ingenuity. An alternative method is called for.

There is a recipe that has been known since antiquity for producing good rational approximations to $\sqrt{2}$. Consider the following sequence of rational numbers:

$$\begin{aligned}
u_1/v_1 &= 1/1 \\
u_2/v_2 &= 3/2 \\
u_3/v_3 &= 7/5 \\
u_4/v_4 &= 17/12
\end{aligned}$$

$$\cdots$$

$$u_{i+1}/v_{i+1} = (u_i + 2v_i)/(u_i + v_i)$$

$$\cdots$$

An induction on i shows that $u_i^2 - 2v_i^2 = (-1)^i$ for all natural numbers i. E.g., $17^2 - 2 \times 12^2 = 289 - 288 = 1 = (-1)^4$. So, for each i, $(u_i/v_i)^2 = 2 + (-1)^i/v_i^2$. Using the methods of the calculus, it follows that u_i/v_i converges to $\sqrt{2}$ as i tends to infinity. Because of this, $a + b\sqrt{2}$ will be positive precisely when $a + (u_i/v_i)b$ is positive for all sufficiently large i. However, while we are *en route* to $\mathbb{R}$, the methods of the calculus are away in the distance. We need a rule for deciding when $a + (u_i/v_i)b$ is positive without appealing to the calculus or even to the existence of real or rational numbers.

Since the v_i are all positive, $a + (u_i/v_i)b$ will be positive precisely when $w_i = v_i a + u_i b$ is positive. Given integers a, and b, let's look at the sequence of numbers w_i:

$$\begin{aligned}
w_1 &= a + b \\
w_2 &= 2a + 3b \\
w_3 &= 5a + 7b \\
w_4 &= 12a + 17b
\end{aligned}$$

$$\cdots$$

If we set $w_0 = b$ to help us get started, the w_i follow a very simple rule:

$$\begin{aligned}
w_0 &= b \\
w_1 &= a + b \\
w_{i+2} &= 2w_{i+1} + w_i
\end{aligned}$$

We have already observed that $a + b\sqrt{2}$ is positive precisely when w_i is positive for all sufficiently large i. From the above rule for the w_i, this will happen precisely when two consecutive values, w_i and w_{i+1} are positive for some i.

In the light of the above, we can now describe an algorithm, which to the best of my knowledge is new, for testing the sign of an element, $\mathbf{x} = (a, b)$ of $\mathbb{Z}[\sqrt{2}]$. To describe the algorithm, we begin by introducing the "sign-test" functions. These are a family of functions, ST_i, one for each natural number i. Each of the sign-test functions maps $\mathbb{Z}[\sqrt{2}]$ to $\mathbb{Z}$. They are defined by the following recurrence equations which hold for any natural number i and integers a and b:

$$ST_0(a,b) = b$$
$$ST_1(a,b) = a + b$$
$$ST_{i+2}(a,b) = 2ST_{i+1}(a,b) + ST_i(a,b)$$

It is easy to verify by induction on i that the sign-test functions are all homomorphisms from the additive group of $\mathbb{Z}[\sqrt{2}]$ to the additive group of $\mathbb{Z}$. I.e., for any natural number i and members $\mathbf{x}$ and $\mathbf{y}$ of $\mathbb{Z}[\sqrt{2}]$ the following equation holds:

$$ST_i(\mathbf{x} + \mathbf{y}) = ST_i(\mathbf{x}) + ST_i(\mathbf{y})$$

Here the addition on the left-hand side is our newly-defined addition in $\mathbb{Z}[\sqrt{2}]$, while the addition on the right is the usual addition in $\mathbb{Z}$. Note this implies that for any integers n, a and b, we have $ST_i(na, nb) = nST_i(a,b)$ and $ST_i(-a, -b) = -ST_i(a,b)$. If $n \in \mathbb{Z}$, and $\mathbf{x} = (a,b) \in \mathbb{Z}[\sqrt{2}]$, we will write $n\mathbf{x}$ for (na, nb). For $n \in \mathbb{N}$, $n\mathbf{x}$ is equal to the iterated addition: $\mathbf{x} + \mathbf{x} + \ldots + \mathbf{x}$, with n appearances of $\mathbf{x}$ (which we take, by convention, to be $\mathbf{0}$ if $n = 0$).

The algorithm for testing the sign of $\mathbf{x} = (a,b) \in \mathbb{Z}[\sqrt{2}]$ is as follows: calculate $w_i = ST_i(\mathbf{x})$ for $i = 0, 1, 2, \ldots$ in turn until one of the following three outcomes occurs: either, *(i)*, $w_i = w_{i+1} = 0$, in which case, as is easy to see, a and b were both equal to 0 to start with and $\mathbf{x} = \mathbf{0}$; *(ii)*, w_i and w_{i+1} are both positive, in which case, as we have already remarked, $\mathbf{x}$ is positive; or, *(iii)*, w_i and w_{i+1} are both negative, in which case $\mathbf{x}$ is negative (because carrying out the calculation using $-\mathbf{x}$ in place of $\mathbf{x}$ would end up in case *(ii)* and show that $-\mathbf{x}$ is positive).

We must prove that this algorithm terminates:

Theorem 1. *For any integers a and b, if we construct the sequence of numbers defined by the equations, $w_0 = b$, $w_1 = a + b$ and $w_{i+2} = 2w_{i+1} + w_i$, ($i = 0, 1, 2, \ldots$), then, for some i, and hence for all sufficiently large i, exactly one of the following three cases will obtain:* (i), $w_i = w_{i+1} = 0$, (ii), $0 < w_i \wedge 0 < w_{i+1}$ *or,* (iii), $w_i < 0 \wedge w_{i+1} < 0$. *I.e., the sign-test algorithm described above always terminates.*

Proof: The absolute values of the integers w_i cannot decrease indefinitely, so there is a k such that $|w_k| \leq |w_{k+1}|$. If $w_{k+1} = 0$, then $w_k = 0$ and the algorithm terminates at or before stage k in case *(i)*. If $w_{k+1} \neq 0$, then because $w_{k+2} = 2w_{k+1} + w_k$ and $|w_k| \leq |w_{k+1}|$, w_{k+2} and w_{k+1} must have the same sign, and the algorithm terminates at or before stage $k + 1$ in case *(ii)* or *(iii)* according as w_{k+1} is positive or negative[11]. ■

We may now define the set, $\mathbf{P}$, of positive elements of $\mathbb{Z}[\sqrt{2}]$. $\mathbf{P}$ is the set of all members of $\mathbb{Z}[\sqrt{2}]$ for which the sign-test algorithm returns a positive result.

---

[11] The same argument will work if we replace the recurrence equation $w_{i+2} = 2w_{i+1} + w_i$, by $w_{i+2} = Aw_{i+1} + Bw_i$, for any integers A and B with $A \geq B > 0$. This can be shown to give routes from $\mathbb{Z}$ to $\mathbb{R}$ via subrings $\mathbb{Z}[\alpha]$ for a variety of real numbers α including all those of the form $\sqrt{m}$ for m any positive integer for which $\sqrt{m} \notin \mathbb{Z}$.

Formally, $\mathbf{P}$ may be defined by either of the following two equations (which are equivalent by our earlier remarks about the sequences w_i):

$$\mathbf{P} = \{\mathbf{x} : \mathbb{Z}[\sqrt{2}] | \exists i : \mathbb{N} \bullet \mathsf{ST}_i(\mathbf{x}) > 0 \wedge \mathsf{ST}_{i+1}(\mathbf{x}) > 0\}$$
$$= \{\mathbf{x} : \mathbb{Z}[\sqrt{2}] | \exists i : \mathbb{N} \bullet \forall j \bullet i \le j \Rightarrow \mathsf{ST}_j(\mathbf{x}) > 0\}$$

Let us record what we now know about the sign-test algorithm and our observations on ordered groups to give the following theorem:

Theorem 2. $\mathbb{Z}[\sqrt{2}]$ *equipped with the ordering defined by taking* $\mathbf{P}$ *as the set of positive elements is an ordered commutative group.*

Proof: What we have to prove is that $\mathbf{P}$ is closed under addition, does not contain $\mathbf{0}$, and, for any element $\mathbf{x}$ of $\mathbb{Z}[\sqrt{2}]$, either $\mathbf{x}$ belongs to $\mathbf{P}$ or $-\mathbf{x}$ belongs to $\mathbf{P}$.

Our discussion of the sign-test algorithm has proved everything except that $\mathbf{P}$ is closed under addition. To see this, let $\mathbf{x}$ and $\mathbf{y}$ be any two members of $\mathbf{P}$, so that $\mathsf{ST}_i(\mathbf{x})$ and $\mathsf{ST}_i(\mathbf{y})$ are positive for all sufficiently large i. Now, $\mathsf{ST}_i(\mathbf{x}+\mathbf{y}) = \mathsf{ST}_i(\mathbf{x}) + \mathsf{ST}_i(\mathbf{y})$, and so $\mathsf{ST}_i(\mathbf{x} + \mathbf{y})$ will be positive for all sufficiently large i (just wait until i is large enough so that $\mathsf{ST}_j(\mathbf{x})$ and $\mathsf{ST}_j(\mathbf{y})$ are *both* positive whenever $j \ge i$). This means that $\mathbf{x} + \mathbf{y}$ will also be a member of $\mathbf{P}$, and so $\mathbf{P}$ is indeed closed under addition as needed to complete the proof of the theorem. ∎

Therefore, the relation $<$ defined on $\mathbb{Z}[\sqrt{2}]$ by saying that $\mathbf{x} < \mathbf{y}$ holds precisely when $\mathbf{y} - \mathbf{x}$ belongs to $\mathbf{P}$ gives a linear ordering on $\mathbb{Z}[\sqrt{2}]$ which is compatible with addition, in the sense that, if $\mathbf{x} < \mathbf{y}$, then $\mathbf{x} + \mathbf{z} < \mathbf{y} + \mathbf{z}$ for any $\mathbf{z}$ in $\mathbb{Z}[\sqrt{2}]$.

5.3 Properties of the Ordering

In this section, we show that the ordering $<$ on $\mathbb{Z}[\sqrt{2}]$ induced by the set of positive elements $\mathbf{P}$ is archimedean and dense. We also show that $\mathbf{P}$ is compatible with multiplication.

The *archimedean property* states that iterated addition of any positive quantity results in a sequence of quantities that increase without bound:

Theorem 3. *Let* $\mathbf{x}$ *be any member of* $\mathbf{P}$ *and* $\mathbf{y}$ *any member of* $\mathbb{Z}[\sqrt{2}]$, *then there is a natural number,* n, *such that* $\mathbf{y} < n\mathbf{x}$.

Proof: By the definition of $\mathbf{P}$, the assumption that $\mathbf{x} \in \mathbf{P}$ means that we can find an i such that two consecutive values, $\mathsf{ST}_i(\mathbf{x})$ and $\mathsf{ST}_{i+1}(\mathbf{x})$, are both positive. Choose a natural number n which is greater than the larger of the absolute values $|\mathsf{ST}_i(\mathbf{y})|$ and $|\mathsf{ST}_{i+1}(\mathbf{y})|$. I claim that n satisfies $\mathbf{y} < n\mathbf{x}$. For $\mathsf{ST}_i(n\mathbf{x} - \mathbf{y}) = n\mathsf{ST}_i(\mathbf{x}) - \mathsf{ST}_i(\mathbf{y}) \ge n - \mathsf{ST}_i(\mathbf{y}) > 0$, since $\mathsf{ST}_i(\mathbf{x}) \ge 1$, and $n > |\mathsf{ST}_i(\mathbf{y})|$ by our choices of i and n, and similarly for $\mathsf{ST}_{i+1}(n\mathbf{x} - \mathbf{y})$. So, $n\mathbf{x} - \mathbf{y}$ is in $\mathbf{P}$, and by definition of $<$, we do have $\mathbf{y} < n\mathbf{x}$, as claimed. ∎

Now for *density*: an ordered group is densely ordered if its set of positive elements has no least element. We now show that this is the case for $\mathbb{Z}[\sqrt{2}]$:

Theorem 4. **P** *has no least element.*

Proof: What we have to show is that, if **y** is any member of **P**, then there is a member **x** of **P** such that $\mathbf{x} < \mathbf{y}$. As $\mathbf{y} \in \mathbf{P}$, then for some i, $\mathsf{ST}_i(\mathbf{y})$ and $\mathsf{ST}_{i+1}(\mathbf{y})$ satisfy $0 < \mathsf{ST}_i(\mathbf{y}) < \mathsf{ST}_{i+1}(\mathbf{y})$. Now consider the recurrence equations that define the ST_j. These equations can be used in the reverse direction to find an **x** such that $\mathsf{ST}_i(\mathbf{x}) = 0$ and $\mathsf{ST}_{i+1}(\mathbf{x}) = 1$, whence $\mathsf{ST}_{i+2}(\mathbf{x}) = 2$, $\mathsf{ST}_i(\mathbf{y} - \mathbf{x}) > 0$ and $\mathsf{ST}_{i+1}(\mathbf{y} - \mathbf{x}) > 0$ so that **x** is in **P** and $\mathbf{x} < \mathbf{y}$ as required. ∎

It is natural at this point to ask about the interplay between order and multiplication in $\mathbb{Z}[\sqrt{2}]$. If we plan to follow the approach of section 4 above, we do not actually need to study this part of the scenery in $\mathbb{Z}[\sqrt{2}]$. However, for completeness, we record the following theorem and give a sketch of a proof:

Theorem 5. $\mathbb{Z}[\sqrt{2}]$ *equipped with the ordering defined by taking* **P** *as the set of positive elements is an ordered ring.*

Proof: An ordered ring is an (additive) ordered group together with a multiplication making it into a ring in such a way that *(i)* the unit element **1** is positive and *(ii)* multiplication by positive elements is order-preserving — if $0 < \mathbf{x}$, and $\mathbf{y} < \mathbf{z}$, then $\mathbf{xy} < \mathbf{xz}$. Equivalently, **1** is positive and the set of positive elements is closed under multiplication.

In our case, it easy to check that $1 \in \mathbf{P}$ directly from the definitions. To check that **P** is closed under multiplication, assume **x** and **y** are members of **P**. By definition, this means that, if we let $s_i = \mathsf{ST}_i(\mathbf{x})$ and $t_i = \mathsf{ST}_i(\mathbf{y})$, then the s_i and t_i are positive for all sufficiently large i. Let $w_i = \mathsf{ST}_i(\mathbf{xy})$, so that what we have to prove is that the w_i are positive for all sufficiently large i.

I claim that the following equation holds for any natural numbers m and n:

$$w_{m+n+1} = s_{m+1}t_{n+1} + s_m t_n$$

Given the equation above, if s_m and t_n are both positive, then w_{m+n+1} is too. As the s_i and t_i are positive for all sufficiently large i, then so are the w_i as required.

It remains to prove the equation. To do this, one first proves by induction on m that the equation holds for any m when $n = 0$, then, using that to provide the base case, one proves the equation for all m and n by induction on n. The inductions involve a little algebra and some care with the subscripts. ∎

5.4   Discussion

The motivation behind the construction in this paper was as follows: given any irrational real number λ, the subgroup $\mathbb{Z} + \lambda\mathbb{Z}$ of $(\mathbb{R}, +)$ generated by 1 and λ is, *(i)*, dense (and so its Dedekind-MacNeille completion will be $\mathbb{R}$) and *(ii)* a free abelian group on the given generators (and so it is algebraically very tractable, in particular, every element has a canonical representation as $a + b\lambda$ for unique integers a and b). In contrast, *(i)*, no finitely generated subgroup of $(\mathbb{Q}, +)$ is dense and, *(ii)*, no dense subgroup of $(\mathbb{Q}, +)$ is free as an abelian group.

The case where λ is a real integral quadratic surd, such as $\sqrt{2}$, looked particularly promising, since in that case $\mathbb{Z} + \lambda\mathbb{Z}$ is actually a subring of $\mathbb{R}$. Of course, to construct $\mathbb{R}$ as the completion of $\mathbb{Z} + \lambda\mathbb{Z}$, we need to understand how the latter group is ordered, but the ordering turns out to be very tractable using the rather simple sign-test algorithm discussed above.

So with $\mathbb{Z}[\sqrt{2}]$, one has simple canonical representations and the minor complication of the sign-test algorithm to decide the ordering. In contrast, to get canonical representations of the elements of $\mathbb{Q}$, one has to appeal to the euclidean algorithm, the theory of which is significantly harder than the theory of the sign-test algorithm presented in this paper. The usual construction of $\mathbb{Q}$ as a set of equivalence classes avoids the need for canonical representations, at the price of proof obligations to justify definitions over the set of equivalence classes.

6   The Actual ProofPower Construction

The actual construction of the real numbers in ProofPower as carried out in November 2000 was significantly harder than the improved approach presented here. Nonetheless, measured in terms of lines of proof scripts, the complexity is about equal with that of Harrison's approach as described in [8].

The reason for the extra complication was simple and pragmatic: I had formulated the proof plan sketched in sections 1.2 and 1.3 above, but the direct approach to specifying the ordering in $\mathbb{Z}[\sqrt{2}]$ looked far from attractive and I had not discovered the easier approach of section 5.2. To leave some room for manoeuvre, I formulated a variant of the construction of the additive structure which requires less algebraic structure than the classical Dedekind construction allows. Under suitable hypotheses, the Dedekind construction can be applied to a monoid[12] rather than a group, and I knew I would be able to construct a suitable monoid. The Dedekind construction turns out to be not much harder than the usual one conceptually, but involves quite a lot more work with supremum arguments.

The monoid used is the multiplicative monoid of dyadic rational numbers. A dyadic rational number is one of the form $m/2^n$ where m and n are integers. Positive dyadic rationals may be identified with the set $\mathbb{N} \times \mathbb{Z}$ under the correspondence $(m, n) \mapsto (2m + 1)/2^n$ and the multiplication operator and ordering relation are not hard to define in terms of this. Verifying the required properties of these is a relatively straightforward but rather lengthy exercise in elementary algebra.

Thus, a combination of luck and design means that the actual construction was "transcendental" rather than just "irrational": the starting point for the Dedekind construction amounted to the monoid of all real numbers $\log(m/2^n)$ with $m > 0$ and n integers and most of these numbers are transcendental.

The theory is formulated so that the actual details of the construction are almost invisible to a user of the theory. What a user sees is a collection of

---

[12] A monoid is a "group without an inverse function", i.e., a set with an associative binary product with an identity element.

constants giving the field operations and ordering relation on ℝ with defining properties that give the usual axiomatisation of ℝ as a complete ordered field.

7   Concluding Remarks

The reader is again referred to [5, 8] for comprehensive surveys of constructions of the real numbers with many additional references. In this paper, there is only space for a few observations about other approaches.

The approach promoted here derives the multiplicative structure of ℝ from its additive structure. This lets us exploit the delightfully simple additive structure of groups such as $\mathbb{Z}[\sqrt{2}]$ which turn out to have a very tractable order structure as well. However, the ring structure is simple too, and it now seems to the author that deriving the multiplicative structure of the reals in the traditional way from the ring structure of $\mathbb{Z}[\sqrt{2}]$ may well be advantageous.

This paper has concentrated on the Dedekind-MacNeille method of completing a dense ordered algebraic system. However, an approach using Cantor's method of fundamental sequences could also take $\mathbb{Z}[\sqrt{2}]$ as a starting point. This would need multiplicative inverses to be defined by a supremum argument rather than by pointwise operations on the fundamental sequences, but the supremum argument is an easy one.

A construction of the real numbers from the integers bypassing the rationals is given by Faltin et al. in [6]. Their method is to use a binary positional representation in which the digits are allowed to be arbitrary integers. This results in a presentation of the real numbers as a quotient of a certain subring of a ring of formal Laurent series. This gives considerable insight into the way carries propagate in infinite binary arithmetic and can be applied to other constructions (such as the p-adic completions of the integers). However, the method is considerably more complicated from an arithmetic point of view than the more traditional constructions.

In [3], Conway gives a construction which embraces ℕ, ℤ, ℚ and ℝ and much more using a uniform representation of numbers as pairs of sets which can be thought of as two-player games. The uniform representation leads to very uniform, if rather recondite, methods of proof. Characterising the real numbers within the Conway numbers is a little tricky but can be done. Unfortunately, in a typed framework such as HOL, identifying a type suitable for carrying out enough of the Conway construction to include ℝ involves a far from trivial exercise in justifying transfinite inductive definitions.

In conclusion, selecting a method of constructing ℝ in a mechanised theorem-proving system involves many trade-offs. The choice will be heavily influenced by what theories are already available and what theories are going to be developed in the future. If, for example, you have plans to do a lot of general commutative algebra, then your best route might be to do the general field-of-fractions construction and the standard material on ideals and quotient rings first and use these big guns to attack the specific problems of constructing ℚ as a field-of-fractions and then ℝ via fundamental sequences. If you only have ℕ, and want to get going on analysis quickly, then Harrison's approach is probably the method of choice. If you have good working theories for $\mathbb{N}$ and $\mathbb{Z}$ then the methods of the present paper are offered for your consideration as a quick and simple route from $\mathbb{Z}$ to $\mathbb{R}$.

Acknowledgments

I am grateful to John Harrison for some very helpful correspondence and, in particular, for drawing the work of Behrend to my attention. I am indebted to the referees for all their comments and suggestions; these were most stimulating and have been of great assistance in revising the paper for publication.

References

1. R.D. Arthan. A Report on ICL HOL. In Myla Archer, Jeffrey J. Joyce, Karl N. Levitt, and Philip J. Windley, editors, *Proceedings of the 1991 International Workshop on the HOL Theorem Proving System and its Applications.* IEEE Computer Society Press, 1992.
2. F.A. Behrend. A Contribution to the Theory of Magnitudes and the Foundations of Analysis. *Mathematische Zeitschrift*, 63:345–362, 1956.
3. John H. Conway. *On Numbers and Games.* A.K. Peters Ltd., Second edition, 2001.
4. B.A. Davey and H.A. Priestley. *Introduction to Lattices and Order.* Cambridge University Press, 1990.
5. H.-D. Ebbinghaus, H. Hermes, F. Hirzebruch, M. Koecher, K. Mainzer, J. Neukirch, A. Prestel, and R. Remmert. *Numbers.* Springer-Verlag, 1990.
6. F. Faltin, N. Metropolis, B. Ross, and G.-C. Rota. The Real Numbers as a Wreath Product. *Advances in Mathematics*, 16, 1975.
7. Michael J.C. Gordon and Tom F. Melham, editors. *Introduction to HOL.* Cambridge University Press, 1993.
8. John Harrison. Theorem Proving with the Real Numbers. Technical report, University of Cambridge Computer Laboratory, 1996.
9. O. Hölder. Die Axiome der Quantität und die Lehre vom Mass. *Ber. Verh. Kon. Sch. Ges. Wiss.*, pages 1–64, 1901.
10. R.B. Jones. Methods and Tools for the Verification of Critical Properties. In R.Shaw, editor, *5th Refinement Workshop*, Workshops in Computing. Springer-Verlag/BCS-FACS, 1992.
11. E. Kamke. *Mengenlehre.* Berlin, 1928. Reprinted by Dover in an English translation by F. Bagemihl as *Theory of Sets.* 1950.
12. D.J. King and R.D. Arthan. Development of Practical Verification Tools. *Ingenuity — the ICL Technical Journal*, 1996.
13. Saunders MacLane and Garrett Birkhoff. *Algebra.* AMS Chelsea Publishing, Third edition, 1999.
14. Walter Rudin. *Principles of Mathematical Analysis.* McGraw-Hill Book Company, 1974.
15. C. T. Sennett. Demonstrating the Compliance of Ada Programs with Z Specifications. In R.Shaw, editor, *5th Refinement Workshop*, Workshops in Computing. Springer-Verlag/BCS-FACS, 1992.

HELM and the Semantic Math-Web

Andrea Asperti, Luca Padovani, Claudio Sacerdoti Coen, and Irene Schena

Department of Computer Science
Via di Mura Anteo Zamboni 7, 40127 Bologna, Italy
asperti@cs.unibo.it

Abstract. The eXtensible Markup Language (XML) opens the possibility to start anew, on a solid technological ground, the ambitious goal of developing a suitable technology for the creation and maintenance of a virtual, distributed, hypertextual library of formal mathematical knowledge. In particular, XML provides a central technology for storing, retrieving and processing mathematical documents, comprising sophisticated web-publishing mechanisms (stylesheets) covering notational and stylistic issues. By the application of XML technology to the large repositories of structured, content oriented information offered by Logical Frameworks we meet the ultimate goal of the Semantic Web, that is to allow machines the sharing and exploitation of knowledge in the Web way, i.e. without central authority, with few basic rules, in a scalable, adaptable, extensible manner.

1 Introduction

Existing logical systems are not suitable for the creation of large repositories of structured mathematical knowledge accessible via Web. In fact, libraries in logical frameworks are usually saved in two formats: a textual one, in the specific tactical language of the proof assistant, and a compiled (proof checked) one in some internal, concrete representation language. Both representations are clearly unsatisfactory, since they are too oriented to the specific application: the information is not directly available, if not by means of the functionalities offered by the system itself. This is in clear contrast with the main guidelines of the modern Information Society, the recent emphasis on *content* and the new frontier of the so called "Semantic Web.[1]" The goal of the Semantic Web is to pass from a "machine readable" to a "machine understandable" encoding of the information: establishing a layer of machine understandable data would allow automated agents, sophisticated search engines and interoperable services and will enable higher degree of automation and more intelligent applications.

In contrast with current encodings of mathematical information (e.g. in digital libraries), which are "machine-readable" but not "machine-understandable", Logical Frameworks offer *huge* repositories of structured, content oriented information, naturally providing a major arena for the Semantic Web and its technologies. The point is to allow access to this mathematical knowledge in the

---

[1] Semantic Web Activity, http://www.w3.org/2001/sw.

R.J. Boulton and P.B. Jackson (Eds.): TPHOLs 2001, LNCS 2152, pp. 59–74, 2001.

"Web way", i.e. without central authority, with few basic rules, in a scalable, adaptable, extensible manner.

The first, mandatory step in this direction is the direct encoding of the libraries in XML, which has recently imposed as the main tool for representation, manipulation, linking and exchange of structured information. But of course the broad goal of the Semantic Web goes far beyond the trivial suggestion to adopt XML as a neutral specification language for the "compiled" versions of the libraries, or even the observation that in this way we could take advantage of a lot of functionalities on XML-documents already offered by standard commercial tools. Here is a short list of the added-value offered by the XML approach:

Standardization. Having a common, application independent, meta-language for mathematical proofs, similar software tools could be applied to different logical dialects, regardless of their concrete nature. This would be especially relevant for all those operations like searching, retrieving, displaying or authoring (just to mention a few of them) that are largely independent of the specific logical system.

Publishing. XML offers sophisticated web-publishing technologies (Stylesheets, MathML, ...) which can be profitably used to solve, in a *standard* way, the annoying notational problems that traditionally afflict formal mathematics.

Searching and Retrieving. The World Wide Web is currently doing a big effort in the Metadata and Semantic Web area. Languages as the Resource Description Framework or XML-Query are likely to produce innovative technological solutions in this field.

Interoperability. If having a common representation layer is not the ultimate solution to all interoperability problems between different applications, it is however a first and essential step in this direction.

Modularity. The "XML-ization" process should naturally lead to a substantial simplification and re-organization of the current, "monolithic" architecture of logical frameworks. All the many different and often loosely connected functionalities of these complex programs (proof checking, proof editing, proof displaying, search and consulting, program extraction, and so on) could be clearly split in more or less autonomous tasks, possibly (and hopefully!) developed by different teams, in totally different languages. This is the new *content-based* architecture of future systems.

In this article we present our project on the use of XML technology for the development and maintenance of distributed repositories of formal mathematical knowledge: the Hypertextual Electronic Library of Mathematics (HELM[2]).

2   The eXtensible Markup Language

Perhaps, the best way to introduce XML in few lines is to take a look at a simple example. The following XML document is a possible encoding of the definition of the inductive type of natural numbers in Coq [3].

---

[2] http://www.cs.unibo.it/helm.

```
<?xml version="1.0" encoding="ISO-8859-1"?>
<!DOCTYPE InductiveDefinition
  SYSTEM "http://www.cs.unibo.it/helm/dtd/cic.dtd">
<InductiveDefinition noParams="0" params="">
 <InductiveType name="nat" inductive="true">
  <arity><SORT value="Set"/></arity>
   <Constructor name="0"><REL value="1" binder="nat"/></Constructor>
   <Constructor name="S">
    <PROD>
     <source><REL value="1" binder="nat"/></source>
     <target><REL value="2" binder="nat"/></target>
    </PROD>
   </Constructor>
 </InductiveType>
</InductiveDefinition>
```

XML gives a method for structuring data in a text file. Roughly speaking, the
XML specification says that a XML document is made of *tags* (words bracketed
by '<' and '>'), *attributes* (of the form name="value") and text. Tags are used to
delimit *elements*. Elements may appear in one of the following two forms: either
they are non-empty elements, as InductiveDefinition or InductiveType (they
can contain other elements or text), or they are empty elements, as SORT or REL.
The previous example contains no text: this is a peculiarity of really *formal*
encodings, where every bit of knowledge has a specific intelligence worth to be
encapsulated in markup.

The XML specification defines a XML document to be well-formed if it meets
some syntactical constraints on the use of tags and attributes. For example, non-
empty elements must be perfectly balanced. For this reason, someone can think
of tags of non-empty elements as labeled brackets for structuring the document.

XML lets the user specify his own grammar by means of a Document Type
Definition (DTD), a document which defines the allowed tags, the related attributes and which is the legal content for each element. The XML specification
just defines the validity of a XML document with respect to a given DTD. This
is why XML is a *meta-language* that can be instantiated to a potentially infinite
set of languages, each with its own DTD.

For example, here is a DTD fragment for the previous XML file:

```
<?xml version="1.0" encoding="ISO-8859-1"?>
...
<!ENTITY % term '(LAMBDA|CAST|PROD|REL|SORT|APPLY|VAR|META|IMPLICIT|
                 CONST|LETIN|MUTIND|MUTCONSTRUCT|MUTCASE|FIX|COFIX)'>
...
<!ELEMENT InductiveDefinition (InductiveType+)>
<!ATTLIST InductiveDefinition
          noParams NMTOKEN #REQUIRED
          params   CDATA   #REQUIRED
          id       ID      #REQUIRED>
<!ELEMENT InductiveType (arity,Constructor*)>
<!ATTLIST InductiveType
          name     CDATA         #REQUIRED
```

```
              inductive (true|false) #REQUIRED>
<!ELEMENT Constructor %term;>
<!ATTLIST Constructor name CDATA #REQUIRED>
...
```

A InductiveDefinition element may contain one or more InductiveType elements, each InductiveType contains an arity followed by a possibly empty sequence of Constructors, and a Constructor is an arbitrary term (an ENTITY is a macro declaration). The attributes of InductiveDefinition are noParams, params and id, while name is the only attribute of Constructor. The keyword REQUIRED states that an attribute cannot be omitted when using its related tag.

References to Documents. Documents and resources in general must have a name in order to be accessible over the Web. This is accomplished via the use of URIs (Universal Resource Identifiers) as defined in [6]. A generic URI is made of a formatted (structured) string of characters whose intended meaning is associated by the applications managing it. URLs (Uniform Resource Locators) are a particular kind of URIs specifically designed to name resources accessed by means of a given standard protocol (for example the HTTP protocol). URLs consist of a first part identifying the protocol and a host followed by a second part to locate the resource on it.

URLs can be resolved by standard processing tools and browsers, but suffer from problems of consistency: moving the target document leads to dangling pointers; moreover, being physical names, they cannot be used to identify a whole set of copies located on different servers for fault-tolerance and load-balancing purposes. URIs, instead, can be designed as logical names, leaving to applications the burden of resolution to physical names. So, for examples, the URI "cic:/Coq/Reals/Rdefinitions/R.con" could be used as a logical name for the axiom which defines the existence of the set R of real numbers in the standard library of the Coq Proof Assistant; then, an application is required to map the URI to a physical name (an URL) as

    http://coq.inria.fr/library/Reals/Rdefinitions/R.con.xml

3   The HELM Project

The overall architecture of our project is depicted in Fig. 1.

Once XML has been chosen as the standard encoding format[3] for the library, we must face the problem of recovering the already codified mathematical knowledge. Hence, we need new modules implementing exporting functionalities toward the XML representation for all the available tools for proof reasoning. Currently, we have just written such a module only for the Coq proof assistant [3]. In the near future, we expect that similar exporting functionalities will be provided by the developers of the other logical systems. We will describe the exporting issues in Sect. 4.

---

[3] A standard *format*, not a standard *language*! In other words, the standardization we are pursuing is not at the *logical* level, but at the *technological* one.

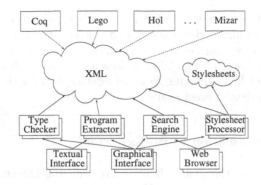

Fig. 1. Architecture of the HELM Project.

To exploit and augment the library, we need several tools to provide all the functionalities given by the current "monolithic" proof assistants, such as type-checking, proof searching, program verification, code extraction and so on. Moreover, we can use the available well-developed and extensible tools for processing, retrieval and rendering of XML-encoded information. In particular, to render the library information, we advocate the use of stylesheets, which are a standard way of associating a presentation to the content of XML files. This allows the user to introduce new mathematical notations by simply writing a new stylesheet. In Sect. 5 we shall briefly discuss our implementation of a type-checking tool, while in Sect. 6 stylesheets are addressed in details.

The user will interact with the library through several interfaces that integrate the different tools to provide an homogeneous view of the functionalities. We are developing two interfaces, described in Sect. 7.

Because of the particular nature of the library, we have also provided a suitable model of distribution, which is discussed in more detail in Sect. 8.

4   Exporting from Coq

Coq is one of the most advanced proof-assistants, based on a very rich logical framework called the Calculus of (Co)Inductive Constructions (CIC). The great number of functionalities (proof editing, proof checking, proof searching, proof extraction, program verification) have made the system, whose last stable release is V6.3.1, very big and complex. In fact, the only practical way to work with the information encoded in Coq is that of writing a new module that extends the system gaining access to its internal representation.

A new release of Coq, called V7, is being now developed with the precise aim to reduce the implementation complexity; notwithstanding this, finding the right information inside the system itself is not a trivial task: first, information is encoded in Coq's data structures which change among different versions of the system; second, the required information is often not directly available. For example, when a file is loaded in V6.3.1, its path is forgotten, while we would like to export files in directories reflecting the logical structure of the library.

In the rest of this section we only focus on the implementation of the exporting module[4] for version 6.3.1 which is a representative example of the difficulties that could be faced when exporting from an existing proof-assistant without the collaboration of its development team.

4.1   Relevant Information to Be Exported

To design the module, the first difficulty has been the identification of which information is worth to be exported. We have chosen not to export:

Parsing and pretty-printing rules. Parsing rules should depend only on the proof engine. To be able to use other proof engines different from Coq we cannot rely on Coq's own rules. Similarly, pretty-printing rules should depend only on the users choice and the type of available browser.

Tactics-related information. These, too, are proof engine dependent. Moreover, we do not think that the tactics used to do a proof are really meaningful to understand the proof itself (surely, they are not the real informative content). In fact, the level of tactics and the level at which a proof should be understood are not the same: what some simple tactics do (as "Auto" that automatically search a proof) is not at all obvious. Moreover, the sequence of tactics used is clearly reflected in the λ-term of the proof; hence it is possible to add as an attribute to a sub term the name and parameters of the tactic used to generate it.

Redundant information added by Coq to the terms of CIC. Coq adds in several places a lot of information to CIC terms in order to speed up the type-checking. For example, during the type-checking of an inductive definition, Coq records which are the recursive parameters of its inductive constructors; this information is then used during the type-checking of fix functions to ensure their termination. This is an example of a clearly redundant information, surely useless for browsing purposes or for indexing, but necessary to every proof-checker implementation. Other times, instead, the added information is important only for browsing purposes. For example, sometimes the user asks the system to infer a type and probably does not want to view the inferred type thereafter.

So, we have decided to export a first core of information, roughly corresponding to the only one available at the logical level, according to a *principle of minimalism*: *no redundant information should be exported*. If the principle were not followed, in every application loading an XML file we would have to add checks to verify the consistency of the redundant (and possibly useless!) information. In Sect. 4.2 we will see how this does not prevent us to link in a precise way additional information to the core one.

---

[4] The module is fully working and has been used to export the whole library provided with the Coq System, yielding about 64 Mb of XML (2 Mb after compression).

The remaining, interesting information could be structured into three different levels that we have clearly separated in the XML representation. The first one is the *level of terms*. Terms (or expressions) can never appear alone, but only as part of an object definition. In Coq, the terms are CIC λ-expressions, i.e. variables (encoded as DeBrujin indexes), λ-abstractions and applications, product types and sorts, augmented with a system of inductive types in the spirit of the ones of Martin-Löf, comprising (co)inductive types and constructors, case analysis operators and inductive and co-inductive function definitions. The whole level is extremely dependent on the logical framework.

The second level, that uses the previous one to encode both bodies and types, is the one of *objects*. Every object is stored into a different file. The files are structured into directories that corresponds to sections in Coq, i.e. delimiters of the scope of a variable. Sections are also used in Coq to structure a large theory into sub-theories. In HELM, the former usage is retained, while theories are described in another way (see the third level). In Coq, the objects are constants, representing definitions, theorems and axioms, (the former two have both a type and a body, while the latter has a type only), variables, (co)inductive definitions (such as **nat** for the natural numbers) and proofs in progress.

The last level is the *level of theories* which is completely independent of the particular logical framework. In our idea, a theory is a (structured) mathematical document containing objects taken almost freely from different sections. Writing a new theory should consist in developing new objects and assembling these new objects and older ones into the mathematical document. It is during the creation of a theory that objects must also be assigned the particular, semantical meaning used to classify them, for example into lemmas, conjectures, corollaries, etc. Theories, that are described in different XML files, do not include the objects directly, but refers to them via their URIs.

The following is an example of theory file with two sections, the first one delimiting the scope of variables A and B.

```xml
<?xml version="1.0" encoding="ISO-8859-1"?>
<!DOCTYPE Theory SYSTEM "http://www.cs.unibo.it/helm/dtd/maththeory.dtd">
<Theory uri="cic:/Coq/Init/Logic">
 <!-- Require Export Datatypes -->
 <DEFINITION uri="True.ind"/>
 <DEFINITION uri="False.ind"/>
 <DEFINITION uri="not.con"/>
 <SECTION uri="Conjunction">
  <DEFINITION uri="and.ind"/>
  <VARIABLE uri="A.var"/>
  <VARIABLE uri="B.var"/>
  <THEOREM id="id1" uri="proj1.con"/>
  <THEOREM id="id2" uri="proj2.con"/>
 </SECTION>
 <SECTION uri="Disjunction">
  <DEFINITION uri="or.ind"/>
 </SECTION>
</Theory>
```

All the URIs, but that of `Theory`, are relative URIs; so, the absolute URI of id1 is "`cic:/Coq/Init/Logic/Conjunction/proj1.con`". In the example you can also see the usage of sections to bound the scope of variables: the scope of A and B is the section `Conjunction`.

It is important to note that at the theory level, sections are not used to structure the document into, for instance, chapters, paragraphs and so on; many kind of (XML) markup languages have just been developed to do so. Accordingly to the spirit of XML, our theory markup will be freely and modularly intermixed with other kinds of markup, such as XHTML;[5] so, our language will play for mathematical theories the same role of MathML for mathematical expressions and SVG[6] for vectorial graphics. The added value of using the theory level (instead of directly embedding the object markup) is that, while enriching the semantics of the objects of the previous level, it could also be used to enforce some constraints as, for example, on the scope of variables or on the links between theorems and lemmas.

4.2   Auxiliary Information and Metadata

In this paragraph we address the problem of the association of additional and possibly redundant information to the one exported using the Coq module. The purpose of this added information is to enable or facilitate specific functionalities such as rendering, searching, indexing and so on.[7]

A simple observation suggests that such information could be naturally associated either to the whole object definition (e.g. the name of the author of a theorem) or to a particular node of a λ-term (e.g. the tactic used to generate it or an informal description of its meaning). So, we can easily store the additional information in a distinct XML file and use XLink technology to relate it to the appropriate XML element in the corresponding logical-level document. Moreover, in the specific case of metadata, we can benefit from the Resource Description Framework (RDF, [11] [12]), which provides a general model for representing metadata as well as a syntax for encoding and exchanging this metadata over the Web. In several cases, this meta-information can be extracted from the document, for instance by means of XSL Transformations. It is important to note that, in this approach, no modification at all is required to the DTDs or to the source document. As a side effect, an application can consult just the XML files holding the information it really needs, without having to parse, check for consistency and finally ignore non-interesting information.

---

[5] `http://www.w3.org/TR/xhtml1`.

[6] `http://www.w3.org/TR/SVG`.

[7] For instance, a major example of such additional information, which is essential for rendering purposes, are the intermediate conclusions inside complex proofs (see [4]), which are typically omitted (as redundant) in a Curry-Howard representation of proofs as λ-terms.

5   Proof-Checker

In order to verify that all the needed core information was exported from Coq, we have developed a stand-alone proof-checker for CIC objects, similar to the Coq one, but fairly simpler and smaller thanks to its independence of the proof engine. It is the first example of a tool working directly on the XML encoding.

With respect to other proof-checkers (as the one of Coq), it is fairly standard but for the peculiar management of the environment: usually, proof-checkers are used to check whole theories, i.e. sequence of definitions or proofs. Each time a definition is checked, it is added to the environment and then it is used in subsequent type-checking. So, every theorem is always checked with the same, statically defined environment. Our proof-checker, instead, builds the environment (a cache, actually) "on-demand": every time a reference to another object not present in the environment is found, the type-checking is interrupted, processing the new object first. Checks are introduced in order to avoid cycles in the definitions, corresponding to an inconsistent environment.

6   XSL Transformations and MathML

XSLT [17] is a language for transforming XML documents into other XML documents. In particular, a stylesheet is a set of rules expressed in XSLT to transform the tree representing a XML document into a result tree. When a pattern is matched against elements in the source tree, the corresponding template is instantiated to create part of the result tree. In this way the source tree can be filtered and reordered, and arbitrary structure can be added. A pattern is an expression of XPath [16] language, that allows to match elements according to their values, structure and position in the source tree.

XSLT is primarily aimed to associate a *style* to a XML document, generating formatted documents suitable for rendering purposes, thus providing a standard tool for processing and transforming XML mathematical document, according to alternative notations and encodings.

A natural encoding for mathematics on the Web is MathML [8], an instance of XML for describing the notation of a mathematical expression, capturing both its structure and content. MathML has, roughly, two categories of markup elements: the presentation markup, which describes the layout structure of mathematical notation, and the content markup, that provides an explicit encoding of the *underlying* mathematical structure of an expression.

Although the target of MathML is the encoding of expressions (so it cannot describe mathematical objects and documents), the MathML Presentation Markup can be considered as a privileged rendering format, providing a standard on the web already implemented by several applications.

The choice of MathML content markup as an intermediate representation between the logic-dependent representation of the mathematical information and its presentation is justified by several reasons:

- Even if the content markup is restricted to the encoding of a particular set of formulas (the ones used until the first two years of college in the United States), it is extensible and flexible.[8]
- Passing through this semi-formal representation will improve the modularity of the overall architecture: many specific logical dialects can be mapped into the same intermediate language (or into suitable extensions of it). Moreover several stylesheets can be written for this single intermediate language to generate specific rendering formats.
- The characteristic of portability of MathML content markup can be exploited for cutting and pasting terms from an application to another.
- MathML content markup can capture the usual *informal* semantics of well-known operators, as for example the disjunction, marking them with the corresponding content elements (e.g. or). Their different formal content is preserved by means of backward pointers to the low level specification.

A feasible alternative to MathML content is provided by OpenMath[9] (see the MathML [8] recommendation for a discussion about the two approaches).

As depicted in Fig. 2, there are two sequential phases of stylesheets application: the first one generates the content representation from the CIC XML one; the second one generates either the MathML presentation markup or the HTML markup (and possibly others presentational formats as well).

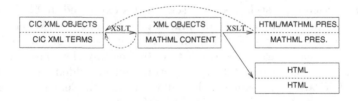

Fig. 2. Transformations of CIC XML Files: The backward arrows represent links from the content and presentation files to the corresponding CIC XML files.

The following is an example of content markup

```
<apply>
<csymbol>app</csymbol>
<ci definitionURL=
    "cic:/Coq/Init/Logic/Conjunction/and_ind.con">and_ind</ci>
<ci>A</ci>
<ci>B</ci>
```

---

[8] The most important element for extensibility purposes is csymbol, defined for constructing a symbol whose semantics is not part of the core content elements provided by MathML, but defined externally.

[9] http://www.openmath.org.

```
<ci>A</ci>
<lambda>
 <bvar><ci>H0</ci><type><ci>A</ci></type></bvar>
 <lambda>
  <bvar><ci>H1</ci><type><ci>B</ci></type></bvar>
  <ci>H0</ci>
 </lambda>
</lambda>
<ci>H</ci>
</apply>
```

The main problems related to the definition of content stylesheets are:

- Objects, in general, cannot be considered as terms. Hence, we have added to the MathML content markup a XML level to describe the level of objects (using different namespaces [9]).
- Operators which are not covered by the MathML content base set are encoded by means of the `csymbol` element.
- The standard semantics of MathML content elements is only informally defined in the specification. In HELM, formal semantics of content elements is enforced, wherever it is possible, by means of pointers to the XML files of their corresponding CIC definitions.

As you can see in Fig. 2, we produce MathML content and presentation in two distinct steps. The only way to combine and link together content and presentation in compliance to the MathML specification consists of using the `semantics` element. This content element is quite ambiguous, a kind of "bridge" between content and presentation; moreover, it is currently ignored by all the browsers supporting MathML. For us, the next natural improvement will consist of having content and the associated presentations in different files, one for the content expression and one for each presentation. Then we need to relate a presentation expression and subexpressions to the respective content expression and subexpressions. This can be achieved in a standard way using the machinery of XLink and XPointer [14,15].

The above solution has been also exploited for the implementation of the links of Fig. 2 for linking the content and presentation markup to the corresponding source CIC XML terms. In this way the user can browse the MathML presentation and also modify it: the changes will have effect on the corresponding CIC XML file.

An example of MathML presentation markup generated after the second phase is:

```
<mrow>
 <mo stretchy="false">(</mo>
 <mi>and_ind</mi><mphantom><mtext>_</mtext></mphantom>
 <mi>A</mi><mphantom><mtext>_</mtext></mphantom>
 <mi>B</mi><mphantom><mtext>_</mtext></mphantom>
 <mi>A</mi><mphantom><mtext>_</mtext></mphantom>
 <mrow>
```

```
<mo color="Red">&lambda;</mo>
<mi>H0</mi> <mo>:</mo> <mi>A</mi> <mo>.</mo>
<mrow>
 <mo color="Red">&lambda;</mo>
 <mi>H1</mi> <mo>:</mo> <mi>B</mi> <mo>.</mo>
 <mi>H0</mi>
</mrow>
</mrow>
<mphantom><mtext>_</mtext></mphantom><mi>H</mi>
<mo stretchy="false">)</mo>
</mrow>
```

To generate presentation markup from the corresponding content markup, we use, among others, a stylesheet, compliant with the last specification of MathML, written by Igor Rodionov.[10] This stylesheet, written in collaboration with the MathML Working Group, transforms MathML content markup in MathML presentation one.

We must solve several problems regarding the presentation output:

- We have had to associate an output to every object and to every `csymbol` defined in the content phase.
- We have modified the MathML stylesheet to implement the policy of line-breaking and alignment for long terms: our choice consists of using tables made of multiple rows. The `mtable` element is specifically designed to arrange expressions in a two-dimensional layout and in particular it provides a set of related elements and attributes to achieve proper alignment and line-breaking.

As we have said above, MathML is not the only format exploited: another presentation format is HTML, due to the wide-spreading of browsers for it and its native hypertextual nature. Thanks to the modular architecture (see Fig. 2), many other formats could be added too.

Finally, note that the general architecture gives the possibility of applying stylesheets of arbitrary complexity. For example, we have developed stylesheets to render proofs in natural language, in the spirit of [5].

We will exploit the same modular architecture of the object level at the level of theories. At this level we can use the same presentation formats of the previous levels; on the contrary, there is no standard language for describing theories at the content level. So we will develop a new (XML) language that will be largely independent of the specific foundational dialect and could aspire to play the same role MathML plays for mathematical expressions. An already existent corresponding proposal for OpenMath is OMDoc [10]. A possibility could consist of achieving the integration of our proposal with an extension to MathML of OMDoc, giving a common standard way to represent the structure of a mathematical document.

---

[10] Computer Science Department of the University of Western Ontario, London, Canada.

7   Interfaces to HELM

Two of the main goals of HELM are the easiness in augmenting and browsing the library:

1. Every user with a small amount of HTTP or FTP space should be able to publish a document.
2. Every user with a common browser should be able to browse the library.

To fullfil these aims, we must face the actual state of technology:

1. Currently, almost all of the Internet users have a web space, but usually without being allowed to run any kind of program on the server, even simple CGIs. So no intelligence can be put on the publisher side.
2. The browser technology is rapidly evolving in such a way that we expect in a few time to have browsers able to understand MathML and, probably, even to apply XSLT stylesheets. At the moment, though, if we require the browser to be standard, then we have to put the intelligence on the other side, i.e. on the server.

Therefore, where can we put the intelligence? A first answer is the creation of *presentation sites* able to retrieve documents from distribution sites, process them (e.g. applying stylesheets) and return them to the users in the user requested format.

In a first prototype of presentation site we relied on the capabilities of Cocoon, a XML server-based web-publishing framework, for the processing of the requested documents. Recently we adopted a more modular and more reusable solution, consisting in having a completely separate component, a servlet indeed, for the application of stylesheets. This component is designed to receive HTTP requests of stylesheet application, sending the result of the transformation as the reply of the request. In this way, ordinary browsing tools can access the processed documents simply by invoking the servlet with a proper URL containing both a reference to the source document to be processed, the list of stylesheets to be applied and possibly a sequence of parameters. In this way the number and order of the stylesheets can be changed at any invocation and their behavior may be affected by the value of the parameters passed by the client. Moreover, the documents, the stylesheets and the DTDs are not constrained to reside on the same host of the processor, thus over-passing the greatest limitation of the Cocoon-based framework.

Though this solution is perfect for browsing[11] and doing simple elaborations, it gives the user too strict interaction possibilities, which are required for more complex tasks (as the creation of new theories, for example). Hence, more advanced interfaces with such capabilities are required. These interfaces must be run on the user's machine and should, at least, be able to provide all the processing functionalities of the presentation servers. At the same time, they should

---

[11] An on-line library of Coq V7 theories can be found at the address http://phd.cs.unibo.it/helm/library/. Each document is rendered on-the-fly either to HTML or to MathML.

also overcome the limitations of standard browsers through the addition of new interaction possibilities.

Since our preferential browsing language is MathML, our interface should at least be able to render its presentation markup. Unfortunately, there are no satisfactory implementations available yet. Moreover, we also need to interact with the MathML rendered files, for example for editing. Not only forms of interaction with this kind of markup have never been proposed before, but we also need to reflect the changes on the source files of the XSLT rendering transformations. This has led us to the development of a brand new engine with rendering and editing capabilities for documents embedding MathML presentation markup. The engine, which is also able to export rendered MathML documents to Postscript, is designed to be stand-alone and it is freely available as a Gtk widget.[12]

We have integrated our widget, the proof-checker and the external XSLT processor into a minimal interface that we are going to extend with editing functionalities.

8   The Model of Distribution

Mathematical documents have some peculiar properties. First of all a mathematical document should be immutable: the correctness of a document A that refers to a document B can be guaranteed only if B does not change. Notwithstanding this, new versions of a mathematical document could be released (for example if a conjecture is actually proved). Secondly, a user cannot be forced to retain a copy of his document forever, even if other documents refer to it. So, it should be possible for everyone to make a copy of a document and also distribute it. When more than a copy is available, the user should be able to download it from any suitable server (for example, from the nearest one). This implies that documents could not be referred to via URLs, but only with logical names in the form of URIs. A particular naming policy should then be adopted to prevent users to publish different documents under the same URI.

To fulfill these requirements, we have adopted almost the same model of distribution of the Debian packaging system APT[13] which has similar requirements (a package could not be modified, but only updated, it is available on different servers, could be downloaded from the user preferred server).

Every document is identified by an URI. For example, the URI that references an inductive definition (".ind") in the subsection Datatypes of the subsection Init of the section Coq is "cic:/Coq/Init/Datatypes/nat.ind". Similarly, the URI "theories:/Coq/Init/Datatypes.theory" refers to the mathematical theory named Datatypes located in the subdirectory Init of the directory Coq.

In order to translate the URI to a valid URL, a particular tool, named *getter*, is needed. It takes in input an ordered list of servers and an URI and returns the URL of the document on the first server in the list supplying it. Each server

---

[12] The widget is now a package of the forthcoming Debian distribution.
See http://www.cs.unibo.it/helm/mml-widget/ for further details.
[13] http://www.debian.org.

publishes a list of the URIs of the documents it provides along with their corresponding URL.

In order to flexibly allow communication between the components of HELM architecture, the interface provided by the getter is the one of an HTTP daemon, pre-dating the ideas of the SOAP working draft [13]: when a document is required, its logical name is resolved in an URL, the document is downloaded, it is processed if needed[14] and finally it is returned to the client and it is possibly locally stored for caching purposes. If the machine hosting the getter is also a distribution site, then, once cached, a document could also be added to the list of documents the server exports. In such a way, often referred to or simply interesting documents spread rapidly over the net, downloading times are reduced and the author can freely get rid of his copy of the document if he does not need it any more. This architecture imposes no constraints on the naming policy: up to now we have not chosen or implemented one yet. To face the issue, one possibility can be the choice of having a centralized naming authority, even if other more distributed scenarios will surely be considered.

9 Conclusions and Further Developments

In this paper we have presented the current status of the HELM project, whose aim is to exploit the potentiality of XML technology for the creation and maintenance of large repositories of structured, content oriented information offered by Logical Frameworks, sharing and processing knowledge in compliance with the main philosophy of Web, i.e. without central authority, with few basic rules, in a scalable, adaptable, extensible manner.

Due to our methodology (HELM is independent of Coq), the extension of the library to other logical frameworks and systems does not look problematic.

We are soon going to develop:

Tools for indexing and retrieval of mathematical documents, based on meta-data specified in the Resource Description Framework (RDF, see [11]). RDF provides a foundation for processing meta-data, complements XML, and improves interoperability between applications that exchange information on the Web.

Tools for the (re)annotation of mathematical objects and terms: the intuitive meaning of these entities is usually lost in their description in a logical framework. Even their automatically extracted presentations in a natural language are often unsatisfactory, being quite different from the typical presentation in a book. We believe that a feasible solution is giving the user the possibility of enriching terms with annotations given in an informal, still structured language.

Tools to provide functionalities missing from monolithic proof assistants, such as proof-extraction of proof-editing.

---

[14] For example, typical processing are deflating compressed files or the resolution of relative URIs contained in the document to absolute ones.

References

1. Asperti, A., Padovani, L., Sacerdoti Coen, C., Schena, I., "Towards a library of formal mathematics". Panel session of the 13th International Conference on Theorem Proving in Higher Order Logics (TPHOLS'2000), Portland, Oregon, USA.
2. Asperti, A., Padovani, L., Sacerdoti Coen, C., Schena, I., "XML, Stylesheets and the re-mathematization of Formal Content", Department of Computer Science, Bologna, Italy, May 2000.
3. Barras, B., et al., "The Coq Proof Assistant Reference Manual, version 6.3.1", http://pauillac.inria.fr/coq/.
4. Coscoy, Y., Kahn, G., Thery, L., *Extracting Text from Proofs*. Technical Report RR-2459, INRIA Sophia Antipolis.
5. Coscoy, Y., "Explication textuelle de preuves pour le Calcul des Constructions Inductives", Phd. Thesis, Université de Nice-Sophia Antipolis, 2000.
6. Berners-Lee, T., "Universal Resource Identifiers in WWW", RFC 1630, CERN, June 1994.
7. Extensible Markup Language (XML) (Second Edition). Version 1.0. W3C Recommendation, 6 October 2000. http://www.w3.org/TR/REC-xml.
8. Mathematical Markup Language (MathML). Version 2.0. W3C Recommendation, 21 February 2001. http://www.w3.org/TR/MathML2/.
9. Namespaces in XML. W3C Recommendation, 14 January 1999.
http://www.w3.org/TR/REC-xml-names/
10. Open Mathematical Documents (OMDoc) 1.0, November 1 2000. http://www.mathweb.org/omdoc/.
11. Resource Description Framework (RDF) Model and Syntax Specification, W3C Recommendation 22 February 1999.
http://www.w3.org/TR/1999/REC-rdf-syntax-19990222/.
12. Resource Description Framework (RDF) Schema Specification 1.0, W3C Candidate Recommendation 27 March 2000. http://www.w3.org/TR/rdf-schema/.
13. Simple Object Access Protocol (SOAP). Version 1.1. W3C Note, 8 May 2000. http://www.w3.org/TR/SOAP/.
14. XML Linking Language (XLink). Version 1.0. W3C Proposed Recommendation, 20 December 2000. http://www.w3.org/TR/xlink/.
15. XML Pointer Language (XPointer). Version 1.0. W3C Working Draft (Last Call), 8 January 2001. http://www.w3.org/TR/xptr/.
16. XML Path Language (XPath). Version 1.0, W3C Recommendation, 16 November 1999. http://www.w3.org/TR/xpath.
17. XSL Transformations (XSLT). Version 1.0, W3C Recommendation, 16 November 1999. http://www.w3.org/TR/xslt/.

Calculational Reasoning Revisited

An Isabelle/Isar Experience

Gertrud Bauer and Markus Wenzel

Technische Universität München
Institut für Informatik, Arcisstrasse 21, 80290 München, Germany
http://www.in.tum.de/~bauerg/
http://www.in.tum.de/~wenzelm/

Abstract. We discuss the general concept of calculational reasoning within Isabelle/Isar, which provides a framework for high-level natural deduction proofs that may be written in a human-readable fashion. Setting out from a few basic logical concepts of the underlying meta-logical framework of Isabelle, such as higher-order unification and resolution, calculational commands are added to the basic Isar proof language in a flexible and non-intrusive manner. Thus calculational proof style may be combined with the remaining natural deduction proof language in a liberal manner, resulting in many useful proof patterns. A case-study on formalizing Computational Tree Logic (CTL) in simply-typed set-theory demonstrates common calculational idioms in practice.

1 Introduction

A proof by calculational reasoning basically proceeds by forming a chain of intermediate results that are meant to be composed by basic principles, such as transitivity of $=/</\leq$ (or similar relations). More advanced calculations may even involve substitution, which in the case of inequalities usually includes monotonicity constraints. In informal mathematics, this kind of proof technique is routinely used in a very casual manner. Whenever mathematicians write down sequences of mixed equalities or inequalities, underline subexpressions to be replaced etc. then it is likely that they are doing calculational reasoning.

In fact, calculational reasoning has been occasionally proposed as simple means to rephrase mathematical proof into a slightly more formal setting (e.g. [2,1]), which does not necessarily include machine-checking of proofs, of course. Observing that logical equivalence and implication may be just as well used in calculations, some have even set out to do away with traditional natural-deduction style reasoning altogether [5], although that discipline does not appeal to everyone.

Nevertheless, calculational reasoning offers a relatively simple conceptual basis to build tools for logical manipulations. The popular Mathʃpad tool supports manipulation of algebraic expressions in a systematic way; it has recently even acquired means for formal proof checking [18], using PVS as the backend.

R.J. Boulton and P.B. Jackson (Eds.): TPHOLs 2001, LNCS 2152, pp. 75–90, 2001.

The Mizar system [17,12,22] focuses on formal proof in common mathematics style in the first place. It also offers a mechanism for iterated equality reasoning, which shall serve here as an example for calculations within a formal setting. The following trivial proof is taken from article #185 of the Mizar library [11].

```
theorem Th1:
  for X,Y being set holds union {X,Y,{}} = union {X,Y}
proof
   let X,Y be set;
   thus union {X,Y,{}} = union ({X,Y} U {{}}) by ENUMSET1:43
                .= union {X,Y} U union {{}} by ZFMISC_1:96
                .= union {X,Y} U {} by ZFMISC_1:31
                .= union {X,Y};
end;
```

In Mizar "thus" indicates that the subsequent statement is meant to solve a pending goal. The continued equality sign ".=" indicates that the actual result shall emerge from a number of individual equations, each being proven separately and the results composed by transitivity behind the scenes.

The present paper discusses quite general concepts of calculational reasoning that may be expressed within the Isabelle/Isar framework for human-readable proof documents [19,20]. Isar provides a high-level view on natural deduction, but is open to incorporate additional derived language elements such as those for calculational reasoning. Thus techniques of natural deduction and calculations may be conveniently used together in the same proof, enabling the writer to apply the most appropriate one for the particular situation at hand.

So the two paradigms may coexist peacefully, and even benefit from each other. There need not be a conflict of natural deduction versus calculational reasoning, as is occasionally raised by followers of Dijkstra's proof format [5].

Before going into further details, we shall see how the above example works out within the Isar proof language.[1] First of all, we observe that it could be easily finished by a single stroke of an automated proof method of Isabelle [13].

theorem $\bigcup\{X, Y, \{\}\} = \bigcup\{X, Y\}$ **by** *auto*

In fact, many calculations in the Mizar library are rather trivial from the perspective of automated proof tools available in Isabelle, HOL, PVS etc., which indicates that Mizar's builtin automation does not handle equality too well. On the other hand, we would usually be less lucky with automated tools, once that the applications get more "realistic". In contrast, well-defined concepts of structured proof (such as calculations) provide means to arrange formal reasoning in a robust and scalable manner, being oriented towards the human reader (and writer) of proof texts, rather than the machine. Automated methods would then find there proper place in solving local proof obligations only.

The subsequent version mimics the original Mizar proof as closely as possible.

---

[1] All formal proofs given in this paper have been processed with Isabelle99-2.

theorem $\bigcup\{X, Y, \{\}\} = \bigcup\{X, Y\}$
proof −
  have $\bigcup\{X, Y, \{\}\} = \bigcup(\{X, Y\} \cup \{\{\}\})$ **by** *auto*
  also have $\ldots = \bigcup\{X, Y\} \cup \bigcup\{\{\}\}$ **by** *auto*
  also have $\ldots = \bigcup\{X, Y\} \cup \{\}$ **by** *auto*
  also have $\ldots = \bigcup\{X, Y\}$ **by** *auto*
  finally show $\bigcup\{X, Y, \{\}\} = \bigcup\{X, Y\}$.
qed

Isar provides an explicit mechanism to finish a calculation (unlike Mizar). In the canonical style of writing calculations this is used to reiterate the final result, sparing readers to determine it themselves. Calculations are not restricted to a fixed scheme, but may be freely composed via a few additional commands (**also** and **finally** encountered above) and the "..." notation for the right-hand side of the most recent statement (see §2.4). Thus the above text merely turns out as an idiomatic expression within a more general language framework (see §3).

We now inspect a bit further how the proof actually proceeds, and recall that the original Mizar proof basically imitates a simplification process. The justifications of intermediate claims (as indicated by **by**) are only of marginal interest here. We look more closely at the transformational process of the equations involved, which is represented at the top level as a plain transitive chain, but essentially performs a few substitution steps. Since Isabelle/Isar handles substitution as well, we may explain these technical details directly within the formal text.

theorem $\bigcup\{X, Y, \{\}\} = \bigcup\{X, Y\}$
proof −
  have $\{X, Y, \{\}\} = \{X, Y\} \cup \{\{\}\}$ **by** *auto*
  also have $\bigcup(\{X, Y\} \cup \{\{\}\}) = \bigcup\{X, Y\} \cup \bigcup\{\{\}\}$ **by** *auto*
  also have $\bigcup\{\{\}\} = \{\}$ **by** *auto*
  also have $\bigcup\{X, Y\} \cup \{\} = \bigcup\{X, Y\}$ **by** *auto*
  finally show $\bigcup\{X, Y, \{\}\} = \bigcup\{X, Y\}$.
qed

Apparently, the result of a calculation need not be the first left-hand side being equal to the last right-hand side, as more general rules get involved.

2   Foundations of Calculational Reasoning

2.1   Logical Preliminaries

We use standard mathematical notation as far as possible; just note that we write lists as $[x_1, \ldots, x_n]$ and $\bar{a} \mathbin{@} \bar{b}$ for appending lists $\bar{a}$ and $\bar{b}$.

Our basic logical foundations are that of the Isabelle/Pure framework [13], a minimal higher-order logic with universal quantification $\bigwedge x.\ P\ x$ and implication $A \implies B$; the underlying term language is that of simply-typed λ-calculus, with application $f\ x$ and abstraction $\lambda x.\ f$. Examples are presented in the object-logic

Isabelle/HOL [13], which extends Pure by common connectives ($\neg$, $\longrightarrow$, $\wedge$, $\vee$, $\forall$, $\exists$ etc.), the classical axiom, and Hilbert's choice operator.

By *theorem* we denote the set of derivable theorems of Pure, we write $\vdash \varphi$ to indicate that proposition φ is a theorem; furthermore let *facts* be the set of lists over *theorem*. Theorems of Pure actually represent (derived) rules of the embedded object logic. The main (derived) operations of Pure are *resolution* (back-chaining, generalized modus ponens) and proof by *assumption* [13] — both are quite powerful primitives as they may involve higher-order unification. We write $r \cdot \bar{a}$ for the resulting theorem of resolving facts $\bar{a}$ in parallel into rule r. A *goal* is represented as a theorem, which is $\vdash \varphi \Longrightarrow \varphi$ initially and gets refined by resolution to become $\vdash \varphi$ eventually [13]; note that Isabelle/Isar is already content with a goal state that is finished up to proof-by-assumption.

2.2   The Isabelle/Isar Proof Language

The Isar proof language provides a general framework for human-readable natural deduction proofs [19,20]; its basic concepts are somewhat oriented towards the basic Isabelle/Pure framework, which happens to offer a good basis for primitive operations of natural deduction (especially resolution $r \cdot \bar{a}$).

The Isar language consists of 12 primitives [20, Appendix A]: "**fix** $x :: \tau$" and "**assume** a: A" augment the context, **then** indicates forward chaining, "**have** a: A" and "**show** a: A" claim local statements (the latter also solves some pending goal afterwards), "**proof** m" performs an initial proof step by applying some method, "**qed** m" concludes a (sub-)proof, **{ }** and **next** manage block structure, "**note** $a = \bar{b}$" binds reconsidered facts, and "**let** $p = t$" abbreviates terms via higher-order matching (the form "(**is** p)" may be appended to any statement).

Basic proof methods are: "$-$" to do nothing, *this* to resolve facts directly (performs *goal* $\cdot$ *this*), and "(*rule r*)" to apply a rule resolved with facts (performs *goal* $\cdot$ ($r \cdot this$)). Arbitrary automated proof tools may be used as well, such as *simp* for Isabelle's Simplifier, and *auto* for a combination of several tools [13].

Standard abbreviations include *?thesis* for the initial claim (head of the proof), and "..." for the right-hand side of the latest (finished) statement; *this* refers the result from the previous step. Default methods are *rule* for **proof**, and "$-$" for **qed**. Further derived proof commands are "**by** m_1 m_2" for "**proof** m_1 **qed** m_2", ".." for "**by** *rule*", "." for "**by** *this*", and "**from** $\bar{a}$" for "**note** $\bar{a}$ **then**".

Isar's natural deduction kernel directly corresponds to the underlying logical framework. A meta-level statement may be established as follows.

> **have** $\bigwedge x\ y\ z.\ A \Longrightarrow B \Longrightarrow C$
> **proof** $-$
>   **fix** $x\ y\ z$ **assume** A **and** B
>   **show** C $\langle proof \rangle$
> **qed**

In reality, such rule statements would typically emerge from a different claim being refined by an initial proof method, used instead of "$-$" encountered here.

2.3   Calculational Sequences

From a syntactical point of view, the essence of a calculational proof is what we shall call a *calculational sequence*: let *calculation* be freely generated by the constructors *start*: *facts* $\rightarrow$ *calculation* and *continue*: *calculation* $\rightarrow$ *facts* $\rightarrow$ *calculation*. Apparently, any *calculation* simply represents a non-empty list of facts. We fine-tune our notation and write canonical calculational sequences *continue* (... (*continue* (*start* a_1) a_2) ... a_n) concisely as $a_1 \circ a_2 \cdots \circ a_n$.

An *interpreted calculation sequence* shall be any *result* achieved by mapping *start* and *continue* in a primitive recursive fashion. We only consider interpretations of *calculation* back into *facts*, i.e. *result*: *calculation* $\rightarrow$ *facts*; we also fix *result* (*start* a) = a. There is only one degree of freedom left to specify *result* ($c \circ a$) in order to give an interpretation of *continue* steps. The following two kinds of calculational steps will be considered within the Isabelle/Isar framework.

(rule-step): specify *result* ($c \circ a$) = $r \cdot$ (*result* c @ a) where r is a suitable rule taken from a given set $\mathcal{T}$ of *transitivity rules*. We produce a (single) result by applying a rule to the current calculational result plus some new facts.

(accumulation-step): specify *result* ($c \circ a$) = *result* c @ a. We simply collect further facts without applying any rule yet.

As a basic example of interpreted calculation sequences, just fix the singleton set $\mathcal{T} = \{\vdash x = y \Longrightarrow y = z \Longrightarrow x = z\}$ of transitivity rules and only perform rule steps; then we have *result* ($\vdash x_1 = x_2 \circ \vdash x_2 = x_3 \circ \vdash x_3 = x_4$) = $\vdash x_1 = x_4$. Thus we may represent canonical chains of equations composed by plain transitivity. Alternatively, only perform accumulation steps to achieve *result* ($\vdash \varphi_1 \circ \vdash \varphi_2 \circ \vdash \varphi_2$) = [$\vdash \varphi_1, \vdash \varphi_2, \vdash \varphi_2$], i.e. simply get a number of facts collected as a single list. As we shall see later on, even the latter case of seemingly degenerate calculational sequences turns out to be quite useful in practice.

2.4   Calculational Elements within the Proof Language

In the next stage we investigate how suitable proof development systems may provide a language interface for the user to compose calculational sequences.

At first sight, the way taken by Mizar [17] seems to be the obvious one: simply invent concrete syntax for the primitive operations of composing calculational sequences, and make the implementation support this directly — probably with some link to the basic mechanisms of stating and proving facts. This way of "making a system do something particular" is usually limited to just the specific feature one had in mind when planning the implementation — no more, no less.

In Isabelle/Isar we do not hardwire calculational reasoning, but figure out how the process of composing calculational sequences may be mapped into the natural flow of reasoning within the existing Isar framework in a non-intrusive fashion. By adding only a few abbreviations and conventions, we achieve a very general framework for calculational reasoning with minimal effort. The resulting space of possible combined proof patterns shall be explored later on.

First of all, we fix a special facts register called *"calculation"* to hold the current state of the (partially interpreted) sequence the user is currently working on. The start of a calculation shall be determined implicitly, as indicated by *calculation* being empty. Whenever a calculation is finished (by an explicit command to be given below), *calculation* will be reset to await the next sequence to start. The result of a finished sequence is exhibited to the subsequent goal statement as explicitly highlighted facts (their actual use in the subsequent proof is not controlled by the calculational process anymore).

We also wish to exploit Isar's inherent block structure to support nested calculations. So any update operation on *calculation* needs to track the current nesting level, in order to commence a new sequence whenever blocks are opened.

The derived Isar proof commands to maintain the *calculation* register are defined as follows, leaving the policies of initializing and resetting the state implicit.

$$\begin{array}{lll}
\textbf{also} \equiv \textbf{note}\ calculation = this & & \text{(initial case)} \\
\textbf{also} \equiv \textbf{note}\ calculation = r \cdot (calculation\ @\ this) & & \text{(for some } r \in \mathcal{T}) \\
\textbf{finally} \equiv \textbf{also from}\ calculation & &
\end{array}$$

$$\textbf{moreover} \equiv \textbf{note}\ calculation = calculation\ @\ this$$
$$\textbf{ultimately} \equiv \textbf{moreover from}\ calculation$$

Here the two main elements are **also** and **moreover**, corresponding to the "rule-steps" and "accumulation-steps" introduced before. The variants of **finally** and **ultimately** finish the current sequence after performing a final step. Due to the forward chaining involved in the **from** operation, the next command has to be a goal statement like **have** or **show** (cf. the Isar semantics given in [19]).

With one more element we arrive at a viable calculational proof language within the Isar framework: the standard term binding "..." refers to right-hand side of the most recent explicit fact statement. This enables the user to include relevant parts of the previous statement in a succinct manner. The "Mizar mode for HOL" [8] provides a similar element, while Mizar [12] uses the ".=" construct.

We may now write the previous examples of calculational sequences as follows.

have $x_1 = x_2$ ⟨*proof*⟩
also have ... = x_3 ⟨*proof*⟩
also have ... = x_4 ⟨*proof*⟩
finally have $x_1 = x_4$.

In the next calculation we use the ultimate list of accumulated facts to prove a result by a certain rule $r = \vdash \varphi_1 \implies \varphi_2 \implies \varphi_3 \implies \varphi_4$.

have φ_1 ⟨*proof*⟩
moreover have φ_2 ⟨*proof*⟩
moreover have φ_3 ⟨*proof*⟩
ultimately have φ_4 **by** (*rule r*)

Certainly, we may rephrase these calculations as basic natural deduction in backwards style, while performing exactly the same inferences internally.

have $x_1 = x_4$
proof (*rule trans*)
  show $x_1 = x_3$
  proof (*rule trans*)
    show $x_1 = x_2$ ⟨*proof*⟩
    show $x_2 = x_3$ ⟨*proof*⟩
  qed
  show $x_3 = x_4$ ⟨*proof*⟩
qed

have φ_4
proof (*rule r*)
  show φ_1 ⟨*proof*⟩
  show φ_2 ⟨*proof*⟩
  show φ_3 ⟨*proof*⟩
qed

2.5 Rules and Proof Search

The philosophy of Isar is to keep automated proof tools out of the basic mechanisms of interpreting the high-level structure proof texts. Only linear search over a limited number of choices plus (higher-order) unification is permitted here.

Reconsidering the commands for outlining calculational sequences in Isar (§2.4), we see that there is a single non-deterministic parameter: the rule $r \in \mathcal{T}$ to be selected by the **also** command. As Isar proof texts are interpreted strictly from left to right [19], the subsequent result *calculation* $= r \cdot$ (*calculation* @ *this*) has to be achieved from the present facts alone, with the rule instance r determined by the system appropriately. As long as $\mathcal{T}$ only holds (mixed) transitivities of $=/</\leq$ the result is already uniquely determined, e.g. providing facts $\vdash x \leq y$ and $\vdash y < z$ invariably yields $\vdash x < z$.

Isar uses the following refined strategy to support more general rule selections. Assume a canonical order on the rule context $\mathcal{T}$, and let $a = calculation$ @ *this* be the input given to the present calculational step. Now enumerate the members r of $\mathcal{T}$, then enumerate the canonical sequences of results $r \cdot a$ as obtained by parallel higher-order unification and back-chaining of a with r. Finally filter this raw result sequence to *disallow mere projections* of a; in other words remove those results b that do not make any actual "progress", in the sense that the conclusion of b is already present in one of the members of the list a.

This strategy subsumes the simple case of unique results considered before, but also does a good job at substitution: let us declare $\vdash P\ x \Longrightarrow x = y \Longrightarrow P\ y$ and $\vdash y = x \Longrightarrow P\ x \Longrightarrow P\ y$ to be tried after the plain transitivities considered so far. The expression $x = y$ only requires plain first-order unification, with a unique most-general result. The critical part is to solve $P\ x$ against the other expression, which is a genuine higher-order problem. Resulting unifiers will assign a certain λ-term to P that abstracts over possible occurrences of sub-expression x. Here the standard strategy [13] is to start with a solution with all occurrences, followed by all possible partial occurrences in a fixed order, and finish with *no* occurrences. Note that the latter case is the only solution if x does not occur at all, which is actually a pathological case for our purpose, as it collapses the substitution rules to $\vdash P \Longrightarrow x = y \Longrightarrow P$ and $\vdash y = x \Longrightarrow P \Longrightarrow P$.

Thus by filtering out mere projections of the original facts, a basic calculational rule-step is able to produce a sensible result, where *all* occurrences of a certain sub-expression may be replaced by an equal one (cf. the final example given in §1). Replacing only some occurrences does *not* work, though, as there is no way to specify the intended result beforehand. In the latter case, it is better to use plain transitivity together with the Simplifier to justify the next step.

Substitution with inequalities (involving additional monotonicity constraints) works as well, see §3 for common patterns. The notion of "progress" in the filtering strategy needs to ignore local premises to detect degenerate cases properly.

3   Idioms of Calculational Reasoning

The space of possible calculational expressions within Isar is somewhat open-ended, due to the particular way that calculational primitives have been incorporated into the proof language. Certainly, creative users of Isabelle/Isar may invent further ways of calculational reasoning at any time. Here we point out possible dimensions of variety, and hint at practically useful idiomatic patterns. Our subsequent categories are guided by the way that primitive calculational sequences (cf. §2.3) may be mapped to Isar proof configurations (cf. §2.4).

3.1   Variation of Rules

The most basic form is a plain transitive chain of equations, cf. the second Isar example in §1. Mixed transitivities may be used as follows; observe that the canonical ending (with a single-dot proof) exhibits the result explicitly.

> **have** $x_1 \leq x_2$ ⟨*proof*⟩
> **also have** $\ldots \leq x_3$ ⟨*proof*⟩
> **also have** $\ldots = x_4$ ⟨*proof*⟩
> **also have** $\ldots < x_5$ ⟨*proof*⟩
> **also have** $\ldots = x_6$ ⟨*proof*⟩
> **finally have** $x_1 < x_6$.

Likewise, we may use further combinations of relations such as antisymmetry, as long as there is a clear functional mapping from facts to the result, and no serious conflict with other rules.

> **have** $x \leq y$ ⟨*proof*⟩ **also have** $y \leq x$ ⟨*proof*⟩
> **finally have** $x = y$.

We have already covered substitution of equals by equals near the end of §1 (and §2.5); with inequalities this works out quite similarly.

> **have** $A = B + x + C$ ⟨*proof*⟩
> **also have** $x \leq y$ ⟨*proof*⟩
> **finally** $- \vdash (\bigwedge x\, y.\ x \leq y \implies B + x + C \leq B + y + C) \implies A \leq B + y + C$
> **have** $A \leq B + y + C$ **by** *simp*

The rule used here is $\vdash a = f\, b \implies b \leq c \implies (\bigwedge u\, v.\ u \leq v \implies f\, u \leq f\, v) \implies a \leq f\, c$, which has 3 premises, but we have only filled in two facts during the calculation; the remaining monotonicity constraint has been left as a hypothesis of the result, which eventually was solved by the final simplification step. The hard part of instantiating the side-condition has already been performed during the calculation, with the relevant propositions given in the text. We see how high-level proof outlining nicely cooperates with dumb automated reasoning.

In very simple cases, one may as well provide all 3 facts in the first place. For example, see the phrase "**moreover note** *AG-mono*" that appears in §4.3.

We may also calculate directly with logical propositions, approaching the original proof style of [5]. The following pattern essentially achieves "light-weight" natural deduction, by implicit use of the *modus ponens* rule.

> **have** $A \longrightarrow B \longrightarrow C$ *⟨proof⟩*
> **also have** A *⟨proof⟩*
> **also have** B *⟨proof⟩*
> **finally have** C .

Certainly, transitivity of "$\longrightarrow$" may be used as well. On the other hand, chaining of implications is more conveniently expressed directly by Isar's **then** primitive (cf. §2.2), circumventing the overhead of explicit logical connectives altogether.

3.2 Variation of Conclusions

Recall that the actual business of managing the calculational process finishes with the concluding **finally** or **ultimately** command, which just offers the result with forward-chaining indicated (cf. §2.4). The next command may be any kind of goal, such **have**, **show**, or even the powerful **obtain** [3,20].

Any such claim has to be followed by a proof. The most basic one is ".", meaning that the goal statement actually reiterates the calculational result directly. Another useful idiom is to feed the result (which may be just a number accumulated facts) into a single rule (with several premises), e.g. see the proof of *AG-AG* in §4.3. One may even generalize this principle to use arbitrary automated methods, resulting in some kind of "big-step" inferences. Without the calculational infrastructure, the latter mode of operation would usually require a lot of name references for intermediate facts, which tend to degrade readability.

3.3 Variation of Facts

In virtually all calculational schemes discussed so far, the facts to be placed into the chain are produced as local statements "**have** φ *⟨proof⟩*". Nevertheless, any Isar language element that produces facts may be used in calculations. This includes **note** to recall existing theorems, or other goal elements such as **show** or **obtain**, or even context commands such as **assume**. See §4.3 for some uses of "**moreover note**", and §4.4 for "**also note**". Combinations with **obtain** are very useful in typical computer-science applications (e.g. [21]) where results about representations of syntactic entities are incrementally put together.

The use of **assume** within a calculation represents the most basic case of combining calculational reasoning and natural deduction, e.g. within an induction.

theorem $(\sum i < n.\ 2 * i + 1) = n^2$
proof (*induct n*)
  show $(\sum i < 0.\ 2 * i + 1) = 0^2$ **by** *auto*
next
    fix n **have** $(\sum i < Suc\ n.\ 2 * i + 1) = 2 * n + 1 + (\sum i < n.\ 2 * i + 1)$ **by** *auto*
    also assume $(\sum i < n.\ 2 * i + 1) = n^2$
    also have $2 * n + 1 + n^2 = (Suc\ n)^2$ **by** *auto*
    finally show $(\sum i < Suc\ n.\ 2 * i + 1) = (Suc\ n)^2$.
qed

The "**also assume**" line indicates substitution with the induction hypothesis.

3.4 Variation of Structure

Calculational sequences are basically linear, but arbitrarily many intermediate steps may be taken until the next fact is produced. This includes further nested calculations, as long as these are arranged on a separate level of block structure. See §4.4 for the very common case of using the implicit block structure induced by local proofs, and §4.3 for explicit blocks indicated by braces.

4 Case-Study: Some Properties of CTL

In order to demonstrate how the idiomatic expressions of calculational reasoning are used in practice, we present a case-study of formalizing basic concepts of Computational Tree Logic (CTL) [10,9] within the simply-typed set theory of HOL.[2] The proofs are mostly by algebraic reasoning over basic set operations.

4.1 CTL Formulae

By using the common technique of "shallow embedding", a CTL formula is identified with the corresponding set of states where it holds. Consequently, CTL operations such as negation, conjunction, disjunction simply become complement, intersection, union of sets. We only require a separate operation for implication, as point-wise inclusion is usually not encountered in plain set-theory.

types α *ctl* $= \alpha$ *set*
constdefs
  imp :: α *ctl* $\Rightarrow \alpha$ *ctl* $\Rightarrow \alpha$ *ctl*   (**infixr** $\rightarrow$ 75)
  $p \rightarrow q \equiv -\ p \cup q$

The CTL path operators are more interesting; they are based on an arbitrary, but fixed model $\mathcal{M}$, which is simply a transition relation over states α.

---

[2] See also `http://isabelle.in.tum.de/library/HOL/CTL/document.pdf`.

consts *model* :: $(\alpha \times \alpha)$ *set* $(\mathcal{M})$

The operators EX, EF, EG are taken as primitives, while AX, AF, AG are defined as derived ones. We denote by EX p the set of states with a successor state s' (with respect to the model $\mathcal{M}$), such that $s' \in p$. The expression EF p denotes the set of states, such that there is a path in $\mathcal{M}$, starting from that state, such that there is a state s' on the path with $s' \in p$. The expression EG p is the set of all states s, such that there is a path, starting from s, such that for all states s' on the path, $s' \in p$. It is well known that EF p and EG p may be expressed using least and greatest fixed points [10].

constdefs

$EX :: \alpha\ ctl \Rightarrow \alpha\ ctl$	(EX - [80] 90)	EX $p \equiv \{s.\ \exists s'.\ (s,\ s') \in \mathcal{M} \wedge s' \in p\}$
$EF :: \alpha\ ctl \Rightarrow \alpha\ ctl$	(EF - [80] 90)	EF $p \equiv lfp\ (\lambda s.\ p \cup \text{EX } s)$
$EG :: \alpha\ ctl \Rightarrow \alpha\ ctl$	(EG - [80] 90)	EG $p \equiv gfp\ (\lambda s.\ p \cap \text{EX } s)$

AX, AF and AG are now defined dually in terms of EX, EF and EG.

constdefs

$AX :: \alpha\ ctl \Rightarrow \alpha\ ctl$	(AX - [80] 90)	AX $p \equiv\ -\ \text{EX } -\ p$
$AF :: \alpha\ ctl \Rightarrow \alpha\ ctl$	(AF - [80] 90)	AF $p \equiv\ -\ \text{EG } -\ p$
$AG :: \alpha\ ctl \Rightarrow \alpha\ ctl$	(AG - [80] 90)	AG $p \equiv\ -\ \text{EF } -\ p$

4.2 Basic Fixed Point Properties

First of all, we use the de-Morgan property of fixed points

lemma *lfp-gfp*: *lfp* $f =\ -\ gfp\ (\lambda s\ .\ -\ (f\ (-\ s)))$ ⟨*proof*⟩

in order to give dual fixed point representations of AF p and AG p:

lemma *AF-lfp*: AF $p = lfp\ (\lambda s.\ p \cup \text{AX } s)$ **by** (*auto simp add: lfp-gfp*)

lemma *AG-gfp*: AG $p = gfp\ (\lambda s.\ p \cap \text{AX } s)$ **by** (*auto simp add: lfp-gfp*)

From the greatest fixed point definition of AG p, we derive as a consequence of the Knaster-Tarski theorem on the one hand that AG p is a fixed point of the monotonic function $\lambda s.\ p \cap \text{AX } s$.

lemma *AG-fp*: AG $p = p \cap \text{AX AG } p$

proof −

  have *mono* $(\lambda s.\ p \cap \text{AX } s)$ ⟨*proof*⟩

  then show *?thesis* ⟨*proof*⟩

qed

This fact may be split up into two inequalities (merely using transitivity of $\subseteq$, which is an instance of the overloaded $\leq$ in Isabelle/HOL).

lemma *AG-fp$_1$*: AG $p \subseteq p$

proof −

  note *AG-fp* **also have** $p \cap \text{AX AG } p \subseteq p$ **by** *auto*

  finally show *?thesis* .

qed

lemma *AG-fp$_2$*: AG $p \subseteq \text{AX AG } p$

proof −

note *AG-fp* **also have** $p \cap$ AX AG $p \subseteq$ AX AG p **by** *auto*
finally show *?thesis* .
qed

On the other hand, we have from the Knaster-Tarski fixed point theorem that
any other post-fixed point of $\lambda s.\ p \cap$ AX s is smaller than AG p. A post-fixed
point is a set of states q such that $q \subseteq p \cap$ AX q. This leads to the following
co-induction principle for AG p.

lemma *AG-I*: $q \subseteq p \cap$ AX $q \Longrightarrow q \subseteq$ AG p
   by (*simp only*: *AG-gfp*) (*rule gfp-upperbound*)

4.3   The Tree Induction Principle

With the most basic facts available, we are now able to establish a few more
interesting results, leading to the *tree induction* principle for *AG* (see below).
We will use some elementary monotonicity and distributivity rules.

lemma *AX-int*: AX $(p \cap q) =$ AX $p \cap$ AX q ⟨*proof*⟩
lemma *AX-mono*: $p \subseteq q \Longrightarrow$ AX $p \subseteq$ AX q ⟨*proof*⟩
lemma *AG-mono*: $p \subseteq q \Longrightarrow$ AG $p \subseteq$ AG q ⟨*proof*⟩

If a state is in the set AG p it is also in AX p (we use substitution of $\subseteq$ with
monotonicity).

lemma *AG-AX*: AG $p \subseteq$ AX p
proof −
   have AG $p \subseteq$ AX AG p **by** (*rule AG-fp$_2$*)
   also have AG $p \subseteq p$ **by** (*rule AG-fp$_1$*) **moreover note** *AX-mono*
   finally show *?thesis* .
qed

Furthermore we show idempotency of the AG operator. The proof is a good
example of how accumulated facts may get used to feed a single rule step.

lemma *AG-AG*: AG AG $p =$ AG p
proof
   show AG AG $p \subseteq$ AG p **by** (*rule AG-fp$_1$*)
next
  show AG $p \subseteq$ AG AG p
  proof (*rule AG-I*)
    have AG $p \subseteq$ AG p ..
    moreover have AG $p \subseteq$ AX AG p **by** (*rule AG-fp$_2$*)
    ultimately show AG $p \subseteq$ AG $p \cap$ AX AG p ..
  qed
qed

We now give an alternative characterization of the AG operator, which describes
the AG operator in an "operational" way by tree induction: AG p is the set of all
states $s \in p$, such that for all reachable states (starting from that state) holds
the following condition: if a state lies in p then also will any successor state.

We use the co-induction principle *AG-I* to establish this in a purely algebraic manner.

theorem *AG-induct*: $p \cap$ AG $(p \rightarrow$ AX $p) =$ AG p
proof
  show $p \cap$ AG $(p \rightarrow$ AX $p) \subseteq$ AG p **(is** *?lhs* $\subseteq$ *?rhs*)
  proof (*rule AG-I*)
    show *?lhs* $\subseteq p \cap$ AX *?lhs*
    proof
      show *?lhs* $\subseteq p$ ..
      show *?lhs* $\subseteq$ AX *?lhs*
      proof −
        {
          have AG $(p \rightarrow$ AX $p) \subseteq p \rightarrow$ AX p **by** (*rule AG-fp₁*)
          also have $p \cap p \rightarrow$ AX $p \subseteq$ AX p ..
          finally have *?lhs* $\subseteq$ AX p **by** *auto*
        } − (1)
        moreover
        {
          have $p \cap$ AG $(p \rightarrow$ AX $p) \subseteq$ AG $(p \rightarrow$ AX $p)$ ..
          also have $\ldots \subseteq$ AX $\ldots$ **by** (*rule AG-fp₂*)
          finally have *?lhs* $\subseteq$ AX AG $(p \rightarrow$ AX $p)$.
        } − (2)
        ultimately have *?lhs* $\subseteq$ AX $p \cap$ AX AG $(p \rightarrow$ AX $p)$ ..
        also have $\ldots =$ AX *?lhs* **by** (*simp only: AX-int*)
        finally show *?thesis* .
      qed
    qed
  qed
next
  show AG $p \subseteq p \cap$ AG $(p \rightarrow$ AX $p)$
  proof
    show AG $p \subseteq p$ **by** (*rule AG-fp₁*)
    show AG $p \subseteq$ AG $(p \rightarrow$ AX $p)$
    proof −
      have AG $p =$ AG AG p **by** (*simp only: AG-AG*)
      also have AG $p \subseteq$ AX p **by** (*rule AG-AX*) **moreover note** *AG-mono*
      also have AX $p \subseteq (p \rightarrow$ AX $p)$ .. **moreover note** *AG-mono*
      finally show *?thesis* .
    qed
  qed
qed

The middle part of this proof provides an example for nested calculations using explicit blocks: the two contributing results (1) and (2), which are established separately by calculations as well, are ultimately put together.

4.4   An Application of Tree Induction

Further interesting properties of CTL expressions may be demonstrated with the help of tree induction; here we show that AX and AG commute.

theorem *AG-AX-commute*: AG AX p = AX AG p
proof –
  have AG AX p = AX p ∩ AX AG AX p **by** (*rule AG-fp*)
  also have ... = AX (p ∩ AG AX p) **by** (*simp only: AX-int*)
  also have p ∩ AG AX p = AG p (**is** *?lhs = ?rhs*)
  proof — (1)
    have AX p ⊆ p → AX p ..
    also have p ∩ AG (p → AX p) = AG p **by** (*rule AG-induct*)
    also note *Int-mono AG-mono* — (2)
    ultimately show *?lhs* ⊆ AG p **by** *auto*
  next — (1)
    have AG p ⊆ p **by** (*rule AG-fp₁*)
    moreover
    {
      have AG p = AG AG p **by** (*simp only: AG-AG*)
      also have AG p ⊆ AX p **by** (*rule AG-AX*)
      also note *AG-mono*
      ultimately have AG p ⊆ AG AX p .
    }
    ultimately show AG p ⊆ *?lhs* ..
  qed — (1)
  finally show *?thesis* .
qed

This is an example for nested calculation with implicit block structure (1), as managed automatically by **proof**/**next**/**qed**. Naturally, users would complain if calculations in sub-proofs could affect the general course of reasoning! Also note that (2) indicates a non-trivial use of ⊆ substitution into a monotone context.

4.5   Discussion

Our theory of CTL serves as a nice example of several kinds of calculational reasoning, mainly due to the high-level algebraic view on set operations. Alternatively, one could have worked point-wise with explicit set membership. Then the proofs would certainly have become more cumbersome, with many primitive natural deduction steps to accommodate quantified statements.

There is an interesting story about this example. Incidently, it has once served as an assignment for the Isabelle course given in summer 2000 at TU Munich. After the students had been exposed to Isabelle for a few weeks (only the crude tactical part!), the instructors intended to pose a relatively simple "realistic" application of set theory, which turned out to be much harder than expected.

The reason was that on the one hand, the instructors simply started off by developing the theory interactively in Isabelle/Isar, using its proper proof language basically to "think aloud formally". This was a relatively leisurely experience, as it involves only a number of algebraic manipulation, as we have presented here. On the other hand, the students only knew traditional tactic scripts, with that strong bias towards hairy natural deduction operations performed in backwards style. This posed a real problem to them; some students would even proclaim that the assignment was impossible to finish with their present knowledge.

In retrospect, it is understandable that rephrasing the kind of algebraic reasoning we have seen here into tactic scripts is quite cumbersome, even for the expert.

5   Conclusion and Related Work

We have seen that calculational reasoning in Isabelle/Isar provides a viable concept for arranging a large variety of algebraic proof techniques in a well-structured manner. While requiring only minimal conservative additions to the basic Isar proof engine, we have been able to achieve a large space of useful patterns of calculational reasoning, including mixed transitivity rules, substitution of equals-by-equals, and even substitution by greater (or equal) sub-expressions. The underlying mechanisms of Isabelle/Isar do not need any advanced proof search, apart from plain (higher-order) unification with a simple filtering scheme.

Interestingly, traditional tactic-based interactive proof systems such as (classic) Isabelle, HOL, Coq, PVS etc. lack support for calculational reasoning altogether. This has been addressed several times in the past. Simons proposes tools to support calculational reasoning within tactical proof scripts [14]. Grundy provides an even more general transformational infrastructure for "window inference" [7]. Harrison's "Mizar mode for HOL" simulates a number of concepts of declarative theorem proving on top of the tactic-based hol-light system [8], including calculational reasoning for mixed transitivity rules.

Concerning the class of theorem proving environments for human-readable proofs, its canonical representative Mizar [17,12] supports a fixed format for iterative equations, with implicit application of both transitivity and general substitution rules. Syme's DECLARE system for declarative theorem proving [15,16] does not address calculations at all. Zammit outlines a generalized version of Mizar-style calculations for SPL [23], but observes that these have not been required for the examples at hand, so it has not been implemented.

For users of Isabelle/Isar, calculational reasoning has become a useful tool for everyday applications — not just the typical "mathematical" ones [3], but also (abstract) system verification tasks [21]. Calculations fit indeed very well into the general high-level natural deduction framework of Isar, so we may say that calculational reasoning [5] and natural deduction [6] have been finally reconciled.

90   Gertrud Bauer and Markus Wenzel

References

1. R.J. Back, J. Grundy, and J. von Wright. Structured calculational proof. *Formal Aspects of Computing*, 9, 1997.
2. R.J. Back and J. von Wright. Structured derivations: A method for doing high-school mathematics carefully. Technical report, Turku Centre for C.S., 1999.
3. G. Bauer and M. Wenzel. Computer-assisted mathematics at work — the Hahn-Banach theorem in Isabelle/Isar. In T. Coquand, P. Dybjer, B. Nordström, and J. Smith, editors, *Types for Proofs and Programs: TYPES'99*, LNCS, 2000.
4. Y. Bertot, G. Dowek, A. Hirschowitz, C. Paulin, and L. Thery, editors. *Theorem Proving in Higher Order Logics: TPHOLs '99*, LNCS 1690, 1999.
5. E.W. Dijkstra and C.S. Scholten. *Predicate Calculus and Program Semantics*. Texts and monographs in computer science. Springer, 1990.
6. G. Gentzen. Untersuchungen über das logische Schließen. *Mathematische Zeitschrift*, 1935.
7. J. Grundy. Window inference in the HOL system. In M. Archer, J. J. Joyce, K. N. Levitt, and P. J. Windley, editors, *Proceedings of the International Workshop on HOL*. ACM SIGDA, IEEE Computer Society Press, 1991.
8. J. Harrison. A Mizar mode for HOL. In J. Wright, J. Grundy, and J. Harrison, editors, *Theorem Proving in Higher Order Logics: TPHOLs '96*, LNCS 1125, 1997.
9. K. McMillan. Lecture notes on verification of digital and hybrid systems. NATO summer school,
   http://www-cad.eecs.berkeley.edu/~kenmcmil/tutorial/toc.html.
10. K. McMillan. *Symbolic Model Checking: an approach to the state explosion problem*. PhD thesis, Carnegie Mellon University, 1992.
11. Mizar mathematical library. http://www.mizar.org/library/.
12. M. Muzalewski. *An Outline of PC Mizar*. Fondation of Logic, Mathematics and Informatics — Mizar Users Group, 1993.
13. L.C. Paulson. *Isabelle: A Generic Theorem Prover*. LNCS 828. 1994.
14. M. Simons. Proof presentation for Isabelle. In E. L. Gunter and A. Felty, editors, *Theorem Proving in Higher Order Logics: TPHOLs '97*, LNCS 1275, 1997.
15. D. Syme. DECLARE: A prototype declarative proof system for higher order logic. Technical Report 416, University of Cambridge Computer Laboratory, 1997.
16. D. Syme. Three tactic theorem proving. In Bertot et al. [4].
17. A. Trybulec. Some features of the Mizar language. Presented at a workshop in Turin, Italy, 1993.
18. R. Verhoeven and R. Backhouse. Interfacing program construction and verification. In J. Wing and J. Woodcock, editors, *FM99: The World Congress in Formal Methods*, volume 1708 and 1709 of *LNCS*, 1999.
19. M. Wenzel. Isar — a generic interpretative approach to readable formal proof documents. In Bertot et al. [4].
20. M. Wenzel. *The Isabelle/Isar Reference Manual*, 2000. Part of the Isabelle distribution, http://isabelle.in.tum.de/doc/isar-ref.pdf.
21. M. Wenzel. Some aspects of Unix file-system security. Isabelle/Isar proof document, http://isabelle.in.tum.de/library/HOL/Unix/document.pdf, 2001.
22. F. Wiedijk. Mizar: An impression. Unpublished paper, 1999.
   http://www.cs.kun.nl/~freek/mizar/mizarintro.ps.gz.
23. V. Zammit. On the implementation of an extensible declarative proof language. In Bertot et al. [4].

Mechanical Proofs about a Non-repudiation Protocol

Giampaolo Bella[1,2] and Lawrence C. Paulson[1]

[1] Computer Laboratory, University of Cambridge
Pembroke Street, Cambridge CB2 3QG (UK)
{gb221,lcp}@cl.cam.ac.uk
[2] Dipartimento di Matematica e Informatica, Università di Catania
Viale A. Doria 6, I-95125 Catania (Italy)
giamp@dmi.unict.it

Abstract. A non-repudiation protocol of Zhou and Gollmann [18] has been mechanically verified. A non-repudiation protocol gives each party evidence that the other party indeed participated, evidence sufficient to present to a judge in the event of a dispute. We use the theorem-prover Isabelle [10] and model the security protocol by an inductive definition, as described elsewhere [1,12]. We prove the protocol goals of *validity of evidence* and of *fairness* using simple strategies. A typical theorem states that a given piece of evidence can only exist if a specific event took place involving the other party.

1 Introduction

A wide variety of techniques are available for verifying cryptographic protocols [3,8,12,14]. Past work has focused largely on two security goals: *confidentiality* (who can read the message?) and *authenticity* (who originated the message?). One direction for further research is to attempt proofs of more esoteric security goals. Traditional protocols help a pair of honest agents to communicate in the presence of an attacker, but in some situations agents may act unfairly and abandon protocol sessions before these terminate. The present work concerns *non-repudiation*, which seeks to prevent a party from abandoning an agreement. Non-repudiation would provide us with a reliable means of making contracts over a network.

The primary goal of a non-repudiation protocol is *validity of evidence*. It must provide each peer with convincing evidence of the other's participation in a protocol session. If one peer falsely denies participating in a session, then the other peer can present his evidence to a judge, who can safely conclude that the other peer did participate. Crucially, the judge does not have to monitor the network traffic, but can make his judgement on the basis of the evidence alone. Some of the evidence is usually referred to as *non-repudiation of origin*, other as *non-repudiation of receipt*. The initiator of a session typically seeks evidence of the first form, and the responder typically looks for evidence of the second form.

An additional goal of some non-repudiation protocols is *fairness*: at no time should one peer hold more evidence than the other does. Although fairness is not

R.J. Boulton and P.B. Jackson (Eds.): TPHOLs 2001, LNCS 2152, pp. 91–104, 2001.

indispensable in all situations, it may be needed for certain e-commerce transactions. For example, if a client C holds evidence that a merchant M received C's request for goods, fairness means that C cannot deny sending the request: M holds the corresponding evidence. Similarly, if M holds evidence that C received the goods, fairness means that C holds evidence that it was M who sent them. In the latter case for example, M could claim the payment for the goods but, should the goods be unsatisfactory, C could demand a refund. Resolving such disputes becomes a matter of cyberlaw; the judge referred to above could be a real judge sitting in a traditional courtroom.

A number of protocols have been designed to achieve non-repudiation, but they are not yet deployed [7,9,18]. Verifying them formally [16,17] might increase their credibility. Proving non-repudiation was one of the the first author's reasons for extending the Inductive Approach to verifying cryptographic protocols [12] with message reception [1] and agents' knowledge [2]. This paper shows that we have now achieved that purpose through the development of simple strategies to prove validity of evidence and fairness. We were pleased to observe that these strategies differ little from those for proving authentication goals [5,6], and that the approach required no extensions. Our proofs were conducted on a popular non-repudiation protocol due to Zhou and Gollmann [18] using the second author's original modelling of agents. An unlimited population of agents can only send messages of the form that the protocol prescribes but can quit a protocol session at any time; the *spy* can send messages of arbitrary form.

This paper is organised as follows. A brief overview of the Inductive Approach (§2) precedes the description of our strategies to proving the non-repudiation goals (§3). The Zhou-Gollmann protocol is described (§4), modelled (§5) and verified without the spy (§6). Then, the verification is repeated in the presence of the spy (§7). Finally, the related work is discussed (§8), and some conclusions are given (§9).

2   The Inductive Approach

The Inductive Approach has been used successfully to analyse Local Area Network protocols [5], Internet protocols [13], e-commerce protocols [4] and smart card protocols [3]. Here, we recall only its main concepts, but a full treatment may be found elsewhere [1,12].

The approach draws from the observation that the goals of security protocols are invariants of the protocol execution, so proving the goals means showing that they are preserved by all protocol steps. The inductive model of a protocol is the set of all possible histories (*traces*) of the network that the protocol execution may produce. There is no limit to the number of agents who may participate. They may also interleave sessions at will.

A trace is a list of network events of the following form:

- Says $A\,B\,X$, indicating that agent A sends a message X to agent B;
- Gets $A\,X$, indicating that A receives X;
- Notes $A\,X$, indicating that A notes down X for future use.

The last event can model an agent's storing a message component or the result of a computation [13].

There are traces in which some events have not taken place although the necessary preconditions are met. Therefore, the protocol model does not force events to happen; messages may be sent but may not be received, and agents may abandon a protocol execution. This captures the unreliability of the communications, and a degree of unfairness of agents. However, the only agent who can build messages other than those prescribed by the protocol is the spy. Also, messages cannot alter during transmission.

Given a trace *evs*, we model the knowledge that agent A acquires during the network history denoted by *evs* as knows A *evs* [2]. This is the set of messages that A sent or received or noted on *evs*. In particular, knows Spy *evs* contains the private signature keys of a set bad of agents and all messages that were sent or received by anyone or noted by bad agents on *evs*.

Three operators can be applied to a message set H:

- parts, yielding all components of messages in H, except encryption keys;
- analz, yielding those components of messages in H whose encryption key is recursively available;
- synth, yielding all messages constructed by concatenation or encryption from messages recursively obtained from H.

The special set synth(analz(knows Spy *evs*)) contains all messages that the spy can synthesise using the components obtained from the analysis of the traffic with the help of bad agents' private keys. The spy can send in the traffic any message derived from that set (§7).

3   Strategies to Proving Non-repudiation

How can a judge who is off-line evaluate the non-repudiation evidence presented by a peer? The judge could perhaps make a decision given a full log of the network traffic, but that would not be practical. Our proofs can help the judge by establishing that a given piece of evidence guarantees that certain critical events occurred. Our proofs are subject to human error (for instance, our model could be too abstract), but they add credibility to the protocol. The judge weighs up these points in making his decision; a Guilty verdict requires the absence of a reasonable doubt.

Each trace of the protocol model is in fact a full log of a network history. So, scanning the trace tells what events have occurred. These observations inspire our strategy to proving validity of evidence, which must be applied for each piece of evidence that an agent presents to the judge. If A presents evidence X, then certainly A holds X; formally: $X \in$ knows A *evs* for some trace *evs*. Our strategy rests on an assumption of that form, and develops through two main types of result:

1. If A holds some evidence X, then A got the evidence from the network, perhaps from the spy.

2. If A got evidence X, then B sent some other evidence Y. Alternatively —
2′. If A got evidence X, then B was entitled to receive some other evidence Y.

Proving a theorem of the form (1) and a theorem of the form (2) typically serves to establish validity of the evidence for non-repudiation of origin. Proving a theorem of the form (1) and a theorem of the form (2′) typically serves to establish validity of the evidence for non-repudiation of receipt.

Proving theorems of the form (1) is novel as it involves reasoning on the knowledge of friendly agents. Since a friendly agent *only* knows what she sends or receives or notes [2], these proofs generate longer case splits than previous proofs [6,12] based on the spy's knowledge, which includes *everything* that is sent or received by anyone or noted by bad agents. By contrast, theorems of the form (2) or (2′) can be proved conventionally, as they resemble authentication theorems [5].

The strategy for proving fairness is simple once the theorems assessing validity of evidence are available. We need to establish is that, if some evidence is available to a peer, then other evidence is available to the other peer. This is in fact a possible way to read the theorems on validity of evidence. Simple lemmas stating that an agent performs an event only if he has performed another one may be sometimes required.

4   A Fair Non-repudiation Protocol

We choose a recent non-repudiation protocol, shown in Fig. 1, that also aims at fairness [18] as a case study to demonstrate our approach. The protocol was designed by Zhou and Gollmann, who also published a version aiming at efficient implementation [19]. One of the motivations for our choice was the existence of significant related work [16,17], which is discussed in the next section. It is useful

$$1.\ A \to B \quad : \quad f_{NRO}, B, L, C, \underbrace{\{f_{NRO}, B, L, C\}_{sK_A}}_{NRO}$$

$$2.\ B \to A \quad : \quad f_{NRR}, A, L, \underbrace{\{f_{NRR}, A, L\}_{sK_B}}_{NRR}$$

$$3.\ A \to \mathsf{TTP} \ : \quad f_{SUB}, B, L, K, \underbrace{\{f_{SUB}, B, L, K\}_{sK_A}}_{sub\_K}$$

$$4.\ B \leftrightarrow \mathsf{TTP} : \quad f_{CON}, A, B, L, K, \underbrace{\{f_{CON}, A, B, L, K\}_{sK_{TTP}}}_{con\_K}$$

$$5.\ A \leftrightarrow \mathsf{TTP} : \quad f_{CON}, A, B, L, K, \underbrace{\{f_{CON}, A, B, L, K\}_{sK_{TTP}}}_{con\_K}$$

Fig. 1. The Fair Zhou-Gollmann Protocol.

to outline the syntax we use:

- A is the initiator of a protocol session with B;
- B is the responder of the session initiated by A;
- TTP is the trusted third party;
- M is the message that A wants to transmit to B;
- K is the key that A chooses to transmit M;
- C is M encrypted with K (the C refers to A's Commitment to B);
- L is a unique label identifying the session between A and B;
- f_* are the non-repudiation flags;
- sK_X is the private signature key of agent X (no syntax is needed for the public verification key of X);
- $\{m\}_{sK_X}$ is the signature of message m by key sK_X.

The protocol intends to transmit a message M from A to B, giving A evidence for non-repudiation of receipt, giving B evidence for non-repudiation of origin, and ensuring fairness. The first protocol step prescribes that A pick a cryptographic key K and a random label L. Then, A uses symmetric cryptography to build C out of M and K, signs $\{f_{NRO}, B, L, C\}$ and sends the result to B along with the unsigned message, which is in general needed for signature verification. Note that A sends M encrypted, so B will not be able to obtain M until he gets K. Upon reception of the first message, B verifies A's signature, signs $\{f_{NRR}, A, L\}$ and sends the result to A. Upon reception of the second message, A lodges K with TTP by sending her signature on $\{f_{SUB}, B, L, K\}$.

Once TTP has successfully verified A's signature on the received message, TTP signs $\{f_{CON}, A, B, L, K\}$ and makes it available in its public directory. This message confirms that the key K concerns the session between A and B that is identified by label L. The last two steps, which are interchangeable, see the peers *ftp get* the message available from TTP. The protocol assumes that nobody can interfere with an *ftp get* operation, but we will relax this assumption below (§7).

Zhou and Gollmann [18] observe that, even if the peers do not want to play fair, they must complete a session in order to get sufficient evidence to win any disputes with each other. Let us informally analyse how to resolve disputes. From B's standpoint, it appears that obtaining *con_K* signifies that A submitted K, bound to label L, to TTP; obtaining *NRO* should signify that A sent C as a commitment bound to label L. In consequence, message M, obtained by decrypting C with K, should have originated with A. From A's standpoint, a similar reasoning seems feasible. If A holds *con_K*, this should guarantee that A lodged K and L with TTP, and so B should be able to get it via *ftp*. If A also holds *NRR*, it should be the case that B accepted commitment C. In consequence, B would be able to obtain M.

This reasoning might resemble that of a judge who is provided with evidence *NRO*, *con_K*, M, C, K, L by agent B, or with a similar evidence (but *NRR* rather than *NRO*) by agent A. It is not trivial to verify such reasoning for all possible network histories. The communication means is unreliable, and the protocol is executed by an unlimited number of agents, each entitled to interleave or quit sessions at will.

5   Modelling a Fair Non-repudiation Protocol

We build our protocol model on the Isabelle theory Public [11] for cryptographic protocols based on asymmetric encryption. The theory models three kinds of network agents: a spy, whom we discuss later (§7), a trusted server, which is renamed as TTP here, and an unlimited population of legitimate agents. Each agent X is endowed with a key pair. His private signature key, priK X, he keeps secret; his public verification key, pubK X, is known to all. The theory also provides a primitive for encryption, Crypt, which we use where the protocol requires a digital signature.

The protocol model is the set of traces zg, whose inductive definition is in Fig. 2. A rule for the base of the induction, stating that the empty trace belongs to zg, is omitted from the figure. Rules ZG1, ZG2 and ZG3 respectively model the first three steps of the protocol. Note that agent A chooses a fresh nonce in rule ZG1 to initiate the protocol with B. Recall that A runs the protocol because she wants to transmit some message M to B. All these messages and the ciphertexts obtained from them by any key constitute the set targetmsgs. We reasonably assume that this set contains none of the other messages (either atomic or compound) exchanged by the protocol. Also, A is free to choose any key to encrypt M, even an old one — we merely assume that she cannot pick private signature keys.

We highlight the important certificates by defining them in the premises, using equations; we use the names so defined in the conclusions. When a certificate is defined in the premises of a rule, then the rule only applies for a certificate of the specified form: informally, the agent verifies it. For example, B must check that NRO in rule ZG2 is signed by A in order to learn the sender of the message just received and address NRR to her.

By contrast, A does not need to check that NRR in rule ZG3 is signed by B because NRR is associated to label L, which A knows to be associated with B. Clearly, the check becomes mandatory in the presence of the spy, who can actively intercept and fake the messages that are in the traffic (§7).

Rule TTP_prepare_ftp models TTP's preparation of the key confirmation con_K. Note that TTP verifies the signature on sub_K to learn the identities of the peers of K. All the components needed to verify that signature are available. The installation of con_K in TTP's public directory can be modelled by a Notes event.

Rules A_ftp and B_ftp model the peers' retrieval of con_K. The two rules are not forced to fire simultaneously, since each peer decides independently whether to terminate the protocol. Rather than introducing a new event to express the *ftp get* operation, we again adopt Notes. Using a Gets event instead would violate the conventions of the message reception model: each Gets event must follow a matching Says event, as established by rule Reception.

ZG1
```
[| evs1 ∈ zg; Nonce L ∉ used evs1; C = Crypt K M;
   M ∈ targetmsgs; K ∉ range priK;
   NRO = Crypt (priK A) {|Number f_nro, Agent B, Nonce L, C|} |]
⟹ Says A B {|Number f_nro, Agent B, Nonce L, C, NRO|} # evs1 ∈ zg
```

ZG2
```
[| evs2 ∈ zg; C ∈ targetmsgs;
   Gets B {|Number f_nro, Agent B, Nonce L, C, NRO|} ∈ set evs2;
   NRO = Crypt (priK A) {|Number f_nro, Agent B, Nonce L, C|};
   NRR = Crypt (priK B) {|Number f_nrr, Agent A, Nonce L, C|} |]
⟹ Says B A {|Number f_nrr, Agent A, Nonce L, NRR|} # evs2 ∈ zg
```

ZG3
```
[| evs3 ∈ zg; C = Crypt K M;
   Says A B {|Number f_nro, Agent B, Nonce L, C, NRO|} ∈ set evs3;
   Gets A {|Number f_nrr, Agent A, Nonce L, NRR|} ∈ set evs3;
   sub_K = Crypt (priK A) {|Number f_sub, Agent B, Nonce L, Key K|} |]
⟹ Says A TTP {|Number f_sub, Agent B, Nonce L, Key K, sub_K|}
      # evs3 ∈ zg
```

TTP_prepare_ftp
```
[| evsT ∈ zg;
   Gets TTP {|Number f_sub, Agent B, Nonce L, Key K, sub_K|} ∈ set evsT;
   sub_K = Crypt (priK A) {|Number f_sub, Agent B, Nonce L, Key K|};
   con_K = Crypt (priK TTP) {|Number f_con, Agent A, Agent B,
                             Nonce L, Key K|} |]
⟹ Notes TTP {|Number f_con, Agent A, Agent B, Nonce L, Key K, con_K|}
      # evsT ∈ zg
```

A_ftp
```
[| evsA ∈ zg;
   Notes TTP {|Number f_con, Agent A, Agent B, Nonce L, Key K, con_K|}
      ∈ set evsA |]
⟹ Notes A {|Number f_con, Agent A, Agent B, Nonce L, Key K, con_K|}
      # evsA ∈ zg
```

B_ftp
```
[| evsB ∈ zg;
   Notes TTP {|Number f_con, Agent A, Agent B, Nonce L, Key K, con_K|}
      ∈ set evsB |]
⟹ Notes B {|Number f_con, Agent A, Agent B, Nonce L, Key K, con_K|}
      # evsB ∈ zg
```

Reception
```
[| evsr ∈ zg; Says A B X ∈ set evsr |] ⟹ Gets B X # evsr ∈ zg
```

Fig. 2. Modelling the Fair Zhou-Gollmann Protocol.

6   Verifying a Fair Non-repudiation Protocol

For the sake of clarity, this section discusses the guarantees proved of the Zhou-Gollmann protocol in a model that allows no spy. The influence of the spy on these guarantees will be the topic of the next section.

6.1   Proving Validity of Evidence

Guarantees for B. Let us verify that, at the end of a session, B holds sufficient evidence to refute a denial by A. We prove that, if B holds con_K, NRO and all other atomic messages, then A cannot deny having sent M.

According to the general strategy (§3), we establish that the only way for B to get hold of con_K is via ftp, namely completing the protocol, as stated by Theorem 1.

Theorem 1.
```
[| evs ∈ zg; con_K ∈ parts (knows B evs);
   con_K = Crypt (priK TTP) {|Number f_con, Agent A, Agent B,
                             Nonce L, Key K|} |]
⟹ Notes B {|Number f_con, Agent A, Agent B, Nonce L, Key K, con_K|}
     ∈ set evs
```

The proof is non-trivial in the Reception case, where Isabelle's simplifier leaves us with the possibility that B knows con_K because he has received it from the network (rather than noted it). In this sub-case, someone must have sent it by a Says event, but we appeal to a lemma stating that nobody ever sends con_K.

Again following the general strategy, we can routinely prove Theorem 2 by induction, which states that if B has con_K then A indeed lodged K with TTP, bound to label L. The proof initially deduces that TTP made con_K available, and then concludes that A sent sub_K.

Theorem 2.
```
[| evs ∈ zg;
   Notes B {|Number f_con, Agent A, Agent B, Nonce L, Key K, con_K|}
     ∈ set evs;
   con_K = Crypt (priK TTP) {|Number f_con, Agent A, Agent B,
                             Nonce L, Key K|};
   sub_K = Crypt (priK A) {|Number f_sub, Agent B, Nonce L, Key K|} |]
⟹ Says A TTP {|Number f_sub, Agent B, Nonce L, Key K, sub_K|} ∈ set evs
```

Theorems 1 and 2 together state that, if B has con_K, then A certainly sent sub_K, binding the key K to the label L. However, some extra evidence is needed to B to refute a denial from A. The evidence is NRO, which (by Theorem 3) B holds only if A sent it to him.

Theorem 3.
```
[| evs ∈ zg; NRO ∈ parts (knows B evs);
   NRO = Crypt (priK A) {|Number f_nro, Agent B, Nonce L, C|} |]
⟹ Says A B {|Number f_nro, Agent B, Nonce L, C, NRO|} ∈ set evs
```

Proving this theorem requires a lemma concluding that B could only receive NRO inside the first message of the protocol, namely that the event

$$\text{Gets } B \text{ } \{\!|\text{Number } f\_nro, \text{Agent } B, \text{Nonce } L, C, NRO|\!\}} \tag{1}$$

occurred. In the Reception case, the simplifier tries to establish whether B might learn NRO by receiving a message of any form, but another lemma states that this is impossible. Event (1) implies that NRO is in the network traffic, and then an authenticity theorem derives that it certainly originated with A, thus concluding the proof. Theorem 3 states that a judge may safely conclude from B's presenting NRO that A sent it, binding the ciphertext C to the label L.

These theorems show that C is bound to the key K via the label L. Hence, if B presents NRO, con_K, C, L and K to a judge, then the judge can conclude that A sent B the message M that is obtained decrypting C by K.

Guarantees for A. Analogous theorems justify A's evidence that B received the plaintext, M. In particular, Theorem 1 can be proved analogously for A, stating that, when con_K is known to A, then A certainly noted it. On this assumption, we easily prove that TTP made con_K publicly available. Combining these two results, we get Theorem 4.

Theorem 4.
```
[| evs ∈ zg; con_K ∈ parts (knows A evs);
   con_K = Crypt (priK TTP) {|Number f_con, Agent A, Agent B,
                             Nonce L, Key K|};
⟹ Notes TTP {|Number f_con, Agent A, Agent B, Nonce L, Key K, con_K|}
   ∈ set evs
```

Following this theorem, when A presents con_K to a judge, she also proves that she has bound the key K to L via TTP. Theorem 5 also states that, if A has NRR, then B certainly received NRO confirming that A associated the ciphertext C to the label L.

Theorem 5.
```
[| evs ∈ zg; NRR ∈ parts (knows A evs);
   NRR = Crypt (priK B) {|Number f_nrr, Agent A, Nonce L, C|};
   NRO = Crypt (priK A) {|Number f_nro, Agent B, Nonce L, C|} |]
⟹ Gets B {|Number f_nro, Agent B, Nonce L, C, NRO|} ∈ set evs
```

The proof resembles that of Theorem 3 to derive that B sent NRR inside an instance of message 2. This, in turn, requires an appeal to an authenticity theorem: once NRR is in the traffic, then it certainly originated with B. A subsidiary lemma stating that B only sends NRR upon reception of NRO concludes.

Theorems 4 and 5 guarantee to a judge that, if A presents NRR, con_K, C, L and K, then B can decrypt C using the key K, which was available with con_K via *ftp*. It is up to B to get con_K, so this may appear a weaker guarantee than the corresponding one for B. However, the protocol authors observe that B is interested in getting con_K in order to win a dispute over A, as confirmed by Theorems 1 and 2.

6.2 Proving Fairness

Guarantees for *B*. Theorem 4 may be read as a guarantee of fairness for *B* because it says that, should *con_K* be known to *A*, then *B* too would be able to obtain it via *ftp* from TTP's public directory. Similarly, Theorem 5 guarantees to *B* that, in case *A* knows *NRR*, then *B* has received the corresponding *NRO*.

Certainly TTP makes *con_K* available only in case it receives a valid instance of message 3. So, on the conclusion of Theorem 4, we can prove that the event

$$\text{Gets TTP } \{\!|\text{Number f\_sub, Agent } B, \text{Nonce } L, \text{Key } K, sub\_K|\!\}$$

occurred. This implies that *sub_K* is in the traffic and therefore, via a suitable authenticity theorem for *sub_K*, that the event

$$\text{Says } A \text{ TTP } \{\!|\text{Number f\_sub, Agent } B, \text{Nonce } L, \text{Key } K, sub\_K|\!\}$$

also occurred. We can now conclude that *A* received a valid instance of message 2, thus learning *NRR*; this verifies the main condition of Theorem 5. The reasoning above is the proof of Theorem 6, which states that *A*'s knowledge of *con_K* enables *B* to retrieve the same certificate from TTP and guarantees *B* to have received *NRO*. The ciphertext *C* being existentially quantified does not weaken the theorem because *C* is also bound to label *L* by the message structure.

Theorem 6.
```
[| evs ∈ zg; con_K ∈ parts (knows A evs);
    con_K = Crypt (priK TTP) {|Number f_con, Agent A, Agent B,
                                Nonce L, Key K|} |]
⟹ Notes TTP {|Number f_con, Agent A, Agent B, Nonce L, Key K, con_K|}
      ∈ set evs ∧
   (EX NRO C.
        Gets B {|Number f_nro, Agent B, Nonce L, C, NRO|} ∈ set evs ∧
        NRO = Crypt (priK A) {|Number f_nro, Agent B, Nonce L, C|})
```

Guarantees for *A*. If *B* holds *con_K*, and it names *A* as the originator, then *con_K* is available to *A* too, who has also received *NRR*. Theorem 7 guarantees this.

Theorem 7.
```
[| evs ∈ zg; con_K ∈ parts (knows B evs);
    con_K = Crypt (priK TTP) {|Number f_con, Agent A, Agent B,
                                Nonce L, Key K|};
   NRR = Crypt (priK B) {|Number f_nrr, Agent A, Nonce L, C|} |]
⟹ Notes TTP {|Number f_con, Agent A, Agent B, Nonce L, Key K, con_K|}
      ∈ set evs ∧
   Gets A {|Number f_nrr, Agent A, Nonce L, NRR|} ∈ set evs
```

The first part of the conclusion derives from proving Theorem 4 on the assumption that *con_K* is known to *B*. The second part derives from an appeal to Theorem 2 and a lemma saying that *A* only sends message 3 upon reception of message 2.

Note that there is no analogue of Theorem 5 for A: B's possession of NRO does not imply A's possession of NRR. Although this suggests that, upon reception of NRO, B has an advantage over A, who holds no evidence, our theorems on validity of the evidence held by B indicate that B cannot win any disputes until he also gets con_K. Theorem 7 concludes that, at that stage, A will hold equivalent evidence.

7 Modelling and Verifying with a Spy

This section discusses how the presence of the spy influences the protocol goals. The protocol definition must be extended by the rule Fake given in Fig. 3. That rule allows the spy to send any of the messages that can be built from the analysis of the traffic using the private signature keys of bad agents [12]. Note that the spy also sees the messages that bad agents retrieve via *ftp*, for those events were modelled in terms of Notes (§2, §5). By contrast, the spy cannot exploit TTP's creation of con_K because TTP is assumed not to be bad.

```
Fake
[| evsF ∈ zg;   X ∈ synth (analz (knows Spy evsF)) |]
⟹ Says Spy B X # evsF ∈ zg
```

Fig. 3. Modelling a Spy.

The rest of the protocol definition requires minor changes. Rule ZG3 must check that NRR truly is B's signature on the expected components, because the spy might have replaced it with a fake signature. Rule TTP_prepare_ftp must check that K is a symmetric key, as the spy might have inserted some bad agent's private key. This attack could not take place in the real world, since private keys are asymmetric, with a typical length of 1024 bits, while a symmetric key is typically no longer that 128 bits. So it is realistic to assume that TTP can reject such substitutions.

Our strategies to proving the non-repudiation goals work as before. However, when proving validity of evidence, the exact form of the message whereby an agent learnt a certificate cannot be stated. The spy could have prevented the delivery of the legal message containing the certificate, extracted the certificate and then forwarded it inside a fake message of unpredictable form.

So, the theorems presented above receive minor variations. For example, Theorem 1 now has the form of Theorem $1'$, which shows that an agent other than the spy who knows con_K has either got it via *ftp* or received it from the network inside some larger message.

Theorem $1'$.
```
[| evs ∈ zg; con_K ∈ parts (knows B evs); B ≠ Spy;
   con_K = Crypt (priK TTP) {|Number f_con, Agent A, Agent B,
                         Nonce L, Key K|} |]
```

$\Longrightarrow$ Notes B {|Number f_con, Agent A, Agent B, Nonce L, Key K, con_K|}
    ∈ set evs ∨
    Gets B X ∈ set evs ∧ con_K ∈ parts {X}

What was Theorem 2 can now be proved on the conclusion of Theorem 1′ via the observation that *con_K* was certainly in the traffic, and therefore originated with TTP. In consequence, combining the two new theorems produces the same guarantee as before, but only for an agent who is not the spy.

Other minor changes concern the authenticity theorems that have been mentioned along the treatment. For example, *NRO* is encrypted by *A*'s private key, so proving that it originated with *A* requires assuming that *A* does not belong to the set bad, otherwise the spy would know *A*'s private signature key priK *A* and could forge the certificate. The same extra condition is needed on *A* when proving that *sub_K* originated with *A*, or on *B* when proving that *NRR* originated with *B*. In consequence, for Theorem 3 to continue to hold, *B* must not be bad. Likewise, Theorem 5 now needs *A* not to be bad, and can only state that *B* gets *NRO* inside a message of some form. Theorem 4 remains unchanged.

The fairness theorems do not need extra assumptions because they rest on the message signed by TTP, which cannot be forged. However, their conclusions cannot state the exact form of the messages that deliver *NRO* and *NRR* respectively. Those messages are now existentially quantified.

Following these considerations, it seems fair to conclude that the Zhou-Gollmann protocol achieves its goals even in the presence of a spy who is allowed to monitor the traffic and to exploit bad agent's private signature keys.

8   Related Work

Schneider was the first to analyse the Zhou-Gollmann protocol formally [16]. He uses the theory of Communicating Sequential Processes (*CSP*) to extend an existing model previously used for authentication protocols with extra channels whereby the peers present their evidence to a judge. His excellent account on validity of evidence and fairness is carried out by pen and paper. The proof strategies are significantly different from ours. Events are enforced by proving that they do not belong to a CSP refusal set. He writes,

> the verifications of the correctness of evidence properties are carried out without reference to the protocol at all, but only with respect to the capabilities and assumptions concerning the participating agents [15, §5]

Schneider allows any agent to send messages of any form using components from the agent's knowledge, but obviously prevents this when proving fairness. By contrast, in our model, all agents must send messages of the form that the protocol prescribes and can arbitrarily decide to quit the protocol; but we have also considered the influence of a powerful spy. This difference between the two models is superficial: it would be trivial to define a set of unfair agents and allow each agent *A* of the set to send messages from synth(analz(knows *A* *evs*)) on any trace *evs*.

Zhou and Gollmann analyse their protocol using a *belief logic* [17]. The approach allows for simple proofs on validity of evidence that only require four axioms and two inference rules. They formalise a judge J and reach the conclusions that, at the end of a session between agents A and B, the following predicates hold:

- J *believes* $(A$ *said* $M)$
- J *believes* $(B$ *received* $M)$

These predicates do not highlight what evidence the peers have to present to convince the judge, but the protocol verifier could understand this from following the proofs more closely. Fairness properties are not considered, and the difficulty in tackling them appears to be a limitation of the approach. The philosophical differences between reasoning on beliefs and reasoning on traces of events are well known. However, it may be interesting to note that also these proofs on validity of evidence closely follow the events of the session. The protocol in fact requires each agent to send certain evidence only upon reception of some other, specific evidence.

Both works discussed here model a judge explicitly. We have chosen not to model a judge because his functioning as well as the peers' interaction with him are external to the non-repudiation protocol. A peer's presenting some evidence to the judge in fact implies that the peer holds the evidence, which our function knows concisely expresses. A desirable consequence is that the current Inductive Approach can be used *with no extensions* to verify non-repudiation goals.

9   Conclusions

A non-repudiation protocol differs from the protocols traditionally studied in that the protocol participants do not trust each other. Every agent is a potential enemy. This change affects our models and our theorems slightly, but not drastically. We plan to enrich the model further, to model more precisely an agent who is trying to subvert the protocol. (The spy behaves too arbitrarily; for instance, he might give away his private keys, as no real villain would). To the best of our knowledge, no one else has proved non-repudiation properties using verification tools.

Acknowledgements

This work was funded by the EPSRC grant GR/R01156/01 *Verifying Electronic Commerce Protocols*.

References

1. G. Bella. Message Reception in the Inductive Approach. Research Report 460, University of Cambridge — Computer Laboratory, 1999.
2. G. Bella. Modelling Agents' Knowledge Inductively. In *Proc. of the 7th International Workshop on Security Protocols*, LNCS 1796. Springer-Verlag, 1999.

3. G. Bella. Mechanising a protocol for smart cards. In *Proc. of International Conference on Research in Smart Cards (e-Smart'01)*, LNCS. Springer-Verlag, 2001. In Press.

4. G. Bella, F. Massacci, L.C. Paulson, and P. Tramontano. Formal Verification of Cardholder Registration in SET. In F. Cuppens, Y. Deswarte, D. Gollmann, and M. Waidner, editors, *Proc. of the 6th European Symposium on Research in Computer Security (ESORICS 2000)*, LNCS 1895, pages 159–174. Springer-Verlag, 2000.

5. G. Bella and L.C. Paulson. Kerberos Version IV: Inductive Analysis of the Secrecy Goals. In J.-J. Quisquater, Y. Deswarte, C. Meadows, and D. Gollmann, editors, *Proc. of the 5th European Symposium on Research in Computer Security (ESORICS'98)*, LNCS 1485, pages 361–375. Springer-Verlag, 1998.

6. G. Bella and L.C. Paulson. Mechanising BAN Kerberos by the Inductive Method. In A. J. Hu and M. Y. Vardi, editors, *Proc. of the International Conference on Computer-Aided Verification (CAV'98)*, LNCS 1427, pages 416–427. Springer-Verlag, 1998.

7. M. Ben-Or, O. Goldreich, S. Micali, and R. Rivest. A Fair Protocol for Signing Contracts. *IEEE Transactions on Information Theory*, 36(1):40–46, 1990.

8. C.A. Meadows. The NRL Protocol Analyzer: An Overview. *Journal of Logic Programming*, 26(2):113–131, 1996.

9. T. Okamoto and K. Ohta. How to Simultaneously Exchange Secrets by General Assumptions. In *Proc. of the 2nd ACM Conference on Computer and Communication Security (CCS'94)*, pages 184–192, 1994.

10. L.C. Paulson. *Isabelle: A Generic Theorem Prover*. LNCS 828. Springer-Verlag, 1994.

11. L.C. Paulson. *Theory for public-key protocols*, 1996.
    http://www4.informatik.tu-muenchen.de/~isabelle/library/
    HOL/Auth/Public.html.

12. L.C. Paulson. The Inductive Approach to Verifying Cryptographic Protocols. *Journal of Computer Security*, 6:85–128, 1998.

13. L.C. Paulson. Inductive Analysis of the Internet protocol TLS. *ACM Transactions on Computer and System Security*, 1999. In press.

14. P.Y.A. Ryan and S.A. Schneider. *The Modelling and Analysis of Security Protocols: the CSP Approach*. Addison-Wesley, 2000.

15. S. Schneider. Verifying Authentication Protocols with CSP. In *Proc. of the 10th IEEE Computer Security Foundations Workshop*, pages 3–17. IEEE Computer Society Press, 1997.

16. S. Schneider. Formal Analysis of a Non-Repudiation Protocol. In *Proc. of the 11th IEEE Computer Security Foundations Workshop*. IEEE Computer Society Press, 1998.

17. G. Zhou and D. Gollmann. Towards Verification of Non-Repudiation Protocols. In *Proc. of the 1998 International Refinement Workshop and Formal Methods Pacific*, pages 370–380. Springer-Verlag, 1998.

18. J. Zhou and D. Gollmann. A Fair Non-Repudiation Protocol. In *Proc. of the 15th IEEE Symposium on Security and Privacy*, pages 55–61. IEEE Computer Society Press, 1996.

19. J. Zhou and D. Gollmann. An Efficient Non-Repudiation Protocol. In *Proc. of the 10th IEEE Computer Security Foundations Workshop*, pages 126–132. IEEE Computer Society Press, 1996.

Proving Hybrid Protocols Correct

Mark Bickford, Christoph Kreitz, Robbert van Renesse, and Xiaoming Liu

Department of Computer Science, Cornell University
Ithaca, NY, U.S.A.
{markb,kreitz,rvr,xliu}@cs.cornell.edu

Abstract. We describe a generic switching protocol for the construction of hybrid protocols and prove it correct with the NUPRL proof development system. For this purpose we introduce the concept of *meta-properties* and use them to formally characterize communication properties that can be preserved by switching. We also identify *switching invariants* that an implementation of the switching protocol must satisfy in order to work correctly.

1 Introduction

Formal methods tools have greatly influenced our ability to increase the reliability of software and hardware systems by revealing errors and clarifying critical concepts. Tools such as extended type checkers, model checkers [9] and theorem provers [2,15,23,25] have been used to detect subtle errors in prototype code and to clarify critical concepts in the design of hardware and software systems. System falsification is already an established technique for finding errors in the early stages of the development of hardware circuits and the impact of formal methods has become larger the earlier they are employed in the design process.

An engagement of formal methods at an early stage of the design depends on the ability of the formal language to naturally and compactly express the ideas underlying the system. When it is possible to precisely define the assumptions and goals that drive the system design, then a theorem prover can be used as a design assistant that helps the designers explore in detail ideas for overcoming problems or clarifying goals. This formal design process can proceed at a reasonable pace, if the theorem prover is supported by a sufficient knowledge base of basic facts about systems concepts that the design team uses in its discussions.

The NUPRL Logical Programming Environment (LPE) [10,3] is a framework for the development of formalized mathematical knowledge that is well suited to support such a formal design of software systems. It provides an expressive formal language and a substantial body of formal knowledge that was accumulated in increasingly large applications, such as verifications of a logic synthesis tool [1] and of the SCI cache coherency protocol [13] as well as the verification and optimization of communication protocols [17,12,18].

We have used the NUPRL LPE and its database of thousands of definitions, theorems and examples for the formal design of an adaptive network protocol for the ENSEMBLE group communication system [28,11,19]. The protocol is realized as a hybrid protocol that *switches* between specialized protocols. Its design

R.J. Boulton and P.B. Jackson (Eds.): TPHOLs 2001, LNCS 2152, pp. 105–120, 2001.

was centered around a characterization of communication properties that can be preserved by switching. This led to a study of *meta-properties*, i.e. properties of properties, as a means for classifying those properties. It also led to the characterization of a *switch-invariant* that an implementation of the switch has to satisfy to preserve those properties.

In this paper we show how to formally prove such hybrid protocols correct. In Section 2 we describe the basic architecture of hybrid protocols that are based on protocol switching. We then discuss the concept of meta-properties and use it to characterize *switchable* properties, i.e. communication properties that can be preserved by switching (Section 3). In Section 4 we give a formal account of communication properties and meta-properties as a basis for the verification of hybrid protocols with the NUPRL system. In Section 5 we develop the switch-invariant and formally prove that switchable properties are preserved whenever the implementation of a switching protocol satisfies this invariant.

2   Protocol Switching

Networking properties such as total order or recovery from message loss can be realized by many different protocols. These protocols offer the same functionality but are optimized for different environments or applications. *Hybrid protocols* can be used to combine the advantages of various protocols, but designing them correctly is difficult, because they require a distributed migration between different approaches to implementing the desired properties.

The ENSEMBLE system [28,11] provides a mechanism for *switching* between different protocols at run-time. So far, however, it was not clear how to guarantee that the result was actually *correct*, i.e. under what circumstances a switch would actually preserve the properties of the individual protocols.

Our new approach to switching is to design a *generic switching protocol* (*SP*) that would serve as a wrapper for a set of protocols with the same functionality. This switching protocol shall interact with the application in a transparent fashion, that is, the application cannot tell easily that it is running on the *SP* rather than on one of the underlying protocols, even as the *SP* switches between protocols. The kinds of uses we envision include the following:

- *Performance.* By using the best protocol for a particular network and application behavior, performance can always be optimal.
- *On-line Upgrading.* Protocol switching can be used to upgrade network protocols or fix minor bugs at run-time without having to restart applications.
- *Security.* System managers will be able to increase security at run-time, for example when an intrusion detection system notices unusual behavior.

In a protocol layering architecture like the one used in ENSEMBLE the switching protocol will reside on top of the individual protocols to be switched, coupled by a multiplexer below them, as illustrated in Figure 1.

The basic idea of the switching protocol is to operate in one of two modes. In *normal mode* it simply forwards messages from the application to the current protocol and vice versa. When there is a request to switch to a different

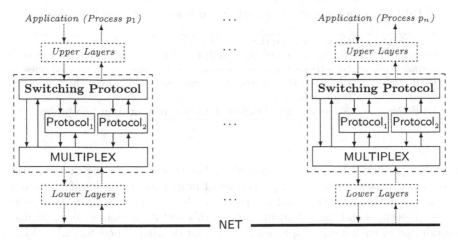

Fig. 1. Generic Switching Protocol for a Protocol Layering Architecture.

protocol, the SP goes into *switching mode*, during which the switching layer at each process will deliver all messages that were sent under the old protocol while buffering messages sent under the new one. The SP will return to normal mode as soon as all messages for the old protocol have been delivered.

The above coarse description, which trivially generalizes to switching between an arbitrary number of protocols, served as the starting point for proving the correctness of the resulting hybrid protocol. The verification proceeded in two phases. We first classified communication properties that are *switchable*, i.e. have the potential to be preserved under switching, and then derived a *switching invariant* that a switching protocol must satisfy to preserve switchable properties. The implementation of the SP (see [19]) was strongly influenced by the latter.

3   Meta-Properties: Classifying Switchable Properties

The main purpose of a switching protocol is to dynamically reconfigure a communication protocol without noticeable effects for the application. This is not possible for switching between arbitrary, functionally equivalent protocols, as the current protocol does not have information about messages that were sent before the switch took place but may need this information to accomplish its task.

A notion of correctness for switching protocols can thus only be expressed relatively to the communication properties that it shall preserve. Because of the broad range of applications there are many interesting properties that one may want a communication system to satisfy. Table 1 lists some examples.

Usually, these properties are expressed as properties of global (systemwide) or local (for one process) traces of *Send/Deliver* events. Reliability, for instance, means that for every *Send* event in the global trace there are corresponding *Deliver* events for all receivers.

Rather than studying the effects of the switching protocol on each communication property separately, we have developed a *characterization* of the ones

Table 1. Examples of Commonly Used Communication Properties.

Reliability:	Every message that is sent is delivered to all receivers
Integrity:	Messages cannot be forged; they are sent by trusted processes
Confidentiality:	Non-trusted processes cannot see messages from trusted ones
Total Order:	Processes that deliver the same messages deliver them in the same order
No Replay:	A message body can be delivered at most once to a process

that are preserved by protocol switching. For this purpose, we introduce the concept of *meta-properties*, i.e. properties of properties, that classify communication properties into those that are preserved by certain communication protocol architectures and those that are not. In this section we will give an intuitive description of such meta-properties (see [19] for details). Their formalization as used in the verification of the switching protocol will be described in section 4.2.

Our verification efforts showed that four meta-properties are important for characterizing the effects of layered communication systems.

Safety.   Safety [4] is probably the best-known meta-property. Safety means that a property does not depend on how far the communication has progressed: if the property holds for a trace, then it also holds for every prefix of that trace. Total order, for instance, is safe since taking events of the end off a trace cannot reorder message delivery. Reliability, however, is not safe since chopping off a suffix containing a *Deliver* event can make a reliable trace unreliable.

Asynchrony.   Any global ordering that a protocol implements on events can get lost due to delays in the send and deliver streams through the protocol layers above it. Only properties that are asynchronous, i.e. do not depend on the relative order of events of different processes, are preserved under the effects of layering. Total order is asynchronous as well, as it does not require an absolute order of delivery events at different processes.

Delayable.   Another effect of layered communication is local: at any process, *Send* events are delayed on the way down, and *Deliver* events are delayed on the way up. A property that survives these delays is called *delayable*. Total order is delayable, since delays do not change the order of *Deliver* event. This meta-property is similar to delay-insensitivity in asynchronous circuits.

Send Enabled.   A protocol that implements a property for the layer above typically does not restrict when the layer above sends messages. We call a property *Send Enabled* if it is preserved by appending new *Send* events to traces. Total order is obviously send enabled. *Send Enabled* and *Delayable* are related, as both are concerned with being unable to control when the application sends messages.

These four meta-properties are sufficient for properties to survive the effects of delay in any layered environment. Since the switching protocol is based on a layered architecture, these meta-properties will be important for a property to be preserved by the switching protocol. However, two additional meta-properties are necessary to describe the specific effects of switching.

Memoryless.   When we switch between protocols, the current protocol may not see part of the history of events that were handled by another protocol. It thus has to be able to work as if these events never happened. A property is *memoryless* if we can remove all events pertaining to a particular message from a trace without violating the property. That is, whether such a message was ever sent or delivered is no longer of importance. This does not imply, however, that a protocol that implements the property has to be *stateless* and must forget about the message. Total order is memoryless, since it only places conditions on events that actually take place, but its implementations are certainly not stateless.

Composable.   Protocol switching causes the traces of several protocols to be glued together. Since we expect the resulting trace to satisfy the same properties as the individual traces, these properties must be *composable* in the sense that if they hold for any two traces that have no messages in common, then they also must hold for the concatenation. Total order is composable, because the concatenation of traces does not change the order of events in either trace.

Using the NUPRL system [3] we have shown that these six meta-properties are sufficient for a communication property to be preserved by the switching protocol: if such a property holds for the traces of the two protocols below the switching protocol, then it also holds for the resulting trace above the switch. In the following sections we will show how this is formally proven.

4   Formalization

A formal verification of the switching protocol with a formal proof system has to be based on an appropriate formalization of the underlying concepts in the language of the proof system. The formal language of the NUPRL proof development system [10,3], an extension of Martin-Löf's intuitionistic Type Theory [22], already provides formalizations of the fundamental concepts of mathematics, data types, and programming.

NUPRL supports conservative language extensions by user-defined concepts via *abstractions* and *display forms*. An abstraction of the form

$$operator\text{-}id(\ parameters\ )\ \equiv\ expression\ with\ parameters$$

defines a new, possibly parameterized term in terms of already existing type-theoretical expressions. Display forms can be used to change the textual representation of this term on the screen or within formal printed documents almost arbitrarily. In particular they can be used to suppress the presentation of implicit assumptions and thus ease the comprehensibility of formal text.

The NUPRL proof development system supports interactive and tactic-based reasoning in a sequent-based formalism, decision procedures, an evaluation mechanism for programs, and an extendable library of verified knowledge from various domains. A *formal documentation* mechanism supports the automated creation of "informal documents" from the formal objects. The technical report [5], containing a complete formal account of the work described in the following sections, for instance, was created entirely from within NUPRL.

4.1   A Formal Model of Communication

To support a formal verification of communication protocols, we have developed a formal model of distributed communication systems and their properties. Our model formalizes notions for the specification of distributed algorithms introduced by Lynch [20] and concepts used for the implementation of reliable network systems [6], particularly of ENSEMBLE and its predecessors [7,27,11].

Messages, Events, and Traces. Processes multicast *messages* that contain a body, a sender, and a unique identifier. We will consider two types of *events*. A *Send(m)* event models that some process p has multicast a message m. A *Deliver(p,m)* event models that process p has delivered message m. A *trace* is an ordered sequence of *Send* and *Deliver* events without duplicate *Send* events.

In order to be able to reason formally about messages, events and traces, we introduce two classes `MessageStruct` and `EventStruct` of formal *message structures* and *event structures*, respectively.

A message structure $M \in$ `MessageStruct` provides a carrier $|M|$ and three functions, content_M, sender_M, and uid_M, which compute the body, sender, and identifier of a message $m \in M$. Two messages m_1 and m_2 are considered equal, denoted by $m_1 =_M m_2$ if they have the same content, sender, and identifier.

Similarly, an event structure $E \in$ `EventStruct` provides a carrier type $|E|$, a message structure MS_E, and three functions, is-send_E, loc_E, and msg_E, where $\text{is-send}_E(e)$ is `true` when the event $e \in |E|$ is a *Send* event (otherwise it is a *Deliver* event); $\text{loc}_E(e)$, the *location* of the event e, is the identifier of the process that sends or receives e; and $\text{msg}_E(e)$ is the message $m \in \text{MS}_E$ contained in the event e. Using the latter we define a binary relation, $e_1 =_E^m e_2$, which holds if the messages contained in the events e_1 and e_2 are equal wrt. $=_M$. For example, e_1 and e_2 might be *Deliver* events of the same message m at two different locations.

Given an event structure E, a trace is just a list of events of type $|E|$. The data type of traces over E is thus defined as

$$\text{Trace}_E \equiv |E| \text{ List}$$

All the usual list operations like length $|tr|$, selecting the i-th element $tr[i]$, concatenation $tr_1 @ tr_2$, prefix relation $tr_1 \sqsubseteq tr_2$, and filtering elements that satisfy a property P, $[e \in tr | P]$, apply to traces as well.

For process identifiers we introduce a (recursively defined) type `PID` that contains tokens and integers and is closed under pairing. A similar type, called `Label`, will be later be used to tag events processed by different protocols.

Properties of Traces. A *trace property* is a predicate on traces that describes certain behaviors of communication. We formalize trace properties as propositions on traces, i.e. as functions from Trace_E to the type $\mathbb{P}$ of logical propositions.

$$\text{TraceProperty}_E \equiv \text{Trace}_E \to \mathbb{P}$$

All traces that we consider must satisfy at least three basic properties.

Every delivered message must have been sent before (*causality*), no message is sent twice, and no message is delivered twice (*replayed*) to the same process. These assumptions are made implicitly in the implementation of communication systems but need to be made explicit in a formal account.

$\text{Causal}_E(tr)$
$\equiv \forall i < |tr| . \exists j < |tr| . \; j \leq i \; \wedge \; \text{is-send}_E(tr[j]) \; \wedge \; tr[j] =_E^m tr[i]$

$\text{No-dup-send}_E(tr)$
$\equiv \forall i,j < |tr| . \; (\text{is-send}_E(tr[i]) \wedge \text{is-send}_E(tr[j]) \wedge tr[j] =_E^m tr[i])$
$\qquad \Rightarrow \; i = j$

$\text{No-replay}_E(tr)$
$\equiv \forall i,j < |tr| . \; (\quad \neg\text{is-send}_E(tr[i]) \; \wedge \; \neg\text{is-send}_E(tr[j])$
$\qquad\qquad\qquad \wedge \; tr[j] =_E^m tr[i] \qquad \wedge \; \text{loc}_E(tr[i]) = \text{loc}_E(tr[j])$
$\qquad\qquad\quad) \; \Rightarrow \quad i = j$

The properties *reliability* (for multicasting), *integrity*, *confidentiality*, and *total order* (c.f. Section 3) can be formalized as follows.

$\text{Reliable}_E(tr)$
$\equiv \forall e \in tr . \; \text{is-send}_E(e) \Rightarrow$
$\qquad \forall p : \text{PID} . \; \exists e_1 \in tr . \; \neg\text{is-send}_E(e_1) \; \wedge \; e =_E^m e_1 \; \wedge \; \text{loc}_E(e_1) = p$

$\text{Integrity}_E(tr)$
$\equiv \forall e \in tr . \; (\neg\text{is-send}_E(e) \wedge \text{trusted}(\text{loc}_E(e))) \Rightarrow$
$\qquad \forall e_1 \in tr . \; (\text{is-send}_E(e_1) \; \wedge \; e =_E^m e_1) \; \Rightarrow \; \text{trusted}(\text{loc}_E(e_1))$

$\text{Confidential}_E(tr)$
$\equiv \forall e \in tr . \; (\neg\text{is-send}_E(e) \wedge \neg\text{trusted}(\text{loc}_E(e))) \Rightarrow$
$\qquad \neg(\exists e_1 \in tr . \; \text{is-send}_E(e_1) \; \wedge \; e =_E^m e_1 \; \wedge \; \text{trusted}(\text{loc}_E(e_1)))$

$\text{TotalOrder}_E(tr)$
$\equiv \forall p,q : \text{PID} . \; tr{\downarrow}p \, \rfloor \, tr{\downarrow}q \; = \; tr{\downarrow}q \, \rfloor \, tr{\downarrow}p$

where $\text{trusted}(p)$ characterizes trusted processes, $tr{\downarrow}p$ is the trace tr delivered at process p (the projection of all $Deliver(p,m)$ events from trace tr), and $tr_1 \, \rfloor \, tr_2$ denotes the restriction of tr_1 to events whose messages also occur in tr_2.

$tr{\downarrow}p \quad \equiv \; [\, e \in tr \mid \neg\text{is-send}_E(e) \wedge \text{loc}_E(e) = p \,]$
$tr_1 \, \rfloor \, tr_2 \quad \equiv \; [\, e_1 \in tr_1 \mid \exists e_2 \in tr_2 . \; e_1 =_E^m e_2 \,]$

In the following investigations we also need a notion of *refinement* on trace properties, which is defined as follows.

$P \rhd Q \; \equiv \; \forall tr : \text{Trace}_E . \; P(\texttt{tr}) \; \Rightarrow \; Q(\texttt{tr})$

4.2   Meta-properties

Meta-properties are predicates on properties that are used to classify which properties are preserved by a protocol layer. In principle, any predicate on properties could be meta-property. But the meta-properties that we are specifically interested in are the ones that describe how passing events through a protocol layer affects the properties of the traces above and below that layer. We say that a reflexive and transitive relation R on traces *preserves* a property P if, whenever two traces tr_1 and tr_2 are related by R, and P holds for trace tr_1, then it also holds for tr_2. A similar definition is also given for ternary relations.

$$R \text{ preserves } P$$
$$\equiv \forall tr_u, tr_l : \text{Trace}_E. \ (P(tr_l) \ \wedge \ tr_u \ R \ tr_l) \ \Rightarrow \ P(tr_u)$$
$$R \text{ preserves}_3 \ P$$
$$\equiv \forall tr_u, tr_1, tr_2 : \text{Trace}_E. \ (P(tr_1) \ \wedge \ P(tr_2) \ \wedge \ R(tr_u, tr_1, tr_2))$$
$$\Rightarrow \ P(tr_u)$$

Preservation by a (binary or ternary) relation R is thus a predicate on properties, i.e. a meta-property. Note that preservation automatically makes the effects of the relation R transitive, even if R is not. Below, we will formalize six such relations that describe the meta-properties discussed in Section 3.

Safety.   Safety means that if the property holds for a trace, then it is also satisfied for every prefix of that trace. The corresponding relation R_{safety} specifies that the trace above the protocol (tr_u) is a prefix of the one below (tr_l).

$$tr_u \ \text{R\_safety}_E \ tr_l \qquad \equiv \qquad tr_u \sqsubseteq tr_l$$

Asynchrony.   A property is asynchronous if it does not depend on the relative order of events at different processes. The corresponding relation R_{asynch} specifies that two traces are related if they can be formed by swapping adjacent events that belong to different processes. Events belonging to the same process may not be swapped.

$$tr_u \ \text{R\_async}_E \ tr_l \qquad \equiv \qquad tr_u \ \text{swap-adjacent}_{[\text{loc}_E(e) \neq \text{loc}_E(e')]} \ tr_l$$

where $tr_1 \ \text{swap-adjacent}_{[c(e;e')]} \ tr_2$ denotes that tr_1 can be transformed into tr_2 by swapping adjacent events e and e' of tr_1 that satisfy the condition $c(e; e')$.

Delayable.   A property is *delayable* if it survives delays of *Send* events on the way down and of *Deliver* events on the way up. The corresponding relation $R_{delayable}$ specifies that adjacent *Send* and *Deliver* events in the lower trace may be swapped in the upper. Events of the same kind or containing the same message may not be swapped.

$$tr_u \ \text{R\_delayable}_E \ tr_l$$
$$\equiv \ tr_u \ \text{swap-adjacent}_{[e \neq_E^m e' \wedge \text{is-send}_E(e) \neq \text{is-send}_E(e')]} \ tr_l$$

Send Enabled.   A property is *Send Enabled* if it is preserved by appending *Send* events to traces. The corresponding relation $R_{send\text{-}enabled}$ specifies that the upper trace is formed by adding *Send* events to the end of the lower trace.

$$tr_u \ \text{R\_send-enabled}_E \ tr_l \equiv \exists e : |E|. \ \text{is-send}_E(e) \ \wedge \ tr_u = tr_l @ [e]$$

Memoryless.   A property is *memoryless* if we can remove all events pertaining to a particular message from a trace without violating the property. The corresponding relation $R_{memoryless}$ defines that the upper trace can be formed from the one below by removing *all* events related to certain messages.

$$tr_u \ \texttt{R\_memoryless}_E \ tr_l \quad \equiv \quad \exists e : |E| . \ tr_u = [\,e_1 \in tr_l \mid e \neq^m_E e_1\,]$$

Composable. A property is *composable* if it is preserved when two traces that have no messages in common are concatenated. The corresponding relation $R_{composable}$ is ternary, as it characterizes the upper trace tr as concatenation of two lower traces without common messages.

$$\texttt{R\_composable}_E(tr_u, tr_1, tr_2) \quad \equiv \quad tr_u = tr_1 @ tr_2 \ \wedge \ \forall e_1 \in tr_1 . \forall e_2 \in tr_2 . \ e_1 \neq^m_E e_2$$

Switchable Properties. The above collection of meta-properties and its formalization is the result of a complex formal analysis of the switching protocol. The formal verification process with the NUPRL proof development system [3] required us to make many assumptions explicit that are usually implicitly present in an informal analysis of communication protocols. This is reflected in the definition of switchable communication properties. A trace property P is *switchable* if it requires the trace to be meaningful and satisfies all of the six meta-properties.

$$
\begin{array}{lllll}
\texttt{switchable}_E(P) & \equiv & P & \triangleright & \texttt{Causal}_E \\
& \wedge & P & \triangleright & \texttt{No-replay}_E \\
& \wedge & \texttt{R\_safety}_E & \texttt{preserves} & P \\
& \wedge & \texttt{R\_async}_E & \texttt{preserves} & P \\
& \wedge & \texttt{R\_delayable}_E & \texttt{preserves} & P \\
& \wedge & \texttt{R\_send-enabled}_E & \texttt{preserves} & P \\
& \wedge & \texttt{R\_memoryless}_E & \texttt{preserves} & P \\
& \wedge & \texttt{R\_composable}_E & \texttt{preserves}_3 & P
\end{array}
$$

In the following section we will show that switchable communcation properties are in fact preserved by the switching protocol.

5   Verification of Hybrid Protocols

In the previous sections we have given an abstract and formal characterization of communication protocols whose properties can be preserved by switching. In a similar way we will now develop an abstract characterization of the switching protocol in terms of a *switching invariant*. We will then prove that every implementation of a switching protocol that satisfies the switching invariant is guaranteed to preserve switchable properties. In this paper, we will focus on the highlights of this proof and the underlying formal theory. A complete account of this theory, which has been developed entirely within the NUPRL proof development system [3], can be found in the technical report that has been created automatically from the formal theory [5].

In order to prove the switching protocol to work correctly for a switchable property P we have to show that if P holds for the traces tr_1 and tr_2 of the two protocols below the switching protocol, then P also holds for the trace tr_u above the switch. That is, an application cannot tell easily that it is running a hybrid protocol with a switch instead of one of the individual protocols.

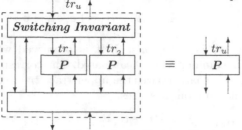

The presence of the switch has two effect on the traces. First, the two traces tr_1 and tr_2 will be merged in some way, and second, the order of some events in the merged trace may be modified due to the effects of layering.

To investigate these effects separately we introduce a *virtual middle trace* tr_m that consists of the events of tr_1 and tr_2. We will study what *local switch invariants* such a trace must satisfy to guarantee that a property, which holds on its subtraces, also hold for the whole trace. We will then link tr_m to tr_1 and tr_2 by merging and to tr_u by introducing global and local delays and additional *Send* events and derive a *global switch invariant*, which models the basic architecture of the switching protocol described in Section 2 and guarantees its correctness.

To be able to identify the origin of events in a merged trace we define a class `TaggedEventStruct` of *tagged event structures* as subtype of `EventStruct`. A tagged event structure $TE \in$ `TaggedEventStruct` provides the same components as any element of `EventStruct` but an additional function tag_{TE} that computes the label $tg \in$ `Label` of an event $e \in |TE|$. By `TaggedEventStruct`$_E$ we denote the subclass of tagged event structures whose components as event structure are identical to those of E. Traces over tagged events are defined as before, but every event of such a trace tr is associated with a tag as well. This enables us to define the subtrace of tr that consists of all events with a given tag tg as

$$tr|_{tg} \ \equiv \ [\text{e} \in tr \mid \text{tag}_{TE}(\text{e}) = tg]$$

Note that the notion $tr|_{tg}$ contains an implicit index TE, whose display is suppressed to simplify the notation.

We will need the following property. It characterizes tagged traces in which events with the same message have the same tag.

$$\text{Tag-by-msg}_{TE}(tr)$$
$$\equiv \ \forall \text{i,j} < |tr|. \ tr[\text{i}] =^m_{TE} tr[\text{j}] \ \Rightarrow \ \text{tag}_{TE}(tr[\text{i}]) = \text{tag}_{TE}(tr[\text{j}])$$

5.1   The Local Switching Invariant

A local switch invariant I on a trace tr shall guarantee that a switchable property P holds for tr whenever P holds for all subtraces $tr|_{\text{tg}}$. If this is the case we say that I *fuses* P:

$$I \text{ fuses } P \equiv \forall tr\text{:Trace}_E.\ I(tr) \Rightarrow (\forall \text{tg:Label}.P(tr|_{\text{tg}})) \Rightarrow P(tr)$$

From the description of the switching protocol we know that if two messages are sent using different protocols, then the second message will be buffered at a location until the first one has been delivered. In other words, if two *Send* events have different tags, then at any location, the first message must have been delivered before the second. This requirement is represented by the following invariant.

$$\text{switch\_inv}_{TE}(tr)$$
$$\equiv\ \forall \text{i,j,k}<|tr|.\ (\text{i}<\text{j}\ \wedge\ \text{is-send}_{TE}(tr[\text{i}])\ \wedge\ \text{is-send}_{TE}(tr[\text{j}])$$
$$\wedge\ \text{tag}_{TE}(tr[\text{i}])\neq\text{tag}_{TE}(tr[\text{j}])\quad \wedge\ tr[\text{j}]\!\downarrow_{TE}tr[\text{k}]\ )$$
$$\Rightarrow\ \exists \text{k'}<\text{k}.\ \text{loc}_{TE}(tr[\text{k'}])=\text{loc}_{TE}(tr[\text{k}])\ \wedge\ tr[\text{i}]\!\downarrow_{TE}tr[\text{k'}]$$

where $e\!\downarrow_{TE}tr[\text{k}]$ denotes that a message related to the event e is delivered at time k in tr:

$$e\!\downarrow_{TE}tr[\text{k}]\ \equiv\ e=_{TE}^{m}tr[\text{k}]\ \wedge\ \neg\text{is-send}_{TE}(tr[\text{k}])$$

switch_inv_{TE} is sufficient to fuse switchable properties, provided the trace describes a meaningful communication, i.e. does not contain duplicate send events.

Theorem 1.

$$\vdash\ \forall \text{TE:TaggedEventStruct}.\ \forall \text{P:TraceProperty}_E.\ \text{switchable}_{TE}(\text{P})$$
$$\Rightarrow (\text{No-dup-send}_{TE}\ \wedge\ \text{switch\_inv}_{TE})\ \text{fuses P}$$

Proof. Theorem 1 is the result of a series of steps that refine the invariants for fusing certain classes of properties until we arrive at the fusion condition for the class of switchable predicates.

1. We begin by proving an invariant for the preservation of all properties P that are memoryless, composable, and safe, denoted by the meta-property $\text{MCS}_{TE}(P)$. A sufficient condition is *single-tag-decomposability*, meaning that any nonempty trace can be decomposed into two traces with no messages in common, such that all events of the (non-empty) second trace have the same tag.

$$\text{single-tag-decomposable}_{TE}(tr)$$
$$\equiv\ tr\neq[]\ \Rightarrow\ \exists \text{tr}_1,\text{tr}_2\text{:Trace}_{TE}.\ tr=\text{tr}_1@\text{tr}_2\ \wedge\ \text{tr}_2\neq[]$$
$$\wedge\ \forall \text{e}_1\in\text{tr}_1.\forall \text{e}_2\in\text{tr}_2.\ \text{e}_1\neq_E^{m}\text{e}_2$$
$$\wedge\ \exists \text{tg:Label}.\ \forall \text{e}_2\in\text{tr}_2.\ \text{tag}_{TE}(\text{e}_2)=\text{tg}$$

By induction over the length of a trace we prove that any single-tag-decomposable safety property is a fusion condition for any MCS property.

$$\vdash\ \forall \text{TE:TaggedEventStruct}.\ \forall \text{P,I:TraceProperty}_{TE}.\ \text{MCS}_{TE}(\text{P})\ \Rightarrow$$
$$\text{R\_safety}_{TE}\ \text{preserves I}\ \wedge\ \text{I}\ \triangleright\ \text{single-tag-decomposable}_{TE}$$
$$\Rightarrow\ \text{I fuses P}$$

2. In the next step we refine single-tag-decomposability to a more constructive condition that we call *switch decomposability*. It says that it must be possible to characterize timing of some send events in a trace (i.e. their indices) by some decidable predicate Q that satisfies a number of closure conditions.

$\texttt{switch-decomposable}_{TE}(tr)$
$\equiv tr = [] \lor \exists Q : \mathbb{IN} \to \mathbb{P}. \ \texttt{decidable(Q)} \ \land \ \exists i < |tr|. \ \texttt{Q(i)}$
$\qquad \land \ \forall i < |tr|. \texttt{Q(i)} \Rightarrow \texttt{is-send}_{TE}(tr[\texttt{i}])$
$\qquad \land \ \forall \texttt{i,j} < |tr|. \texttt{Q(i)} \land \texttt{Q(j)} \Rightarrow \texttt{tag}_{TE}(tr[\texttt{i}]) = \texttt{tag}_{TE}(tr[\texttt{j}])$
$\qquad \land \ \forall \texttt{i} < |tr|. \texttt{Q(i)} \Rightarrow \forall \texttt{i} \leq \texttt{j} < |tr|. \ \texttt{Cl}_{\texttt{Q}}(\texttt{j})$

where $\texttt{Cl}_Q(j)$, the *message closure* of Q at time j is defined as

$\texttt{Cl}_Q(\texttt{i}) \equiv \exists \texttt{k} < |tr|. \ \texttt{Q(k)} \ \land \ tr[\texttt{k}] =^m_E tr[\texttt{i}]$

By partitioning the trace into those events that satisfy $\texttt{Cl}_Q(i)$ and those that don't we can prove that switch-decomposability refines single-tag-decomposability.

$\vdash \forall \texttt{TE:TaggedEventStruct}$
$\qquad (\texttt{switch-decomposable}_{TE} \ \land \ \texttt{Tag-by-msg}_{TE} \ \land \ \texttt{Causal}_{TE} \ \land \ \texttt{No-dup-send}_{TE})$
$\qquad \triangleright \texttt{single-tag-decomposable}_{TE}$

3. In the third step we show that a certain strengthening of $\texttt{switch\_inv}_{TE}$ refines switch-decomposability. For this purpose we have to find a predicate Q that satisfies the five conditions for switch-decomposability.
If the trace satisfies $\texttt{switch\_inv}_{TE}$ and causality, then it must contain a *Send* event. We define Q to hold on all indices that are related to the index $\texttt{ls}$ of the last *Send* event by the transitive closure of the relation $\texttt{R\_switch}_{tr}$, which relates *Send* events whose messages were delivered out of order at some location.

$\texttt{i R\_switch}_{tr} \ \texttt{j} \equiv \ \texttt{is-send}_{TE}(tr[\texttt{i}]) \ \land \ \texttt{is-send}_{TE}(tr[\texttt{j}])$
$\qquad \land \ (\texttt{i} < \texttt{j} \land tr[\texttt{j}] \downarrow^<_{TE} tr[\texttt{i}] \ \lor \ \texttt{j} < \texttt{i} \land tr[\texttt{i}] \downarrow^<_{TE} tr[\texttt{j}])$

where $e \downarrow^<_{TE} tr[\texttt{k}]$ denotes that the event e is delivered at some time before time k. It is fairly easy to prove that Q has the first four of the five required properties. For the fifth, however, we need more than just $\texttt{switch\_inv}_{TE}$ and $\texttt{Causal}_{TE}$. We have to assume that the trace tr has a certain normal form, in which *Send* events occur as late as possible and asynchronous *Deliver* events match the order of their *Send* events. Since the algorithm for generating this normal form can be shown to preserve asynchronous and delayable properties, we call this property an *asynchronous-delayable normal form* or *AD-normal*.

$\texttt{AD-normal}_{TE}(tr)$
$\equiv \ \forall \texttt{i} < |tr|. \ (\texttt{is-send}_{TE}(tr[\texttt{i}]) \land \neg\texttt{is-send}_{TE}(tr[\texttt{i+1}]) \ \Rightarrow \ tr[\texttt{i}] =^m_E tr[\texttt{i+1}]$
$\qquad \land \ (\exists \texttt{j,k} < |tr|. \ \texttt{j} < \texttt{k} \ \land \ \texttt{is-send}_{TE}(tr[\texttt{j}]) \ \land \ tr[\texttt{j}] \downarrow_{TE} tr[\texttt{i+1}]$
$\qquad\qquad\qquad \land \ \texttt{is-send}_{TE}(tr[\texttt{k}]) \ \land \ tr[\texttt{k}] \downarrow_{TE} tr[\texttt{i}] \ )$
$\qquad \Rightarrow \ \texttt{loc}_{TE}(tr[\texttt{i}]) = \texttt{loc}_{TE}(tr[\texttt{i+1}]))$

This property, together with causality and no-duplicate-deliver suffices to prove the fifth property of Q. Thus altogether we have proved the following

$\vdash \forall \texttt{TE:TaggedEventStruct}$
$\qquad (\texttt{switch\_inv}_{TE} \ \land \ \texttt{Causal}_{TE} \ \land \ \texttt{AD-normal}_{TE} \ \land \ \texttt{No-replay}_{TE})$
$\qquad \triangleright \texttt{switch-decomposable}_{TE}$

4. Putting the above results together we can show

$\vdash \forall \texttt{TE:TaggedEventStruct}. \ \forall \texttt{P:TraceProperty}_{TE}.$

$$\text{MCS}_{TE}(\text{P}) \quad \wedge \quad \text{P} \vartriangleright (\text{Causal}_{TE} \ \wedge \ \text{No-replay}_{TE})$$
$$\Rightarrow (\text{switch\_inv}_{TE} \ \wedge \ \text{AD-normal}_{TE} \ \wedge \ \text{No-dup-send}_{TE}) \text{ fuses P}$$

In the last step we prove that the normal form requirement can be removed if we assume the predicate P to be asynchronous and delayable.

For this purpose we apply general theorem about the existence of partially sorted lists. It says that, if swapping adjacent elements e and e' in a list tr for which a decidable predicate $GOOD(e, e')$ does *not* hold increases the number of good pairs, then we may reach a list tr' in which all adjacent pairs satisfy $GOOD$ (proof by induction over the number of bad pairs).

By instantiating $GOOD$ with a localized version of AD-normal_{TE} we can show that a trace can be converted into normal form.

$$\vdash \forall \text{TE}:\text{TaggedEventStruct}. \ \forall \text{tr}:\text{Trace}_{TE}$$
$$\text{switch\_inv}_{TE}(\text{tr}) \ \wedge \ \text{No-dup-send}_{TE}(\text{tr})$$
$$\Rightarrow \exists \text{tr'}:\text{Trace}_{TE}. \ \text{switch\_inv}_{TE}(\text{tr'}) \ \wedge \ \text{AD-normal}_{TE}(\text{tr'})$$
$$\wedge \ \text{tr} \ (\text{R\_delayable}_{TE} \vee \text{R\_asynch}_{TE})^* \ \text{tr'}$$

Since switchable properties are preserved by $\text{R\_delayable}_{TE} \vee \text{R\_asynch}_{TE}$, Theorem 1 follows from the above two results.   □

The proof of Theorem 1 was developed completely within the NUPRL proof development system. Further details can be found in [5].

5.2   Global Correctness of Switching

Theorem 1 states that a switchable property P holds on a tagged event trace tr_m whenever P holds for all subtraces $tr_m|_{\text{tg}}$, provided tr_m satisfies the local switch invariant and does not contain duplicate *Send* events.

The *global switch invariant* expresses that some virtual inner trace tr_m, which is created by merging the traces tr_1 and tr_2 of the protocols below and is linked to the upper trace tr_u by introducing global and local delays and additional *Send* events, must satisfy the local switch invariant and be free of duplicates.

In the formal model, we describe the traces tr_1 and tr_2 by a single lower trace tr_l of tagged events. tr_l is related to tr_m by allowing adjacent events with different tags to be swapped, which accounts for the effects of buffering during *switch mode*. tr_m is related to tr_u by allowing (global and local) delays and enabling *Send* events.

$$\text{R}_{tag} \quad\equiv\quad (\text{swap-adjacent}_{[tag(e)\neq tag(e')]})^*$$
$$\text{R\_layer}_{TE} \equiv (\text{R\_async}_{TE} \vee \text{R\_delayable}_{TE} \vee \text{R\_send-enabled}_{TE})^*$$

where R^* denotes the transitive closure of a relation R. Note that R_layer_{TE} is the same as R_layer_E if $TE \in \text{TaggedEventStruct}_E$.

The definition of the global switch invariant summarizes all the above insights into a single relation between the lower and the upper trace.

$$\text{full\_switch\_inv}_{TE}(\text{tr}_u; \text{tr}_l) \ \equiv \ \exists \text{tr}_m:\text{Trace}_{TE}. \ \text{tr}_l \ \text{R}_{\text{tag}_{TE}} \ \text{tr}_m$$
$$\wedge \ \text{switch\_inv}_{TE}(\text{tr}_m)$$
$$\wedge \ \text{tr}_m \ \text{R\_layer}_{TE} \ \text{tr}_u$$
$$\wedge \ \text{No-dup-send}_E(\text{tr}_u)$$

Switching protocols that implement this invariant, support all protocols that implement switchable properties. Whenever a switchable property P holds for all traces $tr_l|_{tg}$ of the individual protocols below a switching protocol that satisfies the global switching invariant, then it also holds for the trace tr_u above it. In the NUPRL proof development system this theorem, which is an straightforward consequence of Theorem 1, is formalized as follows.

Theorem 2 (Correctness of Switching).

$$\vdash \quad \forall \texttt{E:EventStruct.} \ \forall \texttt{P:TraceProperty}_E. \ \forall \texttt{TE:TaggedEventStruct}_E$$
$$\forall \texttt{tr}_u \texttt{:Trace}_E. \ \forall \texttt{tr}_l \texttt{:Trace}_{TE}.$$
$$(\ \texttt{switchable}_E(\texttt{P}) \ \wedge \ \texttt{full\_switch\_inv}_{TE}(\texttt{tr}_u; \texttt{tr}_l) \ )$$
$$\Rightarrow \ (\forall \texttt{tg:Label.} \ \texttt{P}(\texttt{tr}_l|_{tg})) \ \Rightarrow \ \texttt{P}(\texttt{tr}_u)$$

5.3   Implementation Aspects

The implementation of a switching protocol was developed in parallel to the formal verification efforts, and took into account that the switch has to satisfy the global switch invariant. Together with the fact that switching protocols designed according to the description in Section 2 are *live*, this gives us assurance that the resulting hybrid protocol works correctly.

We have evaluated the performance implications of using the switching protocol by switching between two well-known total order protocols [19], one based on a centralized sequencer [16] and the other using a rotating token with a sequence number [8]. These two protocols have an interesting trade-off. The sequencer-based algorithm has low latency, but the sequencer may become a bottleneck when there are many active senders. The token-based algorithm does not have a bottleneck, but the latency is relatively high under low load. Experiments have shown that having the switch follow a small hysteresis at the cross-over point has the potential of achieving the best of both

6   Conclusion

We have designed a generic switching protocol for the construction of adaptive network systems and formally proved it correct with the NUPRL Logical Programming Environment. In the process we have developed an abstract characterization of communication properties that can be preserved by switching and an abstract characterization of invariants that an implementation of the switching protocol must satisfy in order to work correctly.

There has been a flurry of research on the verification of software systems and communication protocols (see e.g. [14,21,24,26]). But most approaches so far provided only a-posteriori verifications of well-understood algorithms. To our knowledge this is the first case in which a new communication protocol was designed, verified, and implemented in parallel. Because of a team that consisted of both systems experts and experts in formal methods the protocol construction could proceed at the same pace of implementation as designs that are not formally assisted, and at the same time provide a formal guarantee for the correctness of the resulting protocol.

The verification efforts revealed a variety of implicit assumptions that are usually made when reasoning about communication systems and uncovered minor design errors that would have otherwise made their way into the implementation (such as to use switching for arbitrary protocols). This demonstrates that an expressive theorem proving environment with a rich specification language (such as provided by the NUPRL LPE) can contribute to the design and implementation of verifiably correct network software.

So far we have limited ourselves to investigating sufficient conditions for a switching protocol to work correctly. However, some of the conditions on switchable properties may be stricter than necessary. Reliability, for instance, is not a safety property, but we are confident that it is preserved by protocol layering and thus by our hybrid protocol. We intend to refine our characterization of switchable predicates and demonstrate that larger class of protocols can be supported.

Also, we would like to apply our proof methodology to the verification of protocol stacks. To prove that a given protocol stack satisfies certain properties, we have to be able to prove that these properties, once "created" by some protocol, are preserved by the other protocols in the stack. We believe that using meta-properties to characterize the properties preserved by specific communication protocols will make these investigations feasible.

Our case study has shown that formal methods are moving into the design and implementation phases of software construction as well as into the testing and debugging phases. The impact of formal methods is larger the more they are engaged at the earliest stages of design and implementation. We believe that the early use can add value to all subsequent stages, including the creation of informative documentation need for maintenance and evolution of software.

Acknowledgements

This work was supported by DARPA grants F 30620-98-2-0198 (An Open Logical Programming Environment) and F 30602-99-1-0532 (Spinglass).

References

1. M. Aagaard and M. Leeser.   Verifying a logic synthesis tool in Nuprl.   In G. Bochmann and D. Probst, eds., *Workshop on Computer-Aided Verification*, LNCS 663, pages 72–83. Springer, 1993.
2. ACL2 home page. http://www.cs.utexas.edu/users/moore/acl2.
3. S. Allen, R. Constable, R. Eaton, C. Kreitz, L. Lorigo. The Nuprl open logical environment. In D. McAllester, ed., *17th Conference on Automated Deduction*, LNAI 1831, pages 170–176. Springer, 2000.
4. B. Alpern and F. Schneider. Recognizing safety and liveness. *Distributed Computing*, 2(3):117–126, 1987.
5. M. Bickford, C. Kreitz, R. van Renesse. Formally verifying hybrid protocols with the NUPRL logical programming environment. Technical report Cornell CS:2001-1839, Cornell University. Department of Computer Science, 2001.

6. K. Birman. *Building Secure and Reliable Network Applications*. Manning Publishing Co. and Prentice Hall, 1997.
7. K. Birman and R. van Renesse. *Reliable Distributed Computing with the Isis Toolkit*. IEEE Computer Society Press, 1994.
8. J. Chang and N. Maxemchuk. Reliable broadcast protocols. *ACM Transactions on Computer Systems*, 2(3):251–273, 1984.
9. E. M. Clarke, O. Grumberg, D. Peled. *Model Checking*. MIT Press, 1999.
10. R. Constable, S. Allen, M. Bromley, R. Cleaveland, J. Cremer, R. Harper, D. Howe, T. Knoblock, P. Mendler, P. Panangaden, J. Sasaki, S. Smith. *Implementing Mathematics with the NUPRL proof development system*. Prentice Hall, 1986.
11. M. Hayden. *The Ensemble System*. PhD thesis, Cornell University. Department of Computer Science, 1998.
12. J. Hickey, N. Lynch, R. van Renesse. Specifications and proofs for Ensemble layers. In R. Cleaveland, ed., *5th International Conference on Tools and Algorithms for the Construction and Analysis of Systems*, LNCS 1579, pages 119–133. Springer, 1999.
13. D. Howe. Importing mathematics from HOL into NuPRL. In J. von Wright, J. Grundy, J. Harrison, eds., *Theorem Proving in Higher Order Logics*, LNCS 1125, pages 267–282. Springer, 1996.
14. D. Hutter, B. Langenstein, C. Sengler, J. H. Siekmann, W. Stephan, and A. Wolpers. Verification support environment (VSE). *Journal of High Integrity*, 1997.
15. Isabelle home page. http://www.cl.cam.ac.uk/Research/HVG/Isabelle.
16. M. Kaashoek, A. Tanenbaum, S. Flynn-Hummel, H. E. Bal. An efficient reliable broadcast protocol. *Operating Systems Review*, 23(4):5–19, 1989.
17. C. Kreitz, M. Hayden, J. Hickey. A proof environment for the development of group communication systems. In C. and H. Kirchner, eds., *15th Conference on Automated Deduction*, LNAI 1421, pages 317–332. Springer, 1998.
18. X. Liu, C. Kreitz, R. van Renesse, J. Hickey, M. Hayden, K. Birman, R. Constable. Building reliable, high-performance communication systems from components. *Operating Systems Review* 34(5):80–92, 1999.
19. X. Liu, R. van Renesse, M. Bickford, C. Kreitz, R. Constable. Protocol switching: Exploiting meta-properties. In Luis Rodrigues and Michel Raynal, eds., *International Workshop on Applied Reliable Group Communication*. IEEE CS Press, 2001.
20. N. Lynch. *Distributed Algorithms*. Morgan Kaufmann, 1996.
21. Z. Manna and A. Pnueli. *Temporal Verification of Reactive Systems*. Springer, 1995.
22. P. Martin-Löf. *Intuitionistic Type Theory*. Bibliopolis, 1984.
23. Nuprl home page. http://www.cs.cornell.edu/Info/Projects/NuPrl.
24. L. Paulson. The inductive approach to verifying cryptographic protocols. *Journal of Computer Security*, 6:85–128, 1998.
25. PVS home page. http://pvs.csl.sri.com.
26. John Rushby. Systematic formal verification for fault-tolerant time-triggered algorithms. *IEEE Transactions on Software Engineering*, 25(5):651–660, 1999.
27. R. van Renesse, K. Birman, S. Maffeis. Horus: A flexible group communication system. *Communications of the ACM*, 39(4):76–83, 1996.
28. R. van Renesse, K. Birman, M. Hayden, A. Vaysburd, D. Karr. Building adaptive systems using Ensemble. *Software—Practice and Experience*, 1998.

Nested General Recursion and Partiality in Type Theory

Ana Bove[1] and Venanzio Capretta[2]

[1] Department of Computing Science, Chalmers University of Technology
412 96 Göteborg, Sweden
e-mail: bove@cs.chalmers.se
telephone: +46-31-7721020, fax: +46-31-165655
[2] Computing Science Institute, University of Nijmegen
Postbus 9010, 6500 GL Nijmegen, The Netherlands
e-mail: venanzio@cs.kun.nl
telephone: +31+24+3652647, fax: +31+24+3553450

Abstract. We extend Bove's technique for formalising simple general recursive algorithms in constructive type theory to nested recursive algorithms. The method consists in defining an inductive special-purpose accessibility predicate, that characterizes the inputs on which the algorithm terminates. As a result, the type-theoretic version of the algorithm can be defined by structural recursion on the proof that the input values satisfy this predicate. This technique results in definitions in which the computational and logical parts are clearly separated; hence, the type-theoretic version of the algorithm is given by its purely functional content, similarly to the corresponding program in a functional programming language. In the case of nested recursion, the special predicate and the type-theoretic algorithm must be defined simultaneously, because they depend on each other. This kind of definitions is not allowed in ordinary type theory, but it is provided in type theories extended with Dybjer's schema for simultaneous inductive-recursive definitions. The technique applies also to the formalisation of partial functions as proper type-theoretic functions, rather than relations representing their graphs.

1   Introduction

Constructive type theory (see for example [ML84,CH88]) can be seen as a programming language where specifications are represented as types and programs as elements of types. Therefore, algorithms are correct by construction or can be proved correct by using the expressive power of constructive type theory.

Although this paper is intended mainly for those who already have some knowledge of type theory, we recall the basic ideas that we use here. The basic notion in type theory is that of *type*. A type is explained by saying what its objects are and what it means for two of its objects to be equal. We write $a \in \alpha$ for "a is an object of type α".

We consider a basic type and two type formers.

R.J. Boulton and P.B. Jackson (Eds.): TPHOLs 2001, LNCS 2152, pp. 121–135, 2001.

The basic type comprises sets and propositions and we call it Set. Both sets and propositions are inductively defined. A proposition is interpreted as a set whose elements represent its proofs. In conformity with the explanation of what it means to be a type, we know that A is an object of Set if we know how to form its canonical elements and when two canonical elements are equal.

The first type former constructs the type of the elements of a set: for each set A, the elements of A form a type. If a is an element of A, we say that a has type A. Since every set is inductively defined, we know how to build its elements.

The second type former constructs the types of dependent functions. Let α be a type and β be a family of types over α, that is, for every element a in α, $\beta(a)$ is a type. We write $(x \in \alpha)\beta(x)$ for the type of dependent functions from α to β. If f has type $(x \in \alpha)\beta(x)$, then, when we apply f to an object a of type α, we obtain an object $f(a)$ of type $\beta(a)$.

A set former or, in general, any inductive definition is introduced as a constant A of type $(x_1 \in \alpha_1; \ldots; x_n \in \alpha_n)$Set, for $\alpha_1, \ldots, \alpha_n$ types. We must specify the constructors that generate the elements of $A(a_1, \ldots, a_n)$ by giving their types, for $a_1 \in A_1, \ldots, a_n \in A_n$.

Abstractions are written as $[x_1, \ldots, x_n]e$ and theorems are introduced as dependent types of the form $(x_1 \in \alpha_1; \ldots; x_n \in \alpha_n)\beta(x_1, \ldots, x_n)$. If the name of a variable is not important, one can simply write (α) instead of $(x \in \alpha)$, both in the introduction of inductive definitions and in the declaration of (dependent) functions. We write $(x_1, x_2, \ldots, x_n \in \alpha)$ instead of $(x_1 \in \alpha; x_2 \in \alpha; \ldots; x_n \in \alpha)$.

General recursive algorithms are defined by cases where the recursive calls are performed on objects that satisfy no syntactic condition guaranteeing termination. As a consequence, there is no direct way of formalising them in type theory. The standard way of handling general recursion in type theory uses a well-founded recursion principle derived from the accessibility predicate Acc (see [Acz77,Nor88,BB00]). The idea behind the accessibility predicate is that an element a is accessible by a relation $\prec$ if there exists no infinite decreasing sequence starting from a. A set A is said to be well-founded with respect to $\prec$ if all its elements are accessible by $\prec$. Formally, given a set A, a binary relation $\prec$ on A and an element a in A, we can form the set $\mathsf{Acc}(A, \prec, a)$. The only introduction rule for the accessibility predicate is

$$\frac{a \in A \quad p \in (x \in A; h \in x \prec a)\mathsf{Acc}(A, \prec, x)}{\mathsf{acc}(a, p) \in \mathsf{Acc}(A, \prec, a)}.$$

The corresponding elimination rule, also known as the rule of well-founded recursion, is

$$\frac{\begin{array}{c} a \in A \\ h \in \mathsf{Acc}(A, \prec, a) \\ e \in (x \in A; h_x \in \mathsf{Acc}(A, \prec, x); p_x \in (y \in A; q \in y \prec x)P(y))P(x) \end{array}}{\mathsf{wfrec}(a, h, e) \in P(a)}$$

and its computation rule is

$$\mathsf{wfrec}(a, \mathsf{acc}(a, p), e) = e(a, \mathsf{acc}(a, p), [y, q]\mathsf{wfrec}(y, p(y, q), e)) \in P(a).$$

Hence, to guarantee that a general recursive algorithm that performs the recursive calls on elements of type A terminates, we have to prove that A is well-founded and that the arguments supplied to the recursive calls are smaller than the input.

Since Acc is a general predicate, it gives no information that can help us in the formalisation of a specific recursive algorithm. As a consequence, its use in the formalisation of general recursive algorithms often results in long and complicated code. On the other hand, functional programming languages like Haskell [JHe+99] impose no restrictions on recursive programs; therefore, writing general recursive algorithms in Haskell is straightforward. In addition, functional programs are usually short and self-explanatory. However, there is no powerful framework to reason about the correctness of Haskell-like programs.

Bove [Bov01] introduces a method to formalise simple general recursive algorithms in type theory (by simple we mean non-nested and non-mutually recursive) in a clear and compact way. We believe that this technique helps to close the gap between programming in a functional language and programming in type theory.

This work is similar to that of Paulson in [Pau86]. He defines an ordering associated with the recursive steps of an algorithm, such that the inputs on which the algorithm terminates are the objects accessible by the order. Then he defines the algorithm by induction on the order. The proof of termination for the algorithm reduces to a proof that the order is wellfounded. Bove's idea is a translation of this in the framework of type theory in a way more convenient than the straightforward translation. Given the Haskell version of an algorithm f_alg, the method in [Bov01] uses an inductive special-purpose accessibility predicate called fAcc. We construct this predicate directly from f_alg, and we regard it as a characterization of the collection of inputs on which f_alg terminates. It has an introduction rule for each case in the algorithm and provides a syntactic condition that guarantees termination. In this way, we can formalise f_alg in type theory by structural recursion on the proof that the input of f_alg satisfies fAcc, obtaining a compact and readable formalisation of the algorithm.

However, the technique in [Bov01] cannot be immediately applied to nested recursive algorithms. Here, we present a method for formalising nested recursive algorithms in type theory in a similar way to the one used in [Bov01]. Thus, we obtain short and clear formalisations of nested recursive algorithms in type theory. This technique uses the schema for simultaneous inductive-recursive definitions presented by Dybjer in [Dyb00]; hence, it can be used only in type theories extended with such schema.

The rest of the paper is organised as follows. In section 2, we illustrate the method used in [Bov01] on a simple example. In addition, we point out the advantages of this technique over the standard way of defining general recursive algorithms in type theory by using the predicate Acc. In section 3, we adapt the method to nested recursive algorithms, using Dybjer's schema. In section 4, we show how the method can be put to use also in the formalisation of partial functions. Finally, in section 5, we present some conclusions and related work.

2   Simple General Recursion in Type Theory

Here, we illustrate the technique used in [Bov01] on a simple example: the modulo algorithm on natural numbers. In addition, we point out the advantages of this technique over the standard way of defining general recursive algorithms in type theory by using the accessibility predicate Acc.

First, we give the Haskell version of the modulo algorithm. Second, we define the type-theoretic version of it that uses the standard accessibility predicate Acc to handle the recursive call, and we point out the problems of this formalisation. Third, we introduce a special-purpose accessibility predicate, ModAcc, specifically defined for this case study. Intuitively, this predicate defines the collection of pairs of natural numbers on which the modulo algorithm terminates. Fourth, we present a formalisation of the modulo algorithm in type theory by structural recursion on the proof that the input pair of natural numbers satisfies the predicate ModAcc. Finally, we show that all pairs of natural numbers satisfy ModAcc, which implies that the modulo algorithm terminates on all inputs.

In the Haskell definition of the modulo algorithm we use the set N of natural numbers, the subtraction operation <-> and the less-than relation << over N, defined in Haskell in the usual way. We also use Haskell's data type Maybe A, whose elements are Nothing and Just a, for any a of type A. Here is the Haskell code for the modulo algorithm[1]:

```
mod :: N -> N -> Maybe N
mod n 0 = Nothing
mod n m | n << m = Just n
        | not(n << m) = mod (n <-> m) m.
```

It is evident that this algorithm terminates on all inputs. However, the recursive call is made on the argument $n - m$, which is not structurally smaller than the argument n, although the value of $n - m$ is smaller than n.

Before introducing the type-theoretic version of the algorithm that uses the standard accessibility predicate, we give the types of two operators and two lemmas[2]:

$$- \in (n, m \in \mathsf{N})\mathsf{N} \qquad \text{less-dec} \in (n, m \in \mathsf{N})\mathsf{Dec}(n < m)$$
$$< \in (n, m \in \mathsf{N})\mathsf{Set} \qquad \text{min-less} \in (n, m \in \mathsf{N}; \neg(n < \mathsf{s}(m)))(n - \mathsf{s}(m) < n).$$

On the left side we have the types of the subtraction operation and the less-than relation over natural numbers. On the right side we have the types of two lemmas that we use later on. The first lemma states that it is decidable whether a natural number is less than another. The second lemma establishes that if the natural number n is not less than the natural number $\mathsf{s}(m)$, then the result of subtracting $\mathsf{s}(m)$ from n is less than n. [3]

---

[1] For the sake of simplicity, we ignore efficiency aspects such as the fact that the expression n << m is computed twice.

[2] Dec is the decidability predicate: given a proposition P, $\mathsf{Dec}(P) \equiv P \vee \neg P$.

[3] The hypothesis $(n - \mathsf{s}(m) < n)$ is necessary because the subtraction of a larger number from a smaller one is set to be 0 by default.

In place of Haskell's `Maybe` type, we use the type-theoretic disjunction of the set N of natural numbers and the singleton set Error whose only element is error. The type-theoretic version of the modulo algorithm that uses the standard accessibility predicate Acc to handle the recursive call is[4]

$\mathsf{mod}_\mathsf{acc} \in (n, m \in \mathsf{N}; \mathsf{Acc}(\mathsf{N}, <, n))\mathsf{N} \vee \mathsf{Error}$
$\quad \mathsf{mod}_\mathsf{acc}(n, 0, \mathsf{acc}(n, p)) = \mathsf{inr}(\mathsf{error})$
$\quad \mathsf{mod}_\mathsf{acc}(n, \mathsf{s}(m_1), \mathsf{acc}(n, p)) =$
$\qquad \mathbf{case}\ \mathsf{less\text{-}dec}(n, \mathsf{s}(m_1)) \in \mathsf{Dec}(n < \mathsf{s}(m_1))\ \mathbf{of}$
$\qquad \quad \mathsf{inl}(q_1) \Rightarrow \mathsf{inl}(n)$
$\qquad \quad \mathsf{inr}(q_2) \Rightarrow \mathsf{mod}_\mathsf{acc}(n - \mathsf{s}(m_1), \mathsf{s}(m_1), p(n - \mathsf{s}(m_1), \mathsf{min\text{-}less}(n, m_1, q_2)))$
$\qquad \mathbf{end}.$

This algorithm is defined by recursion on the proof that the first argument of the modulo operator is accessible by $<$. We first distinguish cases on m. If m is zero, we return an error, because the modulo zero operation is not defined. If m is equal to $\mathsf{s}(m_1)$ for some natural number m_1, we distinguish cases on whether n is smaller than $\mathsf{s}(m_1)$. If so, we return the value n. Otherwise, we subtract $\mathsf{s}(m_1)$ from n and we call the modulo algorithm recursively on the values $n - \mathsf{s}(m_1)$ and $\mathsf{s}(m_1)$. The recursive call needs a proof that the value $n - \mathsf{s}(m_1)$ is accessible. This proof is given by the expression $p(n - \mathsf{s}(m_1), \mathsf{min\text{-}less}(n, m_1, q_2))$, which is structurally smaller than $\mathsf{acc}(n, p)$.

We can easily define a function $\mathsf{allacc}_\mathsf{N}$ that, applied to a natural number n, returns a proof that n is accessible by $<$. We use this function to define the desired modulo algorithm:

$$\mathsf{Mod}_\mathsf{acc} \in (n, m \in \mathsf{N})\mathsf{N} \vee \mathsf{Error}$$
$$\mathsf{Mod}_\mathsf{acc}(n, m) = \mathsf{mod}_\mathsf{acc}(n, m, \mathsf{allacc}_\mathsf{N}(n)).$$

The main disadvantage of this formalisation of the modulo algorithm is that we have to supply a proof that $n - \mathsf{s}(m_1)$ is accessible by $<$ to the recursive call. This proof has no computational content and its only purpose is to serve as a structurally smaller argument on which to perform the recursion. Notice that, even for such a small example, this accessibility proof distracts our attention and enlarges the code of the algorithm.

To overcome this problem, we define a special-purpose accessibility predicate, ModAcc, containing information that helps us to write a new type-theoretic version of the algorithm. To construct this predicate, we ask ourselves the following question: on which inputs does the modulo algorithm terminate? To find the answer, we inspect closely the Haskell version of the modulo algorithm. We can directly extract from its structure the conditions that the input values should satisfy to produce a basic (that is, non recursive) result or to perform a terminating recursive call. In other words, we formulate the property that an input value must satisfy for the computation to terminate: either the algorithm does

---

[4] The set former $\vee$ represents the disjunction of two sets, and inl and inr the two constructors of the set.

not perform any recursive call, or the values on which the recursive calls are performed have themselves the property. We distinguish three cases:

- if the input numbers are n and zero, then the algorithm terminates;
- if the input number n is less than the input number m, then the algorithm terminates;
- if the number n is not less than the number m and m is not zero[5], then the algorithm terminates on the inputs n and m if it terminates on the inputs $n - m$ and m.

Following this description, we define the inductive predicate ModAcc over pairs of natural numbers by the introduction rules (for n and m natural numbers)

$$\frac{}{\mathsf{ModAcc}(n, 0)}, \quad \frac{n < m}{\mathsf{ModAcc}(n, m)}, \quad \frac{\neg(m = 0) \quad \neg(n < m) \quad \mathsf{ModAcc}(n - m, m)}{\mathsf{ModAcc}(n, m)}.$$

This predicate can easily be formalised in type theory:

$$\mathsf{ModAcc} \in (n, m \in \mathsf{N})\mathsf{Set}$$
$$\mathsf{modacc}_0 \in (n \in \mathsf{N})\mathsf{ModAcc}(n, 0)$$
$$\mathsf{modacc}_< \in (n, m \in \mathsf{N}; n < m)\mathsf{ModAcc}(n, m)$$
$$\mathsf{modacc}_\geq \in (n, m \in \mathsf{N}; \neg(m = 0); \neg(n < m); \mathsf{ModAcc}(n - m, m))$$
$$\qquad \mathsf{ModAcc}(n, m).$$

We now use this predicate to formalise the modulo algorithm in type theory:

$$\mathsf{mod} \in (n, m \in \mathsf{N}; \mathsf{ModAcc}(n, m))\mathsf{N} \vee \mathsf{Error}$$
$$\mathsf{mod}(n, 0, \mathsf{modacc}_0(n)) = \mathsf{inr}(\mathsf{error})$$
$$\mathsf{mod}(n, m, \mathsf{modacc}_<(n, m, q)) = \mathsf{inl}(n)$$
$$\mathsf{mod}(n, m, \mathsf{modacc}_\geq(n, m, q_1, q_2, h)) = \mathsf{mod}(n - m, m, h).$$

This algorithm is defined by structural recursion on the proof that the input pair of numbers satisfies the predicate ModAcc. The first two equations are straightforward. The last equation considers the case where n is not less than m; here q_1 is a proof that m is different from zero, q_2 is a proof that n is not less than m and h is a proof that the pair $(n - m, m)$ satisfies the predicate ModAcc. In this case, we call the algorithm recursively on the values $n - m$ and m. We have to supply a proof that the pair $(n - m, m)$ satisfies the predicate ModAcc to the recursive call, which is given by the argument h.

To prove that the modulo algorithm terminates on all inputs, we use the auxiliary lemma modacc$_{\mathsf{aux}}$. Given a natural number m, this lemma proves $\mathsf{ModAcc}(i, m)$, for i an accessible natural number, from the assumption that $\mathsf{ModAcc}(j, m)$ holds for every natural number j smaller than i. The proof proceeds by case analysis on m and, when m is equal to $\mathsf{s}(m_1)$ for some natural

---

[5] Observe that this condition is not needed in the Haskell version of the algorithm due to the order in which Haskell processes the equations that define an algorithm.

number m_1, by cases on whether i is smaller than $s(m_1)$. The term $nots0(m_1)$ is a proof that $s(m_1)$ is different from 0.

$$\begin{aligned}
modacc_{aux} &\in (m, i \in N; Acc(N, <, i); f \in (j \in N; j < i)ModAcc(j, m)) \\
&\quad ModAcc(i, m) \\
modacc_{aux}&(0, i, h, f) = modacc_0(i) \\
modacc_{aux}&(s(m_1), i, h, f) = \\
&\quad \textbf{case } less\text{-}dec(i, s(m_1)) \in Dec(i < s(m_1)) \textbf{ of} \\
&\quad\quad inl(q_1) \Rightarrow modacc_<(i, s(m_1), q_1) \\
&\quad\quad inr(q_2) \Rightarrow modacc_\geq(i, s(m_1), nots0(m_1), q_2, \\
&\quad\quad\quad\quad\quad\quad\quad f(i - s(m_1), min\text{-}less(i, m_1, q_2))) \\
&\quad \textbf{end}
\end{aligned}$$

Now, we prove that the modulo algorithm terminates on all inputs, that is, we prove that all pairs of natural numbers satisfy $ModAcc$[6]:

$$\begin{aligned}
allModAcc &\in (n, m \in N)ModAcc(n, m) \\
allModAcc&(n, m) = wfrec(n, allacc_N(n), modacc_{aux}(m)).
\end{aligned}$$

Notice that the skeleton of the proof of the function $modacc_{aux}$ is very similar to the skeleton of the algorithm mod_{acc}.

Finally, we can use the previous function to write the final modulo algorithm:

$$\begin{aligned}
Mod &\in (n, m \in N)N \vee Error \\
Mod&(n, m) = mod(n, m, allModAcc(n, m)).
\end{aligned}$$

Observe that, even for such a small example, the version of the algorithm that uses our special predicate is slightly shorter and more readable than the type-theoretic version of the algorithm that is defined by using the predicate Acc. Notice also that we were able to move the non-computational parts from the code of mod_{acc} into the proof that the predicate ModAcc holds for all possible inputs, thus separating the actual algorithm from the proof of its termination.

We hope that, by now, the reader is quite familiar with our notation. So, in the following sections, we will not explain the type-theoretic codes in detail.

3   Nested Recursion in Type Theory

The technique we have just described to formalise simple general recursion cannot be applied to nested general recursive algorithms in a straightforward way. We illustrate the problem on a simple nested recursive algorithm over natural numbers. Its Haskell definition is

```
nest :: N -> N
nest 0 = 0
nest (S n) = nest(nest n).
```

---

[6] Here, we use the general recursor wfrec with the elimination predicate $P(n) \equiv ModAcc(n, m)$.

Clearly, this is a total algorithm returning 0 on every input.

If we want to use the technique described in the previous section to formalise this algorithm, we need to define an inductive special-purpose accessibility predicate NestAcc over the natural numbers. To construct NestAcc, we ask ourselves the following question: on which inputs does the nest algorithm terminate? By inspecting the Haskell version of the nest algorithm, we distinguish two cases:

- if the input number is 0, then the algorithm terminates;
- if the input number is $s(n)$ for some natural number n, then the algorithm terminates if it terminates on the inputs n and $nest(n)$.

Following this description, we define the inductive predicate NestAcc over natural numbers by the introduction rules (for n natural number)

$$\frac{}{\mathsf{NestAcc}(0)}, \qquad \frac{\mathsf{NestAcc}(n) \quad \mathsf{NestAcc}(\mathsf{nest}(n))}{\mathsf{NestAcc}(\mathsf{s}(n))}.$$

Unfortunately, this definition is not correct since nest is not yet defined. Moreover, the purpose of defining the predicate NestAcc is to be able to define the algorithm nest by structural recursion on the proof that its input value satisfies NestAcc. Hence, the definitions of NestAcc and nest are locked in a vicious circle.

However, there is an extension of type theory that gives us the means to define the predicate NestAcc inductively generated by two constructors corresponding to the two introduction rules of the previous paragraph. This extension has been introduced by Dybjer in [Dyb00] and it allows the simultaneous definition of an inductive predicate P and a function f, where f has the predicate P as part of its domain and is defined by recursion on P. In our case, given the input value n, nest requires an argument of type $\mathsf{NestAcc}(n)$. Using Dybjer's schema, we can simultaneously define NestAcc and nest:

$$\mathsf{NestAcc} \in (n \in \mathsf{N})\mathsf{Set}$$
$$\mathsf{nest} \quad \in (n \in \mathsf{N}; \mathsf{NestAcc}(n))\mathsf{N}$$

$$\mathsf{nestacc0} \in \mathsf{NestAcc}(0)$$
$$\mathsf{nestaccs} \in (n \in \mathsf{N}; h_1 \in \mathsf{NestAcc}(n); h_2 \in \mathsf{NestAcc}(\mathsf{nest}(n, h_1)))$$
$$\mathsf{NestAcc}(\mathsf{s}(n))$$

$$\mathsf{nest}(0, \mathsf{nestacc0}) = 0$$
$$\mathsf{nest}(\mathsf{s}(n), \mathsf{nestaccs}(n, h_1, h_2)) = \mathsf{nest}(\mathsf{nest}(n, h_1), h_2).$$

This definition may at first look circular: the type of nest requires that the predicate NestAcc is defined, while the type of the constructor nestaccs of the predicate NestAcc requires that nest is defined. However, we can see that it is not so by analysing how the elements in NestAcc and the values of nest are generated. First of all, $\mathsf{NestAcc}(0)$ is well defined because it does not depend on any assumption and its only element is nestacc0. Once $\mathsf{NestAcc}(0)$ is defined, the result of nest on the inputs 0 and nestacc0 becomes defined and its value is 0. Now, we can apply the constructor nestaccs to the arguments $n = 0$, $h_1 =$

nestacc0 and h_2 = nestacc0. This application is well typed since h_2 must be an element in NestAcc(nest(0, nestacc0)), that is, NestAcc(0). At this point, we can compute the value of nest(s(0), nestaccs(0, nestacc0, nestacc0)) and obtain the value zero[7], and so on. Circularity is avoided because the values of nest can be computed at the moment a new proof of the predicate NestAcc is generated; in turn, each constructor of NestAcc calls nest only on those arguments that appear previously in its assumptions, for which we can assume that nest has already been computed.

The next step consists in proving that the predicate NestAcc is satisfied by all natural numbers:

$$\text{allNestAcc} \in (n \in \text{N})\text{NestAcc}(n).$$

This can be done by first proving that, given a natural number n and a proof h of NestAcc(n), nest(n, h) $\leq n$ (by structural recursion on h), and then using well-founded recursion on the set of natural numbers.

Now, we define Nest as a function from natural numbers to natural numbers:

$$\text{Nest} \in (n \in \text{N})\text{N}$$
$$\text{Nest}(n) = \text{nest}(n, \text{allNestAcc}(n)).$$

Notice that by making the simultaneous definition of NestAcc and nest we can treat nested recursion similarly to how we treat simple recursion. In this way, we obtain a short and clear formalisation of the nest algorithm.

To illustrate our technique for nested general recursive algorithms in more interesting situations, we present a slightly more complicated example: Paulson's normalisation function for conditional expressions [Pau86]. Its Haskell definition is

```
data CExp = At | If CExp CExp CExp

nm :: CExp -> CExp
nm At = At
nm (If At y z) = If At (nm y) (nm z)
nm (If (If u v w) y z)= nm (If u (nm (If v y z)) (nm (If w y z))).
```

To define the special-purpose accessibility predicate, we study the different equations in the Haskell version of the algorithm, putting the emphasis on the input expressions and the expressions on which the recursive calls are performed. We obtain the following introduction rules for the inductive predicate nmAcc (for y, z, u, v and w conditional expressions):

$$\frac{}{\text{nmAcc}(\text{At})}\,,\qquad\qquad \frac{\begin{array}{c}\text{nmAcc}(\text{If}(v,y,z))\\ \text{nmAcc}(\text{If}(w,y,z))\\ \text{nmAcc}(\text{If}(u,\text{nm}(\text{If}(v,y,z)),\text{nm}(\text{If}(w,y,z))))\end{array}}{\text{nmAcc}(\text{If}(\text{If}(u,v,w),y,z))}\,.$$

$$\frac{\text{nmAcc}(y)\quad\text{nmAcc}(z)}{\text{nmAcc}(\text{If}(\text{At},y,z))}\,,$$

---

[7] Since nest(s(0), nestaccs(0, nestacc0, nestacc0)) = nest(nest(0, nestacc0), nestacc0) = nest(0, nestacc0) = 0.

In type theory, we define the inductive predicate nmAcc simultaneously with the function nm, recursively defined on nmAcc:

$$\mathsf{nmAcc} \in (e \in \mathsf{CExp})\mathsf{Set}$$
$$\mathsf{nm} \quad \in (e \in \mathsf{CExp}; \mathsf{nmAcc}(e))\mathsf{CExp}$$

$$\mathsf{nmacc}_1 \in \mathsf{nmAcc}(\mathsf{At})$$
$$\mathsf{nmacc}_2 \in (y, z \in \mathsf{CExp}; \mathsf{nmAcc}(y); \mathsf{nmAcc}(z))\mathsf{nmAcc}(\mathsf{If}(\mathsf{At}, y, z))$$
$$\mathsf{nmacc}_3 \in (u, v, w, y, z \in \mathsf{CExp};$$
$$h_1 \in \mathsf{nmAcc}(\mathsf{If}(v, y, z)); h_2 \in \mathsf{nmAcc}(\mathsf{If}(w, y, z));$$
$$h_3 \in \mathsf{nmAcc}(\mathsf{If}(u, \mathsf{nm}(\mathsf{If}(v, y, z), h_1), \mathsf{nm}(\mathsf{If}(w, y, z), h_2))))$$
$$\mathsf{nmAcc}(\mathsf{If}(\mathsf{If}(u, v, w), y, z))$$

$$\mathsf{nm}(\mathsf{At}, \mathsf{nmacc}_1) = \mathsf{At}$$
$$\mathsf{nm}(\mathsf{If}(\mathsf{At}, y, z), \mathsf{nmacc}_2(y, z, h_1, h_2)) = \mathsf{If}(\mathsf{At}, \mathsf{nm}(y, h_1), \mathsf{nm}(z, h_2))$$
$$\mathsf{nm}(\mathsf{If}(\mathsf{If}(u, v, w), y, z), \mathsf{nmacc}_3(u, v, w, y, z, h_1, h_2, h_3)) =$$
$$\mathsf{nm}(\mathsf{If}(u, \mathsf{nm}(\mathsf{If}(v, y, z), h_1), \mathsf{nm}(\mathsf{If}(w, y, z), h_2)), h_3).$$

We can justify this definition as we did for the nest algorithm, reasoning about the well-foundedness of the recursive calls: the function nm takes a proof that the input expression satisfies the predicate nmAcc as an extra argument and it is defined by structural recursion on that proof, and each constructor of nmAcc calls nm only on those proofs that appear previously in its assumptions, for which we can assume that nm has already been computed.

Once again, the next step consists in proving that the predicate nmAcc is satisfied by all conditional expressions:

$$\mathsf{allnmAcc} \in (e \in \mathsf{CExp})\mathsf{nmAcc}(e).$$

To do this, we first show that the constructors of the predicate nmAcc use inductive assumptions on smaller arguments, though not necessarily structurally smaller ones. To that end, we define a measure that assigns a natural number to each conditional expression:

$$|\mathsf{At}| = 1 \quad \text{and} \quad |\mathsf{If}(x, y, z)| = |x| * (1 + |y| + |z|).$$

With this measure, it is easy to prove that

$$|\mathsf{If}(v, y, z)| < |\mathsf{If}(\mathsf{If}(u, v, w), y, z)|, \quad |\mathsf{If}(w, y, z)| < |\mathsf{If}(\mathsf{If}(u, v, w), y, z)|$$
$$\text{and} \quad |\mathsf{If}(u, v', w')| < |\mathsf{If}(\mathsf{If}(u, v, w), y, z)|$$

for every v', w' such that $|v'| \leq |\mathsf{If}(v, y, z)|$ and $|w'| \leq |\mathsf{If}(w, y, z)|$. Therefore, to prove that the predicate nmAcc holds for a certain $e \in \mathsf{CExp}$, we need to call nm only on those arguments that have smaller measure than e[8].

Now, we can prove that every conditional expression satisfies nmAcc by first proving that, given a conditional expression e and a proof h of $\mathsf{nmAcc}(e)$,

---

[8] We could have done something similar in the case of the algorithm nest by defining the measure $|x| = x$ and proving the inequality $y < \mathsf{s}(x)$ for every $y \leq x$.

$|\mathsf{nm}(e,h)| \leq |e|$ (by structural recursion on h), and then using well-founded recursion on the set of natural numbers.

We can then define NM as a function from conditional expressions to conditional expressions:

$$\mathsf{NM} \in (e \in \mathsf{CExp})\mathsf{CExp}$$
$$\mathsf{NM}(e) = \mathsf{nm}(e, \mathsf{allnmAcc}(e)).$$

4   Partial Functions in Type Theory

Until now we have applied our technique to total functions for which totality could not be proven easily by structural recursion. However, it can also be put to use in the formalisation of partial functions. A standard way to formalise partial functions in type theory is to define them as relations rather than objects of a function type. For example, the minimization operator for natural numbers, which takes a function $f \in (\mathsf{N})\mathsf{N}$ as input and gives the least $n \in \mathsf{N}$ such that $f(n) = 0$ as output, cannot be represented as an object of type $((\mathsf{N})\mathsf{N})\mathsf{N}$ because it does not terminate on all inputs. A standard representation of this operator in type theory is the inductive relation

$$\mu \in (f \in (\mathsf{N})\mathsf{N}; n \in \mathsf{N})\mathsf{Set}$$
$$\mu_0 \in (f \in (\mathsf{N})\mathsf{N}; f(0) = 0)\mu(f, 0)$$
$$\mu_1 \in (f \in (\mathsf{N})\mathsf{N}; f(0) \neq 0; n \in \mathsf{N}; \mu([m]f(\mathsf{s}(m)), n))\mu(f, \mathsf{s}(n)).$$

The relation μ represents the graph of the minimization operator. If we indicate the minimization function by min, then $\mu(f, n)$ is inhabited if and only if $\mathsf{min}(f) = n$. The fact that min may be undefined on some function f is expressed by $\mu(f, n)$ being empty for every natural number n.

There are reasons to be unhappy with this approach. First, for a relation to really define a partial function, we must prove that it is univocal: in our case, that for all $n, m \in \mathsf{N}$, if $\mu(f, n)$ and $\mu(f, m)$ are both nonempty then $n = m$. Second, there is no computational content in this representation, that is, we cannot actually compute the value of $\mathsf{min}(f)$ for any f.

Let us try to apply our technique to this example and start with the Haskell definition of min:

```
min :: (N -> N) -> N
min f | f 0 == 0 = 0
      | f 0 /= 0 = s (min (\m -> f (s m))).
```

We observe that the computation of min on the input f terminates if $f(0) = 0$ or if $f(0) \neq 0$ and min terminates on the input $[m]f(\mathsf{s}(m))$. This leads to the inductive definition of the special predicate minAcc on functions defined by the introduction rules (for f a function from natural numbers to natural numbers and m a natural number)

$$\frac{f(0) = 0}{\mathsf{minAcc}(f)}, \qquad \frac{f(0) \neq 0 \quad \mathsf{minAcc}([m]f(\mathsf{s}(m)))}{\mathsf{minAcc}(f)}.$$

We can directly translate these rules into type theory:

$$\text{minAcc} \in (f \in (\text{N})\text{N})\text{Set}$$
$$\text{minacc0} \in (f \in (\text{N})\text{N}; f(0) = 0)\text{minAcc}(f)$$
$$\text{minacc1} \in (f \in (\text{N})\text{N}; f(0) \neq 0; \text{minAcc}([m]f(\text{s}(m))))\text{minAcc}(f).$$

Now, we define min for those inputs that satisfy minAcc:

$$\min \in (f \in (\text{N})\text{N}; \text{minAcc}(f))\text{N}$$
$$\min(f, \text{minacc0}(f, q)) = 0$$
$$\min(f, \text{minacc1}(f, q, h)) = \text{s}(\min([m]f(\text{s}(m)), h)).$$

In this case, it is not possible to prove that all elements in (N)N satisfy the special predicate, simply because it is not true. However, given a function f, we may first prove $\text{minAcc}(f)$ (that is, that the recursive calls in the definition of min are well-founded and, thus, that the function min terminates for the input f) and then use min to actually compute the value of the minimization of f.

Partial functions can also be defined by occurrences of nested recursive calls, in which case we need to use simultaneous inductive-recursive definitions. We show how this works on the example of the normal-form function for terms of the untyped λ-calculus. The Haskell program that normalises λ-terms is

```
data Lambda = Var N | Abst N Lambda | App Lambda Lambda

sub :: Lambda -> N -> Lambda -> Lambda

nf :: Lambda -> Lambda
nf (Var i) = Var i
nf (Abst i a) = Abst i (nf a)
nf (App a b) = case (nf a) of
                  Var i -> App (Var i) (nf b)
                  Abst i a' -> nf (sub a' i b)
                  App a' a'' -> App (App a' a'') (nf b).
```

The elements of Lambda denote λ-terms: Var i, Abst i a and App a b denote the variable x_i, the term $(\lambda x_i.a)$ and the term $a(b)$, respectively. We assume that a substitution algorithm sub is given, such that (sub a i b) computes the term $a[x_i := b]$.

Notice that the algorithm contains a hidden nested recursion: in the second sub-case of the case expression, the term a', produced by the call (nf a), appears inside the call nf (sub a' i b). This sub-case could be written in the following way, where we abuse notation to make the nested calls explicit:

```
nf (App a b) = nf (let (Abst i a') = nf a in (sub a' i b)).
```

Let Λ be the type-theoretic definition of Lambda. To formalise the algorithm, we use the method described in the previous section with simultaneous induction-recursion definitions. The introduction rules for the special predicate nfAcc, some of which use nf in their premises, are (for i natural number, and a, a', a'' and b λ-terms)

$$\frac{}{\mathsf{nfAcc}(\mathsf{Var}(i))},\qquad \frac{\mathsf{nfAcc}(a)\quad \mathsf{nfAcc}(b)\quad \mathsf{nf}(a)=\mathsf{Var}(i)}{\mathsf{nfAcc}(\mathsf{App}(a,b))},$$

$$\frac{\mathsf{nfAcc}(a)}{\mathsf{nfAcc}(\mathsf{Abst}(i,a))},\qquad \frac{\mathsf{nfAcc}(a)\quad \mathsf{nf}(a)=\mathsf{Abst}(i,a')\quad \mathsf{nfAcc}(\mathsf{sub}(a',i,b))}{\mathsf{nfAcc}(\mathsf{App}(a,b))},$$

$$\frac{\mathsf{nfAcc}(a)\quad \mathsf{nfAcc}(b)\quad \mathsf{nf}(a)=\mathsf{App}(a',a'')}{\mathsf{nfAcc}(\mathsf{App}(a,b))}.$$

To write a correct type-theoretic definition, we must define the inductive predicate nfAcc simultaneously with the function nf, recursively defined on nfAcc:

$$\mathsf{nfAcc} \in (x \in \Lambda)\mathsf{Set}$$
$$\mathsf{nf} \quad \in (x \in \Lambda; \mathsf{nfAcc}(x))\Lambda$$

$$\mathsf{nfacc}_1 \in (i \in \mathsf{N})\mathsf{nfAcc}(\mathsf{Var}(i))$$
$$\mathsf{nfacc}_2 \in (i \in \mathsf{N}; a \in \Lambda; h_a \in \mathsf{nfAcc}(a))\mathsf{nfAcc}(\mathsf{Abst}(i,a))$$
$$\mathsf{nfacc}_3 \in (a,b \in \Lambda; h_a \in \mathsf{nfAcc}(a); h_b \in \mathsf{nfAcc}(b); i \in \mathsf{N}; \mathsf{nf}(a,h_a)=\mathsf{Var}(i))$$
$$\qquad \mathsf{nfAcc}(\mathsf{App}(a,b))$$
$$\mathsf{nfacc}_4 \in (a,b \in \Lambda; h_a \in \mathsf{nfAcc}(a); i \in \mathsf{N}; a' \in \Lambda;$$
$$\qquad \mathsf{nf}(a,h_a)=\mathsf{Abst}(i,a'); \mathsf{nfAcc}(\mathsf{sub}(a',i,b)))$$
$$\qquad \mathsf{nfAcc}(\mathsf{App}(a,b))$$
$$\mathsf{nfacc}_5 \in (a,b \in \Lambda; h_a \in \mathsf{nfAcc}(a); h_b \in \mathsf{nfAcc}(b);$$
$$\qquad a',a'' \in \Lambda; \mathsf{nf}(a,h_a)=\mathsf{App}(a',a''))$$
$$\qquad \mathsf{nfAcc}(\mathsf{App}(a,b))$$

$$\mathsf{nf}(\mathsf{Var}(i),\mathsf{nfacc}_1(i)) = \mathsf{Var}(i)$$
$$\mathsf{nf}(\mathsf{Abst}(i,a),\mathsf{nfacc}_2(i,a,h_a)) = \mathsf{Abst}(i,\mathsf{nf}(a,h_a))$$
$$\mathsf{nf}(\mathsf{App}(a,b),\mathsf{nfacc}_3(a,b,h_a,h_b,i,q)) = \mathsf{App}(\mathsf{Var}(i),\mathsf{nf}(b,h_b))$$
$$\mathsf{nf}(\mathsf{App}(a,b),\mathsf{nfacc}_4(a,b,h_a,i,a',q,h)) = \mathsf{nf}(\mathsf{sub}(a',i,b),h)$$
$$\mathsf{nf}(\mathsf{App}(a,b),\mathsf{nfacc}_5(a,b,h_a,h_b,a',a'',q)) = \mathsf{App}(\mathsf{App}(a',a''),\mathsf{nf}(b,h_b)).$$

5 Conclusions and Related Work

We describe a technique to formalise algorithms in type theory that separates the computational and logical parts of the definition. As a consequence, the resulting type-theoretic algorithms are compact and easy to understand. They are as simple as their Haskell versions, where there is no restriction on the recursive calls. The technique was originally developed by Bove for simple general recursive algorithms. Here, we extend it to nested recursion using Dybjer's schema for simultaneous inductive-recursive definitions. We also show how we can use this technique to formalise partial functions. Notice that the proof of the special predicate for a particular input is a trace of the computation of the original algorithm, therefore its structural complexity is proportional to the number of steps of the algorithm.

We believe that our technique simplifies the task of formal verification. Often, in the process of verifying complex algorithms, the formalisation of the algorithm is so complicated and clouded with logical information, that the formal verification of its properties becomes very difficult. If the algorithm is formalised as we propose, the simplicity of its definition would make the task of formal verification dramatically easier.

The examples we presented have been formally checked using the proof assistant ALF (see [AGNvS94,MN94]), which supports Dybjer's schema.

There are not many studies on formalising general recursion in type theory, as far as we know. In [Nor88], Nordström uses the predicate Acc for that purpose. Balaa and Bertot [BB00] use fix-point equations to obtain the desired equalities for the recursive definitions, but one still has to mix the actual algorithm with proofs concerning the well-foundedness of the recursive calls. In any case, their methods do not provide simple definitions for nested recursive algorithms. Both Giesl [Gie97], from where we took some of our examples, and Slind [Sli00] have methods to define nested recursive algorithms independently of their proofs of termination. However, neither of them works in the framework of constructive type theory. Giesl works in first order logic and his main concern is to prove termination of nested recursive algorithms automatically. Slind works in classical HOL. He uses an inductive principle not available in TT but closely silimar to structural induction over our special purpose accessibility predicate.

Some work has been done in the area of formalising partial functions. Usually type theory is extended with partial objects or nonterminating computations. This is different from our method, in which partiality is realized by adding a new argument that restricts the domain of the original input; the function is still total in the two arguments. In [Con83], Constable associates a domain to every partial function. This domain is automatically generated from the function definition and contains basically the same information as our special-purpose predicates. However, the definition of the function does not depend on its domain as in our case. Based on this work, Constable and Mendler [CM85] introduce the type of partial functions as a new type constructor. In [CS87], Constable and Smith develop a partial type theory in which every type has a twin containing diverging objects. Inspired by the work in [CS87], Audebaud [Aud91] introduces fix-points to the Calculus of Constructions [CH88], obtaining a conservative extension of it where the desired properties still hold.

Acknowledgement

We want to thank Herman Geuvers for carefully reading and commenting on a previous version of this paper.

References

[Acz77]   P. Aczel. An Introduction to Inductive Definitions. In J. Barwise, editor, *Handbook of Mathematical Logic*, pages 739–782. North-Holland Publishing Company, 1977.

[AGNvS94]   T. Altenkirch, V. Gaspes, B. Nordström, and B. von Sydow. *A User's Guide to ALF*. Chalmers University of Technology, Sweden, May 1994. Available on the WWW ftp://ftp.cs.chalmers.se/pub/users/alti/alf.ps.Z.

[Aud91]   P. Audebaud. Partial Objects in the Calculus of Constructions. In *6th Annual IEEE Symposium on Logic in Computer Science, Amsterdam*, pages 86–95, July 1991.

[BB00]   Antonia Balaa and Yves Bertot. Fix-point equations for well-founded recursion in type theory. In Harrison and Aagaard [HA00], pages 1–16.

[Bov01]   A. Bove. Simple general recursion in type theory. *Nordic Journal of Computing*, 8(1):22–42, Spring 2001.

[CH88]   Thierry Coquand and Gérard Huet. The Calculus of Constructions. *Information and Computation*, 76:95–120, 1988.

[CM85]   R. L. Constable and N. P. Mendler. Recursive Definitions in Type Theory. In *Logic of Programs, Brooklyn*, volume 193 of *Lecture Notes in Computer Science*, pages 61–78. Springer-Verlag, June 1985.

[Con83]   R. L. Constable. Partial Functions in Constructive Type Theory. In *Theoretical Computer Science, 6th GI-Conference, Dortmund*, volume 145 of *Lecture Notes in Computer Science*, pages 1–18. Springer-Verlag, January 1983.

[CS87]   R. L. Constable and S. F. Smith. Partial Objects in Constructive Type Theory. In *Logic in Computer Science, Ithaca, New York*, pages 183–193, June 1987.

[Dyb00]   Peter Dybjer. A general formulation of simultaneous inductive-recursive definitions in type theory. *Journal of Symbolic Logic*, 65(2), June 2000.

[Gie97]   J. Giesl. Termination of nested and mutually recursive algorithms. *Journal of Automated Reasoning*, 19:1–29, 1997.

[HA00]   J. Harrison and M. Aagaard, editors. *Theorem Proving in Higher Order Logics: 13th International Conference, TPHOLs 2000*, volume 1869 of *Lecture Notes in Computer Science*. Springer-Verlag, 2000.

[JHe+99]   Simon Peyton Jones, John Hughes, (editors), Lennart Augustsson, Dave Barton, Brian Boutel, Warren Burton, Joseph Fasel, Kevin Hammond, Ralf Hinze, Paul Hudak, Thomas Johnsson, Mark Jones, John Launchbury, Erik Meijer, John Peterson, Alastair Reid, Colin Runciman, and Philip Wadler. Report on the Programming Language Haskell 98, a Non-strict, Purely Functional Language. Available from http://haskell.org, February 1999.

[ML84]   P. Martin-Löf. *Intuitionistic Type Theory*. Bibliopolis, Napoli, 1984.

[MN94]   L. Magnusson and B. Nordström. The ALF proof editor and its proof engine. In *Types for Proofs and Programs*, volume 806 of *LNCS*, pages 213–237, Nijmegen, 1994. Springer-Verlag.

[Nor88]   B. Nordström. Terminating General Recursion. *BIT*, 28(3):605–619, October 1988.

[Pau86]   L. C. Paulson. Proving Termination of Normalization Functions for Conditional Expressions. *Journal of Automated Reasoning*, 2:63–74, 1986.

[Sli00]   K. Slind. Another look at nested recursion. In Harrison and Aagaard [HA00], pages 498–518.

A Higher-Order Calculus for Categories

Mario Cáccamo* and Glynn Winskel

Computer Laboratory, University of Cambridge
{Mario.Caccamo,Glynn.Winskel}@cl.cam.ac.uk

Abstract A calculus for a fragment of category theory is presented. The types in the language denote categories and the expressions functors. The judgements of the calculus systematise categorical arguments such as: an expression is functorial in its free variables; two expressions are naturally isomorphic in their free variables. There are special binders for limits and more general ends. The rules for limits and ends support an algebraic manipulation of universal constructions as opposed to a more traditional diagrammatic approach. Duality within the calculus and applications in proving continuity are discussed with examples. The calculus gives a basis for mechanising a theory of categories in a generic theorem prover like Isabelle.

1 Introduction

A language for category theory [11] together with a calculus to derive natural isomorphisms are presented. We systematise categorical judgements of the kind: an expression is functorial in its free variables; there is an isomorphism between two expressions natural in their free variables. The resulting logic gives the foundations for a mechanisation of category theory in a generic theorem prover like Isabelle [15].

The language is based on the simply typed λ-calculus [2] where types denote categories and expressions functors between categories. We introduce constants, for hom-sets, for example, and binders for ends and coends. Ends are a generalisation of limits and play a central role in the calculus in increasing its expressive power.

The rules of the calculus enable a mechanical manipulation of formulae with ends and their dual coends. This gives a more calculational approach to categories than is usual, and less dependence on diagrams. This approach supplies tools for proving preservation of limits and colimits.

One motivation behind this work is the increasing use of the machinery of category theory in denotational semantics. There categories are often seen as generalised domains. An application of special interest to us is the use of presheaf categories as models for concurrency. A central result there is that functions between presheaf categories which preserve colimits, a form of continuity, preserve open-map bisimulation [9] (see [7] for details).

---

* PhD student at BRICS, Centre of the Danish National Research Foundation.

R.J. Boulton and P.B. Jackson (Eds.): TPHOLs 2001, LNCS 2152, pp. 136–153, 2001.

2   The Language

2.1   Categories as Types

In general, a category $\mathcal{C}$ consists of a class of objects and a class of arrows between any pair of objects A, B, written $\mathcal{C}(A, B)$, which support composition and have identities. If the class of arrows between any pair of objects is a set we say that $\mathcal{C}$ is *locally small* and call $\mathcal{C}(A, B)$ the hom-set for A, B. We will concentrate on locally small categories.

Locally small categories together with *functors*, arrows between categories, themselves form the large category **CAT**. Furthermore, given two locally small categories $\mathcal{C}$ and $\mathcal{D}$, the functors from $\mathcal{C}$ to $\mathcal{D}$ also form a category in which the objects are the functors and the arrows between them are *natural transformations*. We can summarise the rich structure of **CAT** in the diagram

where F and G are functors between locally small categories $\mathcal{C}$ and $\mathcal{D}$, and θ is a natural transformation from F to G.[1] We shall be particularly concerned with those natural transformations between functors which are isomorphisms, so-called *natural isomorphisms*.

The structure of **CAT** suggests a language. Its types will denote locally small categories; so we expect judgements which express the legitimate ways to build up types. Its expressions with free variables will denote functors from the category where the variables range to the category where the expression belongs; there will be judgements saying that expressions are functorial in their free variables. The diagram above suggests terms and judgements for constructing natural transformations. Here we will however restrict attention to just the judgements of there being a natural isomorphism between functors denoted by expressions. We plan to extend this work to a notation for natural transformations. Despite just considering natural isomorphisms, the calculus is surprisingly useful, allowing us to derive, for example, results on preservation of limits.

The constructors for types are interpreted as operations over categories. Given the categories $\mathcal{C}$ and $\mathcal{D}$,

- the opposite $\mathcal{C}^{\mathrm{op}}$ is the category whose objects are the objects of $\mathcal{C}$ and whose arrows are the arrows in $\mathcal{C}$ reversed, *i.e.*, $\mathcal{C}^{\mathrm{op}}(A, B) = \mathcal{C}(B, A)$ for any pair of objects A, B;
- the product $\mathcal{C} \times \mathcal{D}$ is the category whose objects and arrows are ordered pairs of objects and arrows in $\mathcal{C}$ and $\mathcal{D}$;
- the sum $\mathcal{C} + \mathcal{D}$ is the category whose objects and arrows are given by the disjoint union of objects and arrows in $\mathcal{C}$ and $\mathcal{D}$; and

---

[1] In fact, making **CAT** an example of a 2-category.

- the functor category $[\mathcal{C}, \mathcal{D}]$ is the category of functors from $\mathcal{C}$ to $\mathcal{D}$ and the natural transformation between them.

Observe that a functor category built out of locally small categories is not necessarily locally small (Crole discusses this point in [8, page 61]). We constrain the use of functor categories $[\mathcal{C}, \mathcal{D}]$ to the case where $\mathcal{C}$ is small. A locally small category is *small* when the collection of objects is a set. Simple examples of small categories are $\mathbf{0}$ and $\mathbf{1}$, the empty and singleton categories respectively. We write $\mathbb{C}, \mathbb{D}, \mathbb{I}, \mathbb{J}, \cdots$ for small categories.

The syntax for types as locally small categories is

$$\mathcal{C} ::= \mathbf{Set} \mid \mathbf{0} \mid \mathbf{1} \mid \mathcal{C}^{\mathrm{op}} \mid \mathcal{C}_1 \times \mathcal{C}_2 \mid \mathcal{C}_1 + \mathcal{C}_2 \mid [\mathbb{C}, \mathcal{C}] \;.$$

Thus, for the language *locally small category* and *type* are synonymous.

2.2   Syntax for Expressions

The expressions $E_1, E_2, \cdots$ are defined by

$$
\begin{aligned}
E ::=\; & X \mid 1 \mid \lambda X.E \mid E_1(E_2) \mid \mathcal{C}(E_1, E_2) \mid (E_1, E_2) \mid \\
& fst(E) \mid snd(E) \mid inl(E) \mid inr(E) \mid case_{\mathcal{C}+\mathcal{D}}(E_1, E_2, E_3) \mid \\
& E_1 \times E_2 \mid E_1 + E_2 \mid \int_{X \in \mathbb{C}^{\mathrm{op}}, Y \in \mathbb{C}} E \mid \int^{X \in \mathbb{C}^{\mathrm{op}}, Y \in \mathbb{C}} E
\end{aligned}
$$

where $\mathcal{C}$, $\mathcal{D}$ and $\mathbb{C}$ are types, and X is drawn from a countably infinite set of variables. The constant 1 stands for the singleton set.

The syntax is that of the typed λ-calculus with products and sums. The "integral" binders denote ends and coends. Ends extend the concept of limit to functors of mixed variance with domain of the form $\mathbb{C}^{\mathrm{op}} \times \mathbb{C}$. The treatment of ends given in this work supports a mechanical manipulation of these binders whose properties resemble the properties of the integral in mathematical analysis. Ends are discussed later – they are a central notion of the language for categories.

2.3   Functoriality

Not all possible expressions in the language give rise to functors. An example of a non-functorial expression is $\mathcal{C}(X, X)$ for a nontrivial category $\mathcal{C}$; there is no action over arrows matching the action over objects. Well-typed expressions in the language represent those expressions functorial in their free variables.

The syntactic judgement $X_1 : \mathcal{C}_1, \cdots, X_n : \mathcal{C}_n \vdash E : \mathcal{C}$ says that the expression E of type $\mathcal{C}$ is functorial in the free variables occurring in the context $X_1 : \mathcal{C}_1, \cdots, X_n : \mathcal{C}_n$; *i.e.* it denotes a functor from $\mathcal{C}_1 \times \ldots \times \mathcal{C}_n$ to $\mathcal{C}$. In informal mathematical usage one says $E(X_1, \cdots, X_n)$ is functorial in $X_1, \cdots, X_n$. Thus, an expression-in-context has two possible readings: as an object when the free variables are interpreted as objects, and as an arrow when the free variables are interpreted as arrows.

From the typing rules we derive well-typed expressions enforcing functoriality. One example is the rule for hom-expressions:

$$\text{hom} \quad \frac{\Gamma \vdash E_1 : \mathcal{C} \qquad \Gamma' \vdash E_2 : \mathcal{C}}{\Gamma^{\text{op}}, \Gamma' \vdash \mathcal{C}(E_1, E_2) : \textbf{Set}}$$

where Γ and Γ' are contexts[2] and Γ^{op} is obtained from Γ by replacing each occurrence of a type $\mathcal{C}$ by $\mathcal{C}^{\text{op}}$. We insist, also in the syntax, that $(\mathcal{C}^{\text{op}})^{\text{op}} = \mathcal{C}$ and that forming the opposite category respects the type constructions so *e.g.* $(\mathcal{C} \times \mathcal{D})^{\text{op}} = \mathcal{C}^{\text{op}} \times \mathcal{D}^{\text{op}}$ and $[\mathcal{C}, \mathcal{D}]^{\text{op}} = [\mathcal{C}^{\text{op}}, \mathcal{D}^{\text{op}}]$.

The rule for lambda abstraction introduces functor categories:

$$\text{lam} \quad \frac{\Gamma, X : \mathcal{C} \vdash E : \mathcal{D}}{\Gamma \vdash \lambda X.E : [\mathcal{C}, \mathcal{D}]}$$

with the assumption that $\mathbb{C}$ is small. If E is an expression with free variables W, Z, we use the abbreviation $\lambda W, Z.E$ for $\lambda X.E[fst(X)/W, snd(X)/Z]$. There is a symmetric rule for eliminating functor categories:

$$\text{app} \quad \frac{\Gamma \vdash F : [\mathbb{C}, \mathcal{D}] \qquad \Gamma' \vdash E : \mathbb{C}}{\Gamma, \Gamma' \vdash F(E) : \mathcal{D}.}$$

The derivation below shows $X : \mathbb{C} \vdash \lambda Y.\mathbb{C}(X, Y) : [\mathbb{C}^{\text{op}}, \textbf{Set}]$ which denotes the so-called Yoneda functor for $\mathbb{C}$:

$$\cfrac{\cfrac{\overline{Y : \mathbb{C} \vdash Y : \mathbb{C}}\ \text{ass} \qquad \overline{X : \mathbb{C} \vdash X : \mathbb{C}}\ \text{ass}}{X : \mathbb{C}, Y : \mathbb{C}^{\text{op}} \vdash \mathbb{C}(Y, X) : \textbf{Set}}\ \text{hom} + \text{exc}}{X : \mathbb{C} \vdash \lambda Y.\mathbb{C}(Y, X) : [\mathbb{C}^{\text{op}}, \textbf{Set}]}\ \text{lam}$$

where the rule (*exc*) allows us to permute the variables in the contexts (there are rules for weakening and contraction as well).

2.4 Naturality

Given two expressions $E_1(X_1, \cdots, X_n)$ and $E_2(X_1, \cdots, X_n)$ functorial in the variables $X_1, \cdots, X_n$ it is sensible to ask whether the associated functors are naturally isomorphic. When they are, one says

$$E_1(X_1, \cdots, X_n) \cong E_2(X_1, \cdots, X_n)$$

natural in $X_1, \cdots, X_n$. More formally, the syntactic judgement $\Gamma \vdash E_1 \cong E_2 : \mathcal{C}$ says the expressions E_1 and E_2, where $\Gamma \vdash E_1 : \mathcal{C}$ and $\Gamma \vdash E_2 : \mathcal{C}$, are naturally isomorphic in the variables of Γ. The judgement $\Gamma \vdash E_1 \cong E_2 : \mathcal{C}$ asserts the existence of a natural isomorphism between the functors denoted by E_1 and E_2.

The relation defined by isomorphism is an equivalence, and there are rules for reflexivity, symmetry and transitivity. The rules for isomorphisms encode useful facts in category theory. There are, for example, rules for the Yoneda lemma and its corollary:

---

[2] The variables that appear in a context are distinct and different contexts have disjoint set of variables; any conflict is avoided by renaming.

Theorem 1 (Yoneda Lemma). *Let* C *be a locally small category. Then*

$$[\mathcal{C}^{\mathrm{op}}, \mathbf{Set}](\lambda X.\mathcal{C}(X, C), F) \cong F(C)$$

natural in $C \in \mathcal{C}$ *and* $F \in [\mathcal{C}^{\mathrm{op}}, \mathbf{Set}]$.

A special case of the Yoneda lemma is expressed by the rule

$$yon \; \frac{\Gamma, X : \mathbb{C}^{\mathrm{op}} \vdash E : \mathbf{Set}}{\Gamma, Z : \mathbb{C}^{\mathrm{op}} \vdash E[Z/X] \cong [\mathbb{C}^{\mathrm{op}}, \mathbf{Set}](\lambda X.\mathbb{C}(X, Z), \lambda X.E) : \mathbf{Set}} .$$

That the Yoneda functor is full and faithful follows by replacing F in Theorem 1 with the functor $\lambda X.\mathcal{C}(X, D)$ for some D in $\mathcal{C}$. This, together with the fact that full and faithful functors preserve isomorphisms, gives:

Corollary 1. $C \cong D$ *iff* $\lambda X.\mathcal{C}(X, C) \cong \lambda X.\mathcal{C}(X, D)$ *for* $C, D \in \mathcal{C}$.

This is encoded in the calculus by the rule:

$$rep \; \frac{\Gamma, X : \mathcal{C}^{\mathrm{op}} \vdash \mathcal{C}(X, E_1) \cong \mathcal{C}(X, E_2) : \mathbf{Set}}{\Gamma \vdash E_1 \cong E_2 : \mathcal{C}}$$

with the assumption that X is not free in E_1 or E_2. A complete presentation of the rules is postponed until section 4.

3   Ends and Coends

3.1   Representability

The manipulation of ends relies on the theory of representable functors.

Definition 1 (Representable Functor). *A functor* $F : \mathcal{C}^{\mathrm{op}} \to \mathbf{Set}$ *is representable if for some object* C *in* $\mathcal{C}$ *there is an isomorphism* $\mathcal{C}(X, C) \cong F(X)$ *natural in* X.

A *representation* for F is a pair (C, θ) such that $\mathcal{C}(X, C) \overset{\theta X}{\cong} F(X)$ natural in X. There is a dual definition for functors in $[\mathcal{C}, \mathbf{Set}]$. A trivial example of a representable functor is $\lambda X.\mathcal{C}(X, A)$ for some object A in $\mathcal{C}$. Below we see that limits and more generally ends are representations for special functors. The next result is a consequence of the Yoneda functor being full and faithful (see [6] for a proof):

Theorem 2 (Parametrised Representability). *Let* $F : \mathcal{A} \times \mathcal{B}^{\mathrm{op}} \to \mathbf{Set}$ *be a functor such that for every object* A *in* $\mathcal{A}$ *there exists a representation* $(\mathcal{B}(A), \theta^A)$ *for the functor* $\lambda X.F(A, X)$, *then there is a unique extension of the mapping* $A \mapsto \mathcal{B}(A)$ *to a functor* $\lambda X.\mathcal{B}(X) : \mathcal{A} \to \mathcal{B}$ *such that*

$$\mathcal{B}(X, \mathcal{B}(A)) \overset{(\theta^A)X}{\cong} F(A, X)$$

is natural in $A \in \mathcal{A}$ *and* $X \in \mathcal{B}^{\mathrm{op}}$.

This result shows that representations are functorial in their parameters; this will be crucial in justifying the typing rules for end formulae.

3.2   Limits and Ends as Representations

Definition 2 (Limit). *A limit of a functor $F : \mathbb{I} \to \mathcal{C}$ is a representation (L, θ) for $\lambda X.[\mathbb{I}, \mathcal{C}](\lambda Y.X, F) : \mathcal{C}^{\mathrm{op}} \to \mathbf{Set}$, i.e.,*

$$\mathcal{C}(X, L) \overset{\theta_X}{\cong} [\mathbb{I}, \mathcal{C}](\lambda Y.X, F) \tag{1}$$

natural in $X \in \mathcal{C}^{\mathrm{op}}$.

The object L in (1) is often written in the literature as $\varprojlim_{\mathbb{I}} F$ and called the limit of F. The right hand side of (1) is the set of natural transformations from the constant functor $\lambda Y.X$ to F. Given $\gamma \in [\mathbb{I}, \mathcal{C}](\lambda Y.X, F)$ and an arrow $u : I \to J$ in $\mathbb{I}$ the naturality condition ensures that the diagram

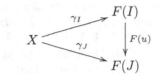

commutes. A natural transformation of this kind is a *cone* from X to F. The isomorphism θ_X in (1) establishes a one-to-one correspondence between arrows from X to L and cones from X to F. From the naturality condition on X we recover the more concrete definition of limits where $\theta_L(\mathrm{id}_L)$ is the universal cone. Dually, a *colimit* for $F : \mathbb{I} \to \mathcal{C}$ is a representation for the functor $\lambda X.[\mathbb{I}, \mathcal{C}](F, \lambda Y.X) : \mathcal{C} \to \mathbf{Set}$.

The notion of end extends that of limit to functors of mixed-variance, *e.g.* with domain $\mathbb{I}^{\mathrm{op}} \times \mathbb{I}$. In this setting, cones are generalised to wedges. Given a functor $G : \mathbb{I}^{\mathrm{op}} \times \mathbb{I} \to \mathcal{D}$, a *wedge* β from X to G is a family of arrows $\langle \beta_I : X \to G(I, I) \rangle_{I \in \mathbb{I}}$ in $\mathcal{D}$ such that for any arrow $u : I \to J$ in $\mathbb{I}$ the diagram

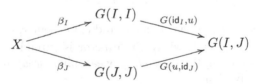

commutes. Just as cones are natural transformations, so are wedges dinatural transformations – see [11, page 218] for the definition of dinatural transformations. Dinatural transformations do not compose in general, but they do compose with natural transformations. So there is a functor $\lambda F, G.\mathbf{Dinat}(F, G) : [\mathbb{I}^{\mathrm{op}} \times \mathbb{I}, \mathcal{D}]^{\mathrm{op}} \times [\mathbb{I}^{\mathrm{op}} \times \mathbb{I}, \mathcal{D}] \to \mathbf{Set}$ where $\mathbf{Dinat}(F, G)$ is the set of dinatural transformations from F to G. A wedge from X to G is an element in $\mathbf{Dinat}(\lambda Y.X, G)$.

Definition 3 (End). *An end of a functor $G : \mathbb{I}^{\mathrm{op}} \times \mathbb{I} \to \mathcal{D}$ is a representation (E, θ) for $\lambda X.\mathbf{Dinat}(\lambda Y.X, G) : \mathcal{D}^{\mathrm{op}} \to \mathbf{Set}$, i.e.,*

$$\mathcal{D}(X, E) \overset{\theta_X}{\cong} \mathbf{Dinat}(\lambda Y.X, G) \tag{2}$$

natural in $X \in \mathcal{D}^{\mathrm{op}}$.

Following a similar analysis to that with limits, we may recover a more concrete definition for ends where $\theta_E(\mathrm{id}_E)$ is the universal wedge. In the language for categories the object E in (2) is written as $\int_{X\in\mathbb{I}^{op}, Y\in\mathbb{I}} G(X,Y)$, and more informally, and economically, as $\int_{Z\in\mathbb{I}} G(Z^-, Z^+)$ where $Z^-{:}\mathbb{I}^{op}$ and $Z^+{:}\mathbb{I}$.

Dually, a *coend* of $G : \mathbb{I}^{op} \times \mathbb{I} \to \mathcal{C}$ is a representation for the functor $\lambda X.\mathbf{Dinat}(G, \lambda Y.X)$. We write $\int^{X\in\mathbb{I}^{op}, Y\in\mathbb{I}} G(X,Y)$ for the coend of G (more informally, $\int^{Z\in\mathbb{I}} G(Z^-, Z^+)$).

3.3   Ends with Parameters

A special case of parametrised representability arises when considering ends as representations. Suppose the functor $F : \mathcal{A} \times \mathbb{I}^{op} \times \mathbb{I} \to \mathcal{B}$ such that for any object A in $\mathcal{A}$ the induced functor $\lambda X, Y.F(A, X, Y) : \mathbb{I}^{op} \times \mathbb{I} \to \mathcal{B}$ has as end the representation $(\int_{Z\in\mathbb{I}} F(A, Z^-, Z^+), \theta^A)$. Then the mapping $A \mapsto \int_{Z\in\mathbb{I}} F(A, Z^-, Z^+)$ extends uniquely to a functor from $\mathcal{A}$ to $\mathcal{B}$ such that

$$\mathcal{B}(X, \int_{Z\in\mathbb{I}} F(A, Z^-, Z^+)) \overset{(\theta^A)_x}{\cong} [\mathbb{I}^{op} \times \mathbb{I}, \mathcal{B}]\big((\lambda Y, W.X), (\lambda Y, W.F(A, Y, W))\big)$$

natural in $A \in \mathcal{A}$ and $X \in \mathcal{B}^{op}$. This is just Theorem 2 applied to the functor $\lambda A, X.[\mathbb{I}^{op} \times \mathbb{I}, \mathcal{B}]\big((\lambda Y, W.X), (\lambda Y, W.F(A, Y, W))\big)$. We conclude that the process of taking ends does not disturb functoriality over the variables which remain free. This justifies the rule for ends:

$$int \; \frac{\Gamma, X : \mathbb{C}^{op}, Y : \mathbb{C} \vdash E : \mathcal{D}}{\Gamma \vdash \int_{X\in\mathbb{C}^{op}, Y\in\mathbb{C}} E : \mathcal{D}}$$

where $\mathcal{D}$ is complete, *i.e.*, $\mathcal{D}$ has all ends (and equivalently, all limits).

Limits correspond to ends where the functor is extended with a "dummy" argument.[3] Thus, by using the rules (*int*), weakening (*wea*) and exchange (*exc*) we can form the derivation:

$$\frac{\dfrac{\Gamma, Y : \mathbb{C} \vdash E : \mathcal{D}}{\Gamma, X : \mathbb{C}^{op}, Y : \mathbb{C} \vdash E : \mathcal{D}} \; wea + exc}{\Gamma \vdash \int_{X\in\mathbb{C}^{op}, Y\in\mathbb{C}} E : \mathcal{D} .} \; int$$

As the variable X is not free in the expression E the last judgement might be abbreviated as just $\Gamma \vdash \int_{Y\in\mathbb{C}} E : \mathcal{D}$. Hence, we can use the integral for both ends and limits.

---

[3] Conversely, an end can be regarded as a limit: given a functor $F : \mathbb{I}^{op} \times \mathbb{I} \to \mathcal{C}$ there is a category $\mathbb{I}^{\S}$ together with a functor $d^{\S} : \mathbb{I}^{\S} \to \mathbb{I}^{op} \times \mathbb{I}$ such that $\int_{I\in\mathbb{I}} F(I^-, I^+) \cong \varprojlim_{\mathbb{I}}(F \circ d^{\S})$; for the details of this construction see [6,11].

3.4   Complete Categories

We restrict the application of rules for ends to complete categories. A category is complete when it has all limits. The category **Set**, for example, is complete.

The set of natural transformations from F to G is characterised by an end expression, the so-called *naturality formula*:

$$[\mathbb{I}, \mathcal{D}](F, G) \cong \int_{I \in \mathbb{I}} \mathcal{D}\big(F(I^-), G(I^+)\big)$$

natural in $F \in [\mathbb{I}, \mathcal{D}]^{\mathrm{op}}$ and $G \in [\mathbb{I}, \mathcal{D}]$. This isomorphism is explained by giving a concrete choice for the end in **Set** (see [6,11] for details). In the calculus there is a rule for this formula:

$$nat \; \frac{\Gamma, X : \mathbb{C} \vdash E_1 : \mathcal{D} \qquad \Gamma', Y : \mathbb{C} \vdash E_2 : \mathcal{D}}{\Gamma^{\mathrm{op}}, \Gamma' \vdash [\mathbb{C}, \mathcal{D}](\lambda X.E_1, \lambda Y.E_2) \cong \int_{X \in \mathbb{C}^{\mathrm{op}}, Y \in \mathbb{C}} \mathcal{D}(E_1, E_2) : \mathbf{Set}} \; .$$

Similarly, there is an end expression for dinatural transformations:

$$\mathbf{Dinat}(F, G) \cong \int_{I \in \mathbb{I}} \mathcal{D}\big(F(I^+, I^-), G(I^-, I^+)\big) \tag{3}$$

natural in $F \in [\mathbb{I}^{\mathrm{op}} \times \mathbb{I}, \mathcal{D}]^{\mathrm{op}}$ and $G \in [\mathbb{I}^{\mathrm{op}} \times \mathbb{I}, \mathcal{D}]$. By composing the isomorphism for the definition of ends (2) with an instance of the *dinaturality formula* (3) where F is a constant functor, we obtain the isomorphism:

$$\mathcal{D}\big(X, \int_{I \in \mathbb{I}} G(I^-, I^+)\big) \cong \int_{I \in \mathbb{I}} \mathcal{D}\big(X, G(I^-, I^+)\big) \tag{4}$$

natural in $X \in \mathcal{D}^{\mathrm{op}}$ and $G \in [\mathbb{I}^{\mathrm{op}} \times \mathbb{I}, \mathcal{D}]$. This formula shows how ends can be moved outside of a hom-expression. To avoid the introduction of special syntax for dinaturals in the language for categories we adopt (4) as the definition for ends:

$$end \; \frac{\Gamma, X : \mathbb{C}^{\mathrm{op}}, Y : \mathbb{C} \vdash E : \mathcal{D}}{\Gamma, W : \mathcal{D}^{\mathrm{op}} \vdash \mathcal{D}\big(W, \int_{X \in \mathbb{C}^{\mathrm{op}}, Y \in \mathbb{C}} E\big) \cong \int_{X \in \mathbb{C}^{\mathrm{op}}, Y \in \mathbb{C}} \mathcal{D}(W, E) : \mathbf{Set}}$$

where $\mathcal{D}$ is complete.

The definition of limits is derivable from (end), (nat) and weakening (wea). First we derive a special case of the naturality formula:

$$\frac{\dfrac{\overline{\rule{2cm}{0.4pt}} \; ass}{W : \mathcal{D} \vdash W : \mathcal{D}}}{W : \mathcal{D}, X : \mathbb{C} \vdash W : \mathcal{D}} \; wea \qquad \begin{array}{c} \vdots \\ \Gamma, Y : \mathbb{C} \vdash E : \mathcal{D} \end{array}}{\Gamma, W : \mathcal{D}^{\mathrm{op}} \vdash [\mathbb{C}, \mathcal{D}](\lambda X.W, \lambda Y.E) \cong \int_{X \in \mathbb{C}^{\mathrm{op}}, Y \in \mathbb{C}} \mathcal{D}(W, E) : \mathbf{Set}} \; nat + exc$$

This is combined by means of transitivity of isomorphism with

$$\Gamma, W : \mathcal{D}^{\mathrm{op}} \vdash \mathcal{D}\big(W, \int_{X \in \mathbb{C}^{\mathrm{op}}, Y \in \mathbb{C}} E\big) \cong \int_{X \in \mathbb{C}^{\mathrm{op}}, Y \in \mathbb{C}} \mathcal{D}(W, E) : \mathbf{Set} \; .$$

Finally (with some rewriting):

$$x\Gamma, W : \mathcal{D}^{\mathrm{op}} \vdash \mathcal{D}\big(W, \int_{Y \in \mathbb{C}} E\big) \cong [\mathbb{C}, \mathcal{D}](\lambda X.W, \lambda X.E) : \mathbf{Set} \; .$$

An important result in reasoning about ends is the *Fubini theorem*:

$$fub \frac{\Gamma, X_1 : \mathbb{I}^{\mathrm{op}}, X_2 : \mathbb{I}, Y_1 : \mathbb{J}^{\mathrm{op}}, Y_2 : \mathbb{J} \vdash E : \mathcal{D}}{\Gamma \vdash \int_{X_1 \in \mathbb{I}^{\mathrm{op}}, X_2 \in \mathbb{I}} \int_{Y_1 \in \mathbb{J}^{\mathrm{op}}, Y_2 \in \mathbb{J}} E \cong \int_{Y_1 \in \mathbb{J}^{\mathrm{op}}, Y_2 \in \mathbb{J}} \int_{X_1 \in \mathbb{I}^{\mathrm{op}}, X_2 \in \mathbb{I}} E : \mathcal{D}}$$

where $\mathcal{D}$ is complete.

3.5   Duality: Coend Formulae

In **CAT**, any functor $F : \mathcal{C} \to \mathcal{D}$ is mirrored by its dual, a functor $F^* : \mathcal{C}^{\mathrm{op}} \to \mathcal{D}^{\mathrm{op}}$ which acts, as a function, in exactly the same way as F on objects and arrows. This dual view also involves natural transformations and is given by applying the 2-functor $(-)^* : \mathbf{CAT} \to \mathbf{CAT}$, which acts

where the components of θ^* are opposites of the components of θ. Note that dualising twice gives the identity. (Although $(-)^*$ reverses natural transformations, this does not have a direct effect in the calculus since we are only concerned with natural isomorphisms.)

Like a mirror, dualising affects our view of things and the way we describe them. A judgement $\Gamma \vdash E : \mathcal{D}$ denotes a functor whose dual is described by a dual form of judgement, $\Gamma^{\mathrm{op}} \vdash E^* : \mathcal{D}^{\mathrm{op}}$, where E^* is the expression obtained by turning ends into coends and coends into ends in E, adjusting the types of the bound variables. For example, the dual form of $Z : \mathcal{C} \vdash \int_{X \in \mathbb{I}^{\mathrm{op}}, Y \in \mathbb{I}} E : \mathcal{D}$ is $Z : \mathcal{C}^{\mathrm{op}} \vdash \int^{Y \in \mathbb{I}^{\mathrm{op}}, X \in \mathbb{I}} E^* : \mathcal{D}^{\mathrm{op}}$ where E is an expression with free variables amongst X, Y, Z. The dual form of a product $E_1 \times E_2$ in **Set** is the sum $E_1^* + E_2^*$ in $\mathbf{Set}^{\mathrm{op}}$. As a consequence of the definition of opposite category it follows that $(E^*)^* = E$. In a similar way we can dualise judgements about the existence of natural isomorphisms, and so embody dualisation in the rules:

$$dua \frac{\Gamma \vdash E : \mathcal{D}}{\Gamma^{\mathrm{op}} \vdash E^* : \mathcal{D}^{\mathrm{op}}} \qquad dual \frac{\Gamma \vdash E_1 \cong E_2 : \mathcal{D}}{\Gamma^{\mathrm{op}} \vdash E_1^* \cong E_2^* : \mathcal{D}^{\mathrm{op}}}.$$

We can now, for example, derive the rule (int^*) for typing coends:

$$\cfrac{\cfrac{\cfrac{\Gamma, X : \mathbb{C}^{\mathrm{op}}, Y : \mathbb{C} \vdash E : \mathcal{D}}{\Gamma^{\mathrm{op}}, Y : \mathbb{C}^{\mathrm{op}}, X : \mathbb{C} \vdash E^* : \mathcal{D}^{\mathrm{op}}} \; dua + exc}{\Gamma^{\mathrm{op}} \vdash \int_{Y \in \mathbb{C}^{\mathrm{op}}, X \in \mathbb{C}} E^* : \mathcal{D}^{\mathrm{op}}} \; end}{\Gamma \vdash \int^{X \in \mathbb{C}^{\mathrm{op}}, Y \in \mathbb{C}} E : \mathcal{D}} \; dua$$

A judgement $\Gamma^{\mathrm{op}}, \Gamma' \vdash \mathcal{C}(E_1, E_2) : \mathbf{Set}$ where $\Gamma \vdash E_1 : \mathcal{C}$ and $\Gamma' \vdash E_2 : \mathcal{C}$ denotes the composition of the functor $\mathcal{C}(-, +) : \mathcal{C}^{\mathrm{op}} \times \mathcal{C} \to \mathbf{Set}$ with the functors

$E_1^* : \Gamma^{\mathrm{op}} \to \mathcal{C}^{\mathrm{op}}$ and $E_2 : \Gamma \to \mathcal{C}$. Notice that, in keeping with practice, an expression occurring on the left of a hom-expression is implicitly dualised. This affects the definition of substitution of expressions for free variables.

The substitution $E_1[E_2/X]$ replaces the negative occurrences of the free variable X (on the left in an odd number of hom-expressions) by E_2^* and other occurrences by E_2. Formally, a substitution $E_1[E_2/X]$ is defined by induction on the structure of E_1 where the defining clause for hom-expressions is

$$\mathcal{C}(E', E'')[X/E_2] = \mathcal{C}(E'[E_2^*/X], E''[E_2/X]).$$

Because $\mathcal{C}(X, Y) \cong \mathcal{C}^{\mathrm{op}}(Y, X)$, for $X : \mathcal{C}^{\mathrm{op}}, Y : \mathcal{C}$, by substitution and dualisation we obtain the rule

$$opp \frac{\Gamma \vdash E_1 : \mathcal{C} \quad \Gamma' \vdash E_2 : \mathcal{C}}{\Gamma^{\mathrm{op}}, \Gamma' \vdash \mathcal{C}(E_1, E_2) \cong \mathcal{C}^{\mathrm{op}}(E_2^*, E_1^*) : \mathbf{Set}.}$$

Thus, there is a derivation

$$\frac{\dfrac{\Gamma, X : \mathbb{C}^{\mathrm{op}}, Y : \mathbb{C} \vdash E : \mathcal{D}}{\Gamma^{\mathrm{op}}, Y : \mathbb{C}^{\mathrm{op}}, X : \mathbb{C} \vdash E^* : \mathcal{D}^{\mathrm{op}}} \; dua + exc}{\Gamma^{\mathrm{op}}, W : \mathcal{D} \vdash \mathcal{D}^{\mathrm{op}}(W, \int_{Y \in \mathbb{C}^{\mathrm{op}}, X \in \mathbb{C}} E^*) \cong \int_{Y \in \mathbb{C}^{\mathrm{op}}, X \in \mathbb{C}} \mathcal{D}^{\mathrm{op}}(W, E^*) : \mathbf{Set}.} \; end$$

Using (opp) twice and transitivity we obtain the derived rule

$$end* \frac{\Gamma, X : \mathbb{C}^{\mathrm{op}}, Y : \mathbb{C} \vdash E : \mathcal{D}}{\Gamma^{\mathrm{op}}, W : \mathcal{D} \vdash \mathcal{D}(\int^{X \in \mathbb{C}^{\mathrm{op}}, Y \in \mathbb{C}} E, W) \cong \int_{Y \in \mathbb{C}^{\mathrm{op}}, X \in \mathbb{C}} \mathcal{D}(E, W) : \mathbf{Set}.}$$

We have chosen to formalise dualisation in rules and then derive rules for coends. By starting out with sufficient extra rules for coends we could eliminate the dualisation rules from any derivation.

4 The Calculus

4.1 Rules for Typing

To avoid the set-theoretic paradoxes, categories are classified according to their size as small and locally small. The formalisation of this distinction demands a form of judgement for types: $\mathcal{C}$ *is small* where $\mathcal{C}$ is any type. Similarly, the rules involving end expressions make assumptions about completeness asking for judgements: $\mathcal{C}$ *is complete* and $\mathcal{C}$ *is cocomplete* where $\mathcal{C}$ is any type.

With a view to keeping the presentation of the rules compact, assumptions about types have been presented rather informally. In Fig. 1, however, the basic set of formal rules is shown. Rules for other constants than **Set** should be added. This point is not elaborated here; a natural extension to this work is to design a richer language for types.

In Fig. 2 we show the typing rules for expressions. The typing rules are interpreted as operations on functors, taking the functors denoted by the premises

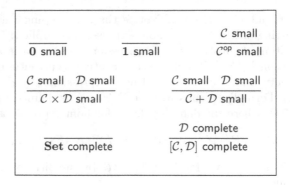

Figure 1. Some Rules for Smallness and Completeness.

to that denoted by the conclusion. Such an interpretation yields a categorical semantics in the usual sense (see [1,5,8]).

The rule for assumption (*ass*) is interpreted as the identity functor which exists for any category. The interpretation of the rule for weakening (*wea*) takes the functor $\Gamma \xrightarrow{E} \mathcal{C}$ denoted by the premise of the rule to the composition $\Gamma \times \Gamma' \xrightarrow{\pi_\Gamma} \Gamma \xrightarrow{E} \mathcal{C}$ which denotes the conclusion. We can interpret the rules for exchange and contraction similarly.

The rule for pairs (*pai*) corresponds to the application of the product functor $- \times - : \mathbf{CAT} \times \mathbf{CAT} \to \mathbf{CAT}$ to the interpretation of E_1 and E_2. The projections (*fst*) and (*snd*) are just the composition with the projection arrows associated to the product. The rules for introduction and elimination of sums are interpreted through the functor $- + - : \mathbf{CAT} \times \mathbf{CAT} \to \mathbf{CAT}$ in a similar fashion.

The rule (*dua*) is peculiar since it not only acts on the expressions but on the judgement as a whole. This is explained through the application of the functor $(-)^*$ to $\Gamma \xrightarrow{E} \mathcal{C}$.

The abstraction rule (*lam*) is interpreted by "currying" the functor denoted by E, *i.e.*, a variable from the context is shifted into the expression. Symmetrically the evaluation functor justifies the rule (*app*). The rule for substitution (*sub*) corresponds to the composition of functors; recall substitution may involve dualisation – see § 3.5.

The rules (*ten*) and (*uni*) have a special status. Products in **Set** are introduced with a view to a more general model given by $\mathcal{V}$-enriched categories, where $\mathcal{V}$ is a monoidal closed category equipped with a tensor product $\otimes$. In the case of **Set**, the tensor product is the categorical product.

4.2   Rules for Natural Isomorphisms

The rules for natural isomorphisms are listed in Fig. 3. The structural rules for weakening, exchange and contraction are defined as usual and not shown. The rules describe how to build natural isomorphisms. For example, the premise of

$$ass \; \frac{}{X : \mathcal{C} \vdash X : \mathcal{C}} \qquad wea \; \frac{\Gamma \vdash E : \mathcal{C}}{\Gamma, \Gamma' \vdash E : \mathcal{C}}$$

$$exc \; \frac{\Gamma \vdash E : \mathcal{C}}{\Pi(\Gamma) \vdash E : \mathcal{C}} \Pi \; \text{permutation} \qquad con \; \frac{\Gamma, X : \mathcal{C}, Y : \mathcal{C} \vdash E : \mathcal{D}}{\Gamma, Z : \mathcal{C} \vdash E[Z/X, Z/Y] : \mathcal{D}} \; Z \; \text{is fresh}$$

$$fst \; \frac{\Gamma \vdash E : \mathcal{C} \times \mathcal{D}}{\Gamma \vdash fst(E) : \mathcal{C}} \qquad snd \; \frac{\Gamma \vdash E : \mathcal{C} \times \mathcal{D}}{\Gamma \vdash snd(E) : \mathcal{D}} \qquad pai \; \frac{\Gamma \vdash E_1 : \mathcal{C} \quad \Gamma' \vdash E_2 : \mathcal{D}}{\Gamma, \Gamma' \vdash (E_1, E_2) : \mathcal{C} \times \mathcal{D}}$$

$$inl \; \frac{\Gamma \vdash E : \mathcal{C}}{\Gamma \vdash inl(E) : \mathcal{C} + \mathcal{D}} \qquad inr \; \frac{\Gamma \vdash E : \mathcal{D}}{\Gamma \vdash inr(E) : \mathcal{C} + \mathcal{D}}$$

$$cas \; \frac{\Gamma \vdash E_1 : \mathcal{C} + \mathcal{D} \quad \Gamma' \vdash E_2 : \mathcal{E} \quad \Gamma'' \vdash E_3 : \mathcal{E}}{\Gamma, \Gamma', \Gamma'' \vdash case_{\mathcal{C}+\mathcal{D}}(E_1, E_2, E_3) : \mathcal{E}} \qquad dua \; \frac{\Gamma \vdash E : \mathcal{D}}{\Gamma^{op} \vdash E^* : \mathcal{D}^{op}}$$

$$lam \; \frac{\Gamma, X : \mathcal{C} \vdash E : \mathcal{D} \quad \mathcal{C} \; \text{small}}{\Gamma \vdash \lambda X.E : [\mathcal{C}, \mathcal{D}]} \qquad app \; \frac{\Gamma \vdash F : [\mathcal{C}, \mathcal{D}] \quad \Gamma' \vdash E : \mathcal{C} \quad \mathcal{C} \; \text{small}}{\Gamma, \Gamma' \vdash F(E) : \mathcal{D}}$$

$$hom \; \frac{\Gamma \vdash E_1 : \mathcal{C} \quad \Gamma' \vdash E_2 : \mathcal{C}}{\Gamma^{op}, \Gamma' \vdash \mathcal{C}(E_1, E_2) : \mathbf{Set}} \qquad sub \; \frac{\Gamma, X : \mathcal{C} \vdash E_1 : \mathcal{D} \quad \Gamma' \vdash E_2 : \mathcal{C}}{\Gamma, \Gamma' \vdash E_1[E_2/X] : \mathcal{D}}$$

$$uni \; \frac{}{\vdash 1 : \mathbf{Set}} \qquad ten \; \frac{\Gamma \vdash E_1 : \mathbf{Set} \quad \Gamma' \vdash E_2 : \mathbf{Set}}{\Gamma, \Gamma' \vdash E_1 \times E_2 : \mathbf{Set}}$$

$$int \; \frac{\Gamma, X : \mathcal{C}^{op}, Y : \mathcal{C} \vdash E : \mathcal{D} \quad \mathcal{D} \; \text{complete} \quad \mathcal{C} \; \text{small}}{\Gamma \vdash \int_{X \in \mathcal{C}^{op}, Y \in \mathcal{C}} E : \mathcal{D}}$$

Figure 2. Typing Rules.

the rule $(lamI)$

$$X_1 : \mathcal{C}_1, \cdots, X_n : \mathcal{C}_n, X : \mathcal{C} \vdash E_1 \cong E_2 : \mathcal{D}$$

means in more informal mathematical notation that there is an isomorphism

$$E_1(X_1, \cdots, X_n, X) \stackrel{\theta_{X_1, \cdots, X_n, X}}{\cong} E_2(X_1, \cdots, X_n, X)$$

natural in $X_1, \cdots, X_n, X$.

Thus we can abstract on the variable X to obtain an isomorphism

$$\lambda X.E_1(X_1, \cdots, X_n, X) \stackrel{\langle \theta_{X_1, \cdots, X_n, X} \rangle_X}{\cong} \lambda X.E_2(X_1, \cdots, X_n, X)$$

$$ref \frac{\Gamma \vdash E : \mathcal{C}}{\Gamma \vdash E \cong E : \mathcal{C}} \qquad sym \frac{\Gamma \vdash E_1 \cong E_2 : \mathcal{C}}{\Gamma \vdash E_2 \cong E_1 : \mathcal{C}}$$

$$tra \frac{\Gamma \vdash E_1 \cong E_2 : \mathcal{C} \quad \Gamma \vdash E_2 \cong E_3 : \mathcal{C}}{\Gamma \vdash E_1 \cong E_3 : \mathcal{C}} \qquad lamI \frac{\Gamma, X : \mathcal{C} \vdash E_1 \cong E_2 : \mathcal{D} \quad \mathcal{C} \text{ small}}{\Gamma \vdash \lambda X.E_1 \cong \lambda X.E_2 : [\mathcal{C}, \mathcal{D}]}$$

$$appI \frac{\Gamma \vdash F \cong G : [\mathcal{C}, \mathcal{D}] \quad \Gamma' \vdash E : \mathcal{C} \quad \mathcal{C} \text{ small}}{\Gamma, \Gamma' \vdash F(E) \cong G(E) : \mathcal{D}} \qquad subI \frac{\Gamma, X : \mathcal{C} \vdash E_1 \cong E_2 : \mathcal{D} \quad \Gamma' \vdash E : \mathcal{C}}{\Gamma, \Gamma' \vdash E_1[E/X] \cong E_2[E/X] : \mathcal{D}}$$

$$intI \frac{\Gamma, X : \mathcal{C}^{\mathrm{op}}, Y : \mathcal{C} \vdash E_1 \cong E_2 : \mathcal{D} \quad \mathcal{C} \text{ small} \quad \mathcal{D} \text{ complete}}{\Gamma \vdash \int_{X \in \mathcal{C}^{\mathrm{op}}, Y \in \mathcal{C}} E_1 \cong \int_{X \in \mathcal{C}^{\mathrm{op}}, Y \in \mathcal{C}} E_2 : \mathcal{D}}$$

$$end \frac{\Gamma, X : \mathcal{C}^{\mathrm{op}}, Y : \mathcal{C} \vdash E : \mathcal{D} \quad \mathcal{C} \text{ small} \quad \mathcal{D} \text{ complete}}{\Gamma, W : \mathcal{D}^{\mathrm{op}} \vdash \mathcal{D}(W, \int_{X \in \mathcal{C}^{\mathrm{op}}, Y \in \mathcal{C}} E) \cong \int_{X \in \mathcal{C}^{\mathrm{op}}, Y \in \mathcal{C}} \mathcal{D}(W, E) : \mathbf{Set}}$$

$$nat \frac{\Gamma, X : \mathcal{C} \vdash E_1 : \mathcal{D} \quad \Gamma', Y : \mathcal{C} \vdash E_2 : \mathcal{D} \quad \mathcal{C} \text{ small}}{\Gamma^{\mathrm{op}}, \Gamma' \vdash [\mathcal{C}, \mathcal{D}](\lambda X.E_1, \lambda Y.E_2) \cong \int_{X \in \mathcal{C}^{\mathrm{op}}, Y \in \mathcal{C}} \mathcal{D}(E_1, E_2) : \mathbf{Set}}$$

$$rep \frac{\Gamma, X : \mathcal{C}^{\mathrm{op}} \vdash \mathcal{C}(X, E_1) \cong \mathcal{C}(X, E_2) : \mathbf{Set}}{\Gamma \vdash E_1 \cong E_2 : \mathcal{C}} X \notin FV(E_1) \cup FV(E_2)$$

$$dualI \frac{\Gamma \vdash E_1 \cong E_2 : \mathcal{D}}{\Gamma^{\mathrm{op}} \vdash E_1^* \cong E_2^* : \mathcal{D}^{\mathrm{op}}} \qquad opp \frac{\Gamma \vdash E_1 : \mathcal{C} \quad \Gamma' \vdash E_2 : \mathcal{C}}{\Gamma^{\mathrm{op}}, \Gamma' \vdash \mathcal{C}(E_1, E_2) \cong \mathcal{C}^{\mathrm{op}}(E_2^*, E_1^*) : \mathbf{Set}}$$

$$uniI \frac{\Gamma \vdash E : \mathbf{Set}}{\Gamma \vdash 1 \times E \cong E : \mathbf{Set}} \qquad com \frac{\Gamma \vdash E_1 : \mathbf{Set} \quad \Gamma' \vdash E_2 : \mathbf{Set}}{\Gamma, \Gamma' \vdash E_1 \times E_2 \cong E_2 \times E_1 : \mathbf{Set}}$$

$$clo \frac{\Gamma \vdash E_1 : \mathbf{Set} \quad \Gamma' \vdash E_2 : \mathbf{Set} \quad \Gamma'' \vdash E_3 : \mathbf{Set}}{\Gamma^{\mathrm{op}}, (\Gamma')^{\mathrm{op}}, \Gamma'' \vdash [E_1 \times E_2, E_3] \cong [E_1, [E_2, E_3]] : \mathbf{Set}}$$

$$cur \frac{\Gamma, X : \mathcal{C}, Y : \mathcal{D} \vdash E_1 : \mathcal{E} \quad \Gamma', X : \mathcal{C}, Y : \mathcal{D} \vdash E_2 : \mathcal{E} \quad \mathcal{C} \text{ small} \quad \mathcal{D} \text{ small}}{\Gamma^{\mathrm{op}}, \Gamma' \vdash [\mathcal{C} \times \mathcal{D}, \mathcal{E}](\lambda X, Y.E_1, \lambda X, Y.E_2) \cong [\mathcal{C}, [\mathcal{D}, \mathcal{E}]](\lambda X.\lambda Y.E_1, \lambda X.\lambda Y.E_2) : \mathbf{Set}}$$

$$yon \frac{\Gamma, X : \mathcal{C}^{\mathrm{op}} \vdash E : \mathbf{Set} \quad \mathcal{C} \text{ small}}{\Gamma, Z : \mathcal{C}^{\mathrm{op}} \vdash E[Z/X] \cong [\mathcal{C}^{\mathrm{op}}, \mathbf{Set}](\lambda X.\mathcal{C}(X, Z), \lambda X.E) : \mathbf{Set}}$$

$$fub \frac{\Gamma, X_1 : \mathcal{C}^{\mathrm{op}}, X_2 : \mathcal{C}, Y_1 : \mathcal{D}^{\mathrm{op}}, Y_2 : \mathcal{D} \vdash E : \mathcal{E} \quad \mathcal{C} \text{ small} \quad \mathcal{D} \text{ small} \quad \mathcal{E} \text{ complete}}{\Gamma \vdash \int_{X_1 \in \mathcal{C}^{\mathrm{op}}, X_2 \in \mathcal{C}} \int_{Y_1 \in \mathcal{D}^{\mathrm{op}}, Y_2 \in \mathcal{D}} E \cong \int_{Y_1 \in \mathcal{D}^{\mathrm{op}}, Y_2 \in \mathcal{D}} \int_{X_1 \in \mathcal{C}^{\mathrm{op}}, X_2 \in \mathcal{C}} E : \mathcal{E}}$$

Figure 3. Rules for Natural Isomorphisms.

natural in $X_1, \cdots, X_n$. This justifies the conclusion of the rule (*lamI*). The rules for end, duality and application are interpreted in a similar way, their soundness resting on the earlier discussion. Just as we could derive the dual rule (*end**) in § 3.5, we can derive dual rules (*intI**), (*rep**) and (*fub**).

The rules (*clo*) and (*com*) derive from the closed structure of **Set**. Notice that we abbreviate hom-expressions over **Set** by using brackets, *e.g.* [A, B] instead of

$\mathbf{Set}(A, B)$. The "closed" structure of **CAT** gives the rule (cur) for currying. A rule for swapping arguments in functors is derivable from (cur), (nat) and (fub).

5 Examples

5.1 Continuity

The two driving notions in the previous sections have been functoriality and natural isomorphism. The example below shows that the calculus is rich enough to prove continuity.

Definition 4 (Preservation of Limits). *Let $F : \mathbb{I} \to \mathcal{C}$ be a functor with limiting cone $\langle k_I : \varprojlim_{\mathbb{I}} F \to F(I) \rangle_{I \in \mathbb{I}}$, a functor $G : \mathcal{C} \to \mathcal{D}$ preserves the limit of F iff $\langle G(k_I) : G(\varprojlim_{\mathbb{I}} F) \to G(F(I)) \rangle_{I \in \mathbb{I}}$ is a limiting cone in $\mathcal{D}$. Preservation of colimits is defined dually.*

We say that G preserves $\mathbb{I}$-index limits if G preserves the limits of all functors in $[\mathbb{I}, \mathcal{C}]$. A functor which preserves all limits is called *continuous*.

One might expect to prove that a given functor preserves limits by showing an isomorphism of objects. This gives, however, a necessary but not sufficient condition.[4] The situation improves when the isomorphism is sufficiently natural however:

Theorem 3. *Assume that the categories $\mathcal{C}$ and $\mathcal{D}$ have limits for all functors with domain $\mathbb{I}$. The functor $G : \mathcal{C} \to \mathcal{D}$ preserves $\mathbb{I}$-indexed limits iff*

$$\varprojlim_{\mathbb{I}}(G \circ F) \cong G(\varprojlim_{\mathbb{I}} F),$$

natural in $F \in [\mathbb{I}, \mathcal{C}]$ (see [6] for a proof.).

This theorem supplies the key to proving continuity within the calculus. For example, that $\mathcal{C}(C, X)$ preserves limits in X is a direct consequence of the naturality formula.

Another result we can prove in the calculus is that right adjoints preserve limits. Given the judgements $X : \mathcal{C} \vdash E_1 : \mathcal{D}$ and $Y : \mathcal{D} \vdash E_2 : \mathcal{C}$ respectively denoting functors $E_1 : \mathcal{C} \to \mathcal{D}$ and $E_2 : \mathcal{D} \to \mathcal{C}$, an adjunction where, as functors, E_1 is the left adjoint and E_2 is the right adjoint consists of an isomorphism

$$X : \mathcal{C}^{\mathrm{op}}, Y : \mathcal{D} \vdash \mathcal{D}(E_1, Y) \cong \mathcal{C}(X, E_2) : \mathbf{Set}.$$

By Theorem 3 is enough to prove $E_2[\int_{I \in \mathbb{I}} H/Y] \cong \int_{I \in \mathbb{I}} E_2[H(I)/Y] : \mathcal{C}$ where $H : [\mathbb{I}, \mathcal{D}]$. The proof proceeds backwards, using (rep) to obtain the goal:

$$X : \mathcal{C}^{\mathrm{op}}, H : [\mathbb{I}, \mathcal{D}] \vdash \mathcal{C}\left(X, E_2[\int_{I \in \mathbb{I}} H(I)/Y]\right) \cong \mathcal{C}\left(X, \int_{I \in \mathbb{I}} E_2[H(I)/Y]\right) : \mathbf{Set}.$$

---

[4] There are examples of functors which preserve limiting objects but don't preserve the limiting cones, see [3, ex. 5.3.16(4)].

The derivation of this goal is sketched in the chain of isomorphisms:

$$\mathcal{C}(X, E_2[\textstyle\int_{I\in\mathbb{I}} H(I)/Y]) \cong \mathcal{D}(E_1, \textstyle\int_{I\in\mathbb{I}} H(I)) \qquad \text{by the adjunction,}$$
$$\cong \textstyle\int_{I\in\mathbb{I}} \mathcal{D}(E_1, H(I)) \qquad \text{by } (end),$$
$$\cong \textstyle\int_{I\in\mathbb{I}} \mathcal{C}(X, E_2[H(I)/Y]) \qquad \text{by the adjunction,}$$
$$\cong \mathcal{C}(X, \textstyle\int_{I\in\mathbb{I}} E_2[H(I)/Y]) \qquad \text{by } (end).$$

We conclude that the functor denoted by $Y : \mathcal{C} \vdash E_2 : \mathcal{D}$ preserves limits.

The dual result, *i.e.* left adjoints preserve colimits, follows from the rules *opp* and *dualI*. From the definition of adjunction and by applying the rule *opp* twice together with transitivity we get

$$X : \mathcal{C}^{\mathrm{op}}, Y : \mathcal{D} \vdash \mathcal{C}^{\mathrm{op}}(E_2^*, X) \cong \mathcal{D}^{\mathrm{op}}(Y, E_1^*) : \mathbf{Set}$$

i.e. an adjunction where the functor denoted by E_1^* is the right adjoint. From the derivation above we can conclude

$$H : [\mathbb{I}^{\mathrm{op}}, \mathcal{C}^{\mathrm{op}}] \vdash E_1^*[\textstyle\int_{I\in\mathbb{I}^{\mathrm{op}}} H(I)/X] \cong \textstyle\int_{I\in\mathbb{I}^{\mathrm{op}}} E_1^*[H(I)/X] : \mathcal{D}^{\mathrm{op}}$$

and by applying the rule *dualI*

$$H : [\mathbb{I}, \mathcal{C}] \vdash E_1[\textstyle\int^{I\in\mathbb{I}} H(I)/X] \cong \textstyle\int^{I\in\mathbb{I}} E_1[H(I)/X] : \mathcal{D}.$$

5.2   The Density Formula

Functor categories of the form $[\mathbb{C}^{\mathrm{op}}, \mathbf{Set}]$ have a number of important properties that give them a special rank in the calculus.[5] From the rules (*yon*) and (*nat*), a functor $X : [\mathbb{C}^{\mathrm{op}}, \mathbf{Set}]$ is expressible as the end formula:

$$X : [\mathbb{C}^{\mathrm{op}}, \mathbf{Set}], W : \mathbb{C}^{\mathrm{op}} \vdash X(W) \cong \textstyle\int_{Y\in\mathbb{C}^{\mathrm{op}}} [\mathbb{C}(Y^-, W), X(Y^+)] : \mathbf{Set} . \qquad (5)$$

There is also a coend formula for X, the so-called *density formula*:

$$X : [\mathbb{C}^{\mathrm{op}}, \mathbf{Set}], W : \mathbb{C}^{\mathrm{op}} \vdash X(W) \cong \textstyle\int^{Y\in\mathbb{C}} \mathbb{C}(W, Y^+) \times X(Y^-) : \mathbf{Set} . \qquad (6)$$

The chain of isomorphisms below sketches a derivation for this formula:

$$[\mathbb{C}^{\mathrm{op}}, \mathbf{Set}](\lambda W. \textstyle\int^{Y\in\mathbb{C}} \mathbb{C}(W, Y^+) \times X(Y^-), Z)$$
$$\cong \textstyle\int_{W\in\mathbb{C}^{\mathrm{op}}}[(\textstyle\int^{Y\in\mathbb{C}} \mathbb{C}(W^-, Y^+) \times X(Y^-), Z(W^+)] \quad \text{by } (nat),$$
$$\cong \textstyle\int_{W\in\mathbb{C}^{\mathrm{op}}} \textstyle\int_{Y\in\mathbb{C}^{\mathrm{op}}}[\mathbb{C}(W^-, Y^+) \times X(Y^-), Z(W^+)] \quad \text{by } (end^*) \text{ and } (intI),$$
$$\cong \textstyle\int_{Y\in\mathbb{C}^{\mathrm{op}}} \textstyle\int_{W\in\mathbb{C}^{\mathrm{op}}}[\mathbb{C}(W^-, Y^+) \times X(Y^-), Z(W^+)] \quad \text{by } (fub),$$
$$\cong \textstyle\int_{Y\in\mathbb{C}^{\mathrm{op}}} \textstyle\int_{W\in\mathbb{C}^{\mathrm{op}}} [X(Y^-), [\mathbb{C}(W^-, Y^+), Z(W^+)]] \quad \text{by } (com) \text{ and } (clo)$$
$$\cong \textstyle\int_{Y\in\mathbb{C}^{\mathrm{op}}} [X(Y^-), \textstyle\int_{W\in\mathbb{C}^{\mathrm{op}}}[\mathbb{C}(W^-, Y^+), Z(W^+)]] \quad \text{by } (end) \text{ and } (intI),$$
$$\cong \textstyle\int_{Y\in\mathbb{C}^{\mathrm{op}}}[X(Y^-), Z(Y^+)] \quad \text{by } (5) \text{ and } (intI),$$
$$\cong [\mathbb{C}^{\mathrm{op}}, \mathbf{Set}](X, Z) \quad \text{by } (nat).$$

The next step applies the rule (*rep**) to yield the isomorphism (6).

---

[5] Such categories are called presheaf categories.

6   Implementation in Isabelle

As part of ongoing research we are carrying out the implementation of the calculus in the theorem prover Isabelle. The calculus is implemented in several user-defined theories which extend the initial theory **Pure**. Basically, **Pure** gives the built-in higher-order logic [14] on top of which we define the object-logic for categories.

There are two meta-level types: **cat** and **exp** for the types and the expressions of the language respectively. The types constructors are defined as constants, for example:

```
Set    :: cat
One    :: cat
Op     :: cat => cat          ("_^op" [10] 10)
FunCat :: [cat, cat] => cat   ("[_,_]") .
```

The syntax for the expressions is defined similarly, for example:

```
Hom  :: [cat,exp,exp]=> exp
Lam  :: (exp=>exp) => exp      (binder "LAM" 10)
Into :: (exp=>exp) => exp      (binder "INTO" 10)
Int  :: (exp=>exp) => exp      (binder "INT" 10) .
```

where **Lam**, **Into** and **Int** give the definition for the binders λ and $\int$. There are two special constants to encode assertions for types and natural isomorphisms:

```
":"    :: [exp,cat] => o        (infixl 7)
NatIso :: [exp,exp,cat] => o    ("_~_:_" [5,5,5] 5) .
```

The constant ":" takes a term and a type as input and returns a truth value, similarly **NatIso** takes two terms and a type a returns a truth value.

The judgements of the calculus correspond to theorems in the meta-logic. For example, $X : \mathcal{C}^{\mathrm{op}}, Y : \mathcal{C} \vdash \mathcal{C}(X, Y) : \mathbf{Set}$ is written in the object-logic for categories as

```
!! X Y. [| X:C^op; Y:C |] ==> Hom(C,X,Y):Set .
```

Notice that the universal quantification prevents a possible instantiation of the meta-variables X and Y enforcing their treatment as variables in the object-logic level. The manipulation of the contexts in the rules is done through lifting. Thus, the definition of the rules is only concerned with the part of the context which changes. For example, the rule for typing end formulae is:

```
int " ( !!X Y. [| X:C^op ; Y:C; C is Small |] ==> E(X,Y):D)
                        ==> INTO X. INT Y. E(X,Y):D" .
```

This approach gives the structural rules for free; the rule (*ass*) corresponds to a proof by assumption, exchange to rotating the assumptions in a subgoal, and so on. We are currently developing an alternative implementation of the calculus in Isabelle/HOL [12] where the contexts are defined explicitly as sets of pairs. This approach should ease the implementation of duality.

7   Conclusions, Related Work, and Future Directions

A calculus which formalises an expressive fragment of category theory has been presented. The rules of the calculus support a calculational approach to universality where the manipulation of ends and coends plays a central role. We have shown how to formalise judgements about functoriality and how to verify isomorphisms. In this setting, we have explored duality and studied applications to encode and prove results on continuous functors. An implementation of the calculus in the theorem prover Isabelle has been outlined briefly.

Previous work in the automation of category theory has followed a somewhat different tack. Takeyama [18] presents a computer checked language with the goal of supplying a categorical framework for type theory and includes an implementation in the theorem prover LEGO [16]. This follows in spirit the work of Rydeheard and Burstall [17] on formalising universal constructions in ML. Beylin and Dybjer [4] formalise monoidal categories and present a proof of the Mac Lane's coherence theorem in Martin Löf's type theory [13].

The interpretation of the rules suggests a language for natural isomorphisms. Observe that in theorem provers like Isabelle where a goal may contain unknowns, a witness for a natural isomorphism may be given as output of the proof search. More generally, a further extension to the calculus is to introduce expressions for natural transformations.

A richer language for types may be considered by adding new constructors like recursion and lifting. For recursive definition of categories we need to extend the language for types to allow expressions with variables. The lifted type $\mathcal{C}_\perp$ would be interpreted as the category $\mathcal{C}$ with an initial object $\perp$ freely adjoined.

The utility of end and coend notation was demonstrated in the pioneering work of Kelly and others in enriched category theory [10]. In emphasising a calculus for categories, a goal has been to make working with functor categories routine. The formalisation here should lend itself to enriched category theory.

Acknowledgments

This work was inspired by Martin Hyland's Cambridge part III lecture course on category theory and its emphasis on end and coend manipulation.

References

1. A. Asperti and G. Longo. *Categories, Types and Structures : An introduction to category theory for the working computer scientist.* Foundations of Computing Series. MIT Press, 1991.
2. H. Barendregt. Lambda calculi with types. In S. Abramsky, D. M. Gabbay, and T. S. E. Maibaum, editors, *Handbook of Logic in Computer Science*, volume 2: Computational Structures. Oxford University Press, 1991.
3. M. Barr and C. Wells. *Category Theory for Computing Science.* C.A.R. Hoare Series Editor. Prentice Hall, second edition, 1996.

4. I. Beylin and P. Dybjer. Extracting a proof of coherence for monoidal categories from a proof of normalization for monoids. *Lecture Notes in Computer Science*, 1158, 1996.
5. T. Braüner. *An Axiomatic Approach to Adequacy*. PhD thesis, BRICS PhD School, 1996.
6. M. Cáccamo, J. M. E. Hyland, and G. Winskel. Lecture notes in category theory. Available from: http://www.brics.dk/~mcaccamo.
7. G. L. Cattani. *Presheaf Models for Concurrency*. PhD thesis, BRICS PhD School, 1999.
8. R. L. Crole. *Categories for Types*. Cambridge Mathematical Textbooks. Cambridge University Press, 1993.
9. A. Joyal, M. Nielsen, and G. Winskel. Bisimulation and open maps. In R. L. Constable, editor, *Proceedings of the 8th Annual IEEE Symposium on Logic in Computer Science*, Montreal, Canada, June 1993. IEEE Computer Society Press.
10. G. M. Kelly. *Basic Concepts of Enriched Category Theory*, volume 64 of *London Mathematical Society Lecture Note Series*. Cambridge University Press, 1982.
11. S. Mac Lane. *Categories for the Working Mathematician*, volume 5 of *Graduate Texts in Mathematics*. Springer-Verlag, second edition, 1998.
12. T. Nipkow and L. Paulson. Isabelle HOL: The tutorial. Documentation included in the official distribution of Isabelle, Feb. 2001.
13. B. Nordström, K. Petterson, and J. Smith. *Programming in Martin-Löf's Type Theory. An Introduction*. Oxford University Press, 1990.
14. L. Paulson. The foundation of a generic theorem prover. *Journal of Automated Reasoning*, 5(3):363–397, 1988.
15. L. C. Paulson. *Isabelle: A Generic Theorem Prover*, volume 828 of *Lecture Notes in Computer Science*. Springer-Verlag, 1994.
16. R. Pollack. *The Theory of LEGO: A Proof Checker for the Extended Calculus of Constructions*. PhD thesis, The University of Edinburgh, 1994.
17. D. Rydeheard and R. Burstall. *Computational Category Theory*. International Series in Computer Science. Prentice Hall, 1988.
18. M. Takeyama. *Universal Structure and a Categorical Framework for Type Theory*. PhD thesis, The University of Edinburgh, 1995.

Certifying the Fast Fourier Transform with Coq

Venanzio Capretta*

Computing Science Institute, University of Nijmegen
Postbus 9010, 6500 GL Nijmegen, The Netherlands
venanzio@cs.kun.nl
telephone: +31+24+3652647, fax: +31+24+3553450

Abstract. We program the Fast Fourier Transform in type theory, using the tool Coq. We prove its correctness and the correctness of the Inverse Fourier Transform. A type of trees representing vectors with interleaved elements is defined to facilitate the definition of the transform by structural recursion. We define several operations and proof tools for this data structure, leading to a simple proof of correctness of the algorithm. The inverse transform, on the other hand, is implemented on a different representation of the data, that makes reasoning about summations easier. The link between the two data types is given by an isomorphism. This work is an illustration of the *two-level approach* to proof development and of the principle of adapting the data representation to the specific algorithm under study. CtCoq, a graphical user interface of Coq, helped in the development. We discuss the characteristics and usefulness of this tool.

1 Introduction

An important field of research in formalized mathematics tackles the verification of classical algorithms widely used in computer science. It is important for a theorem prover to have a good library of proof-checked functions, that can be used both to extract a formally certified program and to quickly verify software that uses the algorithm. The Fast Fourier Transform [8] is one of the most widely used algorithms, so I chose it as a case study in formalization using the type-theory proof tool Coq [2]. Here I present the formalization and discuss in detail the parts of it that are more interesting in the general topic of formal verification in type theory.

Previous work on the computer formalization of FFT was done by Ruben Gamboa [10] in ACL2 using the data structure of powerlists introduced by Jayadev Misra [11], which is similar to the structure of polynomial trees that we use here.

* I worked on the formalization of FFT during a two-month stay at the INRIA research center in Sophia Antipolis, made possible by a grant from the Dutch Organization for Scientific Research (NWO, Dossiernummer F 62-556). I am indebted to the people of the Lemme group for their support and collaboration. In particular, I want to thank Yves Bertot for his general support and for teaching me how to use CtCoq, and Loïc Pottier for his help in formulating the Fast Fourier Transform in type theory.

R.J. Boulton and P.B. Jackson (Eds.): TPHOLs 2001, LNCS 2152, pp. 154–168, 2001.

The Discrete Fourier Transform is a function commuting between two representations of polynomials over a commutative ring, usually the algebraic field $\mathbb{C}$. One representation is in the *coefficient domain*, where a polynomial is given by the list of its coefficients. The second representation is in the *value domain*, where a polynomial of degree $n - 1$ is given by its values on n distinct points. The function from the coefficient domain to the value domain is called *evaluation*, the inverse function is called *interpolation*. The Discrete Fourier Transform (DFT) and the Inverse Discrete Fourier Transform (iDFT) are the evaluation and interpolation functions in the case in which the points of evaluation are distinct n-roots of the unit element of the ring. The reason to consider such particular evaluation points is that, in this case, an efficient recursive algorithm exists to perform evaluation, the Fast Fourier Transform (FFT), and interpolation, the Inverse Fourier Transform (iFT). Let

$$f(x) = a_0 + a_1 x + a_2 x^2 + \ldots + a_{n-1} x^{n-1} = \sum_{i=0}^{n-1} a_i x^i$$

be a polynomial of degree $n - 1$ and ω be a primitive n-root of unity, that is, $\omega^n = 1$ but $\omega^j \neq 1$ for $0 < j < n$. We must compute $f(\omega^j)$ for $j = 0, 1, \ldots, n-1$. First of all we write $f(x)$ as the sum of two components, the first comprising the monomials of even power and the second the monomials of odd power, for which we can collect a factor x:

$$f(x) = f_e(x^2) + x f_o(x^2). \tag{1}$$

The polynomials f_e and f_o have degree $n/2 - 1$ (assuming that n is even). We could apply our algorithm recursively to them and to ω^2, which is an $n/2$-root of unity. We obtain the values

$$f_e((\omega^2)^0), \ f_e((\omega^2)^1), \ \ldots, \ f_e((\omega^2)^{n/2-1});$$
$$f_o((\omega^2)^0), \ f_o((\omega^2)^1), \ \ldots, \ f_o((\omega^2)^{n/2-1}).$$

We have, therefore, $f_e((\omega^2)^i) = f_e((\omega^i)^2)$ for $i = 0, \ldots, n/2-1$ which we can feed into Formula 1. The only problem is that Formula 1 must be evaluated for $x = \omega^i$ when $i = 0, \ldots, n-1$. We are still missing the values for $i = n/2, \ldots, n-1$. Here is where the fact that ω is a primitive n-root of unity comes useful: $\omega^{n/2} = -1$, so for $j = 0, \ldots, n/2 - 1$ we have that

$$\omega^{n/2+j} = \omega^{n/2} \omega^j = -\omega^j$$

and therefore $f_e((\omega^{n/2+j})^2) = f_e((\omega^j)^2)$. So the values of the first term of Formula 1 for $i = n/2, \ldots, n-1$ are equal to the values for $i = 0, \ldots, n/2-1$ and we don't need to compute them. A similar argument holds for f_o. If we measure the algorithmic complexity by the number of multiplications of scalars that need to be performed, we see that the algorithm calls itself twice on inputs of half size and then must still perform n multiplications (multiply x by $f_o(x)$ in Formula 1). This gives an algorithm of complexity $O(n \log n)$, much better than the naive quadratic algorithm.

Vice versa if we are given the values of the polynomial f on the n-roots of unity, $y_0 = f(\omega^0), \ldots, y_{n-1} = f(\omega^{n-1})$, we can compute the vector of coefficients of f by applying DFT to the vector $\langle y_0, \ldots, y_{n-1} \rangle$ with ω^{-1} in place of ω and then divide by n. The proof of this fact is well-known. We will give a type-theoretic version of it in section 5.

One useful application of FFT is the computation the product of two polynomials. If $f(x) = \sum_{i=0}^{n-1} a_i x^i$ and $g(x) = \sum_{i=0}^{n-1} b_i x^i$, we want to compute their product $f(x)g(x) = \sum_{i=0}^{n-1} c_i x^i$. A direct computation of the coefficients would require the evaluation the formula $c_i = \sum_{j+k=i} a_j b_k$ for $i = 0, \ldots, 2n - 2$, for a total of n^2 scalar products. A faster way to compute it is, first, to find the representations of the polynomials in the value domain with FFT: $f(\omega^i)$ and $g(\omega^i)$ for $i = 0, \ldots, 2n - 1$; second, to multiply the corresponding values to obtain the representation of the product in the value domain: $f(\omega^i)g(\omega^i)$; and third, to return to the coefficient domain iFT. In this way we need to perform only $2n$ multiplications plus the $O(n \log n)$ multiplications needed for the conversions. The overall complexity of the multiplication algorithm is then also $O(n \log n)$, instead of quadratic.

The rest of the article describes the formalization of these ideas in type theory, using the proof tool Coq. In Section 2 we discuss the different representations for the data types involved. We choose a tree representation that is specifically designed for FFT. We prove that it is equivalent to a more natural one. In Section 3 we apply the two-level approach (see [3] and [6]) to the tree representation to prove some basic facts about it. Section 4 contains the definition and proof of correctness of FFT. Section 5 introduces iFT and proves its correctness. Finally, Section 6 discusses the tools used in the formalization and some implementation issues.

2   Data Representation

Let us fix the domain of coefficients and values. We need to work in a commutative ring with unity, and in the case of the inverse transform we will need a field. Usually it is required that the domain is an algebraically closed field, because the transform is applied to a polynomial and a root of unity. We will not do that, but just require that, when the algorithm is applied, a proof that its argument is a root of unity is supplied. This covers the useful case in which we want to apply the algorithm to finite fields (that can never be algebraically closed) or finite rings. In type theory an algebraic structure like that of ring is represented by an underlying *setoid*, which is a type with an equivalence relation, plus some operations on the setoid and proofs of the defining properties of the structure. In our case we will have the following data:

K : Set
K_eq : $K \to K \to$ Prop
K_eq_refl : (reflexive K_eq)
K_eq_symm : (symmetric K_eq)
K_eq_trans : (transitive K_eq).

K_eq is thus an equivalence relation that expresses the equality of the objects represented by terms of the type K. We will write $x \equiv y$ for (K_eq a b). The basic ring constants and operations are

$$0, 1 \colon K$$
$$\mathsf{sm}, \mathsf{ml} \colon K \to K \to K$$
$$\mathsf{sm\_inv} \colon K \to K.$$

We will use the notations $x+y$, $x \cdot y$ and $-x$ for (sm x y), (ml x y) and (sm_inv x), respectively. We need to require that they are well behaved with respect to $\equiv$, or, equivalently, that $\equiv$ is a congruence relation with respect to these operations:

$$\mathsf{sm\_congr} \colon \forall x_1, x_2, y_1, y_2 \colon K. x_1 \equiv x_2 \to y_1 \equiv y_2 \to x_1 + y_1 \equiv x_2 + y_2$$
$$\mathsf{ml\_congr} \colon \forall x_1, x_2, y_1, y_2 \colon K. x_1 \equiv x_2 \to y_1 \equiv y_2 \to x_1 \cdot y_1 \equiv x_2 \cdot y_2$$
$$\mathsf{sm\_congr} \colon \forall x_1, x_2 \colon K. x_1 \equiv x_2 \to (-x_1) \equiv (-x_2)$$

The axioms of commutative rings can now be formulated for these operations and for the equality $\equiv$.

We will often require that a certain element $\omega \colon K$ is a primitive n-root of unity. This means that $\omega^n \equiv 1$ (ω is a root) and n is the smallest non-zero element for which this happens (primitivity). At some point we will also need that, if n is even, $\omega^{n/2} \equiv -1$. Note that this fact does not generally follow from ω being a primitive n-root of unity. Indeed, if K is an integral domain, we can prove this from the fact that $\omega^{n/2}$ is a solution of the equation $x^2 \equiv 1$, but cannot be 1 by primitivity of ω. In an integral domain 1 and -1 are the only solutions of the equation. But in a commutative ring this is not always true. For example, take the finite commutative ring $\mathbb{Z}_{15}$ and the value $\omega = 4$, which is a primitive 2-root of unity ($4^2 \equiv 16 \equiv 1$). Nevertheless $4^1 \equiv 4 \not\equiv -1$. So the requirement $\omega^{n/2} \equiv -1$ will have to be stated explicitly when needed.

Polynomials in one variable are usually represented as the vectors of their coefficients. So the polynomial $a_0 + a_1 x + \cdots + a_{n-1} x^{n-1}$ is represented by the vector $\langle a_0, a_1, \ldots, a_{n-1} \rangle$. We can choose to implement such a vector in three standard ways: as a list (in which case there is no restriction on the length), as an element of a type with fixed length, or as a function from the finite type with n elements, $\mathbb{N}_n$, to K. This last representation is the most elastic for a certain number of purposes, specifically for reasoning about summations. It will be useful when prove the correctness of iFT. So we adopt it as our basic implementation of polynomials. The type of polynomials of degree $n-1$ will then be $\mathbb{N}_n \to K$.

However, in the proof of correctness of FFT, a different representation results more useful. A fundamental step of the computation consists in breaking the polynomial f in two parts f_e and f_o, consisting of the even and odd terms, respectively. We apply the algorithm recursively on these two polynomials. The recursion is wellfounded because f_e and f_o have smaller degree than f. This requires the use of course-of-value recursion on the degree of the polynomial, which can be realized in type theory using a general method for wellfounded recursion (see [1]). The formalization of the algorithm that we obtain is more complex than necessary, because it contains the proofs of the fact that the degrees decrease. Simpler algorithms are obtained by using structural recursion in place of wellfounded recursion. To use structural recursion we need that the algorithm calls itself recursively only on structurally smaller arguments.

So we are led to look for a different implementation of polynomials whose structure reflects the steps of the algorithm. A general method to obtain a data type whose structure is derived from the recursive definition of a function is presented in [7]. In our case we obtain the result by representing polynomials as tree structures in which the left subtree contains the even coefficients and the right subtree contains the odd coefficients. This results in the recursive definition

$$\text{Tree} \colon \mathbb{N} \to \text{Set} :=$$
$$\text{Tree}(0) := K$$
$$\text{Tree}(k+1) := \text{Tree}(k) \times \text{Tree}(k).$$

An element of $\text{Tree}(k)$ is a binary tree of depth k whose leaves are elements of the coefficient domain K. We will use the notation $\text{leaf}(a)$ to denote an element $a \colon K$ when it is intended as a tree of depth 0, that is, an element of $\text{Tree}(0) = K$. We will use the notation $\text{node}(t_1, t_2)$ to denote the element $\langle t_1, t_2 \rangle \colon \text{Tree}(k+1) = \text{Tree}(k) \times \text{Tree}(k)$, if t_1 and t_2 are elements of $\text{Tree}(k)$. The number of leaves of such a tree is 2^k. This is not a problem since, for the application of FFT, we always assume that the degree of the input polynomial is one less than a power of 2. Otherwise we adjust it to the closest power of 2 by adding terms with zero coefficients.

The equality $\equiv$ on K is extended to the equality $\cong$ on trees. We say that two elements $t_1, t_2 \colon \text{Tree}(k)$ are equal, and write $t_1 \cong t_2$, when the relation $\equiv$ holds between corresponding leaves. The relation $\cong$ can be formally defined by recursion on k.

A polynomial is represented by putting the coefficients of the even powers of x in the left subtree and the coefficients of the odd powers of x in the right one, and this procedure is repeated recursively on the two subtrees. If we have, for example, a polynomial of degree 7 ($= 2^3 - 1$),

$$f(x) = a_0 + a_1 x + a_2 x^2 + a_3 x^3 + a_4 x^4 + a_5 x^5 + a_6 x^6 + a_7 x^7,$$

we break it into two parts

$$f_e(y) := a_0 + a_2 y + a_4 y^2 + a_6 y^3, \quad f_o(y) := a_1 + a_3 y + a_5 y^2 + a_7 y^3$$

so that $f(x) = f_e(x^2) + x f_o(x^2)$. Recursively $f_e(y)$ and $f_o(y)$ can be broken into even and odd terms

$$f_{ee}(z) := a_0 + a_4 z, \quad f_{eo}(z) := a_2 + a_6 z,$$
$$f_{oe}(z) := a_1 + a_5 z, \quad f_{oo}(z) := a_3 + a_7 z$$

so that $f_e(y) = f_{ee}(y^2) + y f_{eo}(y^2)$ and $f_o(y) = f_{oe}(y^2) + y f_{oo}(y^2)$. With another step we reach single coefficients:

$$f_{eee}(u) := a_0, \quad f_{eeo}(u) := a_4, \quad f_{eoe}(u) := a_2, \quad f_{eoo}(u) := a_6,$$
$$f_{oee}(u) := a_1, \quad f_{oeo}(u) := a_5, \quad f_{ooe}(u) := a_3, \quad f_{ooo}(u) := a_7$$

with $f_{ee}(z) = f_{eee}(z^2) + z f_{eeo}(z^2)$, $f_{eo}(z) = f_{eoe}(z^2) + z f_{eoo}(z^2)$, $f_{oe}(z) = f_{oee}(z^2) + z f_{oeo}(z^2)$, $f_{oo}(z) = f_{ooe}(z^2) + z f_{ooo}(z^2)$. Now we transform each of these polynomials in trees, starting with the single-coefficient ones. We simply obtain

$$t_{eee} := \mathsf{leaf}(a_0) = a_0, \quad t_{eeo} := \mathsf{leaf}(a_4) = a_4,$$
$$t_{eoe} := \mathsf{leaf}(a_2) = a_2, \quad t_{eoo} := \mathsf{leaf}(a_6) = a_6,$$
$$t_{oee} := \mathsf{leaf}(a_1) = a_1, \quad t_{oeo} := \mathsf{leaf}(a_5) = a_5,$$
$$t_{ooe} := \mathsf{leaf}(a_3) = a_3, \quad t_{ooo} := \mathsf{leaf}(a_7) = a_7.$$

The polynomials of degree one are then represented by the trees

$$t_{ee} := \mathsf{node}(t_{eee}, t_{eeo}) = \langle a_0, a_4 \rangle, \quad t_{eo} := \mathsf{node}(t_{eoe}, t_{eoo}) = \langle a_2, a_6 \rangle,$$
$$t_{oe} := \mathsf{node}(t_{oee}, t_{oeo}) = \langle a_1, a_5 \rangle, \quad t_{oo} := \mathsf{node}(t_{ooe}, t_{ooo}) = \langle a_3, a_7 \rangle.$$

The polynomials of degree three are represented by

$$t_e := \mathsf{node}(t_{ee}, t_{eo}) = \langle \langle a_0, a_4 \rangle, \langle a_2, a_6 \rangle \rangle,$$
$$t_o := \mathsf{node}(t_{oe}, t_{oo}) = \langle \langle a_1, a_5 \rangle, \langle a_3, a_7 \rangle \rangle.$$

Finally, the original polynomial is represented by

$$t := \mathsf{node}(t_e, t_o) = \langle \langle \langle a_0, a_4 \rangle, \langle a_2, a_6 \rangle \rangle, \langle \langle a_1, a_5 \rangle, \langle a_3, a_7 \rangle \rangle \rangle.$$

It is clear that the two representations are equivalent, in the sense that the types $\mathsf{Tree}(k)$ and $\mathbb{N}_{2^k} \to K$ are isomorphic, with the isomorphism outlined above.

The type $\mathsf{Tree}(k)$ is similar to the structure of powerlists by Misra [11], used by Gamboa in the verification of FFT in ACL2 [10]. The difference consists in the fact that powerlists are presented as an abstract data type that can be constructed and read in two different ways: by concatenation or by interleaving. It is not specified how powerlists are actually represented. One could implement them as simple lists or as a structure like $\mathsf{Tree}(k)$. The important fact is that there are functions doing and undoing the two different construction methods, and that we have corresponding recursion and induction principles. Here we made the choice of committing to the particular representation $\mathsf{Tree}(k)$ and keep it both for polynomials and for argument lists, avoiding costly representation transformations. Instead of using the normal list operations we have then to define equivalent ones for the tree types.

We go on to the definition of DFT. It is defined simply as the vector of evaluations of a polynomial on the powers of an argument, that is, if f is a polynomial of degree $2^k - 1$ and w is an element of K, we want that $\mathsf{DFT}(f, w) = \langle f(w^0), f(w^1), f(w^2), \ldots, f(w^{2^k - 1}) \rangle$. For consistency we also want that this result vector is represented in the same form as the polynomials, that is, as an element of $\mathbb{N}_{2^k} \to K$ in the first representation and as an element of $\mathsf{Tree}(k)$ in the second representation with the values interleaved in the same way as the coefficient. For example if $k = 3$ we want that

$$\mathsf{DFT}(f, w) = \langle \langle \langle f(w^0), f(w^4) \rangle, \langle f(w^2), f(w^6) \rangle \rangle, \langle \langle f(w^1), f(w^5) \rangle, \langle f(w^3), f(w^7) \rangle \rangle \rangle.$$

The proof that the two definitions of DFT for the two representations are equivalent via the isomorphism of the types $\mathsf{Tree}(k)$ and $\mathbb{N}_{2^k} \to K$ is straightforward.

3   The Two-Level Approach for Trees

We need some operations on the type of trees and tools that facilitate reasoning about them. First of all, we define the mapping of the operations of the domain K on the trees: When we write $t_1 \circ t_2$ with $t_1, t_2 \colon \mathsf{Tree}(k)$ and $\circ$ one of the binary operations of K $(\cdot, +, -)$, we mean that the operation must be applied to pairs of corresponding leaves on the two trees, to obtain a new tree of the same type. Similarly, the unary operation of additive inversion $(-)$ will be applied to each leaf of the argument tree. Multiplication by a scalar, also indicated by $\cdot$, is the operation that takes an element a of K and a tree t and multiplies a for each of the leaves of t.

We denote the evaluation of a polynomial with $(t \xrightarrow{e} w)$, meaning "the value given by the evaluation of the polynomial represented by the tree t in the point w":

$$(\_ \xrightarrow{e} \_) \colon \mathsf{Tree}(k) \times K \to K$$
$$(\mathsf{leaf}(a) \xrightarrow{e} w) := a$$
$$(\mathsf{node}(t_1, t_2) \xrightarrow{e} w) := (t_1 \xrightarrow{e} w^2) + w \cdot (t_2 \xrightarrow{e} w^2).$$

The evaluation operation can be extended to evaluate a polynomial in all the leaves of a tree. This extension is achieved by mapping $\xrightarrow{e}$ to the trees in a way similar to the basic ring operations,

$$(\_ \xrightarrow{e}\!\!\!\to \_) \colon \mathsf{Tree}(k) \to \mathsf{Tree}(h) \to \mathsf{Tree}(h).$$

Two other operations that we need are the duplication of the leaves of a tree, in which every leaf is replaced by a tree containing two copies of it, and a duplication with change of the sign of the second copy:

$$\Downarrow \colon \mathsf{Tree}(k) \to \mathsf{Tree}(k+1) \qquad\qquad \pm \colon \mathsf{Tree}(k) \to \mathsf{Tree}(k+1)$$
$$\Downarrow \mathsf{leaf}(a) := \mathsf{node}(a, a) \qquad\qquad \pm\, \mathsf{leaf}(a) := \mathsf{node}(a, -a)$$
$$\Downarrow \mathsf{node}(t_1, t_2) := \mathsf{node}(\Downarrow t_1, \Downarrow t_2), \qquad \pm\, \mathsf{node}(t_1, t_2) := \mathsf{node}(\pm t_1, \pm t_2).$$

We use $\pm$ also as a binary operator: We write $t_1 \pm t_2$ for $\Downarrow t_1 + (\pm t_2)$.

Given any scalar $x \colon K$, we want to generate the tree containing the powers of x in the interleaved order. So, for example for $k = 3$, we want to obtain

$$\langle\langle\langle x^0, x^4\rangle, \langle x^2, x^6\rangle\rangle, \langle\langle x^1, x^5\rangle, \langle x^3, x^7\rangle\rangle\rangle.$$

This is achieved by the function

$$(\_\Uparrow\!\!\text{-}) \colon K \times \mathbb{N} \to \mathsf{Tree}(k)$$
$$(x\Uparrow^0) := \mathsf{leaf}(1)$$
$$(x\Uparrow^{k+1}) := \mathsf{node}(t, x \cdot t) \text{ with } t := (x^2\Uparrow^k).$$

To facilitate reasoning about trees, we use the method known as *the two-level approach* (see, for example, [3] and [6]). It is a general technique to automate the proof of a class of goals by internalizing it as an inductive type. Suppose we want to implement a decision procedure for a class of goals $\mathcal{G} \subseteq \mathsf{Prop}$. First of all we define a type of codes for the goals, goal: Set, and an interpretation function $[\![\_]\!]$: goal $\rightarrow$ Prop, such that the image of the whole type goal is $\mathcal{G}$. Then we define a decision procedure as a function dec: goal $\rightarrow$ bool and we prove that it is correct, that is, correctness: $\forall g$: goal.dec(g) = true $\rightarrow$ $[\![g]\!]$. As a consequence, whenever we want to prove a goal $P \in \mathcal{G}$, we can do it with just one command, correctness(g)(eq_refl(true)), where g is the code corresponding to P. In the case of equational reasoning the method can be further refined. We have a certain type of objects T: Set, and a certain number of operations over it. We want to be able to prove the equality of two expressions of type T build from constants and variables using the operations. We define a type code^T: Set of codes for such expressions. It is defined as an inductive type having as basis names for the constants and variables, and as constructors names for the operations. Then we define an interpretation function that associate an object of T to a code under a certain assignment of values to the variables, that is, if α is an assignment that associates an element of T to every variable, and c: code^T is a code, we obtain an element $[\![c]\!]_\alpha$: T. We can now use the syntactic level code^T to implement different tactics to decide equality of terms. For example, we may have a simplifying function simplify: code^T $\rightarrow$ code^T. If we prove that the simplification does not change the interpretation of the term, $\forall c$: code^T.$\forall \alpha.[\![c]\!]_\alpha$ = $[\![$simplify$(c)]\!]_\alpha$, then we can easily prove the equality of two terms by simply checking if the simplifications of their codes are equal.

A very helpful use of the two-level approach consists in proving equalities obtained by substitution of equal elements in a context. Suppose that we need to prove $C[\cdots a \cdots] = C[\cdots b \cdots]$ for a certain context $C[\cdots]$ and two objects a and b of which we know that they are equal. If the equality considered is Leibniz equality, then the goal can be proved by rewriting. But if we are using a defined equality (a generic equivalence relation), this method will not work and we will have to decompose the context $C[\cdots]$ and apply various times the proofs that the operations preserve equality. If the context is complex, this may result in very long and tedious proofs. We want to be able to solve such goals in one step. This can be done by simply encoding the context as an element of code^T containing a variable corresponding to the position of the objects a and b. If we have a proof that the interpretation of a code does not change when we assign equal values to a variable, we are done.

We apply this general method to trees. The objects that we are considering, trees, do not form a single type but a family of types indexed on the natural numbers according to their depth. This means that also the type of tree codes needs to be parameterized on the depth. Also the variables appearing inside a tree expression can have different depths, not necessarily equal to the depth of the whole expression. Having expressions in which several variables of different depth may appear would create complications that we do not need or desire. Instead we implement expressions in which only one variable appears, in other words, we formalize the notion of a context with a hole that can be filled with different trees. Be careful not to confuse this kind of variable, a hole in the context, from a regular variable of type Tree(k), that at the syntactic level is treated as a constant. We could call the hole variables *metavariables*, but contrary to usual metavariables, there can be occurrences of at most one hole variable in a term. Here is the definition of tree expressions, it has two natural-number parameters, the first for the depth of the metavariable, the second for the depth of the whole tree:

Inductive Tree_exp: $\mathbb{N} \to \mathbb{N} \to$ Set :=

trex_var(k): (Tree_exp k k)	for k: $\mathbb{N}$
trex_const(h, k, t): (Tree_exp h k)	for h, k: $\mathbb{N}$; t: Tree(k)
trex_leaf(h, x): (Tree_exp h 0)	for h: $\mathbb{N}$; x: K
trex_node(h, k, e_1, e_2): (Tree_exp h $k+1$)	for h, k: $\mathbb{N}$; e_1, e_2: (Tree_exp h k)
trex_sm(h, k, e_1, e_2): (Tree_exp h k)	for h, k: $\mathbb{N}$; e_1, e_2: (Tree_exp h k)
trex_ml(h, k, e_1, e_2): (Tree_exp h k)	for h, k: $\mathbb{N}$; e_1, e_2: (Tree_exp h k)
trex_mn(h, k, e_1, e_2): (Tree_exp h k)	for h, k: $\mathbb{N}$; e_1, e_2: (Tree_exp h k)
trex_sc_ml(h, k, x, e): (Tree_exp h k)	for h, k: $\mathbb{N}$; x: K; e: (Tree_exp k h)
trex_pow(h, k, x, e): (Tree_exp h k)	for h: $\mathbb{N}$; x: K; k: $\mathbb{N}$
trex_dupl(h, k, e): (Tree_exp h $k+1$)	for h, k: $\mathbb{N}$; e: (Tree_exp h k)
trex_id_inv(h, k, e): (Tree_exp h $k+1$)	for h, k: $\mathbb{N}$; e: (Tree_exp h k)
trex_sm_mn(h, k, e_1, e_2): (Tree_exp h $k+1$)	for h, k: $\mathbb{N}$; e_1, e_2: (Tree_exp h k)
trex_eval(h, k_1, k_2, e_1, e_2): (Tree_exp h k_2)	for h, k_1, k_2: $\mathbb{N}$; e_1: (Tree_exp h k_1);
	e_2: (Tree_exp h k_2).

Each of the constructors of Tree_exp corresponds to an operation on trees, except trex_var, that introduces a metavariable, and trex_const that *quotes* an actual tree inside an expression. We now define the interpretation function that takes a tree expression, a tree in which the metavariable must be interpreted, of depth equal to the first argument of the tree expression type, and gives a tree as a result. We omit the first two arguments of the function, the natural-number parameters h and k, because they can be inferred from the types of the other arguments.

$$\llbracket \_ \rrbracket\_ : (h, k: \mathbb{N})(\text{Tree\_exp } h\ k) \to \text{Tree}(h) \to \text{Tree}(k)$$
$$\llbracket \text{trex\_var}(k) \rrbracket_s := s$$
$$\llbracket \text{trex\_const}(h, k, t) \rrbracket_s := t$$
$$\llbracket \text{trex\_leaf}(h, x) \rrbracket_s := \text{leaf}(x) = x$$
$$\llbracket \text{trex\_node}(h, k, e_1, e_2) \rrbracket_s := \text{node}(\llbracket e_1 \rrbracket_s, \llbracket e_2 \rrbracket_s) = \langle \llbracket e_1 \rrbracket_s, \llbracket e_2 \rrbracket_s \rangle$$
$$\llbracket \text{trex\_sm}(h, k, e_1, e_2) \rrbracket_s := \llbracket e_1 \rrbracket_s + \llbracket e_2 \rrbracket_s$$
$$\llbracket \text{trex\_ml}(h, k, e_1, e_2) \rrbracket_s := \llbracket e_1 \rrbracket_s \cdot \llbracket e_2 \rrbracket_s$$
$$\llbracket \text{trex\_mn}(h, k, e_1, e_2) \rrbracket_s := \llbracket e_1 \rrbracket_s - \llbracket e_2 \rrbracket_s$$
$$\llbracket \text{trex\_sc\_ml}(h, k, x, e_2) \rrbracket_s := x \cdot \llbracket e_2 \rrbracket_s$$
$$\llbracket \text{trex\_pow}(h, x, k) \rrbracket_s := x{\uparrow}{\uparrow}^k$$
$$\llbracket \text{trex\_dupl}(h, k, e) \rrbracket_s := {\Downarrow} \llbracket e \rrbracket_s$$
$$\llbracket \text{trex\_id\_inv}(h, k, e) \rrbracket_s := \pm \llbracket e \rrbracket_s$$
$$\llbracket \text{trex\_sm\_mn}(h, k, e_1, e_2) \rrbracket_s := \llbracket e_1 \rrbracket_s \pm \llbracket e_2 \rrbracket_s$$
$$\llbracket \text{trex\_eval}(h, k_1, k_2, e_1, e_2) \rrbracket_s := (\llbracket e_1 \rrbracket_s \overset{e}{\twoheadrightarrow} \llbracket e_2 \rrbracket_s)$$

The most important use of this setup is in proving equality of substitutions inside a context.

Theorem 1 (Tree Reflection). *Let* $h, k \colon \mathbb{N}$; *for every context, given as a tree expression* $e \colon (\mathsf{Tree\_exp}\ h\ k)$, *and for every pair of trees* $t_1, t_2 \colon \mathsf{Tree}(h)$; *if* $t_1 \cong t_2$, *then the interpretations of the context under* t_1 *and* t_2 *are equal,* $[\![e]\!]_{t_1} \cong [\![e]\!]_{t_2}$.

Proof: A routine induction on the structure of e, using the proofs that the various operations considered preserve tree equality.

This theorem has been formalized in Coq with the name tree_reflection and is the most powerful tool in the development and proof of correctness of FFT. Whenever we need to prove a goal in the form $C[\cdots a \cdots] \cong C[\cdots a \cdots]$ with trees a and b for which we have a proof $p \colon a \cong b$, we can do it with the single command tree_reflection(h, k, e, a, b, p), where e is an encoding of C as an element of $(\mathsf{Tree\_exp}\ h\ k)$.

This method has been repeatedly used in the formal proofs of the following lemmas, important steps towards the proof of correctness of FFT.

Lemma 1 (scalar_ml_tree_ml). *For every* $x_1, x_2 \colon K$ *and for every pair of trees* $t_1, t_2 \colon \mathsf{Tree}(k)$,

$$(x_1 \cdot x_2) \cdot (t_1 \cdot t_2) \cong (x_1 \cdot t_1) \cdot (x_2 \cdot t_2).$$

(The operator $\cdot$ *is overloaded and has three different meanings.)*

Lemma 2 (tree_ml_tree_ml). *For every quadruple of trees* $t_1, t_2, s_1, s_2 \colon \mathsf{Tree}(k)$,

$$(t_1 \cdot t_2) \cdot (s_1 \cdot s_2) \cong (t_1 \cdot s_1) \cdot (t_2 \cdot s_2).$$

Lemma 3 (pow_tree_square). *For every* $k \colon \mathbb{N}$ *and* $x \colon K$,

$$(x \cdot x)\Uparrow^k \cong (x\Uparrow^k \cdot x\Uparrow^k).$$

(Here also $\cdot$ *has a different meaning on the left-hand and right-hand side.)*

Lemma 4 (eval_duplicate). *For every polynomial represented as a tree* $t \colon \mathsf{Tree}(k)$ *and for every vector of arguments represented as a tree* $u \colon \mathsf{Tree}(h)$, *the evaluation of* t *on the tree obtained by duplicating the leaves of* u *is equal to the tree obtained by duplicating the leaves of the evaluation of* t *on* u,

$$(t \overset{e}{\twoheadrightarrow} \underset{}{\Downarrow} u) \cong \underset{}{\Downarrow}(t \overset{e}{\twoheadrightarrow} u).$$

Lemma 5 (tree_eval_step). *A polynomial represented by the tree composed of its even and odd halves,* $t = \mathsf{node}(t_e, t_o) \colon \mathsf{Tree}(k+1)$ *is evaluated on a tree of arguments* $u \colon \mathsf{Tree}(h)$ *by the equality*

$$(\mathsf{node}(t_e, t_o) \overset{e}{\twoheadrightarrow} u) \cong (t_e \overset{e}{\twoheadrightarrow} u \cdot u) + u \cdot (t_o \overset{e}{\twoheadrightarrow} u \cdot u).$$

(Note that this rule is simply the recursive definition of evaluation when we have a single element of K *as argument, but it needs to be proved when the argument is a tree.)*

Lemma 6. *Let* k: $\mathbb{N}$, t, t_1, t_2, s_1, s_2: $\mathsf{Tree}(k)$, *and* x: K. *The following equalities hold:*

$$\begin{aligned}
\mathsf{sm\_mn\_duplicate\_id\_inv}: &\quad t_1 \pm t_2 \cong (\Downarrow t_1) + (\pm t_2); \\
\mathsf{ml\_id\_inv\_duplicate}: &\quad \pm t_1 \cdot \Downarrow t_2 \cong \pm(t_1 \cdot t_2); \\
\mathsf{scalar\_ml\_in\_inv}: &\quad x \cdot (\pm t) \cong \pm(x \cdot t); \\
\mathsf{scalar\_ml\_duplicate}: &\quad x \cdot (\Downarrow t) \cong \Downarrow(x \cdot t); \\
\mathsf{node\_duplicate}: &\quad \mathsf{node}(\Downarrow t_1, \Downarrow t_2) \cong \Downarrow \mathsf{node}(t_1, t_2).
\end{aligned}$$

The method of tree reflection and the above lemmas are extensively used in the following sections.

4   Definition and Correctness of FFT

We have build enough theory to obtain a short formulation of FFT and to prove its correctness.

Definition 1 (FFT). *The algorithm computing the Fast Fourier Transform of a polynomial represented by a tree* t: $\mathsf{Tree}(k)$ *(polynomial of degree* $2^k - 1$*) on the roots of unity generated by a primitive* 2^k*-root* w: K *is given by the type-theoretic function*

$$\begin{aligned}
&\mathsf{FFT}: (k: \mathbb{N})\mathsf{Tree}(k) \to K \to \mathsf{Tree}(k) \\
&\mathsf{FFT}(0, \mathsf{leaf}(a_0), w) := \mathsf{leaf}(a_0) \\
&\mathsf{FFT}(k+1, \mathsf{node}(t_1, t_2), w) := \mathsf{FFT}(k, t_1, w^2) \pm (w{\Uparrow}^k \cdot \mathsf{FFT}(k, t_2, w^2))
\end{aligned}$$

We actually do not require that w is a root of unity, but we allow it to be any element of K to keep the definition of the algorithm simple. The correctness statement will hold only when w is a primitive root of unity and states that FFT computes the same function as DFT.

Definition 2 (DFT). *The Discrete Fourier Transform of a polynomial represented by a tree* t: $\mathsf{Tree}(k)$ *(polynomial of degree* $2^k - 1$*) on the roots of unity generated by a primitive* 2^k*-root* w: K *is given by the evaluation of the polynomial on every root*

$$\begin{aligned}
&\mathsf{DFT}: (k: \mathbb{N})\mathsf{Tree}(k) \to K \to \mathsf{Tree}(k) \\
&\mathsf{DFT}(k, t, w) := t \overset{e}{\twoheadrightarrow} w{\Uparrow}^k
\end{aligned}$$

The fundamental step in the proof of equivalence of the two functions consists in proving that DFT satisfies the equality expressed in the recursion step of FFT. The equivalence follows by induction on the steps of FFT, that is, by induction on the tree structure of the argument.

Lemma 7 (DFT_step). *Let* t_1, t_2: $\mathsf{Tree}(k)$ *and* ω *be a* 2^{k+1} *principal root of unity such that* $\omega^{2^k} = -1$; *then*

$$\mathsf{DFT}(k+1, \mathsf{node}(t_1, t_2), \omega) \cong \mathsf{DFT}(k, t_1, \omega^2) \pm (\omega{\Uparrow}^k \cdot \mathsf{DFT}(k, t_2, \omega^2)).$$

Proof: We prove the equality through the intermediate steps

$$\mathsf{DFT}(k+1, \mathsf{node}(t_1, t_2), \omega) \cong (t_1 \xrightarrow{e} \omega^2 \Uparrow^{k+1}) + \omega \Uparrow^{k+1} \cdot (t_2 \xrightarrow{e} \omega^2 \Uparrow^{k+1})$$
$$\cong \Downarrow (t_1 \xrightarrow{e} \omega^2 \Uparrow^k) + \omega \Uparrow^{k+1} \cdot \Downarrow (t_2 \xrightarrow{e} \omega^2 \Uparrow^k)$$
$$\cong \Downarrow \mathsf{DFT}(k, t_1, \omega^2) + \omega \Uparrow^{k+1} \cdot \Downarrow \mathsf{DFT}(k, t_2, \omega^2)$$
$$\cong \mathsf{DFT}(k, t_1, \omega^2) \pm (\omega \Uparrow^k \cdot \mathsf{DFT}(k, t_2, \omega^2)).$$

The first step follows from the definition of DFT and Lemma tree_eval_step. The other steps are proved using the lemmas from the previous section, the method of tree reflection, and induction on the structure of trees. In the last step the hypothesis $\omega^{2^k} = -1$ must be used.

Theorem 2 (FFT_correct). *Let* $k \colon \mathbb{N}$, $t \colon \mathsf{Tree}(k)$ *representing a polynomial, and* ω *be a principal* 2^k-*root of unity with the property that* $\omega^{2^{k-1}} = -1$; *then*

$$\mathsf{FFT}(k, t, \omega) \cong \mathsf{DFT}(k, t, \omega).$$

Proof: By straightforward induction on the structure of t using the previous lemma in the recursive case.

5 The Inverse Fourier Transform

We formulate and prove the correctness of iFT. We need that K is a field, not just a commutative ring. This means that we assume that there is an operation

$$\mathsf{ml\_inv} \colon (x : K)x \not\equiv 0 \to K$$

satisfying the usual properties of multiplicative inverse. We can therefore define a division operation

$$\mathsf{dv} \colon (x, y \colon K)y \not\equiv 0 \to K.$$

Division is a function of three arguments: two elements of K, x and y, and a proof p that y is not 0. We use the notation x/y for $(\mathsf{dv}\ x\ y\ p)$, hiding the proof p.

The tree representation for polynomials is very useful for the verification of FFT, but the proof of correctness of iFT is easier with the function representation: A polynomial $f(x) = a_0 + a_1 x + a_2 x^2 + \cdots + a_{n-1} x^{n-1}$ is represented as a function $a \colon \mathbb{N}_n \to K$, and we write a_i for the value $a(i)$. We already proved in Section 2 that the two representations are equivalent, so we can freely switch between the two to develop our proofs. Let then DFT^f be the version of the Discrete Fourier Transform for the functional representation of polynomials. Here is the definition of the inverse transform.

Definition 3. *The* Inverse Discrete Fourier Transform *is the function that applies* DFT *to the multiplicative inverse of a root of unity and then divides by the degree:*

$$\mathsf{iDFT}^f \colon (n : \mathbb{N})(\mathbb{N}_n \to K) \to (\omega \colon K)\omega \not\equiv 0 \to (\mathbb{N}_n \to K)$$
$$\mathsf{iDFT}^f(n, a, \omega, p) := \tfrac{1}{n}\mathsf{DFT}(n, a, \omega^{-1}).$$

Our goal is to prove that this function is indeed the inverse of DFT^f, that is, $\mathsf{iDFT}^f(n, \mathsf{DFT}(n, a, \omega), \omega) = a$. The proof of this fact follows closely the standard proof given in the computer algebra literature, so we do not linger over its details. We only point out the passages where extra work must be done to obtain a formalization in type theory. First of all, we need to define the summation of a vector of values of K. The vector is represented by a function $v \colon \mathbb{N}_n \to K$. The summation $\sum v$ is defined by recursion on n. The main reason for choosing the representation $\mathbb{N}_n \to K$, in place of $\mathsf{Tree}(k)$, is that we often need to exchange the order of double summations, that is, we need the equality

$$\sum_{i=0}^{n-1}\sum_{j=0}^{m-1} a_{ij} = \sum_{j=0}^{m-1}\sum_{i=0}^{n-1} a_{ij}.$$

With the function notation, this becomes very easy: $a \colon \mathbb{N}_n \to \mathbb{N}_m \to K$ and the equality is written

$$\sum \lambda i \colon \mathbb{N}_n. \sum a(i) \equiv \sum \lambda j \colon \mathbb{N}_m. \sum \lambda i \colon \mathbb{N}_n a(i)(j).$$

We can easily define a summation function for $\mathsf{Tree}(k)$, but in that case it becomes much more complicated to formulate a double summation. A matrix of values like $\{a_{ij}\}$ would have to be represented as a tree having trees for leaves. Then the swap of the indexes in the summation would correspond to lifting the tree structure of the leaves to the main tree and lowering the main tree structure to the leaves. This would require much more work than simply changing representation.

In the proof we make essential use of the formula for the summation of a geometric series, expressed in type theory by

Lemma 8 (geometric_series). *For every* $n \colon \mathbb{N}$, $x \colon K$ *such that* $x \not\equiv 1$,

$$\sum \lambda i \colon \mathbb{N}_n.x^i \equiv \frac{x^n - 1}{x - 1}$$

where we simplified notation treating i as an element of $\mathbb{N}$ (we should really write $x^{(\mathsf{fin\_to\_nat}(i))}$ in place of x^i, where $\mathsf{fin\_to\_nat} \colon \mathbb{N}_n \to \mathbb{N}$ is an embedding function).

Proof: Standard.

Lemma 9 (summation_root_delta). *For* $n \colon \mathbb{N}$, $\omega \colon K$ *a primitive n-root of unity, and* $k, j \colon \mathbb{N}_n$,

$$\sum \lambda i \colon \mathbb{N}_n.(\omega^i)^j \cdot ((\omega^{-1})^k)^i \equiv n\delta_{jk}$$

where δ_{ij}, the Kronecker symbol, is 1 if $i = j$, 0 otherwise. Once again we abused notation leaving out the application of the conversion function $\mathsf{fin\_to\_nat}$. On the right-hand side we used juxtaposition of the natural number n to an element of K to indicate the function giving the n-fold sum in K.

Proof: Standard.

Finally we can prove the correctness of the inverse transform.

Theorem 3 (inverse_DFT). *Let* $n\colon \mathbb{N}$, $a\colon \mathbb{N}_n \to K$, $\omega\colon K$ *a primitive* n-*root of unity; then for every* $k\colon \mathbb{N}_n$,

$$\mathsf{DFT}^f(n, \mathsf{DFT}^f(n, a, \omega), \omega^{-1})_k \equiv n \cdot a_k.$$

Proof: Standard using the previous lemmas.

Once iDFT has been defined and proved correct for the functional representation of polynomials, we can use the equivalence of the two representations to obtain a proof of correctness of the version of the inverse transform for trees using the fast algorithm:

$$\mathsf{iFT}(n, t, \omega) := \frac{1}{n}\mathsf{FFT}(n, t, \omega^{-1}).$$

6 Conclusion

The definition and the proof of correctness for FFT and iFT have been completely formalized using the proof tool Coq. I have used the graphical interface CtCoq [4] to develop the formalization. CtCoq was extremely useful for several reasons. It affords extendable notation which allows the printing of terms in nice mathematical formalism, hiding parts that have no mathematical content (for example the applications of the commutation function fin_to_nat or the presence of a proof that the denominator is not zero in a division). The technique of *proof-by-pointing* [5] allows the user to construct complicated tactics with a few clicks of the mouse. It is easy to search for theorems and lemmas previously proved and apply them by just pressing a key. I found that the use of CtCoq increased the efficiency and speed of work, and I could complete the whole development in just a couple of months.

The proof uses two main techniques. First, instead of using the most natural data type to represent the objects on which the algorithm operates, we chose an alternative data type that makes it easier to reason about the computations by structural recursion. Second, we used the two-level approach to automate part of the generation of proofs of equality for tree expressions.

Future work will concentrate in controlling more carefully how the algorithm exploits time and space resources. It is known that FFT runs in $O(n \log n)$ time, but we didn't prove it formally in Coq. The problem here is that there is no formal study of algorithmic complexity in type theory. In general it is difficult to reason about the running time of functional programs, since the reduction strategy is not fixed. A solution could be achieved by translating FFT into a development of imperative programming and then reasoning about its complexity in that framework. Another point is the use of memory. One important feature of FFT is that it can be computed *in place*, that means that the memory occupied by the input data can be reused during the computation, without the need of extra memory. Also memory management is a sore point in functional programming. I think it is possible to use the *uniqueness* types of the programming language Clean [9] to force the algorithm to reuse the space occupied by the data.

References

1. Antonia Balaa and Yves Bertot. Fix-point equations for well-founded recursion in type theory. In J. Harrison and M. Aagaard, editors, *Theorem Proving in Higher Order Logics: 13th International Conference, TPHOLs 2000*, volume 1869 of *Lecture Notes in Computer Science*, pages 1–16. Springer-Verlag, 2000.
2. Bruno Barras, Samuel Boutin, Cristina Cornes, Judicaël Courant, Yann Coscoy, David Delahaye, Daniel de Rauglaudre, Jean-Christophe Filliâtre, Eduardo Giménez, Hugo Herbelin, Gérard Huet, Henri Laulhère, César Muñoz, Chetan Murthy, Catherine Parent-Vigouroux, Patrick Loiseleur, Christine Paulin-Mohring, Amokrane Saïbi, and Benjanin Werner. *The Coq Proof Assistant Reference Manual. Version 6.3*. INRIA, 1999.
3. G. Barthe, M. Ruys, and H. P. Barendregt. A two-level approach towards lean proof-checking. In S. Berardi and M. Coppo, editors, *Types for Proofs and Programs (TYPES'95)*, volume 1158 of *LNCS*, pages 16–35. Springer, 1995.
4. Yves Bertot. The CtCoq system: Design and architecture. *Formal aspects of Computing*, 11:225–243, 1999.
5. Yves Bertot, Gilles Kahn, and Laurent Théry. Proof by pointing. In *Symposium on Theoretical Aspects Computer Software (STACS), Sendai (Japan)*, volume 789 of *LNCS*. Springer, April 1994.
6. Samuel Boutin. Using reflection to build efficient and certified decision procedures. In Martín Abadi and Takayasu Ito, editors, *Theoretical Aspects of Computer Software. Third International Symposium, TACS'97*, volume 1281 of *LNCS*, pages 515–529. Springer, 1997.
7. Ana Bove and Venanzio Capretta. Nested general recursion and partiality in type theory. http://www.cs.kun.nl/ venanzio/publications/nested.ps.gz, 2001.
8. James W. Cooley and John W. Tukey. An algorithm for the machine calculation of complex Fourier series. *Mathematics of Computation*, 19(90):297–301, April 1965.
9. Paul de Mast, Jan-Marten Jansen, Dick Bruin, Jeroen Fokker, Pieter Koopman, Sjaak Smetsers, Marko van Eekelen, and Rinus Plasmeijer. *Functional Programming in Clean*. Computing Science Institute, University of Nijmegen.
10. Ruben A. Gamboa. The correctness of the Fast Fourier Transform: a structured proof in ACL2. *Formal Methods in System Design, Special Issue on UNITY*, 2001. in print.
11. Jayadev Misra. Powerlist: a structure for parallel recursion. *TOPLAS*, 16(6):1737–1767, November 1994.

A Generic Library for Floating-Point Numbers and Its Application to Exact Computing

Marc Daumas[1], Laurence Rideau[2], and Laurent Théry[2]

[1] CNRS, Laboratoire de l'Informatique du Parallélisme
UMR 5668 - ENS de Lyon - INRIA
Marc.Daumas@ens-lyon.fr
[2] INRIA, 2004 route des Lucioles, 06902 Sophia Antipolis France
{Laurence.Rideau,Laurent.Thery}@sophia.inria.fr

Abstract. In this paper we present a general library to reason about floating-point numbers within the Coq system. Most of the results of the library are proved for an arbitrary floating-point format and an arbitrary base. A special emphasis has been put on proving properties for exact computing, i.e. computing without rounding errors.

1 Introduction

Building a reusable library for a prover is not an easy task. The library should be carefully designed in order to give direct access to all key properties. This work is usually underestimated. Often libraries are developed for a given application, so they tend to be incomplete and too specific. This makes their reuse problematic. Still we believe that the situation of proving is similar to the one of programming. The fact that the programming language Java was distributed with a quite complete set of libraries has been an important factor to its success.

This paper presents a library for reasoning about floating-point numbers within the Coq system [18]. There has already been several attempts to formalize floating-point numbers in other provers. Barrett [2] proposed a formalization of floating-point numbers using the specification language Z [33]. Miner [25] was the first to provide a proving environment for reasoning about floating-point numbers. It was done for PVS [30]. More recently Harrison [16] and Russinoff [31] have developed libraries for HOL [14] and ACL2 [21] respectively and applied them successfully to prove the correctness of some algorithms and hardware designs. When developing our library we have tried to take a generic approach. The base of the representation and the actual format of the mantissa and of the exponent are parameterized. We still use the key property of correct rounding and the clean ideas of the IEEE 754 and 854 standards [35,7,13].

The paper is organized as follows. We first present some basic notions and their representation in Coq. Then we spend some time to explain how we have defined the central notion of rounding. In Section 4, we give examples of the kind of properties that are in the library and how they have been proved. Section 5 details the proof of correctness of a program that is capable to detect the

R.J. Boulton and P.B. Jackson (Eds.): TPHOLs 2001, LNCS 2152, pp. 169–184, 2001.

base of an arbitrary arithmetic. Finally we show an application of this library to floating-point expansions. These expansions were presented in [11] first and more formally in [28,32]. The technique can be specialized for the predicates of computational geometry [5,19] or to small-width multiple precision arithmetic [1,9], among other applications.

2   Floating-Point Format and Basic Notions

2.1   Definitions

Our floating-point numbers are defined as a new type composed by records:

Record. *float*: *Set* := *Float* {*Fnum*:$\mathbb{Z}$; *Fexp*:$\mathbb{Z}$}

This command creates a new type *float*, a constructor function *Float* of type $\mathbb{Z} \to \mathbb{Z} \to float$ and two destructor functions *Fnum* and *Fexp* of type *float* $\to \mathbb{Z}$. The fact that *float* is of type *Set* indicates that *float* is a datatype. The component *Fnum* represents the mantissa and *Fexp* the exponent. In the following we write (*Float x y*) simply as $\langle x, y \rangle$ and (*Fnum p*) and (*Fexp p*) as $n[p]$ and $e[p]$ respectively.

In order to give a semantics to this new type, we have to relate our *float* to their value as a real. The reals in Coq are defined axiomatically [24] as the smallest complete archimedian field. We define the function *FtoR* of type *float* $\to \mathbb{R}$ as:

Definition. $FtoR := \lambda p: float. \, n[p] * \beta^{e[p]}$.

This definition is parameterized over an arbitrary base β. We suppose that the base is an integer strictly greater than one. Our notation differs from the IEEE standard notation [35] and even from the pre-standard notation [6]. The mantissa is an integer and $\beta^{e[x]}$ is one unit in the last place of the float x or the weight of its least significant bit.

Having the type *float* as a separate type instead of a subtype of the real numbers as in [16] implies that we have to manipulate two notions of equality. The usual Leibniz equality $p = q$ means that p and q have the same components as a record. The equality over $\mathbb{R}$ (*FtoR p*) = (*FtoR q*) means that they represent the same real. In the following this last equality will be denoted $p == q$ and the function *FtoR* is used implicitly as a coercion between our floating-point numbers and the reals, so $0 < p$ should be understood as $0 < (FtoR \, p)$. The two notions of equality are related. For example we have the following theorems:

Theorem. $FtoREqInv_1 : \forall p, q: float. \, \neg p == 0 \Rightarrow p == q \Rightarrow n[p] = n[q] \Rightarrow p = q$.

Theorem. $FtoREqInv_2 : \forall p, q: float. \, p == q \Rightarrow e[p] = e[q] \Rightarrow p = q$.

On the type *float*, we can define the usual operations that return an element of type *float* such as:

Definition. $Fplus := \lambda p, q: float.$
$$\langle n[p] * (\beta^{e[p]-min(e[p],e[q])}) + n[q] * (\beta^{e[q]-min(e[p],e[q])}), min(e[p], e[q]) \rangle$$

Definition. $Fop := \lambda p: float. \langle -n[p], e[p] \rangle.$

Definition. $Fabs := \lambda p: float. \langle |n[p]|, e[p] \rangle.$

Definition. $Fminus := \lambda p, q: float. (Fplus\ p\ (Fop\ q)).$

Definition. $Fmult := \lambda p, q: float. \langle n[p] * n[q], e[p] + e[q] \rangle.$

For each of these functions we have proved a theorem of correctness. For addition this theorem looks like:

Theorem. $Fplus\_correct: \forall p, q: float. (Fplus\ p\ q) == p + q.$

where the rightmost addition is the usual addition on real numbers. Note that since we do not have uniqueness of representation, these functions just pick a possible representant of the result. In the following we write $+, -, |\ |, -, *$ for *Fplus, Fop, Fabs, Fminus, Fmult* respectively.

2.2 Bounded Floating-Point Numbers

As it is defined, the type *float* contains too many elements. In order to represent machine floating-point numbers we need to define the notion of bound:

Record. $Fbound: Set := Bound\ \{vNum{:}\mathbb{N};\ dExp{:}\mathbb{N}\}$

We use this notion of bound to parameterize our development over an arbitrary bound b. In the following, we write $(vNum\ b)$ and $(dExp\ b)$ as $N[b]$ and $E[b]$. With this arbitrary bound we can define a predicate *Fbounded* to characterize bounded floating-point numbers:

Definition. $Fbounded := \lambda p: float. - N[b] \leq n[p] \leq N[b] \wedge -E[b] \leq e[p].$

In the following we write $(Fbounded\ p)$ as $\mathcal{B}[p]$. A real that has a bounded floating-point number equivalent is said to be *representable*. Note that we do not impose any upper bound on the exponent. This allows us to have a more uniform definition of rounding since any real is always between two bounded floating-point numbers.

In existing systems, overflows generate combinatorial quantities like infinities, errors (NaN) and so on. Having the upper bound would force us to treat these non-numerical quantities at each theorem. The bound should rather be added only to the final data type. Only the high level theorems will be proved both for numerical and for combinatorial values.

Removing the lower bound is not admissible as it will hide the difficult question of the subnormal numbers. As can be seen for example in [10], the lower bound is used to prove properties through the full set of floating-point numbers and not uniquely on small numbers.

2.3 Canonical Numbers

So far the bound on the mantissa is arbitrary. In practice, it is set so that any number is represented with a fixed width field. The width of the field is called the *precision*. We define an arbitrary integer variable *precision* that is supposed not null and we add the following hypothesis:

Hypothesis. *pGivesBound*: $N[b] = \beta^{precision} - 1$.

This insures that the number of digits of the mantissa is at most *precision* in base β. We can also define a notion of *canonical* representant.

We first define the property of a floating-point number to be *normal* if it is bounded and the number of digits of its mantissa is exactly the precision:

Definition. *Fnormal* := λp: *float*. $\mathcal{B}[p] \wedge digit(p) = precision$.

where *digit* is a function that returns the number of radix-β digits in the integer $n[p]$ (no leading zeros). All bounded numbers do not have a normal equivalent, take for example $\langle 0, 0 \rangle$. For numbers near zero, we define the property of being *subnormal* by relaxing the constraint on the number of digits:

Definition. *Fsubnormal* := λp: *float*. $\mathcal{B}[p] \wedge e[p] = -E[b] \wedge digit(p) < precision$.

We can now define what it is for a number to be *canonic* as:

Definition. *Fcanonic* := λp: *float*. $(Fnormal\ p) \vee (Fsubnormal\ p)$.

In the following the properties $(Fnormal\ p)$, $(Fsubnormal\ p)$, $(Fcanonic\ p)$ will be denoted as $\mathcal{N}[p]$, $\mathcal{S}[p]$, and $\mathcal{C}[p]$ respectively. It is easy to show that normal, subnormal and canonic representations are unique:

Theorem. *FnormalUnique*: $\forall p, q$: *float*. $\mathcal{N}[p] \Rightarrow \mathcal{N}[q] \Rightarrow p == q \Rightarrow p = q$.

Theorem. *FsubnormalUnique*: $\forall p, q$: *float*. $\mathcal{S}[p] \Rightarrow \mathcal{S}[q] \Rightarrow p == q \Rightarrow p = q$.

Theorem. *FcanonicUnique*: $\forall p, q$: *float*. $\mathcal{C}[p] \Rightarrow \mathcal{C}[q] \Rightarrow p == q \Rightarrow p = q$.

In order to compute the canonical representant of a bounded number, we build the following function:

Definition. *Fnormalize* := λp: *float*.
    `if` $n[p] = 0$ `then` $\langle 0, -E[b] \rangle$
    `else let` $z = min(precision - digit(p), |E[b] + e[p]|)$ `in` $\langle n[p] * \beta^z, e[p] - z \rangle$.

The following two theorems insure that what we get is the expected function:

Theorem. *FnormalizeCorrect*: $\forall p$: *float*. $(Fnormalize\ p) == p$.

Theorem. *FnormalizeCanonic*: $\forall p$: *float*. $\mathcal{B}[p] \Rightarrow \mathcal{C}[(Fnormalize\ p)]$.

With the function *Fnormalize*, it is possible to capture the usual notion of *unit in the last place* with the following definition:

Definition. *Fulp* := λp: *float*. $\beta^{e[(Fnormalize\ p)]}$.

Working with canonical representations not only do we get that equality is the syntactic one but also the comparison between two numbers can be interpreted directly on their components with lexicographic order on positive numbers:

Theorem. *FcanonicLtPos*: $\forall p, q$: *float*. $\mathcal{C}[p] \Rightarrow \mathcal{C}[q] \Rightarrow$
    $0 \leq p < q \Rightarrow (e[p] < e[q]) \vee (e[p] = e[q] \wedge n[p] < n[q])$.

We have a similar theorem for negative floating-point numbers. These two theorems give us a direct way to construct the successor of a canonical number:

Definition. *FSucc* := λp: *float*.
  if $n[p] = N[b]$ then $\langle \beta^{precision-1}, e[p] + 1 \rangle$
  else if $n[p] = -\beta^{precision-1}$ then
    if $e[p] = -E[b]$ then $\langle n[p] + 1, e[p] \rangle$ else $\langle -N[b], e[p] - 1 \rangle$
  else $\langle n[p] + 1, e[p] \rangle$

To be sure that this function is the expected one, we have proved the three following theorems:

Theorem. *FSuccCanonic*: $\forall p$: *float*. $\mathcal{C}[p] \Rightarrow \mathcal{C}[(FSucc\ p)]$.

Theorem. *FSuccLt*: $\forall p$: *float*. $p < (FSucc\ p)$.

Theorem. *FSuccProp*: $\forall p, q$: *float*. $\mathcal{C}[p] \Rightarrow \mathcal{C}[q] \Rightarrow p < q \Rightarrow (FSucc\ p) \leq q$.

The function *FPred* that computes the preceeding canonical number can also be defined in a similar way.

3   Rounding Mode

Rounding plays a central role in any implementation of floating-point numbers. Following the philosophy of the IEEE standard, all operations on floating-point numbers should return the rounded value of the result of the exact operation. The logic of Coq is constructive: every function definition has to be explicit. In such a context defining a rounding function is problematic. We overcome this problem by defining rounding as a relation between a real number and a floating-point number. Rounding is defined abstractly. The first property a rounding must verify is to be total:

Definition. *TotalP* := λP: $\mathbb{R} \to$ *float* $\to$ *Prop*. $\forall r$: $\mathbb{R}$. $\exists p$: *float*. $(P\ r\ p)$.

In Coq, propositions are of type *Prop*, so an object P of type $\mathbb{R} \to$ *float* $\to$ *Prop* is a relation between a real and a floating-point number. Another property that is needed is the compatibility:

Definition. *CompatibleP* := λP: $\mathbb{R} \to$ *float* $\to$ *Prop*. $\forall r_1, r_2$: $\mathbb{R}$. $\forall p, q$: *float*.
  $(P\ r_1\ p) \Rightarrow r_1 = r_2 \Rightarrow p == q \Rightarrow \mathcal{B}[q] \Rightarrow (P\ r_2\ q)$.

Although we defined a canonical representation of floating-point numbers, we will not specify that the rounded value of a floating-point number should be canonical. This is definitely not needed at this point and we will see later that being more general allows us to build easier proofs. We specify that the rounding must be monotone:

Definition. *MonotoneP* := λP: $\mathbb{R} \to$ *float* $\to$ *Prop*. $\forall r_1, r_2$: $\mathbb{R}$. $\forall p, q$: *float*.
  $r_1 < r_2 \Rightarrow (P\ r_1\ p) \Rightarrow (P\ r_2\ q) \Rightarrow p \leq q$.

Finally looking for a projection, we set that the rounded value of a real must be one of the two floats that are around it. When the real to be rounded can be represented by a bounded floating-point number, the two floating-point numbers around it are purposely equal. We define the ceil (*isMin*) and the floor (*isMax*) relations and the property for a rounded value to be either a ceil or a floor:

Definition. $isMin := \lambda r\colon \mathbb{R}.\ \lambda min\colon float.$
  $\mathcal{B}[min] \wedge min \leq r \wedge \forall p\colon float.\ \mathcal{B}[p] \Rightarrow p \leq r \Rightarrow p \leq min.$

Definition. $isMax := \lambda r\colon \mathbb{R}.\ \lambda max\colon float.$
  $\mathcal{B}[max] \wedge r \leq max \wedge \forall p\colon float.\ \mathcal{B}[p] \Rightarrow r \leq p \Rightarrow max \leq p.$

Definition. $MinOrMaxP := \lambda P\colon \mathbb{R} \to float \to Prop.$
  $\forall r\colon \mathbb{R}.\ \forall p\colon float.\ (P\ r\ p) \Rightarrow (isMin\ r\ p) \vee (isMax\ r\ p).$

Using the previous definitions, we can define what is a rounding mode:

Definition. $RoundedModeP := \lambda P\colon \mathbb{R} \to float \to Prop.$
  $(TotalP\ P) \wedge (CompatibleP\ P) \wedge (MinOrMaxP\ P) \wedge (Monotone\ P).$

Having defined the rounding abstractly gives us for free the possibility of proving general properties of rounding. An example is the property that the rounding of a bounded floating-point number is the number itself. It can be stated as:

Definition. $ProjectorP := \lambda P\colon \mathbb{R} \to float \to Prop.$
  $\forall p,\ q\colon float.\ \mathcal{B}[p] \Rightarrow (P\ p\ q) \Rightarrow p == q.$

Theorem. $RoundedProjector\colon \forall P\colon \mathbb{R} \to float \to Prop.$
  $(RoundedModeP\ P) \Rightarrow (ProjectorP\ P).$

As a matter of fact we could have replaced in the definition of $RoundModeP$ the property $MinOrMax$ by $ProjectorP$.

We can now define the usual rounding modes. First of all, the two relations $isMin$ and $isMax$ are rounding:

Theorem. $MinRoundedModeP\colon (RoundedModeP\ isMin).$

Theorem. $MaxRoundedModeP\colon (RoundedModeP\ isMax).$

The rounding to zero is defined as follows:

Definition. $ToZeroP := \lambda r\colon \mathbb{R}.\ \lambda p\colon float.$
  $(0 \leq r \wedge (isMin\ r\ p)) \vee (r \leq 0 \wedge (isMax\ r\ p)).$

Theorem. $ToZeroRoundedModeP\colon (RoundedModeP\ ToZeroP).$

Similarly we define the rounding to infinity:

Definition. $ToInfinityP := \lambda r\colon \mathbb{R}.\ \lambda p\colon float.$
  $(r \leq 0 \wedge (isMin\ r\ p)) \vee (0 \leq r \wedge (isMax\ r\ p)).$

Theorem. $ToInfinityRoundedModeP\colon (RoundedModeP\ ToInfinityP).$

While the preceeding roundings are really functions, we take advantage of having a relation to define rounding to the closest:

Definition. $Closest := \lambda r\colon \mathbb{R}.\ \lambda p\colon float.\ \mathcal{B}[p] \wedge \forall f\colon float.\ \mathcal{B}[f] \Rightarrow |p - r| \leq |f - r|.$

Theorem. $ClosestRoundedModeP\colon (RoundedModeP\ Closest).$

For the real in the middle of two successive bounded floating-point numbers there are two possible closest. So a tie-break rule is usually invoked. In our presentation, we simply accept these two points as a rounding value since uniqueness is not required. This gives us the possibility of both proving properties that are true independently of a particular tie-break rule and investigating properties relative to a particular tie-break rule like in [29].

4 Basic Results

It is well known in any formalization that before being able to derive any interesting result, it is necessary to prove a number of elementary facts. An example of such elementary facts is the compatibility of the complement with the property of being bounded:

Theorem. *oppBounded*: $\forall x$: *float*. $\mathcal{B}[x] \Rightarrow \mathcal{B}[-x]$.

This fact is a direct consequence of our definition of the mantissa. It would not be true if we used β's complement instead of the usual sign-magnitude notation for the mantissa.

One of the first interesting result is that the difference of relatively close numbers can be done exactly with no rounding error. This property was first published by Sterbenz [34]. It has been expressed in our formalization as follows:

Theorem. *Sterbenz*: $\forall p, q$: *float*. $\mathcal{B}[p] \Rightarrow \mathcal{B}[q] \Rightarrow 1/2 * q \leq p \leq 2 * q \Rightarrow \mathcal{B}[p - q]$.

This theorem is interesting for several reasons. First of all, it contains the magic number 2. As this result is often presented and proved in binary arithmetic [13], it is not obvious if in the generic case, one has to replace 2 with β or not. For example, another property that is often used in binary arithmetic is:

Theorem. *plusUpperBound*: $\forall P$: $\mathbb{R} \rightarrow$ *float* $\rightarrow$ *Prop*. $\forall p, q, r$: *float*.
    (*RoundedModeP P*) $\Rightarrow$ (P ($p + q$) r) $\Rightarrow \mathcal{B}[p] \Rightarrow \mathcal{B}[q] \Rightarrow |r| \leq 2 * max(|p|, |q|)$.

In binary arithmetic this is a direct consequence of the monotony of rounding since $|p + q| \leq 2 * max(|p|, |q|)$ and $2 * max(|p|, |q|)$ is always representable in binary arithmetic. This is not the case for an arbitrary base. Take for example $\beta = 10$ with two digits of precision, rounding to the closest and $p = q = 9.9$. We have $2 * max(|p|, |q|) = 19.8$ but (*Closest* ($p + q$) 20).

The Sterbenz property is also interesting by the way its proof relies on the previous definitions. The proof proceeds as follows. First of all, we restrict ourselves to the case $q \leq p \leq 2 * q$ because of the symmetry of the problem. By definition of *Fminus*, an exponent of $p - q$ is $min(e[p], e[q])$, so it is greater than or equal to $-N[b]$ since both p and q are bounded. For the mantissa, we do a case analysis on the value of $min(e[p], e[q])$. If it is $e[q]$, the initial equation can be rewritten as $0 \leq p - q \leq q$ and since $p - q$ and q have identical exponent we obtain $0 \leq n[p - q] \leq n[q]$. As q is bounded, $n[q] \leq N[b]$ allows us conclude. Similarly if $min(e[p], e[q]) = e[p]$, we rewrite the initial equation as $0 \leq p - q \leq q \leq p$ and since $p - q$ and p have same exponent we have $0 \leq n[p - q] \leq n[p]$.

Another property that we have proved is the one concerning intervals proposed by Priest [28]. If we take two bounded positive floating-point numbers p and q and if $q - p$ can be represented exactly, then for all the floating-point numbers r inside the interval $[p, q]$, the value $r - p$ can also be represented exactly.

This is stated in our library as follows:

Theorem. $ExactMinusInterval: \forall P: \mathbb{R} \to float \to Prop. \forall p, q, r: float.$
$(RoundedModeP\ P) \Rightarrow \mathcal{B}[p] \Rightarrow \mathcal{B}[q] \Rightarrow \mathcal{B}[r] \Rightarrow 0 \leq p \leq r \leq q \Rightarrow$
$(\exists r': float. \mathcal{B}[r'] \wedge r' == q - p) \Rightarrow (\exists r': float. \mathcal{B}[r'] \wedge r' == r - p).$

This is a nice property but more interestingly this is the only theorem in our library that requires an inductive proof. Our proof follows the steps given by Priest. The cases where $p \leq 2 * q$ or $r \leq 2 * p$ can be proved easily using the Sterbenz property. For the other cases, we take an arbitrary r in $]2 * p, q]$ and show that if the property holds for r it holds for $(FPred\ r)$.

5   An Example

In order to show how the library can be used effectively, we sketch the proof that we have done to derive the correctness of a simple test program. This program is supposed to detect the radix of the arithmetic on which it is running. It was first proposed by Malcolm [23]. Here is its formulation in a Pascal-like syntax:

```
x := 1.0;
y := 1.0;
while ((x + 1.0) - x) = 1.0 do x := 2.0 * x;
while ((x + y) - x) != y do y := y + 1.0;
```

The claim is that the final value of y is the base of the arithmetic. Of course this program would make no sense if the computations were done exactly. It would never leave the first loop since its test is always true, and it would never enter the second loop. The proof of correctness of this program relies on two main properties. The first one insures that by increasing the mantissa of any bounded floating-point number we still get a bounded floating-point number:

Theorem. $FboundNext: \forall p: float. \mathcal{B}[p] \Rightarrow \exists q: float. \mathcal{B}[q] \wedge q == \langle n[p] + 1, e[p] \rangle.$

In the case of the program, we use this property with $e[p] = 0$ to justify the fact that till $x \leq N[b]$, x+1.0 is computing with no rounding error, so the test is true.

The second property is more elaborate. It uses the fact that in a binade $[\langle \beta^{precision-1}, e \rangle, \langle N[b], e \rangle]$ two successive floating-point numbers are separated by exactly β^e. So if we add something less than β^e to a floating-point number, we are still between this number and its successor. So the rounding is necessarily one of the two. This is expressed by the following theorem:

Theorem. $InBinade: \forall P: \mathbb{R} \to float \to Prop. \forall p, q, r: float. \forall e: \mathbb{Z}. - E[b] \leq e \Rightarrow$
$(RoundedModeP\ P) \Rightarrow \mathcal{B}[p] \Rightarrow \mathcal{B}[q] \Rightarrow \langle \beta^{precision-1}, e \rangle \leq p \leq \langle N[b], e \rangle \Rightarrow$
$0 < q < \beta^e \Rightarrow (P\ (p+q)\ r) \Rightarrow r == p \vee r == p + \beta^e$

In the case of the program we use the previous theorem only for $e = 1$. It can be rewritten as:

Theorem. $InBinade_1: \forall P: \mathbb{R} \to float \to Prop. \forall p, q, r: float.$
$(RoundedModeP\ P) \Rightarrow \mathcal{B}[p] \Rightarrow \mathcal{B}[q] \Rightarrow N[b] + 1 \leq p \leq \beta * N[b] \Rightarrow 0 < q < \beta \Rightarrow$
$(P\ (p+q)\ r) \Rightarrow r == p \vee r == p + \beta.$

This explains why we exit the first loop as soon as $N[b] < $ x. In that case the test reduces to $0 = 1.0$ or $\beta = 1.0$. In a similar way, it explains why we remain in the second loop when $y < \beta$, the test reducing to $0 \mathrel{!\!=} y$ or $\beta \mathrel{!\!=} y$.

In order to prove the program correct, we use the possibility of annotating the program with assertions as proposed in [12]. The complete program has the following form:

```
x := 1.0;
y := 1.0;
while (x+1.0)-x = 1.0 do
    {invariant :  ∃m: ℕ. 1 ≤ m ≤ β * N[b] ∧ m = x ∧ B[x]
        variant :  β * N[b] − (Int_part x) for < }
    x:= 2.0 * x;
{∃m: ℕ. N[b] + 1 ≤ m ≤ β * N[b] ∧ m = x ∧ B[x] }
while (x+y)-x != y do
    {invariant :  ∃m: ℕ. 1 ≤ m ≤ β ∧ m = y ∧ B[y]
        variant :  β − (Int_part y) for < }
    y:= y + 1.0;
{y == β}
```

In the assertions we can refer to the variables of the program freely. For the first loop, we simply state the invariant that x represents an integer in the interval $[1, \beta * N[b]]$. The variant insures that at each iteration x becomes closer to $\beta * N[b]$. The function Int_part takes a real and returns its integer part. It is used to have the variant in $\mathbb{N}$. At the end of the first loop, x represents an integer in the interval $[N[b] + 1, \beta * N[b]]$. We have a similar invariant for the second loop but this time for the interval $[1, \beta]$. At the end of the program we have the expected conclusion. We can go one step further, adding an extra loop to get the precision:

```
n := 0;
x := 1.0;
while (x+1.0)-x = 1.0 do
    {invariant :  ∃m: ℕ. 1 ≤ m ≤ β * N[b] ∧ m = x ∧ B[x]
        variant :  β * N[b] − (Int_part x) for < }
    begin
        x:= y * x;
        n:= n + 1;
    end
{n = precision}
```

This game can be played even further. Programs like Paranoia [20], that includes Malcolm's algorithm, have been developed to check properties of floating-point arithmetics automatically.

6   Floating-Point Expansion

While computing with floating point numbers, we are usually going to accumulate rounding errors. So at the end of the computation, the result will be more or less accurate. Countless techniques exist to estimate the actual errors on the result [17]. One of the most popular methods is to use the so-called $1 + \epsilon$ property.

This property just expresses that all operations are performed with a relative error of ϵ, i.e if we have an operation $\cdot$ and its equivalent with rounding $\odot$ we have the following relation:

$$\forall a, b: float.\, a \odot b = (a \cdot b) * (1 + \epsilon)$$

Given a computation, it is then possible to propagate errors and take the main term in ϵ to get an estimation of the accuracy. What is presented in this section is an orthogonal approach where one tries to give an exact account of computations while using floating-point arithmetic.

6.1   Two Sum

An interesting property of the four radix-2 IEEE implemented operations with rounding to the closest is that the error is always representable [4]. This property, independent of the radix, was already clear for the addition in [22] inspired by [27,26]. We take the usual convention that $+$ and $-$ are the exact functions, and $\oplus$ and $\ominus$ are the same operations but with rounding. This property holds:

Theorem. $errorBoundedPlus{:}\,\forall p, q, r{:}\,float.\,\mathcal{B}[p] \Rightarrow \mathcal{B}[q] \Rightarrow$
$(Closest\ (p+q)\ r) \Rightarrow \exists error{:}\,float.\,error == (p+q) - r \wedge \mathcal{B}[error].$

In order to prove it, we rely on a basic property of rounding:

Theorem. $RoundedModeRep{:}\,\forall P{:}\,\mathbb{R} \to float \to Prop.\,\forall p, q{:}\,float.$
$(RoundedModeP\ P) \Rightarrow (P\ p\ q) \Rightarrow \exists m{:}\,\mathbb{Z}.\,q == \langle m, e[p]\rangle.$

This simply says that the rounding of an unbounded floating-point number can always be expressible with the same exponent, i.e by rounding we only lose bits. This means in particular that we can find a floating-point number $error$ equal to $(p+q) - r$ whose exponent is either the one of p or the one of q. To prove that this number is bounded we just need to verify that its mantissa is bounded. To do this, we use the property of the rounding to the closest

$$\forall f{:}\,float.\,\mathcal{B}[f] \Rightarrow |(p+q) - r| \leq |(p+q) - f|$$

with $f = p$ and $f = q$ to get $|error| \leq |q|$ and $|error| \leq |p|$ respectively. As the exponent of $error$ is the one of either p or q, we get that the $error$ is bounded.

To compute effectively the error of a sum, one possibility is to use the program proposed by Knuth [22] copied here with Shewchuk's presentation [32]. It is composed of 6 operations:

$\mathsf{TwoSum_k}\,(a, b) =$

1	$x := a \oplus b$
2	$b_v := x \ominus a$
3	$a_v := x \ominus b_v$
4	$b_r := b \ominus b_v$
5	$a_r := a \ominus a_v$
6	$error := a_r \oplus b_r$

There exist several proofs that this program is correct. Shewchuk gives a proof for binary arithmetic with the extra condition that precision is greater than or equal to 3. Priest sets his proof in a general framework similar to ours but with the extra condition

$$\forall a: float. \, |a \oplus a| \leq 2|a|.$$

His proof is rather elegant as it makes use of general properties of arithmetic. It is the one we have formalized in our library. Knuth gives a more general proof in [22] since it does not have the extra condition given by Priest. Unfortunately his proof is very intricate and due to time constraint it has not yet been formalized in our library.

It is possible to compute the error of a sum with less than 6 operations, if we have some information on the operands. In particular, if we have $|a| \leq |b|$ Dekker [11] proposes the following 3 operations:

TwoSum$_d(a, b) =$

   1     $x := a \oplus b$

   2    $a_v := x \ominus b$

   3 $error := a \ominus a_v$

As a matter of fact, we can loosen a bit more the condition in binary arithmetic and only require that the inputs have a bounded representation such that $e[a] \leq e[b]$. This proof is not usually found in the literature, so we detail how it has been obtained in our development. First of all, the only problematic situation is when $|b| < |a|$ and $e[a] \leq e[b]$. But in this case, we can just reduce the problem to $|b| < |a|$ and $e[a] = e[b]$ and by symmetry we can suppose a positive. If b is negative, a and b being of opposite sign with same exponent, their sum is exact. When the first sum is exact, the correctness is insured because we have $a_v = a$ and $error = 0$. So we can suppose $0 \leq b \leq a$. If $n[a] + n[b] \leq N[b]$, the sum of a and b is computed exactly. So we are left with $N[b] + 1 \leq n[a] + n[b] < 2 * N[b]$. In that case it is easy to show that the second operation is performed without any rounding error, i.e. $a_v = (a \oplus b) - b$. This means that $a - a_v = (a+b) - (a \oplus b)$ which is rounding exactly as we know that the quantity on the right is representable.

The condition $e[a] \leq e[b]$ was raised in [8] by an algorithm that was working on tests but that cannot be proved with the usual condition of $|a| \leq |b|$. Giving the condition would have been more difficult had we decided to hide all the equivalent floating-point numbers behind the unique canonical representant. For this reason, Knuth only proved his theorem under the condition that the *canonical representations* of the inputs verify $e[a] \leq e[b]$ [22].

6.2   Expansion

In the previous section we have seen that in floating-point arithmetic with rounding to the closest it is possible to represent exactly a sum by a pair composed of the rounded sum and the error. Expansions are a generalisation of this idea, trying to represent a multiple precision floating-point number as a list of bounded floating-point numbers.

This technique is very efficient when multiple precision is needed for just a few operations, the inputs are floating-point numbers and the output is either a floating-point number or a boolean value. Using a conventional high radix multiple precision package such as GMP [15] would require a lot of work for converting the input from floating-point number to the internal format. On the contrary, the best asymptotic algorithms are only available with a conventional notation. As the intermediate results need more words to be stored precisely and the number of operations grows, conventional multiple precision arithmetic will turn out to be better than expansions.

To give an exact account on the definition of expansion, we first need to define the notion of *most significant bit* and *least significant bit*. The most significant bit is represented by the function:

Definition. $MSB\!: float \rightarrow \mathbb{Z} := \lambda p\!: float.\, digit(p) + e[p]$.

The characteristic property of this function is the following:

Theorem. $ltMSB\!: \forall p\!: float.\, \neg(p == 0) \Rightarrow \beta^{(MSB\ p)} \leq |p| < \beta^{(MSB\ p)+1}$.

For the least significant bit, we need an intermediate function $maxDiv$ that, given a floating-point number p, returns the greatest natural number n smaller than *precision* such that β^n divides $n[p]$. With this function, we can define the least significant bit as:

Definition. $LSB\!: float \rightarrow \mathbb{Z} := \lambda p\!: float.\, maxDiv(p) + e[p]$.

One of the main properties of the least significant bit is the following:

Theorem. $LSBrep\!: \forall p, q\!: float.$
$\quad \neg(q == 0) \Rightarrow (LSB\ p) \leq (LSB\ q) \Rightarrow \exists z\!: \mathbb{Z}.\, q == \langle z, e[p] \rangle$.

Expansions are defined as lists of bounded floating-point numbers that do not overlap. As arithmetic algorithms manipulating expansions usually need the components to be sorted, our lists are arbitrarily sorted from the smallest number to the largest one. Also, zero elements are allowed at any place in the expansion. This is done in order not to have to necessarily insert a test to zero after every elementary operation. It also simplifies the presentation of the algorithms. Using the Prolog convention to denote list, we have the following definition:

Inductive. $IsExpansion\!: (list\ float) \rightarrow Prop :=$
$\quad Nil : (IsExpansion\ [])$
$\mid\quad Single : \forall p\!: float.\, \mathcal{B}[p] \Rightarrow (IsExpansion\ [p])$
$\mid\quad Top_1 : \forall p\!: float.\, \forall L\!: (list\ float).$
$\qquad \mathcal{B}[p] \Rightarrow p == 0 \Rightarrow (IsExpansion\ L) \Rightarrow (IsExpansion\ [p|L])$
$\mid\quad Top_2 : \forall p, q\!: float.\, \forall L\!: (list\ float).$
$\qquad \mathcal{B}[p] \Rightarrow \mathcal{B}[q] \Rightarrow q == 0 \Rightarrow (IsExpansion\ [p|L]) \Rightarrow (IsExpansion\ [p, q|L])$
$\mid\quad Top : \forall p, q\!: float.\, \forall L\!: (list\ float).\, \mathcal{B}[p] \Rightarrow \mathcal{B}[q] \Rightarrow (IsExpansion\ [q|L]) \Rightarrow$
$\qquad \neg p == 0 \Rightarrow \neg q == 0 \Rightarrow (MSB\ p) < (LSB\ q) \Rightarrow (IsExpansion\ [p, q|L])$

It is direct to associate an expansion with the value it represents by the following function:

Fixpoint. $expValue\,[L:\ (list\ float)]:\ \ float:=$
    Cases. L **of**
          $[]\ \Longrightarrow\ \langle 0, -E[b]\rangle$
      $|\ [p|L_1]\ \Longrightarrow p\ +\ (expValue\ L_1)$
    end.

Finally, every unbounded floating-point number that has a representation with an exponent larger than $-E[b]$ has an expansion representation. It is sufficient to break its large mantissa into smaller ones. For example, if we take the number $\langle 11223344, 0\rangle$ with an arithmetic in base 10 and 2 digits of precision, a possible expansion is $[\langle 44, 0\rangle, \langle 33, 2\rangle, \langle 22, 4\rangle, \langle 11, 6\rangle]$. We can see this construction as a recursive process. $\langle 11, 6\rangle$ is the initial number rounded to zero and $[\langle 44, 0\rangle, \langle 33, 2\rangle, \langle 22, 4\rangle]$ is the expansion representing the error done by rounding to zero. Using this process we get the following theorem:

Theorem. $existExp\!:\forall p\!:\ float.$
    $-E[b] \le (LSB\ p) \Rightarrow \exists L\!:\ (list\ float).\,(IsExpansion\ L) \wedge p == (expValue\ L).$

A similar result could be obtained using rounding to the closest.

6.3   Adding Two Expansions

Once we have expansions, we can start writing algorithms to manipulate them. Here we present a relatively simple but not too naive way of adding expansions given in [32] and formalized using our library. This algorithm does not use any comparison. In a deeply pipelined processor, a branch prediction miss costs many clock cycles. When the number of components of the inputs is relatively small, we get better results with this algorithm compared to asymptotically faster algorithms.

    To build this adder, we suppose the existence of a function TwoSum that takes two floating-point numbers p and q and returns a pair of floating-point numbers (h, c) such that $h == p \oplus q$ and $c == (p + q) - (p \oplus q)$. Using this basic function, we first define a function that adds a single number to an expansion:

Fixpoint. $growExp\,[p:\ float;\ L:(list\ float)]:\ \ (list\ float):=$
    Cases. L **of**
          $[]\ \Longrightarrow\ [p]$
      $|\ [q|L_1]\ \Longrightarrow$ **let** $(h, c) = (TwoSum\ p\ q)$ **in** $[c|(growExp\ h\ L_1)]$
    end.

It is quite direct to see that this function returns an expansion and is correct:

Theorem. $growExpIsExp\!:\forall L\!:\ (list\ float).\,\forall p\!:\ float.\,\mathcal{B}[p] \Rightarrow$
    $(IsExpansion\ L) \Rightarrow (IsExpansion\ (growExp\ p\ L)).$

Theorem. $growExpIsVal\!:\forall L\!:\ (list\ float).\,\forall p\!:\ float.\,\mathcal{B}[p] \Rightarrow$
    $(IsExpansion\ L) \Rightarrow (expValue\ (growExp\ p\ L)) == p + (expValue\ L).$

The naive algorithm for adding two expansions is to repeatedly add all the elements of the first expansion to the second using $growExp$. In fact, because expansions are sorted, we can do slightly better:

Fixpoint. $addExp [L_1, L2 : (list\ float)] :$ $(list\ float) :=$
  Cases. L_1 **of**
      $[] \Longrightarrow L_2$
    $| [p|L_1'] \Longrightarrow$ **Cases.** $(growExp\ p\ L_2)$ **of**
          $[] \Longrightarrow L_1'$
        $[q|L_2'] \Longrightarrow [q|(addExp\ L_1'\ L_2')]$
      end
  end.

The recursive call can be seen as an optimised form of the naive recursive call ($addExp\ L_1'\ [q|L_2']$). Because q is at most comparable with p, q is 'smaller' than any element of L_1' and 'smaller' than any element of L_2', so it appears first and unchanged by the addition. This is the key result to prove that addition returns an expansion, while the correctness is direct:

Theorem. $addExpIsExp: \forall L_1, L_2: (list\ float)$.
  $(IsExpansion\ L_1) \Rightarrow (IsExpansion\ L_2) \Rightarrow (IsExpansion\ (addExp\ L_1\ L_2))$.

Theorem. $addExpIsVal: \forall L_1, L_2: (list\ float).\ (IsExpansion\ L_1) \Rightarrow (IsExpansion\ L_2) \Rightarrow$
  $(expValue\ (addExp\ L_1\ L_2)) == (expValue\ L_1) + (expValue\ L_2)$.

7 Conclusion

We hope that what we have presented in this paper shows how effectively our floating-point library can already be used to do some verification tasks. Compared to previous works on the subject, the main originality is its genericity. No base and no format are pre-supposed and rounding is defined abstractly. Other libraries such as [16,31] follow the IEEE 754 standard and are restricted to base 2. An exception is [25] where the IEEE 784 standard is formalized, so it accommodates bases 2 and 10. We believe that most of the proofs in these libraries do not rely on the actual value of the base. This is the case, for example, in [25] where one could remove the assumption on the base and rerun the proofs without any problem. The situation is somewhat different for rounding. Other libraries define rounding as one of the four usual rounding modes. We are more liberal as we only ask for some specific properties to be met by the rounding. For example, the program in Section 5 is proved correct for an arbitrary rounding mode. Also some properties have been proved for rounding to the closest independently of a particular tie-break rule.

The core library represents 10000 lines of code for 60 definitions and 400 theorems. It is freely available from `http://www-sop.inria.fr/lemma/AOC/coq`. It is difficult to compare our library with others. Libraries such as [16,31] have been intensively used for large verification works. Most probably they are more complete than ours. Still some basic results needed for reasoning about expansions can only be found in our library.

Working on this library makes us realize that proofs really depend on the domain of application. Most proofs have been done without using any induction principle and consist mainly of nested case analysis. This clearly indicates a limit to the generic approach of provers like Coq and the need for the development of specific tools. This is especially true for the presentation of proofs. Tactic-based theorem proving is not adequate to represent proof scripts. A more declarative approach à la Isar [36] would be more than needed in order to be able to communicate our proofs to non-specialists of Coq.

Finally, we are aware that building a library is a never-ending process. New applications could give rise to new elementary results and a need for some global reorganization of the library. In order to get a more stable and complete core library, we plan to work further on expansions. Recent works such as [32,9] have proposed elaborated algorithms to manipulate expansions. Getting a computer-checked version of these algorithms is a challenging task.

References

1. David H. Bailey, Robert Krasny, and Richard Pelz. Multiple precision, multiple processor vortex sheet roll-up computation. In *Proceedings of the Sixth SIAM Conference on Parallel Processing for Scientific Computing*, pages 52–56, Philadelphia, Pennsylvania, 1993.
2. Geoff Barrett. Formal Methods Applied to a Floating-Point Number System. *IEEE Transactions on Software Engineering*, 15(5):611–621, 1989.
3. Yves Bertot, Gilles Dowek, André Hirschowitz, Christine Paulin, and Laurent Théry, editors. *Theorem Proving in Higher Order Logics: 12th International Conference, TPHOLs'99*, number 1690 in LNCS, Nice, France, September 1999. Springer-Verlag.
4. Gerd Bohlender, Wolfgang Walter, Peter Kornerup, and David W. Matula. Semantics for exact floating point operations. In Peter Kornerup and David W. Matula, editors, *Proceedings of the 10th Symposium on Computer Arithmetic*, pages 22–26, Grenoble, France, 1991. IEEE Computer Society Press.
5. C. Burnikel, R. Fleischer, K. Mehlhorn, and S. Schirra. Efficient exact geometric computation made easy. In *Proceedings of the 15th Annual ACM Symposium on Computational Geometry*, pages 341–350, Miami, Florida, 1999.
6. William J. Cody. Static and dynamic numerical characteristics of floating point arithmetic. *IEEE Transactions on Computers*, 22(6):598–601, 1973.
7. William J. Cody, Richard Karpinski, et al. A proposed radix and word-length independent standard for floating point arithmetic. *IEEE Micro*, 4(4):86–100, 1984.
8. Marc Daumas. Multiplications of floating point expansions. In Israel Koren and Peter Kornerup, editors, *Proceedings of the 14th Symposium on Computer Arithmetic*, pages 250–257, Adelaide, Australia, 1999.
9. Marc Daumas and Claire Finot. Division of Floating-Point Expansions with an application to the computation of a determinant. *Journal of Universal Computer Science*, 5(6):323–338, 1999.
10. Marc Daumas and Philippe Langlois. Additive symmetric: the non-negative case. *Theoretical Computer Science*, 2002.
11. T. J. Dekker. A Floating-Point Technique for Extending the Available Precision. *Numerische Mathematik*, 18(03):224–242, 1971.
12. Jean-Christophe Filliâtre. Proof of Imperative Programs in Type Theory. In *International Workshop, TYPES '98, Kloster Irsee, Germany*, number 1657 in LNCS. Springer-Verlag, March 1998.

13. David Goldberg. What every computer scientist should know about floating point arithmetic. *ACM Computing Surveys*, 23(1):5–47, 1991.
14. Michael J. C. Gordon and Thomas F. Melham. *Introduction to HOL : a theorem proving environment for higher-order logic*. Cambridge University Press, 1993.
15. Tobjörn Granlund. *The GNU multiple precision arithmetic library*, 2000. Version 3.1.
16. John Harrison. A Machine-Checked Theory of Floating Point Arithmetic. In Bertot et al. [3], pages 113–130.
17. Nicholas J. Higham. *Accuracy and stability of numerical algorithms*. SIAM, 1996.
18. Gérard Huet, Gilles Kahn, and Christine Paulin-Mohring. The Coq Proof Assistant: A Tutorial: Version 6.1. Technical Report 204, INRIA, 1997.
19. V. Karamcheti, C. Li, I. Pechtchanski, and Chee Yap. A core library for robust numeric and geometric computation. In *Proceedings of the 15th Annual ACM Symposium on Computational Geometry*, pages 351–359, Miami, Florida, 1999.
20. Richard Karpinski. PARANOIA: a floating-point benchmark. *Byte*, 10(2):223–235, 1985.
21. Matt Kaufmann, Panagiotis Manolios, and J Strother Moore. *Computer-Aided Reasoning: An Approach*. advances in formal methods. Kluwer Academic Publishers, 2000.
22. Donald E. Knuth. *The art of computer programming: Seminumerical Algorithms*. Addison Wesley, 1973. Second edition.
23. Michael A. Malcolm. Algorithms to reveal properties of floating-Point Arithmetic. *Communications of the ACM*, 15(11):949–951, 1972.
24. Micaela Mayero. The Three Gap Theorem: Specification and Proof in Coq. Technical Report 3848, INRIA, 1999.
25. Paul S. Miner. Defining the IEEE-854 floating-point standard in pvs. Technical Memorandum 110167, NASA, Langley Research Center, 1995.
26. Ole Møller. Note on quasi double-precision. *BIT*, 5(4):251–255, 1965.
27. Ole Møller. Quasi double-precision in floating point addition. *BIT*, 5(1):37–50, 1965.
28. Douglas M. Priest. On Properties of Floating Point Arithmetics: Numerical Stability and the Cost of Accurate. Phd, U.C. Berkeley, 1993.
29. John F. Reiser and Donald E. Knuth. Evading the drift in floating point addition. *Information Processing Letter*, 3(3):84–87, 1975.
30. John M. Rushby, Natajaran Shankar, and Mandayam Srivas. PVS: Combining specification, proof checking, and model checking. In *CAV '96*, volume 1102 of *LNCS*. Springer-Verlag, July 1996.
31. David M. Russinoff. A Mechanically Checked Proof of IEEE Compliance of the AMD K5 Floating-Point Square Root Microcode. *Formal Methods in System Design*, 14(1):75–125, January 1999.
32. Jonathan Richard Shewchuk. Adaptive Precision Floating-Point Arithmetic and Fast Robust Geometric Predicates. *Discrete & Computational Geometry*, 18(03):305–363, 1997.
33. Mike J. Spivey. *Understanding Z: A Specification Language and its Formal Semantics*. Cambridge Tracts in Theoretical Computer Science. Cambridge University Press, 1988.
34. Pat H. Sterbenz. *Floating point computation*. Prentice Hall, 1974.
35. David Stevenson et al. An american national standard: IEEE standard for binary floating point arithmetic. *ACM SIGPLAN Notices*, 22(2):9–25, 1987.
36. Markus Wenzel. A Generic Interpretative Approach to Readable Formal Proof Documents. In Bertot et al. [3], pages 167–184.

Ordinal Arithmetic: A Case Study for Rippling in a Higher Order Domain

Louise A. Dennis and Alan Smaill

Division of Informatics, University of Edinburgh
80 South Bridge, Edinburgh, EH1 1HN, UK
louised@dai.ed.ac.uk, A.Smaill@ed.ac.uk

Abstract. This paper reports a case study in the use of proof planning in the context of higher order syntax. Rippling is a heuristic for guiding rewriting steps in induction that has been used successfully in proof planning inductive proofs using first order representations. Ordinal arithmetic provides a natural set of higher order examples on which transfinite induction may be attempted using rippling. Previously Boyer-Moore style automation could not be applied to such domains. We demonstrate that a higher-order extension of the rippling heuristic is sufficient to plan such proofs automatically. Accordingly, ordinal arithmetic has been implemented in $\lambda Clam$, a higher order proof planning system for induction, and standard undergraduate text book problems have been successfully planned. We show the synthesis of a fixpoint for normal ordinal functions which demonstrates how our automation could be extended to produce more interesting results than the textbook examples tried so far.

1 Introduction

This paper reports on using $\lambda Clam$ to plan proofs about ordinal arithmetic, making use of higher order features. Ordinal arithmetic is of interest, among other things, for its use in aiding termination proofs (see [7]), and in classifying proof-theoretic complexity.

The system was used to attempt to plan proofs of examples appearing in a number of text books [21,9,14] with encouraging results. We were also able to synthesize a fixpoint for a normal function. The emphasis is on the automated control of proof search, and we aim for both a declarative account of this control, and the construction of mathematically natural proofs. As far as we know this is the first time that automation of such proofs has been attempted in a fully higher-order fashion.

It was found that no modifications of the existing proof plan for induction and theory of rippling were needed to plan these higher order proofs. This result supports the generality of the rippling approach, and its ability to generate mathematically natural proofs.

This paper begins with an overview of ordinal arithmetic (§2) and proof planning focusing on the proof plan for induction using the ripple heuristic as implemented in $\lambda Clam$ (§3). We then discuss the modifications we had to make

R.J. Boulton and P.B. Jackson (Eds.): TPHOLs 2001, LNCS 2152, pp. 185–200, 2001.

to this in order to handle ordinal arithmetic (§4) and evaluate our results (§5). Finally we consider some options for further work (§6).

2   Ordinal Arithmetic: A Higher Order Family of Problems

First we present the background to the problem area. Traditionally the theory of ordinals is presented within set theory; a machine-checked presentation following this route is given in [17]. We instead present a computationally more direct theory of ordinals in which to reason.

Ordinals can be thought of as (equivalence classes of) well-ordered linear orders, i.e. orders where each non-empty set has a least element. As such they are a generalisation of the usual natural numbers. We work with so-called *ordinal notations*, as in [15]. These notations give us a language that allows us to speak about some (but not all) of the ordinals. The underlying formal language here is a constructive type theory with a general mechanism for introducing inductively defined types[1]. An inductively defined type for ordinal notations is given by Coquand in [8] as follows:

```
datatype ordinal = 0 | s of ordinal | lim of (nat -> ordinal)
```

where we understand s as a successor operation, and lim to refer to the least upper bound of the ordinals in the range of its argument. This definition yields corresponding induction and recursion schemes as follows.

Theorem 1 (Induction for Ordinal Notations). *Suppose that*

1. $\phi(0)$;
2. *for every* α, *if* $\phi(\alpha)$ *then* $\phi(s(\alpha))$;
3. *for every function* f : *nat→ordinal, if for every* n : *nat,* $\phi(f(n))$ *then* $\phi(lim(f))$.

Then for every ordinal notation α, $\phi(\alpha)$.

This makes ordinals a credible test case for inductive theorem provers. Proofs using this principle are naturally higher-order, as we will see.

A corresponding iteration principle is then available to us, allowing us to define operations involving ordinal notations. Suppose that for some type T we have $a : T$, $G : T \rightarrow T$ and $H : (nat \rightarrow T) \rightarrow T$. Then the iteration principle yields a function $F : ordinal \rightarrow T$ such that:

$$F(0) = a, \tag{1}$$
$$F(s(x)) = G(F(x)), \tag{2}$$
$$F(\lim(f)) = H(f). \tag{3}$$

---

[1] Specifically, the extended calculus of constructions as formulated in the Lego proof system [12].

Note that equality here is between ordinal notations – this is a finer equality than that between ordinals where isomorphic orders are identified. However, it is sufficient for present purposes.

To take a particular example, addition for ordinals is defined as follows:

$$x + 0 = x, \tag{4}$$
$$x + s(y) = s(x + y), \tag{5}$$
$$x + \lim(f) = \lim(\lambda n.\, x + f(n)). \tag{6}$$

We can embed the natural numbers in the ordinals in the obvious way via a function *embed*; the ordinal ω, the first infinite ordinal, is then denoted by *lim(embed)*.

Since for an infinite order, tacking an extra element at the beginning or at the end can give different results, in the sense of having different properties as orders, not all the arithmetic identities for natural numbers still hold for ordinals (commutativity of addition fails for example), and we have to be more careful about the arguments used for recursive definitions. Halmos [13] gives a good account of the ideas involved.

In brief, ordinal arithmetic presents itself as an area where induction applies but one which contains higher order aspects. Not all theorems in standard arithmetic hold for ordinal numbers making it genuinely distinct from the finite case.

3   Proof Planning

Proof planning was first suggested by Bundy [4]. A proof plan is a proof of a theorem, at some level of abstraction, presented as a tree. A proof plan is generated using AI-style planning techniques. The planning operators used by a proof planner are the *proof methods*. These are defined by their pre- and post-conditions which are used by the planner to form the proof plan. The defining feature of a proof method is this presentation in terms of pre- and post- conditions. Methods themselves need not contain any guarantee of soundness and generally refer to a tactic in an LCF-style theorem prover which can be run to create a sound proof. In principle a method could directly include a justification function etc. in which case it would be both a method and a tactic. There is, in our opinion, no reason why methods and tactics must necessarily be distinct. On the other hand proof methods are a general framework for coordinating proof steps and so are not specifically tied to the LCF paradigm.

The first and most famous proof plan is that for induction with the associated rippling heuristic (a form of rewriting constrained to be terminating by meta-logical annotations). This was implemented in the *Clam* proof planner. $\lambda Clam$ [19] is a higher order descendant of *Clam* and was the chosen system for this case study.

3.1   Proof Planning in λ*Clam*

Proof planning in λ*Clam* works as follows: A goal is presented to the system. This goal is a sequent and several of the methods embody standard sequent calculus inference rules. There are two sorts of method; compound and atomic. A compound method is a *methodical expression* built from methods and *methodicals*. Methodicals are analogous to tacticals in an LCF setting. They specify that, for instance, one method should be applied then another, or a method should be repeated as many times as possible. Each compound method thus imposes a structure on its *submethods*. In this way the step_case method for induction attempts to ripple (rewrite) the induction conclusion at least once and does not attempt any other theorem proving method (thus reducing the search space at this point) and then tries to fertilise (exploit the induction hypothesis) once it is no longer possible to rewrite the conclusion. Atomic methods have the normal preconditions and effects (postconditions)[2] presentation. If all of an atomic method's preconditions are satisfied then it is applied and the effects are used to determine the new goal on which planning should be attempted.

λ*clam*[3] is implemented in λProlog, a higher order, strongly typed, modular logic programming language. λProlog is used to provide a declarative language for method precondition descriptions.

3.2   The Proof Strategy for Induction and Rippling

The proof strategy for induction can be seen in figure 1. This is implemented as a selection of atomic and compound methods. The diagram shows a top level repeat which attempts a disjunction of methods. These include basic propositional logic, generalisation of common subterms and also symbolic evaluation and the induction strategy (ind_strat). Within the induction strategy, the induction method performs ripple analysis [6] to choose an induction scheme (from a selection specified in λ*Clam*'s theories) and produces subgoals for base and step cases. The base cases are passed out to the repeat of the top level strategy. The step cases are annotated with *skeletons* and *embeddings* (described below) and then the wave method is repeatedly applied to them followed by fertilisation (exploitation of the induction hypothesis). Annotations are then removed. The methods (set_up_ripple and post_ripple) which place and remove annotations are omitted from the diagram. The results are then passed out to the top level strategy again. The process terminates when all subgoals have been reduced to *true* (or *false* in the case of failure).

We will discuss the wave_method in more detail since it was a new formulation of this method we wished to investigate. The wave method embodies the

---

[2] In λ*Clam* method postconditions are entirely concerned with generating the next subgoal (the output) – hence they are frequently called effects to illustrate their more restricted role.

[3] Details of λ*Clam* are at http://dream.dai.ed.ac.uk/systems/lambda-clam/. The current implementation can be obtained by emailing dream@dai.ed.ac.uk.

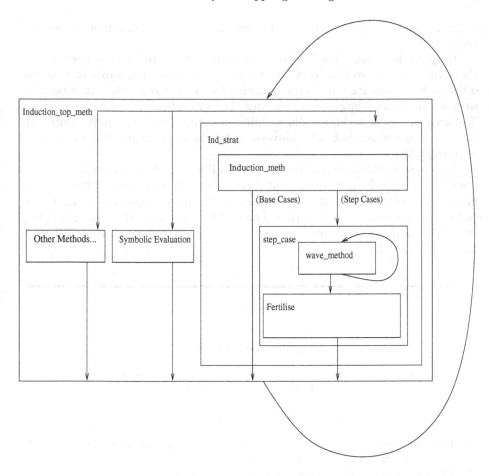

Fig. 1. The Proof Strategy for Induction.

rippling heuristic. Rippling was first introduced in [5]. We use the theory as presented by Smaill & Green [20] who proposed a version that naturally coped with higher-order features. Rippling steps apply rewrite rules to a target term which is associated with a skeleton and an embedding that relates the skeleton to the target term (e.g. rippling rewrites an induction conclusion which has an induction hypothesis embedded in it). In the present context, we make use of higher order rewriting, following the style of Felty [11]. The rewriting is implemented as a method; a rewriting step may correspond to a series of inference steps in the underlying object-logic system.

After rewriting a new embedding of the skeleton into the rewritten term is calculated. There is a measure on embeddings and any rewriting step must reduce this *embedding measure* (written as $<_\mu$). This is a generalisation of the original version of rippling that used annotated *wave rules* to rewrite annotated terms.

Rippling is terminating [2]. Rippling either moves differences outwards in the term structure so that they can be cancelled away or inwards so that the differences surround a universally quantified variable (or *sink*). If it is possible to move differences inwards in this way the embedding is said to be *sinkable*. The measure on embeddings allows differences that are being moved outwards to be moved inwards but not vice versa – this is at the heart of the guarantee of termination.

The `wave_method` method has five preconditions. It finds a rewrite rule that rewrites the goal. It then checks that there is still an embedding of the skeleton into the rewritten goal and that this new embedding is less, according to the embedding measure, than the original embedding. It checks that the embedding is sinkable and that any conditions for the application rule are trivial. This is shown in figure 2.

Input

$$ripple\_goal(H \vdash G, S, E).$$

where $ripple\_goal$ is a triple of a sequent, a skeleton, S and an embedding, E, of that skeleton into the goal, G.

Preconditions

1. The conditional rewrite rule $Rule$, $Cond \rightarrow X :\Rightarrow Y$ instantiated with some substitution σ, applies to G and rewrites it to G'.
2. There is an embedding E' that embeds S in G'.
3. $E' <_\mu E$.
4. $\sigma(Cond) = True$ or $\sigma(Cond) \in H$.
5. E' is sinkable.

Output

$$ripple\_goal(H \vdash G', S, E')$$

Fig. 2. The Wave Method.

The method will backtrack in order to try to satisfy all requirements, and if it is successful returns a new goal.

The main advantages of rippling is that it allows an equation to be treated as a rewrite in both directions without loss of termination and provides useful information for automatically patching failed proof attempts. These abilities were not required in this case study and all the proofs went through automatically using symbolic evaluation instead of rippling. However, our intention was to test the higher-order presentation of rippling *not* to justify its necessity in the case of ordinals.

Embeddings. We review here the notion of embeddings from Smaill & Green [20]. These provide a the higher-order framework for rippling used in this paper, in conjunction with higher-order rewriting introduced above.

Embeddings are described by a tree data structure. Embedding trees describe how a *skeleton* embeds in a term, called the *erasure*. The nodes in an embedding tree can be viewed as labels on the nodes in the term tree of the skeleton. These labels contain addresses and directions. The directions are used during rippling as outlined above. The addresses are the addresses of nodes in the term tree of the erasure which correspond to that node in the skeleton. Term trees represent function application and λ-abstraction explicitly as nodes with constant and variables symbols appearing only at the leaves of the tree. Our implementation also contains tuple nodes for lists of arguments to functions but these are not necessary to the theory. Embeddings do not annotate λ-abstraction nodes. Where an embedding matches a variable in the skeleton to one in the erasure it indicates that they are α-convertible. It is the ability to coherently handle λ-abstractions which was particularly valuable in this experiment. The ability to handle difference occurring within functions as well as the arguments to functions is also an extension of the previous calculus.

Example 1. Consider embedding the term $\lambda x.\ f(x)$ into the term $\lambda y.\ \lambda x.\ (f(y)+ x)$. We do this as in figure 3. The two terms are shown as trees with branches represented by solid lines. The address of each node is given (λ-abstraction nodes do not carry addresses). The embedding appears between them as an embedding tree with dashed lines – the address label of the nodes is also shown. The dotted arrows illustrate how the embedding tree links the two terms.

The embedding tree for this is (node [1, 2] [(leaf [1, 1, 1]) (leaf [2, 1, 2])])). This states that the function application at the top of $f(x)$ matches with the node at address [1, 2] of $f(y) + x$ (i.e. the application involving + has been bypassed), that the function symbol f matches the sub term at [2,1,1] (i.e. f) and x matches y (i.e. the bound variables can be consistently renamed in either (or both) terms so that they are identical).

The annotations originally used in rippling are still useful for presentation. Annotations consist of contexts (expressions with holes) indicated by a wave front (box) with a directional arrow. The holes in the context are wave holes (i.e. they are filled with an expression which is underlined). The skeleton is everything that appears outside wave fronts, or in wave holes. So the above embedding can be presented as

$$\lambda x.\ \boxed{\lambda y.\ \underline{f(y)} + x}^{\uparrow}.$$

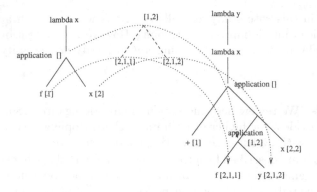

Fig. 3. An Embedding.

NB. It is important to remember that the annotations do not actually exist in the implementation which records instead the skeleton and embedding[4]. In some cases it is less easy to use the traditional annotations to represent embeddings, particularly when dealing with λ-abstractions which are ignored by the embedding trees. You can see that in the above the bound variables in the skeleton are assumed to have been appropriately renamed already. These annotations are just a presentational convenience.

4   Proof Planning Ordinal Arithmetic

To implement ordinal arithmetic in λ*Clam* we faced a number of tasks.

1. Provide a representation of ordinals, encompassing limit operations.
2. Provide, as rewrite rules, definitions for the standard arithmetical operators.
3. Determine an appropriate small set of support lemmas and provide these as additional rewrite rules.
4. Provide one or more induction schemes for transfinite induction.

The notion of rewriting here is higher-order, in the sense of Baader & Nipkow [1]. Thus variables in rewrite rules may be of functional type.

4.1   Representing Ordinals in λ*Clam*

It is simple to supply new constants and types for λ*Clam* in an appropriate module.

We know that 0 is an ordinal and that there are two ways of forming larger ordinals, either by applying the successor function, or taking the supremum

---

[4] In fact λ*Clam* maintains a list of possible embeddings during rippling since there may be more than one way to embed the induction hypotheses into the conclusion. For convenience we assume here there is only one.

(limit) of an indexed set of ordinals. So we were able to use these as constructors for a type *ordl*.

We chose to use the notation lim (the "limit" of a function) in the implementation. In fact, the definitional rewrite rules for plus etc. express the continuity of the standard operations, with respect to the standard topology on ordinals; however, the reader should understand uses of lim in what follows to correspond to the traditional supremum or set-theoretic union.

4.2   Defining the Arithmetical Operators

The first two clauses in the definition of plus are similar to the standard definition for natural numbers except that the recursion is defined on a non-standard argument:

$$x + 0 = x, \tag{7}$$
$$x + s(y) = s(x + y), \tag{8}$$

These become the rewrite rules

$$X + 0 \Leftarrow:\Rightarrow X, \tag{9}$$
$$X + s(Y) \Leftarrow:\Rightarrow s(X + Y), \tag{10}$$

in $\lambda Clam$. The symbol $\Leftarrow:\Rightarrow$ is used to indicate a pair of rewrite rules. These rules can be used in either direction during rippling but only from left to right in symbolic evaluation.

$\lambda Clam$ allows a user to state exactly which lemmas and definitions they wish to use. So the definitions were simply presented to the system as axioms in a special module for ordinals. This does place a burden on the user, however, to use only a consistent set of rewrites. We ensured this with a Lego construction of our rules. Our proof methods are all consistent with constructive type theory so the resulting plans represent proofs in constructive logic.

The final defining equation for addition is as follows:

$$x + \lim f = \lim \lambda n. \ (x + f(n)). \tag{11}$$

This then yields the rewrite rule

$$X + \lim F \Leftarrow:\Rightarrow \lim \lambda y. \ (X + F(y)) \tag{12}$$

in $\lambda Clam$. The following rewrites come from the similar defining equations for multiplication and exponentiation.

$$x \cdot 0 \Leftarrow:\Rightarrow 0, \tag{13}$$
$$x \cdot s(y) \Leftarrow:\Rightarrow (x \cdot y) + x, \tag{14}$$
$$x \cdot \lim f \Leftarrow:\Rightarrow \lim \lambda n. \ (x \cdot f(n)). \tag{15}$$

$$x^0 \Leftarrow:\Rightarrow s(0), \tag{16}$$
$$x^{s(y)} \Leftarrow:\Rightarrow (x^y) \cdot x, \tag{17}$$
$$x^{\lim f} \Leftarrow:\Rightarrow \lim \lambda n. \ (x^{f(n)}). \tag{18}$$

4.3   Defining Support Lemmas

We attempted to use as minimal a set of consistent support lemmas as possible. These are as follows.

First, reflexivity of equality: $(X = X) \Leftarrow:\Rightarrow true$.

The following rewrites are derived from implications not equations and so may only be used in one direction during proof. Three cancellation rewrites follow simply from the functionality of the operators concerned:

$$s(X) = s(Y) :\Rightarrow X = Y$$
$$X + Z = Y + Z :\Rightarrow X = Y$$
$$X \cdot Z = Y \cdot Z :\Rightarrow X = Y$$

Finally, we also introduced the following new rewrite that corresponds to a basic property of the lim operation.

$$\lim F = \lim G :\Rightarrow (\forall n : nat. \ F(n) = G(n)). \tag{19}$$

4.4   An Induction Scheme for Transfinite Induction

The induction scheme used follows from the definition of the data-type of ordinal notations and was developed in Lego. For reference this is:

$$\frac{\vdash P(0) \quad P(x) \vdash P(s(x)) \quad \forall n : nat. \ P(f(n)) \vdash P(\lim \lambda x. \ f(x))}{\vdash \forall \alpha : ordl. \ P(\alpha)} \tag{20}$$

This was added into the system in the ordinal module.

5   Evaluation

This machinery was enough to plan automatically the following goals. The times given are for a Sun E450 server dual processor machine with 2G of memory.

Theorem	Time Taken (CPU mins:secs)
$\forall \alpha : ordl. \ 0 + \alpha = \alpha,$	3.8
$\forall \alpha : ordl. \ \alpha + 1 = s(\alpha),$	0.8
$\forall \alpha, \beta, \gamma : ordl. \ (\alpha + \beta) + \gamma = \alpha + (\beta + \gamma),$	18.1
$\forall \alpha : ordl. \ 1 \cdot \alpha = \alpha,$	7.2
$\forall \alpha : ordl. \ \alpha \cdot 1 = \alpha,$	7.2
$\forall \alpha : ordl. \ \alpha \cdot 2 = \alpha + \alpha,$	5.0
$\forall \alpha, \beta, \gamma : ordl. \ \alpha \cdot (\beta + \gamma) = \alpha \cdot \beta + \alpha \cdot \gamma,$	1:09.5
$\forall \alpha, \beta, \gamma : ordl. \ (\alpha \cdot \beta) \cdot \gamma = \alpha \cdot (\beta \cdot \gamma),$	2:20.9
$\forall \alpha : ordl. \ \alpha^1 = \alpha,$	8.3
$\forall \alpha : ordl. \ \alpha^2 = \alpha \cdot \alpha,$	8.7
$\forall \alpha, \beta, \gamma : ordl. \ \alpha^{\beta + \gamma} = \alpha^\beta \cdot \alpha^\gamma,$	4:49.0
$\forall \alpha, \beta, \gamma : ordl. \ \alpha^{\beta \cdot \gamma} = \alpha^{\beta^\gamma}.$	7:04.9

These were drawn from exercises in three undergraduate text books [21,9,14]. They represent examples of ordinal arithmetic listed in those books which use only transfinite induction and the definitions of the arithmetical operators (i.e. which don't also use some set theoretic reasoning based on the definitions of ordinals) except for those involving the order relation. They were planned using only the given induction scheme, definitions and lemmas mentioned in section 4. Note that no use is made of earlier theorems in planning later ones in this list, which would of course reduce the timings substantially; this is because our aim is to achieve a significant amount of automation.

5.1   The Distributivity of Multiplication over Addition

As a sample of the sort of plan produced by λ *Clam* for these examples we present the plan for the distributivity of multiplication over addition. It is presented in a natural language way, but each step performed by the proof planner is marked.

Example 2. **Goal:**
λ *Clam* performs backwards proof so it starts with the initial goal.

$$\forall \alpha, \beta, \gamma : ordl. \, \alpha \cdot (\beta + \gamma) = \alpha \cdot \beta + \alpha \cdot \gamma. \tag{21}$$

`induction_top_meth` is applied to this. This tries each of its submethods in turn. Only one of these succeeds, `ind_strat`, because its submethod, `induction_meth` succeeds. Ripple analysis[5] suggests the use of induction on γ. This splits the goal into three subgoals; one base case and two step cases.
    Case 1:

$$\alpha \cdot (\beta + 0) = \alpha \cdot \beta + \alpha \cdot 0. \tag{22}$$

This is a base case and so is returned to `induction_top_meth` unaltered. This time symbolic evaluation succeeds and performs the following sequence of rewrites:

$$\alpha \cdot \beta = \alpha \cdot \beta + \alpha \cdot 0, \tag{23}$$
$$\alpha \cdot \beta = \alpha \cdot \beta + 0, \tag{24}$$
$$\alpha \cdot \beta = \alpha \cdot \beta, \tag{25}$$
$$true. \tag{26}$$

Case 2:
This is identical to the step case that would be produced in an attempt to proof plan the theorem using the traditional form of rippling.

$$\alpha \cdot (\beta + x) = \alpha \cdot \beta + \alpha \cdot x \vdash$$
$$\alpha \cdot (\beta + s(x)) = \alpha \cdot \beta + \alpha \cdot s(x). \tag{27}$$

---

[5] Ripple analysis analyses possible rewrites and chooses the variable most likely to promote extensive rewriting.

This is annotated and rippled as follows:

$$\alpha \cdot (\beta + \boxed{s(\underline{x})}^{\uparrow}) = \alpha \cdot \beta + \alpha \cdot \boxed{s(\underline{x})}^{\uparrow}, \tag{28}$$

$$\alpha \cdot \boxed{s(\beta + \underline{x})}^{\uparrow} = \alpha \cdot \beta + \alpha \cdot \boxed{s(\underline{x})}^{\uparrow}, \tag{29}$$

$$\boxed{\alpha \cdot (\beta + \underline{x}) + \alpha}^{\uparrow} = \alpha \cdot \beta + \alpha \cdot \boxed{s(\underline{x})}^{\uparrow}, \tag{30}$$

$$\boxed{\alpha \cdot (\beta + \underline{x}) + \alpha}^{\uparrow} = \alpha \cdot \beta + \boxed{(\underline{\alpha \cdot x} + \alpha)}^{\uparrow}. \tag{31}$$

Weak fertilisation (using the induction hypothesis as a rewrite rule) then returns the goal

$$(\alpha \cdot \beta + \alpha \cdot x) + \alpha = \alpha \cdot \beta + (\alpha \cdot x + \alpha). \tag{32}$$

Two generalise steps convert the goal to

$$(\delta + \zeta) + \alpha = \delta + (\zeta + \alpha). \tag{33}$$

The proof then continues as a proof for the associativity of plus, using a second induction.

Case 3:

The third case is the "new" step case containing the limit operation.

$$\begin{aligned} \alpha \cdot (\beta + f(n)) = \alpha \cdot \beta + \alpha \cdot f(n) \vdash \\ \alpha \cdot (\beta + \lim(\lambda x.\ f(x))) = \alpha \cdot \beta + \alpha \cdot \lim(\lambda x.\ f(x)). \end{aligned} \tag{34}$$

The induction assumption embeds in the conclusion, giving an annotation which is shown below. The notation $\lfloor \ \rfloor$ shows that there is a sink in the skeleton at this point.

$$\alpha \cdot (\beta + \boxed{\lim(\lambda x.\ f(\lfloor x \rfloor))}^{\uparrow}) = \alpha \cdot \beta + \alpha \cdot \boxed{\lim(\lambda x.\ f(\lfloor x \rfloor))}^{\uparrow}. \tag{35}$$

This ripples (using (12) – definition of +) to

$$\alpha \cdot \boxed{\lim(\lambda x.\ \underline{\beta + f(\lfloor x \rfloor)})}^{\uparrow} = \alpha \cdot \beta + \alpha \cdot \boxed{\lim(\lambda x.\ f(\lfloor x \rfloor))}^{\uparrow}. \tag{36}$$

The proof then proceeds rewriting with the definition of multiplication (15),

$$\boxed{\lim(\lambda x.\ \alpha \cdot \underline{(\beta + f(\lfloor x \rfloor))})}^{\uparrow} = \alpha \cdot \beta + \alpha \cdot \boxed{\lim(\lambda x.\ f(\lfloor x \rfloor))}^{\uparrow}. \tag{37}$$

$\lambda Clam$ then rewrites using (15) again,

$$\boxed{\lim(\lambda x.\ \alpha \cdot \underline{(\beta + f(\lfloor x \rfloor))})}^{\uparrow} = \alpha \cdot \beta + \boxed{\lim(\lambda x.\ \alpha \cdot f(\lfloor x \rfloor))}^{\uparrow} \tag{38}$$

λ*Clam* then rewrites using (12),

$$\boxed{\lim(\lambda x.\ \underline{\alpha \cdot (\beta + f(\lfloor x \rfloor)))}}^{\uparrow} = \boxed{\lim(\lambda x.\ \underline{\alpha \cdot \beta + \alpha \cdot f(\lfloor x \rfloor))}}^{\uparrow} \tag{39}$$

λ*Clam* then rewrites using (19),

$$\boxed{\forall n : nat.\ \underline{\alpha \cdot (\beta + f(\lfloor n \rfloor)) = \alpha \cdot \beta + \alpha \cdot f(\lfloor n \rfloor))}}^{\uparrow} . \tag{40}$$

Notice here that the formula has been β-reduced implicitly. This then succeeds by strong fertilisation (i.e. the conclusion is now follows simply from the induction hypothesis by manipulation of the universal quantifiers). It is no coincidence that the hypothesis and conclusion match at this point. The rippling heuristic is explicitly designed to bring this about. This whole proof has been automated in λ*Clam*.

5.2   The Synthesis of a Fixpoint for a Normal Function

One of our primary interests in creating λ*Clam* was to investigate the use of least-commitment reasoning in order to perform synthesis proofs. By this we mean placing uninstantiated meta-variables in proof goals which become instantiated during the course of the proof and generate an existential witness. We looked at a simple case where this style of reasoning could be using in the ordinal domain. This synthesis proof was performed automatically in λ*Clam*. It made no use of induction succeeding with the symbolic evaluation method alone.

Definition 1. *A function, ϕ, from ordinals to ordinals that is strictly increasing (preserves the order) and continuous is called* normal.

Theorem 2. *Any normal ϕ has a fixed point:*

$$\exists \eta.\ \phi(\eta) = \eta. \tag{41}$$

The continuity of ϕ is expressed by the rewrite

$$\phi(\lim(\lambda z.\ F(z))) \Longleftarrow:\Longrightarrow \lim \lambda z.\ \phi(F(z)). \tag{42}$$

We were able to synthesize such a fixed point using symbolic evaluation and the lemmas:

$$\lim \lambda n.\ F(s(n)) \Longleftarrow:\Longrightarrow \lim \lambda n.\ F(n), \tag{43}$$
$$\lambda n.\ F(F^n(A)) \Longleftarrow:\Longrightarrow \lambda n.\ F^{s(n)}(A) \tag{44}$$

where the second is simply a defining property of the iteration of function application, and the former holds for increasing functions.

The final planning proceeds as follows. Here, capital letters indicate meta-variables whose instantiation is refined during the planning process.

$$
\begin{aligned}
\exists \eta.\ \phi(\eta) &= \eta \\
\phi(E) &= E & \text{Exists Introduction} \\
\lim \lambda z.\ \phi(F(z)) &= \lim \lambda z.\ F(z) & \text{Rewriting LHS with (42)} \\
\lim \lambda z.\ \phi^{s(z)}(A) &= \lim \lambda z.\ \phi^{z}(A) & \text{Rewriting LHS with (44)} \\
\lim \lambda z.\ \phi^{z}(A) &= \lim \lambda z.\ \phi^{z}(A) & \text{Rewriting LHS with (43)} \\
\mathit{true}. & & \text{Rewriting the identity}
\end{aligned}
$$

As can be seen the system gradually instantiates the meta-variable, E, as it rewrites the terms. The plan shows that $\lim \lambda z.\ \phi^{z}(A)$ is a fixed point; as A is a meta-variable here, this shows that the proof will hold for *any* instantiation of A.

This plan is found with the small but appropriately chosen set of definitions and lemmas shown in this section. We feel it demonstrates the possible applications for higher-order proof planning systems in the ordinal domain.

6   Related and Further Work

Different mechanisations of reasoning about ordinals and cardinals have been carried out previously. For example, Paulson [17] introduces ordinals in the course of a development of set theory. While providing the foundational assurance of a development from first principles, this work assumes a fair amount of user interaction in building up proofs. A further development in this style is in [18]. Closer in spirit to our presentation is the introduction of ordinals in the Coq system, though again user guidance is assumed in building proofs as a new datatype.

The system, ACL2, described by Boyer & Moore [3] makes use of induction over ordinals to strengthen the proof system. However, this feature is hidden in the system's "black box" treatment used to check termination of user-defined functions, and is not directly accessible by the user. Following this work, PVS [16] also contains a construction of the ordinals up to ϵ_0 and an axiomatisation asserting well-foundedness for the associated order.

There are a number of extensions we would like to make to this case study. At a basic level we should like to include definitions for sums and products as presented by Suppes [21] and attempt to plan theorems with them. We should also like to implement the work on transitivity which allowed proofs involving order relations to be planned in *Clam* in λ*Clam* in order to plan theorems about the order on ordinals.

Moving on from this there are a number of more challenging theorems (as illustrated by our trial synthesis of a fixed point for a continuous function) to which our theory could be extended and which we believe would be a fruitful area of study for mechanised higher order proof.

7   Conclusion

We have chosen to examine ordinal arithmetic as a test case for the extension of the ideas of rippling and proof planning in a higher order setting. Our aim was to maintain the natural higher-order presentation of the ordinals while retaining full automation of the proof generation process.

We were greatly helped in our case study by the higher order features built into λProlog which removed the need for explicitly stating β-reduction as a rewrite rule and allowed side-conditions preventing variable capture to be left to the underlying language to handle.

With a small amount of theory building we were able to successfully plan standard undergraduate textbook examples and exercises. We were also able to demonstrate how proof planning, in particular least commitment devices such as the use of meta-variables, could have a part to play in the mechanisation of proof theoretic results in the ordinal domain. These results were confirmation that λ*Clam* can naturally handle higher order examples and that λProlog is a suitable language in which to express such mathematical concepts.

Thus, we claim to have identified common patterns of proof search that extend automated inductive theorem proving to the mathematically interesting higher order domain of ordinals and ordinal functions.

Acknowledgements

This research was funded by EPSRC grant Gr/m45030. We thank members of the Mathematical Reasoning Group, and especially Alan Bundy for input to this work. The presentation has benefited from the comments of the anonymous referees.

References

1. F. Baader and T. Nipkow. *Term Rewriting and All That*. Cambridge University Press, 1998.
2. David Basin and Toby Walsh. A calculus for and termination of rippling. *Journal of Automated Reasoning*, 16(1–2):147–180, 1996.
3. R. S. Boyer and J S. Moore. *A Computational Logic Handbook*. Academic Press, 1988. Perspectives in Computing, Vol 23.
4. A. Bundy. The use of explicit plans to guide inductive proofs. In R. Lusk and R. Overbeek, editors, *9th International Conference on Automated Deduction*, pages 111–120. Springer-Verlag, 1988. Longer version available from Edinburgh as DAI Research Paper No. 349.
5. A. Bundy, A. Stevens, F. van Harmelen, A. Ireland, and A. Smaill. Rippling: A heuristic for guiding inductive proofs. *Artificial Intelligence*, 62:185–253, 1993. Also available from Edinburgh as DAI Research Paper No. 567.
6. Alan Bundy. The automation of proof by mathematical induction. In A. Robinson and A. Voronkov, editors, *Handbook of Automated Reasoning*. Elsevier., 1998. Forthcoming.
7. A. Cichon and H. Touzet. An ordinal calculus for proving termination in term rewriting. In *Proceedings of CAAP'96, Coll. on Trees in Algebra and Programming*, number 1059 in Lecture Notes in Computer Science. Springer, 1996.
8. Th. Coquand. *Une Théorie des Constructions*. PhD thesis, University of Paris VII, 1985.

9. Herbert B. Enderton. *Elements of Set Theory*. Academic Press, 1977.
10. W. M. Farmer, J. D. Guttman, and F. J. Thayer. IMPS : an interactive mathematical proof system. *Journal of Automated Reasoning*, 9(11):213–248, 1993.
11. A. Felty. A logic programming approach to implementing higher-order term rewriting. In L-H Eriksson et al., editors, *Second International Workshop on Extensions to Logic Programming*, volume 596 of *Lecture Notes in Artificial Intelligence*, pages 135–61. Springer-Verlag, 1992.
12. Lego group. Lego home page. http://www.dcs.ed.ac.uk/home/lego/.
13. P. Halmos. *Naive Set Theory*. Van Nostrand, Princeton, NJ, 1960.
14. A. G. Hamilton. *Numbers, sets and axioms: the apparatus of mathematics*. Cambridge University Press, 1982.
15. Jean-Pierre Jouannaud and Mitsuhiro Okada. Satisfiability of systems of ordinal notations with the subterm property is decidable. In *Proceedings of the Eighteenth EATCS Colloquium on Automata, Languages and Programming*, Madrid, Spain, 1991.
16. S. Owre, J. M. Rushby, and N. Shankar. PVS : An integrated approach to specification and verification. Tech report, SRI International, 1992.
17. L.C. Paulson. Set theory for verification: II. induction and recursion. *Journal of Automated Reasoning*, 15:353–389, 1995.
18. L.C. Paulson and K. Grabczewski. Mechanizing set theory: cardinal arithmetic and the axiom of choice. *Journal of Automated Reasoning*, pages 291–323, 1996.
19. J.D.C Richardson, A. Smaill, and Ian Green. System description: proof planning in higher-order logic with LambdaCLAM. In Claude Kirchner and Hélène Kirchner, editors, *15th International Conference on Automated Deduction*, volume 1421 of *Lecture Notes in Artificial Intelligence*, pages 129–133, Lindau, Germany, July 1998.
20. Alan Smaill and Ian Green. Higher-order annotated terms for proof search. In Joakim von Wright, Jim Grundy, and John Harrison, editors, *Theorem Proving in Higher Order Logics: 9th International Conference, TPHOLs'96*, volume 1275 of *Lecture Notes in Computer Science*, pages 399–414, Turku, Finland, 1996. Springer-Verlag. Also available as DAI Research Paper 799.
21. P. Suppes. *Axiomatic Set Theory*. Van Nostrand, Princeton, NJ, 1960.

Abstraction and Refinement
in Higher Order Logic*

Matt Fairtlough, Michael Mendler, and Xiaochun Cheng **

Department of Computer Science, The University of Sheffield
Regent Court, 211 Portobello Street, Sheffield S1 4DP, UK
{matt,michael}@dcs.shef.ac.uk

Abstract. We develop within higher order logic (HOL) a general and flexible method of abstraction and refinement, which specifically addresses the problem of handling constraints. We provide a HOL interpretation of first-order Lax Logic, which can be seen as a modal extension of deliverables. This provides a new technique for automating reasoning about behavioural constraints by allowing constraints to be associated with, but formally separated from, an abstracted model. We demonstrate a number of uses, *e.g.* achieving a formal separation of the logical and timing aspects of hardware design, and systematically generating timing constraints for a simple sequential device from a formal proof of its abstract behaviour. The method and proofs have been implemented in Isabelle as a definitional extension of the HOL logic which extends work by Jacobs and Melham on encoding dependent types in HOL. We assume familiarity with HOL but not detailed knowledge of circuit design.

1 Introduction

In this paper we develop within HOL a general method of abstraction and refinement, and apply it, by way of an instructive example, to the problem of synthesising timing constraints in sequential circuit design. Fig. 1 illustrates our general approach: we view the abstraction process as one of *separation of concerns*, which involves splitting a concrete model or theory into two dimensions which we term the *deductive* and *constraint* dimensions. Along the deductive dimension we *deduce* abstract consequences of our theory, and this process corresponds to traditional abstraction

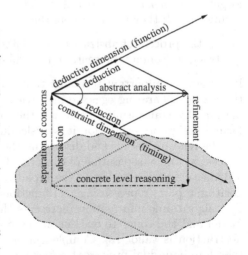

Fig. 1. Diagram of Our Method.

* This work was partially supported by EPSRC under grant GR/L86180.
** Department of Computer Science, Reading University. x.cheng@reading.ac.uk.

methods in Artificial Intelligence as presented, for example, in [16]. Along the constraint dimension we track the discrepancies between the abstract and concrete models by computing and *reducing* the constraints under which the abstraction is valid: our method is of practical use insofar as this process can be automated for the constraint domain involved. A key ingredient in our method is an algorithm for recombining the two dimensions at any point, a process implicit in [10] and strongly related to realizability [17] which we term *refinement*. It is this constraint dimension and the associated concept of refinement that appears to be missing in the AI literature. If we perform an abstraction on a concrete model, develop an abstract analysis and then refine the result, we obtain a concrete consequence which could have been obtained by concrete level reasoning alone; however we argue that the abstraction mechanism will often make it easier to obtain the desired result. In our main example we apply the method to the generation of timing constraints for an RS latch, addressing an open problem raised in [8] and by [9]: a formal proof of circuit behaviour is produced (deduction) at an abstract level at which timing details are elided; an interpretation of the proof as a *constraint λ-term* then yields a concrete proof of correctness incorporating the necessary timing constraints (reduction). The key difference to the previous works is that the constraints are systematically synthesised and do not need to be anticipated at the outset.

Abstraction in Artificial Intelligence. Abstraction techniques have been extensively applied and studied in Artificial Intelligence. See for example [16, 7]. In [7] Walsh and Guinchiglia present a very general method to analyse the uses of abstraction in a number of different fields such as theorem proving, planning, problem solving and approximate reasoning. They give an informal definition of abstraction as a process which "allows people to consider what is *relevant* and forget a lot of *irrelevant* details which would get in the way of what they are trying to do"; they go on to note that

> ... the process of abstraction is related to the process of *separating*, extracting from a representation an "abstract" representation ...

It is however important to realize that separation does not just involve extraction; after separating eggs we may wish to use the white as well as the yolk, perhaps by transforming both and then recombining them. In the context of formal design or verification it is misleading to think of abstraction as extracting the relevant details and discarding the rest as irrelevant; rather we view the process as one of separation of concerns: for example, a system can be split into a deductive part, relating to the broad functionality of the system, and an algorithmic part, representing non-functional aspects such as timing properties. The algorithmic information represents the offset between the abstract system model and the concrete one, *i.e.* it represents the *constraints* under which the abstraction is valid [13]. Complementing the abstraction process there should therefore be a dual process of *refinement*, in which the areas of concern are recombined and constraints are (re-)generated. In the examples we present in this paper, the result of refinement is a concrete-level statement that the system has the required functionality provided the constraints are satisfied.

Abstraction and Constraints in Hardware Verification. There is a substantial amount of work on the use of abstraction techniques in formal hardware verification. We cite [5, 6, 1] and [12] as early publications. A fundamental obstacle to the sound use of abstraction techniques is that the associated constraints accumulate in the opposite direction to the proof effort, whether forward or goal-directed proof methods are used. Thus a situation typically arises where it is not known at the outset what exactly needs to be proved. A knock-on effect of the presence of constraints is a loss of compositionality or modularity with respect to refinement.

Although pervasive, this problem of non-compositionality has not often been clearly delineated in the literature. A notable exception is [1]. In his discussion of hierarchical design methods, Eveking presents an example which "...shows that, in the general case, one has to make a *complete reanalysis* of a switch-level network even if the correctness of the fragments was proven". Our research shows how such a painful reanalysis may be mitigated, since a lack of attention to lower level constraints is a major stumbling block to the successful decomposition of systems at an abstract level.

In [12] Melham takes two approaches to the problem of handling the constraints involved in the abstraction process. The first process he calls "abstraction within models", and involves theorems of the form $\vdash C \supset M \underset{F}{\text{sat}} S$ where M represents the implementation, S the specification and C the constraints under which the implementation satisfies the specification. F is an abstraction function that serves to relate *e.g.* concrete information to its abstract counterpart. Constraints are handled using explicit rules. In our approach, the abstraction is explicit and the associated constraint rules are implicit, being generated from the abstraction itself. This may prove to be more convenient and flexible in applications.

Melham's second abstraction process is called "abstraction between models" and involves a formal proof of a relationship between hardware models which may be seen as saying "provided certain design rules are followed, the abstract model is a valid description of concrete behaviour". The relevant constraints are automatically satisfied for any correct combination of basic components. [5] takes essentially the same approach. The approach has two limitations: firstly the concrete model at least must be represented by a deep embedding in the object logic, and secondly an adequate set of design rules must be discovered and formalised. While this approach can be highly effective, in general it is not possible to find such a set of design rules, or they are deliberately broken to optimise designs. In contrast, our approach does not require a deep embedding of the concrete model or a formalised set of design rules.

Our Contribution. Our approach involves maintaining a close connection between abstraction (the deductive dimension) and constraints (the algorithmic dimension). The algorithmic aspect corresponds to the *calculation* of constraints, and in accordance with this principle we record the "irrelevant" information as sets of constraint λ-terms. Let us consider a small example to explain our approach. We define three concrete formulas as follows

$$\psi_1 = \forall s.(s \geq 5) \supset (P_1 \, a \, \underline{s}) \qquad \psi_2 = \forall s, y.(s \geq 9 \cdot y) \supset (P_2 \, (f \, y) \, \underline{s})$$

$$\psi_3 = \forall t, y_1, y_2.(\exists s.(t \geq s + 35) \wedge (P_1 \, y_1 \, \underline{s}) \wedge (P_2 \, y_2 \, \underline{s})) \supset (Q \, (g(y_1, y_2)) \, \underline{t}).$$

These formulas can be seen as representing three components linked together: ψ_1 represents a component P_1 which constantly delivers an output a once 5 time units have elapsed, ψ_2 represents a component P_2 which non-deterministically outputs a value $f(y)$ once $9 \cdot y$ time units have elapsed, and ψ_3 represents their connection to a component Q which takes the outputs from P_1 and P_2 and transforms them using function g, producing the result after a delay of 35 time units. In order to separate the functional and timing aspects, we choose to abstract parameters s from P_1 and P_2 and t from Q, treating the formulas $s \geq 5$, $s \geq 9 \cdot y$ and $t \geq s + 35$ as constraints which should also be hidden at the abstract, functional level. We have indicated the fact that certain parameters and formulas are to be abstracted by underlining them. We use s and t for time variables and y, y_1 and y_2 for data variables. The results of applying the abstraction process to these formulas ψ_i are then

$$\psi_1^{\sharp} = \lambda s.s \geq 5 : \bigcirc_\forall (P_1 \, a) \qquad \psi_2^{\sharp} = \lambda y, s.s \geq 9 \cdot y : \forall y.\bigcirc_\forall (P_2 \, (f \, y))$$

$$\psi_3^{\sharp} = \lambda y_1, y_2, z, t.(\pi_1 z = \pi_2 z \wedge t \geq \pi_1 z + 35) :$$

$$\forall y_1, y_2.((P_1 \, y_1) \wedge (P_2 \, y_2)) \supset \bigcirc_\forall (Q \, (g(y_1, y_2)))$$

Each new expression $\psi_i^{\sharp}$ is of the form $\psi_i^{\sharp_1} : \psi_i^{\sharp_2}$ where $\psi_i^{\sharp_1}$ is a *constraint* λ-*term* and $\psi_i^{\sharp_2}$ is an *abstract formula*. We shall see later that the : constructor and the modal operator $\bigcirc_\forall$ used in these expressions may be *defined* within HOL so that ψ_i is equivalent to $\psi_i^{\sharp}$ for $1 \leq i \leq 3$. Thus, our abstraction method is a definitional extension of HOL. Informally, the occurrence of the modal operator $\bigcirc_\forall$ in the abstract formula $\bigcirc_\forall (P_1 \, a)$ can be explained by reading the formula as: *under some constraint $C \, s$ on the hidden parameter s, $P_1 \, a \, s$ holds*, formally $\forall s.C \, s \supset P_1 \, a \, s$. In other words, $\bigcirc_\forall (P_1 \, a)$ indicates that $P_1 \, a$ is to be *weakened* by some constraint on the implicit constraint parameter s. Later, we shall see that it is convenient to have a dual modal operator $\bigcirc_\exists (P_1 \, a)$ to express a *strengthening* constraint $\exists s \, . \, C \, s \wedge P_1 \, a \, s$. The simplest form of abstraction occurs when $C \, s$ is an equality constraint $s = d$ for some term d. Then both $\forall s. \, s = d \supset P_1 \, a \, s$ and $\exists s.s = d \wedge P_1 \, a \, s$ are equivalent to $P_1 \, a \, d$. In this case we may simply write $d : P_1 \, a$ as an abstraction of $P_1 \, a \, d$, i.e. the constraint λ-term is the parameter term d itself.

Having performed an abstraction, we will want to use formal reasoning to deduce abstract properties of the system under consideration. It turns out that the higher order nature of the $\bigcirc_\forall$ modality allows us in many instances to confine our reasoning to a first-order (modal) framework. In section 2 we present a set of rules which are derivable within HOL when extended by abstraction and refinement equations (Fig. 4 for interpreting formulas of the form $p : M$. We may use the rules to deduce abstract consequences of our abstract theory $\Psi^{\sharp} = \psi_1^{\sharp}, \psi_2^{\sharp}, \psi_3^{\sharp}$, for example there is a constraint λ-term p such that

$$\Psi^{\sharp} \vdash p : \exists v.\bigcirc_\forall Q(v). \tag{1}$$

The crucial point here is that the derivation of (1) may be obtained by proceeding along two independent and well-separated dimensions of reasoning: some steps may manipulate the abstract formulas on right-hand side of :, which in this case pertain to functional aspects; other steps may focus on the constraint λ-terms on the left-hand side of :, which contain constraint information. While the analysis of constraint terms, which is done by equational reasoning may in certain domains be decidable and automatic, the abstract formulas require proper logical deduction, which in general is interactive and undecidable. The fact that both aspects are clearly separated by the colon : allows us to benefit from this methodological distinction. At any point, however, the two parts of an abstract conclusion $p : \exists v.\bigcirc_\forall Q(v)$ (whether or not it has been obtained in this structured fashion) may be re-combined to give a concrete-level formula. Note that p is playing a dual role: on the one hand it can be seen as a proof term witnessing how the abstract conclusion $\exists v.\bigcirc_\forall Q(v)$ has been reached; on the other hand it can be seen as a constraint (realiser) for refining the conclusion into a concrete level consequence of the theory Ψ. This is achieved by applying the equivalences in section 2 which allow us to calculate that $p : \exists v.\bigcirc_\forall Q(v)$ is equivalent to the concrete level formula stating that the value $g(a, f(a))$ must appear on the output of Q after at most $(\max 5 (9 \cdot f(a))) + 35$ time units:

$$\forall u.u \geq (\max 5 (9 \cdot f(a))) + 35 \supset (Q (g(a, f(a))) u).$$

2   Higher-Order Framework: Technical Details

We take as *base logic* a polymorphic classical higher order logic such as is implemented in Isabelle. We also assume a suitably closed subset Φ of formulas of higher order logic to act as constraints. In our general implementation, we allow arbitrary formulas of HOL, while a restricted set of formulas might be used in more specialised settings. These constraints can appear in λ-terms, as we saw earlier, and indeed it is this feature that gives our approach bite. We use the notation $T \vdash_B M$ to express the fact that M is a consequence of formulas T in the base logic and $\Delta \vdash_B t :: \alpha$ to express the fact that the HOL term t has type α in the context Δ of typed variables.

Abstraction and Refinement. We introduce the notation $p : M$ as a syntactic abbreviation in the base logic, where the first component p is a constraint λ-term and M is an abstract formula. Fig. 2 gives the raw (*i.e.* untyped) syntax of constraint λ-terms p and the syntax of the abstract language to which M must belong. The formula $p : M$ will only be well-formed under certain conditions on p and M. In order to define when a pair $p : M$ is properly formed, we give a mapping from formulas M of our abstract language into refinement types $|M|$ of higher order logic according to Fig. 3 and require that $\vdash_B p :: |M|$. We refer to $|M|$ as the *refinement type* of M.

Note that the mapping removes any dependency of types on object level terms, *i.e.* $|M| = |M\{\sigma\}|$ for any substitution σ of terms for object level variables of M. Also note that both *false* and *true* are mapped to the unit type $\mathbf{1}$. We

$$p ::= z \mid * \mid c \mid (p,p) \mid \pi_1(p) \mid \pi_2(p) \mid$$
$$\quad \text{case } p \text{ of } [\iota_1(z_1) \to p, \iota_2(z_2) \to p] \mid \iota_1(p) \mid \iota_2(p) \mid$$
$$\quad \lambda z.p \mid p\,p \mid \text{val}_\forall(p) \mid \text{val}_\exists(p) \mid \text{let}_\forall z \Leftarrow p \text{ in } p \mid \text{let}_\exists z \Leftarrow p \text{ in } p$$
$$\quad \langle p \mid x \rangle \mid \pi_t\,p \mid \iota_t(p) \mid \text{case } p \text{ of } [\iota_x(z) \to p]$$
$$M ::= A \mid \text{false} \mid \text{true} \mid M \wedge M \mid M \vee M \mid M \supset M \mid$$
$$\quad \bigcirc_\forall M \mid \bigcirc_\exists M \mid \forall x.\,M \mid \exists x.\,M$$

x ranges over object variables, z, z_1, z_2 over proof variables, t over well-formed object-level terms and c over constraint formulas in Φ. A is a meta-variable for atomic formulas $R\,t_1 \ldots t_n$. Negated formulas $\neg M$ are defined by $M \supset \text{false}$.

Fig. 2. Syntax of Constraint λ-Terms and Abstract Formulas.

choose a non-empty type for each formula as empty types are inconsistent with our base logic. The meaning of a well-formed pair $p : M$ is now given by Fig. 4 by

$\|P\| := \alpha$ if $P :: \alpha \Rightarrow \mathbb{B}$	$\|M_1 \wedge M_2\| := \|M_1\| \times \|M_2\|$	$\|\bigcirc_\exists M\| := \|M\| \Rightarrow \mathbb{B}$
$\|true\| := \mathbf{1}$	$\|M_1 \vee M_2\| := \|M_1\| + \|M_2\|$	$\|\bigcirc_\forall M\| := \|M\| \Rightarrow \mathbb{B}$
$\|false\| := \mathbf{1}$	$\|M_1 \supset M_2\| := \|M_1\| \Rightarrow \|M_2\|$	$\|\forall x :: \alpha.M\| := \alpha \Rightarrow \|M\|$
		$\|\exists x :: \alpha.M\| := \alpha \times \|M\|$

Fig. 3. Refinement Types of Abstract Formulas.

recursion on the structure of M. We can read these equations in either direction: from left to right they are used to refine an abstract proof/formula pair into the concrete base logic by zipping p and M together to produce $(p : M)^\flat$, thereby completely eliminating the colon. We call this process *refinement*. From right to left, they can be used to completely separate a formula M into a constraint term $M^{\sharp_1}$ and an abstract formula $M^{\sharp_2}$. The process of generating the pair $M^\sharp = M^{\sharp_1} : M^{\sharp_2}$ we call *abstraction*. Let us first look at ψ_1 from the introduction.

$$(p : true) = true \quad \text{and} \quad (p : false) = false$$
$$(p : P) = P\,p \quad \text{if } P :: \alpha \Rightarrow \mathbb{B} \text{ and } p :: \alpha$$
$$(p : M \wedge N) = (\pi_1(p) : M) \wedge (\pi_2(p) : N)$$
$$(p : M \vee N) = \text{case } p \text{ of } [\iota_1(x) \to (x : M), \iota_2(y) \to (y : N)]$$
$$(p : M \supset N) = \forall z :: \|M\|.\,(z : M) \supset (p\,z : N)$$
$$(p : \forall x :: \alpha.\,M) = \forall u :: \alpha.\,(p\,u : M\{u/x\})$$
$$(p : \exists x :: \alpha.\,M) = \pi_2(p) : M\{\pi_1(p)/x\}$$
$$(p : \bigcirc_\exists M) = \exists z :: \|M\|.\,p\,z \wedge (z : M)$$
$$(p : \bigcirc_\forall M) = \forall z :: \|M\|.\,p\,z \supset (z : M)$$

Fig. 4. Equations for Abstraction and Refinement.

We can apply the following sequence of equivalences from Fig. 4 and standard equations of higher order logic to generate the abstraction $\psi_1{}^\sharp$: $\forall s . (s \geq 5) \supset (P_1\, a\, s) \equiv \forall s . (s \geq 5) \supset (s : P_1\, a) \equiv \forall s . (\lambda s . s \geq 5)\, s \supset (s : P_1\, a) \equiv \lambda s . s \geq 5 : (\bigcirc_\forall (P_1\, a))$. The next example shows that we can pull an arbitrary constraint formula c into a proof term: $c \equiv c \wedge true \equiv \exists z :: \mathbf{1} . ((\lambda z . c)\, z \wedge z : true) \equiv \lambda z . c : \bigcirc_\exists true$. Finally, we can pull arbitrary terms out of disjunctions as follows: $M\, p \vee N\, q \equiv p : M \vee q : N \equiv \exists z . |M| + |N| . \mathsf{case}\ z\ \mathsf{of}\ [\iota_1(x_1) \rightarrow x_1 = p,\ \iota_2(x_2) \rightarrow x_2 = q] \wedge z : (M \vee N) \equiv \lambda z . \mathsf{case}\ z\ \mathsf{of}\ [\iota_1(x_1) \rightarrow x_1 = p,\ \iota_2(x_2) \rightarrow x_2 = q] : \bigcirc_\exists (M \vee N)$. In a similar way, we can abstract out of conjunctions, implications and quantifiers. In essence, we can abstract out arbitrary sub-terms or formulas out of first-order syntax, which generalises both parameter abstraction [16] and constraint abstraction [13].

Lemma 1 (Conservativity over HOL). *Our definitions and equations for formulas of the form $p : M$ are a conservative extension of HOL.*

In fact, our implementation in Isabelle/HOL provides a purely definitional extension using a non-recursive encoding of a new set of logical operators, from which the equations of Fig. 4 are derived. We return to this point in our conclusions.

Abstract Reasoning (Deduction). In Fig. 5 we present a set of rules to be used to progress an abstract analysis along the deductive dimension, driven only by the right hand side of :. These rules are a variant of QLL [3, 4] and are derivable in the base logic from the equations of Fig. 4. They represent a standard first-order, constructive logic with proof terms extended by two modalities $\bigcirc_\exists$ and $\bigcirc_\forall$ which correspond to two independent strong monads, extrapolating the Curry-Howard correspondence between formulas and types.

Constraint Reasoning (Reduction). Constraint reasoning proceeds by equational rewriting of the constraint λ-terms on the left hand side of :. This involves both the standard β, η equations of λ-calculus and special constraint simplifications that can be generated from the equations 6. These latter equations in fact provide a computational semantics for the proof term constructors such as $\mathsf{case}\ p_1\ \mathsf{of}\ [\iota_1(z_1) \rightarrow p_2,\ \iota_2(z_2) \rightarrow p_3]$ or $\mathsf{val}_\forall(p)$ which are special to our constraint λ-calculus. These equations, called γ-equations in [2], are justified by the definition of $p : M$ as an abbreviation in HOL.

3   Our Method in Practice

We give three examples of practical applications of our method. The first provides an extension of constraint logic programming (CLP), the second is an example of a simple combinational circuit with inductive structure and the third is the latch case study first verified by Herbert in [9].

Returning to the example specification of the introduction, we observe that the formulas of Ψ are in fact (equivalent to) Horn clauses. The standard resolution rules for logic programming can be extended by lax resolution rules which

$$\frac{}{\Gamma, z : M, \Gamma' \vdash z : M} \, I \qquad \frac{\Gamma, z : M, \Gamma' \vdash q : N}{\Gamma, p : M, \Gamma' \vdash q\{p/x\} : N} \, Subst \quad (p :: |M|)$$

$$\frac{\Gamma \vdash p : M \quad \Gamma \vdash q : N}{\Gamma \vdash (p,q) : M \wedge N} \, \wedge_I \qquad \frac{\Gamma \vdash r : M \wedge N}{\Gamma \vdash \pi_1(r) : M} \, \wedge_\varepsilon \qquad \frac{\Gamma \vdash r : M \wedge N}{\Gamma \vdash \pi_2(r) : N} \, \wedge_\varepsilon$$

$$\frac{\Gamma \vdash r : M \vee N \quad \Gamma, y : M \vdash p : K \quad \Gamma, z : N \vdash q : K}{\Gamma \vdash \text{case } r \text{ of } [\iota_1(y) \to p, \, \iota_2(z) \to q] : K} \, \vee_\varepsilon$$

$$\frac{\Gamma \vdash p : M}{\Gamma \vdash \iota_1(p) : M \vee N} \, \vee_I \qquad \frac{\Gamma \vdash q : N}{\Gamma \vdash \iota_2(q) : M \vee N} \, \vee_I$$

$$\frac{\Gamma, z : M \vdash p : N}{\Gamma \vdash \lambda z. p : M \supset N} \, \supset_I \qquad \frac{\Gamma \vdash p : M \supset N \quad \Gamma \vdash q : M}{\Gamma \vdash p \, q : N} \, \supset_\varepsilon$$

$$\frac{\Gamma \vdash p : M}{\Gamma \vdash \text{val}_Q(p) : \bigcirc_Q M} \, \bigcirc_I \quad \text{if } Q = \forall \text{ or } Q = \exists$$

$$\frac{\Gamma \vdash p : \bigcirc_Q M \quad \Gamma, z : M \vdash q : \bigcirc_Q N}{\Gamma \vdash \text{let}_Q \, z \Leftarrow p \text{ in } q : \bigcirc_Q N} \, \bigcirc_\varepsilon \quad \text{if } Q = \forall \text{ or } Q = \exists$$

$$\frac{\Gamma \vdash p : M}{\Gamma \vdash \langle p \mid x \rangle : \forall x. M} \, \forall_I \quad (x \text{ not free in } \Gamma) \qquad \frac{\Gamma \vdash p : \forall x. M}{\Gamma \vdash \pi_t(p) : M[t/x]} \, \forall_\varepsilon$$

$$\frac{\Gamma \vdash p : M[t/x]}{\Gamma \vdash \iota_t(p) : \exists x. M} \, \exists_I \qquad \frac{}{\Gamma \vdash * : true} \, true_I$$

$$\frac{\Gamma \vdash r : \exists x. M \quad \Gamma, z : M \vdash p : K}{\Gamma \vdash \text{case } r \text{ of } [\iota_x(z) \to p] : K} \, \exists_\varepsilon \quad (x \text{ not free in } K \text{ or } \Gamma)$$

Fig. 5. Natural Deduction Rules for Abstract Logic.

$$\begin{aligned} \langle p \mid x \rangle &= \lambda x. p & \pi_t(p) &= p \, t \\ \iota_t(p) &= (t, p) & \text{case } r \text{ of } [\iota_x(z) \to p] &= p\{\pi_1(r)/x, \pi_2(r)/z\} \\ \text{val}_Q(x) &= \lambda y. x = y & (\text{let}_Q \, z \Leftarrow p \text{ in } q) &= \lambda x. \exists z. p \, z \wedge q \, x \\ c &= d \quad (c, d \in \Phi, \, \vdash_B c \Longleftrightarrow d) \end{aligned}$$

Fig. 6. Interpretation of Proof Terms.

also handle the modality $\bigcirc_\forall$ (and in fact, $\bigcirc_\exists$ also). For example,

$$\frac{\Gamma \vdash p : \bigcirc_Q M \quad \Gamma \vdash q : \bigcirc_Q N}{\Gamma \vdash \wedge_\bigcirc(p,q) : \bigcirc_Q(M \wedge N)} \, \wedge_\bigcirc \qquad \frac{\Gamma \vdash r : M \supset N \quad \Gamma \vdash p : \bigcirc_Q M}{\Gamma \vdash \supset_\bigcirc(r,p) : \bigcirc_Q N} \, \supset_\bigcirc.$$

The first rule states that a constraint p for M and a constraint q for N can be combined to form a constraint $\wedge_\bigcirc(p,q) = \lambda(w,z). p \, w \wedge q \, z$ for $M \wedge N$, while the second that a constraint p for M can be propagated through an implication $r : M \supset N$. The resulting constraint $\supset_\bigcirc(r,p)$ is provably equal to $\lambda z. \exists m. p \, m \wedge z = r \, m$. The second rule also has a variant more useful in resolution in which the first premise has the form $\Gamma \vdash r : M \supset \bigcirc_Q N$. In [2] we have shown that the standard semantics for CLP can be faithfully represented by a resolution strategy including lax versions of the usual resolution rules. More precisely, the execution of a CLP program corresponds to a lax resolution strategy for proofs and the CLP constraint analysis corresponds to the reduction of proof terms in our framework. This means that we can use our abstraction method to separate the constraints from any CLP program, producing an abstract lax logic program and a separate constraint table. The abstract program may be run using a lax form of SLD resolution and the corresponding constraints generated from the table. We conjecture that our results can be extended to higher order hereditary Harrop formulas.

The second example is taken from [13] where Mendler sets himself the task of realising the abstract successor function at the concrete level of bit vectors. He defines $Inc_w :: \mathbb{B}^w \Rightarrow \mathbb{B}^w$ as a cascade of w half-adders which implements the successor function provided the result can be encoded as a word of at most w bits. This overflow constraint is constructed by a recursion mirroring the recursive construction of the incrementor itself. The abstract goal to prove is

$$\forall w, n . \bigcirc_{\forall} ((\alpha_w \circ Inc_w \circ \rho_w) n = n + 1)$$

where $\alpha_w :: \mathbb{B}^w \Rightarrow \mathbb{N}$ and $\rho_w :: \mathbb{N} \Rightarrow \mathbb{B}^w$ are the abstraction and realisation mappings that translate from bit vectors to numbers and conversely. The constraint generated by the lax proof of the goal is $\lambda w, n . f \, w \, n \, true$ where f is defined recursively by $f \, 0 \, n \, c = (n = 0 \wedge \neg c)$ and $f \, (k+1) \, n \, c = f \, k \, (n \div 2) \, (n = 1$ $(mod \, 2) \wedge c)$. This constraint has computational behaviour, but it can also be shown to be equivalent to a flattened version $n + 1 < 2^w$. The key difference lies in the fact that in certain contexts the recursive version may *evaluate* to the trivial constraint, while the flattened version would have to be *proved* trivial. Note that the inductive basis of the constraint $f \, w \, n \, true$ when $w = 0$, which is $(n = 0 \wedge \neg true)$, is not only unsatisfiable, but in fact inconsistent. In other words, the abstract proof started from an inconsistent base case. Nevertheless, the lax proof returns a satisfiable constraint, since there are solutions to the constraint $n + 1 < 2^w$ for any fixed $w > 0$.

Finally we apply our method to the RS latch, which is illustrated in Fig. 7. The latch is the simplest of three memory devices verified by Herbert in [9]. He verifies the device in the HOL system at a detailed timing level, using a discrete model of time and a transport model of basic component behaviour. For example, he defines a NOR gate as

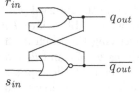

Fig. 7. RS Latch.

NOR2(in0, in1, out, del) := $\forall t. \, \text{out} \, (t + del) =$ $\neg(\text{in0} \, t \, \vee \, \text{in1} \, t)$ and the latch as NOR2(r_{in}, $\overline{q_{out}}$, d_1, q_{out}) $\wedge$ NOR2(s_{in}, q_{out}, d_2, $\overline{q_{out}}$) . It is clear that the proofs he presents are the result of several iterations which were needed to discover the exact timing constraints necessary to prove them. Similar problems were reported in the work by Hanna and Daeche [8]. The main improvement yielded by our approach is that we do not need to make repeated attempts to prove the memory properties, because the timing constraints are synthesised in the course of the abstract analysis.

Our previous work *e.g.* [15, 14] in this area was focussed on combinational devices. The analysis of the system represented by Ψ in the introduction illustrates the basic idea, namely the extraction of a data-dependent timing delay from an abstract proof of functional behaviour. On the other hand, the functional behaviour of sequential devices such as latches depends on timing properties in an essential manner. Thus it is not immediately clear if the same approach will work. We shall however see that it does. The essential idea is to introduce an abstract induction axiom $Ind_P^{\sharp 1} : P \supset (P \supset \bigcirc_\forall P) \supset \bigcirc_\forall P$ which captures the reasoning behind proofs of memory effects. These effects depend on the existence of at least one self-sustaining feedback loop. Given proof terms $p : P$ representing an initial impulse and $q : P \supset \bigcirc_\forall P$ representing the propagation of the impulse through a feedback loop then $Ind_P^{\sharp 1} \, p \, q : \bigcirc_\forall P$ represents the constraints under which the loop is self-sustaining, $i.e.$ produces a memory effect.

We verify one of the transitions in fundamental mode, namely the transition that resets the latch: the input r_{in} is held high for a period of time and the output s_{in} is held low for that period and for ever after. Provided that r_{in} is held high for long enough and the intertiality of at least one NOR gate is non-zero, then, after a suitable delay, the output on q_{out} is permanently low. Our specification of the latch and its input excitation, given in Fig. 8, follows Herbert's fairly closely.

The inputs r_{in}, s_{in}, and outputs q_{out}, $\overline{q_{out}}$ of the latch are modelled as signals, $i.e.$ functions from $\mathbb{N}$ to $\mathbb{B}$. We lift the negation operation $\neg :: \mathbb{B} \Rightarrow \mathbb{B}$ to signals r by defining $]r$ to be $\lambda t :: \mathbb{N} . \neg(r\,t)$. In his proofs Herbert uses a predicate $During$ which has type

$$\theta_1 = \forall s, t . (\!|r_{in}|\!)(s,t) \supset (\!]q_{out}|\!)(s+d_1, t+D_1)$$

$$\theta_2 = \forall s_1, t_1, s_2, t_2 . ((\!]s_{in}|\!)(s_1, t_1) \wedge (\!]q_{out}|\!)(s_2, t_2))$$
$$\supset (\!|\overline{q_{out}}|\!)((\max s_1 s_2) + d_2, (\min t_1 t_2) + D_2)$$

$$\theta_3 = \forall s, t . (\!|\overline{q_{out}}|\!)(s,t) \supset (\!]q_{out}|\!)(s+d_1, t+D_1)$$

$$\theta_{p1} = (\!|r_{in}|\!)(s_a, t_a)$$

$$\theta_{p2} = \forall t \geq s_a . (\!]s_{in}|\!)(s_a, t)$$

Fig. 8. Latch Theory.

$(\mathbb{N} \Rightarrow \mathbb{B}) \Rightarrow \mathbb{N} \times \mathbb{N} \Rightarrow \mathbb{B}$. For a signal r of type $\mathbb{N} \Rightarrow \mathbb{B}$ and pair (s, t) of type $\mathbb{N} \times \mathbb{N}$ the meaning of $During\, r\,(s, t)$ is that r is high (has value $true$) on the whole of the interval $[s, t]$. Thus $During\,]r\,(s, t)$ expresses the fact that r is low (has value $false$) on the interval $[s, t]$. To save space in the presentation of the latch analysis below, we abbreviate $During\, r$ to $(\!|r|\!)$. Fig. 8 3 gives three base logic axioms specifying the latch itself and two assumptions on the inputs to the latch. The axioms θ_1, θ_2 and θ_3 express the behaviour of the circuit, while θ_{p1} expresses the fact that the input r_{in} is high in the interval $[s_a, t_a]$ and θ_{p2} the fact that the input s_{in} is low in the interval $[s_a, \infty)$. In the formal proof, the parameters s_a, t_a, d_1, d_2, D_1 and D_2 are universally quantified and the assumptions θ_{p1} and θ_{p2} incorporated into the statement of the theorem proved. Currently, the mechanism used is that of Isabelle's locales, which allow a formal development that closely matches our informal presentation. The main difference to Herbert is that we specify both a delay and an inertiality for each gate. For instance, the clause θ_1 specifies that if the signal r_{in} is high throughout the interval $[s, t]$ then the signal q_{out} is low throughout the interval $[s + d_1, t + D_1]$. The value d_1 represents the maximal delay before the input is reflected in the output, while D_1 represents the minimal length of time the gate continues to propagate the input after it is no longer present. One reason for generalising the system specification in this way is that it is electronically more realistic than the transport model.

Applying the equations of Fig. 4 in reverse and some simple optimisations, we obtain the following abstractions of our circuit theory $\Theta = \{\theta_1, \theta_2, \theta_3, \theta_{p1}, \theta_{p2}\}$:

$$\theta_1{}^\sharp = \theta_1{}^{\sharp_1} : (\!|r_{in}|\!) \supset (\!|\,]q_{out}|\!) \qquad \theta_1{}^{\sharp_1} = \lambda(z_1, z_2).(z_1 + d_1, z_2 + D_1)$$

$$\theta_2{}^\sharp = \theta_2{}^{\sharp_1} : ((\!|\,]s_{in}|\!) \wedge (\!|\,]q_{out}|\!)) \supset (\!|\overline{q_{out}}|\!) \quad \theta_2{}^{\sharp_1} = \lambda((z_{11}, z_{12}), (z_{21}, z_{22})).$$
$$((\max z_{11} z_{21}) + d_2, (\min z_{12} z_{22}) + D_2)$$

$$\theta_3{}^\sharp = \theta_3{}^{\sharp_1} : (\!|\overline{q_{out}}|\!) \supset (\!|\,]q_{out}|\!) \qquad \theta_3{}^{\sharp_1} = \lambda(z_1, z_2).(z_1 + d_1, z_2 + D_1)$$

$$\theta_{p1}{}^\sharp = \theta_{p1}{}^{\sharp_1} : (\!|r_{in}|\!) \qquad\qquad \theta_{p1}{}^{\sharp_1} = (s_a, t_a)$$

$$\theta_{p2}{}^\sharp = \theta_{p2}{}^{\sharp_1} : \bigcirc_\forall (\!|\,]s_{in}|\!) \qquad\qquad \theta_{p2}{}^{\sharp_1} = \lambda(s, t).s_a \leq s \wedge s \leq t$$

in which the functional and timing aspects have been separated completely from each other.

Induction Principles for Latching Proof. To prove the latching property for the reset transition we will use the following interval induction principle for properties of intervals $I \subseteq \mathbb{N}$: If P holds on an initial interval $I_0 = [b_1, b_2]$ and, whenever $I = [b_1, t_1]$ extends I_0 and P holds on I, then P also holds on an interval properly overlapping I on the right (*i.e.* an interval $[s_2, t_2]$ such that $b_1 \leq s_2 \leq t_1 < t_2$), then P holds on all intervals $[b_1, t]$. This principle is valid for any property P that satisfies $P(I) \wedge P(J) \supset P(I \cup J)$ for all intervals I and J. For convenience we will identify closed intervals $[b_1, b_2]$ with pairs of endpoints (b_1, b_2). As an abstraction of this induction principle we therefore propose the following proof-formula pair:

$$Ind_P^\sharp = (Ind_P^{\sharp_1} : Ind_P^{\sharp_2})$$
$$= (\lambda(b_1, b_2).\lambda R.\lambda(s, t).s = b_1 \wedge b_1 \leq t \wedge Prog\, R\,(b_1, b_2)$$
$$: P \supset (P \supset \bigcirc_\forall P) \supset \bigcirc_\forall P),$$

where $P :: \mathbb{N} \times \mathbb{N} \Rightarrow \mathbb{B}$ is any binary relation on natural numbers and $Prog\, R\,(b_1, b_2)$ means that R is *progressive* on (b_1, b_2), *i.e.* whenever (b_1, t_1) is an interval extending (b_1, b_2) then there is an interval (s_2, t_2) strictly overlapping (b_1, t_1) on the right such that (b_1, t_1) and (s_2, t_2) are related by R:

$$Prog\, R\,(b_1, b_2) = (\forall t_1.t_1 \geq b_2 \supset$$
$$(\exists s_2, t_2.b_1 \leq s_2 \leq t_1 < t_2 \wedge R\,(b_1, t_1)\,(s_2, t_2))).$$

$Ind_P^\sharp$ is a sound induction axiom for any property P of the form $(\!|Q|\!)$, which can be seen once we have refined it (using the equations in Fig. 4):

$$Ind_P^\sharp = \forall(b_1, b_2).((b_1, b_2) : P) \supset$$
$$\forall R.(\forall(x_1, x_2).(x_1, x_2) : P \supset \forall(y_1, y_2).R(x_1, x_2)(y_1, y_2) \supset (y_1, y_2) : P) \supset$$
$$\forall(s, t).(s = b_1 \wedge b_1 \leq t \wedge (\forall t_1.t_1 \geq b_2$$
$$\supset (\exists s_2, t_2.b_1 \leq s_2 \leq t_1 < t_2 \wedge R\,(b_1, t_1)\,(s_2, t_2)))) \supset (s, t) : P.$$

This formula is in fact equivalent to the interval induction property presented above. To further clarify the meaning of $Ind_P^\sharp$ we say P is *invariant* under a binary relation $R :: (\mathbb{N} \times \mathbb{N}) \Rightarrow (\mathbb{N} \times \mathbb{N}) \Rightarrow \mathbb{B}$, written $Inv\,P\,R$, when P and R satisfy $\forall s_1, t_1, s_2, t_2\,.\,(P(s_1, t_1) \wedge R\,(s_1, t_1)\,(s_2, t_2)) \supset P(s_2, t_2)$. Then $Ind_P^\sharp$ may be directly re-formulated as

$$\forall b_1, b_2\,.\,P(b_1, b_2) \supset \forall R\,.\,Inv\,P\,R \supset Prog\,R\,(b_1, b_2) \supset \forall t \geq b_1\,.\,P(b_1, t),$$

i.e. if P holds in some initial interval (b_1, b_2), and P is invariant under a relation R that is progressive on (b_1, b_2), then P must hold in the infinite interval (b_1, ∞). Now if $R\,(s_1, t_1)\,(s_2, t_2)$ is chosen to mean that $P(s_1, t_1) \supset P(s_2, t_2)$ then P is trivially invariant under R and the statement $Prog\,R\,(b_1, b_2)$ amounts to the condition that whenever $I = [b_1, t_1]$ extends $[b_1, b_2]$ to the right and P holds on I, then P also holds on an interval properly overlapping I on the right. Thus we see that the interval induction principle for P is a consequence of $Ind_P^\sharp$; $Ind_P^\sharp$ is a mild generalisation which in our implementation we prove in the form $\forall Q\,.\,Ind_{(\![Q]\!)}^\sharp$.

Verifying the Latch.

Let us use our abstractions to carry through an abstract proof and see how the latching constraint comes in. The strategy is to find a proof-formula pair $p_l : \bigcirc_\forall (\![q_{out}]\!)$ which can then be refined to give the timing constraint C under which the output q_{out} is low: $\forall s, t\,.\,C(s, t) \supset (\![q_{out}]\!)(s, t)$. We want to find a persistent memory property, that is, one that arises from a (single) self-sustaining feedback loop around the latch. This requirement is satisfied by choosing a single application of the abstract induction rule to $(\![q_{out}]\!)$. The application $Ind^\sharp\,(\![q_{out}]\!)$ is then $ind : (\![q_{out}]\!) \supset ((\![q_{out}]\!) \supset \bigcirc_\forall (\![q_{out}]\!)) \supset \bigcirc_\forall (\![q_{out}]\!)$ where $ind = \lambda(b_1, b_2)\,.\,\lambda R\,.\,\lambda(s, t)\,.\,s = b_1 \wedge b_1 \leq t \wedge Prog\,R\,(b_1, b_2)$. So we find proof terms $(q_1, q_2) : (\![q_{out}]\!)$ and $R : (\![q_{out}]\!) \supset \bigcirc_\forall (\![q_{out}]\!)$ and then apply the abstract rule $\supset_\mathcal{E}$ of Fig. 5 twice; we obtain $p_l : \bigcirc_\forall (\![q_{out}]\!)$ where p_l is the composition $ind\,(q_1, q_2)\,R$ which reduces to $\lambda(s, t)\,.\,s = q_1 \wedge q_1 \leq t \wedge Prog\,R\,(q_1, q_2)$. The abstract proof tree is as follows, where most of the proof terms and the subproof with proof term R have been elided:

$$
\cfrac{
  \cfrac{
    \cfrac{ind}{\cfrac{(\![q_{out}]\!) \supset}{\cfrac{((\![q_{out}]\!) \supset \bigcirc_\forall(\![q_{out}]\!))}{\supset \bigcirc_\forall(\![q_{out}]\!)}}}
    \qquad
    \cfrac{\cfrac{\theta_1^\sharp}{(\![r_{in}]\!) \supset (\![q_{out}]\!)} \qquad \cfrac{\theta_{p1}^\sharp}{(\![r_{in}]\!)}}{(q_1, q_2) : (\![q_{out}]\!)}\supset_\mathcal{E}
  }{((\![q_{out}]\!) \supset \bigcirc_\forall(\![q_{out}]\!)) \supset \bigcirc_\forall(\![q_{out}]\!)}\supset_\mathcal{E}
  \qquad
  \cfrac{\vdots}{R : \; (\![q_{out}]\!) \supset \bigcirc_\forall(\![q_{out}]\!)}
}{\bigcirc_\forall(\![q_{out}]\!)}\supset_\mathcal{E}
$$

Now for the details: in the following we will compose formulas and proof terms at the same time in a forward fashion, so that the constraint corresponding to p_l is computed in an incremental manner. In our Isabelle implementation, in contrast, this is carried out in a goal-oriented fashion. Note, however, in either case the constructions can be done in a single direction, no mix-up of forward and backward steps is forced. To find (q_1, q_2) we start with axiom $\theta_{p1}^\sharp = (s_a, t_a) : (\![r_{in}]\!)$ and compose this with the implication axiom $\theta_1^\sharp$ to obtain $(q_1, q_2) = (s_a + d_1, t_a + D_1) : (\![q_{out}]\!)$, where we have already performed the β-normalisation of the proof term. This is our base case. For the step case we assume (as an hypothesis) we have a proof $(s_1, t_1) : (\![q_{out}]\!)$. We will need to lift this to a proof

$\mathsf{val}_\forall(s_1, t_1) = (\lambda z \,.\, z = (s_1, t_1)) : \bigcirc_\forall(\lceil\rceil q_{out}\rceil)$ using rule $\bigcirc_{\mathcal{I}}$. Applying $\wedge_\bigcirc$ to the axiom $\theta_{p2}{}^\sharp$ and $\mathsf{val}_\forall(s_1, t_1) : \bigcirc_\forall(\lceil\rceil q_{out}\rceil)$ we derive

$$q = (\lambda((s, t), (u, v)) \,.\, s_a \le s \le t \wedge u = s_1 \wedge v = t_1) : \bigcirc_\forall((\lceil\rceil s_{in}\rceil) \wedge (\lceil\rceil q_{out}\rceil)). \quad (2)$$

We may use $\supset_\bigcirc$ to propagate this through the implication $\theta_2{}^\sharp$ to obtain $\supset_\bigcirc(r_2, q)$: $\bigcirc_\forall(\lceil\overline{q_{out}}\rceil)$ where $r_2 = \lambda((z_{11}, z_{12}), (z_{21}, z_{22})) \,.\, ((\max z_{11} z_{21}) + d_2, (\min z_{12} z_{22}) + D_2)$, which after β-normalisation and a little simplication yields:

$$\lambda(z_1, z_2) \,.\, \exists m_{11}, m_{12} \,.\, s_a \le m_{11} \le m_{12}$$
$$\wedge\ z_1 = (\max m_{11} s_1) + d_2 \wedge z_2 = (\min m_{12} t_1) + D_2 : \bigcirc_\forall(\lceil\overline{q_{out}}\rceil). \quad (3)$$

The next step is to use $\supset_\bigcirc$ to feed (3) through the implication $\theta_3{}^\sharp$, and simplify:

$$\lambda(z_1, z_2) \,.\, \exists m_{11}, m_{12} \,.\, s_a \le m_{11} \le m_{12} \wedge z_1 = (\max m_{11} s_1) + d_2 + d_1$$
$$\wedge\ z_2 = (\min m_{12} t_1) + D_2 + D_1 \ : \ \bigcirc_\forall(\lceil\rceil q_{out}\rceil). \quad (4)$$

We derived this under the assumption $(s_1, t_1) : (\lceil\rceil q_{out}\rceil)$, which we now discharge:

$$\lambda(s_1, t_1), (z_1, z_2) \,.\, \exists m_{11}, m_{12} \,.\, s_a \le m_{11} \le m_{12}$$
$$\wedge\ z_1 = (\max m_{11} s_1) + d_2 + d_1 \wedge z_2 = (\min m_{12} t_1) + D_2 + D_1$$
$$: (\lceil\rceil q_{out}\rceil) \supset \bigcirc_\forall(\lceil\rceil q_{out}\rceil). \quad (5)$$

We have generated the proof term R for the induction step. The abstract proof tree is as follows:

Now we can take the induction base $(s_a + d_1, t_a + D_1)$ and step function R as arguments of the induction rule $Ind^\sharp(\lceil\rceil q_{out}\rceil)$ to obtain $\lambda(s, t) \,.\, s = s_a + d_1 \wedge s_a + d_1 \le t \wedge Prog\, R\,(s_a + d_1, t_a + D_1) : \bigcirc_\forall(\lceil\rceil q_{out}\rceil)$. Expanding, we obtain

$$\lambda(s, t) \,.\, s = s_a + d_1 \wedge s_a + d_1 \le t \wedge$$
$$(\forall t_1 \,.\, t_1 \ge t_a + D_1 \supset$$
$$(\exists s_2, t_2 \,.\, s_a + d_1 \le s_2 \le t_1 < t_2 \wedge R\,(s_a + d_1, t_1)\,(s_2, t_2)))$$
$$: \bigcirc_\forall(\lceil\rceil q_{out}\rceil), \quad \text{where} \quad (6)$$
$$R\,(s_a + d_1, t_1)\,(s_2, t_2) = \exists m_{11}, m_{12} \,.\, s_a \le m_{11} \le m_{12}$$
$$\wedge\ s_2 = (\max m_{11} s_a + d_1) + d_2 + d_1 \wedge t_2 = (\min m_{12} t_1) + D_2 + D_1.$$

Again, we have β-normalised to keep the expressions as simple as possible. It is now time again to do some constraint simplifications. The two equations for s_2

and t_2 allow us to eliminate the $\exists s_2, t_2$ quantifiers, a computation that would be part of simple constraint analysis, *i.e.* incorporated into constraint simplifications.

$$\lambda(s,t).\, s = s_a + d_1 \wedge s_a + d_1 \leq t \wedge$$
$$(\forall t_1.\, t_1 \geq t_a + D_1 \supset (\exists m_{11}, m_{12}.\, s_a \leq m_{11} \leq m_{12}$$
$$s_a + d_1 \leq (\max m_{11} s_a) + d_1 + d_2 + d_1 \leq t_1 < (\min m_{12} t_1) + D_2 + D_1))$$
$$: \bigcirc_\forall(\!|\, q_{out}|\!)\,. \tag{7}$$

The constraint computation will detect that $t_1 < (\min m_{12} t_1) + D_2 + D_1$ is equivalent to $D_2 + D_1 > 0$; that $\max m_{11} s_a$ is the same as m_{11} and hence $(\max m_{11} s_a) + d_1 + d_2 + d_1 \leq t_1$ is equivalent to $m_{11} + 2 \cdot d_1 + d_2 \leq t_1$; and that $s_a + d_1 \leq (\max m_{11} s_a) + d_1 + d_2 + d_1$ is always trivially satisfied. Thus, we end up with

$$\lambda(s,t).\, s = s_a + d_1 \wedge s_a + d_1 \leq t \wedge$$
$$(\forall t_1 \geq t_a + D_1.\, \exists m_{11} \geq s_a.\, m_{11} + 2d_1 + d_2 \leq t_1 \wedge D_2 + D_1 > 0)$$
$$: \bigcirc_\forall(\!|\, q_{out}|\!)\,. \tag{8}$$

At this point, now, it appears we need one slightly more sophisticated argument to deal with the $\forall t_1$ and $\exists m_{11}$ quantifiers: the condition $\forall t_1 \geq t_a + D_1.\, \exists m_{11} \geq s_a \cdot m_{11} + 2d_1 + d_2 \leq t_1$ is logically equivalent to $t_a + D_1 \geq s_a + 2d_1 + d_2$. Given such reasoning is built into constraint simplifications, we are looking at the solution form:

$$\lambda(s,t).\, s = s_a + d_1 \wedge s_a + d_1 \leq t \wedge$$
$$t_a + D_1 \geq s_a + 2d_1 + d_2 \wedge D_2 + D_1 > 0 : \bigcirc_\forall(\!|\, q_{out}|\!)\,. \tag{9}$$

When (9) is refined back into the base logic we have the desired result:

$$(t_a + D_1 \geq s_a + 2d_1 + d_2 \wedge D_2 + D_1 > 0) \supset \forall t \geq s_a + d_1.\, (\!|\, q_{out}|\!)\, (s_a + d_1, t).$$

The predicate $t_a + D_1 \geq s_a + 2d_1 + d_2$ is the external hold constraint: input r_{in} must remain high for a period of length at least $2d_1 + d_2 - D_1$ for the latch fully to reset; the second part $D_2 + D_1 > 0$ is the internal memory constraint that at least one of the gates must have non-zero inertia; finally, the third component $t \geq s_a + d_1$ of the overall constraint states that the propagation delay is d_1.

4   Conclusions

We have presented a conservative extension to higher order logic reasoning that allows for general shallow abstractions and an inverse refinement operation. Our method subsumes some abstraction techniques used in AI, for instance propositional abstraction [16], and can be used for data and structural abstractions as well as for the timing abstractions on which we have concentrated.

The extension uses a computational lambda calculus to represent constraint information that is factored out by the abstraction. The combination between these constraint terms and abstract formulas (syntactically separated by the colon : operator) is a realisability interpretation of constructive logic which formally extends the "deliverables" approach of [11], and is implemented much as described in [10], although the motivation of these papers and the theory of [11] is rather different from ours. It is important to stress that the method does not depend on a constructive (intuitionistic) version of higher-order logic. However, the abstraction process applies constructive principles, within HOL.

Our approach to organising proofs in HOL allows for the clean and yet sound separation of algorithmic (constraint λ-calculus) and non-algorithmic reasoning (abstract formulas). Abstraction by realisability separation should also open up new avenues for developing heuristic techniques for proof search in HOL, borrowing ideas from AI and constraint programming (CLP). The method yields a natural embedding and generalisation of CLP within HOL. To support our claims we have applied the technique here to the verification of a memory device and demonstrated how abstract functional verification can be combined with constraint synthesis, in one and the same derivation. This solves a methodological problem in the verification of memory devices as highlighted in the work of Hanna and Daeche [8] or Herbert [9]. We are *not* proposing our approach as a replacement for the many other effective approaches to verifying hardware in HOL, but we do suggest that it is compatible with them and is especially useful where the handling of differing levels of abstraction is involved.

We have implemented our method in the Isabelle theorem prover and synthesised and analysed the timing constraints for the latch and the incrementor example. Our priority is now to develop a set of tactics to automate constraint simplification. Space permits discussion of only one point of detail: the reader may have noticed that the connectives in the abstract formulas of Fig. 4 do not have their expected types. For example, if $P :: \alpha \Rightarrow \mathbb{B}$, $Q :: \beta \Rightarrow \mathbb{B}$, $p :: \alpha$ and $q :: \beta$ then $P\,p \wedge Q\,q = ((p,q) : P \wedge Q)$ which forces the second occurrence of $\wedge$ to have type $(\alpha \Rightarrow \mathbb{B}) \Rightarrow (\beta \Rightarrow \mathbb{B}) \Rightarrow (\alpha \times \beta) \Rightarrow \mathbb{B}$ instead of the usual $\mathbb{B} \Rightarrow \mathbb{B} \to \mathbb{B}$. In our implementation we have defined a new set of logical connectives $\sqcup, \sqcap, \sqsupset, \ldots$ to connect abstract formulas and used this definition to *derive* the rules of Fig. 4. This is very straightforward to do following the example of [10], *e.g.* we define the abstract version of conjunction by $P \sqcap Q := \lambda(p,q).p : P \wedge q : Q$, where $p : P$ can now be simply defined as $P\,p$.

Acknowledgements

We are grateful to Tom Melham for his encouragement and advice and to the anonymous referees for their comments and suggestions.

References

[1] H. Eveking. Behavioural consistency between register-transfer- and switch-level descriptions. In D. A. Edwards, editor, *Design Methodologies for VLSI and Computer Architecture*. Elsevier Science, B. V., 1989.

[2] M. Fairtlough, M. Mendler, and M. Walton. First-order Lax Logic as a Framework for CLP. Technical Report MIPS-9714, Passau University, Department of Mathematics and Computer Science, 1997.

[3] M. Fairtlough and M. V. Mendler. Propositional Lax Logic. *Information and Computation*, 137(1):1–33, August 1997.

[4] M. Fairtlough and M. Walton. Quantified Lax Logic. Technical Report CS-97-11, Sheffield University, Department of Computer Science, 1997.

[5] M.P. Fourman. Proof and design. Technical Report ECS-LFCS-95-319, Edinburgh University, Department of Computer Science, 1995.

[6] M.P. Fourman and R.A. Hexsel. Formal synthesis. In G. Birtwistle, editor, *Proceedings of the IV Higher Order Workshop, Banff, 1990*, 1991.

[7] F. Giunchiglia and T. Walsh. A theory of abstraction. *Artificial Intelligence*, 57:323–389, 1992.

[8] F.K. Hanna and N. Daeche. Specification and verification using higher order logic: A case study. In G. M. Milne and P. A. Subrahmanyam, editors, *Formal Aspects of VLSI design, Proc. of the 1985 Edinburgh conf. on VLSI*, pages 179–213. North-Holland, 1986.

[9] J. Herbert. Formal reasoning about timing and function of basic memory devices. In Dr. Luc Claesen, editor, *IMEC-IFIP International Workshop on Applied Formal Methods for Correct VLSI Design, Volume 2*, pages 668–687. Elsevier Science Publishers, B.V., 1989.

[10] B. Jacobs and T. Melham. Translating dependent type theory into higher order logic. In *Typed Lambda Calculi and Applications, TLCA'93*, pages 209–229. Springer LNCS 664, 1993.

[11] J.H. McKinna. *Deliverables: A Categorical Approach to Program Development in Type Theory*. PhD thesis, Edinburgh University, Department of Computer Science, 1992.

[12] T.F. Melham. *Higher Order Logic and Hardware Verification*. Cambridge University Press, 1993.

[13] M. Mendler. *A Modal Logic for Handling Behavioural Constraints in Formal Hardware Verification*. PhD thesis, Edinburgh University, Department of Computer Science, ECS-LFCS-93-255, 1993.

[14] M. Mendler. Timing refinement of intuitionistic proofs and its application to the timing analysis of combinational circuits. In P. Miglioli, U. Moscato, D. Mundici, and M. Ornaghi, editors, *Proc. 5th Int. Workshop on Theorem Proving with Analytic Tableaux and Related Methods*, pages 261–277. Springer, 1996.

[15] M. Mendler and M. Fairtlough. Ternary simulation: A refinement of binary functions or an abstraction of real-time behaviour? In M. Sheeran and S. Singh, editors, *Proc. 3rd Workshop on Designing Correct Circuits (DCC'96)*. Springer Electronic Workshops in Computing, 1996.

[16] D.A. Plaisted. Theorem proving with abstraction. *Artificial Intelligence*, 16:47–108, 1981.

[17] A.S. Troelstra. Realizability. In S. Buss, editor, *Handbook of Proof Theory*. Elsevier Science B.V., 1998.

A Framework for the Formalisation of Pi Calculus Type Systems in Isabelle/HOL

Simon J. Gay*

Department of Computing Science, University of Glasgow
Glasgow, G12 8QQ, UK
simon@dcs.gla.ac.uk

Abstract. We present a formalisation, in the theorem proving system Isabelle/HOL, of a linear type system for the pi calculus, including a proof of runtime safety of typed processes. The use of a uniform encoding of pi calculus syntax in a meta language, the development of a general theory of type environments, and the structured formalisation of the main proofs, facilitate the adaptation of the Isabelle theories and proof scripts to variations on the language and other type systems.
Keywords: Types; pi calculus; automatic theorem proving; semantics.

1 Introduction

Static type systems are an established feature of programming languages, and the range of type systems is growing. The general principle is that a program which has been typechecked (at compile time) is guaranteed to satisfy a particular runtime property: for example (traditionally) that all functions are called with the correct number and type of arguments, or (more exotically) that some security property, such as secrecy, holds. In order for typechecking to give a proper guarantee of some form of program correctness, it is essential to prove, with respect to a well-defined semantics, that execution of typed programs is well-behaved.

Proofs of type soundness have traditionally been carried out by hand, which is feasible for small theoretical languages but much more difficult for real programming languages such as Java. The proofs are characterised by large inductions over the syntax of the language, the definition of the typing rules, and the definition of the operational semantics; many cases must be considered, which often differ in subtle ways and are very sensitive to the precise formulation of the syntax and the typing rules. Modifications of the language require proofs to be redone, often with only minor variations but it is dangerous to assume that previously-established properties will survive.

For these reasons, the idea of formalising proofs of type soundness (and other aspects of programming language theory, such as program equivalence, but this is not the concern of the present paper) within an automatic theorem proving system is very attractive. As part of a research project investigating type systems

---

* Partially supported by EPSRC grants GR/L75177 and GR/N39494.

R.J. Boulton and P.B. Jackson (Eds.): TPHOLs 2001, LNCS 2152, pp. 217–232, 2001.

for the control of concurrent communication, we are interested in concurrent programming languages based on the pi calculus. The pi calculus provides a core concurrent programming notation, dealing with inter-process communication along named channels. We have developed a formalisation within Isabelle/HOL of the pi calculus and the linear type system proposed by Kobayashi et al. [12]. Our aim has been not simply to formalise a particular type system, but to develop a flexible framework within which a variety of type systems can be investigated, with as much re-use of existing theory and proof as possible. Our formalisation of the linear type system is a step towards a treatment of a language [5] based on the pi calculus and combining session types [10, 24] with subtyping [20].

We should emphasise that the purpose of this formalisation is to prove properties of the type system itself, principally type soundness, rather than to support typechecking. However, given the formalisation of a pi calculus type system it should be straightforward to construct proofs that particular processes are typable.

Related Work

The following table summarises work on formalisation of the pi calculus by a number of researchers, including the present paper. The parameters are: the theorem proving system used; the style of pi calculus (monadic or polyadic); the approach to binding (names, de Bruijn indices [1], higher order abstract syntax (HOAS) [19], McKinna and Pollack's [13] approach (MP), Gabbay and Pitts' [4] FM-sets approach (GP)); the style of operational semantics (labelled transition system (LTS) or reduction relation (RED)); the focus on bisimulation ($\sim$) or typing ($\vdash$).

Author	Prover	Calculus	Binding	Semantics	Focus
Melham [14]	HOL	monadic	names	LTS	$\sim$
Hirschkoff [9]	Coq	polyadic	de Bruijn	LTS	$\sim$
Honsell et al. [11]	Coq	monadic	HOAS	LTS	$\sim$
Röckl et al. [22]	Isabelle/HOL	monadic	HOAS	-	syntax
Röckl [21]	Isabelle/HOL	monadic	GP	-	syntax
Henry-Gréard [8]	Coq	monadic	MP	LTS	$\vdash$
Despeyroux [2]	Coq	monadic	HOAS	LTS	$\vdash$
This paper	Isabelle/HOL	polyadic	de Bruijn	RED	$\vdash$

There are two main novelties of the formalisation reported in the present paper. First, we formalise an operational semantics based on a reduction relation rather than a labelled transition system; this is because the language which we set out to formalise uses the reduction semantics. Second, we use a meta language rather than a direct formalisation of pi calculus syntax. More technically, the introduction of a type system for the meta language (see Section 8) is also new. The meta language approach supports our goal of developing a general framework in which a variety of languages and type systems can be formalised; we return to this point in Section 12.

Formalisations of other programming language type systems have been carried out, notably for Java [26, 23] and Standard ML [3]. The present paper concentrates on concurrent languages in the style of the pi calculus; the ambitious goal of applying our meta language approach to a wider range of language paradigms is left for future work.

2 Pi Calculus

We assue some familiarity with the pi calculus [16, 17] but summarise its syntax and semantics in this section.

The following grammar defines *processes* P; variables x stand for channel names; $\tilde{x}$ is a list of variables. There are two binding operators: the variables $\tilde{x}$ are bound in $(\nu\tilde{x})P$ and in $x?[\tilde{x}] . P$. All other variable occurrences are free.

$$
\begin{array}{llll}
P ::= & \mathbf{0} & \text{(nil)} & \mid \ (\nu\tilde{x})P \quad \text{(restriction)} \\
& \mid \ P\mid P & \text{(parallel)} & \mid \ x?[\tilde{x}] . P \ \text{(input)} \\
& \mid \ !P & \text{(replication)} & \mid \ x![\tilde{x}] . P \ \text{(output)} \\
& \mid \ P + P & \text{(choice)}
\end{array}
$$

The operational semantics of the pi calculus is defined in two stages. The *structural congruence* relation axiomatises some basic process equivalences, and the *reduction relation* axiomatises inter-process communication.

The structural congruence relation, denoted by $\equiv$, is defined inductively as the smallest equivalence relation which is additionally a congruence (i.e. is preserved by the process constructors) and is closed under a number of rules. These rules include α-equivalence, basic properties of parallel composition and choice (commutativity, associativity, the fact that $\mathbf{0}$ is a unit), and some less trivial equivalences. Chief among these are a rule which captures the meaning of replication:

$$!P \equiv P|!P$$

and the *scope extrusion* rule:

$$P \mid (\nu\tilde{x})Q \equiv (\nu\tilde{x})(P \mid Q) \qquad \text{if none of the } \tilde{x} \text{ are free in } P.$$

The reduction relation is also defined inductively, by the following rules. The first rule uses substitution to express transmission of channel names during communication; only substitution of variables for variables is required.

$$
\frac{length(\tilde{y}) = length(\tilde{z})}{x?[\tilde{y}] . P \mid x![\tilde{z}] . Q \longrightarrow P\{\tilde{z}/\tilde{y}\} \mid Q}
\qquad
\frac{P \longrightarrow P'}{(\nu\tilde{x})P \longrightarrow (\nu\tilde{x})P'}
$$

$$
\frac{P' \equiv P \quad P \longrightarrow Q \quad Q \equiv Q'}{P' \longrightarrow Q'}
\qquad
\frac{P \longrightarrow P'}{P \mid Q \longrightarrow P' \mid Q}
\qquad
\frac{P \longrightarrow P'}{P + Q \longrightarrow P'}
$$

Communication between an input and an output of different arities is not defined, and the appearance of such a miscommunication during the execution of a process can be interpreted as a runtime error, analogous to calling a function with the wrong number of arguments. The simple type system [15, 25] for the pi calculus allows such errors to be eliminated by static typechecking; other type systems, such as Kobayashi *et al.*'s linear type system [12] which we formalise in this paper, additionally check other properties of processes. Many pi calculus type systems have the following general features. The syntax of the language is modified so that bound variables are annotated with types, in the Church style. Typing judgements of the form $\Gamma \vdash P$ are used, where Γ is a list $x_1 : T_1, \ldots, x_n : T_n$ of typed variables and P is a process, and the set of valid judgements is defined inductively. Note that a process is either correctly typed or not; processes themselves are not assigned types.

Linear Types

Kobayashi *et al.* [12] proposed a linear [6] type system for the pi calculus, in which certain channels must be used for exactly one communication. The main motivation was the observation that many pi calculus programming idioms involve single-use channels, and making this information available to a compiler by means of the type system could permit many useful optimisations. If a particular channel is used for exactly one communication, it must occur once in an input position and once in an output position. It therefore becomes necessary to consider the two ends of a channel separately, and enforce linear use of each end.

   Kobayashi *et al.* introduce a system of *multiplicities*: 1 for linear and ω for non-linear, and *polarities*: subsets of $\{i, o\}$ representing input and output capabilities. Types are defined by $T ::= p^m[\tilde{T}]$ and the abbreviations $\updownarrow = \{i, o\}$, $? = \{i\}$, $! = \{o\}$, $| = \{\}$ are used for polarities.

   If $x : ?^1[\tilde{T}]$ appears in an environment Γ then a process typed in Γ must use the input capability of x, either by receiving a tuple of values (of types $\tilde{T}$) along x, or by sending x to another process as part of a tuple of values. Similarly, there are two possible ways of using the output capability of a channel. If $x : \updownarrow^1[\tilde{T}]$ appears in Γ, then a process typed in Γ must use both capabilities of x.

   The typing rule for parallel composition is

$$\frac{\Gamma \vdash P \quad \Delta \vdash Q}{\Gamma + \Delta \vdash P \mid Q} \text{ T-Par}$$

where the $+$ operation combines the capabilities of the channels in Γ and Δ; it is defined on single types (and undefined for unequal multiplicities) by

$$p^\omega + q^\omega = (p \cup q)^\omega$$
$$p^1 + q^1 = (p \cup q)^1 \text{ if } p \cap q = \emptyset$$

and extended to environments with equal domains by

$$(\Gamma_1, x : p^m[\tilde{T}]) + (\Gamma_2, x : q^n[\tilde{T}]) = (\Gamma_1 + \Gamma_2), x : (p^m + q^n)[\tilde{T}].$$

The $+$ operation is also used to add a single capability to a channel in an environment: $(\Gamma, x : p^m[\tilde{T}]) + x : q^n[\tilde{T}] = \Gamma, x : (p^m + q^n)[\tilde{T}]$.

The typing rules for input and output are

$$\frac{\Gamma, \tilde{y} : \tilde{T} \vdash P}{\Gamma + x : !^m[\tilde{T}] \vdash x?[\tilde{y} : \tilde{T}] . P} \text{ T-In} \qquad \frac{\Gamma \vdash P}{\Gamma + x : !^m[\tilde{T}] + \tilde{y} : \tilde{T} \vdash x![\tilde{y}]P} \text{ T-Out}$$

Because + is a partial operation, all typing rules implicitly carry the additional hypothesis that all uses of + are defined.

The uniform definition of + on linear and non-linear types means that the same typing rule covers (say) output on both linear and non-linear channels. In the non-linear case, it is possible for Γ to already contain x and $\tilde{y}$, in which case the hypothesis that + is defined reduces to a check that x and $\tilde{y}$ have the correct types in Γ.

Because **0** uses no channels, it is only typable in an environment in which all linear channels have polarity $|$. Such an environment is said to be *unlimited*. Replication can only be used in an unlimited environment, otherwise the possibility would be created of using linear channels more than once.

The typing rule for choice has an *additive* (in the terminology of linear logic [6]) form:

$$\frac{\Gamma \vdash P \quad \Gamma \vdash Q}{\Gamma \vdash P + Q} \text{ T-Sum}$$

This is because executing $P + Q$ means executing *either P or Q*, so the capabilities in Γ will only be used once.

For example, a process which sends the output end of a linear channel along a non-linear channel can be typed as follows, where T is an arbitrary type; note that Γ is unlimited.

$$\frac{\Gamma = x : \updownarrow^\omega[!^1[T]], y : |^1[T] \vdash \mathbf{0}}{\Gamma + x : !^\omega[!^1[T]] + y : !^1[T] \vdash x![y] . \mathbf{0}} \text{ T-Out}$$

The final typing judgement is

$$x : \updownarrow^\omega[!^1[T]], y : !^1[T] \vdash x![y] . \mathbf{0}.$$

The process $x![y] . \mathbf{0}$ delegates the responsibility for using the output capability of y to whichever process receives it.

We formalise a language slightly different from that of Kobayashi *et al.*: we use output prefix rather than asynchronous output, choice rather than a conditional construct (and therefore drop the boolean type), and replication rather than replicated input. These differences do not change the nature of the type soundness proofs, but simplify some details.

3   Overview of the Formalisation

We have formalised the linear type system for the pi calculus within the theorem prover Isabelle/HOL [18]. Isabelle is a generic theorem proving system; one of the logics which it implements is HOL, or higher-order logic. Defining a theory in Isabelle/HOL feels very much like programming in a functional language with a rich type system including polymorphism, algebraic datatypes, and extensible record types. Additionally, it is possible to define sets inductively (we make essential use of this feature) or coinductively, and to use (possibly non-computable) logical operators within definitions. Isabelle provides powerful automatic proof tactics, including simplification (generalised equational rewriting), classical reasoning, various kinds of resolution, induction, and case-analysis.

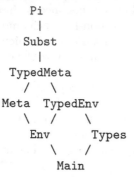

All the definitional mechanisms are associated with appropriate proof rules: making an inductive definition of a set automatically defines elimination rules and an induction rule to support proofs by case-analysis or induction. As well as using the proof tactics defined by Isabelle, it is possible to define (by programming in Standard ML) new tactics; this is made easy by Isabelle's provision of a range of *tacticals*, or combinators for tactics, such as THEN for sequencing and REPEAT for repetition.

The formalisation consists of a hierarchy of Isabelle theories. Each theory has a definition file and a proof file. The hierarchy is as shown; each theory depends on the theories below it. Main is predefined and provides all the definitional facilities mentioned above. In the following sections, we describe each theory in turn. Wherever possible, the theories are defined in a sufficiently general way to support the formalisation of different pi calculus type systems.

The theory files and proof scripts are available from the following web address: http://www.dcs.gla.ac.uk/~simon. The complete formalisation consists of approximately 650 lines of theory definitions and 6500 lines of proof script.

4   The Theory Types

Types is a generic theory of linear and non-linear types, which accounts for multiplicities and polarities but does not specify that the content of a message is a tuple of channel names. Kobayashi *et al.* exploit the fact that linear and non-linear channel types differ only in their multiplicity, and give a unified presentation in which every type consists of a polarity, a multiplicity and a message type. In order to be able to generalise our formalisation to type systems in which linear and non-linear types might differ in more substantial ways (particularly *session types* — see Section 11), we take a different approach. The linear and non-linear cases are defined as separate constructors for the polymorphic type vty, which represents the type of a variable in an environment.

```
datatype ('a,'b) vty = LinV ('a linv) | NLinV 'b
```

Ultimately we use the instantiation (lty,nlty) vty where lty is the type of linear channel types and nlty is the type of non-linear channel types.

The type `linv` is a record with two fields, `pos` and `neg`, representing the positive (output) and negative (input) occurrences of a variable.

```
record 'a linv =   pos :: 'a oty    neg :: 'a oty
```

The type `oty` is defined by

```
datatype 'a oty = Zero | One 'a
```

and the constructors represent non-use or use of a capability. For example, the type $?^1 T$ is represented in an environment by the type

```
LinV (| pos = Zero , neg = One T |).
```

For non-linear types, we drop the polarities and do not distinguish between the two ends of a channel.

The operation `addt` (addition of types), the predicate `canaddt` (testing definedness of addition), the predicate `unlim` (testing whether an individual type is unlimited, which is later extended to a predicate `unlimited` on environments), and several others, can be defined at this stage. Later, in the theory `Pi`, we define the (mutually recursive) types

```
datatype lty  = LChan   ((lty,nlty) vty list)
and       nlty = NLChan  ((lty,nlty) vty list)
```

and use `(lty,nlty) vty list` as the type of an environment.

Our departure from the unified presentation of linear and non-linear types means that when formalising the typing rules we need separate rules for input on linear and non-linear channels, and similarly for output, but the extra generality of the theory `Types` compensates for this complication in the theory `Pi`.

Another way in which our formalisation differs from the presentation of Kobayashi *et al.* is that when defining addition of linear types, we check the disjointness condition on the polarities but do not require the message types to be equal. This makes it easier to generalise to session types, but requires us eventually to impose a global condition that the environments of typed processes be *balanced*, which means that every linear type in the environment has the same message type associated with its positive and negative ends.

A large number (over 60) of essential basic theorems about types can be proved independently of the specific definitions of linear and non-linear types. A typical example is commutativity of addition of types:

```
canaddt t u ==> addt t u = addt u t
```

The function `addt` should be partial, but for convenience is defined as a total function in Isabelle; in the unwanted cases, its value is arbitrary. To make sure that these arbitrary values do not interfere with the properties of `addt`, the predicate `canaddt` is used to check that arguments to `addt` are within its domain of definition.

The types of `t` and `u` are `vty`. The proofs of these theorems require case-analysis on `t` and `u`, using the exhaustion theorem (automatically supplied by

Isabelle) for the datatype `vty`; use of Isabelle's tactic `record_split_tac` to decompose goals involving variables of type `linv`; and further case-analysis using the exhaustion theorem for the datatype `oty`. Simplification is also used at each stage.

All of these theorems are proved in essentially the same way, and we have implemented a specialised tactic, `Types_tac`, for this purpose. Unfortunately, when applying case-analysis it is necessary to provide the name of the variable involved. This means that `Types_tac` only works if the theorems are stated in terms of the variables `t`, `u`, `v`, `w` or a subset of these; none of the theorems involve more than 4 variables. Furthermore, the second round of case-analysis depends on the exact names of variables which are introduced by Isabelle during the first round. The behaviour of `Types_tac`, in terms of the number of subgoals generated and the time taken by simplification, depends on the order in which variables are considered in the second round of case-analysis. In practice, `Types_tac` works well and proves all but two of the theorems in `Types`. The remaining theorems are proved by a variation of `Types_tac` which considers variables in a different order. The dependence on particular variable names, particularly internally-generated names, means that `Types_tac` is not robust and this is somewhat unsatisfactory. We are still trying to find a better way of expressing the proofs in this theory.

5   Environments

The theories `Env` and `TypedEnv` define operations on environments. An environment is a list of types, and variable indices refer to positions within an environment. `Env` defines all operations which can be expressed independently of `Types`, for example the function `typeof` which returns the type at a particular position in an environment. The operations defined by `Env` are either polymorphic operations on lists, which will later be applied to environments, or operations manipulating positions within environments, which are therefore functions on integers or lists of integers.

`TypedEnv` defines, in terms of `addt`, operations associated with addition of types and environments: `addtypetoenv`, which adds a capability to the type at a given position within an environment; `addtoenv`, which adds a list of capabilities to the types at a list of positions; and `addenv`, which adds environments. All of these operations are partial, because `addt` is partial. Each operation therefore has an associated predicate, for example `canaddenv`, which is used in the hypotheses of theorems about the partial operations. For example, the theorem that addition of environments is commutative is

```
canaddenv G H ==> addenv G H = addenv H G.
```

This theorem is proved by induction on `G` and case-analysis on `H`, using the corresponding theorem about `addt` (mentioned in Section 4).

6   The Meta Language

Rather than define a representation of pi terms directly, we use a meta language, which is a lambda calculus with constants. This approach has a number of advantages.

- Once basic properties of the meta language (e.g. injectivity of constructors) have been proved, the corresponding properties of the pi calculus are easily proved by Isabelle's automatic tactics, and it is trivial to transfer the proofs to extensions or variations of the calculus.
- The meta language is simpler (has fewer constructors) than the pi calculus. This means that some key theorems, whose proofs are complex, are easier to prove for the meta language and lift to the pi calculus than to prove for the pi calculus directly; see Section 8.
- Both of the n-ary binding operators of the pi calculus are represented in terms of a single unary binding operator in the meta language; issues to do with variable binding are therefore concentrated into a single, relatively simple, area.

We represent variables by de Bruijn indices [1], to avoid the complications of reasoning about α-conversion and freshness of variable names in substitutions [7]. Theory Meta defines the following datatype, parameterised by a type of constants.

```
datatype 'a meta =
    mCon 'a                          (* constant *)
  | mVar var                         (* variable *)
  | mAbs ('a meta)                   (* abstraction *)
  | mApp ('a meta) ('a meta)         (* application *)
  | mAdd ('a meta) ('a meta)         (* additive application *)
```

The type var is a record type with fields index, of type nat, and tag, whose type is an enumeration with possible values Pos, Neg or Both. The index field is the de Bruijn index of the variable occurrence. The tag field distinguishes between positive and negative occurrences of linear variables and occurrences of non-linear variables (which have tag Both). This explicit tagging of variable occurrences simplifies some proofs by making it easier to determine which end of a linear channel is being transmitted by an output. In a practical language this information could probably be obtained by type inference, and it might be possible to eliminate it from our formalisation in the future. More generally, we anticipate other uses of the tag field when adapting our formalisation to other type systems; for example, Pierce and Sangiorgi's proof of type soundness for the pi calculus with subtyping [20] uses an auxiliary syntax in which variable occurrences are tagged with runtime types.

The de Bruijn index of a variable occurrence counts the number of abstractions between the occurrence and the abstraction which binds it. Indices so large that they point outside all abstractions refer to positions in a notional list of free variables; this list is, in effect, an untyped environment for the term. For example, if the environment of free variables is taken to be u, v (the order is arbitrary), and if we pretend that `var = nat` and omit the `mVar` constructors, then the term

$$\lambda x.u(\lambda y.u(x(yv)))$$

is represented by `mAbs (mApp 1 (mAbs (mApp 2 (mApp 1 (mApp 0 3)))))`.

It is slightly misleading to think of the meta language as a lambda calculus. Because we never apply β-reduction to meta language terms, `mAbs` and `mApp` are unrelated; in particular, the order of the arguments of `mApp` is unimportant. Note the inclusion of a second "application", called `mAdd`, which will be used when representing additive linear operators; it is convenient for multiplicative and additive operators to use different meta language constructors.

In order to support the n-ary binding operators of the pi calculus, and to represent output (which involves a list of variables), we define `mABS` for iterated abstraction and `mAPP` which applies `mApp` repeatedly to the elements of a list.

7   Substitution

Substitution is defined for the meta language in theory `Meta` and lifted to the pi calculus in theory `Pi`. In order to define substitution appropriately, we consider the key case in the proof of the subject reduction theorem. The derivation

$$\frac{\dfrac{\Gamma \vdash P}{\Gamma + x : !^1[\tilde{T}] + \tilde{y} : \tilde{T} \vdash x![\tilde{y}] \,.\, P} \quad \dfrac{\Delta, \tilde{z} : \tilde{T} \vdash Q}{\Delta + x : ?^1[\tilde{T}] \vdash x?[\tilde{z} : \tilde{T}] \,.\, Q}}{\Gamma + \Delta + x : \updownarrow^1[\tilde{T}] + \tilde{y} : \tilde{T} \vdash x![\tilde{y}] \,.\, P \mid x?[\tilde{z} : \tilde{T}] \,.\, Q}$$

types the process

$$x![\tilde{y}] \,.\, P \mid x?[\tilde{z} : \tilde{T}] \,.\, Q$$

which reduces to

$$P \mid Q\{\tilde{y}/\tilde{z}\}$$

and we must therefore derive a typing for the latter process. If we have

$$\Delta + \tilde{y} : \tilde{T} \vdash Q\{\tilde{y}/\tilde{z}\}$$

then we can derive

$$\Gamma + \Delta + \tilde{y} : \tilde{T} \vdash P \mid Q\{\tilde{y}/\tilde{z}\}$$

which is sufficient; note that the linear input and output capabilities of x were used by the communication and are not needed in order to type $P \mid Q\{\tilde{y}/\tilde{z}\}$. This example shows that the variables $\tilde{z}$ do not appear in the environment of $Q\{\tilde{y}/\tilde{z}\}$, but that the types of $\tilde{z}$ must be added to the environment as extra capabilities for $\tilde{y}$. Theory `Subst` defines a function `substenv` which calculates the typed environment for a substituted term, and a predicate `oksubst` which tests definedness of this environment.

We have already noted that it is sufficient to define substitution of variables (not arbitrary terms) for variables. Furthermore, because it is only necessary to substitute for input-bound variables, we can assume that the variables being replaced are distinct from each other and from the variables replacing them; it is therefore possible to define the simultaneous substitution of a list of variables as a sequence of substitutions of single variables. This is different from other pi calculus formalisations (for example, Melham's [14]) which define simultaneous substitution directly, but given that we are using de Bruijn indices it represents a very significant simplification. Because substitution in a typed process requires a change in the environment, the variable indices throughout the process must be adjusted. This adjustment would be rather complex to define for simultaneous substitutions, but is much more straightforward for a single substitution. Similarly, proofs about simultaneous substitution use induction to extend results about single substitution to lists, and this is simpler than reasoning directly about simultaneous substitution. Reasoning about the adjustment of indices in single substitutions is facilitated by Isabelle's recently-introduced tactic `arith_tac`, which is based on a decision procedure for linear arithmetic.

8   The Typed Meta Language

Another novel feature of our formalisation is that we define a type system for the meta language, which keeps track of linear variable use. The rules (omitting tags, and presented informally) are shown in Figure 1.

$$\frac{\Gamma \text{ unlimited}}{\Gamma + v : \texttt{LinV } (|\texttt{ pos } = \texttt{One } T \texttt{ , neg } = \texttt{Zero } |) \vdash_m \texttt{mVar } v} \qquad \frac{\Gamma \text{ unlimited}}{\Gamma \vdash_m \texttt{mCon } c}$$

$$\frac{\Gamma \text{ unlimited}}{\Gamma + v : \texttt{LinV } (|\texttt{ pos } = \texttt{Zero } \texttt{ , neg } = \texttt{One } T \texttt{ |) } \vdash_m \texttt{mVar } v} \qquad \frac{\Gamma, x : T \vdash_m t}{\Gamma \vdash_m \texttt{mAbs } t}$$

$$\frac{\Gamma \text{ unlimited}}{\Gamma + v : \texttt{NLinV } T \vdash_m \texttt{mVar } v} \qquad \frac{\Gamma \vdash_m t \quad \Delta \vdash_m u}{\Gamma + \Delta \vdash_m \texttt{mApp } t \, u} \qquad \frac{\Gamma \vdash_m t \quad \Gamma \vdash_m u}{\Gamma \vdash_m \texttt{mAdd } t \, u}$$

Fig. 1. Typing Rules for the Meta Language.

A few technical theorems are proved at this stage, for example:

If $\Gamma \vdash_m p$ and $\Delta \vdash_m p$ and $\Gamma + \Delta$ is defined and Γ is unlimited then Δ is unlimited.

The proof of this theorem is simpler for the typed meta language than it would be for the typed pi calculus, because the meta language has fewer constructors. In the theory `Pi` we prove that every typing rule for the pi calculus is a derived rule for the meta language type system. Hence this theorem, and others like it, can be lifted very easily to the pi calculus level, and extended easily to variations of the pi calculus. This particular theorem is used in the proof that structural congruence preserves typability (Section 10).

This technique only applies to theorems whose conclusions do not mention the typing relation. Correct typing of (the representation of) a pi calculus term as a meta language term does not imply corect typing of the pi calculus term — the pi calculus typing rules have extra hypotheses which are not captured by the meta language typing rules. Nevertheless, we have found the introduction of the meta language type system to be a useful structuring technique which very significantly simplifies the proofs of the theorems to which it is applicable.

9   Formalising the Pi Calculus

The theory `Pi` defines specific linear and non-linear channel types and a specialised type of environments, as mentioned in Section 4. A specific type `con` of constants for the meta language is defined, and representations of pi calculus terms are defined as meta language terms of type `pi = con meta`. For example,

```
OUT x n xs p == mAPP (mApp (mCon (Out n)) p) (map mVar (x # xs))
```

represents $x![xs].p$ where $length(xs) = n$.

The structural congruence relation, the reduction relation and the typing relation are all defined inductively. The de Bruijn representation affects some rules: for example, the scope extrusion rule for structural congruence (Section 2) becomes (`SCONG` is an inductively-defined subset of `pi * pi`, formalising the structural congruence relation, so that `(p,q):SCONG` means $p \equiv q$)

```
(PAR p (NEW n ts q) , NEW n ts (PAR (lift 0 n p) q)) : SCONG
```

where `lift 0 n p` adjusts the indices of the free variables of p to take account of the insertion of n variables at position 0 in the environment. The definition of `lift` guarantees that the first n variables in the environment, corresponding to $\tilde{x}$, do not occur in `lift 0 n p`, so the condition on free variables disappears.

As indicated in Section 7, if $\Gamma \vdash P$ and $P \longrightarrow Q$ by a communication on a linear channel, then Q is typed in an environment in which the polarity of that channel has been reduced to $|$. It is therefore necessary to label a reduction with the name of the channel involved (or τ if the channel is hidden by an enclosing ν), represented by type `redch`. The reduction $P \xrightarrow{x} Q$ is formalised by (`P , x , Q) : RED` where `RED` is an inductively defined subset of `pi * redch * pi`.

Defining pi terms via a meta language rather than directly as a datatype means that distinctness and injectivity theorems need to be proved explicitly for the pi calculus constructors. The number of such theorems is fairly large (the square of the number of constructors), but they are all proved by Isabelle's automatic tactics.

Theorems about substitution on pi terms are also proved automatically, for example (note the addition of n due to changing environments):

```
(NEW n ts p)[x//i] = NEW n ts p[x+n // i+n].
```

Similarly, theorems about `lift` on pi terms are proved automatically.

Theorems stating that the pi typing rules are derived rules for the typed meta language are proved, as mentioned in Section 8. Each theorem is simply a pi typing rule with the pi typing relation replaced by the meta typing relation. The proofs are short, the only complexity being some explicit use of theorems about environments.

10   Type Soundness

The key to proving soundness of the type system is the *subject reduction theorem*, which states that reduction of a typed process yields a typed process. We prove

```
[| G |- p ; (p, x, q) : RED ; balanced G |] ==> usechan x G |- q
```

by induction on the reduction relation, `RED`. As discussed in Section 7, q is typed not in G but in an environment in which the capability of the channel x has been used, if its type is linear.

As we also saw in Section 7, we need to prove a *substitution lemma*:

```
[| G |- p ; oksubst x i G |] ==> substenv x i G |- p[x//i]
```

for substitutions of single variables and extend it by induction to substitutions of lists of variables. Here we use the induction principle derived from the inductive definition of the typing relation. The proof breaks down into a number of cases, one for each pi calculus constructor. In order to make it easier to extend the language later, we prove a lemma for each case and then combine them with a "driver" proof which simply applies the induction rule to generate the cases and then applies the appropriate lemma to each case. Once the proof is structured in this way, it is easy to see how to extend it if new constructors are added. All of our proofs about the typing relation are similarly modularised.

Because structural congruence can be used when deriving reductions, we prove that structural congruence preserves typability:

```
[| G |- p ; (p , q) : SCONG |] ==> G |- q.
```

The proof is by induction on the definition of `SCONG`, and as with the inductive proofs about `|-`, we structure the proof by extracting the cases as separate lemmas. The congruence cases are almost trivial and are all proved by a simple specialised tactic, `SCONG_tac`, which uses Isabelle's classical reasoner to search for a proof involving the introduction and elimination rules arising from the inductive definition of the typing relation. Most of the other cases are straightforward, involving application of the typing rules and some reasoning about addition of environments. Some of the cases dealing with replication and restriction are more complex, requiring (for replication) the fact about unlimited environments mentioned in Section 8 and (for restriction) the following *weakening lemma*:

```
[| G |- p ; length ts = n ; unlimited ts ; m <= length G |] ==>
ins ts m G |- lift m n p
```

in which `ins ts m G` is the environment obtained by inserting the types `ts` into `G` at position `m`. Another form of weakening adds capabilities to types which are already in the environment. We prove

```
[| G |- p ; unlimited H ; canaddenv G H |] ==> addenv G H |- p
```

by induction on the typing relation, again structuring the proof into a lemma for each case.

The subject reduction theorem states that reductions of typed processes yield typed processes, but because reduction is not defined for communications with an arity mismatch, we need to prove that these incorrect communications cannot occur in typed processes. Following Kobayashi *et al.* we prove that if a typed process contains a term $x![\tilde{z}] . P \mid x?[\tilde{y} : \tilde{T}] . Q$ then $length(\tilde{y}) = length(\tilde{z})$ and the type of x (in the environment or in an enclosing restriction) has polarity $\updownarrow$. We also prove their theorems about correct use of linear and non-linear channels, for example that if a typed process contains a term $x![\tilde{z}] . P \mid x![\tilde{z}] . Q$ then the type of x is non-linear.

11   Extension to Session Types

Honda *et al.* [10, 24] have proposed *session types*, which allow successive communications on a channel to carry different message types. Branching is also allowed, so that the transmission of a particular value (from a finite range) can determine the type of the subsequent interaction. Consider, for example, a server for mathematical operations, which initially offers a choice between equality testing and negation. A client must choose an operation and then send the appropriate number of arguments to the server, which responds by sending back the result. All communications take place on a single session channel called x; the type of the server side of this channel is

$$S = \&\langle \mathsf{eq} : ?[\mathsf{int}] . ?[\mathsf{int}] . ![\mathsf{bool}] . \mathsf{end}, \mathsf{neg} : ?[\mathsf{int}] . ![\mathsf{int}] . \mathsf{end}\rangle.$$

The author and Malcolm Hole [5] have defined a notion of subtyping for session types, proposing a language whose type system allows the description of backward-compatible upgrades to client-server systems. Ultimately we aim to formalise the type system of this language.

To avoid runtime type errors, a session channel must be shared by exactly two processes, one at each end. Within each process, however, the channel must be used for as many communications as are specified by its type. Session types therefore require an interesting mixture of linear and non-linear (but bounded) control and this will require a generalisation of our present theory **Types**. Addition of a capability to a session type should mean prefixing a new communication to the existing type, for example extending ![int] . end to ?[int] . ![bool] . end.

Using Pierce and Sangiorgi's [20] technique, proving type soundness for the system with subtyping requires the definition of an auxiliary language in which variable occurrences are tagged with runtime types. Our formalisation will have to define two different, although related, languages, and our structured approach should make it easy to achieve this, especially as we have already included support for tagging of variable occurrences.

12 Conclusions

We have formalised a linear type system for the pi calculus, and a proof of its soundness, as a step towards a formalisation of a more complex type system incorporating session types and subtyping.

Our work differs from other formalisations of the pi calculus in several significant ways. One is that we concentrate on reasoning about the reduction relation and type systems, including systems with linear features, rather than labelled transition systems and bisimulation. More importantly, mindful of our desire to extend this work to a more complex language, we have aimed to develop a methodology and general framework for the formalisation of type systems for languages based on the pi calculus, rather than simply to formalise a particular type system. The use of a typed meta language (Sections 6 and 8), the development of a generic theory of linear and non-linear types (Section 4) and environments (Section 5), and the modular structure of the proofs about the pi calculus typing relation (Section 10), are all intended to facilitate the transfer of our techniques to other languages.

Acknowledgements

The author is grateful to Tom Melham and the anonymous referees for many valuable comments, to Malcolm Hole for discussions of pi calculus type soundness proofs, and to Simon Ambler for discussions of formalisations of operational semantics.

References

[1] N. G. deBruijn. Lambda calculus notation with nameless dummies. *Indagationes Mathematicae*, 34:381–392, 1972.

[2] J. Despeyroux. A higher-order specification of the pi-calculus. In *Proceedings of the IFIP International Conference on Theoretical Computer Science*, 2000.

[3] C. Dubois. Proving ML type soundness within Coq. In M. Aagaard and J. Harrison, editors, *Proceedings of TPHOLs2000, the 13th International Conference on Theorem Proving in Higher Order Logics*, LNCS, pages 126–144. Springer, 2000.

[4] M. J. Gabbay and A. M. Pitts. A new approach to abstract syntax with variable binding. *Formal Aspects of Computing*, 2001.

[5] S. J. Gay and M. J. Hole. Types and subtypes for client-server interactions. In S. D. Swierstra, editor, *ESOP'99: Proceedings of the European Symposium on Programming Languages and Systems*, number 1576 in Lecture Notes in Computer Science, pages 74–90. Springer-Verlag, 1999.

[6] J.-Y. Girard. Linear Logic. *Theoretical Computer Science*, 50(1):1–102, 1987.

[7] A. D. Gordon and T. Melham. Five axioms of alpha conversion. In J. von Wright, J. Grundy, and J. Harrison, editors, *Theorem Proving in Higher Order Logics: 9th International Conference, TPHOLs'96*, volume 1125 of *Lecture Notes in Computer Science*, pages 173–190. Springer-Verlag, 1996.

[8] L. Henry-Gréard. Proof of the subject reduction property for a π-calculus in COQ. Technical Report 3698, INRIA Sophia-Antipolis, May 1999.

[9] D. Hirschkoff. A full formalisation of π-calculus theory in the calculus of constructions. In *Proceedings of the Tenth International Conference on Theorem Proving in Higher Order Logics*, volume 1275 of *Lecture Notes in Computer Science*, pages 153–169. Springer-Verlag, 1997.

[10] K. Honda, V. Vasconcelos, and M. Kubo. Language primitives and type discipline for structured communication-based programming. In *Proceedings of the European Symposium on Programming*, Lecture Notes in Computer Science. Springer-Verlag, 1998.

[11] F. Honsell, M. Miculan, and I. Scagnetto. π-calculus in (co)inductive type theory. *Theoretical Computer Science*, 253(2):239–285, 2001.

[12] N. Kobayashi, B. C. Pierce, and D. N. Turner. Linearity and the Pi-Calculus. *ACM Transactions on Programming Languages and Systems*, 21(5):914–947, September 1999.

[13] J. McKinna and R. Pollack. Some lambda calculus and type theory formalized. *Journal of Automated Reasoning*, 23(3), 1999.

[14] T. F. Melham. A mechanized theory of the π-calculus in HOL. *Nordic Journal of Computing*, 1(1):50–76, 1994.

[15] R. Milner. The polyadic π-calculus: A tutorial. Technical Report 91-180, Laboratory for Foundations of Computer Science, Department of Computer Science, University of Edinburgh, 1991.

[16] R. Milner. *Communicating and Mobile Systems: the π-calculus*. Cambridge University Press, 1999.

[17] R. Milner, J. Parrow, and D. Walker. A calculus of mobile processes, I and II. *Information and Computation*, 100(1):1–77, September 1992.

[18] L. C. Paulson. *Isabelle — A Generic Theorem Prover*, volume 828 of *Lecture Notes in Computer Science*. Springer-Verlag, 1994.

[19] F. Pfenning and C. Elliott. Higher-order abstract syntax. In *Proceedings of the ACM SIGPLAN '88 Symposium on Programming Language Design and Implementation*. ACM Press, 1988.

[20] B. C. Pierce and D. Sangiorgi. Types and subtypes for mobile processes. In *Proceedings, Eighth Annual IEEE Symposium on Logic in Computer Science*. IEEE Computer Society Press, 1993.

[21] C. Röckl. A first-order syntax for the pi-calculus in Isabelle/HOL using permutations. Technical report, Département d'Informatique, École Polytechnique Fédérale de Lausanne, 2001.

[22] C. Röckl, D. Hirschkoff, and S. Berghofer. Higher-order abstract syntax with induction in Isabelle/HOL: Formalizing the pi-calculus and mechanizing the theory of contexts. In F. Honsell and M. Miculan, editors, *Proceedings of FOSSACS'01*, number 2030 in Lecture Notes in Computer Science, pages 364–378. Springer-Verlag, 2001.

[23] D. Syme. Proving Java type soundness. In J. Alves-Foss, editor, *Formal Syntax and Semantics of Java*, volume 1523 of *LNCS*. Springer, 1999.

[24] K. Takeuchi, K. Honda, and M. Kubo. An interaction-based language and its typing system. In *Proceedings of the 6th European Conference on Parallel Languages and Architectures*, number 817 in Lecture Notes in Computer Science. Springer-Verlag, 1994.

[25] D. N. Turner. *The Polymorphic Pi-Calculus: Theory and Implementation*. PhD thesis, University of Edinburgh, 1996.

[26] D. von Oheimb and T. Nipkow. Machine-checking the Java specification: Proving type-safety. In J. Alves-Foss, editor, *Formal Syntax and Semantics of Java*, volume 1523 of *LNCS*, pages 119–156. Springer, 1999.

Representing Hierarchical Automata in Interactive Theorem Provers

Steffen Helke and Florian Kammüller

Technische Universität Berlin
Institut für Softwaretechnik und Theoretische Informatik

Abstract. Hierarchical Automata represent a structured model of statecharts. They are formalized in Isabelle/HOL. The formalization is on two levels. The first level is the set-based semantics; the second level exploits the tree-like structure of the hierarchical automata to represent them using Isabelle's datatypes and primitive recursive functions. Thereby the proofs about hierarchical automata are simplified. In order to ensure soundness of this twofold approach we define a mapping from the latter to the former representation and prove that it preserves the defining properties of hierarchical automata.

1 Introduction

Statecharts [HN96] are a popular formalism for describing dynamic systems. Most recently they have even been incorporated as a separate view into the unified modelling language (UML). In this paper we want to report on an approach to formalizing statecharts in the theorem prover Isabelle/HOL [Pau94].

One of our interests is to find abstraction concepts for the simplification of the data contained in statecharts. Abstraction is a means to enable model checking [CGP99] of infinite state systems. Another interest is the integration of static and dynamic views of a system. Current trends in Software engineering – like UML — lack a clean semantical foundation for such combinations [KH00].

For both goals we need to be able to transfer properties proved for a statechart to an aggregation or to related statecharts at other levels of abstraction. In other words, we need to be able to compose and abstract properties and proofs. That is, we have to find a model that supports compositionality of properties and modular reasoning.

To that end, we use a structured model for representing statecharts: hierarchical automata (HA). This representation is used by Mikk [Mik00] as an intermediate language for connecting STATEMATE to the modelchecking tools SPIN and SMV. Hence, as a by-product of formalizing HA instead of the classical statecharts semantics [HN96] we can exploit the results of [Mik00] by feeding our formalization in a one-to-one manner into model checkers — once they become sufficiently small by abstraction and decomposition.

One major drawback of most model checking approaches is the restriction to finite state spaces. Therefore, to use model checkers one has to first simplify the system that has to be verified. This hand-made abstraction process is naturally

R.J. Boulton and P.B. Jackson (Eds.): TPHOLs 2001, LNCS 2152, pp. 233 248, 2001.

error-prone: unless this is done on paper there is no rigorous proof that the simplified model used in the model checker does actually correspond to the real system. This problem may be overcome by embedding a formalism in a theorem prover and combine it with a model checker. Our formalization of HA in higher order logic offers rigorous mechanical support for this first simplification step.

Another motivation for our work is to further the semantical foundation of statecharts — statecharts semantics are known to contain a lot of subtleties [vdB94]. Other work on formalizing statecharts in higher order logic has been performed by Day [DJ93]. The emphasis of this formalization is on building a front-end to the HOL/VOSS model checker rather than on building a basis for abstract reasoning about the structure.

Although there are formalizations from the designers of statecharts [HN96] these are often not satisfactory as they are not suited for precise semantical descriptions crucial for rigorous analysis. Other approaches to formalize diagrammatic models for dynamic systems and combine them with model checkers includes the work by Müller and Nipkow on I/O-Automata [MN95] – based on some earlier mechanizations by Nipkow and Slind [NS95].

The combination of model checking and theorem proving using abstraction has been studied, e.g. [SS99]. It uses, as many other approaches, theoretical concepts based on Galois connections for abstract interpretation [CC77] which we studied in the context of this work discovering a foundational error [BKS01].

The expressive strength of higher order logic enables an adequate formalization of HA. In Section 2 the formalization of a set based semantics similar to the one given in [Mik00] is described in Isabelle/HOL. This formalization of the semantics in higher order logic gives rise to a more efficient representation of the automata that uses a recursive tree-like datatype definition for the composition function; this approach is described in Section 3. We illustrate how the latter representation is mapped onto the former validating the efficient representation; the two representations are related via a function that is proved to preserve the defining properties of the HA. In Section 4 we describe the behaviour of statecharts by configurations and statuses.

2   Hierarchical Automata

As a first step to defining statecharts we formalize sequential automata (SA). Those will then be assembled in a structured way to build HA. Section 2.2 presents this representation of SA and HA. To provide an intuitive understanding of statecharts, we start this section with an example statechart modelling a car-audio-system that served at our university as an exercise for students. This example will accompany us throughout the paper.

2.1   Example Specification: Car-Audio-System

First we introduce the problem domain. The following picture illustrates the user interface of the car-audio-system.

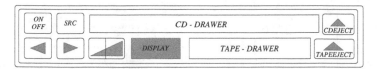

It has just a minimal control panel. We have not considered volume control, display of internal informations, and programming of a channel storage. The system has three signal sources (tuner, tape-deck and cd-player) and consists of the following sensing devices.

- ON/OFF: switches the system on and off.
- SRC: changes the signal source.
- ▶: changes the channel selection of the radio, spools the tape forward, or selects the next title of the disc.
- ◀: changes the channel selection of the radio, spools the tape backward or returns to the former track of the disc.

Figure 1 shows the statecharts specification of the car-audio-system. After starting the system — represented by the event O — the $TUNER\_MODE$ is initially activated. By pressing the key SRC we can change the activated signal mode in a determined order. If there is no disc available in the addressed subsystem the next signal mode is selected by the controller. Inserting a medium cannot change the current mode. The $TUNER\_MODE$ consists of four channels, which can be selected cyclically by pressing the keys ▶ and ◀. When the $TAPE\_MODE$ is activated, then the tape-deck immediately starts playing. When the end of the tape is reached the tuner mode is activated again. Pressing the keys ▶ and ◀ spools the tape forward and backward. By pressing a contrary key we can interrupt the spooling process. If the beginning of the tape is reached by spooling backward the system changes into the playing mode. If the CD_MODE is activated the cd-player immediately starts playing. After the last title the first one is selected by the system. By pressing the keys ▶ and ◀ we can jump to next or previous titles. After selecting a new title, the system must again adapt the position of the read head. The termination of this process is modelled by an internal event $READY$.

In [Mik00] it was shown that a statecharts specification can be adequately represented by a hierarchical automata. The HA of the car-audio-system in figure 2 gives a first impression of this representation. In the following paragraph we describe a function-based formalization of HA in Isabelle.

2.2   Function-Based Formalization

A hierarchical automaton (HA) is built from sequential automata (SA). The SA are composed in a tree-like fashion; the composition is defined as a function γ from states to sets of SA. The SA contained in $\gamma(s)$ for some state s of a HA are supposed to be parallel automata refining the state s. As in statecharts the communication happens through events which are immediately visible throughout the hierarchical automaton. A hierarchical automaton performs steps by executing transitions. During a step, events may be consumed and new events may be generated.

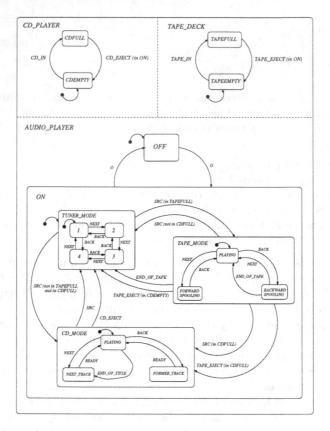

Fig. 1. Statecharts Specification of a Car-Audio-System.

Definition 1 (Sequential Automata (SA)). *A sequential automaton is a quadruple* (Σ, s_0, L, δ) *where* Σ *is a set of states,* s_0 *is the initial state,* L *is a set of transition labels and* $\delta \subseteq \Sigma \times L \times \Sigma$ *is a transition relation. A label* l *is a tuple* (ex, ac) *where* ex *is a proposition over event and state names (constant true, primitive events, and states connected with* $\wedge$, $\vee$, $\neg$) *and* ac *is a set of event names.*

We use an Isabelle type definition to create the type of SA as an abstraction over the set

$$(\sigma, \varepsilon) \text{ seqauto } \equiv_{df} \{(S,I,L,D) \mid (S::\sigma \text{ set}) \ (I::\sigma) \ (L::((\sigma,\varepsilon)\text{label}) \text{ set})$$
$$(D::((\sigma,\varepsilon)\text{trans}) \text{ set}). \text{ SeqAuto S I L D} \}$$

where `SeqAuto` is precisely the predicate defined in Definition 1. For simple access to the constituents of an SA we define the projections `States`, `Init`, `Labels`, `TransRel`, and `Events`, based on the representation injection that is created automatically by Isabelle with the type definition.

The expression part ex of a label represents the guard and ac is the action that is produced by the transition. Expressions are evaluated with respect to a tuple (C, E) where C is a set of (current) states and E is a set of (current) events (cf. Section 4). For expressions we define a simple expression language using a datatype definition.

```
datatype (σ,ε)expr = true | In σ | En ε | Not((σ,ε)expr)
                   | And((σ,ε)expr)((σ,ε)expr)
                   | Or((σ,ε)expr)((σ,ε)expr)
```

Associated primitive recursive definitions model the evaluation of expressions with respect to a current status (C, E) by mapping the expression language to higher order logic. For example, evaluation of an And expression is defined by the primitive recursion

```
primrec  "eval sc (And e1 e2) = ((eval sc e1) ∧ (eval sc e2))"
```

We define the convenient syntax $(C, E) \vDash ex$ for $\texttt{eval}(C, E)\ ex$.

Basically SA are flat automata, which describe individual levels of a modular hierarchy. We can build an HA from several SA by a composition function, which has to satisfy the following properties.

Definition 2 (Composition Function γ). *Let* F *be a set of SA. Then a partial function γ is a composition function iff*

1. *there exists an unique root automaton called γ_{root},*

   ```
   ∃¹ A. A ∈ F ∧ A ∉ ⋃ ran γ
   ```

2. *γ is a partial function[1] mapping states of the SA in* F *to sets of SA that do not contain γ_{root},*

   ```
   dom γ = ⋃ A ∈ F. States A ∧
   ⋃ (ran γ) = F - {γroot F γ}
   ```

3. *the set* F *has mutually distinct sets of states,*

   ```
   ∀ A ∈ F. ∀ B ∈ F. A ≠ B --> (States A) ∩ (States B) = {}
   ```

4. *each* F $\neq \gamma_{root}$ *has exactly one ancestor state,*

   ```
   ∀ A ∈ (F - {γroot F G}).
   ∃¹ s. s ∈ (⋃ A' ∈ F - {A}. States A') ∧ A ∈ the (γ s)
   ```

5. *and γ contains no cycles[2].*

   ```
   ∀ S ∈ ℙ (⋃ A ∈ F. States A). S ≠ {} -->
   ∃ s ∈ S. S ∩ ⋃ A ∈ the(γ s). States A = {}
   ```

The previous definition is summarized in the predicate `IsCompFun`.

Using Definitions 1 und 2 we can now formally describe an HA.

---

[1] We use the partial functions from the theory `Map` of Isabelle which models them via the option type.

[2] The constructor `the` is the evaluation for partial functions (maps).

Definition 3 (Hierarchical Automata (HA)). *A hierarchical automaton is a triple* (F,E,γ) *where* F *is a finite set of SA,* γ *is a composition function and* E *is a set of events, which contains all events defined in the automata of* F.

```
HierAuto F E γ ≡_df ⋃ A ∈ F. Events A ⊆ E ∧ finite F ∧ IsCompFun F γ
```

As for SA we can now define the following type `hierauto` for HA.

```
(σ,ε) hierauto ≡_df {(F,E,γ) |
                     (F::((σ,ε) seqauto set))
                     (E::(ε set))
                     (γ::(σ ~=> ((σ,ε) seqauto set))). HierAuto F E γ }
```

The corresponding projections of this type to its constituents F, E, and γ are called `SAs`, `Events`, and `CompFun`. For convenience in following definitions and proofs we furthermore define

```
States HA ≡_df ⋃ A ∈ (SAs HA). States A
TransRel HA ≡_df ⋃ F ∈ (SAs HA). TransRel F
Init HA   ≡_df ⋃ A ∈ (SAs HA). {Init A}
Root HA   ≡_df γ_root (SAs HA) (CompFun HA)
```

Figure 2 illustrates how our running example is represented using HA.

The composition function γ of the HA `CAS` of the car-audio-system is given by:

```
CompFun CAS ≡_df { AUDIO_SYSTEM ↦ {AUDIO_PLAYER, CD_PLAYER, TAPE_DECK},
              ON ↦ {AUDIO_CTRL}, TUNER_MODE ↦ {TUNER_CTRL},
              CD_MODE ↦ {CD_CTRL}, TAPE_MODE ↦ {TAPE_CTRL} }
        ⋃ { s ↦ {} | s ∈ {OFF, CDFULL, CDEMPTY, TAPEFULL, TAPEEMPTY,
              1, 2, 3, 4, CD_CTRL.PLAYING, NEW_TRACK, FORMER_TRACK,
              TAPE_CTRL.PLAYING, FORWARD_SPOOLING, BACKWARD_SPOOLING} }
```

The presented formalization is derived directly from the ideas of [Mik00]. We will see in the next paragraph that this approach has some disadvantages.

2.3   Well-Formedness of HA

When applying our formalization we have to check according to the definition of HA all its defining properties to ensure that our application is indeed a well formed HA. This may be cumbersome as there are some rather complex parts of the property `IsCompFun`. For example, the check that there are no cycles (Definition 2.5) involves checking for some nonempty intersections for all subsets of the union of all states of a HA — $2^{|\text{States HA}|}$ possibilities. In our small example of the car-audio-system we would have to derive 1048576 different proof obligations. The expenditure is exponential in the number of states. Here we need to exploit the tree-like structure of an HA. We define a constructor [+] that adds an SA at a specified position s to an HA extending the constituents of the HA.

```
HA [+] SAS ≡_df let (s,SA) = SAS;
                   SANew = insert SA (SAs HA);
                   ENew  = Events HA ⋃ Events SA;
```

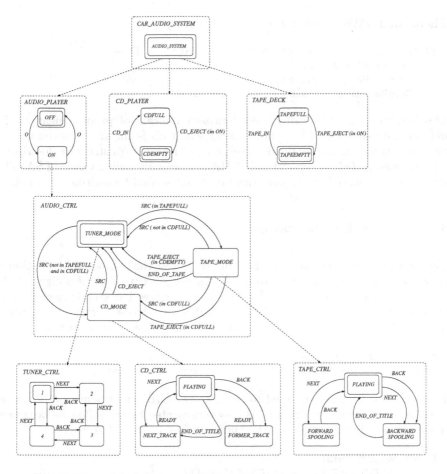

Fig. 2. Hierarchical Automata Representation of a Car-Audio-System.

$$\gamma\text{New} \;=\; \text{CompFun HA } [\text{f+] (s,SA)}$$

in

$$\text{Abs\_hierauto(SANew,ENew,}\gamma\text{New)}$$

The subexpression `CompFun HA [f+] (s,SA)` extends the partial function γ by s $\mapsto$ ($\{$SA$\}$ $\cup$ `CompFun HA s`) and $\{$s' $\mapsto$ $\{\}$ | s' $\in$ `States SA`$\}$. The injection `Abs_hierauto` creates a new element of the type `hierauto`. Preserving the defining properties of HA can now be checked more efficiently by proving theorems that reduce the defining properties of HA to simpler ones sufficient for [+]. The conditions `States SA` $\cap$ `States HA` = $\{\}$ and s $\in$ `States HA` are sufficient conditions to prove that the triple (SANew,ENew,γNew) corresponds to an element of type `hierauto` as is shown in the following theorem.

Theorem 1 (Well-Formedness of Addition).

```
[| (States SA ∩ States HA) = {}; s ∈ States HA |] ==>
   (insert SA (SAs HA),
    Events HA ∪ Events SA,
    CompFun HA [f+] (s,SA) ) ∈ hierauto
```

This construction results in a considerable reduction of proof obligations for well-formedness of an HA — now the expenditure is linear in the number of involved sequential automata. However, considering the constructive description implemented in [+] we recognize that HA are actually built as *trees* of SA. This structure is exploited even more strongly in our second formalization of HA.

3   Efficient Formalization

The complexity of the mechanization of HA lies in the composition function γ. As we have seen there is a way to tackle the complexity of proof obligations by building up a HA step by step with [+] using the tree-like structure of γ. Now, we develop a second model of HA that makes that tree-like structure explicit. Instead of a function γ we start off with a recursive datatype comptree.

```
datatype (σ,ε)comptree ≡df
        NodeG "(σ,ε)sequuto" "(σ * (σ,ε)comptree) list"
```

This tree-type may now be used to replace the third constituent of a HA. Considering our example its structure is now represented by the following comptree (for a graphical illustration see also the right hand side of Figure 3).

```
NodeG CAR_AUDIOSYSTEM
        [(AUDIO_SYSTEM, NodeG CD_PLAYER []),
         (AUDIO_SYSTEM, NodeG TAPE_DECK []),
         (AUDIO_SYSTEM, NodeG AUDIO_PLAYER
                         [(ON, NodeG AUDIO_CTRL
                              [(TUNER_MODE, NodeG TUNER_CTRL []),
                               (CD_MODE, NodeG CD_CTRL []),
                               (TAPE_MODE, NodeG TAPE_CTRL [])])])])]
```

With this representation the criteria for a composition function corresponding to Definition 2 can be expressed algorithmically as primitive recursions on the type comptree.

First, we introduce a predicate that checks whether the references in the tree are correct: $\mathtt{ValidReference}_t$ is true iff the ancestor states of the sets of SA in T are states of the ancestor SA in T. We define it as a primitive recursive function[3].

---

[3] The actual function definition in Isabelle needs a third clause for matching the pair. We omit this here as it seems to us a temporary flaw in the recent versions (99-1/2). The operator # is the Isabelle notation for list append.

```
ValidReference_t (NodeG SA L) =
     (set (map (λ p. fst p) L)) ⊆ (States SA)) ∧
     (ValidReferenceList_t L)

ValidReferenceList_t [] = True
ValidReferenceList_t (ST#L) = let (s,T) = ST
          in ValidReference_t T ∧ ValidReferenceList_t L
```

Furthermore, we define now a primitive recursive predicate $\texttt{MutuallyDistinct}_t$ ensuring that the sets of states of the SA are mutually distinct (cf. Definition 2.2), a predicate $\texttt{RootEx}_t$ defining the unique existence of a root automaton (cf. Definition 2.1), and a primitive recursive function $\texttt{SAs}_t$ collecting the SA of a comptree. With these preparations we can describe the characteristics of composition trees similar to the definition of composition functions (Definition 2).

Definition 4 (Composition Tree γ_t). *A tree γ_t of the recursive datatype* comptree *is a composition tree iff*

   $\texttt{ValidReference}_t \; \gamma_t \; \wedge \; \texttt{MutuallyDistinct}_t \; \gamma_t \; \wedge \; \texttt{RootEx}_t \; \gamma_t$

Now we can define a tree-based hierarchical automaton.

Definition 5 (Tree-Based Hierarchical Automata (HA_t)). *A tree-based hierarchical automaton is a tuple* (E,γ_t) *where γ_t is a composition tree and E is a set of events, which contains all events defined in the automata of* $\texttt{SAs}_t \; \gamma_t$.

This definition is summarized again in a predicate $\texttt{HierAuto}_t$, which is used to define the following type $\texttt{hierauto}_t$.

```
(σ,ε) hierauto_t ≡_df { (E,γ_t) |
                       (E::(ε set))
                       (γ_t::((σ,ε)comptree)). HierAuto_t E γ_t }
```

The definition of HA_t is a much simpler notion than the HA from Definition 3, in particular since the notion of composition tree is much less complex. Moreover, we will show now that it is sound to use this definition instead of HA. We define the following transformation $\texttt{HALift}$ lifting HA_ts to HA.

```
HALift HA_t ≡_df
     Abs_hierauto (SAs_t (CompTree HA_t), Events_t HA_t, Fun (CompTree HA_t))
```

The transformation $\texttt{Fun}$ builds a function that maps a state s to the set of SA paired with s in the list L of $\texttt{NodeG s L}$, which is the set of SA in γ s in the HA. If it does not find such a node it is "undefined", i.e. it maps to $\texttt{None}$.

```
Fun (NodeG SA L) s = if s ∈ (States SA) then
                       Some (set (map (λ p . Head (snd p))
                                      (filter (λ p . s = (fst p)) L)))
                     else FunList L s

FunList [] s = None
```

```
FunList (ST#L) s = let (s',T) = ST
                   in  if (s ∉ (Dom_t T)) then FunList L s
                       else Fun T s
```

The constructor Dom_t is the union of the states of all SA in a comptree and Head returns the SA of a NodeG element. The constants Some and None are the constructors of the option type. We can prove that for any composition tree the application of Fun produces a composition function. This theorem can then be lifted to the types hierauto and $hierauto_t$, summarized in the following theorem.

Theorem 2 (Hierarchical Automata Consistency).

$(SAs_t$ (CompTree HA_t), $Events_t$ HA_t, Fun (CompTree HA_t)) ∈ hierauto

Note, that the representation of a composition function as a composition tree is ambiguous: since we use lists in the type comptree there are various trees representing the same function. However, the function Fun can be seen as an appropriate partition of these different representations into classes of equivalent trees[4]. Theorem 2 guarantees that any tree-based HA is actually a well-formed HA thereby ensuring that a property proved for an HA_t does actually hold for the corresponding HA. However, to be able to infer that properties do hold *for all* HA while proving them for HA_t, we need to show that the efficient representation is complete: we may show that HALift is surjective. We have not done so, but will do so in due course. We have already been able to define an inverse for HALift constructively.

Similar to the first approach we redefine also the addition function [+] and obtain a function called [t+] that adds an SA to an HA and extends the comptree of HA_t accordingly.

Although the second formalization of HA using comptree is much more efficient it is still worthwhile keeping the first one in order to transport theorems. The first formalization in terms of a composition function corresponds directly to the semantics of HA as described in [Mik00] and serves as an input language for various model checkers. Thereby, we validate our efficient encoding of HA with respect to the mathematical semantics and make it at the same time compatible to other methods. In other words, we have in one formalization a semantics — given by the function based representation of HA — and an efficient encoding.

In the following we will describe the behaviour of HA defined by configurations and statuses. We will first describe the behaviour using the formalization of the semantics and then point out how we can integrate it with our efficient encoding.

4   Semantics of HA

The semantics of HA is described by configurations and statuses. Similar to the previous sections we will first present a semantical formulation close to [Mik00] and then a more efficient one on trees.

---

[4] A function partitions its domain into equivalence classes by the relation $x \sim y \equiv_{df} fx = fy$.

4.1 Configurations and Statuses

Configurations are basically sets of current states C describing the state of the entire system. Configurations are accompanied by sets of current events E.

Definition 6 (Configuration). *A set* C $\subseteq$ States HA *is a configuration iff there is a unique element of the configuration in* γ_{root} *and* s $\in$ C *corresponds to a unique* s' $\in$ C *for all SA in* γ s. [5] *Hence, the set of all configurations is defined as*

```
Conf HA ≡df {C. C ⊆ States HA ∧
              (∃¹ s. s ∈ States(Root HA) ∧ s ∈ C) ∧
              (∀ s ∈ States HA. (∀ A ∈ the(CompFun HA s).
              if (s ∈ C) then ∃¹ s'. s' ∈ States A ∧ s' ∈ C)
              else ∀ s ∈ States A. s ∉ C))}
```

A status of a HA is a configuration combined with a set E of events.

Definition 7 (Status). *A status of a HA comprises the HA, a configuration, and a set of events.*

```
Status HA C E ≡df E ⊆ Events HA ∧ C ∈ Conf HA
```

We use the previous predicate for the definition of a type **status**.

Configurations and accordingly statuses change when active transitions are executed. In order to define a step relation on statuses we need to define a notion of "firing" of transitions. By defining maximal non-conflicting sets of transitions we determine sets of enabled transitions. A step of a HA is modelled by firing enabled transitions of a configuration to generate a new status. To determine maximal non-conflicting sets of transitions we need a cascade of notions summarized in the following definition.

Definition 8 (Highest Priority Transitions (HPT)).

1. *The **successor relation** χ of an HA is defined based on γ.*

```
χ ≡df {(s,s'). s ∈ States HA ∧
       ∃ A ∈ (SAs HA). A ∈ the(CompFun HA s) ∧ s' ∈ States A }
```

   By χ^{+} and χ^{*} we denote the irreflexive and reflexive transitive closure of χ.

2. *We define transitions of an SA to be **enabled in** Status S if their origin is in the current configuration and the expression in their label is valid.*

```
EnabledTrans S SA ≡df {t. t ∈ TransRel SA ∧
                       source t ∈ Conf S ∧
                       (Conf S,Events S) ⊨ Expr t }
```

   The functions HA, Conf, *and* Events *are the projections of type* Status, source t *is the source of transition* t . *By* ET S *we denote the set of enabled transitions in* S *as the enabled transition contained in some SA of the HA.*

```
ET S ≡df UN A ∈ SAs (HA S). EnabledTrans S A
```

---

[5] Note that our definition differs from [Mik00]: to guarantee upwards-closedness of configurations the defining predicate has to be an equivalence — not just an implication as in [Mik00] — here expressed using "if".

3. *A set of transitions* trs *of a HA is called* **maximal non-conflicting** *iff each SA of the HA contributes at most one transition and for each* t ∈ trs *there is no transition with higher priority in* trs — *a notion based on* χ.

```
MaxNonConflict S trs ≡df trs ⊆ ET S ∧
                    ∀ A ∈ (SAs HA S). | trs ∩ TransRel A | ≤ 1 ∧
                    ∀ t ∈ trs. ¬ ∃ t'∈ ET S.
                                (source t', source t) ∈ χ⁺ HA
```

4. *Let* HPT S *denote the set of maximal non-conflicting sets in status* S.

The fact that there may be more than one maximal non-conflicting set of transitions trs reflects the non-determinism of statecharts: if there are several transitions that may fire in a status of an HA then each of these transitions is part of a different set trs ∈ HPT S.

Finally, we can define what it means for a HA to perform a step.

Definition 9 (Step Function[6]). *We define an* **initial status** *and a* **step function** *on statuses and transition sets.*

1. *The initial status is produced by starting from the initial state of* γ_{root} *and incorporating all predecessors using* χ^*. *The set of events is empty.*

```
InitStatus HA ≡df let
                SO = Init (Root HA)
                CO = ((Init HA × UNIV) ∩ χ* HA) ^^ {SO}
            in Abs_status(HA, CO, {}))
```

2. *A next status is derived by eliminating all predecessor states from each source of an enabled transition and adding the target state and all its initial predecessors. The events are obtained by collecting all actions produced by firing transitions.*

```
StepStatus ST trs ≡df let (A, C, E) = Rep_status ST
                    C' = C - (χ* A ^^ (Source trs)) ∪ (Target trs)
                            ∪ ((χ⁺ A ^^ (Target trs)) ∩ Init A )
                    E' =  Action(Label(trs))
                in Abs_status(A, C', E')
```

The projections Source, Target, *and* Action *build sets of the corresponding items.*

In principle one could prove now in the theorem prover the closure of statuses with respect to StepStatus [Mik00, Prop. 7]: for every status S and transition set trs ∈ HPT S the application StepStatus S trs is of type status again. However, this proof is awkward using the set based semantical definition. Assuming that the closure property holds, we can define the set of all reachable statuses as the inductive set

---

[6] Note, that the step "function" is only a function, because we consider the set trs as additional parameter.

```
inductive "ReachStatuses A"
    Status0       "InitStatus A : ReachStatuses A"
    StatusStep    "[| S : ReachStatuses A; trs : HPT S |]
                   ==> StepStatus S trs : ReachStatuses A"
```

However, the semantical representation is still not very well suited for mechanical reasoning. Following the idea of efficient representation of HA (see Section 3) we will in the following again use the full infrastructure of Isabelle/HOL simplifying the matter.

4.2 Configuration Trees

Following the ideas from Section 3 we can make the structure in configurations more explicit: as the HA are tree-structured, obviously this structure must also be present in the sets of states forming configurations. Reconsidering Definition 6, we see that a configuration is a tree as well. It is simpler than a comptree as nodes are just states. Each sequential automaton beginning from the root that is "active" in a status contributes exactly one state to this configuration tree.

Instead of a set of states we use the following recursive datatype conftree for n-ary trees of states in order to represent configurations.

datatype σ conftree $\equiv_{df}$ NodeC "σ" "(σ conftree) list"

With this representation the criteria for a configuration tree similar to Definition 6 can be expressed algorithmically as a primitive recursive predicate IsConfTree on the type conftree. This algorithm is based on the structural relationship between the γ_t of a HA$_t$ and a configuration tree illustrated in figure 3. The

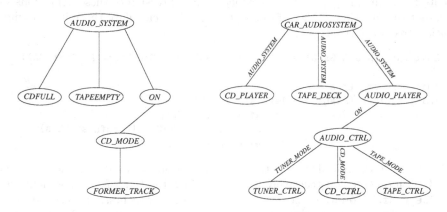

Fig. 3. Relationship between a γ_t of a HA$_t$ and a Configuration Tree.

levels of both trees are explored top-down step by step such that for each state of the configuration tree exactly one sequential automaton has to be found at the same level of hierarchy of γ_t. Furthermore, the algorithm inspects whether the successor relation for states in the configuration tree respects the successor relation for automata in γ_t. Based on the introduced configuration trees we obtain now an alternative definition for statuses (cf. Definition 7).

Definition 10 (Tree-Based Status). *A status of a* $\mathrm{HA_t}$ *comprises the* $\mathrm{HA_t}$, *a configuration tree, and a set of events.*

$$\mathrm{Status_t}\ \mathrm{HA_t}\ C_t\ E \equiv_{df} E \subseteq \mathrm{Events_t}\ \mathrm{HA_t} \wedge \mathrm{IsConfTree}\ (\mathrm{CompTree}\ \mathrm{HA_t})\ C_t$$

We use this predicate to define a type $\mathrm{status_t}$. Similar to the described procedure in Section 3, a tree-based status can be transformed into a "flat" status, i.e. the previously defined status with configurations as sets with no information on hierarchical structure. The definition of the semantical relationship between the two status types is on the one hand relevant for the validation of our encoding, on the other hand it is helpful for defining constitutive theories, as for example for classical temporal logics, which are usually defined on flat models. One can prove the following proof obligation similarly to Theorem 2 where the function Set maps a configuration tree to a flat set of states.

Theorem 3 (Status Consistency).

$$(\mathrm{HALift}\ (\mathrm{HA_t}\ S_t),\ \mathrm{Events_t}\ S_t,\ \mathrm{Set}\ (\mathrm{Conf_t}\ S_t)) \in \mathrm{status}$$

In order to obtain a notion of "firing" of transitions for tree-based statuses we have defined a predicate $\mathrm{MaxNonConflict_t}$ algorithmically by primitive recursions on the type $\mathrm{conftree}$. Based on this predicate we have derived the transition set $\mathrm{HPT_t}$, which reflects the non-determinism of "tree-based" statecharts. Definition 9 can be expressed by primitive recursions on the type $\mathrm{conftree}$ as well. However, these recursive functions are quite technical and will not be presented fully in this paper. To give at least an impression of these definitions we present the function $\mathrm{InitConf_t}$ here. It is used to calculate the initial configuration tree for a given γ_t.

```
InitConf_t (NodeG SA L) = NodeC (Init SA) (InitConfList_t L (Init SA))

InitConfList_t [] s = []
InitConfList_t (ST#L) s = let (s',T) = ST
                          in  if (s = s') then
                                  (InitConf_t T)#(InitConfList_t L s)
                              else InitConfList_t L s
```

Starting with the initial state of the root automaton we can determine the initial configuration tree constructively by gradual investigation of γ_t. The definition of $\mathrm{StepConf_t}$ — omitted here — is based on a similar recursive procedure calculating a new configuration tree for a given set of transitions trs. This algorithm determines first all subtrees of the current configuration tree, in which root states coincide with source states of individual transitions from trs. Afterwards these subtrees are replaced by initial configuration trees, which are derived from the target states of the transitions. Finally we obtain an inductive definition of sets for reachable statuses, which are derived directly from a $\mathrm{HA_t}$. The corresponding closure theorem (cf. Section 4.1) can now be proved much more efficiently.

In general we believe that this efficient representation of the semantics of statecharts — in addition to their efficient structural representation — is a further important ingredient in order to derive theorems for compositional reasoning effectively.

5   Conclusion

We have formalized a hierarchical semantics of statecharts in Isabelle/HOL. As a first step we followed the mathematical description as it is given in [Mik00].

The logic proved to be strong enough to capture all the structural concepts and enabled the formulation of the dynamic behaviour of these automata expressed as configurations. It was feasible to encode the simple expression language of a guard language. Here, mightier languages may be plugged in later. As usual the process of formalization revealed some minor inconsistencies in the original definitions.

However, as became apparent during the process of formalizing the tree-structured hierarchical automata we could employ much more powerful construction mechanisms of HOL: datatypes and primitive recursion. Since Isabelle/HOL is a mature proof environment we were able to deviate from the classical way of encoding an object language using merely the basic mathematical toolset of sets, relations, and closures. The obvious representation of the composition function as a recursive tree is an intuitive, efficient, and — since it is based on the rigorous construction methods of HOL — a sound formalization of HA.

Nevertheless, to validate our efficient encoding of tree-based hierarchical automata as the type $\mathtt{hierauto}_t$, we preserved the set-based formalization and mapped the $\mathtt{HA}_t$ to this mathematical semantics. This shows the well-formedness of elements of $\mathtt{HA}_t$. Rather than just being an academic challenge this has the effect that we may now use the set-based semantics to interface our formalization to model checkers as this semantics was defined for that purpose. Although not yet fully accomplished it is clear that we will be able to prove surjectivity of the translation function $\mathtt{HALift}$. If we show in addition that $\mathtt{HALift}$ respects the step function we will be able to lift general proof obligation for HA to our efficient representation and solve them there.

In comparison to other formalizations of statecharts (e.g. [DJ93]) the approach we have chosen has some advantages. Since it is structured it is very natural to decompose automata — as has already been illustrated in this paper. Furthermore, the modular fashion of the automata promises to support decomposition of properties along with the automata — a feature particularly relevant for reducing properties to make them accessible to model checking. Another advantage of our formalization is that through the explicit modelling of hierarchy we can express multi-level transitions (cf. [Mik00]). Also, we have already developed — though not yet integrated in the formalization — ideas to express history connectors. This is particularly simple in our formalization as it formalizes configurations as trees and those can be stored as histories even over multiple layers.

It is an interesting experience to discover that paradigms of programming, i.e. datatypes and recursive function, do actually apply to mathematics, i.e. semantics, and cause a considerable simplification of representation and proof.

Acknowledgements

We would like to thank Andre Nordwig for providing us with the car-audio-system example, Thomas Santen for very valuable discussions, and the anonymous referees for their suggestions.

References

[BKS01]   J. Burghardt, F. Kammüller, J. Sanders. *On the Antisymmetry of Galois Embeddings*. Information Processing Letters, **79**:2, Elsevier, June 2001.

[CC77]   P. Cousot and R. Cousot. *Abstract Interpretation*. In Principles of Programming Languages, ACM Press, 1977.

[CGP99]   Edmund M. Clarke, Orna Grumberg, and Doron A. Peled. *Model Checking*. The MIT Press, Cambridge, Massachusetts, 1999.

[DJ93]   Nancy Day and Jeffrey Joyce. *The Semantics of Statecharts in HOL*. In International Meeting on Higher-Order Logic Theorem Proving and its Applications. *Springer LNCS*, **780**:338-351, 1993.

[HN96]   D. Harel and D. Naamad. *A STATEMATE semantics for statecharts*. ACM Trans. on Software Engineering and Methodology, 5(4):293–333, Oct 1996.

[KH00]   F. Kammüller and S. Helke. *Mechanical Analysis of UML State Machines and Class Diagrams*. In Defining Precise Semantics for UML, Sophia Antipolis, France, June 2000. Satellite Workshop, ECOOP 2000.

[Mik00]   E. Mikk. *Semantics and Verification of Statecharts*. PhD thesis, Christian-Albrechts-Universität, Kiel. Bericht Nr. 2001, October 2000.

[MN95]   Olaf Müller and Tobias Nipkow. Combining Model Checking and Deduction for I/O Automata. In *TACAS'95, Tools and Algorithms for the Construction and Analysis of Systems*, *Springer LNCS*, **1019**:1–16, 1995.

[NS95]   T. Nipkow and K. Slind. I/O Automata in Isabelle/HOL. In Types for Proofs and Programs, *Springer LNCS*, **996**:101–119, 1995.

[Pau94]   L. C. Paulson. *Isabelle: A Generic Theorem Prover, Springer LNCS*, **828**, 1994.

[SS99]   Hassen Saïdi and Natarajan Shankar. Abstract and Model Check While You Prove. In N. Halbwachs and D. Peled, editors, *11th International Conference on Computer Aided Verification, CAV'99, Springer LNCS*, **1633**, 1999.

[vdB94]   M. von der Beeck. *A Comparison of Statechart Variants*. In Formal Techniques in Real-Time and Fault-Tolerant Systems. *Springer LNCS*, **863**: 128–148, 1994.

Refinement Calculus for Logic Programming in Isabelle/HOL

David Hemer[1], Ian Hayes[2], and Paul Strooper[2]

[1] Software Verification Research Centre
The University of Queensland, Australia
hemer@svrc.uq.edu.au
[2] School of Computer Science and Electrical Engineering
The University of Queensland, Australia

Abstract. This paper describes a deep embedding of a refinement calculus for logic programs in Isabelle/HOL. It extends a previous tool with support for procedures and recursion. The tool supports refinement in context, and a number of window-inference tactics that ease the burden on the user. In this paper, we also discuss the insights gained into the suitability of different logics for embedding refinement calculii (applicable to both declarative and imperative paradigms). In particular, we discuss the richness of the language, choice between typed and untyped logics, automated proof support, support for user-defined tactics, and representation of program states.

1 Introduction

In this paper we present a deep embedding of a refinement calculus for logic programs [8] based on the Isabelle/HOL logic [13,1]; this embedding forms part of the Marvin tool. The refinement calculus includes a wide-spectrum language, a declarative semantics for the language, and a collection of refinement laws. The wide-spectrum language includes executable constructs such as sequential conjunction, disjunction, existential quantification, procedures and recursion; the language also includes a number of specification constructs, including assumptions, specifications, parallel conjunction and universal quantification. The semantics of the language is described in terms of *executions*, which are mappings between initial and final states. Refinement laws have been proven in terms of the semantic framework, including: algebraic properties of the language; monotonicity rules; rules for lifting predicate connectives to the command level; rules for introducing commands; and rules for manipulating specifications and assumptions. These laws are applied by the user to refine programs to implementable code. Marvin lets the user write procedures, that can be called within other procedures or recursively. When introducing recursive calls, Marvin ensures the recursion terminates by insisting that the arguments to the recursive procedure are strictly decreasing with respect to a well-founded relation.

In embedding the refinement calculus we have two main choices : a *shallow* or a *deep* embedding. A shallow embedding avoids explicitly defining a separate

R.J. Boulton and P.B. Jackson (Eds.): TPHOLs 2001, LNCS 2152, pp. 249–264, 2001.

syntax for the language. Rather it embeds the language directly in the host syntax and expresses the semantics of the language in terms of this representation. A deep embedding, on the other hand, explicitly represents an abstract syntax of the language and provides an explicit function to map the syntax to the semantics as defined in the host language. Thus it decouples issues of syntactic equality from semantic equality. In this paper we describe a deep embedding of a refinement calculus.

Marvin supports refinement in context, where information about the program environment and local assumptions are automatically passed down to subcommands. This context information can then be used in the refinement of these subcommands. The approach used in Marvin is similar to *program window inference*, developed by Nickson and Hayes [12]. This approach allows context information to be handled separately from the rest of the command. Marvin also includes several window-inference-like tactics that support step-wise refinement of programs, thereby greatly reducing the number and complexity of individual refinement steps.

In providing tool support for the refinement calculus we were initially faced with the question of what logic/proof tool to embed the calculus in. Prototype tools had been developed in several different logics prior to the version described in this paper. An earlier prototype [5] — based on a different semantic framework [7] — includes a shallow embedding of the calculus in the Ergo 4 theorem prover [19], a prover based on the window-inference paradigm. Two more embeddings (also based on the earlier semantics) were done in Ergo 5 [20] (a generic theorem prover based on sequent calculus) and Isabelle/ZF as part of a comparative study [9]. Finally, before settling on the current version, an embedding, based on the current semantics, was investigated in HOL-Z [11] (an embedding of the Z specification language in Isabelle/HOL).

At first, the choice of logic seemed rather arbitrary, but after experimenting with the different logics, we found several features of refinement calculi that have a fundamental effect on the choice of logics. Before choosing a logic, several questions need to be answered:

1. Can the constructs that model the syntax and semantics of the wide-spectrum language be easily represented in the logic?
2. Do the semantics include types?
3. To what extent does the proof tool automate proof of properties of the semantics and refinement laws, as well as the proof obligations that arise during refinement?
4. Can tactics be implemented to assist the user during the refinement process?
5. How readily can program states be represented in the logic?

In this paper, we discuss how the answers to these questions affect the choice of logic, using the embedding of the logic program refinement calculus as an example. Section 2 gives details of an embedding of the calculus in Isabelle/HOL. In Section 3 we illustrate the tool by showing the refinement of a simple program. We then show how this appears in the tool for the first couple of steps. In Section 4 we discuss how the questions raised above affect the choice of logic.

2 Refinement Calculus for Logic Programs in Isabelle/HOL

2.1 Preliminary Definitions

The semantics of our wide-spectrum language are defined in terms of a relationship between the initial and final states of a program. A state consists of a set of bindings, where a binding is a function that maps each variable to a value. The type `Val` represents the values that program variables can take; we wish to associate these with Isabelle types in some manner. To do this we represent `Val` as a type sum (using a datatype declaration):

```
Bnds == Var → Val
State == ℙ Bnds
datatype Val ==
    natV nat | listV (nat list) | setV (nat set) | pairV Val Val
```

The building blocks of our language are terms and predicates. A term is defined as either a variable or a function application to a list of terms. The functions `evallist` and `eval` evaluate a list of terms and a term respectively for a particular binding. Terms are evaluated to an element of `Val`. Predicates are modelled using a datatype; they are evaluated, with respect to a binding, by the function `evalp`, a boolean-valued result is returned.

```
datatype rterm == varT Var | funT (rterm list)

evallist : rterm list × Bnds → Val list
eval : rterm × Bnds → Val

datatype pred == pred ∧ pred | pred ∨ pred | pred ⇒ pred
    | pred ⇔ pred | rterm = rterm | rterm < rterm
    | ¬ pred | ∃ Var pred | ∀ Var pred | true | false
    | isNat Var | isList Var | isSet Var | isPair Var

evalp :: pred × Bnds → bool
```

2.2 Wide-Spectrum Language

The wide spectrum language includes both logic programming language and specification constructs. It allows constructs that may not be executable, allowing gradual refinement without the need for notational changes during the refinement process. The syntax of the commands in the wide-spectrum language is defined by the datatype `Cmd`.

```
datatype Cmd == ⟨ pred ⟩      -- specification
    | { pred }         -- assumption
    | Cmd ∧ Cmd        -- parallel conjunction
    | Cmd ∨ Cmd        -- parallel disjunction
    | Cmd , Cmd        -- sequential conjunction
    | ∃ Var • Cmd      -- existential quantification
    | ∀ Var • Cmd      -- universal quantification
    | PIdent(rterm)    -- procedure call
```

A specification $\langle P \rangle$ represents a set of instantiations of free variables of P that satisfy P. An assumption $\{A\}$ formally states the context in which a program is called. If an assumption does not hold, the program fragment in which it appears may abort. Aborting includes program behaviour such as nontermination and abnormal termination due to exceptions like division by zero (the latter being distinct from a procedure that fails if the divisor is zero), as well as termination with arbitrary results.

Sequential conjunction (S, T) evaluates S before T. The parallel conjunction $(S \wedge T)$ evaluates S and T independently and forms the intersection of their respective results on completion. The disjunction of two programs $(S \vee T)$ computes the union of the results of the two programs. Disjunction is generalised to an existential quantifier $(\exists X \bullet S)$, which computes the union of the results of S for all possible values of X. Similarly, the universal quantifier $(\forall X \bullet S)$ computes the intersection of the results of S for all possible values of X. A procedure can be called by referring to the procedure identifier and applying it to a term, e.g., $pid(T)$ applies the procedure named pid to the term T.

Parameterised commands are defined as a separate datatype $PCmd$ consisting of two entries: non-recursive commands and recursive commands.

```
datatype PCmd == Var :- Cmd | re PIdent • PCmd er
```

A command can be parameterised over a variable; it has the form $v : -S$, where v is a variable and S is a wide-spectrum program. A parameterised command is instantiated by applying it to a term — the result is a command.

Recursive calls are introduced within a recursion block. A recursion block has the form **re** $id \bullet pc$ **er**, where id names the block and pc is a parameterised command. Within recursion blocks, recursive calls of the form $id(T)$ can be used, provided certain termination conditions are met. We associate a well-founded relation with the arguments of the recursive call, and prove that the arguments are strictly decreasing with respect to the relation.

Procedures are defined by associating a procedure identifier, pid, with a parameterised command, e.g., $pid \mathrel{\widehat{=}} v : -S$.

2.3   Execution Semantics

The semantics of the wide-spectrum language is defined in terms of the function `exec`, which maps each command to a partial mapping between initial and final states (so-called *executions*). The mapping is partial because programs may not defined for all initial states.

We begin by defining the type `StateMap`, representing the set of partial mappings between initial and final states. Partial mappings are defined in Isabelle/HOL in terms of total functions. The labels `Some` and `None` are used to distinguish defined and undefined values. More precisely, for a partial mapping f and element x, if x is in the domain of f then there exists a y such that $f(x)$ = `Some` y, otherwise $f(x)$ = `None`.

```
StateMap == State ↛ State
```

We define the type `Exec`, as a subtype of `StateMap`, using Isabelle's `typedef` facility. The three conditions in the set comprehension correspond to the three healthiness conditions for executions [8].

```
Exec == {e: StateMap | dom(e) = P {b. {b} ∈ dom(e)}
        ∧ ∀ s ∈ dom(e). the e(s) ⊆ s
        ∧ ∀ s ∈ dom(e). e(s) = Some {b. b ∈ s & (e({b}) = Some {b})}}}
```

These conditions characterise useful properties of our wide-spectrum language that allow us to consider the effect of language constructs on a single binding rather than having to look at the effect on an entire state. The first condition states that the domain of an execution is equivalent to those states formed by merging states consisting of a single binding in the domain of the execution. Effectively the domain of an execution is closed under union and intersection (of states in the domain). The second condition states that executions are restricted to those mappings for which the output state is a subset of the input state. The third condition states that for an input state, the output state can be determined by considering the effect of the execution on each singleton binding in the input state, and then forming the union of the results.

The `typedef` facility defines `Exec` as a meta-level type, as well as an object level set. In defining a type in Isabelle/HOL, we must exhibit that the set is non-empty which is easily established by showing that the element $\{\varnothing \mapsto \varnothing\}$ is in the set.

The definition of `Exec` illustrates the overhead that is involved in representing partial functions in Isabelle/HOL. The second line of the definition requires the function "`the`", used in this case to strip away the label `Some` associated with `e(s)`. Conversely, in the third line we must include the label `Some`.

Programs are refined in the context of a program environment, describing any predefined procedures. The type `Env` is a mapping from procedure identifiers to their corresponding parameterised executions. Parameterised executions are defined as mappings from terms to executions, and provide the semantics of parameterised commands. Note that in this case `Exec` is used as a meta-level type.

```
PExec == rterm → Exec
Env == PIdent ↛ PExec
```

The function `exec`, used to define the semantics of the wide-spectrum language, is declared as a function mapping an environment and a command to a state mapping.

```
exec : Env × Cmd → StateMap
```

The translation of the `exec` into Isabelle/HOL was straightforward, with two exceptions. Firstly, to define `exec` for sequential conjunction, we needed to define composition of partial functions. Secondly, in defining `exec` for procedure calls we needed to perform a type coercion between the type `StateMap` (the expected type) and the type `Exec` (the actual type). This was done by introducing a call to the auxiliary function *Rep_Exec* (created by the `typedef` facility), that maps an abstract type to its representative type.

Having defined the `exec` function, we prove that for any environment ρ and command c, (`exec` ρ c) is of type *Exec*, and thus satisfies the three healthiness properties above. This is proved by structural induction on the command c. Notice in this case we are using *Exec* as an object level set. Defining types using Isabelle/HOL's `typedef` facility allows this dual usage.

The number of proof steps for this theorem was significantly less than the same proof in an earlier embedding in HOL-Z. This can be attributed to the fact that the HOL-Z proof involved large amounts of type checking (the types in HOL-Z are modelled as sets at the object level, and therefore do not make use of Isabelle/HOL's built-in type checker), as well as the fact that the automated proof tactics were more effective in Isabelle/HOL.

2.4   Refinement

We define the refinement relations $\sqsubseteq$ and $\sqsupseteq$ for state mappings (and consequently for executions).

```
e1 ⊑ e2 == dom(e1) ⊆ dom(e2) ∧ (∀ s: dom(e1). e1(s) = e2(s))
e1 ⊒ e2 == (e1 = e2)
```

The above definition states that an execution can be refined by extending the set of initial states for which it is defined. Next we define the notion of refinement for commands, including the context in which the commands are refined. The context includes the environment, `env`, under which the commands are refined.

```
env ρ ⊢ c1 ⊒ c2 == (exec ρ c1) ⊒ (exec ρ c2)
env ρ ⊢ c1 ⊑ c2 == (exec ρ c1) ⊑ (exec ρ c2)
```

Refinement of a command is defined in terms of its underlying execution. A command is refined by extending the set of initial states for which we can associate a final state, effectively removing undefinedness. "⊑" is a preorder and "⊒" is an equivalence relation. These properties are exploited to perform step-wise refinement.

Refinement laws for the wide-spectrum language have been proven in terms of the underlying execution semantics. When performing program refinement, these refinement laws are used to prove the correctness of individual refinement steps, rather than apply the definition of refinement directly.

The collection of rules include: algebraic properties for the propositional constructs; monotonicity rules for the language constructs; rules for lifting predicate connectives appearing in specifications to corresponding program constructs; rules for introducing and eliminating program constructs; and rules for manipulating specifications and assumptions.

Monotonicity. The wide-spectrum language is monotonic with respect to refinement in that a command can be refined by refining one or more of its subcommands. Consider, for example the law **sand-right-mono** given as:

$$\frac{env\ \rho\ \Vdash\ c1\ \sqsubseteq\ c2}{env\ \rho\ \Vdash\ c3\ ,\ c1\ \sqsubseteq\ c3\ ,\ c2}$$

This law states that the command "$c3$, $c1$" can be refined by refining the second command $c1$.

Predicate Lifting. Predicate lifting laws are used to lift predicate connectives contained in specifications to their program construct counterparts. For example the rule `lift-exists` lifts an existential quantifier within a specification to a command-level existential quantifier:

$$env\ \rho\ \Vdash\ \langle \exists\ V \bullet P \rangle\ \sqsubseteq\ \exists\ V \bullet \langle P \rangle$$

Note that the existential quantifier symbol $\exists$ is overloaded in the above law. The first occurence is the predicate quantifier, while the second occurence is the command quantifier.

Table 1 gives a comparison of the number of steps required to prove various refinement laws in Isabelle/HOL and HOL-Z. The table shows the reduction in proof steps in Isabelle/HOL, which can be attributed to the built-in type checker and improved automated proof support.

Table 1. Comparison of Proof Steps to Prove Refinement Laws.

Law	Isabelle/HOL	HOL-Z
lift-exists	4	75
por-mono	26	37
distribute-pand-over-por	4	8
left-distribute-sand-over-por	3	122
weaken-assume	5	54

2.5   Assumption Context

We have already seen that commands are refined in the context of a program environment ρ. In this section we describe a second kind of context, the so-called *assumption context* (based on the "**pre**" context used in the program window inference of Nickson and Hayes [12]), assumptions are introduced with the keyword "`assume`". Consider the command "$\{A\}$, S". In refining S and its subcommands we may use the assumption A. Rather than having to propagate the assumption throughout S and its subcommands, we add the assumption A to the context of the refinement. Refinement of commands in the context of assumptions extends the definition of command refinement given in Section 2.4.

$$env\ \rho\ \textbf{assume}\ A\ \Vdash\ c1\ \sqsubseteq\ c2\ ==\ env\ \rho\ \Vdash\ \{A\}, c1\ \sqsubseteq\ \{A\}, c2$$

Extending refinement to include assumption contexts allows us to prove refinement laws that use assumption contexts to manipulate specifications and assumptions. The equivalent-spec law states that a specification can be replaced by one that is equivalent under the assumptions in context:

$$\frac{A \;\Rightarrow\; (P \Leftrightarrow Q)}{env \; \rho \; assume \; A \;\Vdash\; \langle P \rangle \;\sqsubseteq\; \langle Q \rangle}$$

where $\Rightarrow$ is the entails operator, mapping two predicates to a boolean, defined as:

$$(p1 \Rightarrow p2) \Leftrightarrow (\forall b \bullet p1(b) \Rightarrow p2(b))$$

For example, under the assumption $X = []$, the specification "$\langle Y = lenX \rangle$" can be refined to "$\langle Y = 0 \rangle$", by observing that $X = [] \Rightarrow Y = \texttt{len } X \Leftrightarrow Y = 0$.

We have also proved laws for extending the assumption context. For example, the assumption context can be extended by using the law assumpt-in-context, a specialisation of the (right) monotonicity law for sequential conjunction.

$$\frac{env \; \rho \; assume \; A \wedge B \;\Vdash\; c1 \sqsubseteq c2}{env \; \rho \; assume \; A \;\Vdash\; \{B\}, c1 \sqsubseteq \{B\}, c2}$$

Similarly the law spec-in-context states that specifications can be used to extend the assumption context:

$$\frac{env \; \rho \; assume \; A \wedge P \;\Vdash\; c1 \sqsubseteq c2}{env \; \rho \; assume \; A \;\Vdash\; \langle P \rangle, c1 \sqsubseteq \langle P \rangle, c2}$$

2.6   Supporting Window Inference

The window-inference proof paradigm [14] (on which Ergo 4 is based) provides support for stepwise refinement. To support window inference in Isabelle/HOL we have implemented four tactics — optac, close, transtac and trans_inst_tac — which can all be applied regardless of the underlying refinement relation. Each tactic operates on the first subgoal, with any newly created subgoals moving to the top of the subgoal stack. These tactics are described in more detail separately below.

Tactic optac supports monotonic refinement, where a command is refined by refining one of its components. The subcommand to be refined is indicated by a list of numbers; for example, for the command "$S, (T \wedge U)$", [1] refers to the subcommand S and [2,2] refers to the subcommand U. Tactic optac updates the assumption context by calling rules such as assumpt_in_context and spec_in_context where appropriate. Consider the subgoal:

1. $env \; \rho \; assume \; A \;\Vdash\; \langle P \rangle, (T, U) \sqsubseteq \; ?x$

where $?x$ is a meta-variable used to represent the as yet to be determined refined command. Focusing on the subcommand T (by calling optac [2,1]), adds P to the context for T. The refinement of T becomes the first subgoal, with T being replaced by the program it is refined to in the original command, i.e.,

```
1. env ρ assume A ∧ P ⊩ T ⊑ ?y
2. env ρ assume A ⊩ ⟨P⟩ , (?y , U) ⊑ ?x
```

Tactic `close` applies an appropriate reflexivity rule to instantiate an unknown on the right-hand side of a refinement relation to the command on the left-hand side, effectively removing the first subgoal. For example, applying `close` to

```
1. env ρ assume A ⊩ S ⊑ ?x
```

removes subgoal 1 from the subgoal stack, and instantiates ?x to S.

Tactic `transtac` implements step-wise refinement; it transforms the current program to an intermediate program by applying a single refinement law. The context information is passed to the new intermediate program. If the refinement law includes any assumptions, then a proof obligation is generated to show that the assumptions are satisfied in the current context.

Consider the subgoal

```
1. env ρ assume A ⊩ S ⊑ ?x
```

applying `transtac` to a law of the form

$$\frac{C(\rho, A)}{\text{env } \rho \text{ assume } A \Vdash S \sqsubseteq T}$$

replaces the above subgoal with

```
1. C(ρ, A)
2. env ρ assume A ⊩ T ⊑ ?x
```

Tactic `transtac` applies Isabelle/HOL's simplification tactics to the proof obligation in the first subgoal. In most cases, where the proof obligation is valid, the proof obligation is discharged automatically.

Often the refinement law that we want to apply involves $\sqsupseteq$ instead of $\sqsubseteq$. In this case, `transtac` will weaken the law by replacing $\sqsupseteq$ by $\sqsubseteq$. Similarly, in some cases we want to apply a law containing $\sqsupseteq$ in the reverse direction, in this case `transtac` will attempt to apply such a rule in both directions.

Tactic `trans_inst_tac` is similar to `transtac`, except that it also allows the user to instantiate some or all of the meta-variables that occur in the law.

3   Example

In this section, we illustrate `Marvin` by showing the refinement of a simple example for testing list membership by recursively traversing the list. The refinement process begins by supplying a top-level program:

$$(X, L) :\text{-} \{isList(L)\} , \langle X \in elems(L) \rangle$$

The program, parameterised over the variables X and L, includes assumptions that L is a list. The specification states that X is in the set of elements that appear in the list.

The individual refinement steps shown here correspond to those used in Marvin. However, we use a more readable notation, based on the structured calculational proof notation described in [2]. The notation is indented to represent the depth of the subcommand that is currently being refined; 'n •' and '.' represent the beginning and end respectively of a refinement of a subcommand (where n is the depth of the subcommand). The notation $\llcorner S \lrcorner$ represents opening on the subcommand S (using optac). Application of refinement laws (using transtac or trans_inst_tac) is represented by a refinement relation ($\sqsubseteq$ or $\sqsubseteq$) followed by the name of the rule. The individual assumptions that make up the assumption context are labelled as they are introduced. Closing subcommands (using close) is represented by removal of indentation. Appendix A gives listing of the laws used in this example that have not been described earlier.

The refinement of the membership program starts by setting up the framework for introducing recursive calls. We apply the recursion-intro law to introduce a recursion block, Member. Included is an assumption stating that specifications of the form $\langle X1 \in elems(L1) \rangle$ can be refined to the procedure call Member(X1,L1), provided $L1$ is a list, and the length of $L1$ is strictly less than the length of L. The last condition ensures the recursive procedure terminates.

$(X, L) \mathbin{:-} \{isList(L)\}, \langle X \in elems(L) \rangle$
$\sqsubseteq$ recursion-intro: $<$ is well-founded on $\mathbb{N}$
   re $Member$ • $(X, L) \mathbin{:-}$
     $\{\forall X1, L1$ • env ρ ass $\#L1 < \#L \wedge isList(L1)$
       $\Vdash \langle X1 \in elems(L1) \rangle \sqsubseteq Member(X1, L1)\}$,
     $\{isList(L)\}, \llcorner \langle X \in elems(L) \rangle \lrcorner$
   er

Focusing on the specification, we can assume the assumptions prior to the specification:

    Assumption 1: $\forall X1, L1$ • env ρ ass $\#L1 < \#L \wedge isList(L1)$
         $\Vdash \langle X1 \in elems(L1) \rangle \sqsubseteq Member(X1, L1)$
    Assumption 3: $isList(L)$
    1 • $\langle X \in elems(L) \rangle$
    $\sqsubseteq$ intro-spec
       $\llcorner \langle L = [] \vee \exists H, T$ • $L = cons(H, T) \rangle \lrcorner \wedge \langle X \in elems(L) \rangle$
       2 • $\langle L = \langle \rangle \vee \exists H, T$ • $L = cons(H, T) \rangle$
       $\sqsubseteq$ lift-por
          $\langle L = [] \rangle \vee \langle \exists H, T$ • $L = cons(H, T) \rangle$
      . $\langle L = [] \rangle \vee \langle \exists H, T$ • $L = cons(H, T) \rangle \wedge \langle X \in elems(L) \rangle$
    $\sqsubseteq$ right-distribute-pand-over-por
       $\llcorner \langle L = [] \rangle \wedge \langle X \in elems(L) \rangle \lrcorner \vee \langle \exists H, T$ • $L = cons(H, T) \rangle \wedge \langle X \in elems(L) \rangle$

Next we focus on the subcommand on the left of the disjunction, firstly converting the parallel conjunction to sequential conjunction, then replacing the specification $\langle X \in elems(L) \rangle$ with $\langle false \rangle$ using the assumption context.

      2 • $\langle L = [] \rangle \wedge \langle X \in elems(L) \rangle$
      $\sqsubseteq$ pand-to-sand

$\langle L = [\,] \rangle , \llcorner \langle X \in elems(L) \rangle \lrcorner$
Assumption 4: $L = [\,]$
3 • $\langle X \in elems(L) \rangle$
$\sqsubseteq$ equivalent-spec $L = [\,] \Rightarrow X \in elems(L) \Leftrightarrow false$
  $\langle false \rangle$
. $\langle L = [\,] \rangle , \langle false \rangle$
$\sqsubseteq$ sand-false
 $\langle false \rangle$

We now focus on the subcommand on the right of the disjunction. We begin by lifting the existential quantifiers in the specification to the command level, then expand the scope of these quantifiers over the parallel conjunction (the rules lift-existsx2 and expand-scope-existsx2 correspond to lift-exists and expand-scope-exists except they apply to programs quantified over two variables). The parallel conjunction is then replaced by sequential conjunction.

2 • $\llcorner \langle \exists H, T \bullet L = cons(H, T) \rangle \lrcorner \wedge \langle X \in elems(L) \rangle$
3 • $\langle \exists H, T \bullet L = cons(H, T) \rangle$
$\sqsubseteq$ lift-existsx2
 $\exists H, T \bullet \langle L = cons(H, T) \rangle$
. $(\exists H, T \bullet \langle L = cons(H, T) \rangle) \wedge \langle X \in elems(L) \rangle$
$\sqsubseteq$ expand-scope-existsx2
 $\exists H, T \bullet \llcorner \langle L = cons(H, T) \rangle \wedge \langle X \in elems(L) \rangle \lrcorner$
 4 • $\langle L = cons(H, T) \rangle \wedge \langle X \in elems(L) \rangle$
 $\sqsubseteq$ pand-to-sand
  $\langle L = cons(H, T) \rangle , \llcorner \langle X \in elems(L) \rangle \lrcorner$

The specification $\langle X \in elems(L) \rangle$ is replaced by noting that under the assumption $L = cons(H, T)$, either X equals the first element of L, or X is an element of the remainder of the list. The introduced disjunction is then lifted to the command level. Finally we replace the specification $\langle X \in elems(T) \rangle$ by $Member(X, T)$ using Assumption 1, and noting that from the assumption $L = cons(H, T)$ it follows that $\#T < \#L$.

Assumption 5: $L = cons(H, T)$
5 • $\langle X \in elems(L) \rangle$
$\sqsubseteq$ equivalent-spec, assumption 5
 $\langle X = H \vee X \in elems(T) \rangle$
$\sqsubseteq$ lift-por
 $\langle X = H \rangle \vee \llcorner \langle X \in elems(T) \rangle \lrcorner$
 6 • $\langle X \in elems(T) \rangle$
 $\sqsubseteq$ Assumption 1
  $Member(X, T)$
. $\langle X = H \rangle \vee Member(X, T)$

Putting this all together, removing assumptions, using remove-assumpt, and removing the first specification $\langle false \rangle$, using por-false we get:

re *Member* • (X, L) :-
  $(\exists\, H,\, T \bullet \langle L = cons(H,\, T)\rangle\,,\, (\langle X = H \rangle \lor Member(X,\, T)))$
er

The resulting program is now at a sufficiently concrete level to be readily translated into code in a language such as Prolog or Mercury.

4 Discussion

There are a number of different embeddings of refinement calculi in theorem provers [3]. While these embeddings differ in many ways, there are a number of fundamental issues for each. In this section we present these issues, comparing the solutions presented in this paper to solutions presented elsewhere.

4.1 Richness of Language

The first issue relates to the richness of the syntax of the logic. Can the syntax and semantics of the refinement language be conveniently expressed in the logic? In particular, when the language has already been specified using some formal language (such as Z), can this specification be readily translated (by hand or indeed automatically) into the notation used by the logic?

The semantics of our language [8] are formally specified using the Z specification language [15]; this in turn is based on Zermelo Frankel set theory. Therefore it was relatively straightforward to translate the semantics into HOL-Z and Isabelle/ZF notation. However, while the translation to Isabelle/HOL notation required a little more effort, we found that in reference to the other issues raised below, the extra effort up front was more than rewarded later on. We conclude here that we need to be wary of selecting a logic primarily because of its richness without considering the other factors. Also note that while in this case ZF and HOL-Z were closer to the specification language than HOL, this is not necessarily always the case. For example users of higher-order logics might specify their calculus using a language that is closer to HOL.

4.2 Typed versus Untyped Logics

The second issue involves the choice of an untyped or typed logic. Embedding refinement calculi in logics such as HOL-Z or Isabelle/ZF requires that any types in the semantics be expressed at the object level (as sets). The result of this is that large parts of proofs involve discharging type constraints. These same type constraints are handled automatically by a built-in type checker in the typed Isabelle/HOL logic.

Isabelle/HOL is a typed logic, meaning that types used in our semantics can be modelled at the meta-level. Isabelle/HOL employs a built-in type checker that automatically checks type constraints, therefore simplifying proofs. New types are introduced using either type synonyms or type definitions. The type system available in Isabelle/HOL is not as rich as those used in the untyped logics (where types are modelled as sets). However it does include the basic types required to model our semantics; including natural numbers, lists, sets and functions.

4.3 Automated Proof Support

The third issue relates to the fact that embeddings of refinement calculi involve a large amount of proof. An embedding will typically involve establishing some general properties of the language and proving refinement laws. Automated proof support to take care of the mundane proof steps is useful here. However it is worth noting that embedding the calculus is a one-off process usually performed by somebody with expertise in theorem proving; of more importance is automatically discharging proof obligations that arise during refinement of programs. The extra importance here is twofold: firstly refinement of programs is an ongoing process, and secondly the user of the tool is not necessarily an expert in theorem proving.

We found that Isabelle/HOL gave us a better level of automation (and consequently fewer proof steps) than the other logics, in both setting up and using the tool. This is despite the fact that Isabelle/ZF and HOL-Z both employ the same tactics as Isabelle/HOL. The decreased performance for these two logics can be partly explained by the fact that the tactics struggled to discharge type constraints[1]. For HOL-Z, we also note that the tactics have been set up for the HOL logic, but have not been extended to provide support for the HOL-Z theories.

An earlier report [9] shows that the tactics employed by Ergo 4 and Ergo 5 were in turn significantly less effective than those used in Isabelle/ZF.

4.4 User-Defined Tactics

In relation to tactics, we observe that significant reductions in both the number and complexity of refinement steps can be achieved by using a window-inference paradigm. Some theorem provers, most notably Ergo 4 [19], provide native support for window inference. The majority, however, are based on other proof paradigms, in which case it is important to be able to emulate the window-inference paradigm through the use of tactics [6,16]. Only those provers that offer user-extensionality, usually in the form of tactics, are suitable in this case.

As we have seen earlier in the paper, it was a straightforward task to define tactics in Isabelle/HOL that emulate the window inference paradigm. Indeed we were able to write (or adapt) tactics that emulate window inference in all of the logics that we have trialed. The approach used here is similar to that used by [16] in Isabelle/ZF, except we provide better support for context, based on program window inference [12].

---

[1] We used an earlier version of Isabelle/ZF. The most recent version includes tactics for discharging type constraints and we have not evaluated the effectiveness of these tactics.

4.5   Representing Program State

Finally, we need to consider how we can model the state of programs within a particular logic. More precisely, given that a state associates program variables with values, we need to consider what range of values can be modelled, i.e., how do we model the type of values? Earlier embeddings tended to ignore the issue by only allowing the set of natural numbers as values. However, this severely restricts the application of the tool.

States are represented in our embedding as sets of bindings, which are in turn mappings from variables to values. The type of values is represented as a sum of Isabelle types (including lists, sets, naturals and pairs). This sum of types is static, therefore introducing a new value type can only be done by reworking the semantics. This would be of no use if we wanted to introduce data abstraction, where users can introduce new value types on the fly.

Von Wright [21] represents states as a tuple of values, with each state component (program variable) corresponding to a value in the tuple. Each state is assigned product of types, with one type for each variable. Staples [17] notes some limitations of this approach, in particular the fact that variables are not explicitly named.

Staples's [17,18] solution to these problems is to represent states as dependently typed functions from variable names to under-specified families of types. This function is dynamically extendible, meaning that arbitrary abstract types for local program variables can be introduced during the refinement.

5   Conclusions

Using an embedding of a refinement calculus in a theorem prover leads to greater assurance that any proof obligations for individual refinement steps have been satisfied. The more mundane proof obligations can often be discharged automatically by the prover. In this paper we presented a deep embedding of a refinement calculus for logic programs in the Isabelle/HOL logic, including support for parameterised procedures and recursion. The embedding includes support for refinement in context, based on program window inference [12]. In comparison to other embeddings of (imperative) refinement calculi [6,18,4,21], the embedding presented here makes use of Isabelle/HOL's datatypes, primitive recursive definitions and type definitions to provide a deep embedding.

In developing **Marvin**, we formulated a number of criteria that are fundamental in choosing a logic for embedding refinement calculi (or other similar semantic models [10]). These criteria were gathered by tracing the problems encountered during the embedding back to deficiencies in the logics. Against these criteria, Isabelle/HOL scored well. In particular, we found:

- Isabelle/HOL notation was rich enough to represent our Z specified semantics with only minimal adaptations required.
- The type system significantly reduced the amount of proof in comparison to the untyped logics (cf. Table 1).

- Automated proof support performed better than for the other provers.
- Window-inference-like tactics could be easily written using Isabelle's tactic language.

One remaining concern is with representing program state. Our solution only allows state variables to range over a fixed product of types.

Acknowledgements

We would like to thank Robert Colvin for his comments on earlier drafts of this paper. The work reported in this paper is supported by Australian Research Council grant number A49937007 : *Refinement Calculus for Logic Programming*.

References

1. Isabelle home page.
   http://www.cl.cam.ac.uk/Research/HVG/Isabelle/index.html.
2. Ralph Back, Jim Grundy, and Joakim von Wright. Structured calculational proof. *Formal Aspects of Computing*, 9(5–6):469–483, 1997.
3. D. Carrington, I. Hayes, R. Nickson, G. Watson, and J. Welsh. A review of existing refinement tools. Technical report 94-08, Software Verification Research Centre, The University of Queensland, Brisbane 4072. Australia, June 1994.
4. D. Carrington, I. Hayes, R. Nickson, G. Watson, and J. Welsh. A program refinement tool. *Formal Aspects of Computing*, 10:97–124, 1998.
5. R. Colvin, I. Hayes, R. Nickson, and P. Strooper. A tool for logic program refinement. In D. J. Duke and A. S. Evans, editors, *Second BCS-FACS Northern Formal Methods Workshop*, Electronic Workshops in Computing. Springer Verlag, 1997.
6. J. Grundy. A window inference tool for refinement. In C.B. Jones, R.C. Shaw, and T. Denvir, editors, *Fifth Refinement Workshop*, Workshops in Computing, pages 230–254. BCS FACS, Springer-Verlag, 1992.
7. I. Hayes, R. Nickson, and P. Strooper. Refining specifications to logic programs. In J. Gallagher, editor, *Logic Program Synthesis and Transformation. Proceedings of the 6th International Workshop, LOPSTR'96, Stockholm, Sweden, August 1996*, volume 1207 of *Lecture Notes in Computer Science*, pages 1–19. Springer Verlag, 1997.
8. I. Hayes, R. Nickson, P. Strooper, and R. Colvin. A declarative semantics for logic program refinement. Technical Report 00-30, Software Verification Research Centre, The University of Queensland, October 2000.
9. D. Hemer. Building tool support for a refinement calculus for logic programming: A comparison of interactive theorem provers. Technical Report 00-06, Software Verification Research Centre, The University of Queensland, March 2000.
10. P. Homeier and D. Martin. Mechanical verification of mutually recursive procedures. In M.A. McRobbie and J.K. Slaney, editors, *Proceedings of the 13th International Conference on Artificial Deduction (CADE-13)*, number 1104 in Lecture Notes in Artificial Intelligence, pages 201–215. Springer-Verlag, 1996.
11. Kolyang, T. Santen, and B. Wolff. A structure preserving encoding of Z in Isabelle/HOL. In J. von Wright, J. Grundy, and J. Harrison, editors, *Theorem Proving in Higher Order Logics — 9th International Conference*, LNCS 1125, pages 283–298. Springer Verlag, 1996.

12. R. Nickson and I. Hayes. Supporting contexts in program refinement. *Science of Computer Programming*, 29:279–302, 1997.
13. L.C. Paulson. *Isabelle - A Generic Theorem Prover*, volume 828 of *Lecture Notes in Computer Science*. Springer-Verlag, 1994.
14. P.J. Robinson and J. Staples. Formalising the hierarchical structure of practical mathematical reasoning. *Journal of Logic and Computation*, 3(1):47–61, February 1993.
15. J.M. Spivey. *The Z Notation: a Reference Manual*. Prentice-Hall, New York, 1989.
16. M. Staples. Window inference in Isabelle. In L. Paulson, editor, *Proceedings of the First Isabelle User's Workshop*, volume 379 of *University of Cambridge Computer Laboratory Technical Report*, pages 191–205, September 1995.
17. M. Staples. *A Mechanised Theory of Refinement*. PhD thesis, Computer Laboratory, University of Cambridge, 1998.
18. M. Staples. Representing WP Semantics in Isabelle/ZF. In *TPHOLs '99*, volume 1690 of *Lecture Notes in Computer Science*, pages 239–254, September 1999.
19. M. Utting and K. Whitwell. Ergo user manual. Technical Report 93-19, Software Verification Research Centre, The University of Queensland, Brisbane, QLD 4072, Australia, March 1994. Describes Version 4.0 of Ergo.
20. Mark Utting. The Ergo 5 generic proof engine. Technical Report 97-44, Software Verification Research Centre, The University of Queensland, 1997.
21. J. von Wright. Program refinement by theorem proving. In D. Till, editor, *Sixth Refinement Workshop*, Workshops in Computing, pages 121–150. BCS FACS, Springer-Verlag, 1994.

A   Refinement Laws

This section contains a listing of rules used in the example that have not been described earlier.

The law *introduce_recursion* lets the user introduce recursion by replacing a parameterised command with a recursion block, and states conditions under which a recursive call can be made.

$$\text{env } \rho \text{ ass } A \Vdash pc \ \square$$
$$\text{re } pid \ . \ (V) :- \{\forall y \bullet \text{env } \rho \text{ ass } y \prec V \Vdash pc(y) \sqsubseteq pid(y)\} \ , \ pc(V)$$
$$\text{er}$$

To ensure termination, we must show that the recursive argument is strictly decreasing with respect to a well-founded relation $\prec$.

expand-scope-exists
$$\frac{X \text{ nfi } c_2}{(\exists X \bullet c_1) \wedge c_2 \ \square \ (\exists X \bullet c_1 \wedge c_2)}$$

remove-assumpt
$$\{A\} \, , c \sqsubseteq c$$

por-false
$$\langle false \rangle \vee c \ \square \ c$$

sand-false
$$c \, , \langle false \rangle \sqsubseteq \langle false \rangle$$

pand-to-sand
$$c_1 \wedge c_2 \sqsubseteq c_1 \, , c_2$$

right-distribute-pand-over-por
$$(c1 \vee c2) \wedge c3 \ \square \ (c1 \wedge c3) \vee (c2 \wedge c3)$$

lift-por
$$\langle c1 \vee c2 \rangle \ \square \ \langle c1 \rangle \vee \langle c2 \rangle$$

intro-spec
$$\frac{A \Rrightarrow P}{\text{env } \rho \text{ ass } A \Vdash c \ \square \ \langle P \rangle \wedge c}$$

Predicate Subtyping with Predicate Sets

Joe Hurd*

Computer Laboratory
University of Cambridge
joe.hurd@cl.cam.ac.uk

Abstract. We show how PVS-style predicate subtyping can be simulated in HOL using predicate sets, and explain how to perform subtype checking using this model. We illustrate some applications of this to specification and verification in HOL, and also demonstrate some limits of the approach. Finally we report on the effectiveness of a subtype checker used as a condition prover in a contextual rewriter.

1 Introduction

HOL [4] and PVS [13] are both interactive theorem-provers extending Church's simple type theory [1]: in HOL with Hindley-Milner polymorphism [11]; and in PVS with parametric theories[1] and predicate subtyping [14]. In this paper we will focus on PVS predicate subtyping, and show how it can be simulated in HOL.

Predicate subtyping allows the creation of a new subtype corresponding to an arbitrary predicate, where elements of the new type are also elements of the containing type. As a simple illustration of this, the type of real division ($/$) in HOL is $\mathbb{R} \to \mathbb{R} \to \mathbb{R}$, and in PVS is $\mathbb{R} \to \mathbb{R}^{\neq 0} \to \mathbb{R}$, where $\mathbb{R}$ is the type of real numbers and $\mathbb{R}^{\neq 0}$ is the predicate subtype of non-zero real numbers, expressed by the predicate $\lambda x.\ x \neq 0$.

This extension of the type system allows more information to be encoded in types, leading to benefits for specification and verification such as:

- The ability to express dependent types, for example a type for natural number subtraction that prevents the second argument from being larger than the first argument, or a type representing lists of a fixed length in order to model arrays.
- Greater use of types to express side-conditions of theorems, for example the PVS rewrite rule

$$\vdash_{\text{PVS}} \forall x : \mathbb{R}^{\neq 0}.\ x/x = 1 \tag{1}$$

In HOL this would have to be expressed

$$\vdash \forall x : \mathbb{R}.\ (x \neq 0) \Rightarrow (x/x = 1) \tag{2}$$

---

* Supported by an EPSRC studentship.
[1] Parametric theories allow polymorphism at the granularity of the theory (think C++ templates), whereas Hindley-Milner polymorphism operates at the granularity of the declaration (think ML functions).

R.J. Boulton and P.B. Jackson (Eds.): TPHOLs 2001, LNCS 2152, pp. 265–280, 2001.

and the extra condition must be proved each time the rule is applied.[2]
- More errors can be found in specifications during type-checking, giving greater confidence that the goal is correct before a verification is embarked upon. Mokkedem [12] has observed this to be very effective in a large network protocol verification performed in PVS. Many specifications are not verified at all, and in that case the extra confidence is especially valuable.

However, there are also some costs:

- Type-checking becomes undecidable, so (potentially human) effort must be expended to allow terms to be accepted into the system.
- Type-correctness depends on the current logical context, imposing an extra burden on term operations to keep careful track of what can be assumed at each subterm. In the case of users wishing to program their own tactics this merely steepens the learning curve; for term operations in the logical kernel faulty implementations have produced a string of soundness bugs.[3]

In the literature there are papers arguing for and against predicate subtyping. Shankar [17] gives many examples of their utility, while Lamport [9] gives an example where the costs must be paid without much benefit, in his case because predicate subtypes cannot naturally encode the desired invariant.

In this paper we describe our efforts to gain the functionality of predicate subtypes in HOL, without altering the logic in any way. Instead of creating a first-class type associated with a particular predicate P, we reason with the subset of elements that satisfy P. With this substitution, it is possible to simulate the extra reasoning power needed to automatically prove HOL side-conditions that would be expressed in PVS using predicate subtypes (such as the condition of Theorem 2 above). Using the same technology, we can also perform an analogue of predicate subtype-checking for terms, although as we shall see the HOL logic imposes certain limitations on this.

The structure of the paper is as follows: in Section 2 we lay out the details of our formalism and explain how to perform subtype-checking; Section 3 describes some tools that have been built using this technology, and reports on their effectiveness in a case study; in Section 4 we consider some fundamental logical limits of this approach; and finally in Sections 5, 6 and 7 we conclude, examine future prospects, and look at related work.

1.1   Notation

We use sans serif font to notate HOL constants, such as the function power operator funpow, the real number function inv (multiplicative inverse or reciprocal)

---

[2] Analogously, typed logics such as HOL and PVS enjoy this advantage over an untyped logic such as ZF set theory, in which the theorem $\vdash \forall n : \mathbb{N}. \; n + 0 = n$ must be expressed $\vdash \forall n. \; n \in \mathbb{N} \Rightarrow (n + 0 = n)$.

[3] Shankar [17] writes "these bugs stem largely from minor coding errors rather than foundational issues or complexities". However, the extra complexity generated by predicate subtyping does play a part in this: there have been very few soundness bugs found in HOL over the years.

and the list functions length and mem. This font is also used for predicate sets such as nzreal and posreal, in contrast to types (either HOL simple types or PVS predicate subtypes) which are written in mathematical font. Examples of simple types are α, β (type variables), $\alpha \times \beta$ (pairs), α^* (lists), $\mathbb{B}$ (booleans) and $\mathbb{R}$ (the real numbers); whereas $\mathbb{R}^{\neq 0}$ and $\mathbb{R}^{\geq 0}$ are predicate subtypes.

2 The Formalism

2.1 Subtypes

A predicate set is a function $P : \alpha \to \mathbb{B}$ which represents the set of elements $x : \alpha$ for which $P\,x = \top$. Note that P is parameterized by the type α, and we shall use the terminology 'α predicate set' (or just 'α set') when we wish to make this dependency explicit. Predicate sets are a standard modelling of sets in higher-order logic, and we can define polymorphic higher-order constants representing all the usual set operations such as $\in$, $\cup$ and image. In addition, for each α there exists a universe set $\mathcal{U}_\alpha = (\lambda\, x : \alpha.\ \top)$ that contains every element of type α.[4]

As examples, consider the following definitions of predicate sets that we will make use of:

$$\mathsf{nzreal} = \lambda\, x : \mathbb{R}.\ x \neq 0 \tag{3}$$

$$\mathsf{posreal} = \lambda\, x : \mathbb{R}.\ 0 < x \tag{4}$$

$$\mathsf{nnegreal} = \lambda\, x : \mathbb{R}.\ 0 \leq x \tag{5}$$

$$\forall n : \mathbb{N}.\ \mathsf{lenum}\ n = \lambda\, m : \mathbb{N}.\ m \leq n \tag{6}$$

$$\forall n : \mathbb{N}.\ \mathsf{nlist}\ n = \lambda\, l : \alpha^*.\ \mathsf{length}\ l = n \tag{7}$$

$$\forall p : \alpha \to \mathbb{B}.\ \mathsf{list}\ p = \lambda\, l : \alpha^*.\ \forall x : \alpha.\ \mathsf{mem}\ x\ l \Rightarrow x \in p \tag{8}$$

$$\forall p : \alpha \to \mathbb{B}.\ \forall q : \beta \to \mathbb{B}.$$
$$\mathsf{pair}\ p\ q = \lambda\, x : \alpha \times \beta.\ \mathsf{fst}\ x \in p \wedge \mathsf{snd}\ x \in q \tag{9}$$

Definitions 3–5 are straightforward, each representing the set of real numbers that are mapped to $\top$ by the predicate on the right hand side of the definition. Definitions 6–9 are all parameterized by various terms: in the case of lenum n by a natural number n so that $\mathsf{lenum}\ n = \{0, 1, \ldots, n\}$. Definitions 7–9 are polymorphic too, which of course is just another way of saying they are parameterized by types as well as terms. The set nlist n contains all α-lists having length n; the set list p contains all α-lists satisfying the condition that each member must lie in the parameter set p; and finally the set pair $p\ q$ contains all $(\alpha \times \beta)$-pairs (x, y) where x lies in the first parameter set p and y lies in the second parameter set q.

---

[4] Since the HOL logic specifies that all types are disjoint, so must be these universe sets.

2.2   Subtype Constructors

The definitions of list (8) and pair (9) in the previous subsection illustrated 'lifting': an α set is lifted to an α-list set using list, and an α set and a β set are lifted to a $(\alpha \times \beta)$ set using pair. We might thus call list and pair subtype constructors, and we can similarly define subtype constructors for every datatype. The automatic generation of these constuctors might be a worthwhile addition to the datatype package.

We can also define a subtype constructor for the function space $\alpha \to \beta$:

$$\forall p : \alpha \to \mathbb{B}. \ \forall q : \beta \to \mathbb{B}.$$
$$p \overset{\cdot}{\to} q = \lambda f : \alpha \to \beta. \ \forall x : \alpha. \ x \in p \Rightarrow f\,x \in q \tag{10}$$

The type annotations slightly obscure this definition, without them it looks like this: $\forall p, q. \ p \overset{\cdot}{\to} q = \lambda f. \ \forall x \in p. \ f\,x \in q.$[5] Given sets p and q, f is in the set $p \overset{\cdot}{\to} q$ iff it maps every element of p to an element of q.

We can illustrate this function subtype constructor with the following theorems that follow from the definitions so far:[6]

$$\vdash (\lambda x : \mathbb{R}. \ x^2) \in \mathsf{nzreal} \overset{\cdot}{\to} \mathsf{nzreal} \tag{11}$$

$$\vdash (\lambda x : \mathbb{R}. \ x^2) \in \mathcal{U}_{\mathbb{R}} \overset{\cdot}{\to} \mathsf{nnegreal} \tag{12}$$

$$\vdash \forall f, p. \ f \in p \overset{\cdot}{\to} \mathcal{U}_{\mathbb{R}} \tag{13}$$

$$\vdash \forall f, q. \ f \in \emptyset \overset{\cdot}{\to} q \tag{14}$$

$$\vdash \forall f, p. \ f \in p \overset{\cdot}{\to} \emptyset \iff p = \emptyset \tag{15}$$

There is an alternative subtype constructor for function spaces, defined like so:

$$\forall p : \alpha \to \mathbb{B}. \ \forall q : \alpha \to \beta \to \mathbb{B}.$$
$$p \overset{*}{\to} q = \lambda f : \alpha \to \beta. \ \forall x : \alpha. \ x \in p \Rightarrow f\,x \in q\,x \tag{16}$$

The difference here is that q is a parameterized set, where the parameter comes from the set p. This allows us to model dependent predicate subtypes with predicate sets, such as the following subtype containing natural number subtraction:

$$\mathcal{U}_{\mathbb{N}} \overset{*}{\to} (\lambda n. \ \mathsf{lenum}\ n \overset{\cdot}{\to} \mathsf{lenum}\ n)$$

Recall that $\mathcal{U}_{\mathbb{N}}$ is the universe set for the type $\mathbb{N}$ of natural numbers. We should therefore read the above subtype as the set of functions that: given any natural number n return a function from $\{0, \ldots, n\}$ to $\{0, \ldots, n\}$. One last thing to note: if the parameterized set q is of the form $\lambda x. \ q'$ where q' does not contain any

---

[5] The notation $\forall x \in p. \ M\,x$ is a restricted universal [18], and expands to $\forall x. \ x \in p \Rightarrow M\,x$. There are restricted versions of all the usual HOL quantifiers.

[6] Note that $\overset{\cdot}{\to}$ associates to the right and has tighter binding than $\in$, so $f \in p \overset{\cdot}{\to} q \overset{\cdot}{\to} r$ means the same as $f \in (p \overset{\cdot}{\to} (q \overset{\cdot}{\to} r))$. Also x^2 here means x squared.

occurrences of the bound variable x, then $p \xrightarrow{*} q = p \xrightarrow{\cdot} q'$: this shows that Definition 16 is more general than Definition 10.

PVS also has two function space subtypes, covering the dependent and non-dependent cases. It also allows dependent products, which cannot be expressed using our pair notation. However, analogously to $\xrightarrow{*}$ it would be simple to define a dependent pair constructor dpair $p\ q$, taking a set $p : \alpha \to \mathbb{B}$ and a parameterized set $q : \alpha \to \beta \to \mathbb{B}$.

2.3 Subtype Rules

Now that we have defined the form of subtype sets, we shall show how to derive subtypes of a HOL term. Given a term t, we say that p is a subtype of t if we can prove the subtype theorem $\vdash t \in p$. This is the major difference between our model and PVS: here subtypes are theorems, whilst in PVS subtypes are types.

Milner's type inference algorithm [11] for simply-typed terms is structural: a single bottom-up pass of a well-formed term suffices to establish the most general type.[7] We also use a single bottom-up pass to derive sets of subtype theorems, though the algorithm is complicated by two factors:

- two rules to break down terms (covering function applications and λ-abstractions) are no longer sufficient since we also need to keep track of logical context;
- there is no concept of a 'most general set of subtype theorems',[8] so instead we perform proof search up to some fixed depth and return all the subtype theorems that we can prove.

To keep track of logical context, we create subtype rules similar to the congruence rules of a contextual rewriter. Here are some examples:

$$\vdash \forall c : \mathbb{B}.\ \forall a : \alpha.\ \forall b : \alpha.\ \forall p : \alpha \to \mathbb{B}.$$

$$(c \in \mathcal{U}_{\mathbb{B}}) \wedge (c \Rightarrow a \in p) \wedge (\neg c \Rightarrow b \in p) \Rightarrow (\text{if } c \text{ then } a \text{ else } b) \in p \quad (17)$$

$$\vdash \forall a, b : \mathbb{B}.\ (b \Rightarrow a \in \mathcal{U}_{\mathbb{B}}) \wedge (a \Rightarrow b \in \mathcal{U}_{\mathbb{B}}) \Rightarrow (a \wedge b) \in \mathcal{U}_{\mathbb{B}} \quad (18)$$

$$\vdash \forall f : \alpha \to \beta.\ \forall a : \alpha.\ \forall p : \alpha \to \mathbb{B}.\ \forall q : \alpha \to \beta \to \mathbb{B}.$$

$$(f \in p \xrightarrow{*} q) \wedge (a \in p) \Rightarrow f\ a \in q\ a \quad (19)$$

$$\vdash \forall f : \alpha \to \beta.\ \forall p : (\alpha \to \beta) \to \mathbb{B}.$$

$$(\forall x : \alpha.\ f\ x \in p\ x) \Rightarrow (\lambda x.\ f\ x) \in (\mathcal{U}_\alpha \xrightarrow{*} p) \quad (20)$$

These rules are rather long, but fortunately can be read easily from left to right. For example the conditional subtype rule (17) reads: "if we can show c to be in $\mathcal{U}_{\mathbb{B}}$; and assuming c we can show a to be in a subtype p; and assuming $\neg c$ we can show b to be in the same subtype p; then the combined term if c then a else b must also be an element of p." In this way we can build up logical context. Note that

---

[7] Though not completely avoiding all difficulty: Mairson [10] has shown that the most general simple type of a term can be exponentially large in the size of the term.

[8] Theoretically we could intersect all subtypes that a term t satisfies, but then we would just end up with $\{t\}$ if the logical context was consistent, or $\emptyset$ if it was not!

c is trivially in the universe set $\mathcal{U}_{\mathbb{B}}$, the only purpose of retaining this condition is to force the subtype checker to recurse into c and check all its subterms. The conjunction rule (18) similarly ensures that subterms are covered by the subtype checker, while building the correct logical context.[9] Also shown are the subtype rules for function application (19) and abstraction (20), the main point to note is that they both use the more general dependent version $\xrightarrow{*}$ of the subtype constructor for function spaces.

For each constant that propagates logical information, we need a subtype rule of the above form. Therefore the set of subtype rules used is not fixed, rather we allow the user to add rules for new constants.

Subtype rules tell us how to derive subtypes for a term by combining the subtypes of smaller terms, but they leave two questions unanswered: how do we calculate the subtypes of base terms (variables and constants); and how do we unify the (possibly higher-order) subtypes of the smaller terms, for example to match the two occurrences of p in the antecedent of the conditional subtype rule (17)? These questions are answered in the next two sections.

2.4   Subtypes of Constants

To calculate subtypes of a base term $t : \alpha$, we maintain a dictionary of constant subtypes.[10] If the term we are focussed on is a constant that appears in the dictionary, we return the subtype theorem listed there. If the term is a variable or a constant that is not in the dictionary, we return the default subtype theorem $\vdash t \in \mathcal{U}_\alpha$.[11]

Here are some miscellaneous entries in the dictionary:

$$\vdash \mathsf{inv} \in (\mathsf{nzreal} \xrightarrow{\cdot} \mathsf{nzreal} \cap \mathsf{posreal} \xrightarrow{\cdot} \mathsf{posreal} \cap \mathsf{negreal} \xrightarrow{\cdot} \mathsf{negreal}) \tag{21}$$

$$\vdash \mathsf{sqrt} \in (\mathsf{nnegreal} \xrightarrow{\cdot} \mathsf{nnegreal} \cap \mathsf{posreal} \xrightarrow{\cdot} \mathsf{posreal}) \tag{22}$$

$$\vdash \forall n : \mathbb{N}.\ - \in \mathcal{U}_{\mathbb{N}} \xrightarrow{*} (\lambda n.\ \mathsf{lenum}\ n \xrightarrow{\cdot} \mathsf{lenum}\ n) \tag{23}$$

$$\vdash \forall p : \alpha \to \mathbb{B}.\ \mathsf{funpow} \in (p \xrightarrow{\cdot} p) \xrightarrow{\cdot} \mathcal{U}_{\mathbb{N}} \xrightarrow{\cdot} p \xrightarrow{\cdot} p \tag{24}$$

$$\vdash \forall p : \alpha \to \mathbb{B}.\ [] \in (\mathsf{list}\ p \cap \mathsf{nlist}\ 0) \tag{25}$$

$$\vdash \forall p : \alpha \to \mathbb{B}.\ \forall n : \mathbb{N}.$$

---

[9] A version of the conjunction rule that does not always return the universe set $\mathcal{U}_{\mathbb{B}}$ is as follows:

$$\vdash \forall a, b : \mathbb{B}.\ \forall p, q : \mathbb{B} \to \mathbb{B}.\ (b \Rightarrow a \in p) \wedge (a \Rightarrow b \in q) \Rightarrow (a \wedge b) \in (\{\bot\} \cup (p \,\dot\wedge\, q))$$

where $\dot\wedge$ is a lifted version of $\wedge$ that operates on sets of booleans instead of booleans. However, the version we present is much simpler to work with and usually all that is required in practice.

[10] It is up to the user to add constant subtypes to the dictionary: as yet there is no mechanism to automatically generate these for newly defined constants, though this further work is briefly discussed in Section 6.

[11] Note that when we come to use the subtypes of t later on, other subtypes may also be deduced from the logical context.

$$\mathsf{cons} \in p \overset{\cdot}{\to} (\mathsf{list}\ p \cap \mathsf{nlist}\ n) \overset{\cdot}{\to} (\mathsf{list}\ p \cap \mathsf{nlist}\ (\mathsf{suc}\ n)) \tag{26}$$

$$\vdash \forall f : \alpha \to \beta.\ \forall p : \alpha \to \mathbb{B}.\ \forall q : \beta \to \mathbb{B}.\ \forall n : \mathbb{N}.$$

$$\mathsf{map} \in (p \overset{\cdot}{\to} q) \overset{\cdot}{\to} (\mathsf{list}\ p \cap \mathsf{nlist}\ n) \overset{\cdot}{\to} (\mathsf{list}\ q \cap \mathsf{nlist}\ n) \tag{27}$$

$$\vdash \forall p : \alpha \to \mathbb{B}.\ \forall q : \beta \to \mathbb{B}.\ \forall n : \mathbb{N}. \tag{28}$$

$$\mathsf{zip} \in (\mathsf{nlist}\ n \cap \mathsf{list}\ p) \overset{\cdot}{\to} (\mathsf{nlist}\ n \cap \mathsf{list}\ q) \overset{\cdot}{\to} (\mathsf{nlist}\ n \cap \mathsf{list}\ (\mathsf{pair}\ p\ q))$$

The universal quantification allows variables in the types of constants, and exactly like 'forall types' in functional programming, these generate fresh variables at every instance of the constant.

This dictionary corresponds to the constant judgement mechanism of PVS, whereby the type-checker can be told that for the purpose of calculating type correctness conditions, particular constants are also elements of more specific subtypes than their principal subtype.

2.5 Subtype Judgements

Suppose we have a subtype rule that we are committed to using, and we have recursively derived subtype theorems for the terms in the antecedent of the rule. We must now deduce[12] from these subtype theorems, aiming to find a consistent set of subtype theorems that is matched by the antecedent of the rule.

Example 1. Suppose our term is $f\ a$ (where f has simple type $\mathbb{R} \to \mathbb{R}$); we are using the function application rule (19); and we have recursively shown that $\vdash f \in \mathsf{nzreal} \overset{\cdot}{\to} \mathsf{nzreal}$ and $\vdash a \in \mathsf{posreal}$. However, in order to apply the rule we must find instantiations of the variables p and q such that

$$(f \in p \overset{*}{\to} q)\ \wedge\ (a \in p)$$

is a theorem. We present this goal to our prover, which performs bounded proof search and returns some instantiations, one of which corresponds to the following theorem:

$$\vdash (f \in \mathsf{nzreal} \overset{*}{\to} (\lambda x.\ \mathsf{nzreal}))\ \wedge\ (a \in \mathsf{nzreal})$$

Now we can apply the rule to conclude that $\vdash f\ a \in (\lambda x.\ \mathsf{nzreal})\ a$, which can in turn be simplified to $\vdash f\ a \in \mathsf{nzreal}$.

In this example, the prover needed to show $a \in \mathsf{posreal} \Rightarrow a \in \mathsf{nzreal}$. Steps like these are achieved using subtype judgements: theorems that are manually

---

[12] Deciding the logical context in which we should perform this deduction is quite delicate. It is sound to use the current logical context, but not complete. A more careful approach is to use the (possibly larger) logical context of a subterm whenever we manipulate the subtypes of that subterm. In this way if we can deduce $\vdash 1 \in \mathsf{nzreal}$ and $\vdash \neg \top \Rightarrow 0 \in \mathsf{nzreal}$ then we will be able to deduce $\vdash (\mathsf{if}\ \top\ \mathsf{then}\ 1\ \mathsf{else}\ 0) \in \mathsf{nzreal}$ using the conditional rule.

added to the top-level logical context, and are available for use in deriving subtypes.[13] These will be theory specific, and can be extended by the user at any time. Examples are:

$$\vdash \mathsf{posreal} \subset \mathsf{nzreal} \tag{29}$$

$$\vdash \forall p, q : \alpha \to \mathbb{B}. \ p \subset q \ \Rightarrow \ \mathsf{list} \ p \subset \mathsf{list} \ q \tag{30}$$

From the example we can see that a suitable prover must be: higher-order to deal with parameterized types; able to find multiple instantiations of a goal ('prolog-style'); and able to perform bounded proof search. Any prover that satisfies these criteria will be able to plug in at this point and enable subtype derivation.

However, since there are not many provers available that can satisfy all these requirements, we have implemented one to test our subtype derivation algorithm. Robinson [15] presents an approach to higher-order proving by converting all terms to combinatory form.[14] Together with translation to CNF this conversion leaves terms in a normal form that simplifies the writing of automatic proof search tools. For our application we implement a version of model elimination (mostly following Harrison's presentation [5], with some higher-order extensions), since that is able to return multiple instantiations of goals and we can use a simple depth-bound to limit the search. More powerful normalization means that it can compete with the HOL first-order prover `MESON_TAC` on some first-order problems, and results on higher-order problems are basic but promising. It is under active development, and a paper will soon be available describing its operation in more detail.

2.6   Subtype Derivation Algorithm

To summarize this section, we present the complete algorithm to derive subtypes of a term.

Inputs: A term t having simple type α; a logical context C initialized with a set of assumptions and the current subtype judgements; a set R of subtype rules; and a dictionary D of constant subtypes.

Outputs: A set P of subtype theorems.

1. If t is a variable, return $[\vdash t \in \mathcal{U}_\alpha]$.
2. If t is a constant, look in the dictionary D to see if there is an entry (t, p). If so, return $[\vdash t \in p]$, otherwise return $[\vdash t \in \mathcal{U}_\alpha]$.
3. Otherwise find a subtype rule in R matching t.[15] The rule will have the form

$$\vdash \forall \boldsymbol{v}. \left(\bigwedge_{1 \le i \le n} \forall \boldsymbol{v_i}. \ a_i[\boldsymbol{v_i}] \Rightarrow t_i[\boldsymbol{v_i}] \in p_i[\boldsymbol{v_i}, \boldsymbol{v}] \right) \Rightarrow t \in p[\boldsymbol{v}] \tag{31}$$

---

[13] The name 'subtype judgements' was borrowed from PVS, which contains results used for exactly the same purpose.

[14] Many thanks to John Harrison for drawing my attention to this paper.

[15] If there is more than one rule that matches, return the rule that was most recently added to R: this is almost always the most specific rule too.

4. For each $1 \leq i \leq n$, create the logical context C_i by adding the assumption $a_i[\boldsymbol{v_i}]$ to C and recursively apply the algorithm using C_i to t_i to find a set of subtypes

$$P_i = \{\vdash t_i[\boldsymbol{v_i}] \in p_{i0}[\boldsymbol{v_i}], \ \ldots, \ \vdash t_i[\boldsymbol{v_i}] \in p_{in_i}[\boldsymbol{v_i}]\}$$

5. Find consistent sets of subtypes by calling the following search function with counter $i \leftarrow 1$ and instantiation $\sigma \leftarrow id$.
   (a) If $i > n$ then return σ.
   (b) Using the subtype theorems in P_i and the logical context C_i, use the higher-order prover to find theorems of the form $\vdash t_i[\boldsymbol{v_i}] \in \sigma(p_i[\boldsymbol{v_i}, \boldsymbol{v}])$.
   (c) For each theorem returned, let σ_i be the returned instantiation. Recursively call the depth-first search function with counter $i \leftarrow i + 1$ and instantiation $\sigma \leftarrow (\sigma_i \circ \sigma)$.
6. Each instantiation σ returned by depth-first search corresponds to a specialization of the subtype rule (31) for which we have proven the antecedent. We may thus deduce the consequent by modus ponens, and we add this to the result set P of subtype theorems.

3 Applications

3.1 Predicate Set Prover

An obvious application for the subtype derivation algorithm is to prove set membership goals. Supposing the current goal is $t \in p$, we can derive a set P of subtype theorems for t, and then invoke the higher-order prover once again with the top-level context and the set P to tackle the goal directly.

Example 2. To illustrate the two steps, consider the goal $3 \in$ nzreal.[16] Subtypes are derived for the term 3 (of type $\mathbb{R}$), and the following list of subtype theorems are returned:

$$[\vdash 3 \in \mathsf{K} \text{ posreal } 3, \ \vdash 3 \in \mathsf{K} \text{ nnegreal } 3]$$

(where $\mathsf{K} = \lambda x. \, \lambda y. \, x$). Next these two theorems are passed to the higher-order prover along with the top-level logical context containing type-judgements, and it quickly proves the goal $\vdash 3 \in$ nzreal.

We package up the predicate set prover into a HOL tactic, which calls the prover with the current subgoal as argument: if successful the resulting theorem will match the subgoal and can be dispatched. We can prove some interesting goals with this tactic:

$$\vdash \text{map inv (cons } (-1) \text{ (map sqrt } [3, 1])) \in \text{list nzreal}$$

$$\vdash (\lambda x \in \text{negreal. funpow inv } n \, x) \in \text{negreal} \xrightarrow{\cdot} \text{negreal}$$

---

[16] This is not quite as trivial as it looks, since the real number '3' in HOL is really the complex term real_of_num (numeral (bit1 (bit1 0))).

One optimization that is effective even with this basic tactic is to maintain a cache of the subtypes that have already been derived for HOL constants.[17] For example, the innocuous-looking term '3' used in the above example is actually composed of 4 nested function applications! Rederiving subtypes for constants is unnecessary and inefficient.

Another optimization arises naturally from certain subtype rules, such as the conjunction rule (18), repeated here:

$$\forall a, b : \mathbb{B}. \ (b \Rightarrow a \in \mathcal{U}_{\mathbb{B}}) \wedge (a \Rightarrow b \in \mathcal{U}_{\mathbb{B}}) \Rightarrow (a \wedge b) \in \mathcal{U}_{\mathbb{B}}$$

The set $\mathcal{U}_{\mathbb{B}}$ is the universe set $\mathcal{U}_{\mathbb{B}}$ of booleans, so we can immediately prove $\vdash b \Rightarrow a \in \mathcal{U}_{\mathbb{B}}$ and $\vdash a \Rightarrow b \in \mathcal{U}_{\mathbb{B}}$ without recursing into the structure of the subterms a and b. Note that if we were deriving subtypes in order to check the term for subtype correctness then we would be obliged to carry out this recursion step to check a and b, but if our goal is proving set membership then we can safely skip this.

3.2 Proving Conditions During Rewriting

We can use the predicate set prover as a condition prover in a contextual rewriter, and there are several reasons why it is useful to integrate these tools:

- There is a trend to incorporate tools into contextual rewriters because of the automatic subterm traversal and context accumulation. The logical context built up by the contextual rewriter is easily transferred to the predicate set prover, and the subterm traversal allows us to attempt a proof of all occurrences of $t \in p$ in the goal term.[18]
- Many rewrites have side conditions that can be expressed very naturally using restricted quantifiers, and these generate goals for the predicate set prover when the rewrite is applied.
- Subtype judgements, rules and constants can be stored with the simplification set of a theory, thus reducing the administration burden of theory-specific rules.

Here are some miscellaneous rewrite rules that make use of subtype conditions:

$$\vdash \ \forall x \in \mathsf{nzreal}. \ x/x = 1 \tag{32}$$

$$\vdash \ \forall n. \ \forall m \in \mathsf{lenum} \ n. \ m + (n - m) = n \tag{33}$$

$$\vdash \ \forall n \in \mathsf{nznum}. \ n \ \mathrm{mod} \ n = 0 \tag{34}$$

$$\vdash \ \forall s \in \mathsf{finite}. \ \forall f \in \mathsf{injection} \ s. \ |\mathrm{image} \ f \ s| = |s| \tag{35}$$

$$\vdash \ \forall G \in \mathsf{group}. \ \forall g \in \mathsf{set} \ G. \ \mathrm{id}_G *_G g = g \tag{36}$$

$$\vdash \ \forall G \in \mathsf{group}. \ \forall g, h \in \mathsf{set} \ G. \ (g *_G h = h) = (g = \mathrm{id}_G) \tag{37}$$

---

[17] Here 'constant' means any term having no free variables.

[18] When subtype derivation is applied to a subterm it accumulates context in much the same way as a contextual rewriter. However, despite this similarity, the two tools are orthogonal and are best implemented separately: we tried both approaches.

Using rule 32, a term like $5/5 = 3/3$ is straightforwardly rewritten to $\top$.

An effective optimization for this tool is to make adding assumptions into the subtype logical context a lazy operation. This delays their conversion to combinatory form and CNF normalization until the predicate set prover is invoked on a goal, which might not happen at all.

The last two examples above come from a body of computational number theory that we have recently formalized [6], which provided a test of the utility of our predicate set prover as a condition prover in a contextual rewriter. The properties that were targeted in the development were group membership (e.g., $g *_G h \in$ set G), simple natural number inequalities (e.g., $0 < n$ or $1 < mn$) and nonemptiness properties of lists and sets (e.g., $s \neq \emptyset$).

In theory, the architecture laid out in the previous section can establish much more exotic properties than these, but the predicate subtype prover was found to be most useful and robust on these relatively simple properties that come up again and again during conditional rewriting. These properties naturally propagate upwards through a term, being preserved by most of the basic operations, and in such situations the predicate set prover can be relied upon to show the desired condition (albeit sometimes rather slowly). This tool lent itself to more efficient development of the required theories, particularly the group theory where almost every theorem has one or more group membership side-conditions.

If the predicate set prover had not been available, it would have been possible to use a first-order prover to show most of the side-conditions, but there are three reasons why this is a less attractive proposition: firstly it would have required effort to find the right 'property propagation' theorems needed for the each goal; secondly the explicit invocations would have led to more complicated tactics; and thirdly some of the goals that can be proved using our specialized tool would simply have been out of range of a more general first-order prover.

3.3   Debugging Specifications

How can we use our algorithm for deriving subtypes to find errors in a specification? We do this by invoking the algorithm on the specification, and generating an exception whenever the algorithm would return an empty set of subtypes for a subterm.

Consider the following family of specifications:

$$(\text{inv } x) * x = 1 \tag{38}$$

$$x \in \text{nzreal} \Rightarrow (\text{inv } x) * x = 1 \tag{39}$$

$$\text{inv } x \in \text{nzreal} \Rightarrow (\text{inv } x) * x = 1 \tag{40}$$

$$\text{inv} \in \mathcal{U}_{\mathbb{R}} \xrightarrow{\cdot} \text{nzreal} \Rightarrow (\text{inv } x) * x = 1 \tag{41}$$

$$\text{inv} \in \mathcal{U}_{\mathbb{R}} \xrightarrow{\cdot} \mathcal{U}_{\mathbb{R}} \Rightarrow (\text{inv } x) * x = 1 \tag{42}$$

The subtype checker will generate an exception for specification 38, complaining that it could not derive a type for the subterm inv x. Why does it say this? The exception is raised because the algorithm could not find a consistent set of subtypes for the subterms inv and x, when using the subtype rule (19) for function application. And this we see to be true, because without any additional knowledge of x we cannot show it to be in any of the sets nzreal, posreal or negreal that the subtype (21) of the constant inv demands.

Specification 39 shows the right solution: add a guard to stop x from taking the illegal value of 0. And this solves the problem, the subtype checker can now derive a subtype of nzreal for the subterm inv x (and a subtype of $\mathcal{U}_\mathbb{B}$ for the whole term).

This is how we would expect the subtype checker to be used in practice. A specification is entered and subtype checked, the errors are corrected by adding the necessary guards, and only then is verification started. This could potentially save much wasted effort and act as a valuable teaching tool.

Specifications 40–42 represent various attempts to subvert the subtype checker. Specification 40 is a silly attempt: now the inv x in the antecedent fails to subtype check! However, even if the antecedent were added unchecked to the logical context, the consequent would still not subtype check: an extra subtype for inv x does not help at all in the search to find consistent subtypes for inv and x using the rule for function application. Specification 41 steps up a level in the arms race by assuming a subtype for inv, and now this term does subtype check since the higher-order prover just needs to show that $x \in \mathcal{U}_\mathbb{R}$: a triviality. However, we may take consolation in the fact that this antecedent is unprovable. Finally Specification 42 is the most worrying attack: the term subtype checks, and we can use Theorem 13 to prove the condition.

4   Logical Limits

The final example of the previous section showed how to subvert the subtype checker that we implement. Unfortunately, this is not just an inadequacy of the subtype checker, but rather an inescapable consequence of reasoning with predicate sets in the HOL logic. Since HOL is a logic of total functions, given any function $f : \alpha \to \beta$ we can prove the theorem

$$\vdash f \in \mathcal{U}_\alpha \dot{\to} \mathcal{U}_\beta \tag{43}$$

since this just expands to $\vdash \forall x.\ x \in \mathcal{U}_\alpha \Rightarrow f\ x \in \mathcal{U}_\beta$, which is true by the definition of the universal set $\mathcal{U}_\beta$.

This means that enforceable predicate subtyping using predicate sets cannot exist as a layer on top of the existing HOL kernel, since Theorem 43 is true even for restricted constants (such as inv), and can be used by the subtype checker to allow the application of such constants to any argument.

Example 3. Even if the user is not trying to subvert the system, it might happen accidentally. If we are subtype checking the following specification

$$P \Rightarrow Q\ (\text{inv } 0)$$

then when we subtype check the consequent Q (inv 0) we add the antecedent P to the logical context, and it might transpire that P somehow causes the higher-order prover to deduce inv $\in \mathcal{U}_\mathbb{R} \dot{\to} \mathcal{U}_\mathbb{R}$,[19] which then allows Q (inv 0) to be successfully subtype checked.

PVS is also a logic of total functions, but the ability to make a first-class type of non-zero reals means that if inv is declared to have type $\mathbb{R}^{\neq 0} \to \mathbb{R}$ then the type-system can stop the function from being 'lifted' to a larger type. Essentially the PVS logic implements a logic of partial functions, but by insisting that a type is available for every function's domain can avoid all questions of definedness.

5 Conclusion

We have shown how predicate subtyping can be modelled in HOL using predicate sets, explained how to perform subtype checking using our framework, and illustrated some applications of this to specification and verification in HOL.

It is helpful to divide the benefits of predicate subtyping into two categories: negative features, which consist of spotting and disallowing type-incorrect terms; and positive features, which consist of allowing properties to be (more quickly) deduced that help prove theorems.

In this paper we have shown that we can gain many of the positive benefits of predicate subtyping,[20] and in some ways we can even do better: our system does not only calculate with principal subtypes but rather with any subtype that the term can be shown to satisfy using the rules. This was shown to provide an effective proof procedure on a body of formalized mathematics.

In our experience the model is also quite robust when used for the negative features of predicate subtyping, and finds most typical errors that predicate subtyping is designed to prevent. Unfortunately, we have shown that in certain situations it can be subverted, and so we cannot claim to match the PVS level of type safety. However, it is worth remarking that specifications that are provable must possess this level of type safety,[21] so a guarantee is most valuable if the specification will never be verified. If verification is our goal, then any debugging that can be performed in advance will speed up the process, but an absolute guarantee is not necessary. In conclusion, predicate subtyping using predicate sets should be seen as an extra box of tools to aid verification.

6 Further Work

On the basis of our case study, we can seek to improve the predicate set prover by making it faster and more robust on simple and ubiquitous subtypes. One obvious approach to this would be to improve the underlying higher-order prover.

---

[19] After all, it is a theorem!

[20] Although almost certainly the performance using our model is worse than genuine predicate subtyping: keeping subtypes with the terms so they never have to be derived must provide a boost. We also experimented with this kind of architecture, but dropped it in favour of the system presented in the current paper to simplify the design and increase interoperability with existing tools.

[21] That is, if restricted constants are underspecified outside their domain.

In particular the handling of equality and reasoning with total orders could be much more effective; perhaps we could interface to a linear decision procedure to speed up the latter.

Another, more speculative, line of research would be to use subtype checking to perform subtype inference of new constants. If it could be made to work this would be extremely useful: currently for each constant which we would like to add to the constant subtype dictionary, we must specify and prove a result of the form of Theorems 21–28. The idea is to initially enter the type of the new constant c as $c \in p$ where p is a variable; during subtype checking we collect constraints on p; and finally at the top-level we try to solve these constraints: the solutions being subtypes for c.

7 Related Work

The model of predicate subtyping using predicate sets builds upon Wong's [18] restricted quantifier library in HOL88, and the exact details of the predicate subtyping in our model attempts to follow the PVS architecture. For the full details of the semantics and implementation of subtyping in PVS, refer to Owre [14].

Previous work in this area has been done by Jones [7], who built a tool in HOL to specify the subtype of constants and subtype check terms with respect to the subtypes. Given a term t, the tool sets up HOL goals that, if proved, would correspond to the term being subtype-correct. The user is then free to use these extra theorems during verification. Our model extends Jones' by the introduction of subtype rules for generating type-correctness conditions, the higher-order prover to automatically prove conditions, and the integration of the tool into a rewriter to aid interactive proof.

A comparison of HOL and PVS was made by Gordon [3], from the perspectives of logic, automatic proof and usability. Our work is only relevant to part of this comparison, and enthusiastically takes up some of the suggestions for modelling PVS-style constructs in HOL.

ACL2 uses guards [8] to stop functions from being applied outside their domain; these generate proof obligations when new functions are defined in terms of guarded functions. When the proof obligations have been satisfied the new function is given a 'gold' status, and can be safely executed without causing run-time type errors. This is very similar to the way PVS type-checks terms before admitting them into the system.

Saaltink [16] has also implemented a system of guard formulas in Z/EVES, which both aids formal Z proofs and has found some errors in Z specifications. The Z logic allows terms to be 'undefined', but the system of guard formulas imposed will flag the situations that can result in undefinedness, allowing classical reasoning on the partial logic. Since Z is based on set theory, this use of guards does not suffer from the logical limitations we outlined in Section 4, and can provide strong guarantees about a checked specification. However, whereas our subtype rules propagate all available logical information around the term, Saaltink chooses a "left-to-right system of interpretation" that is not complete, but works well in most practical situations and simplifies guard conditions.

Finally, there has been a huge amount of work on subtyping and polymorphism in various λ-calculi, used to model object-orientated programming languages. Some concepts from this field are related to our work, in particular the notion of intersection types corresponds to finding multiple subtypes of a term. Campognoni's thesis [2] provides a good introduction to this area.

Acknowledgements

My Ph.D. supervisor, Mike Gordon, got me started on this topic and helped bring the project to a successful conclusion. I had many valuable conversations about predicate subtyping with Judita Preiss, Konrad Slind and Michael Norrish, and their comments on this paper (particularly Konrad's keen eye) helped remove many potential misunderstandings. John Harrison gave me help with implementing the higher-order prover, and Ken Larsen should be credited as the local ML guru. Finally, the comments of the TPHOLs referees improved this paper tremendously.

References

1. Alonzo Church. A formulation of the simple theory of types. *Journal of Symbolic Logic*, 5:56–68, 1940.
2. Adriana B. Compagnoni. *Higher-Order Subtyping with Intersection Types*. PhD thesis, Catholic University, Nigmegen, January 1995.
3. M. J. C. Gordon. Notes on PVS from a HOL perspective. Available from the University of Cambridge Computer Laboratory web server.
4. M. J. C. Gordon and T. F. Melham. *Introduction to HOL (A theorem-proving environment for higher order logic)*. Cambridge University Press, 1993.
5. John Harrison. Optimizing proof search in model elimination. In M. A. McRobbie and J. K. Slaney, editors, *13th International Conference on Automated Deduction*, volume 1104 of *Lecture Notes in Computer Science*, pages 313–327, New Brunswick, NJ, 1996. Springer-Verlag.
6. Joe Hurd. Verification of the Miller-Rabin probabilistic primality test. Submitted as a Category B paper to TPHOLs 2001, May 2001.
7. Michael D. Jones. Restricted types for HOL. In *TPHOLs 1997 Category B papers*, 1997.
8. Matt Kaufmann and J. S. Moore. Industrial strength theorem prover for a logic based on Common Lisp. *IEEE Transactions on Software Engineering*, 23(4):203–213, April 1997.
9. Leslie Lamport and Lawrence C. Paulson. Should your specification language be typed? *ACM Transactions on Programming Languages and Systems*, 21(3):502–526, May 1999.
10. Harry G. Mairson. Deciding ML typability is complete for deterministic exponential time. In *Conference Record of the Seventeenth Annual ACM Symposium on Principles of Programming Languages*, pages 382–401. ACM SIGACT and SIGPLAN, ACM Press, 1990.
11. R. Milner. A theory of type polymorphism in programming. *Journal of Computer and System Sciences*, 17:348–375, December 1978.

12. Abdel Mokkedem and Tim Leonard. Formal verification of the Alpha 21364 network protocol. In Mark Aagaard and John Harrison, editors, *Theorem Proving in Higher Order Logics: 13th International Conference, TPHOLs 2000*, volume 1869 of *Lecture Notes in Computer Science*, pages 443–461, Portland, OR, August 2000. Springer-Verlag.

13. S. Owre, N. Shankar, J. M. Rushby, and D. W. J. Stringer-Calvert. *PVS System Guide*. Computer Science Laboratory, SRI International, Menlo Park, CA, September 1999.

14. Sam Owre and Natarajan Shankar. The formal semantics of PVS. Technical Report SRI-CSL-97-2, Computer Science Laboratory, SRI International, Menlo Park, CA, August 1997.

15. J. A. Robinson. A note on mechanizing higher order logic. *Machine Intelligence*, 5:121–135, 1970.

16. Mark Saaltink. Domain checking Z specifications. In C. Michael Holloway and Kelly J. Hayhurst, editors, *LFM' 97: Fourth NASA Langley Formal Methods Workshop*, pages 185–192, Hampton, VA, September 1997.

17. Natarajan Shankar and Sam Owre. Principles and pragmatics of subtyping in PVS. In D. Bert, C. Choppy, and P. D. Mosses, editors, *Recent Trends in Algebraic Development Techniques, WADT '99*, volume 1827 of *Lecture Notes in Computer Science*, pages 37–52, Toulouse, France, September 1999. Springer-Verlag.

18. Wai Wong. *The HOL res_quan library*. HOL88 documentation.

A Structural Embedding of Ocsid in PVS

Pertti Kellomäki

Tampere University of Technology, Tampere, Finland
pertti.kellomaki@tut.fi
http://www.cs.tut.fi/~pk

Abstract. We describe a *structural embedding* of the Ocsid specification language into the logic of the PVS theorem prover. A front end tool is used to manipulate the structural elements of the language, while the expression language is directly borrowed from the theorem prover.
The structural embedding allows us to express and verify invariant properties of distributed systems in an abstract form. An invariant can be verified once, and reused multiple times by discharging a set of relatively simple proof obligations.

1 Introduction

In [25], Muñoz and Rushby advocate *structural embeddings*, where a formal method (e.g. B [2] or VDM [12]) provides the outer level structural elements and means to manipulate them, while a general purpose verification system (e.g. PVS [26] or HOL [14]) provides the semantics for expressions within the structural elements, as well as mechanized means of reasoning about them. We describe an application of this approach, namely an embedding of the Ocsid specification language using the PVS theorem prover.

The Ocsid specification language is an experimental variant of the DisCo [18,21] language, essentially a proof of concept for a new way of structuring superposition. Since we did not want to spend too much effort on uninteresting implementation work in the exploratory phase, we decided to implement the Ocsid compiler as a front end that delegates as much of the work as possible to existing tools. To this end, we use the existing DisCo tool set [1] for visualization and animation of Ocsid specifications, and the PVS theorem prover for type checking and verification. The focus of this paper is on how Ocsid utilizes PVS.

The main motivation behind this work has been independent verification of superposition steps. In our earlier work [19,20] on mechanical verification of DisCo specifications it became painfully obvious that many proofs in the verification of distributed systems are really instances of more abstract proofs, but the DisCo language lacks the expressive power required for expressing these abstractions. The Ocsid language provides mechanisms for expressing behavior in a more abstract fashion, and PVS parametric theories provide the required mechanism for instantiating proofs.

Defining the semantics of a specification language by giving a tool that maps it to the input language of another tool may not be very elegant, but from a

R.J. Boulton and P.B. Jackson (Eds.): TPHOLs 2001, LNCS 2152, pp. 281–296, 2001.
© Springer-Verlag Berlin Heidelberg 2001

pragmatic point of view it has proved to be a good design decision. The front end compiler (about 3000 lines of Haskell) provides features explicitly targeted at the specific problem domain, in our case reactive distributed systems. Sharing the expression language with PVS makes mapping from Ocsid to PVS straightforward, and removes the possibility of subtle errors caused by small differences between the logics of the specification language and the verification system.

The type system of PVS is rich enough to allow a fairly straightforward mapping from Ocsid to the PVS logic. It handles the issue of undefined values, it is used for modeling inheritance hierarchies, and it is also used to express scoping rules for variables embedded within states of hierarchical state machines.

The rest of the paper is structured as follows. Section 2 describes the Ocsid specification language, and Sections 3 and 4 describe the structural embedding. Related work is discussed Section 5, and conclusions are presented in Section 6.

2   The Ocsid Language

Ocsid is based on *superposition*, originally used as a design technique for distributed algorithms without any specific syntactic support (e.g. [13,11,9]). As a syntactic construct, superposition has been used at least in the DisCo [18,21] and Unity [10] languages. In superposition, the underlying program or specification is augmented with new statements or other elements in such a way that some properties of interest of the original are retained.

Ocsid also allows for composition of independent branches of specification. This part of the language is still under development and it is not addressed here.

The semantics of Ocsid is based on the joint action [6,7] formalism of Back and Kurki-Suonio, which can further be mapped to Lamport's Temporal Logic of Actions [22]. The world consists of a set of objects, which are containers of state variables. State variables can only be changed in *joint actions* in which some combinations of objects, the *participants* of the action, synchronize and modify their state variables. An action execution may also involve *parameters*, which are similar to participants but denote values instead of mutable objects. A *behavior* is a sequence of states resulting from atomic executions of joint actions.

Like DisCo, Ocsid is targeted at formal specification of reactive distributed systems. Early focus on collective behavior and atomicity addresses concerns that are especially relevant for systems with a large degree of concurrency and asynchrony.

In Ocsid, the unit of modularity is a *layer*. A layer describes a syntactic transformation that can be applied to a specification, provided that the specification satisfies the assumptions of the layer. The *requires* section of a layer specifies what entities (types, classes, actions) are assumed to be present in a specification to which the layer is applied. The *provides* section introduces new entities and extends the existing ones.

Superposition in Ocsid preserves safety properties by construction. When a layer introduces a new state variable, all assignments to it must be given. New assignments cannot be given in later superposition steps.

The empty specification is the starting point for any Ocsid specification. It contains the empty class and the stuttering action, from which all classes and actions are derived. Figure 1 gives a simple layer, which can be superimposed on the empty specification, yielding a specification of a system in which two nodes may exchange the values of their ax attributes. [1]

```
layer swap_l
requires
provides
    new class node;
    new class bus;
    class extension node is ... ax : integer; y : integer; end;
    new action swap;
    new action change_y;
    action extension swap by ... p1 : node; p2 : node; b : bus
    when ... do ... p1.ax := p2.ax; p2.ax := p1.ax; end
    action extension change_y(... new_y : integer)
    by ... p : node when ... do ... p.y := new_y; end;
end;
```

Fig. 1. A Simple Layer.

The syntactic forms *new class* and *new action* introduce new classes and actions that are disjoint from any other classes and actions. Extension transforms an existing class or action by augmenting it with the new elements. The ellipsis "..." stands for the elements in the class or action being transformed.

New specifications are derived by superimposing layers on existing specifications. Superposition is done with the *superimpose* syntactic form:

specification swap_spec **is**
superimpose(swap_l, the_empty_specification);

Layer *distribution_l* in Figure 2 illustrates how a layer makes assumptions about the specification on which it is superimposed. In order for *distribution_l* to be applicable to a specification, the specification must contain a type T, an action *communicate*, and a class C containing a state variable *abstract_var*. The invariant provided by the layer states that *abstract_var* is a "shadow" variable whose value can always be computed from other variables. The variable need not be present in an implementation, and no synchronizations are needed for referencing it.

The *requires* section describes a closed world; any other actions in the specification may not change the state variable *abstract_var*, and action *communicate*

---

[1] Class *bus* and state variable y do not serve any useful purpose in the layer, they are included for illustrating superposition in Section 4.

in the specification must be a refinement of action *communicate* in the *requires* part. Section 4 discusses this in more detail. The section enables us to verify temporal properties for layers by making use of the closed world assumption and the refinement assumptions for actions.

Each state variable is guarded by a predicate, indicated by square brackets. A variable may only be accessed when its guarding predicate is true. To provide a hierarchical structure similar to that of Statecharts [15], state variables of enumeration types implicitly define predicates that can be used as guarding predicates. For example, the declaration

$$status : (valid, \ invalid);$$

defines predicates *status'valid* and *status'invalid*, used in

$$[status'valid].concrete\_var;$$

Omitting the guarding predicate is equivalent to a guarding predicate that is identically true. In a well-typed specification, variables are only accessed when their guarding predicates are true. Section 3 explains how we use the PVS type system to guarantee this property.

An underscore as the right hand side of an assignment denotes an arbitrary change. Thus the *requires* section allows action *communicate* to change *abstract_var* in an arbitrary way. The backquote " ' " is used to denote the primed value of a variable, i.e. its value in the next state.[2]

A layer can be adapted to a specification by renaming classes, actions, etc. and substituting named types with type expressions. This decouples layers from specifications, and enables the use of layers as abstract specifications of collective behavior. An Ocsid layer is a template that can be used multiple times by giving different substitutions. In terms of object-oriented design methods, an Ocsid layer can be seen as a design pattern.

The following substitution adapts *distribution_l* to be applicable to *swap_spec*:

> **substitution s is**
>   **layer** distribution_l := **layer** swap_dist_l;
>   **type** T := **type** integer;
>   **class** C([status'valid],[ ].abstract_var,[status'valid].concrete_var)
>   := **class** node([status'valid],[ ].ax,[status'valid].x);
>   **action** communicate( ) := **action** swap( );
> **end**;

By using the substitution, we can then apply *distribution_l* to *swap_spec* to derive a specification of distributed swapping:

> **specification** distributed_swap **is**
>   **superimpose**(**substitute**(distribution_l,s),swap_spec);

---

[2] The quote character would be more consistent with standard temporal logic notation. However, since the quote character is used in DisCo to refer to values of enumeration types, we use it in Ocsid for the same purpose.

layer distribution_1
requires
  type T;
  class C **is** abstract_var : T; **end**;
  action communicate
  by p1 : C; p2 : C **when** true
  do p1.abstract_var := _; p2.abstract_var := _;
  end;
provides
  new class message;
  class extension C **is** ...
    status : (valid, invalid); [status'valid].concrete_var : T;
  end;
  class extension message **is** ...
    exists_as : (no_message, a_message); [exists_as'a_message].concrete_var : T;
    represents : ref C;
  end;
  initially init **is**
    ($\forall$ (cc : C, m : message) :
      cc.status = valid $\land$ m.exists_as = no_message
      $\land$ cc.abstract_var = cc.[status'valid].concrete_var))
    $\land$ ($\forall$ (m1, m2:message): m1.represents = m2.represents $\Rightarrow$ ref(m1) = ref(m2)));
  new action send_message; **new action** receive_message;
  action extension send_message **by** ... p1 : C; m : message
  when ... p1.status = valid $\land$ m.exists_as = no_message $\land$ m.represents = ref(p1) **do** ...
    p1.status := invalid; m.exists_as := a_message;
    m.[exists_as'a_message].concrete_var := p1.[status'valid].concrete_var;
  end;
  action extension communicate **by** ... m : message
  when ... p2.status = valid $\land$ m.exists_as = a_message $\land$ m.represents = ref(p1) **do** ...
    p2.[status'valid].concrete_var := 'p2.abstract_var;
    m.[exists_as'a_message].concrete_var := 'p1.abstract_var;
  end;
  action extension receive_message **by** ... p1 : C; m : message
  when ... m.exists_as = a_message $\land$ m.represents = ref(p1) **do** ...
    p1.status := valid;
    p1.[status'valid].concrete_var := m.[exists_as'a_message].concrete_var;
    m.exists_as := no_message;
  end;
  invariant abstract_var_implemented
    ($\forall$(n : C, m : message) :
      (m.represents = ref(n)) $\Rightarrow$
        $\neg$ (n.status = valid $\land$ m.exists_as = a_message)
        $\land$ ((n.status = valid $\Rightarrow$ n.abstract_var = n.[status'valid].concrete_var)
        $\land$ (m.exists_as = a_message $\Rightarrow$ n.abstract_var = m.[exists_as'a_message].concrete_var))
      $\land$ ($\forall$ (m1, m2 : message): m1.represents = m2.represents $\Rightarrow$ ref(m1) = ref(m2)));
end;

Fig. 2. Distribution of an Action as a Layer.

3   Base Ocsid in PVS

In this section we describe the small amount of infrastructure needed for embedding Ocsid in PVS. We also describe how the basic building blocks of Ocsid are mapped to PVS.

3.1   Infrastructure

A small number of PVS definitions are needed to support the structural embedding. They define the empty specification and some temporal logic.

All Ocsid specifications are derived from the empty specification, which defines the empty class and the stuttering action. Figure 3 gives the PVS theory corresponding to the empty specification. Axiom Object_unique_ref models the assumption that each Ocsid object has a unique reference accessed with the function ref.

PVS theory temporal_operators in Figure 4 specifies some linear time temporal logic for reasoning about invariants. The predefined function suffix is the expected operation on infinite sequences.

3.2   Actions in PVS

An Ocsid action is mapped to a PVS function whose arguments are the current state, the next state, and the parameters and participants of the action. The function is composed of the guard of the action, the assignments in the action body, and universally quantified formulas specifying that no other changes take place. We refer to such functions as *action functions* in the following. Section 4 explains how action functions are used for superposition and temporal reasoning.

In temporal logic, an action is a boolean function of two states. An action function is converted to an action by existentially quantifying over the parameters and participants of the action.

3.3   Ocsid Classes in PVS

Ocsid classes are represented as subtypes of Ocsid_object. Ocsid classes form a subclass hierarchy, which is mirrored in PVS as a subtype hierarchy, where each Ocsid class C gives rise to a PVS predicate C. An Ocsid declaration *cc: C* maps to PVS as cc: (C), where (C) denotes a subtype of Ocsid_object whose values satisfy predicate C.

Subtypes offer a convenient way to encode the class hierarchy. A subclass inherits the ability to participate in a role declared to be of the base type. In PVS, participation corresponds to existential quantification, and quantification over a base type also includes the values of any of its subtypes.

In a logic without subtypes we would either need to simulate them axiomatically, or to make explicit all the possible combinations of classes of participants. The latter approach is not practical, since the number of combinations grows fast.

```
the_empty_specification: THEORY
  BEGIN
    state: TYPE+
    Ocsid_object: TYPE+
    Ocsid_object_ref: TYPE+
    ref: [Ocsid_object → Ocsid_object_ref]
    Stutter(now, next: state): bool = TRUE
    INIT(now: state): bool = TRUE
    Object_unique_ref: AXIOM
        ∀ (a, b: ocsid_object): ref(a) = ref(b) ⇒ a = b
  END the_empty_specification
```

Fig. 3. The Empty Specification.

```
temporal_operators[state: TYPE+]: THEORY
  BEGIN
    behavior: TYPE = [nat → state]
    temporal_formula: TYPE = [behavior → bool]
    state_predicate: TYPE = [state → bool]
    action: TYPE = [state, state → bool]
    □(F: temporal_formula, b: behavior): bool = ∀ (n: nat): F(suffix(b, n))
    statepred2temporal(P: state_predicate): temporal_formula =
        λ (b: behavior): P(b(0))
    action2temporal(A: action): temporal_formula =
        λ (b: behavior): A(b(0), b(1))
    invariant(P, I: state_predicate, A: action): bool =
      ∀ (b: behavior):
          I(b(0)) ∧ □(action2temporal(A), b) ⇒ □(statepred2temporal(P), b)
    preserves(single_action: action, P: state_predicate): bool =
        ∀ (now, next: state): P(now) ∧ single_action(now, next) ⇒ P(next)
  END temporal_operators
```

Fig. 4. Temporal Operators.

Let action $\mathcal{A}(C, D)$ be defined for objects of classes C and D respectively. Introducing subclasses $C1$ and $D1$ already gives rise to additional actions $\mathcal{A}(C1, D)$, $\mathcal{A}(C, D1)$ and $\mathcal{A}(C1, D1)$.

Predicate subtypes are used to express guarding predicates of state variables. Each state variable is represented as a function from a predicate subtype to the type of the variable. For example, class *message* and its variable [*exists_as'a_message*].*concrete_var* map to PVS as

```
message: [Ocsid_object → bool]
exists_as_a_message(x: (message), s: state): bool =
    exists_as(x, s) = a_message
exists_as_a_message_concrete_var:
    [(exists_as_a_message) → integer]
```

PVS then generates proof obligations to show that whenever exists_as_a_message_concrete_var(x, s) is referenced, exists_as_a_message(x, s) is true.

3.4   Initial Conditions and Invariants

Initial conditions are state predicates, so they are mapped to PVS as boolean functions of state. The proposed invariants of a specification are mapped to boolean functions of state as well. In addition, each invariant gives rise to a theorem that states that the boolean function is an invariant of the specification.

4   Superposition

In this section we describe how specifications, layers and superposition are mapped to PVS.

4.1   Layers

Each Ocsid layer corresponds to a single PVS theory, parameterized by the types, classes and actions of the *requires* part of the layer (in PVS syntax, theory parameters appear in square brackets immediately after the theory name). The theory consists of assumptions about the formal parameters, definitions of action extension functions, definitions of the initial condition and actions of the layer, and finally theorems that state that the initial state and the actions imply the proposed invariants. Figure 5 depicts the PVS theory corresponding to layer *distribution_l*, given in Figure 2.

We next explain how actions are extended, using *communicate* as an example. The relevant parts of the theory are indicated in bold typeface. Each required action A gives rise to a theory parameter named A, and an assumption

A_refinement : ASSUMPTION
    ∀ (now, next: state,   *parameters and participants*):
        A(now, next, *parameters and participants*) ⇒
            guard and body of A as given in the requires section

When the theory is instantiated, the actual parameter corresponding to the action must have the correct type as indicated by the theory parameter. PVS also generates a proof obligation to show that the parameter satisfies the assumption. In Figure 5, the relevant theory parameter is communicate, and the assumption is communicate_refinement.

Extension of an action A gives rise to a PVS function A_extension, which describes how the action affects the new state variables introduced in the layer. The function consists of the new guard conjuncts, the new assignments, and universally quantified formulas that state that the rest of the world remains unchanged with respect to the new state variables.

The vertical bar "|" in the parameter list of communicate_extension indicates that the actual parameters corresponding to now, next, p_2 and p_1 must satisfy

distribution_l[*omitted parameters,*
              nonrefined_actions: [[state, state] → bool], T: TYPE+,
              Ocsid_object: TYPE+, C: [Ocsid_object→bool],
              abstract_var: [[(C), state] → T],
              communicate: [[state, state, (C), (C)] → bool]]:
THEORY BEGIN ASSUMING
  communicate_parent(now, next: state, p_2, p_1: (C)): bool =
    ¬ (ref(p_2) = ref(p_1)) ∧
    (∀ (C?var: (C)): ¬ ((C?var ∈ (: p_1, p_2 :))) ⇒
        abstract_var(C?var, next) = abstract_var(C?var, now))
  communicate_refinement: ASSUMPTION ∀(now,next:state,p_2:(C),p_1:(C)):
    communicate(now,next,p_2,p_1) ⇒ communicate_parent(now,next,p_2,p_1)
further assumptions ENDASSUMING
IMPORTING temporal_operators[state]
init(now: state): bool = *definition of the initial condition*
abstract_var_implemented(now: state): bool = *definition of the invariant*
further definitions omitted
  communicate_extension(now, next: state, p_2, p_1: (C), m: (message)
        | communicate_parent(now, next, p_2, p_1)): bool =
    status(p_2, now) = valid ∧ exists_as(m, now) = a_message
    ∧ represents(m, now) = ref(p_1) ∧ ¬ (ref(p_2) = ref(p_1))
    ∧ status(p_2, next) = status(p_2, now)
    ∧ status_valid_concrete_var(p_2, next) = abstract_var(p_2, next)
    ∧ status(p_1, next) = status(p_1, now)
    ∧ (status(p_1, now) = valid ∧ status(p_1, next) = valid ⇒
        status_valid_concrete_var(p_1,next)=status_valid_concrete_var(p_1,now))
    ∧ exists_as(m, next) = exists_as(m, now)
    ∧ exists_as_a_message_concrete_var(m, next) = abstract_var(p_1, next)
    ∧ represents(m, next) = represents(m, now)
    ∧ (∀ (C?var: (C)):
              status(C?var, next) = status(C?var, now))
    ∧ *further conjuncts giving values in the next state*
further definitions omitted
refined_communicate(now, next: state): bool =
    ∃ (p_2: (C), p_1: (C), m: (message)):
      communicate(now, next, p_2, p_1) ∧
      communicate_extension(now, next, p_2, p_1, m)
LAYERINIT(now: state): bool = init(now)
LAYERACTIONS(now, next: state): bool =
    (nonrefined_actions(now, next) ∧ Stutter_extension(now, next))
    ∨ refined_Stutter(now, next) ∨ **refined_communicate**(now, next)
    ∨ refined_send_message(now, next) ∨ refined_receive_message(now, next)
abstract_var_implemented_invariance: THEOREM
    invariant(abstract_var_implemented, LAYERINIT, LAYERACTIONS)
END distribution_l

Fig. 5. PVS Theory Corresponding to Layer *distribution_l*.

the predicate following the vertical bar. This condition is needed e.g. when the new conjuncts refer to a state variable guarded by a predicate, and the assumed guard of the action being extended ensures that the predicate is true.

Similar extension functions are created for all actions extended in the layer. The theory also defines a stuttering extension that leaves the new state variables unchanged.

For each action A, a PVS function refined_A is constructed as follows:

refined_A(now, next : state) : bool =
$\exists$(*new parameters and participants*) :
A(now, next, *old parameters and participants*)
$\wedge$ A_extension(now, next, *new parameters and participants*) .

LAYERINIT is defined to be the conjunction of the initial conditions introduced in the layer, here consisting of init, and LAYERACTIONS is defined to be the disjunction of the refined actions. Actions that are not explicitly extended in the layer are extended using Stutter_extension to preserve the values of the new state variables. Each invariant I declared in an Ocsid layer maps to a theorem

I_invariance : THEOREM
invariant(I, LAYERINIT, LAYERACTIONS) .

Verification of the invariance of I is then just standard invariant reasoning. However, instead of reasoning about a fixed set of state variables, one reasons about state variables residing in objects. Consider an action $\mathcal{A}(p, q)$ and an invariant $\forall(r, s) : P(r, s)$. In order to verify that $\mathcal{A}$ preserves P, one has to consider all the possible ways (p, q) and (r, s) can overlap. This makes invariant proofs of joint action specifications somewhat laborious, and reuse of verification an especially attractive proposition.

4.2   Specifications

An Ocsid specification is constructed by applying a layer to a parent specification. A PVS theory corresponding to an Ocsid specification imports the theory corresponding to the parent specification, and an instance of the theory corresponding to the layer being applied. Figure 6 depicts the theory resulting from

specification distributed_swap **is**
superimpose(**substitute**(distribution_l,s),swap_spec);

Substitution of *integer* for T, *node* for C etc. is done by matching actual and formal parameters.

The *requires* section of an Ocsid layer describes a closed world, so any actions not mentioned in the *requires* part are assumed to be stuttering relative to the required state variables. When an instance of a layer is superimposed on a specification, the actual parameter corresponding to theory parameter nonrefined_actions

distributed_swap: THEORY BEGIN
  IMPORTING swap_spec
  message: [Ocsid_object → bool]
  status_enum: TYPE = {valid, invalid}
  status: [(λ (x: (node), s: state): TRUE) → status_enum]
  status_valid(x: (node), s: state): bool = status(x, s) = valid
  status_valid_x: [(status_valid) → integer]
  further declarations of state variables

  swap_dist_l: LIBRARY
  distribution_l[*omitted actual parameters*,
                (λ (now, next: state):
                    ∃ (new_y: integer, p: (node)):
                        swap_spec.change_y(now, next, new_y, p)),
                integer, Ocsid_object, node, ax,
                (λ (now, next: state, p_2: (node), p_1: (node)):
                    ∃ (b: (bus)): swap_spec. **swap**(now, next, b, p_2, p_1))]

  swap(now, next: state, b: (bus), p_2, p_1: (node), m: (message)): bool =
    swap_spec.swap(now, next, b, p_2, p_1)
    ∧ swap_dist_l.communicate_extension(now, next, p_2, p_1, m)

  change_y(now, next: state, new_y: integer, p: (node)): bool =
    swap_spec.change_y(now, next) ∧ swap_dist_l.Stutter_extension(now, next)

  send_message(now, next: state, m: (message), p_1: (node)): bool =
    swap_spec.Stutter(now, next)
    ∧ swap_dist_l.send_message_extension(now, next, m, p_1)

  further definitions of action functions

  INIT(now: state): bool =
    swap_spec.INIT(now) ∧ swap_dist_l.LAYERINIT(now)

  ACTIONS(now, next: state): bool =
    (Stutter(now, next))
    ∨ (∃ (b: (bus), p_2: (node), p_1: (node), m: (message)):
        swap(now, next, b, p_2, p_1, m))
    ∨ (∃ (new_y: integer, p: (node)): change_y(now, next, new_y, p))
    ∨ (∃ (m: (message), p_1: (node)): send_message(now, next, m, p_1))
    ∨ (∃ (m: (message), p_1: (node)): receive_message(now, next, m, p_1))

  abstract_var_implemented_invariance: THEOREM
    invariant(swap_dist_l.abstract_var_implemented, INIT, ACTIONS)
END distributed_swap

Fig. 6. PVS Theory Corresponding to Ocsid Specification *distributed_swap*.

is a disjunct of all actions that do not match any action in the *requires* section. The ASSUMING part contains an assumption that nonrefined_actions does not change any of the variables mentioned in the *requires* section.

In the case of *distributed_swap*, action *swap* is matched with *communicate*, so only *change_y* is not matched with any of the required actions. The expression provided as the actual parameter for nonrefined_actions is thus

$$\lambda \text{ (now, next: state):}$$
$$\exists \text{ (new\_y: integer, } p \text{: (node)):}$$
$$\text{swap\_spec.change\_y(now, next, new\_y, } p \text{)}.$$

The required action *communicate* has two participants, while action *swap* has three. To make *swap* compatible with *communicate*, it is wrapped in a lambda form, and the extra participant b is existentially quantified:

$$\lambda \text{ (now, next: state, } p_2 \text{: (node), } p_1 \text{: (node)):}$$
$$\exists \text{ (}b\text{: (bus)): swap\_spec.swap(now, next, } b, p_2, p_1 \text{)}.$$

When constructing the action functions for the new specification, an action function from the parent specification is conjoined with an extension function from the instantiated theory. For the actions extended in the layer, the corresponding extension is used, and for all other actions the stuttering extension is used.

ACTIONS is defined to be the disjunct of actions so constructed, and the initial condition INIT is the conjunction of the initial condition of the parent specification and the initial condition of the layer. In terms of temporal logic, the specification is

$$\text{INIT} \wedge \Box \text{ACTIONS}.$$

Let I be an invariant property provided by a layer. The theorem verified for the corresponding theory is

$$invariant(I, \text{LAYERINIT, LAYERACTIONS}) \tag{1}$$

while the theorem we are interested in is

$$invariant(I, \text{INIT, ACTIONS}). \tag{2}$$

From the way INIT is constructed, we know that it implies LAYERINIT, as the latter is a conjunct in the former. ACTIONS also implies LAYERACTIONS by construction. These are meta-level theorems as far as our embedding is concerned, so we have to resort to using (1) as a lemma when proving (2).

The structure of the formulas makes the proof straightforward. An action A_S in a specification is the conjunct of a base action A_B in the parent specification, and an extension E from the layer being superimposed. The corresponding action A_L in the layer is the conjunct of the formal parameter A_F and the extension E. When the layer is instantiated, A_B is matched with A_F, possibly by existentially quantifying some parameters and participants. The action implication $A_S \Rightarrow A_L$

is then verified by skolemizing the existentially quantified variables in A_S and instantiating the corresponding existentially quantified variables in A_L with the skolem constants, and rewriting the definitions of action functions.

5 Discussion

There is a plethora of work on the theme "X in Y" where X is a specification language and Y is a verification system [4,3,16,5,29,8,23,20]. Most of this work (including our own) suffers from the problem pointed out in [25]: a mismatch between the logic of X and the logic of Y, which unnecessarily complicates the translation and hinders efficient mechanization. By defining the logic of Ocsid to be the logic of PVS, we avoid the mismatch. Ease of mapping to the logic of PVS has been an explicit goal when designing the Ocsid language.

Compared to embeddings of Unity such as [5,28], our goals are much more modest and pragmatic. We are only interested in safety properties, invariants in particular. The reason for this is that superposition as used in DisCo and Ocsid may invalidate liveness properties in refinement. We have opted for giving the translation from Ocsid to PVS as an auxiliary tool instead of defining the semantics of the specification language using the logic of PVS. The justification is that we are interested in verifying properties of Ocsid specifications instead of reasoning about the language itself. In our experience, verification is much more straightforward with a shallow embedding than with a deep embedding.

Our work is related with the structural embeddings of a tabular notation [27] and the B-method [24] in PVS. The latter is especially close to our work, as it is implemented as a front end tool for PVS.

We originally started to develop a deep embedding, in which one could verify the theorem that links an invariance property of a layer with an invariance property in its application. However, it turns out that the shallow structural embedding gives most of the benefits we would get from a deep embedding. The shallow embedding also makes it easier to utilize the PVS type system as the type system of the specification language, and is less cumbersome when verifying actual specifications.

The drawback of using a shallow embedding is that even though we can use the verification system for proving that the translation of the Ocsid specification implies the translation of the invariants, the question remains whether these are equivalent to the Ocsid specification and its invariants. We plan to utilize a deep embedding for checking this. Let sem be the semantic function that maps a syntactic construct to its meaning, S an Ocsid specification expressed as a set of layers, superpositions and compositions, and S_t the translation of S from Ocsid to PVS. Establishing

$$sem(S) \Leftrightarrow S_t \tag{3}$$

would then suffice for showing that the invariants verified for S_t are in fact invariants of S. We speculate that proving (3) may not be too difficult, because if the translation is correct, then the structure of S is identical to that of S_t. The verification would be laborious but completely mechanical, consisting mostly of rewriting *sem* and the definitions of action functions.

The main thrust of our work has been the recognition of common abstractions in distributed systems. With Ocsid layers, we are able to specify and verify these abstractions, and to reuse both design and verification effort. An Ocsid layer can be utilized in a specification by verifying a set of action refinements, which in our experience are easily handled by the heuristics of PVS.

Many relevant invariant properties are not inductive, i.e. strong enough to be verified using deductive methods. Successful verification needs additional invariants, which easily leads to large invariants that are extremely tedious to verify. When an invariant property has been packaged in a reusable layer, this reasoning can be done once and for all.

The Ocsid compiler is still under development, so we have not applied it to more sizeable problems. However, we have experimented with the ideas using the DisCo specification language. For example, specifying the Recoverable Distributor pattern [17] in DisCo reveals many opportunities for extracting and reusing abstract collective behavior.

6   Conclusions

We have described a structural embedding of the Ocsid specification language in the logic of the PVS theorem prover. The specification language consists of a structuring mechanism peculiar to Ocsid, and an expression language that is defined to be the expression language of PVS.

The structuring mechanism allows us to specify and verify collective behavior of distributed objects in an abstract way. The syntactic unit of specification is a layer, which describes a superposition step (transformation) that derives a more concrete specification from a more abstract specification. The implementation effort for Ocsid has been relatively small, only a few thousand lines of Haskell code. We feel that this implementation work has paid off rather well.

Invariant properties can be expressed and verified for layers, and reused by discharging a set of proof obligations related to action refinement. Potentially expensive temporal reasoning is then reused by verifying relatively simple proof obligations. In the example given in the paper, temporal reasoning took approximately 160 seconds, while the proof obligations were proved in 9 seconds.

Our future plan is to investigate whether one could define a pattern language for distributed systems based on archived superposition steps.

Acknowledgments

Part of this work was carried out when the author was visiting University of Dortmund on a grant from the Academy of Finland. Financial support has also come from Academy of Finland project 757473. Comments from the anonymous reviewers were helpful in improving the presentation.

References

1. Timo Aaltonen, Mika Katara, and Risto Pitkänen. DisCo toolset – the new generation. *Journal of Universal Computer Science*, 7(1):3–18, 2001. http://www.jucs.org.
2. Jean-Raymond Abrial. *The B Book - Assigning Programs to Meanings*. Cambridge University Press, August 1996.
3. S. Agerholm and J. Frost. An isabelle-based theorem prover for VDM-SL. In *Proc. 10th International Theorem Proving in Higher Order Logics Conference*, pages 1–16, 1997.
4. Sten Agerholm, Juan Bicarregui, and Savi Maharaj. On the verification of VDM specification and refinement with PVS. In Juan Bicarregui, editor, *Proof in VDM: Case Studies*, FACIT (Formal Approaches to Computing and Information Technology), chapter 6, pages 157–190. Springer-Verlag, London, UK, 1997.
5. F. Andersen, K. D. Petersen, and J. S. Petterson. Program verification using HOL-UNITY. In J. J. Joyce and C.-J.H Seger, editors, *International Workshop on Higher Order Logic and its Applications*, volume 780 of *Lecture Notes in Computer Science*, pages 1–16, 1994.
6. R. J. R. Back and R. Kurki-Suonio. Distributed cooperation with action systems. *ACM Transactions on Programming Languages and Systems*, 10(4):513–554, October 1988.
7. R. J. R. Back and R. Kurki-Suonio. Decentralization of process nets with a centralized control. *Distributed Computing*, (3):73–87, 1989.
8. J. Bowen and M. J. C. Gordon. Z and HOL. In J. Bowen and A. Hall, editors, *Z User Workshop*, Workshops in Computing, pages 141–167. Springer-Verlag, Cambridge, 1994.
9. K. M. Chandy and L. Lamport. Distributed snapshots: determining the global state of distributed systems. *ACM Transactions on Computer Systems*, 3(1):63–75, 1985.
10. K. M. Chandy and J. Misra. *Parallel Program Design: A Foundation*. Addison-Wesley, 1988.
11. K. Mani Chandy, Jayadev Misra, and Laura M. Haas. Distributed deadlock detection. *ACM Transactions on Computer Systems*, 1(2):144–156, May 1983.
12. John Dawes. *The VDM-SL Reference Guide*. Pitman, 1991. ISBN 0-273-03151-1.
13. Edsger W. Dijkstra and C. S. Scholten. Termination detection for diffusing computations. *Information Processing Letters*, 11(1):1–4, August 1980.
14. Michael J. C. Gordon. HOL: A proof generating system for higher-order logic. In Graham Birtwistle and P. A. Subrahmanyam, editors, *VLSI Specification, Verification and Synthesis*, pages 73–128. Boston Kluwer Academic Publishers, 1988.
15. David Harel. Statecharts: A visual formalism for complex systems. *Science of Computer Programming*, 8(3):231–274, June 1987.
16. Barbara Heyd and Pierre Crégut. A modular coding of UNITY in COQ. In J. von Wright, T. Grundy, and J. Harrison, editors, *Proceedings of the 9th International Conference on Theorem Proving in Higher Order Logics*, volume 1125 of *Lecture Notes in Computer Science*, pages 251–266, 1996.
17. Nayeem Islam and Murthy Devarakonda. An essential design pattern for fault-tolerant distributed state sharing. *Communications of the ACM (CACM)*, 39(10):65–74, October 1996.
18. H.-M. Järvinen, R. Kurki-Suonio, M. Sakkinen, and K. Systä. Object-oriented specification of reactive systems. In *Proceedings of the 12th International Conference on Software Engineering*, pages 63–71. IEEE Computer Society Press, 1990.

19. Pertti Kellomäki. *Mechanical Verification of Invariant Properties of DisCo Specifications*. PhD thesis, Tampere University of Technology, 1997.
20. Pertti Kellomäki. Verification of reactive systems using DisCo and PVS. In John Fitzgerald, Cliff B. Jones, and Peter Lucas, editors, *FME'97: Industrial Applications and Strengthened Foundations of Formal Methods*, number 1313 in Lecture Notes in Computer Science, pages 589–604. Springer–Verlag, 1997.
21. Reino Kurki-Suonio. Fundamentals of object-oriented specification and modeling of collective behaviors. In H. Kilov and W. Harvey, editors, *Object-Oriented Behavioral Specifications*, pages 101–120. Kluwer Academic Publishers, 1996.
22. Leslie Lamport. The temporal logic of actions. *ACM Transactions on Programming Languages and Systems*, 16(3):872–923, May 1994.
23. Thomas Långbacka. A HOL formalization of the temporal logic of actions. In T. F. Melham and J. Camilleri, editors, *Higher Order Logic Theorem Proving and Its Applications*, volume 859 of *Lecture Notes in Computer Science*, Valetta, Malta, 1994. Springer Verlag.
24. César Muñoz. PBS: Support for the B-method in PVS. Technical Report SRI-CSL-99-1, Computer Science Laboratory, SRI International, Menlo Park, CA, February 1999.
25. César Muñoz and John Rushby. Structural embeddings: Mechanization with method. In Jeannette Wing and Jim Woodcock, editors, *FM99: The World Congress in Formal Methods*, volume 1708 of *Lecture Notes in Computer Science*, pages 452–471, Toulouse, France, September 1999. Springer-Verlag.
26. S. Owre, J. M. Rushby, and N. Shankar. PVS: A prototype verification system. In Deepak Kapur, editor, *11th International Conference on Automated Deduction*, volume 607 of *Lecture Notes in Artificial Intelligence*, pages 748–752. Springer Verlag, 1992.
27. Sam Owre, John Rushby, and N. Shankar. Integration in PVS: Tables, types, and model checking. In Ed Brinksma, editor, *Tools and Algorithms for the Construction and Analysis of Systems TACAS '97*, number 1217 in Lecture Notes in Computer Science, pages 366–383, Enschede, The Netherlands, April 1997. Springer-Verlag.
28. Paulson. Mechanizing UNITY in isabelle. *ACM Transactions on Computational Logic*, 1(1), 2000.
29. S. Kalvala. A Formulation of TLA in Isabelle. In E.T. Schubert, P.J. Windley, and J. Alves-Foss, editors, *8th International Workshop on Higher Order Logic Theorem Proving and its Applications*, volume 971 of *Lecture Notes in Computer Science*, pages 214–228, Aspen Grove, Utah, USA, September 1995. Springer-Verlag.

A Certified Polynomial-Based Decision Procedure for Propositional Logic

Inmaculada Medina-Bulo[1], Francisco Palomo-Lozano[1],
and José A. Alonso-Jiménez[2]

[1] Department of Computer Languages and Systems. University of Cádiz
Esc. Superior de Ingeniería de Cádiz. C/ Chile, s/n. 11003 Cádiz. Spain
{francisco.palomo,inmaculada.medina}@uca.es
[2] Department of Comp. Sciences and Artificial Intelligence, University of Sevilla
Fac. de Informática y Estadística. Avda. Reina Mercedes, s/n. 41012 Sevilla, Spain
jalonso@cica.es

Abstract. In this paper we present the formalization of a decision procedure for Propositional Logic based on polynomial normalization. This formalization is suitable for its automatic verification in an applicative logic like ACL2. This application of polynomials has been developed by reusing a previous work on polynomial rings [19], showing that a proper formalization leads to a high level of reusability. Two checkers are defined: the first for contradiction formulas and the second for tautology formulas. The main theorems state that both checkers are sound and complete. Moreover, functions for generating models and counterexamples of formulas are provided. This facility plays also an important role in the main proofs. Finally, it is shown that this allows for a highly automated proof development.

1   Introduction

In this paper we present the main results obtained through the development of an automated proof of the correctness of a polynomial-based decision procedure for Propositional Logic in ACL2 [14,15,16]. ACL2 [1] is the successor of NQTHM [3,5], the Boyer-Moore theorem prover. A concise description of ACL2 can be found in [14]. In order to understand ACL2, it is necessary to consider it under three different perspectives:

1. From a logic viewpoint, ACL2 is an untyped quantifier-free first-order logic of total recursive functions with equality. However, its *encapsulation* principle allows for some kind of higher-order reasoning.
2. From a programming language viewpoint, ACL2 is an applicative programming language in which the result of the application of a function is uniquely determined by its arguments. Every ACL2 function admitted under the definitional principle is a LISP function, so you can obtain both verified and executable software.

---

[1] A Computational Logic for Applicative Common Lisp.

R.J. Boulton and P.B. Jackson (Eds.): TPHOLs 2001, LNCS 2152, pp. 297–312, 2001.

3. From a reasoning system viewpoint, ACL2 is an automated reasoning system and it behaves as a heuristic theorem prover.

Representation issues play a major role in this work. We have represented Propositional Logic formulas in terms of just one Boolean function symbol: the three-place conditional construct present in most programming languages. This is discussed in Sect. 2.1. Definitions related with Boolean polynomials are presented in Sect. 2.2.

Surprisingly, polynomial-based theorem proving has a long history. According to H. Zhang [28], Boole himself [2] was the first to use Boolean polynomials to represent logical formulas and Herbrand described a polynomial-based decision procedure in his thesis. Later, in 1936, M. Stone [23] stated the strong relation existing between Boolean algebras and Boolean rings. Analogous results had been discovered, independently, in 1927 by I. I. Zhegalkin [29].

This relation is at the basis of the modern "algebraic methods" of logical deduction. The algebraic approach began with the development by J. Hsiang of a canonical term-rewriting system for Boolean algebras with applications to first-order theorem proving [11,12]. Concurrently, D. Kapur and P. Narendran used Gröbner bases and Buchberger's algorithm for the same purpose [17].[2] This last method has been extended to many-valued propositional logics [7,26] and it has been recently applied to knowledge based systems verification [18].

Several decision procedures for propositional logic that produce a verifiable proof log have been implemented. For example, [9,10] report the development of BDDs and Stålmarck's algorithm as HOL derived rules. On the other hand, actual formal verifications of decision procedures are less common. The classical work from [3] contains a verified decision procedure in NQTHM using IF-expressions. A similar procedure has been extracted from a COQ proof in [22]. Another decision procedure obtained via proof extraction in NUPRL is described in [6]. However, none of them is based on polynomial normalization.

We have not considered the possibility of integrating the decision procedure into the theorem prover via reflection, though this is feasible in ACL2 thanks to its metatheoretical extensibility capabilities [4]. A reflected decision procedure has been developed in [1] with NUPRL. See also [8] for a critical survey of reflection in theorem proving from a theoretical and practical viewpoint.

Section 2.3 presents a translation algorithm from formulas into polynomials. Once that suitable evaluation functions have been defined, this translation is shown to be interpretation-preserving. In Sect. 3, we review Hsiang's canonical term-rewriting system (TRS) for Boolean algebras. A normalization algorithm that is not based in term-rewriting is also presented. In Sect. 4, we prove the correctness of the decision procedure for Propositional Logic. As the involved algorithms are written in an applicative subset of COMMON LISP, they are intrinsically executable. Some examples of execution are shown in Sect. 5.

Finally, we will discuss the degree of automation achieved and we will also analyze some possible extensions of this work.

---

[2] See also [13,28,27].

2   IF-Formulas and Boolean Polynomials

In [20] an ACL2 formalization of IF-Formulas and Boolean polynomials is proposed. Next, the notion of Stone polynomial of an IF-formula is easily defined. We review here the main results obtained with some improvements.

As the conditional construct IF is functionally complete, we can regard our Propositional Logic formulas as IF-formulas without loss of generality. In fact, the NQTHM Boyer-Moore logic and its descendant ACL2 define the usual propositional connectives after axiomatizing IF. IF-formulas are also related with the OBDD algorithm as can be seen in [21]. A BDD manager has been recently formalized in ACL2 [24].

2.1   IF-Formulas

The underlying representation of IF-formulas is based on the notion of IF-cons. IF-conses are weaker than IF-formulas in the sense that they may not represent well-formed formulas. We use record structures to represent IF-conses. This provides us with a weak recognizer predicate that we strengthen to develop a recognizer for well-formed formulas.

Boolean constants, nil and t, are recognized by the ACL2 booleanp predicate. The set of propositional variables could be then represented by the set of atoms not including the Boolean constants. However, if we represent variables using natural numbers then it is easier to share the same notion of variable in formulas and polynomials. Thus, we define our variable recognizer, variablep, to recognize just natural numbers.

Our notion of IF-cons is captured by an ACL2 structure. An IF-cons is just a collection of three objects (the *test*, and the *then* and *else* branches). The predicate if-consp will recognize terms constructed with if-cons, while the functions test, then and else act as destructors. Well-formed IF-formulas can be recognized by the following total recursive ACL2 predicate:

```
(defun formulap (f)
  (or (booleanp f) (variablep f)
      (and (if-consp f)
           (formulap (test f))
           (formulap (then f))
           (formulap (else f)))))
```

An assignment of values to variables can be represented as a list of Booleans.[3] Thus, the value of a variable with respect to an assignment is given by the element which occupies its corresponding position.

```
(defun truth-value (v a)
  (nth v a))
```

---

[3] Remember each Boolean variable is represented as a natural number.

The value of a formula under an assignment is defined recursively by the following function. To make the valuation function total, we assign an arbitrary meaning to non-formulas.

```
(defun value (f a)
  (cond ((booleanp f) f)
        ((variablep f) (truth-value f a))
        ((if-consp f)
         (if (value (test f) a)
             (value (then f) a)
           (value (else f) a)))
        (t nil)))                        ; for completeness
```

The following theorem states a simple but important property. It says that the value of a formula under an assignment is true if and only if the value of the negation of that formula under the same assignment is false. Why this property is important will become clear in Sect. 4.

```
(defthm duality
  (implies (and (formulap f) (assignmentp a))
           (iff (equal (value f a) t)
                (equal (value (if-cons f nil t) a) nil))))
```

2.2   Boolean Polynomials

In order to represent polynomials with Boolean coefficients, we can use the Boolean ring given by $\langle \{0,1\}, \oplus, \wedge, 0, 1 \rangle$ where $\oplus$ is the logical exclusive disjunction (exclusive-or), $\wedge$ is the logical conjunction and 0 and 1 are regarded as truth-values (false and true). In the following definitions, let $B = \{0,1\}$ and $\neg$, $\vee$ stand for logical negation and logical disjunction, respectively.

Although it suffices with a polynomial Boolean ring for our current purposes, where monomials do not need coefficients, we have implemented monomials with coefficients and terms to reuse part of a previous work on polynomial rings [19].

Definition 1. *A Boolean term on a finite set* $V = \{v_1, \ldots, v_n\}$ *of Boolean variables with an ordering relation* $<_V = \{(v_i, v_j) : 1 \le i < j \le n\}$ *is a finite product of the form:*

$$\bigwedge_{i=1}^{n} (v_i \vee \neg a_i) \qquad \forall i \; a_i \in B \; . \tag{1}$$

We obtain a quite simple representation of a Boolean term on a given set of variables by using the Boolean sequence $\langle a_1, \ldots, a_n \rangle$, namely, v_i appears in the term if and only if $a_i = 1$. The main results that we have proved in ACL2 on our Boolean term formalization may be summed up in the following points:

1. Boolean terms form a commutative monoid with respect to a suitable multiplication operation.
2. Lexicographical ordering on terms is well-founded.

As we usually work with Boolean terms defined on the same set of variables, their sequences will have the same length. In this case they are said to be *compatible*.

Definition 2. *We define the multiplication of two compatible terms as the following operation:*

$$\bigwedge_{i=1}^{n}(v_i \vee \neg a_i) \cdot \bigwedge_{i=1}^{n}(v_i \vee \neg b_i) = \bigwedge_{i=1}^{n}(v_i \vee \neg(a_i \vee b_i)) \ . \tag{2}$$

Having chosen the set of variables, it suffices to "or" their sequences element by element to compute the multiplication of two compatible terms. A proof of terms having a commutative monoid structure with respect to the previous operation is easily obtained.

To order terms it is only necessary to take into account their associated sequences. The obvious choice is to set up a *lexicographical ordering* among them. In the case of compatible terms, this definition is straightforward, since the sequences involved have the same length.

Definition 3. *The lexicographical ordering on compatible Boolean terms is defined as the following relation:*

$$\langle a_1, \ldots, a_n \rangle < \langle b_1, \ldots, b_n \rangle \equiv \exists i \ (\neg a_i \wedge b_i \wedge \forall j < i \ a_j = b_j) \ . \tag{3}$$

Definition 4. *A Boolean monomial on V is the product of a Boolean coefficient and a Boolean term.*

$$c \wedge \bigwedge_{i=1}^{n}(v_i \vee \neg a_i) \qquad c \in B \quad \forall i \ a_i \in B \ . \tag{4}$$

In the same way as happened to terms, it is suitable to define a compatibility relation on monomials. We say that two monomials are *compatible* when their underlying terms are compatible.

A multiplication operation is defined and then it is proved that monomials have a monoid commutative structure with respect to it.

Due to technical reasons it is convenient to extend compatibility of monomials to polynomials. To achieve this we first say that a polynomial is *uniform* if all of its monomials are compatible each other. Henceforth, we will assume uniformity.

Definition 5. *A Boolean polynomial on V is a finite sum of monomials.*

$$\bigoplus_{i=1}^{m}\left[c_i \wedge \bigwedge_{j=1}^{n}(v_j \vee \neg a_{ij})\right] \qquad \forall i, j \ c_i, a_{ij} \in B \ . \tag{5}$$

Now, the definition of compatibility between polynomials arises in a natural way. Two polynomials are *compatible* if their monomials are compatible too.

Finally, we have proved that Boolean polynomials have a ring structure. To achieve this, only coefficients and terms had to be changed from the formalization described in [19]. These changes are reported in [20].

2.3   Interpretation Preserving Translation

Next, we use the relation between Boolean rings and Boolean algebras to derive the translation algorithm. Let us consider a Boolean algebra and the following three place Boolean function if, defined on it:

$$\forall a, b, c \in B \ if(a, b, c) = (a \wedge b) \vee (\neg a \wedge c) \ . \tag{6}$$

We can build an associated if function in the corresponding Boolean ring:

$$if(a, b, c) = a \cdot b \cdot (a + 1) \cdot c + a \cdot b + (a + 1) \cdot c = a \cdot b + a \cdot c + c \ .$$

The following ACL2 functions use this to compute the polynomial associated to a formula (Stone polynomial). The function `variable->polynomial` transforms a propositional variable into a suitable polynomial. The underlying polynomial Boolean ring is represented by ⟨`polynomialp`, `+`, `*`, `null`, `identity`⟩. The argument of the function `identity` is a technical detail that guarantees the uniformity of the resulting polynomial.

```
(defun stone (f)
  (stone-aux f (max-variable f)))

(defun stone-aux (f n)
  (cond ((booleanp f) (if f (identity (LISP::+ n 1)) (null)))
        ((variablep f) (variable->polynomial f n))
        ((if-consp f)
         (let ((s-test (stone-aux (test f) n))
               (s-then (stone-aux (then f) n))
               (s-else (stone-aux (else f) n)))
           (+ (* s-test (+ s-then s-else)) s-else)))
        (t (null))))                      ; for completeness
```

Then, a function, `ev`, to evaluate a polynomial with respect to an assignment is defined. Finally, it is proved that the translation of formulas into polynomials preserves the interpretation:

```
(defthm interpretation-preserving-translation
  (implies (and (formulap f) (assignmentp a))
           (iff (value f a) (ev (stone f) a))))
```

The hard part of the work is dealing with the theorems about the evaluation function and polynomial operations.

3   Normalization

In this section, we review the Hsiang's Canonical TRS and develop a straight-forward normalization procedure for Boolean polynomials. Unlike disjunctive and conjunctive normal forms, polynomial normalization allows us to associate a unique polynomial to each Propositional Logic Formula.

3.1   Hsiang's Canonical TRS for Boolean Algebras

A Boolean ring with identity $\langle B, +, \cdot, 0, 1 \rangle$ is a ring that is idempotent with respect to $\cdot$. It is a known fact that every Boolean ring is nilpotent with respect to $+$ and commutative. Hsiang [11,12] derives his canonical term-rewriting system for Boolean algebras by first generating a canonical system for Boolean rings. Firstly, he considers the Boolean ring axioms:[4]

A1.	$a + (b + c) = (a + b) + c$	(associativity of $+$).
A2.	$a + b = b + a$	(commutativity of $+$).
A3.	$a + 0 = a$	(right identity of $+$).
A4.	$a + (-a) = 0$	(right inverse of $+$).
A5.	$(a \cdot b) \cdot c = a \cdot (b \cdot c)$	(associativity of $\cdot$).
A6.	$a \cdot (b + c) = a \cdot b + a \cdot c$	(distributivity of $\cdot$ over $+$).
A7.	$a \cdot 1 = a$	(right identity of $\cdot$).
A8.	$a \cdot a = a$	(idempotency of $\cdot$).
T1.	$a + a = 0$	(nilpotency of $+$).
T2.	$a \cdot b = b \cdot a$	(commutativity of $\cdot$).

By executing the AC-completion procedure on these rules, he obtains the BR canonical TRS for Boolean rings. Then, BR can be completed[5] by adding rules for transforming the usual Boolean algebraic operations into Boolean ring operations, obtaining the BA canonical TRS for Boolean algebras.

BR: BA:

$$a + 0 \longrightarrow a,$$
$$a \cdot (b + c) \longrightarrow a \cdot b + a \cdot c,$$
$$a \cdot 0 \longrightarrow 0,$$
$$a \cdot 1 \longrightarrow a,$$
$$a \cdot a \longrightarrow a,$$
$$a + a \longrightarrow 0,$$
$$-a \longrightarrow a \ .$$

$$a \vee b \longrightarrow a \cdot b + a + b,$$
$$a \wedge b \longrightarrow a \cdot b,$$
$$\neg a \longrightarrow a + 1,$$
$$a \implies b \longrightarrow a \cdot b + a + 1,$$
$$a \iff b \longrightarrow a \cdot b \cdot 1,$$
$$a + 0 \longrightarrow a,$$
$$a \cdot (b + c) \longrightarrow a \cdot b + a \cdot c,$$
$$a \cdot 0 \longrightarrow 0,$$
$$a \cdot 1 \longrightarrow a,$$
$$a \cdot a \longrightarrow a,$$
$$a + a \longrightarrow 0 \ .$$

---

[4] Note that, T1 and T2 are not axioms, but theorems that are added so that the AC-unification algorithm can be used.

[5] The $-a \longrightarrow a$ rule is discarded since the inverse of $+$ has no significant meaning in Boolean algebras.

Therefore, the irreducible form of any Boolean algebra term is the normal expression defined by the BA TRS above, and it is unique (since BA is a canonical TRS). This implies that a formula from Propositional Logic is a tautology if and only if its irreducible expression is 1, and it is a contradiction if and only if its irreducible expression is 0.

3.2   A Straightforward Normalization Algorithm

An algorithm can be developed to avoid the overhead associated to Hsiang's TRS. Instead of rewriting modulo BA, formulas are translated to polynomials and then polynomial normalization is used. Once we have defined an order on terms, we can say that a polynomial is in normal form if and only if their monomials are strictly ordered by the decreasing term order and none of them is null. This definition implies the absence of identical monomials in a normalized uniform polynomial. We divide the specification of the normalization function in two steps:

1. A function capable of adding a monomial to a polynomial. This must be a normalization-preserving function.
2. A normalization function stable for normalized null polynomials that adds the first monomial to the normalization of the remaining monomials by using the previous function.

The normalization function is easy to define: if the polynomial is null, it is already in normal form, otherwise, it suffices to normalize the rest of the polynomial and then add the first monomial to the result.

```
(defun nf (p)
  (cond ((or (not (polynomialp p)) (nullp p)) (null))
        (t (+-monomial (first p) (nf (rest p))))))
```

In order to make +-monomial total we need to complete, taking the utmost care, the values that it returns when it is not applied to a polynomial.

Next, we show the most important part of the definition of +-monomial function. It takes a monomial m and a polynomial p as its arguments.

1. If m is null, p is returned.
2. If p is null, the polynomial composed of m is returned.
3. If m and the first monomial of p have the same term, both monomials are added. If the result is null then the rest of p is returned, otherwise a polynomial consisting of the resulting monomial and the rest of p is returned.
4. If m is greater than the first monomial of p, a polynomial consisting of m and p is returned.
5. Otherwise, a polynomial consisting of the first monomial of p and the result of recursively adding m to the rest of p is returned.

Important properties of the normalization function have been proved, such as that it meets its specification,

```
(defun nfp (p)
  (equal (nf p) p))

(defthm nfp-nf
  (nfp (nf p)))
```

and that polynomial uniformity is preserved under normalization.

```
(defun uniformp (p)
  (or (nullp p) (nullp (rest p))
      (and (MON::compatiblep (first p) (first (rest p)))
           (uniformp (rest p)))))

(defthm uniformp-nf
  (implies (uniformp p)
           (uniformp (nf p))))
```

One relevant result states that the normal form of a polynomial is strictly decreasingly ordered with respect to the lexicographical order defined on terms.

```
(defthm orderedp-nf
  (orderedp (nf p)))
```

In order to obtain this, we define the function `orderedp` by using the lexicographical order defined on terms.

```
(defun term-greater-than-leader (m p)
  (or (nullp p) (TER::< (MON::term (first p)) (MON::term m))))

(defun orderedp (p)
  (and (polynomialp p)
       (or (nullp p)
           (and (not (MON::nullp (first p)))
                (term-greater-than-leader (first p) (rest p))
                (orderedp (rest p))))))
```

4   A Decision Procedure

In this section, our main aim is to construct a polynomial-based procedure for deciding whether a propositional logic formula is a tautology and prove its correctness.

A formula is a tautology if and only if the value of the formula under every possible assignment of values to variables is true. So, the following first-order formula states the correctness of a tautology-checker:

$$\forall f \ [(\texttt{tautology-checker } f) \iff \forall a \ (\texttt{value } f \ a) = \texttt{t}] \qquad (7)$$

However, it is not possible to write directly this theorem in ACL2, due to the lack of quantifiers. For example, the following "theorem" does not capture our idea:

```
(defthm flawed-tautology-checker-correctness
  (iff (tautology-checker f) (equal (value f a) t)))
```

The problem is that its first-order interpretation is the following:

$$\forall f, a \, [\text{(tautology-checker } f) \iff \text{(value } f \ a) = \text{t}] \qquad (8)$$

which is rather different from (7).

A possible solution to this problem in ACL2 is to use defun-sk to introduce an intermediate function whose body has an outermost quantifier. Internally, defun-sk uses defchoose which is implemented by using the encapsulation principle.

An equivalent approach is to divide the proof in two parts: soundness and completeness. This is the approach used in [3].

$$\forall f, a \, [\text{(tautology-checker } f) \implies \text{(value } f \ a) = \text{t}] \quad \text{(sound)}$$
$$\forall f \, [\neg\text{(tautology-checker } f) \implies \exists a \, \text{(value } f \ a) = \text{nil}] \quad \text{(complete)}$$

The existential quantifier in the second formula can be relieved by substituting a proper function for a. This enforces the constructive character of the ACL2 logic: an explicit function providing a counterexample for a non-tautological formula is constructed in order to prove that the tautology-checker is complete.

On the other hand, it is a bit easier to formalize a contradiction-checker than a tautology-checker when using the polynomial-based approach. Thus, we begin by defining a contradiction-checker. Soundness and completeness for this kind of checker are defined analogously to the tautological case.

4.1   Contradiction-Checker

The contradiction-checker proceeds by transforming a formula into a polynomial, then computing its normal form and, finally, checking if the resulting normal form is the null polynomial.

So, we are trying to prove that a formula is a contradiction if the polynomial in normal form associated to the formula is the null polynomial. First, we introduce the function contradiction-checker.

```
(defun contradiction-checker (f)
  (equal (nf (stone f)) (null)))
```

Second, we prove that the contradiction-checker is sound.

```
(defthm contradiction-checker-is-sound
  (implies (and (formulap f) (assignmentp a) (contradiction-checker f))
           (equal (value f a) nil)))
```

The proof outline is as follows:

1. The translation from formulas to polynomials is interpretation-preserving allowing us to transform (value f a) into (ev (stone f) a).

2. The evaluation of a polynomial is stable under normalization, so we can replace (ev (stone f) a) by (ev (nf (stone f)) a).
3. The term (nf (stone f)) is known to be the null polynomial by the hypothesis (contradiction-checker f). But the evaluation of the null polynomial is nil under every possible assignment.

Therefore, we only need to show that the evaluation of a polynomial is equal to the evaluation of its normal form.[6]

```
(defthm ev-nf
  (implies (and (polynomialp p) (assignmentp a))
           (equal (ev p a) (ev (nf p) a))))
```

In order to prove completeness, we have to compute an explicit model for the formula in case of the formula not being a contradiction. We construct the model from the associated polynomial because it is simpler to find than from the formula itself.

In fact, it suffices to take an assignment such that the least term of the normalized polynomial evaluates to true. It is clear that each of the greater terms must be false, because the least term lacks (at least) a variable appearing in the remaining terms.

As we use the same representation for terms and assignments, this observation is supported by the following theorem. Therefore, the value of the formula is true with respect to the assignment given by the least term of its associated normalized polynomial.

```
(defthm ev-term-<
  (implies (and (TER::termp t1) (TER::termp t2)
                (TER::compatiblep t1 t2) (TER::< t2 t1))
           (equal (ev-term t1 t2) nil)))
```

Next, we define the function that computes such a term. Recall that normalized polynomials remain ordered with respect to the lexicographical order defined on terms. The null polynomial is a special case: it corresponds to a contradiction, which has no models.

```
(defun least-term (p)
  (cond ((nullp p) (TER::null 0))              ; for completeness
        ((nullp (rest p)) (MON::term (first p)))
        (t (least-term (rest p)))))

(defun model (f)
  (least-term (nf (stone f))))
```

Then, it is proved that the contradiction-checker is complete.

---

[6] In fact, the definition of this theorem is completed with syntactic restrictions to prevent the infinite application of its associated rewrite rule.

```
(defthm contradiction-checker-is-complete
  (implies (and (formulap f) (not (contradiction-checker f)))
           (equal (value f (model f)) t)))
```

The proof outline is as follows:

1. Let m be (model f).
2. The translation from formulas to polynomials is interpretation-preserving allowing us to transform (value f m) into (ev (stone f) m).
3. The evaluation of a polynomial is stable under normalization, so we can replace (ev (stone f) m) by (ev (nf (stone f)) m).
4. But the evaluation of (nf (stone f)) is t under m, by induction on the structure of (nf (stone f)), which is known to be an ordered polynomial.

Some lemmas are needed for the last step. The main lemma asserts that whenever least-term is applied to a non-null ordered uniform polynomial, it computes an assignment that makes its evaluation t.

```
(defthm ev-least-term
  (implies (and (polynomialp p) (uniformp p) (orderedp p)
                (not (equal p (null))))
           (equal (ev p (least-term p)) t)))
```

4.2   Tautology-Checker

Once we have certified the contradiction-checker, the definition and certification of a tautology-checker is considerably easier. We proceed by constructing the IF-formula corresponding to the negation of the input formula, then it is only necessary to check whether the resulting IF-formula is a contradiction.

```
(defun tautology-checker (f)
  (equal (nf (stone (if-cons f nil t))) (null)))
```

Let us consider the duality property stated in Sect. 2.1. This important result reduces the problem of determining whether a formula is a tautology to the dual problem of determining whether the negation of this formula is a contradiction. Using this result, we can easily show that the tautology-checker is sound.

```
(defthm tautology-checker-is-sound
  (implies (and (formulap f) (assignmentp a) (tautology-checker f))
           (equal (value f a) t)))
```

But counterexamples of a formula are just models of its negation. Therefore, we can state the completeness of the tautology-checker in the following way:

```
(defun counterexample (f)
  (model (if-cons f nil t)))
```

```
(defthm tautology-checker-is-complete
  (implies (and (formulap f) (not (tautology-checker f)))
           (equal (value f (counterexample f)) nil)))
```

Consequently, the proof of this theorem is simply reduced to the completeness of the contradiction-checker, which we have proven before.

5   Execution Examples

For the sake of simplicity, we are assuming in this section the following macro definitions. In order to prevent name conflicts, we do this in a new package, EX.

```
(defmacro not (a)   `(if-cons ,a nil t))
(defmacro and (a b) `(if-cons ,a (if-cons ,b t nil) nil))
(defmacro or (a b)  `(if-cons ,a t (if-cons ,b t nil)))
(defmacro imp (a b) `(if-cons ,a (if-cons ,b t nil) t))
(defmacro iff (a b) `(if-cons ,a (if-cons ,b t nil) (if-cons ,b nil t)))
```

This is just a bit of syntactic sugar to avoid cumbersome IF-notation when writing formulas from Classical Propositional Logic. In fact, these macros are proved to do the correct thing, though we omit the details here. Basically, the proof consist of stating that the interpretation of the formula built by each macro agree with its corresponding truth-table.

Next, we are going to enumerate some formulas as we discuss their characters by means of the execution of the corresponding functions in an ACL2 session. Let us recall that "false" and "true" are represented by 0 and 1, but they are implemented with nil and t. Variables are represented by natural numbers so that, for example, we can think of p_0, p_1 and p_2 as 0, 1 and 2, respectively.

Although we have not discussed it, we have specified and verified suitable guards for every presented function. Thanks to guard verification we can be sure that execution will not abort[7] if functions are applied to data in their intended (guarded) domain.

◇   The formula $\neg((p_0 \implies p_1) \iff (\neg p_1 \implies \neg p_0))$ is a contradiction.

```
EX !> (contradiction-checker (not (iff (imp 0 1) (imp (not 1) (not 0)))))
T
```

◇   The formula $\neg(p_0 \implies p_1) \lor (p_1 \implies p_0)$ is not a tautology ($p_0 = 0$, $p_1 = 1$ is a counterexample), nor a contradiction ($p_0 = p_1 = 0$ is a model). Its corresponding Boolean polynomial in normal form is $(p_0 \land p_1) \oplus p_1 \oplus 1$.

```
EX !> (tautology-checker (or (not (imp 0 1)) (imp 1 0)))
NIL
EX !> (counterexample (or (not (imp 0 1)) (imp 1 0)))
(NIL T)
EX !> (contradiction-checker (or (not (imp 0 1)) (imp 1 0)))
NIL
EX !> (model (or (not (imp 0 1)) (imp 1 0)))
(NIL NIL)
EX !> (nf (stone (or (not (imp 0 1)) (imp 1 0))))
((T (T T)) (T (NIL T)) (T (NIL NIL)))
```

---

[7] As long as there are enough resources to do the computation.

⋄   The formula $((p_0 \vee p_1) \implies (p_0 \vee p_2)) \iff (p_0 \vee (p_1 \implies p_2))$ is a tautology.

```
EX !> (tautology-checker (iff (imp (or 0 1) (or 0 2)) (or 0 (imp 1 2))))
T
```

⋄   The formula $(p_0 \vee (p_1 \wedge p_2)) \wedge ((p_0 \vee p_1) \wedge (p_0 \vee p_2))$ is not a tautology ($p_0 = p_1 = p_2 = 0$ is a counterexample), nor a contradiction ($p_0 = 0$, $p_1 = p_2 = 1$ is a model). Its corresponding Boolean polynomial in normal form is $(p_0 \wedge p_1 \wedge p_2) \oplus p_0 \oplus (p_1 \wedge p_2)$.

```
EX !> (tautology-checker (and (or 0 (and 1 2)) (and (or 0 1) (or 0 2))))
NIL
EX !> (counterexample (and (or 0 (and 1 2)) (and (or 0 1) (or 0 2))))
(NIL NIL NIL)
EX !> (contradiction-checker (and (or 0 (and 1 2)) (and (or 0 1) (or 0 2))))
NIL
EX !> (model (and (or 0 (and 1 2)) (and (or 0 1) (or 0 2))))
(NIL T T)
EX !> (nf (stone (and (or 0 (and 1 2)) (and (or 0 1) (or 0 2)))))
((T (T T T)) (T (T NIL NIL)) (T (NIL T T)))
```

⋄   The formula $((p_0 \iff p_1) \iff p_2) \iff (p_0 \iff (p_1 \iff p_2))$ is a tautology.

```
EX !> (tautology-checker (iff (iff (iff 0 1) 2) (iff 0 (iff 1 2))))
T
```

6   Conclusions and Further Work

A decision procedure for Propositional Logic in ACL2 has been presented. This includes a contradiction-checker and a tautology-checker together with their proofs of soundness and completeness. Functions for finding counterexamples and models for formulas are also provided. They are useful not only to compute but also to prove the main theorems stating the correctness of the checkers. These results are by no means trivial and we think that this work is testimonial to the high level of automation that can be reached in ACL2 when a proper formalization is used.

All the functions and theorems presented here have been collected in ACL2 books to increase their reusability. Moreover, we have specified and verified suitable guards for every presented function. So, we can be sure that execution will not abort if functions are applied to data in their intended (guarded) domain.

This decision procedure is based in Boolean polynomial normalization, but instead of applying Hsiang's canonical term-rewriting system for Boolean algebras, a straightforward normalization algorithm is used. This application of polynomials has been developed by reusing a previous work on polynomial rings [19]. The formalization presented there is modified to accommodate polynomials with rational coefficients to Boolean polynomials. These modifications are presented in [20].

Previously, formulas are translated into polynomials by using the relation between Boolean algebras and Boolean rings. This translation is interpretation-preserving with respect to a suitable valuation function for formulas and a suitable evaluation function for polynomials. This and other properties were formalized in [20].

The whole formalization consists of (roughly) 40 pages of ACL2 source code. 23 pages are devoted to the formalization of Boolean polynomials and 17 to the formalization of the decision procedures. The automation degree that we have obtained is high, though some technical lemmas and hints were required.

As polynomial formalization has been the most time-consuming task, some of our future work will be devoted to the study of better formalization techniques for generic polynomials.

One important method of logical deduction is the "algebraic method" which also uses the idea of translating formulas into polynomials. This technique transforms the logical problem into an algebraic problem, polynomial ideal membership, what reduces the problem to the computation of Gröbner bases.

The first step to achieve this would consist of certifying Buchberger's algorithm for Gröbner bases computation in ACL2. A work from L. Théry [25], achieves this goal in COQ. Nevertheless, ACL2 and COQ logics differ in many aspects. Automated certification of Buchberger's algorithm in ACL2 remains a challenging project.

The reduction relation defined for Buchberger's algorithm is a subset of the ordering on polynomials. Once we have stated an ordering between terms, it can be extended to polynomials. Therefore, defining a term order is required prior to the definition of the concepts associated with Buchberger's algorithm and, particularly, to its termination. We have already formalized a suitable lexicographical order on terms and proved its well-foundedness in ACL2.

References

1. Aitken, W. E., Constable, R. L., Underwood, J. L.: Metalogical Frameworks II: Developing a Reflected Decision Procedure. J. Automated Reasoning **22**(2) (1999)
2. Boole, G. The Mathematical Analysis of Logic. Macmillan (1847)
3. Boyer, R. S., Moore, J S.: A Computational Logic. Academic Press (1978)
4. Boyer, R. S., Moore, J S.: Metafunctions: Proving Them Correct and Using Them Efficiently as New Proof Procedures. In: Boyer, R. S., Moore, J S. (eds.): The Correctness Problem in Computer Science. Academic Press (1981)
5. Boyer, R. S., Moore, J S.: A Computational Logic Handbook. Academic Press. 2nd edn. (1998)
6. Caldwell, J. L.: Classical Propositional Decidability via Nuprl Proof Extraction. 11th International Conference on Theorem Proving in Higher Order Logics. LNCS **1479** (1998)
7. Chazarain, J., Riscos, A., Alonso, J. A., Briales, E.: Multi-Valued Logic and Gröbner Bases with Applications to Modal Logic. J. Symbolic Computation **11** (1991)
8. Harrison, J.: Metatheory and Reflection in Theorem Proving: A Survey and Critique. SRI International Cambridge Computer Science Research Centre. Technical Report CRC–053 (1995)

9. Harrison, J.: Binary Decision Diagrams as a HOL Derived Rule. The Computer Journal **38** (1995)
10. Harrison, J.: Stålmarck's Algorithm as a HOL Derived Rule. 9th International Conference on Theorem Proving in Higher Order Logics. LNCS **1125** (1996)
11. Hsiang, J.: Refutational Theorem Proving using Term-Rewriting Systems. Artificial Intelligence **25** (1985)
12. Hsiang, J.: Rewrite Method for Theorem Proving in First-Order Theory with Equality. J. Symbolic Computation **3** (1987)
13. Hsiang, J., Huang, G. S.: Some Fundamental Properties of Boolean Ring Normal Forms. DIMACS series on Discrete Mathematics and Computer Science: The Satisfiability Problem. AMS (1996)
14. Kaufmann, M., Moore, J S.: An Industrial Strength Theorem Prover for a Logic Based on Common Lisp. IEEE Trans. on Software Engineering **23**(4) (1997)
15. Kaufmann, M., Manolios, P., Moore, J S.: Computer-Aided Reasoning: An Approach. Kluwer Academic Publishers (2000)
16. Kaufmann, M., Manolios, P., Moore, J S.: Computer-Aided Reasoning: ACL2 Case Studies. Kluwer Academic Publishers (2000)
17. Kapur, D., Narendran, P.: An Equational Approach to Theorem Proving in First-Order Predicate Calculus. 9th International Conference on Artificial Intelligence (1985)
18. Laita, L. M., Roanes-Lozano, E., Ledesma, L., Alonso, J. A.: A Computer Algebra Approach to Verification and Deduction in Many-Valued Knowledge Systems. Soft Computing **3**(1) (1999)
19. Medina-Bulo, I., Alonso-Jiménez, J. A., Palomo-Lozano, F.: Automatic Verification of Polynomial Rings Fundamental Properties in ACL2. ACL2 Workshop 2000 Proceedings, Part A. The University of Texas at Austin, Department of Computer Sciences. Technical Report TR–00–29 (2000)
20. Medina-Bulo, I., Palomo-Lozano, F., Alonso-Jiménez, J. A.: A Certified Algorithm for Translating Formulas into Polynomials. An ACL2 Approach. International Joint Conference on Automated Reasoning (2001)
21. Moore, J S.: Introduction to the OBDD Algorithm for the ATP Community. Computational Logic, Inc. Technical Report 84 (1992)
22. Paulin-Mohring, C., Werner, B.: Synthesis of ML Programs in the System Coq. J. Symbolic Computation **15**(5–6) (1993)
23. Stone, M.: The Theory of Representation for Boolean Algebra. Trans. AMS **40** (1936)
24. Sumners, R.: Correctness Proof of a BDD Manager in the Context of Satisfiability Checking. ACL2 Workshop 2000 Proceedings, Part A. The University of Texas at Austin, Department of Computer Sciences. Technical Report TR–00–29 (2000)
25. Théry, L. A Machine-Checked Implementation of Buchberger's Algorithm. J. Automated Reasoning **26** (2001)
26. Wu, J., Tan, H.: An Algebraic Method to Decide the Deduction Problem in Propositional Many-Valued Logics. International Symposium on Multiple-Valued Logics. IEEE Computer Society Press (1994)
27. Wu, J.: First-Order Polynomial Based Theorem Proving. In: Gao, X., Wang, D. (eds.): Mathematics Mechanization and Applications. Academic Press (1999)
28. Zhang, H.: A New Strategy for the Boolean Ring Based Approach to First Order Theorem Proving. Department of Computer Science. University of Iowa. Technical Report (1991)
29. Zhegalkin, I. I.: On a Technique of Evaluation of Propositions in Symbolic Logic. Mat. Sb. **34** (1927)

Finite Set Theory in ACL2

J Strother Moore*

Department of Computer Sciences, University of Texas at Austin
Taylor Hall 2.124, Austin, Texas 78712
moore@cs.utexas.edu   telephone: 512 471 9568
http://www.cs.utexas.edu/users/moore

Abstract. ACL2 is a first-order, essentially quantifier free logic of computable recursive functions based on an applicative subset of Common Lisp. It supports lists as a primitive data structure. We describe how we have formalized a practical finite set theory for ACL2. Our finite set theory "book" includes set equality, set membership, the subset relation, set manipulation functions such as union, intersection, etc., a choice function, a representation of finite functions as sets of ordered pairs and a collection of useful functions for manipulating them (e.g., domain, range, apply) and others. The book provides many lemmas about these primitives, as well as macros for dealing with set comprehension and some other "higher order" features of set theory, and various strategies or tactics for proving theorems in set theory. The goal of this work is not to provide "heavy duty set theory" – a task more suited to other logics – but to allow the ACL2 user to use sets in a "light weight" fashion in specifications, while continuing to exploit ACL2's efficient executability, built in proof techniques for certain domains, and extensive lemma libraries.

1 Introduction

Doesn't ACL2 [4,3] already provide sets? It contains such standard Lisp functions as member, subsetp, union and intersection. These operate on lists, ignoring duplication and order. For example, consider the two lists (1 2) and (2 1). Both lists can be used to represent the set $\{1,2\}$. Member can be used to determine that 1 and 2 are elements of both lists and that 3 is an element of neither. Subsetp can be used to determine that each list is a subset of the other and so we can say they are "set equal."

But these primitives are like their set theory counterparts only on sets of atoms. For example, (2 1) is not a member of ((1 2)) even though $\{2,1\}$ is a member of $\{\{1,2\}\}$. That is because member compares elements with Lisp's equal, not "set equality." We wish to define finite sets in such a way that sets can be elements of other sets.

Extensive set theory work has been done in both the Isabelle and the Mizar communities. For example, Paulson [9,10] describes a formalization of Zermelo-

---

* This work was supported in part by Compaq Systems Research Center, Palo Alto, CA.

R.J. Boulton and P.B. Jackson (Eds.): TPHOLs 2001, LNCS 2152, pp. 313 328, 2001.

Fraenkel set theory and proves Cantor's Theorem and Ramsey's Theorem. Paulson and Grabczewski develop ZF to the point of proving equivalent twenty different formulations of the Axiom of Choice. The Mizar system is essentially based on Tarski Grothendieck set theory and virtually all of the extensive results proved by the Mizar community and published in their *Journal of Formalized Mathematics* (`http://www.mizar.org/JFM`) may be thought of as set theoretic in nature. See especially [1] and the other articles in Volume 1 of the Journal. There is a little set theory work in HOL [2]. If one's goal is to check the results of set theory, we would recommend Isabelle or Mizar.

But our goal is not "heavy duty set theory." Our goal is to provide sets to the ACL2 user. A typical use of ACL2 is to build an executable model of some system. Execution speed is essential. The ACL2 model of the microprocessor described by Greve and Wilding in [3] executes at 3 million simulated instructions per second (on a 733 MHz machine). Lisp's data structures are excellent for this. But now imagine that in formalizing some property, the ACL2 user wishes to speak of the set of all the states visited during some execution or the powerset of the set of all scheduled threads. A little "light weight" set theory is clearly useful here, whether efficiently executable or not.

We could, of course, adopt a system like Isabelle or Mizar and formalize all of ACL2's objects as sets. For example, we could adopt the von Neumann coding and represent the number 1 as the set containing the empty set, say. Then natural number addition has a straightforward set theoretic definition. But the elementary arithmetic functions are already defined in ACL2 and they do not treat {{}} as the multiplicative identity. So, without some kind of reflection principle, we are forced by this embedding to abandon ACL2's native objects and the functions for manipulating them, in favor of a set theoretic treatment of everything. That also means abandoning ACL2's execution efficiency, built in decision procedures, and existing lemma libraries.

But we want to preserve those things. So we want sets of native ACL2 objects – integers, rationals, strings, symbols and lists representing all manner of other computational objects such as bit vectors, frames, stacks, class tables, superclass hierarchies, etc. We want to be able to load libraries defining various computational objects and functions for manipulating them and theorems relating those functions, and we want to collect those objects together into sets. (Our approach also allows ACL2 objects to contain (objects to be treated as) sets. Since ACL2 is untyped, the functions manipulating those objects must "know" when a component is to be treated as a set and use the set theory functions to manipulate it.)

Having established the need to do *something* to provide first-class finite sets in ACL2 while preserving ACL2's native objects, here is a quick sketch of what we will do.

We are going to develop what might be called the "hereditarily finite sets built from the ACL2 universe of objects." That is, the base elements, or "urelements," of our sets will be the ACL2 objects and the elements of all sets will be these ur-elements or other such sets.

ACL2 does not support the introduction of new data types. So we will represent the set theory individuals (e.g., ur-elements and all the sets we can build) as ACL2 objects. We define an equivalence relation, =, on these ACL2 objects so that two objects are equivalent precisely if they represent the same set theory individual.[1] We define "set theory functions and predicates" that treat objects as though they were the set theory individuals they represent. These functions and predicates enjoy the expected algebraic properties of their set theory counterparts. Throughout this paper we use " = " to mean this new equivalence relation, not the normal Leibniz identity, which we denote as "=". Once we get going, the distinction is not germane to this paper.

So that we do not redefine existing Lisp functions, we do all of our work in a new symbol package named "S" (for "sets"). Common Lisp provides packages so users can have disjoint name spaces. We "import" into our "S" package all of the standard ACL2 symbols except for `union`, `intersection`, `subsetp`, `add-to-set`, `functionp`, `=`, and `apply`, and use "S" as the selected (implicit) package in this paper. This means that when we use a familiar Lisp symbol, such as `car`, we are referring to its standard Lisp meaning. That is, `car` is just shorthand for the symbol whose full name is `lisp::car`. But when we use one of the imported symbols above we are referring to the symbol of that name in our "S" package, e.g., by `union` we mean `s::union`.

The primitive set theory predicates and functions, such as `member` and `union`, are defined so that = is a congruence relation for each argument position. A unary function f admits = as a congruence relation if $u = v \rightarrow f(u) = f(v)$. This notion is extended to functions and predicates of arbitrary arity and to different equivalence relations in the hypothesis and conclusion. Thus, $u = v \rightarrow (\mathrm{p}(x, u) \leftrightarrow \mathrm{p}(x, v))$ is a congruence rule. It tells us that $\mathrm{p}(x, u)$ is equivalent (in "$\leftrightarrow$" sense of propositional equivalence) to $\mathrm{p}(x, v)$ when u is equivalent (in the "=" sense) to v.

The ACL2 theorem prover contains special provisions for dealing with user-defined equivalence relations and congruence rules. When ACL2 rewrites a term, it maintains a given sense of equivalence, specified by an equivalence relation. That goal equivalence relation and the known congruence rules determine the equivalences that may be used as rewrite rules. For example, suppose the system is rewriting $\mathrm{p}(\gamma, \mathrm{union}(\alpha, \beta))$, maintaining the goal equivalence "$\leftrightarrow$". Then the above congruence rule allows the system to shift from "$\leftrightarrow$" to " = " while rewriting the second argument of p. That, in turn, allows it to use theorems concluding with " = " as rewrite rules. For example, $\mathrm{union}(x, y) = \mathrm{union}(y, x)$ is such a rule. Using it, the rewriter may replace the $\mathrm{union}(\alpha, \beta)$ here by $\mathrm{union}(\beta, \alpha)$, even though the two terms are not necessarily equal (in the "=" sense of Leibniz identity native to the logic).

---

[1] In ACL2, true and false are denoted by the objects T and NIL. "Relations" and "predicates" are defined as Boolean valued functions, i.e., functions that return either T or NIL. By proving that a relation is an equivalence relation the user may cause the ACL2 theorem prover to manipulate it with special techniques described below.

In ACL2, a collection of definitions and theorems is called a "book." Books may be included into an ACL2 session to configure the theorem prover. Our set theory book is available at

http://www.cs.utexas.edu/users/moore/publications/finite-set-theory. In this paper we present our formulas in an abstract syntax rather than ACL2's concrete syntax.

Why might this work be of interest outside the ACL2 user community? First, it highlights the importance of certain general theorem proving techniques supported by ACL2 (especially congruence based rewriting). Second, we explore a variety of issues that arise in any attempt to embed one mathematical formalism in another, e.g., identity versus equivalence, mutual recursion versus canonicalization, useful definitional schemes, transparency with respect to existing proof techniques, etc. Third, if one takes the view that all we have done is *implement* finite set theory in a programming language and prove that the implementation satisfies the standard algebraic laws, then the paper represents an interesting challenge to any software verification system. Fourth, if your theorem prover provides set theory, define the powerset function recursively and see if your system can do the proofs required in Section 9 with less guidance than ACL2 requires.

2   Basics

Definitions. The *ACL2 universe* consists of all ACL2 numbers (rationals and complex rationals), characters, strings, symbols, and conses of objects in the ACL2 universe. These notions are made clear in [4]; informally, these are the objects the ACL2 programmer can construct and manipulate. The elements of the ACL2 universe are called *ACL2 objects*.

Definition. An *ur-element* is an ACL2 object other than the keyword symbol :UR-CONS.

To motivate what follows, now imagine some construction of finite sets allowing us to distinguish non-empty sets from ACL2 objects and identifying the empty set with the ACL2 object NIL. We are interested in all the finite sets containing ur-elements and/or other such finite sets.

Definition. The *hereditarily finite ACL2 sets* is the smallest set S with the property that a set s is an element of S precisely if s is finite and every element of s is either an ur-element or is some element of S.

Definition. The *ACL2 set theory universe* consists of all the ur-elements and all the hereditarily finite ACL2 sets. An element of the ACL2 set theory universe is called an *ACL2 set theory individual*. Note that not every set theory individual is a set, e.g., some are numbers, strings, etc.

We are interested in representing the ACL2 set theory individuals. In particular, each such individual can be represented by an ACL2 object, often in multiple ways.

Definition. Let x be an ACL2 set theory individual. We define a *representative* of x recursively as follows. If x is an atomic ur-element (a number, character, string or symbol), then a (in fact, the) representative of x is x itself. If x is a cons, then a (the) representative of x is (:UR-CONS x). If x is the empty set, a representative is NIL. Otherwise, x is a non-empty set containing some element e. In this case, a representative of x is the cons whose car is a representative of e and whose cdr is a representative of the set $x \setminus \{e\}$.

In our set theory book we define an equivalence relation = with the following property: two ACL2 objects are equivalent under = precisely if they represent the same ACL2 set theory individual. We do not show the definition here. Our equivalence relation is insensitive to the order in which elements of sets are presented and in fact allows duplications of elements. Our elimination of the symbol :UR-CONS as an ur-element makes our representation of sets non-ambiguous. The = relation can distinguish ur-elements from each other and from sets. Two sets are = precisely when they are subsets of one another.

Henceforth, we speak of ACL2 objects as though they were the ACL2 set theory individuals they represent. For example, here are three example sets.

- The set containing the symbolic names of the first three days of the week, which ordinarily might be written {SUNDAY, MONDAY, TUESDAY}, may be written (SUNDAY MONDAY TUESDAY). Equivalently (in the "=" sense), it may be written (MONDAY SUNDAY TUESDAY SUNDAY).
- The set of digits, as integers, may be written (0 1 2 3 4 5 6 7 8 9).
- The set consisting of the set of even digits and the set of odd digits may be written ((0 2 4 6 8) (1 3 5 7 9)).

When an ACL2 list, e.g., a machine state, thread, stack, etc., is used as an ur-element, it must be embedded in the :UR-CONS form so it is not treated as a set. Here is a set that contains the set of even digits, the set of odd digits, the list of even digits in ascending order and the list of odd digits in ascending order.

```
((0 2 4 6 8)
 (1 3 5 7 9)
 (:UR-CONS (0 2 4 6 8))
 (:UR-CONS (1 3 5 7 9)))
```

Because ACL2's is a syntactically untyped language it is possible to use ur-elements where sets are expected. We deal with this with a sweeping convention. **The Non-Set Convention.** If a non-NIL ur-element is used where a set is expected, all set theory functions shall behave as though the empty set had been used instead.

For example, our answer to the question "does 3 occur as an element in the set 5?" is "no," because 5 is not a set and hence the question is treated as though it had been "does 3 occur as an element in the set {}?" This should not concern the reader since such "ill-formed" questions are never asked. We tend to ignore such issues in this paper.

Following the normal rules of Lisp, it is necessary to quote values when they are used as literal constants in terms. For example, cardinality('(1 2 3)) denotes the application of the function `cardinality` to (a constant representing) the set $\{1, 2, 3\}$.

3   Set Theoretic Functions and Theorems Proved

In Figure 1 we name some of the functions and macros defined in the "S" package. We discuss below how other operations can be defined.

Since numbers in ACL2 set theory are just ACL2's numbers and all the ACL2 arithmetic functions and predicates (except =) are imported into the "S" package, the arithmetic functions of ACL2 set theory are exactly the arithmetic functions of ACL2.

In Figure 2 we list some of the theorems available in the set theory book. These theorems have some subtle attractive properties that one can appreciate only by considering alternative formulations of set theory in ACL2. One is that most are not burdened by hypotheses restricting them to sets or individuals. Another is the use of = as the only sense of equivalence. Any theorem concluding with an = could be used as a rewrite rule (under certain restrictions imposed by ACL2's rewriter). Still another is that the proofs of most of these theorems are extraordinarily simple. We omit many of our theorems (especially duals) for brevity.

4   The Choice Function

In order to allow us to define certain functions on sets, such as extracting the components of an ordered pair represented by $\{x, \{x, y\}\}$, we must be able to obtain an element of a non-empty set. We therefore defined `choose`.

Key properties of `choose`(s) are that it admits = as a congruence, i.e., the choice is independent of the representation or presentation of s, and `choose`(s) is a member of s if s is non-empty. Ideally, perhaps, nothing else need be said about `choose`. But it is in fact quite specifically defined. We simply opt seldom to expose its other properties. But logically speaking those properties are present and important.

`Choose` is computable. For example, `choose`('(1 2 3 4)) is 4. Our definition of `choose` chooses the largest element of the set, where the ordering is a certain (arbitrarily defined but unspecified here) total ordering on our objects.

Our definition of `choose` allows us to prove the following property.

Weak Choose-Scons Property:
`choose`($\mathtt{scons}(e, a)$) $= e \lor$ `choose`($\mathtt{scons}(e, a)$) $=$ `choose`(a).

That is, `choose` on $\mathtt{scons}(e, a)$ is either e or the choice from a. Of course, it is possible to say exactly which of these cases obtains: `choose`($\mathtt{scons}(e, a)$) is e, if e dominates `choose`(a), and is `choose`(a) otherwise. We call this stronger statement the *Strong Choose-Scons Property*. The strong property requires mention of the total order while the weak property does not. Since this can complicate proofs, we avoid the use of the strong property when possible.

ur-elementp(a)	T or NIL according to whether a is an ur-element.
setp(a)	T or NIL according to whether a is a set.
scons(e, a)	$\{e\} \cup a$.
brace($\alpha_1, \ldots, \alpha_k$)	The set whose elements are given by the values of the k expressions; this is known as "roster notation".
$a = b$	If a and b are the same individual, then T, otherwise, NIL.
mem(e, a)	$e \in a$. Both arguments are treated as sets.
subsetp(a, b)	$a \subseteq b$.
cardinality(a)	$|a|$.
nats(n)	$\{i \mid i \in \mathbf{N} \wedge 0 \leq i \leq n\}$.
union(a, b)	$a \cup b$.
intersection(a, b)	$a \cap b$.
diff(a, b)	$a \setminus b$.
choose(a)	An element of the set a, if a is non-empty.
pair(x, y)	A set representing the ordered pair $\langle x, y \rangle$. We call such a set simply a *pair*. Pair(x, y) is defined to be brace(x, brace(x, y)).
pairp(a)	T or NIL according to whether a is a pair.
hd(a)	If a is the pair $\langle x, y \rangle$, then x; otherwise, NIL.
tl(a)	If a is the pair $\langle x, y \rangle$, then y; otherwise, NIL.
pairps(s)	T or NIL according to whether s is a set of pairs.
functionp(f)	If f is a set of pairs and no two elements of f have the same hd, then T; otherwise, NIL. If a function f contains pair(e, v), then we say v is the *value* of f on e.
domain(f)	$\{e \mid \exists x(x \in f \wedge e = \text{hd}(x))\}$.
range(f)	$\{e \mid \exists x(x \in f \wedge e = \text{tl}(x))\}$.
apply(f, e)	If f is a function and e is in its domain, then the value of f on e.
except(f, e, v)	If f is a function then the function that is everywhere equal to f except on e where the value is v.
restrict(f, a)	The image of f on those elements of a in the domain of f.
sequencep(s)	T if s is a function whose domain is $\{1, \ldots, |s|\}$, otherwise NIL. Generally, ACL2 lists serve more directly but we formalized sequences as an application.
shift(i, j, f, d)	If i and j are integers, then the function obtained by mapping $k + d$ to apply(f, k), for every $i \leq k \leq j$. If i or j is not an integer, the result is NIL.
concat(r, s)	union(r, shift(1, cardinality(s), s, cardinality(r))).

Fig. 1. Some Functions of Our Set Theory.

- subsetp(x, x).
- subsetp$(a, b) \wedge$ subsetp$(b, c) \rightarrow$ subsetp(a, c).
- mem$(e, a) \wedge$ subsetp$(a, b) \rightarrow$ mem(e, b).
- setp$(a) \wedge$ setp$(b) \rightarrow ((a = b) \leftrightarrow ($subsetp$(a, b) \wedge$ subsetp$(b, a)))$.
- $\neg$ mem(e, e).
- mem$(e, $union$(a, b)) \leftrightarrow (mem(e, a) \vee$ mem$(e, b))$.
- subsetp$(a, $union$(a, b))$.
- subsetp$(a_1, a_2) \rightarrow$ subsetp$($union$(a_1, b), $union$(a_2, b))$.
- union$(a, b) = $union$(b, a)$.
- union$($union$(a, b), c) = $union$(a, $union$(b, c))$.
- cardinality$(a) \leq$ cardinality$($union$(a, b))$.
- cardinality$(a) = 0 \leftrightarrow$ ur-elementp(a).
- intersection$(a, b) = $NIL
      $\rightarrow$ cardinality$($union$(a, b)) = $cardinality$(a) + $cardinality$(b)$.
- mem$($choose$(a), a) \leftrightarrow \neg$ ur-elementp(a).
- choose$($scons$(e, a)) = e \vee$ choose$($scons$(e, a)) = $choose$(a)$.
- choose$($scons$(e, NIL)) = e$.
- cardinality$(x) = 1 \wedge$ mem$(e, x) \rightarrow$ scons$(e, NIL) = x$.
- mem$(e, $diff$(a, b)) \leftrightarrow (mem(e, a) \wedge \neg$ mem$(e, b))$.
- subsetp$(a_1, a_2) \rightarrow$ subsetp$($diff$(a_1, b), $diff$(a_2, b))$.
- subsetp$(a, b) \wedge$ subsetp$(b, c) \rightarrow$ union$($diff$(b, a), $diff$(c, b)) = $diff$(c, a)$.
- cardinality$($diff$(a, b)) \leq$ cardinality(a).
- intersection$($diff$(b, c), a) = $diff$($intersection$(a, b), c)$.
- hd$($pair$(x, y)) = x$.
- tl$($pair$(x, y)) = y$.
- pairp$($pair$(x, y))$.
- pairp$(a) \rightarrow$ pair$($hd$(a), tl(a)) = a$.
- pair$(x_1, y_1) = $pair$(x_2, y_2) \leftrightarrow (x_1 = x_2 \wedge y_1 = y_2)$.
- functionp$(f) \rightarrow$ functionp$($except$(f, x, v))$.
- apply$($except$(f, x, v), y) = ($if $x = y$ then v else apply$(f, y))$.
- pairps$(f) \rightarrow$ domain$($except$(f, x, v)) = $scons$(x, $domain$(f))$.
- subsetp$($range$($except$(f, x, v)), $scons$(v, $range$(f)))$.
- domain$($union$(f, g)) = $union$($domain$(f), $domain$(g))$.
- range$($union$(f, g)) = $union$($range$(f), $range$(g))$.
- cardinality$($domain$(f)) \leq$ cardinality(f).
- cardinality$($range$(f)) \leq$ cardinality(f).
- functionp$(f) \wedge$ functionp$(g) \wedge$ intersection$($domain$(f), $domain$(g)) = $NIL
      $\rightarrow$ functionp$($union$(f, g))$.
- domain$($restrict$(f, s)) = $intersection$(s, $domain$(f))$.
- functionp$(f) \wedge$ functionp$(g) \wedge$ intersection$($domain$(f), $domain$(g)) = $NIL
      $\rightarrow$ apply$($union$(f, g), x)$
        $= ($if mem$(x, $domain$(f))$ then apply(f, x) else apply$(g, x))$.
- sequencep$(a) \wedge$ sequencep$(b) \wedge$ sequencep(c)
      $\rightarrow$ concat$($concat$(a, b), c) = $concat$(a, $concat$(b, c))$.

Fig. 2. Some Theorems Proved.

ACL2 allows the user to constrain undefined functions to satisfy arbitrary properties, provided some function (a "witness") can be shown to have those properties. Using this feature of ACL2, it is possible to introduce an undefined choice function, ch, which admits = as a congruence and which selects a member of a non-empty set, without otherwise constraining the choice made. Our choose can be used as a witness to introduce ch.

It should be noted that ch does not enjoy the analogue of the *Weak Choose-Scons Property*. That is, it is impossible to prove from the properties of ch above that ch(scons(e, s)) is either e or ch(s). For example, ch might choose the largest element of the set if the cardinality of the set is odd and the smallest element if the cardinality is even. Such a ch would have the required properties and furthermore ch(scons(1, '(2 3))) would be 3, which is neither 1 nor ch('(2 3)), which is 2.

Therefore, even when using only the weak property, we assume more about choose than we could about an arbitrary choice function. Most importantly, our choose is executable, which means that functions defined in terms of it are also executable. Such functions include pair, hd, tl and apply.

5 Behind the Scenes

Two sets are equal if and only if they are subsets of one another. If we *define* set equality this way, then equality, membership and subset are mutually recursive: set equality is defined in terms of subset, membership is iterated set equality, and subset is iterated membership. ACL2 supports mutual recursion. But mutual recursion can be awkward when dealing with induction. To prove an inductive theorem about one function in a clique of mutually recursive functions, one must often prove a conjunction of related theorems about the other functions of the clique. While ACL2 can often manage the proofs, the user must state the conjunction of theorems in order for the conjecture to be strong enough to be provable. We found this often inconvenient, especially in the early going when nothing but the definitions of the functions are available.

We considered many ways around this obstacle. The eventual solution, which was supported by some work done concurrently by Pete Manolios, was to introduce the notion of canonical forms. Without engaging in mutual recursion it is possible to

- define a total order on our objects,
- canonicalize lists so that their elements are presented in this order and without duplicates,
- define set equality to compare sets in canonical form,
- define membership as iterated set equality,
- define subset as iterated membership, and
- prove that two sets are set equal iff they are subsets of one another.

This program actually has at least two interpretations and we explored both. The interpretation initially favored was to keep lists representing sets in canonical form all the time. That is, the basic set constructor, e.g., scons(e, x), inserts e (if it is not already there) at the position in x at which it belongs. This has the powerful attraction that set equality, =, is Leibniz identity, =.

But we found this approach to complicate set construction to a degree out of proportion to its merits. In particular, functions like union and intersection, which are quite easy to reason about in the list world (where order and duplication matter but are simply ignored), become quite difficult to reason about in the set world, where most of the attention is paid to the sorting of the output with respect to the total ordering. In the end we abandoned this approach and adopted a second interpretation of the program above: lists representing sets are created and manipulated in non-canonical form and are canonicalized only for determining whether two sets are equal. This was quite effective. Scons is cons (with appropriate treatment of :UR-CONS), union is essentially append, etc. ACL2 is designed to prove theorems about these kinds of functions.

Another question that drew our attention was: what are the "ur-elements" of our set theory? The first attack was to formalize hereditarily finite sets: finite sets built entirely from the empty set. Initially we felt that the details of the set theory were irrelevant to the user, since the high level individuals with which the user would deal — numbers, sequences, functions, etc., — would be abstractly represented. According to this thinking, proofs about these high level individuals would be conducted more or less algebraically, using theorems provided by the set theory book.

However, we found the use of hereditarily finite sets to be too cumbersome.

- Concrete examples of sets representing naturals, pairs, etc., were practically impossible to read and comprehend. Here is 3 in the von Neumann representation of the naturals {{{{}}{}}{{}}{}}. It was hard to test definitions and conjectures.
- The need to embed everything as sets forced ACL2 to spend its resources unraveling the embedding rather than dealing with the gist of the user's problem. This was particularly evident when dealing with arithmetic.

In the final view of this project, we saw the objective as to produce a set theory that was "natural" to ACL2's mode of reasoning, so that its power would be spent at the core of the user's problem, not on getting down there. Arithmetic in our set theory is just ACL2's arithmetic. Arbitrary ACL2 objects can be collected into sets. The set primitives are simple and their definitions are usually easily manipulated to derive clean versions of the algebraic laws of set theory. Because of support for congruences, these laws can then be used in the normal way to manipulate set expressions without regard for how sets are actually represented, provided certain basic conventions are followed. The main conventions are that = be used to compare sets and that every time a new set generating function is introduced the appropriate congruence rules are proved establishing that the function admits set equality as a congruence relation.

6   Codified Proof Strategies

The set theory book includes several proof strategies particular to set theory. Such strategies are convenient because they overcome ACL2's lack of quantification.

To prove $\alpha = \beta$, where α and β are two set theory expressions that produce sets (as opposed to ur-elements), it is sometimes convenient to prove that $(e \in \alpha) \leftrightarrow (e \in \beta)$. That is, a set is entirely determined by its elements. This fact may be formalized in set theory as $(\forall e : e \in a \leftrightarrow e \in b) \rightarrow a = b$.

But ACL2 does not have the quantificational power to express this fact directly.[2] We have defined an ACL2 macro (named defx) that allows the user to direct the theorem prover to prove a theorem using a specified strategy. When defx is used to prove $\gamma \rightarrow \alpha = \beta$ with the "set equivalence" strategy it generates two subgoals, $\gamma \wedge \text{mem}(e, \alpha) \rightarrow \text{mem}(e, \beta)$ and its symmetric counterpart, and then proves the main theorem by "functional instantiation" [5] of a general theorem. (The general theorem can be described as follows. Suppose that alpha and beta are two 0-ary functions satisfying the constraint $\text{mem}(e, \text{alpha}()) \rightarrow \text{mem}(e, \text{beta}())$. Then $\text{subsetp}(\text{alpha}(), \text{beta}())$ is a theorem.)

Another special strategy, called "functional equivalence," is useful when α and β are functions: prove that applying them produces identical results. Four subgoals are produced, (a) $\text{functionp}(\alpha)$, (b) $\text{functionp}(\beta)$, (c) $\text{domain}(\alpha) = \text{domain}(\beta)$, and (d) $\text{mem}(e, \text{domain}(\alpha)) \rightarrow \text{apply}(\alpha, e) = \text{apply}(\beta, e)$. Proof obligation (d) could be simplified by dropping the hypothesis; we included it simply because it weakens the proof obligation. The previously mentioned theorem

● $\text{sequencep}(a) \wedge \text{sequencep}(b) \wedge \text{sequencep}(c)$
$\rightarrow \text{concat}(\text{concat}(a, b), c) = \text{concat}(a, \text{concat}(b, c))$

is proved with the functional equivalence strategy. (Sequences in this set theory are functions. We would expect the ACL2 user to prefer to use the native lists, but we formalized sequences-as-functions to test the library.) The two concat expressions are equivalent because they yeild the same results when applied to arbitrary indices.

Defx is defined in a general way that allows the user to add new strategies. (Hint to ACL2 *cognoscenti*: define each strategy as a macro. Defx forms expand to calls of the strategy.) The defx form provides a uniform appearance in command files ("books") and allows the continued use of Emacs' tag feature for indexing names. This use of macros is novel to most ACL2 users.

7   Recursive Functions on Sets

The first order nature of ACL2, combined with the absence of quantification, prevents the formalization of set comprehension in its general form. That is, it is impossible in ACL2 to formalize with complete generality such notation as "$\{x \mid \phi(x)\}$." We have implemented some macros to mitigate the problem.

---

[2] Actually, ACL2 does provide full first-order quantification via defun-sk, but that is no more convenient that what we are about to describe.

The first step is to consider only notation such as $\{x \mid x \in s \wedge \phi(x)\}$, where s is a (finite) set. It is then possible to map over s with a recursive function to identify the appropriate elements. But because ACL2 is first-order, we cannot define a function that takes ϕ as an argument.[3] So the second step is to define a recursive function, f, for any given ϕ, to compute the above set from s.

The most obvious disadvantages of this approach are (a) one must introduce a function symbol f to capture each use of set-builder notation, (b) one must prove "the same" theorems about each such f, and (c) one must prove theorems that relate any two such f's that become entwined in the same problem. Much of this can be handled by macros. We therefore deal with the most fundamental issues here.

The general scheme for defining a recursive function to extract the ϕ subset from a set s is:

Def $f(s) = $ **if** ur-elementp(s)
           then NIL
           else if $\phi($scar$(s))$
              then scons$($scar$(s), f($scdr$(s)))$
              else $f($scdr$(s))$.

The test on whether s is an ur-elementp is the standard way to enforce the Non-Set Convention. This test recognizes NIL, but also all other ur-elements, as the base case of the recursion. They are all treated equivalently.

Otherwise, s is a non-empty set and we define f in terms of scar(s) and scdr(s). We have not previously mentioned these functions because they are not pure "set theory" functions: they do not admit = as a congruence relation. It is best to think of scar and scdr as working on a presentation of a set. Scar returns the first element presented and scdr returns the set containing all the others. But a set may have multiple presentations. For example, '(1 2) = '(2 1) but scar('(1 2)) is 1 while scar('(2 1)) is 2.

In fact, ur-elementp, scar, scdr, and scons are exactly analogous to atom, car, cdr, and cons, except that conses marked with :UR-CONS are treated as atoms. Ignoring the issue raised by :UR-CONS, the definition of f above is

Def $f(s) = $ **if** atom(s)
           then NIL
           else if $\phi($car$(s))$
             then cons$($car$(s), f($cdr$(s)))$
             else $f($cdr$(s))$.

It thus computes a list, not a set.[4] It may seem counterintuitive to prefer recursive definitions of set theory functions in terms of functions that expose the

---

[3] Using apply we could, of course, define the ACL2 function that takes a set s and a finite predicate f represented as a set, and returns the subset of the former satisfying the latter.

[4] Of course it computes a list: sets are lists in ACL2. More precisely, it presents the set in an order determined by the presentation of its arguments.

underlying representation. But this is a deliberate choice and is perhaps the key discovery made in the project. (We discuss what we call "recursion by choose" in [7]. This recursive scheme is entirely set theoretic in nature but makes inductive proofs a little more awkward because of the issues surrounding choose and scons.)

The main appeal of using scar and scdr is that it usually makes it straightforward to prove inductively the fundamental theorems about newly defined recursive set theory functions. Such proofs are generally isomorphic to the proofs of analogous theorems about the analogous list processing functions. The latter kind of theorems are ACL2's "bread and butter." We illustrate a recursive definition of a set in Section 9.

8   The Defmap Macro

We have defined a macro to make it easy to define functions corresponding to two common set builder forms. Each use of the macro not only defines a function but also proves certain theorems about the new function.

> **Def** $f(v_1, \ldots, v_k) =$ **for** x **in** v_i **such_that** ϕ
> defines $f(v_1, \ldots, v_k)$ to be $\{x \mid x \in v_i \land \phi\}$.
> **Def** $f(v_1, \ldots, v_k) =$ **for** x **in** v_i **map** ϕ
> defines $f(v_1, \ldots, v_k)$ to be $\{e \mid \exists x(x \in v_i \land e = \phi)\}$.

For example, in the case of the first form above, the lemmas proved about f include that it produces a set, that x is a member of the answer iff x is in v_i and satisfies ϕ, that the answer is a subset of v_i, that the function admits = as a congruence, and that union and intersection (in the ith argument) distribute over f. Analogous theorems are proved about the other form.

9   Example

Set theory is so rich that the book described here barely scratches the surface. A relevant question though is whether we can build on this foundation. In this section we show a complete development of a simple book that defines the powerset of a set and proves two facts about it: that its elements are precisely the subsets of the set and that our definition admits set equality as a congruence. The theorems in this section are proved automatically by ACL2 (given the hints below) after including the set theory book. The book is shown in the abstract syntax used throughout this paper, but every Lisp form in the book is represented somehow below.

in-package("S")

Here is the definition of powerset.
Def scons-to-every$(e, s) =$ **for** x **in** s **map** scons(e, x).
Def powerset$(s) =$

```
  if ur-elementp(s)
     then brace(NIL)
     else union(powerset(scdr(s)),
               scons-to-every(scar(s), powerset(scdr(s)))).
```

Powerset *builds a set.*

Lemma
setp(powerset(s)).

In fact, it builds a set of sets. But to say that we must define set-of-setsp *and prove that it admits* = *as a congruence.*

Def set-of-setsp(p) =
  if ur-elementp(p)
     then T
     else setp(scar(p)) $\wedge$ set-of-setsp(scdr(p)).

We use the standard defx *strategy for proving congruence for a predicate.*

Defx ...
    $a = b \rightarrow$ set-of-setsp(a) = set-of-setsp(b).

Powerset *builds a set of sets.*

Lemma
set-of-setsp(powerset(s)).

Here is the fundamental fact about membership in scons-to-every.

Lemma
setp(p) $\wedge$ set-of-setsp(p) $\wedge$ setp(s_1)
$\rightarrow$ (mem(s_1,scons-to-every(e, p))
   $\leftrightarrow$
   (mem(e, s_1) $\wedge$ (mem(s_1, p) $\vee$ mem(diff(s_1,brace(e)),p))))

The following function is used to tell ACL2 how to induct in the next theorem. It says: induct on b and assume two inductive hypotheses.

Def induction-hint(a, b) =
  if ur-elementp(b)
     then list(a, b)
     else list(induction-hint(a,scdr(b)),
               induction-hint(diff(a,brace(scar(b))),scdr(b))).

The powerset *contains precisely the subsets. This is our main theorem here.*

Theorem
setp(e) $\rightarrow$ (mem(e,powerset(s)) $\leftrightarrow$ subsetp(e, s)).
Hint:: Induct according to induction-hint(e, s).

The next lemma is needed for the final defx *command.*

Lemma
set-of-setsp(s) $\wedge$ subsetp(s,powerset(b)) $\wedge$ mem(e, b)
$\rightarrow$ subsetp(scons-to-every(e, s),powerset(b)).
Hint: Induct according to scons-to-every(e, s).

We use the standard defx *strategy for proving congruence for a set builder.*
Defx ...
  $a = b \rightarrow$ powerset(a) = powerset(b).

10   Conclusions

An early version of the finite set theory book is part of the general distribution of ACL2 but this is still a work in progress.

The main application of the set theory book is an ongoing experiment by Pacheco [8], of the Department of Computer Sciences, University of Texas at Austin, involving the translation of proof obligations from Leslie Lamport's TLA [6] into ACL2. TLA is based on set theory and thus requires more than "a little set theory" since the notation used in the TLA model frequently uses set constructor notation. To preserve ACL2's reasoning power, we represent TLA numbers, strings and certain other objects with their ACL2 counterparts rather than with Lamport's (unspecified) set representatives. Thus, the TLA experiment involves a mixture of sets and native ACL2 objects.

The TLA experiment has uncovered a few omitted lemmas about functions in our set theory book. More problematically, it has exposed a wealth of well-developed concepts in set theory that are definable but not defined in our book, such as powersets, cross products between sets, the functions between two sets, etc. Such concepts must not only be defined but the highly interconnected web of theorems linking them must be developed. Finally, the TLA experiment has highlighted the need for more support of set comprehension, a feature which gives set theory much of its expressive power. Pacheco has produced prototype macro definitions providing some additional support but much more remains. The whole issue of "faking" higher order expressions in ACL2's first order language will probably require additional low-level support in the ACL2 system itself, such as extensions to our macro feature and connections between macros and the output routines of ACL2.

Set theory is so expressive and so well developed that such problems are not surprising. But the TLA experiment, so far, has not led us to abandon or seek to change the basic representational decisions discussed here. Indeed, we are encouraged by the experiment's success.

Acknowledgments

I thank Pete Manolios for his help in exploring the issues concerning mutual recursion in the definitions of the set theory primitives. I am also grateful to

Carlos Pacheco for his willingness to dive into the undocumented set theory book and begin to use it. Finally, I am grateful to Yuan Yu and Leslie Lamport for helping clarify the goals of the set theory work.

References

1. Grzegorz Bancerek. A model of ZF set theory language. *Journal of Formalized Mathematics*, 1, 1989. http://mizar.org/JFM/Vol1/zf_lang.html.
2. M. J. C. Gordon.   Higher order logic, set theory or both?   In http://www.cl.cam.ac.uk/~mjcg/papers/holst/index.html.   Invited   talk, TPHOLs 96, Turku, Finland, August 1996.
3. M. Kaufmann, P. Manolios, and J S. Moore, editors. *Computer-Aided Reasoning: ACL2 Case Studies*. Kluwer Academic Press, 2000.
4. M. Kaufmann, P. Manolios, and J S. Moore. *Computer-Aided Reasoning: An Approach*. Kluwer Academic Press, 2000.
5. M. Kaufmann and J S. Moore. Structured theory development for a mechanized logic. *Journal of Automated Reasoning*, 26(2):161–203, 2001.
6. L. Lamport. The temporal logic of actions. *ACM Trans. on Programming Languages and Systems*, 16(3):872–923, May 1994.
7. J S. Moore. Recursion by choose. In http://www.cs.utexas.edu/users/moore/publications/finite-set-theory/ recursion-by-choose.lisp. Department of Computer Sciences, University of Texas at Austin, 2000.
8. Carlos Pacheco.   Reasoning about TLA actions.   Technical Report CS-TR-01-16, Computer Sciences, University of Texas at Austin, May 2001. http://www.cs.utexas.edu/ftp/pub/techreports/tr01-16.ps.Z.
9. L. C. Paulson. Set theory for verification: I. from foundations to functions. *Journal of Automated Reasoning*, 11:353–389, 1993.
10. L. C. Paulson. Set theory for verification: Ii. induction and recursion. *Journal of Automated Reasoning*, 15:167–215, 1995.

The HOL/NuPRL Proof Translator
A Practical Approach to Formal Interoperability*

Pavel Naumov[1], Mark-Oliver Stehr[2], and José Meseguer[2]

[1] Pennsylvania State University, Middletown, PA 17057, USA
naumov@psu.edu
[2] SRI International, Menlo Park, CA 94025, USA
{stehr,meseguer}@csl.sri.com

Abstract. We have developed a proof translator from HOL into a classical extension of NuPRL which is based on two lines of previous work. First, it draws on earlier work by Doug Howe, who developed a translator of theorems from HOL into a classical extension of NuPRL which is justified by a hybrid set-theoretic/computational semantics. Second, we rely on our own previous work, which investigates this mapping from a proof-theoretic viewpoint and gives a constructive meta-logical proof of its soundness. In this paper the logical foundations of the embedding of HOL into this classical extension of NuPRL as well as technical aspects of the proof translator implementation are discussed.

1 Introduction

During the last couple of decades we have witnessed an appearance of several dominant theorem proving systems that have attracted considerable attention and have gradually found their way into applications. Simultaneously, the same process has fragmented the research community and has made work and results of any one group almost useless for the rest. The main reason for this fragmentation is the fact that a majority of modern theorem provers have been designed as stand-alone products that can not share formal results with other systems. Partially this can be explained by the fact that different systems are based on quite different logical foundations, which makes any translation a non-trivial mathematical problem. But probably even more importantly, the designers have seldom seen the need for such compatibility. Their goal was to explore new approaches, not to form standards. The need for compatibility appeared when the leading systems accumulated substantial libraries of formal theories produced by joint work of many users. Reproducing such theories in systems where they are not available would be a very tedious and time-consuming task. At the same time, those other systems have unique and interesting features that make them

---

* The first author was supported by DARPA grant F30602-98-2-0198 on the initial stage of this work that was done at Cornell University, Ithaca, NY. We furthermore gratefully acknowledge support for the work conducted at SRI by DARPA and NASA (Contract NAS2-98073), by Office of Naval Research (Contract N00014-96-C-0114), by NSF Grant (CCR-9633363), and by a DAAD grant in the scope of HSP-III.

R.J. Boulton and P.B. Jackson (Eds.): TPHOLs 2001, LNCS 2152, pp. 329–345, 2001.
© Springer-Verlag Berlin Heidelberg 2001

attractive for some users. As a result, the need for proof translation tools has become apparent.

1.1   Two Kinds of Translators

A translation of formal results from one system into another can be carried out at two different levels. First, one can translate *statements* of proven theorems from a source system into a target system. Secondly, one can translate the *proofs* themselves.

The first approach is obviously easier to implement, but it forces the target system to trust the correctness of the source system. In addition, since systems are usually based on different logical foundations, the user has to rely completely on an (informal) meta-logical proof of the fact that the translator is based on a logically sound mapping. Besides, one can raise doubts about the validity of the code of the translator that can have bugs or, for technical reasons, may slightly deviate from the mapping used in the soundness proof. All these problems can be avoided with the second approach, but the need to translate proofs makes the implementation much harder.

Ideally, there is a close connection between the soundness of the mapping between the two formal systems and proof translation: If $\mathcal{L}$ and $\mathcal{L}'$ are the source and target logics, respectively, and α is the mapping of $\mathcal{L}$ into $\mathcal{L}'$ then *soundness*[1] is the property that $\Gamma \vdash_{\mathcal{L}} P$ implies $\alpha(\Gamma) \vdash_{\mathcal{L}'} \alpha(P)$ for any set Γ of axioms and any formula P. Hence, a proof of soundness would demonstrate that for each proof of P from Γ in $\mathcal{L}$ there is a corresponding proof of $\alpha(P)$ from $\alpha(\Gamma)$ in $\mathcal{L}'$. Furthermore, if the soundness proof is conducted in a constructive way, it implicitly contains a description of the translation algorithm that we need. In fact, in our case the proof translator from HOL into NuPRL is an algorithm, which is essentially extracted from a mathematical proof of soundness.

Obviously, soundness of the underlying mapping is the main theoretical requirement for the correctness of the proof translator. Notice, however, that soundness can always be achieved by extending the target system by additional axioms and inference rules, as it is often necessary in practice. Of course, such an extension could make the target system inconsistent, which is why the soundness proof is meaningful only in the presence of a consistency proof of the target system. Typically, such a consistency proof is done using an abstraction of the target system, e.g. by construction of a semantic model. In a more general setting, where we work relative to arbitrary theories, a suitably general *model preservation* property[2] property is that each model M of $\mathcal{L}$ can be obtained from a model M' of $\mathcal{L}'$ by a mapping β such that $\beta(M') \models_{\mathcal{L}} P$ iff $M' \models_{\mathcal{L}'} \alpha(P)$. Although a proof of model preservation is generally important for the translation mapping to be semantically meaningful, it is of little use for the implementation of the proof translator itself which typically relies on proof-theoretic constructions.

---

[1] Soundness is the central property of a map of entailments systems, which represent the notion of derivability in general logics [14].

[2] This property is usually expressed in the context of a map of institutions [8], which constitute the model-theoretic component of general logics [14].

1.2   Previous Results

Some early work on translating formal results between theorem provers was conducted by Doug Howe and Amy Felty. In [12] Howe defined a mapping from HOL [9] into a classical extension of NuPRL [3] and gave a semantic justification for the admissibility of this translation, essentially by constructing a hybrid set-theoretic/computational semantics for the classical extension of NuPRL[3], where HOL models appear as submodels of somewhat richer NuPRL models [10]. Later, Howe developed a translator [11] based on this mapping, which translates *statements* of HOL theorems. Since Howe gave only a semantic justification, extending it to a proof translation is a non-trivial task. The practical usefulness of Howe's HOL/NuPRL connection has been demonstrated in [7], where his translator is used to produce HOL/NuPRL hybrid proofs. In [17] the first author applied a similar approach to built a translator from Isabelle's higher-order logic [19] into NuPRL. This work also sketched a soundness proof, which was so straightforward that in [18] he has been able to formalize it in NuPRL. A corresponding soundness proof can also be given for Howe's original mapping from HOL into NuPRL. In fact, we gave a detailed constructive proof in [22] using general logics terminology [14]. In this paper we present a proof translator from HOL to a classical extension of NuPRL which is based on this proof. Comparison to other closely related works is done in the end of the paper.

1.3   Why Translating from HOL to NuPRL?

There are at least three factors to consider when selecting the source and the target systems for a proof translator to be useful in practice: (1) The source logic should be supported by a well-established theorem proving system that has accumulated a substantial amount of non-trivial results. (2) The target logic should be sufficiently expressive to serve as a target for the translation, so that the translation is natural in the sense that, say, results about standard data types in the source logic can be interpreted as results about the corresponding data types in the target logic. (3) The target logic should be equipped with a semantics that allows us to establish a close relationship to the semantics of the source logic. Taking into account the previous results we think that the pair HOL/NuPRL is a good choice for the source and the target systems from the viewpoint of these three requirements.

1.4   Challenges

There are two major obstacles that we faced in the context of this work: On the theoretical level, the main challenge was to supplement Howe's semantic justification by a proof of soundness on which the translator could be potentially based. The primary concern here is that HOL inference rules, taken literally, are

---

[3] We always use "NuPRL" to refer to Howe's variant of NuPRL which enjoys this hybrid set-theretic/computational semantics. Howe's classical extension of NuPRL is then obtained by adding type-theoretic version of the law of the excluded middle.

not sound in NuPRL. On the implementation level, a technical difficulty has
been the lack of proof objects in HOL. Hence, it was necessary to equip the
HOL system with an explicit notion of proof objects and support for exporting
such objects.

1.5   Paper Outline

We begin in Section 2 by giving a brief introduction to the logical foundations
of HOL and NuPRL and their implementations. Section 3 discusses the classical
extension of NuPRL that we are using and sketches the translation of formulas
and proofs. Section 4 gives a high-level description of the translator and complements it with a discussion of some implementation details and some practical
experience that we have found to be interesting. We compare our work with recent work by Ewen Denney [6] on translating proofs from HOL to Coq in Section
5. Finally, we present some conclusions in Section 6.

2   Overview of the Theorem Provers

This section gives a brief introduction to the HOL and NuPRL proof development systems and their underlying formal logics and type theories.

2.1   The HOL System

Logic. HOL [9] is an interactive theorem prover based on a Gentzen-style formalization of higher-order logic over a simply typed lambda calculus extended by
Hindley-Milner polymorphism, which admits types with (implicitly quantified)
type variables.

Syntactically, HOL clearly distinguishes two kinds of entities: types and
terms. Types are built from type variables and type constants, which include
type operators and regular type constants:

$$Type := TypeVar \mid TypeConst(Type_1, \ldots, Type_n)$$

HOL terms are constructed from free and bound variables as well as constants
using application and typed λ-abstraction:

$$Term := FVar_{Type} \mid BVar \mid Const_{Type} \mid Term\,Term \mid \lambda\,Type\,.\,Term$$

Notice that HOL terms carry explicit type information embedded into them. This
is done by specifying free variables and constants together with their types. Since
bound variables are implemented using de Bruijn indices [5], bound variables are
just natural numbers, but their types can be extracted from the type of the λ-
term they refer to. In HOL all terms used in theories and rules are well-typed,
and, as a result, the unique type of any HOL term can be recursively computed.
In spite of the use of de Bruijn indices in the HOL system we prefer to use names
in the following for better readability.

Formulas of HOL, which we also refer to as propositions, are terms of the primitive propositional type `bool`. In addition to this type constant, the inference rules of HOL, which are given in Fig. 1, presuppose only two other primitive constants, namely polymorphic equality and boolean implication. The fact that `bool` is actually the boolean data type with negation, conjunction, disjunction, polymorphic universal and existential quantifiers and a polymorphic version of Hilbert's ϵ-operator is ensured axiomatically by the logical theory of which all user-defined theories are extensions. It is interesting to note that the inference rules which define the formal system of HOL are independent of the logical theory,[4] which is a theory like any other theory. In fact, it is the logical theory which makes the logic of HOL classical.

$$\frac{}{A \vdash A} \text{ (ASSUME)} \qquad \frac{}{\vdash (\lambda y.M)N = M[N/y]} \text{ (β-CONV)}$$

$$\frac{G \vdash A \quad H \vdash A \Rightarrow B}{H, G \vdash B} \text{ (MP)} \qquad \frac{H_i \vdash M_i = N_i \quad i \in \{1,\ldots,n\} \quad G \vdash A[\overline{M}/\overline{z}]}{H_1,\ldots,H_n, G \vdash A[\overline{N}/\overline{z}]} \text{ (SUBST)}$$

$$\frac{H, A \vdash B}{H \vdash A \Rightarrow B} \text{ (DISCH)} \qquad \frac{H \vdash M = N}{H \vdash (\lambda y : \tau.M) = (\lambda y : \tau.N)} \text{ (ABS)}$$

$$\frac{}{\vdash M = M} \text{ (REFL)} \qquad \frac{H \vdash A}{H \vdash A[\overline{\tau}/\overline{\alpha}]} \ \overline{\alpha} \text{ do not occur in } H \text{ (INST\_TYPE)}$$

Fig. 1. Primitive Inference Rules of HOL.

System Design. HOL is implemented in SML [15] and the type `thm` of theorems is defined as an abstract SML type. The only information a theorem contains is essentially its sequent, i.e. the hypotheses and the conclusion. Typechecking ensures that SML functions can only produce elements of `thm` using constructors corresponding to the inference rules of HOL. Such functions have to be executed in order to actually generate a provable theorem, but the evidence of provability is not stored anywhere in the system.

Wai Wong [23] added a proof recording mechanism to HOL.[5] Each time an inference rule is called, all parameters of this rule are passed to a special proof recording function that can be defined at a user's discretion. In our work this proof recording mechanism is used to construct a proof object.

2.2 The NuPRL System

Logic. NuPRL is based on a variant of Martin-Löf's polymorphic and extensional type theory [13,20], which in contrast to HOL is constructive. NuPRL is a type theory which is naturally equipped with a higher-order logic via a propositions-as-types interpretation. Each formula, which we also refer to as a

---

[4] Although in the HOL implementation we discovered a subtle (and somewhat ugly) dependency of the modus ponens rule on the definition of negation.

[5] Another approach to proof terms for Isabelle/HOL is described in [2].

proposition, can be interpreted as a type, and provability of this formula corresponds to the fact this type is inhabited. Unlike some other type theories such as the Calculus of Constructions [4] the elements of such propositional types should not be interpreted as proofs, since type checking in NuPRL is not decidable, but merely represents the computational contents of the associated proposition.

Both types and their elements are represented in NuPRL by terms. These terms are untyped in the sense that there is in general no effective procedure to reconstruct types of NuPRL terms, which is why NuPRL is sometimes called an "untyped type theory". Syntactically, a NuPRL term is build from so-called abstractions, where each abstraction has an identifier, a list of parameters, and a list of subterms with binders. A subterm with binder is a term with an attached list of variables bound by it. The abstraction identifier (such as var, int, add, lambda, etc.) is the main descriptor, but sometimes an abstraction requires extra parameters to be specified. For example, each variable is represented as an abstraction var together with its name as a parameter. As one can see, the type information is not a fixed part of the NuPRL term structure, and reflecting the polymorphic nature of NuPRL, some terms, such as the λ-abstraction $\lambda x.x$, represent elements of many different types. The NuPRL abstraction mechanism is a powerful tool, which in connection with NuPRL's user-definable display forms, provides syntactic flexibility and readability. In most cases abstractions are introduced by specifying them through existing ones, but it is also possible to introduce an abstraction that is not associated with a definition, in which case we refer to it as a primitive abstraction. A special case of abstractions are constants, which do not have any associated subterms.

The flexibility of NuPRL's polymorphism and the fact that NuPRL does not impose computability of types in any sense enables NuPRL to use a rich and open-ended type theory, which has a predicative cumulative hierarchy of type universes, dependent function types, subset types, parametrized inductive types, quotient types, and other features not present in HOL. As one would expect, most features of NuPRL are not essential for representing HOL theories. In fact, only a few abstractions and inference rules of NuPRL will be used by our proof translator. A detailed description of a fragment of NuPRL sufficient for our work can be found in [21].

System Design. NuPRL is implemented in a hybrid programming framework of Common Lisp and Classic ML. Core parts of the system are written in Lisp, and ML is mostly used as the language to express theorem proving tactics. Data structures for NuPRL terms and proofs are defined in Lisp but are accessible via an ML interface. As a result, dealing with the Lisp part of NuPRL is rarely necessary. In fact, we have implemented the main part of the proof translator entirely in Classic ML on the top of NuPRL.

Unlike HOL, NuPRL uses an explicit representation of proofs as trees. A proof of a theorem consists of the theorem itself, a justification which allows us to infer this theorem, and a list of subproofs, containing one proof for each premise needed by the justification. The justification can either be an instance of a NuPRL inference rule, or, more generally, a NuPRL tactic. To emphasize the style of backward-reasoning employed in NuPRL, we refer to the theorems of the proof and its subproofs also as the goal and its subgoals, respectively.

3   Logical Foundations of the Translator

In [21] we have shown that the mapping from HOL to the classical extension of NuPRL can be understood in the framework of general logics [14] as a composition of two stages: The first stage is a *translation* of an *axiomatic theory of HOL* into an *axiomatic theory of the classical extension of NuPRL*. The use of the term "axiomatic" emphasizes the fact that the theories are not necessarily only definitional extensions of the base logic. The second stage is the *interpretation* of an axiomatic theory inside the classical extension of NuPRL.[6] Whereas the translation stage is of meta-logical nature, the interpretation stage can take place inside the logic of NuPRL in a formally rigorous way. However, since there are many possible choices for the interpretation of translated HOL theories in NuPRL theories, and certain proofs, namely of the NuPRL axioms resulting from the translation of HOL axioms, to be carried out, the user might need to intervene before each separate HOL theory is translated.

3.1   A Classical Extension of NuPRL

Unlike HOL, NuPRL is based on a constructive type theory. Hence, valid HOL theorems like the law of the excluded middle $\forall P.P \vee \neg P$ and logical extensionality $\forall P.(P \Leftrightarrow Q) \Leftrightarrow (P = Q)$ are not provable in NuPRL. There are at least three potential ways to set up the translation:

- First, one can look for a translation that maps HOL into the constructive type theory of NuPRL. For instance, Gödel's double-negation translation (see, for example, [16], p.98) is known to do just that. Unfortunately, double negation or any similar translation would not be very useful for connecting theorem proving systems. The results translated under a non-trivial mapping are difficult to use as lemmas in the target system. Notice also that this translation would still require logical extensionality as an axiom.
- Second, one can consider a stronger non-conservative extension of the constructive type theory of NuPRL by the axiom of the excluded middle, and consider the most straightforward mapping of HOL in this classical extension of NuPRL. Under such a mapping, HOL propositions are translated into NuPRL propositions and logical HOL operators into their NuPRL counterparts. Unfortunately, this approach does not lead to a general solution. The difficulty is that HOL is an impredicative higher-order logic, but NuPRL has a predicative higher-order logic, which is inherited from its predicative type theory via the Curry-Howard isomorphism. As a consequence, the propositional type `bool` of HOL is closed under universal quantification, whereas

---

[6] By means of an interpretation we can often obtain a *computationally meaningful* theory which makes only use of the constructive sublanguage of the classical extension of NuPRL that we consider in this paper.

in NuPRL the use of universal quantification over a proposition in $\mathbb{P}_i$ can result in a proposition from a higher propositional universe $\mathbb{P}_{i+1}$. Hence, there is no single propositional universe in NuPRL that is a suitable image of HOL's propositional type `bool` under this translation. Still, this partial solution could be useful to translate certain predicative developments from HOL into NuPRL.[7] On the other hand, such an approach provides a simple and general solution for the embedding of HOL into an impredicative type theory such as the Calculus of Inductive Constructions (cf. Section 5).

- Third, following Howe [12] one can translate HOL's propositional type `bool` into the boolean type $\mathbb{B}$ of NuPRL. The type $\mathbb{B}$ is not one of the NuPRL primitive types, but is defined as a disjoint union of two single-element types, and all the operators of boolean logic and their (classical) properties are derived, including the law of the excluded middle and logical extensionality. Clearly, $\mathbb{B}$ is a model of classical boolean logic inside NuPRL's constructive type theory, and therefore an obvious candidate for the image of the HOL type `bool`. The only problem is that it lacks some of the features needed for the translation, namely a polymorphic boolean-valued equality, a polymorphic boolean-valued universal quantifier, and a polymorphic version of Hilbert's ε-operator which uses boolean-valued predicates.

In our work we have followed the third approach, since it seems to be the best solution in terms of usability and generality. To fill the remaining gap between the propositional type `bool` of HOL and the boolean type $\mathbb{B}$ of NuPRL we extended NuPRL by new primitive abstractions and axioms as follows.

- HOL equality is a boolean predicate, unlike the standard NuPRL equality $x =_T y$ which is a type living in some propositional univese $\mathbb{P}_i$. In order to translate HOL equality statements into NuPRL terms of type $\mathbb{B}$, we define in NuPRL a new primitive abstraction $x =_T^b y$ which stands for boolean-valued equality of elements of a type T. The following two axioms, that we have added to NuPRL, state that we have a boolean-valued equality that precisely mirrors NuPRL's propositional equality:

$$\forall T : \mathbb{U}_i. \ \forall x, y : T. \ x =_T^b y \in \mathbb{B}$$

$$\forall T : \mathbb{U}_i. \ \forall x, y : T. \ (\uparrow (x =_T^b y)) \Leftrightarrow x =_T y$$

(where $\uparrow b$ stands for the proposition $b =_\mathbb{B} true$)
- We dealt similarly with the universal quantifier which has type $\mathbb{P}_i$ in NuPRL, i.e. we introduced a boolean counterpart $\forall_b$ with the following axioms:

$$\forall T : \mathbb{U}_i. \ \forall b : T \to \mathbb{B}. \ (\forall_b x : T. \ b(x)) \in \mathbb{B}$$

$$\forall T : \mathbb{U}_i. \ \forall b : T \to \mathbb{B}. \ (\uparrow \forall_b x : T. \ b(x)) \Longleftrightarrow (\forall x : T \uparrow b(x))$$

---

[7] Notice, however that we cannot assume logical extensionality in NuPRL, since this would be inconsistent with NuPRL's nontrivial data types, which cannot be distinguished from propositional types.

– Finally, we added a non-constructive ε-operator in order to interpret the corresponding HOL operator. The axiom for this operator is:

$$\forall T : \mathbb{U}.\ \forall b : T \rightarrow \mathbb{B}.\ T \Rightarrow (\varepsilon x : T.\ b(x)) \in T$$

For the understanding of the last axiom recall that NuPRL is based on propositions-as-types paradigm and, as a result, any type T is simultaneously a proposition which asserts non-emptiness of this type.

In [12] it is shown that the operators and axioms given above can all be derived from a simple extension of NuPRL by the axiom of the excluded middle $\forall P.P \vee \neg P$ (more precisely, its type-theoretic version). Assumption of this axiom in NuPRL means, according to the propositions-as-types interpretation, that the corresponding dependent type is inhabited by a function which "decides" for each type P if P is inhabited and returns one of its elements if this is the case. In fact, Howe uses this axiom to define a function $\downarrow_b$ that casts propositions into booleans, and then defines boolean equality and the boolean universal quantifier by lifting their NuPRL counterparts using $\downarrow_b$. Another function, that can be obviously derived from the axiom of the law of the excluded middle, selects an element from a given non-empty type. Howe uses such a function to define the ε-operator.

3.2   Translation of Formulas

The translation of formulas of HOL into propositions of NuPRL is a straightforward recursive procedure once HOL constants are mapped into corresponding NuPRL constants. The mapping of constants, which we call a *dictionary*, has to be provided by the user. The translation is then a natural extension of this mapping to a mapping from the types and terms of HOL into the terms of NuPRL: Type operators of HOL are mapped to functions operating on type universes. Typed λ-abstractions of HOL are translated to λ-abstractions in NuPRL (although the latter are untyped, we decided to keep the type information for better readability). Furthermore, implicitly polymorphic functions (and their types) in HOL are translated to explicitly polymorphic functions (and corresponding types) in NuPRL, and suitable explicit type arguments are generated on the NuPRL side when such functions are applied.

The proof translator requires that the dictionary is an injective mapping of HOL constants into NuPRL constants.[8] For example, the HOL type `bool` is mapped to the NuPRL type $\mathbb{B}$ by an entry

$$\alpha(bool) = \mathbb{B}\ .$$

In some cases we would like to map an HOL constant to a more complicated NuPRL term. For instance, the HOL conjunction $\wedge$ is a function of type `bool` $\rightarrow$

---

[8] In the theoretical treatment [21] we have abstracted from renaming issues by using names of HOL constants directly for NuPRL constants.

bool $\rightarrow$ bool, whereas in NuPRL conjunction $\wedge$ is an abstraction with two subterms but not a constant. Hence, we would like to have a translation:

$$\alpha(\wedge) = \lambda p, q.p \wedge q$$

To this end we exploit the flexibility provided by the interpretation stage mentioned before, that is we introduce an explicit NuPRL counterpart for each HOL constant, which in this case would be a new NuPRL constant $\wedge_h$ and we interpret this constant by adding a definition $\wedge_h := \lambda p, q.p \wedge q$. That makes the corresponding dictionary entry a simple renaming, namely $\alpha(\wedge) = \wedge_h$, and enhances readability of the result of the translation. In a similar way we deal with other HOL constants such as $\vee_h$, $\rightarrow_h$, $=_h$, etc.

After an HOL formula is translated into a NuPRL formula it becomes a term of type $\mathbb{B}$. In order to treat this term as a NuPRL theorem, we have to cast it into a propositional type. To this end, we use the standard NuPRL function assert $\uparrow$, which is defined as $\uparrow b := (b =_{\mathbb{B}} true)$. In addition, since, unlike HOL, NuPRL does not allow free variables in theorem statements, we bind all such variables by an appropriate universal quantifier. For instance, the HOL theorem $x_\sigma = x_\sigma$ (provable in one step using the REFL rule), is translated into the NuPRL statement

$$\forall \alpha(\sigma) : \mathsf{S}. \ \forall x : \alpha(\sigma) \ \ \uparrow (=_h \ x \ x)$$

where S is a type of all representations of HOL types.[9] Note that in most cases translated HOL theorems can be lifted to NuPRL propositions by propagating $\uparrow$ through boolean quantifiers, connectives, and equalities. This transforms these boolean operations into their regular NuPRL (propositional) counterparts. We have developed a NuPRL tactic to perform this transformation.

3.3   Translation of Inference Rules

HOL inference rules, taken literally, are not valid in the classical extension of NuPRL, because they are missing explicit well-formedness conditions. These conditions are implicit in HOL because a built-in type checking mechanism guarantees that each HOL term is well-formed. Because of its open-ended type system, NuPRL imposes much weaker a priori conditions on its terms. In fact, any syntactically valid expression is a term in NuPRL. In the inference rules of NuPRL well-formedness is usually enforced through extra premises which give rise to so-called well-formedness subgoals during a proof. For the standard types of NuPRL these subgoals can be proven automatically by NuPRL's `Auto` tactic in the majority of cases.

To translate inference rules from HOL into NuPRL we have to come up with *derived* rules in NuPRL that match HOL rules as closely as possible and have

---

[9] In order to interpret the HOL axiom for the ε-operator in NuPRL, all translations of HOL types have to be nonempty. In the present version of the proof translator we ignore nonemptiness condition and just use $\mathbb{U}_i$ for S (instead of the subtype of non-empty types described in [12,21]), since most HOL proofs do not depend on this condition. We think that in the future the proof translator should support both possibilities.

suitable well-formedness subgoals to reflect the fact that only well-typed terms occur in the rule. Our proof translator redirects well-formedness subgoals to the Auto tactic. Although in general these extra subgoals might not be provable by Auto tactic (or even false), in the case when the derived rules are applied to the translation of HOL formulas, well-formedness subgoals are provable by a slightly modified version of the Auto tactic.

4   Implementation of the Proof Translator

4.1   Adding Proof Objects to HOL

The generation of new HOL theorems from existing ones is done in ML by HOL inference rules which are ML functions with an arbitrary number of arguments of type thm and a result of the same type. Many actual proofs are written in terms of tactics which are, essentially, ML programs combining several applications of inference rules.

Once an ML term of type thm is parsed by the system, verified by the type checker, and executed successfully, the value of the term (representing the theorem) becomes available and can be used as a lemma in other proofs, but there is no way to reconstruct the proof from the resulting theorem.

Clearly, in order to translate HOL proofs into NuPRL we first have to recover those proofs. Our initial idea was to extract the proofs from the files containing the ML code that generated them. Unfortunately, this is not an easy task. Since HOL tactics could potentially make use of the full power of Standard ML, which is the tactic-language of HOL, the proof translator would need to include a general compiler or interpreter from Standard ML into Classic ML, which is used in NuPRL as the tactic language.

A simpler approach, that we have eventually adopted, is to modify the HOL abstract data type thm in such a way that every element of this type stores additional information about how it has been constructed. To achieve this, we have changed the HOL definition of the thm type from

```
datatype thm = THM of Term.term list * Term.term
```
to
```
datatype thm = THM of Term.term list * Term.term
                     * (string * just_arg list)
```

where an element of type string represents the name of the inference rule that created this theorem and the list over just_arg stores additional arguments that determine the instance of the inference rule which was actually used. For example, if a theorem $H \vdash (\lambda y.M) = (\lambda y.N)$ was proven using the HOL abstraction rule

$$\frac{H \vdash M = N}{H \vdash (\lambda y.M) = (\lambda y.N)} \text{ (ABS)}$$

then it will have ABS as the name of the inference rule and the variable y and theorem $H \vdash M = N$ as its arguments[10]. We have modified all HOL theorem

---

[10] We are using Wong's [23] just_arg type to store inference rule arguments.

constructors that operate on the type thm to work correspondingly. Of course, once each theorem keep track of its parents theorems, the entire proof tree can be reconstructed recursively.

After these modifications to HOL, we have recompiled the system to make every theorem in every HOL theory aware of its proof. Although, this modification drastically increases the size of thm objects, we have not observed a noticeable degradation in the system performance.

4.2   Translating Rules as Tactics

Since HOL and NuPRL have different sets of primitive inference rules, typically several NuPRL rules have to be used to imitate one HOL rule. In the previous section we have expressed this idea by saying that there are derived NuPRL rules that closely match HOL rules. Technically, since NuPRL does not have an explicit concept of derived rules, we have written special NuPRL tactics that combine several primitive inference rule to mimic one derived rule application.

In most cases it was possible to define such tactics using existing NuPRL tactics such as the backchaining tactic BLemma together with a suitable theorem to model HOL inference rules. For example, the HOL inference rule

$$\frac{H, A \vdash B}{H \vdash A \Rightarrow B} \text{ (DISCH)}$$

is imitated by our translator essentially via backchaining through the lemma

$$\forall p, q : \mathbb{B}. (\uparrow p \Rightarrow \uparrow q) \Rightarrow \uparrow (\Rightarrow_h p q)$$

followed by a decomposition of implication using the tactic D 0 and a call to NuPRL's Auto tactic to eliminate potential well-formedness subgoals as discussed earlier:

```
let DISCH = BLemma 'DISCH_lemma' THENM D 0 THENW Auto;;
```

4.3   Dealing with Derived Rules of HOL

Our work was substantially complicated by the status of HOL derived rules. In spite of Gordon's original intention [9] that all the HOL derived rules are reduced to primitive inference rules, in the version 90.10 of HOL that we have used the majority of originally derived rules are represented in the HOL system as new constructors for the thm type.[11] Hence, the majority of derived rules are essentially proclaimed to be new primitive rules. Our understanding is that this change has been done at some point in the past for efficiency reasons.

To face the reality of the HOL implementation we decided to construct NuPRL equivalents for these derived rules the same way as we have done it

---

[11] Although the HOL system contains deactivated ML code that is supposed to define derived rules via primitive rules, an inspection of this code indicated that it is no longer compatible with the current version of HOL.

for primitive rules. On the positive side, the higher level of abstraction provided by the derived rules allows us to avoid reducing logical operators (in particular conjunction and the existential quantifier) to terms involving the ϵ-operator. This does not only lead to more readable proofs, but more importantly the ϵ-operator is only needed in cases where it is explicitly used in a theory.[12]

4.4   Implementation Details

The proof translator is implemented as a pair of functions (`export`, `import`) in two different dialects of ML. The function `export` is written in Standard ML and is integrated into the HOL system. When this function is called in the HOL environment on any theorem named `theorem`, a separate file `theorem.ml` is created and a description of the theorem's proof is stored in the file in what we call *portable theorem format*. Essentially, this file contains a theorem together with its associated proof tree written in Classic ML. When the `theorem.ml` file is loaded into the NuPRL environment this tree is re-created as a Classic ML data structure. The second function `import`, written in Classic ML, takes this structure as an argument, translates the theorem into a NuPRL proposition, proves it by invoking the NuPRL tactics corresponding to the HOL inference rules given by the proof, and adds the new result to the NuPRL library.

  Although the translation process itself does not require user intervention, it relies on the user-defined dictionary in order to translate HOL constants into their NuPRL counterparts. The dictionary not only allows the user to choose meaningful names for the translation of HOL constants, but it is also needed to avoid name clashes which can occur, since in the current version (4.2) NuPRL has a flat name space, and the names for the translated constants could have been already used in one of the theories the user is working with.

4.5   Efficiency Issues

Although the translated proofs that the proof translator produced in a number of small examples of logical nature are valid NuPRL proofs, we were surprised by their sizes. In many cases, a few lines of HOL proofs, invoking just a few tactic calls, turned out to hide thousands of HOL inference rule applications (see Figure 2). Since every HOL inference rule call is translated into a NuPRL tactic call, which itself normally requires several inference rule applications, the resulting NuPRL proofs even for basic propositional theorems are unexpectedly long. From our experience, it takes NuPRL several minutes just to check the validity of the produced proof.

5   Related Work

The translation of proofs between higher-order logic theorem provers is a relatively new field which has both practical potential and interesting theoretical

---

[12] The current version of our proof translator can deal with nearly all basic inference rules and most of the derived rules mentioned above. In this point we are extending the theoretical treatment [21] which uses the HOL logic as presented in [9].

Theorem Name	Statement	HOL rule invocations
DISJ_ASSOC	$\forall A, B, C.\ A \vee B \vee C = (A \vee B) \vee C$	3218
DE_MORGAN_THM	$\forall A, B.\ (\neg(A \wedge B) = \neg A \vee \neg B) \wedge$	
	$\wedge (\neg(A \vee B) = \neg A \wedge \neg B)$	4733
LEFT_AND_OVER_OR	$\forall A, B, C.\ A \wedge (B \vee C) = A \wedge B \vee A \wedge C$	4215
EQ_EXPAND	$\forall t1, t2.\ (t1 = t2) = t1 \wedge t2 \vee \neg t1 \wedge \neg t2$	2618
COND_ABS	$\forall b, f, g.\ (\lambda x.b \Rightarrow (fx)|(gx)) = (b \Rightarrow f|g)$	1368
COND_RATOR	$\forall b, f, g, x.\ (b \Rightarrow f|g)x = (b \Rightarrow (fx)|(gx))$	1357

Fig. 2. Sample HOL Proof Sizes.

aspects. Apart from our own work [21,22], which heavily draws on earlier work by Howe [12], we are only aware of one further implementation of a higher-order logic proof translator, namely the translator from HOL into Coq [1] developed by Ewen Denney and described in [6]. Another piece of work which is related to ours from an implementation point of view is the work by Wai Wong [23] on rechecking HOL proofs using an external HOL proof checker. Our implementation makes use of the basic infrastructure that he provides, but we use our own internal and external proof format to facilitate the connection with NuPRL.

Concerning the proof translator from HOL to Coq [6] there are a number of similarities and differences to our work that we briefly discuss here. Both Coq and NuPRL are goal-oriented theorem provers based on expressive type theories and following the propositions-as-types paradigm. Coq is based on the Calculus of Inductive Constructions with a number of extensions. In contrast to the rich open-ended, predicative and polymorphic type theory of NuPRL [3], the Calculus of Constructions [4] is a monomorphic and impredicative type theory with dependent function types as the central concept, and the Calculus of Inductive Constructions [1] extends it by a predicative universe hierarchy and inductive definitions.

Coq uses the impredicative universe Prop for logical propositions, and due to its impredicativity the HOL/Coq translator can directly use this universe to represent the propositional type bool of HOL. Consequently, [6] assumes the axiom of the excluded middle for propositions in Prop. This is quite different from our approach, which clearly separates HOL propositions from NuPRL propositions, so that we are actually using NuPRL as a hybrid logic. Since, the Coq/HOL translator is already based on a non-conservative extension of Coq, one would expect that it also assumes logical extensionality of propositions in Prop to mirror logical extensionality of bool. However, [6] explicitly avoids this axiom by transforming boolean equality of HOL into an equivalence on Coq propositions, which is somewhat unsatisfactory, since the HOL type bool does not only represent propositions, but more importantly the well-known boolean data type, and Prop does not have the status of a data type in Coq due to the lack of suitable elimination principles over uninformative types. Although [6] does not give any meta-logical results to justify the design choices, we believe that in particular in view of the treatment of HOL equality, the translation deserves a careful study, since functions in HOL clearly respect equality, but the corresponding equivalence in Coq does not in general enjoy the Leibnitz property.[13]

In spite of these foundational differences, we found many similarities on the practical side, namely that both translators make use of an intermediate portable proof format for exchanging proofs between the two provers, and they both use mostly backchaining via suitable lemmas to model applications of HOL primitive inference rules. A unique feature of the HOL/Coq translator is the use of the DAG representation of the proof in the intermediate format and an automated "factoring out" of lemmas in the final proof. We think that this is an interesting idea worth considering also for the HOL/NuPRL translator which could partially solve the inefficiency issues we have discussed before.

Apart from the differences in the choice of the theorem provers and the mapping, there is a more important methodological difference between these two lines of research. Our starting point was the semantic justification that Howe gave for the mapping from HOL into NuPRL [12] together with our proof-theoretic soundness proof for this mapping [21] from which we essentially derived the proof translator. The work [6], however, neither gives a corresponding soundness proof for the mapping from HOL to Coq nor a semantic justification. We think that in general such meta-logical justifications are important to obtain a better understanding of the translation mapping. On the other hand, since Coq is based on a monomorphic and impredicative type theory in contrast to NuPRL which is polymorphic and predicative, the intuitive distance between HOL and Coq is smaller than the distance between HOL and NuPRL, both from a type-theoretic and from a semantic point of view, which makes such meta-theoretical justifications probably more critical for the HOL/NuPRL translator.

6 Conclusions

We have discussed the design principles and the implementation of a proof translator from HOL to NuPRL. The design of the translator is based on our mathematical proof of soundness for a mapping of HOL theories to NuPRL theories [21]. The mapping at the level of theories agrees with Howe's translation [12], but our justification is proof-theoretic whereas Howe's is semantic. Both approaches complement each other. Furthermore, the proof-theoretic nature of our result provides a method for the translation of HOL proofs into NuPRL proofs. In summary, we have designed and implemented a translator based on strong meta-logical justifications, both semantic (thanks to Howe) and proof-theoretic (our own) which in addition generates proofs as internal justifications in the target logic. Further work is required to cover some additional inference rules and to reduce the size of proofs, so that translation of large developments becomes feasible.

---

[13] An issue that remains unclear in [6] is how non-emptiness of HOL types is reflected. In practice, we found that most HOL proofs do not need this assumption, although it is needed for the interpretation of the logical theory of HOL.

Acknowledgements

We would like to thank Robert Constable and Stuart Allen for several discussions on the particularities of NuPRL and the issue of logic translation. We also would like to thank Doug Howe, since this project draws on his earlier work and would not have been possible without his support. He made not only the source code of the HOL/NuPRL connection available to us, but he also gave us the opportunity to discuss with him our initial ideas on a proof-theoretic soundness result.

References

1. B. Barras et al. The Coq Proof Assistant Reference Manual: Version 6.1. Technical Report RT-0203, INRIA, May 1997.
2. S. Berghofer and T. Nipkow. Proof terms for simply typed higher order logic. In M. Aagaard and J. Harrison, editors, *13th International Conference on Theorem Proving in Higher Order Logics*, volume 1869 of *Lecture Notes in Computer Science*, pages 38–52, Portland, Oregon, August 2000. Springer.
3. R.L. Constable et al. *Implementing Mathematics with Nuprl Proof Development System*. Prentice Hall, 1986.
4. T. Coquand and G. Huet. The calculus of constructions. *Information and Computation*, 76(2/3):95–120, 1988.
5. N.G. de Bruijn. Lambda calculus notation with nameless dummies, a tool for automatic formula manipulation, with application to the Church-Rosser theorem. *Indag. Math.*, 34:381–392, 1972.
6. E. Denney. A Prototype Proof Translator from HOL to Coq. In M. Aagaard and J. Harrison, editors, *The 13th International Conference on Theorem Proving in Higher Order Logics*, volume 1869 of *Lecture Notes in Computer Science*, pages 108–125, Portland, Oregon, August 2000. Springer-Verlag.
7. A.P. Felty and D.J. Howe. Hybrid interactive theorem proving using Nuprl and HOL. In W. McCune, editor, *Automated Deduction – CADE-14*, volume 1249 of *Lecture Notes in Artificial Intelligence*, pages 351–365, Berlin, 1997. Springer-Verlag.
8. J. Goguen and R. Burstall. Institutions: Abstract model theory for specification and programming. *Journal of the ACM*, 39(1):95–146, 1992.
9. M.J.C. Gordon and T.F. Melham. *Introduction to HOL – A Theorem Proving Environment for Higher Order Logic*. Cambridge University Press, 1993.
10. D. J. Howe. A classical set-theoretic model of polymorphic extensional type theory. Manuscript.
11. D.J. Howe. Importing mathematics from HOL into Nuprl. In J. von Wright, J. Grundy, and J. Harrison, editors, *Theorem Proving in Higher Order Logics*, volume 1125 of *Lecture Notes in Computer Science*, pages 267–282, Berlin, 1996. Springer-Verlag.
12. D.J Howe. Semantics foundation for embedding HOL in Nuprl. In M. Wirsing and A. Nivat, editors, *Algebraic Methodology and Software Technology*, volume 1101 of *Lecture Notes in Computer Science*, pages 85–101, Berlin, 1996. Springer-Verlag.
13. P. Martin-Löf. *Intuitionistic Type Theory*. Bibliopolis, Napoli, 1984.
14. J. Meseguer. General logics. In H.-D. Ebbinghaus et al., editor, *Logical Colloquium, 1987*, pages 275–329. North-Holland, 1989.
15. R. Milner, M. Tofte, R.M. Harper, and D.B. MacQueen. *The Definition of Standard ML (Revised)*. MIT Press, Cambridge, 1997.

16. G. Mints. *A Short Introduction to Intuitionistic Logic.* Kluwer Academic/Plenum Publishers, 2000.
17. P. Naumov. Importing Isabelle Formal Mathematics into NuPRL. In *Supplemental proceedings of the 12th International Conference on Theorem Proving in Higher Order Logics*, Nice, France, September 1999.
18. P. Naumov. Formalization of Isabelle Meta Logic in NuPRL. In *Supplemental proceedings of the 13th International Conference on Theorem Proving in Higher Order Logics*, pages 141–156, Portland, OR, August 2000.
19. L.C. Paulson. *Isabelle – A Generic Theorem Prover*, volume 828 of *Lecture Notes in Computer Science*. Springer-Verlag, Berlin, 1994.
20. K. Petersson, J. Smith, and B. Nordstroem. *Programming in Martin-Löf's Type Theory. An Introduction.* International Series of Monographs on Computer Science. Oxford: Clarendon Press, 1990.
21. M.-O. Stehr, P. Naumov, and J. Meseguer. A proof-theoretic approach to HOL-Nuprl connection with applications to proof translation (full version). http://cs.hbg.psu.edu/~naumov/Papers/holnuprl.ps, March 2000.
22. M.-O. Stehr, P. Naumov, and J. Meseguer. A proof-theoretic approach to HOL-Nuprl connection with applications to proof translation. In *15th International Workshop on Algebraic Development Techniques*, Genova, Italy, April 2001. To appear. See [21] for the full version.
23. W. Wong. Validation of HOL proofs by proof checking. *Formal Methods in System Design: An International Journal*, 14(2):193–212, 1999.

Formalizing Convex Hull Algorithms

David Pichardie[1] and Yves Bertot[2]

[1] ENS Cachan-Bretagne
David.Pichardie@eleves.bretagne.ens-cachan.fr
[2] INRIA Sophia Antipolis
Yves.Bertot@inria.fr

Abstract. We study the development of formally proved algorithms for computational geometry. The result of this work is a formal description of the basic principles that make convex hull algorithms work and two programs that implement convex hull computation and have been automatically obtained from formally verified mathematical proofs. A special attention has been given to handling degenerate cases that are often overlooked by conventional algorithm presentations.

1 Introduction

Algorithms to compute the convex hull of a collection of points in two or three dimensions abound. The complexity of this problem is known to be approximately the same as for a sorting algorithm in the worst case, but the average complexity depends very much on the distribution of data: some algorithms actually have a complexity of the form $n \times h$, where n is the total number of points and h is the number of points on the convex hull. These algorithms will be more efficient than $nlog(n)$ when few points are on the convex hull. This makes it useful to have several algorithms around.

We have studied two algorithms. The first is an incremental algorithm, where new points are progressively added to the input data. If the new point is outside the convex hull, then it is necessary to add two new edges to the convex hull and remove some others. The second algorithm is known as the package-wrapping algorithm: it follows the intuition of tying a band around the collection of points. At the nth step, the band is already in contact with a few points and the algorithm proceeds by computing what the next point is going to be: if with the band turning clockwise around the points, the next point in the hull is going to be the leftmost remaining point.

All these algorithms rely on an orientation predicate that expresses whether the points of a triangle are enumerated clockwise or counter-clockwise. This orientation predicate is easily computed using the coordinates of the points, but it is meaningless when the points are aligned. Usual presentation of convex hulls algorithms assume that three points in the input data are never aligned.

The structure of convex hull algorithms rely on the fact that the orientation predicate satisfies some properties: for instance the triangles built with four

R.J. Boulton and P.B. Jackson (Eds.): TPHOLs 2001, LNCS 2152, pp. 346–361, 2001.

points have to be oriented in a consistent manner. Knuth [8] describes the minimal properties of the orientation predicates and calls them *axioms*.

Knuth's approach of axioms for convex hulls has the nice property of separating concerns about the properties of arithmetic expressions containing point coordinates and the control structure of algorithms. It has proved a good organization principle for our description and proof development.

Thus, our work contains distinct parts. The first part is about the axioms, and showing that they hold for an implementation predicate. This part involves some numerical computation. The second part describes the main structure of the algorithms based on the axioms, with numeric computation completely avoided. In the last part, we revisit the algorithms to make them robust with respect to degenerate data.

All our proofs have been mechanically checked using the Coq system [2].

1.1 Related Work

Automatic theorem proving and geometry have been in contact for some time. The work in this domain that we are better aware of is that of Chou [5]. In this development, theorems about basic geometric figures like straight lines, triangles and circles are proved automatically, but there is no result about computational geometry *per se*, since algorithms are not the object of the study, but there are other similarities. This work introduces a clever reasoning methods based on surfaces of triangles and ratios of lengths to establish many results (more than 400 theorems, whose proofs are done automatically, are described in the book). This approach using triangle areas is related to the one in this paper, because the determinant we compute actually correspond to the "oriented area" of the triangle being observed. For instance, Axiom 4 can simply be interpreted as the size of triangle being the sum of sub-triangles that compose it. Thus, Chou's work shows before ours the benefit there is to find a different level of abstraction to reason on geometry.

Puitg and Dufourd [9], used the Coq proof system to describe notions of planarity. Work on finding minimal axioms to describe geometric concepts has also been done in constructive proof theory by Jan von Plato [11] and formalized in Coq by Gilles Kahn [7]. Last, we should refer to all the work done on computational geometry, but this domain is far too large to be cited entirely, we can only refer to the books we have used as reference, [6], [3], and [10].

2 Knuth's "Axioms" for Convex Hulls

In what follows, we assume that points are taken from a set P and we describe the orientation predicate as a predicate over three points p, q, r in P, which we denote $\widehat{pqr}$.

Knuth's axioms describe the various ways in which triangles can be looked at and arranged on the plane. The first axiom expresses that when enumerating the points of a triangle, one may start with any of them:

Axiom 1. $\forall p, q, r.\quad \widehat{pqr} \Rightarrow \widehat{qrp}.$

As a corollary of this axiom one also has $\widehat{pqr} \Rightarrow \widehat{rpq}$. This axiom is "cyclic" it can be repeated indefinitely on the same data. For this reason, it impedes automatic proof search procedures.

The second axiom expresses that if a triangle is oriented counter-clockwise, then the same triangle with two points transposed is in fact oriented clockwise.

Axiom 2. $\forall p, q, r.\quad \widehat{pqr} \Rightarrow \neg\widehat{prq}.$

An immediate consequence of the first two axioms is that three points are oriented only if they are pairwise distinct:

$$\forall p, q, r.\quad \widehat{pqr} \Rightarrow p \neq q \wedge q \neq r \wedge r \neq p$$

Many of the lemmas appearing in our development therefore rely on the assumptions that the points being considered are pairwise distinct. We also have a predicate on lists of points expressing that they contain pairwise distinct points.

The third axiom expresses that a triangle is either oriented clockwise or counter-clockwise.

Axiom 3. $\forall p, q, r.\quad p \neq q \Rightarrow q \neq r \Rightarrow p \neq r \Rightarrow \widehat{pqr} \vee \widehat{prq}.$

This affirmation voluntarily overlooks the fact that points may be aligned. This is a tradition of computational geometry that algorithms can be studied without taking care of what are called *degenerate* cases. We will have to study this more carefully later.

The fourth axiom expresses that the four triangles obtained with four arbitrary points may not be oriented in an arbitrary manner: there has to be some sort of consistency, easily understood by observing figure 1.

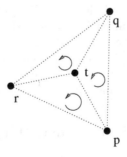

Fig. 1. Axiom 4: Consistent Orientation for Four Triangles.

Axiom 4. $\forall p, q, r, t.\quad \widehat{tqr} \wedge \widehat{ptr} \wedge \widehat{pqt} \Rightarrow \widehat{pqr}.$

The fifth axiom expresses that the orientation predicate may be used to sort points in some way, with a notion that is similar to transitivity. Still one has to be careful to avoid going in circles, this is the reason why this axiom uses 5 points, see figure 2. Clever algorithms use this transitivity-like property to avoid looking at all points.

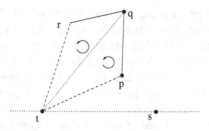

Fig. 2. Axiom 5: Sorting Points in a Half Plane.

Axiom 5. $\forall p, q, r, s, t. \quad \widehat{tsp} \wedge \widehat{tsq} \wedge \widehat{tsr} \wedge \widehat{tpq} \wedge \widehat{tqr} \Rightarrow \widehat{tpr}$

The first three orientation properties express that the three points p, q, and r are in the same half plan. The other three orientation predicates express transitivity: from the point of view of t, if q is left of p and r is left of q, then r is left of p.

There is a variant to this axiom, that can actually be proved using axioms 1, 2, 3, and 5, and which we will refer to by the name *axiom 5'*.

Axiom 5' $\forall p, q, r, s, t. \quad \widehat{stp} \wedge \widehat{stq} \wedge \widehat{str} \wedge \widehat{tpq} \wedge \widehat{tqr} \Rightarrow \widehat{tpr}$

Knuth shows that these axioms are independent. For the case of general positions, these axioms are enough, but if we want our algorithms to be robust for possibly aligned points in the input, there are two possibilities. The first one is to introduce notions that are meaningful for triplets of points that are aligned. In this case, we also use segments and the property that a point belongs to a segment given by its two extremities. This adds up to 9 more axioms, which we do not describe here for the moment. The second solution is to find a way to extend orientation to aligned points in a way that still satisfies the axioms. Perturbation methods as described in [1] provide a satisfactory approach to this.

2.1   Proving the Axioms

When points are given as elements of $\mathbb{R}^2$, the orientation predicate is given by observing the sign of a determinant:

$$\widehat{pqr} \equiv \begin{vmatrix} x_p & y_p & 1 \\ x_q & y_q & 1 \\ x_r & y_r & 1 \end{vmatrix} > 0.$$

In the following we will write $|pqr|$ for this determinant. Knuth's axioms are not proper axioms anymore, they become simple consequences of the properties of addition and multiplication of real numbers.

The proof of Axioms 1 and 2 is given by two equations:

$$|pqr| = |qrp|, \qquad |pqr| = -|prq|.$$

From a mechanical proof point of view, the proofs of these equalities is done painlessly by the usual confluent rewriting system for ring structures, as implemented by the `Ring` tactic in Coq. Axiom 3 simply does not hold in general. When points are aligned, the determinant is null. A common solution to this problem is to consider only data that are in *general position*, that is, assume that no three points given in the problem are ever aligned. We will first follow this practice to get a better idea of the algorithms. In a later section, we will see different solutions to the problem of considering degenerate cases.

In man-made proofs, Axiom 4 relies on an equality obtained from a 4-by-4 determinant that is obviously null, since it has 2 identical columns.

$$\begin{vmatrix} x_p & y_p & 1 & 1 \\ x_q & y_q & 1 & 1 \\ x_r & y_r & 1 & 1 \\ x_t & y_t & 1 & 1 \end{vmatrix} = |pqr| - |tqr| - |ptr| - |pqt| = 0.$$

Proving the right-hand side equality is also a simple matter of equality in a ring structure. Now, if $|tqr|$, $|ptr|$, $|pqt|$ are all strictly positive, then $|pqr|$ is.

Verifying Axiom 5 also relies on an equation, known as Cramer's equation, which has the following form:

$$|stq||tpr| = |tqr||stp| + |tpq||str|$$

Here again, automatically proving this equation is a simple matter of ring based computations.

The conclusion of this section on the orientation predicate is twofold. First numeric computation can be done in a ring rather than in a complete field. This is important as one of the reasons for problems in geometric algorithms is the loss of precision in floating point arithmetic. For convex hulls, floating points are not required. The points may be given by integer coordinates in a small grid. If floating points are used, one may notice that, since the determinant basically is a polynomial of degree two in the coordinates of the three points being considered, it is only necessary to compute the orientation predicate with a precision that is double the precision of the input data.

2.2   The Specification

What is the convex hull of a set of points S? One definition is to describe it as a minimal subset $S' \subset S$, such that all points in S can be described as positive linear combinations of points in S'.

An alternative description of the convex hull uses oriented edges. A possibly open line (i.i. a list of points) S' *encompasses* a set of points S if for any point p in S and any two consecutive points t_i, t_{i+1} in S', $\widehat{t_i t_{i+1} p}$ or $p \in \{t_i t_{i+1}\}$ holds. We consider that a list l is a convex hull of S if l is included in S, l is non-empty if S is not, l contains no duplicates, and if t is the last element of l, then $t \cdot l$, formed by adding t at the head of l, encompasses S. In other terms, the convex hull is defined as a minimal intersection of half-planes.

When a data set is the empty set, a singleton, or a pair, then the convex hull is simply the list enumerating the set's elements.

Knuth chooses the second definition in his monograph. We will also, for several reasons. First, lists are a natural data-structure in the functional programming language we use in our proofs. Second, this definition also relies on the orientation predicate, thus making it possible to forget everything about numerical computation in the main structure of algorithm. Third, most algorithms to compute convex hulls naturally rely on the fact that the intermediary data they construct already is a list of points included in S.

The three parts of the specification are given using inductive definitions on lists (actually we also consider that the input data is given as a list of points).

Still, we have made an effort to establish a bridge between the two definitions. We have mechanically verified a proof that if S' is a convex hull of S and p is an arbitrary point in S, then there exists three points t_i, t_j, and $t_k \in S'$ such that p is inside the triangle formed by t_i, t_j and t_k. This is expressed by the following three orientation predicates:

$$\widehat{t_i t_j p} \quad \widehat{t_j t_k p} \quad \widehat{t_k t_i p}$$

The proof by induction on the length of a convex polygon S' encompassing p works as follows. First, S' cannot be empty, since it encompasses p. If S' is a singleton or a pair, the degenerate p, p, p will do. If the convex polygon contains at least three points, first check whether p is equal to t_1, t_2, or t_3, then compute $\widehat{t_1 t_3 p}$. If any of these conditions holds, then take $t_1 t_2 t_3$. If none of these conditions holds, then p is actually inside the convex polygon defined by $t_1 t_3 \ldots$ You can use an induction hypothesis on this smaller convex polygon to reach the result.

Once you have the three points encompassing p it is possible to show that the coordinates of p are a positive linear combination of the coordinates of the three points. This is simply because the coordinates of p verify the following equation:

$$p \times |t_i t_j t_k| = t_i \times |t_j t_k p| + t_j \times |t_k t_i p| + t_k \times |t_i t_j p|$$

This equation is easily verified using the ring decision procedure.

If $\widehat{t_i t_j p}$, $\widehat{t_j t_k p}$, and $\widehat{t_k t_i p}$ hold, then the three determinants on the right-hand side are positive and by Axiom 4 the determinant on the left-hand side also is. Dividing by this determinant is legitimate and p really is obtained by a positive linear combination of the t's. The cases where the convex hull contains less than three points are also easy to prove. Notice that this proof requires that we work in a field.

2.3   Finding Initial Data

Some algorithms require that one should be able to find one or two points that are already present in the convex hull to start with. The package-wrapping algorithm is among them. The usual technique is to look for the minimal point using a lexical ordering on the coordinates.

If t is the minimal point for the lexical ordering on coordinates, and if p, q, and r are points distinct to t and forming a triangle encompassing t, where the first coordinates of p, q, and r are such $p_1 \geq r_1$ then it is necessary that $r_1 \geq q_1$. Using this result again, we have $p_1 \geq r_1 \Rightarrow r_1 \geq p_1$. Thus all three first coordinates must be equal. But if they are, the points are aligned and cannot constitute a proper triangle.

Once we have the point t whose coordinates are minimal for the lexicographic order, we find its right neighbor by finding the point that is minimal for the order $\prec$ defined by:

$$p \prec q \Leftrightarrow \widehat{tpq}$$

The relation $\prec$ is transitive on the input data, because t is minimal for the lexical order.

3   Proving Algorithms

In this section we review the descriptions and proofs for the abstract setting: positions are general (no three points are aligned) and all numerical computation is hidden behind the orientation predicate and the function producing initial points.

3.1   The Incremental Algorithm

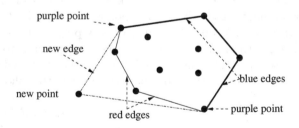

Fig. 3. Red and Blue Edges in the Incremental Algorithm.

The incremental algoritm works by taking the points of the input data one by one and constructing the convex hull of all the points seen so far. At each step, either the new point already lies inside the current convex hull and one can directly proceed to the next, or some edges need to be removed and two edges need to be added. All tests rely on the orientation predicate.

The edges from the previous convex hull are sorted into two categories, called *blue* and *red* edges (see figure 3). Blue edges represent edges, for which the new point lies on the good side. In our description we also say that an edge is blue if the new point is one of the extremities. Red edges are the other. When all edges are blue, the point is inside. All edges cannot be red at the same time and red edges are contiguous. We actually work with lists of points, but we view them as list of edges, considering the edges between successive points.

When looking for red edges there may be four cases:

1. no red edges (including no edges at all),
2. the edge between the last point of the list and the first point of the list (the closing edge) is red, but the last edge of the list is not,
3. the closing edge is red and the last edge too,
4. the closing edge is blue.

In the first case, nothing needs to be done. In the second case, the list of edges can be viewed as the concatenation of two lists, l_r and l_b, such that l_r contains only red edges l_b contains only blue edges, and the edge between the last element in l_r and the first element in l_b is red. This relies on the property that the list describing the convex hull has no duplicates. In this case, the result is the list $p \cdot l_b$. To prove this, we need to show that p is not already in the list (easy), that the new point p is in the input data (easy), that p is left of all the edges in the convex hull (easy, since the edges that are kept are all blue, and the two new edges have p at the extremity), and that all the data considered so far is left of the edges tp and pt', where t and t' are the purple points, the last and first elements of l_b, respectively. The point t is different from t' because there is a red edge (see figure 4). Since t and t' are distinct, there exists a t_k distinct from t

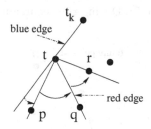

Fig. 4. Using Axiom 5′ to Justify Adding an Edge.

that is last-but-one in l_b. Let q be the other extremity of the first red edge, and let r be an arbitrary point among those that have already been processed. By construction, we have $\widehat{t_k t r}$, $\widehat{t_k t q}$, and $\widehat{t q r}$. Because tq is red we don't have $\widehat{t q p}$. By Axiom 3, this gives $\widehat{t p q}$. Because $t_k t$ is blue, we have $\widehat{t_k t p}$. All hypotheses are present to use Axiom 5' and conclude that $\widehat{tpr}$ holds. The proof for $\widehat{pt'r}$ has the same structure, but uses Axiom 5.

The two other cases are solved by rotating the convex hull to return to the second case. Rotating a convex hull is simply decomposing this convex hull as the concatenation of two lists. In the following, we will denote concatenation of two lists l_1 and l_2 as $l_1 \bullet l_2$. Since concatenation is a simple structural recursive function (recursive over the first argument), it is a simple matter of structural recursion over l_1 to show that rotation preserves inclusion in another list, that it preserves the absence of duplicate elements, and that it preserves encompassing. Thus, if $l_2 \bullet l_1$ is a convex hull of l, $l_1 \bullet l_2$ also is.

For the third case, one traverses down the list representing the convex hull until one finds the first point t_j such that $t_{j-1}t_j$ is blue and t_jt_{j+1} is red. In that case the rotation is given by $l_2 = t_j \cdots t$ and $l_1 = t_1 \cdots t_j$. If t_i is the first point in l_1 such that the edge $t_{i-1}t_i$ is red and the edge t_it_{i+1} is blue, then one has: $l_r = t_j \cdots t \bullet (t_1 \cdots t_{i-1})$ and $l_b = t_{i+1}t_j$.

The fourth case is symmetric to the third one. One also needs to find the two *purple* points that are boundaries between blue and red edges but they are in reverse order.

The main algorithm repeats this computation for each point. It is programmed as a simple structural recursion over the list of inputs.

3.2   The Package-Wrapping Algorithm

The package-wrapping algorithm relies on the possibility to find an initial edge that is known to be part of the convex hull, then it proceeds by constructing an open encompassing list l of pairwise distinct points, included in the data, finding the right neighbour of the first element in the list at each step. At each step one compares the right neigbour with the last element of the list. When the two points are equal, the algorithm terminates without adding the current list. When the two points are different, the right neigbour is added to the list and recursion restarts (see figure 5). During the recursion the list always has at least

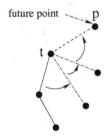

Fig. 5. Intermediary Iteration for the Package-Wrapping Algorithm.

two elements, let t be the head and s be the second element. Finding t's right neighbour is done by finding the greatest element for the relation $\prec$ defined by

$$p \prec q \Leftrightarrow \widehat{tpq}.$$

This relation is not reflexive, but its reflexive closure is a total order, thanks to Axioms 2, 3, and 5. Finding the least element of a list for an arbitrary order is an easy piece of functional programming, and it is also easily proved correct. If p is this greatest element, $\widehat{tqp}$ holds for every point in the input data, and by Axiom 1 $\widehat{ptq}$ also holds. Thus the input data is left of the edge pt and the list $p \cdot l$ also encompasses the input data.

A key ingredient to proving the termination of the algorithm is to ensure that the list being constructed never contains duplicate elements and is included in the input data. The hardest part is to show that checking that p is distinct from the last element of l is enough to ensure that p does not belong to l. In fact, if t is the head of the list, t' is the last element and q is another element of the list, one needs to show that $\widehat{tqt'}$ holds. This is done by recursion over the length of list l but there are many intricacies with base cases, because the proof relies on Axiom 5, which needs 5 distinct points. Let us have a look at this proof.

First assume q is the second element of the list, $\widehat{tqt'}$ comes easily from the fact that the list encompasses the input data and t' is in the input data. Then if q is not the second element of the list, let t_1 be this second element. We do the proof by structural recursion over the list $q \cdots t'$. If this list is reduced to 0 or 1 element, this is contradictory with our hypotheses, if this list has two elements, then qt' is an edge from the list, and $\widehat{qt't}$ holds because t is in the input data. The result then comes from Axiom 1. If the list $q \cdots t'$ has more than two elements, let q' be the second element, one has $\widehat{tq't'}$ by induction hypothesis, $\widehat{tqq'}$ because qq' encompasses the input data and thanks to Axiom 1. Moreover, the properties $\widehat{tt_1q}$, $\widehat{tt_1q'}$, and $\widehat{tt_1t'}$ hold, because q, q', and t' are in the input data. This is enough to use axiom 5 and conclude.

Now, the package-wrapping algorithm is not structural recursive. The termination argument is that the size of the list l is bounded by the size of the input data, because all its elements are pairwise distinct, and that this size increases at each step. For this reason, the function is defined using Coq's solution for defining well-founded recursive functions. This means that we have to exhibit a set containing the principal argument of the recursive function and a well-founded order on this set and show that recursive calls are done only on smaller terms.

The set L_S we exhibit is the set of lists that are included in the input data S and contain no duplicates. In Coq's type theory, this set is described as a type using dependently typed inductive types. We show that the length of a list in in this set is always smaller than the size N of the input data S. We define the order $<_S$ to be :

$$l <_S l' \Leftrightarrow N - length(l) < N - length(l').$$

Proving that this order is well-founded is a simple application of theorems about composing well-founded orders with functions provided in Coq's libraries. In other theorem provers where the termination of recursive functions is ensured by exhibiting measure functions, the measure function to exhibit is the following one:

$$f : l \mapsto N - length(l).$$

At each recursive step, the main argument is l and the argument for the next recursive call is $p \cdot l$ such that $p \cdot l \in L_S$, therefore one has $length(p) < length(p \cdot l) \leq N$ and $f(p \cdot l) < f(l)$.

4   Degenerate Cases

If we want to allow for aligned points in the input data, we need to review our technique. One solution is to change Axiom 3, since it is the one that assumes that a triple of points can always be viewed as a triangle. If we do that, any decision taken with respect to orientation in the algorithms must be reviewed and replaced by a new decision taking extra cases into account. The structure of the algorithm remains, but all the details of its control-flow are deformed by this constraint.

A second solution is to change the orientation predicate so that it satisfies all five axioms even in the presence of aligned triples. This solution somehow imposes that one changes the definition of convex hulls, since our definition relies on the orientation predicate. We shall see that both solutions actually require that we relax our definition of a convex hull.

4.1   Segments

When three distinct points are aligned, one of them lies between the two other. We introduce a new predicate, written $]pqr[$ to express that q occurs inside the segment pr. Axiom 3 is changed to obtain the following formulation:

Axiom 3 $\forall p, q, r. \quad p = q \lor q = r \lor p = r \lor \widehat{pqr} \lor \widehat{prq} \lor]pqr[\lor]qrp[\lor]rpq[.$

In Knuth's work, Axioms 1-5 express a form of internal consistency for the orientation predicate. We need to have the same kind of internal consistency for the segment predicate and between segments and oriented triangles. The first two axioms describe internal consistency for three aligned points.

Axiom 6. $\forall p, q, r. \quad]pqr[\Rightarrow]rqp[.$

Axiom 7. $\forall p, q, r. \quad]pqr[\Rightarrow \neg]qpr[.$

The next five axioms describe consistency between segments and triangles.

Axiom 8. $\forall p, q, r. \quad]pqr[\Rightarrow \neg \widehat{pqr}.$

Axiom 9. $\forall p, q, r, t. \quad \widehat{pqr} \land]ptq[\Rightarrow \widehat{ptr}.$

Axiom 10. $\forall p, q, r, t. \quad \widehat{pqr} \land]pqt[\Rightarrow \widehat{ptr}.$

Axiom 11. $\forall p, q, r, t. \quad \widehat{pqr} \land]ptq[\Rightarrow \widehat{tqr}.$

Axiom 12. $\forall p, q, r, t.\ \widehat{pqr} \wedge \rceil tpq\lceil \Rightarrow \widehat{tqr}.$

The last two axioms describe internal consistency of segments for four aligned points.

Axiom 13. $\forall p, q, r, t.\ \rceil qrt\lceil \wedge \rceil pqt\lceil \Rightarrow \rceil prt\lceil.$

Axiom 14. $\forall p, q, r, t.\ \rceil qrt\lceil \wedge \rceil pqr\lceil \Rightarrow \rceil prt\lceil.$

With these new notions, we change the specification of a convex hull for a set S to be a list of points $t_1 \ldots t_k$ such that for every p in S and every t_i, t_j such that $t_j = t_{i+1}$ or $t_j = t_1$ if $t_i = t_k$ one has $\widehat{t_i t_j p} \vee \rceil t_i p t_j\lceil.$

4.2   The Working Horse Predicate

In the new setting we use a new predicate that combines orientation and segment membership. For the rest of the paper, we will denote this predicate $\overline{pqr}$, with the following meaning:

$$\overline{pqr} \Leftrightarrow \widehat{pqr} \vee r \in \{p, q\} \vee \rceil prq\lceil.$$

Generalizing our algorithms to the degenerate cases works by replacing the orientation predicate by the new predicate wherever it occurs and adding a few equality tests to take care of degeneracies. What matters really is that equivalents of Axiom 5 still hold:

$$\forall p, q, r, s, t.\ \overline{tsp} \wedge \overline{tsq} \wedge \overline{tsr} \wedge \neg\overline{qtp} \wedge \overline{qtr} \Rightarrow \overline{ptr}$$

$$\forall p, q, r, s, t.\ \overline{stp} \wedge \overline{stq} \wedge \overline{str} \wedge \neg\overline{tqp} \wedge \overline{tqr} \Rightarrow \overline{tpr}.$$

Thus, if t is known to be on the convex hull, we keep the property that the order $\prec'$ can be used to find minimal and maximal elements, when this order is defined as follows:

$$p \prec' q \Leftrightarrow \overline{tpq}.$$

4.3   Perturbations

An alternative approach is to change the orientation predicate so that Axiom 3 always holds. This option seems awkward: if we change the orientation predicate how can we be sure that we actually compute the same convex hull? The answer is to make sure that we change the orientation predicate in a manner that remains consistent with the general orientation predicate, so that the convex hull computed in non-degenerate cases is unchanged.

The solution we are going to present is based on the idea that if points are aligned, then moving one of the points only slightly will remove the degeneracy. This make it possible to compute an approximation of the hull. However, points are not actually moved, and all points that should appear on the convex hull will be guaranteed to appear in the approximation we compute. Imprecisions will occur only for points that are on the segment between two legitimate vertices of the convex hull. For these points, this method may or may not include them in the resulting convex hull.

The solution is to consider that all points are moving in a continuous manner and that the configuration that is being studied is the snapshot at date $t = 0$. The determinants used to compute the orientation predicate also are continuous functions in t, that may have the value 0 when $t = 0$. The orientation predicate is continuous for all unaligned triples. However, if the perturbation function can be viewed as a polynomial function in t it is possible to ensure that $\lim_{t \to 0+}$ is either positive or negative. If the points are not aligned, the limit is the same as the value in 0, if there are aligned points, taking a value of t that is small enough will always return the same sign, so that we do not even have to predict the value of t: the sign can be predicted from the signs of the polynomial coefficient.

We use a function taken from [1] to indicate how all points move. The coordinates of the point p actually are given by the formula $x_p + t \times y_p, y_p + t \times (x_p^2 + y_p^2)$. The orientation predicate for points x, y, z then becomes the following term:

$$\begin{vmatrix} x_p + t \times y_p & y_p + t \times (x_p^2 + y_p^2) & 1 \\ x_q + t \times y_q & y_q + t \times (x_q^2 + y_q^2) & 1 \\ x_r + t \times y_r & y_r + t \times (x_r^2 + y_r^2) & 1 \end{vmatrix} = D_1 + D_2 \times t + D_3 \times t^2,$$

where D_1, D_2, and D_3 are the determinants defined as follows:

$$D_1 = \begin{vmatrix} x_p & y_p & 1 \\ x_q & y_q & 1 \\ x_r & y_r & 1 \end{vmatrix}, \qquad D_2 = \begin{vmatrix} x_p & x_p^2 + y_p^2 & 1 \\ x_q & x_q^2 + y_q^2 & 1 \\ x_r & x_r^2 + y_r^2 & 1 \end{vmatrix}, \qquad D_3 = \begin{vmatrix} y_p & x_p^2 + y_p^2 & 1 \\ y_q & x_q^2 + y_q^2 & 1 \\ y_r & x_r^2 + y_r^2 & 1 \end{vmatrix}.$$

The proof that not all three determinants can be zero is formalized using the sketch provided in [1] and relies very much on deciding equalities in a ring, plus a lot of painful reasoning on equalities. However, we work on polynomials and all our proofs are done in an ordered archimedian field: the field of rational numbers suffices so that our model is adequate for arithmetic numbers as they are implemented in computers.

If the first determinant is 0, then the three points are aligned. There exists three numbers m_1, m_2, and m_3 such that $m_1 \times x = m_2 \times y + m_3$ is the equation of the line containing the three points. As these points are distinct, m_1 and m_2 cannot both be null. There are two cases, depending on whether $m_1 = 0$.

If $m_1 = 0$, then $y_p = y_q = y_r$, the second determinant is equal to the following determinant:

$$\begin{vmatrix} x_p & x_p^2 + y_p^2 & 1 \\ x_q & x_q^2 + y_q^2 & 1 \\ x_r & x_r^2 + y_r^2 & 1 \end{vmatrix} = \begin{vmatrix} x_p & x_p^2 & 1 \\ x_q & x_q^2 & 1 \\ x_r & x_r^2 & 1 \end{vmatrix}$$

$$= (x_p - x_q)(x_q - x_r)(x_r - x_p). \tag{1}$$

This value can only be zero if one of the factors is 0, in which case two of the points have both coordinates equal: they are the same.

If $m_1 \neq 0$, $D_2 = 0$ if and only if $m_1 \times D_2 = 0$.

$$m_1^2 \times \begin{vmatrix} y_p & x_p^2 + y_p^2 & 1 \\ y_q & x_q^2 + y_q^2 & 1 \\ y_r & x_r^2 + y_r^2 & 1 \end{vmatrix} = (m_1^2 + m_2^2) \begin{vmatrix} y_p & y_p^2 & 1 \\ y_q & y_q^2 & 1 \\ y_r & y_r^2 & 1 \end{vmatrix}$$

$$= (m_1^2 + m_2^2)(y_p - y_q)(y_q - y_r)(y_r - y_p) \qquad (2)$$

Here again, at least two of the points must have the same vertical coordinate for the determinant to be 0.

The same reasoning applies to the third determinant, which is symmetric with the second one, replacing x coordinates with y coordinates and vice-versa.

Now for every triple of points, the values D_1, D_2, and D_3 cannot be 0 at the same time. We can then show that for every triple p, q, r in the input data, there exists a number ϵ_{pqr} such that the perturbed determinant never becomes 0 in the interval $]0, \epsilon_{pqr}[$. Let $|x|$ be the absolute value of x. If D_1 is non null, then we can choose ϵ_{pqr} to be the following value:

$$\epsilon_{pqr} = min\left(1, \left|\frac{D_1}{2 \times D_2}\right|, \left|\frac{D_1}{2 \times D_3}\right|\right)$$

If $D_2 = 0$ or $D_3 = 0$, just ignore the corresponding term in the computation.

If $D_1 = 0$ and $D_3 \neq 0$, then we can choose ϵ_{pqr} to be the following value:

$$\epsilon_{pqr} = min\left(1, \left|\frac{D_2}{D_3}\right|\right).$$

If $D_1 = 0$ and $D_3 = 0$ we can take any positive value for ϵ_{pqr}.

This concludes the proof of existence of ϵ_{pqr}. This proof was also made only using axioms that are fulfilled by the field of rational numbers.

We could now replace the orientation predicate used in the previous section by a new orientation predicate, noted $\overline{\overline{pqr}}$ and defined in the following manner:

$$\overline{\overline{pqr}} = \begin{vmatrix} x_p & y_p & 1 \\ x_q & y_q & 1 \\ x_r & y_r & 1 \end{vmatrix} > 0$$

$$\vee \begin{vmatrix} x_p & y_p & 1 \\ x_q & y_q & 1 \\ x_r & y_r & 1 \end{vmatrix} = 0 \wedge \begin{vmatrix} y_p & x_p^2 + y_p^2 & 1 \\ y_q & x_q^2 + y_q^2 & 1 \\ y_r & x_r^2 + y_r^2 & 1 \end{vmatrix} > 0$$

$$\vee \begin{vmatrix} x_p & y_p & 1 \\ x_q & y_q & 1 \\ x_r & y_r & 1 \end{vmatrix} = \begin{vmatrix} y_p & x_p^2 + y_p^2 & 1 \\ y_q & x_q^2 + y_q^2 & 1 \\ y_r & x_r^2 + y_r^2 & 1 \end{vmatrix} = 0 \wedge \begin{vmatrix} x_p & x_p^2 + y_p^2 & 1 \\ x_q & x_q^2 + y_q^2 & 1 \\ x_r & x_r^2 + y_r^2 & 1 \end{vmatrix} > 0$$

Note that the ϵ_{pqr} are never computed, we only show their existence to show that the computation of these three determinants is enough to predict the orientations for a general position that is arbitrarily close to the input data. It is not necessary to return a convex hull composed of perturbed points: the points from the input data are correct, since they can be shown to be arbitrarily closed to a legitimate convex hull (we have not done this proof yet).

It is also interesting that the convex hull computation done in this manner returns exactly the same result as the computation described in previous section if the input data is not degenerate. If the input data is degenerate and the convex hulls are required to contain no aligned points, a trivial traversal of the list of points may be needed to remove the useless points. The cost of this traversal should be proportional to the total cost.

It is remarkable that testing the sign of the D_2 can be done by simply combining the signs of the terms $(y_p - y_q)$, $(y_q - y_r)$, $(y_r - y_p)$, according to equations (1) and (2). In fact, D_2 is strictly positive if and only if the line carrying the three points is not horizontal, the point r is outside the segment pq, and the points p and q are ordered in their first coordinate, similarly for D_3. As a result, testing the sign of D_2 and D_3 is equivalent to testing whether r is outside the segment pq and whether p and q are ordered lexicographically. Thus, we have a program that computes $\overline{(pqr)}$ without computing the larger determinants above. This algebraic reasoning brings an elegant justification to the use of segment predicates and lexical ordering in combination with traditional orientation.

5   Conclusion

The development of certified algorithms is well suited to domains where it is easy to have a mathematical formulation of the data and the specifications. Computational geometry is one of these domains. Euclidean geometry makes it easy to connect the various notions encountered in computational geometry to real analysis and algebra. In our experiment, the presence of a decision procedure for ring equalities has been instrumental, although it has also been quite annoying that this decision procedure was not complete, at least for the version we used. This decision procedure Ring, a tactic based on a reflective approach [4].

The problem of numeric computation also deserves some thoughts. We have performed our proofs with an "axiomatized" set of numbers for the coordinates. The axioms we have taken were carefully chosen to make them accurate as a representation of computer numbers used in exact computation. These numbers live in an archimedian field. The model for the field that is needed to express the correction of the algorithm is the field of rational numbers. However, the algorithm does not actually use numbers in the whole field. It only computes a polynomial expression of degree two, so that if the numbers describing input data are bounded, the set of numbers needed for the algorithm to work is much smaller. It could be useful to express the difference between the "concrete" arithmetic used in the algorithm, and the "abstract" arithmetic used in the proof. This is actually the spirit of the work of Laurent Théry and his colleagues in a project to study computer arithmetics.

Perturbation methods are used in other parts of computational geometry, for instance for Delaunay triangulation, where degenerate positions occur when four points are cocyclic. They seem very well adapted as a method to make algorithms robust to degeneracy without changing their structure. Still, one has to be aware that we changed the specification of the problem when we changed the orientation predicate, since the specification is expressed using this predicate.

We actually heard about the perturbation method after having done most of the proofs for the algorithm based on the extended axioms combining the traditional orientation and segment predicates. Still both developments are useful in their own right, since the first development can be tuned to include or exclude colinear points from the convex hull at will, while the second is not as flexible.

We would like to acknowledge the help of several researchers from the computational geometry group at INRIA Sophia Antipolis. In particular, Mariette Yvinec pointed us to Knuth's work on axioms and Olivier Devillers described us the perturbation method.

References

1. Pierre Alliez, Olivier Devillers, and Jack Snoeyink. Removing degeneracies by perturbing the problem or the world. *Reliable Computing*, 6:61–79, 2000. Special Issue on Computational Geometry.
2. Bruno Barras, Samuel Boutin, Cristina Cornes, Judicael Courant, Yann Coscoy, David Delahaye, Jean-Christophe Filliatre Daniel de Rauglaudre, Eduardo Gimenez, Hugo Herbelin, Gerard Huet, Cesar Munoz, Chetan Murthy, Catherine Parent, Christine Paulin-Mohring, Amokrane Saibi, and Benjamin Werner. *The Coq Proof Assistant User's Guide. Version 6.3.1.* INRIA, December 1999.
3. Jean-Daniel Boissonnat and Mariette Yvinec. *Algorithmic geometry*. Cambridge University Press, 1995.
4. Samuel Boutin. Using reflection to build efficient and certified decision procedures. In *Theoretical Aspects of Computer Science*, number 1281 in Lecture Notes in Computer Science. Springer-Verlag, 1997.
5. S.C. Chou, X.S. Gao, and J.Z. Zhang. *Machine Proofs in Geometry*. World Scientific, Singapore, 1994.
6. Thomas H. Cormen, Charles E. Leiserson, and Ronald L. Rivest. *Introduction to algorithms*. MIT-Press, 1990.
7. Gilles Kahn. Elements of constructive geometry group theory and domain theory, 1995. Available as a Coq contribution at http://coq.inria.fr/contribs-eng.html.
8. Donald Knuth. *Axioms and Hulls*. Number 606 in Lecture Notes in Computer Science. Springer-Verlag, 1991.
9. François Puitg and Jean-François Dufourd. Formal specification and theorem proving breakthroughs in geometric modeling. In *Theorem Proving in Higher-Order Logics*, volume 1479 of *Lecture Notes in Computer Science*, pages 410–422. Springer-Verlag, 1998.
10. Robert Sedgewick. *Algorithms*. Addison-Wesley, 1988.
11. Jan von Plato. A constructive theory of ordered affine geometry. *Indagationes Mathematicae*, 9:549–562, 1998.

Experiments with Finite Tree Automata in Coq[*]

Xavier Rival[1,2] and Jean Goubault-Larrecq[1,3]

[1] GIE Dyade, INRIA Rocquencourt
Domaine de Voluceau B.P. 105, 78153 Le Chesnay Cedex, France
[2] Ecole Normale Supérieure
45, rue d'Ulm, 75005 Paris, France
[3] LSV, ENS Cachan
61, av. du président-Wilson, 94235 Cachan Cedex, France

Abstract. Tree automata are a fundamental tool in computer science. We report on experiments to integrate tree automata in Coq using shallow and deep reflection techniques. While shallow reflection seems more natural in this context, it turns out to give disappointing results. Deep reflection is more difficult to apply, but is more promising.

1 Introduction

Finite-state automata, and more generally tree automata [7], are of fundamental importance in computer science, and in particular in hardware or software verification (see e.g. [12]). One particular domain of interest to the authors is cryptographic protocol verification, where tree automata [13] and slight extensions of them [9] have been used with success. In this domain in particular—but this is already true to some extent in verification in general—it is important to *document* the process by which verification is deemed to be complete, as well as to be able to *convince* any third party that the result of verification is correct. Both goals can be achieved by producing a formal proof in some trusted proof assistant. Our aim in this paper is to report on experience we gained in producing formal proofs of correctness of computations on tree automata in Coq [1]. As we shall see, there are many possible approaches to this apparently simple problem, and several unexpected pitfalls to each.

We survey related work in Section 2, recall the features of Coq that we shall use in Section 3, and give a short introduction to finite tree automata in Section 4. We study the most promising technique to check tree automata computations done by an external tool in Coq, namely *shallow reflection*, in Section 5. Rather surprisingly, this yields disastrous performance. We discuss reasons for this failure at the end of this section. This prompts us to investigate *deep reflection* in Section 6: in deep reflection, the algorithms themselves are coded, proved, and run in the target proof assistant. While this is a complex task to engage in, and seems to provide little return on investments, it is worthwhile to investigate, considering the results of Section 5. We shall see in Section 6 that this actually yields encouraging results. We conclude in Section 7.

---

[*] This work was done as part of Dyade, a common venture between Bull S.A. and INRIA.

R.J. Boulton and P.B. Jackson (Eds.): TPHOLs 2001, LNCS 2152, pp. 362–377, 2001.

2   Related Work

There does not seem to have been any work yet on integrating automata-theoretic techniques with proof assistants. Works like [14] are notable exceptions, and deal with extended automata that really are concurrent programs which a proof assistant is called to reason about. We rather wish to use automata as a means of augmenting the capabilites of proof assistants, using external tools. This is *shallow reflection*, where the external tool constructs a trace of its verification, which can then be checked by the given proof assistant. For instance, this is how Harrison [10,11] integrates computations done by an external binary decision diagram package, resp. an implementation of Stålmarck's algorithm into HOL. Similarly, the model-checker of Yu and Luo [18] outputs a proof that can be checked by Lego.

Shallow reflection has many advantages. First, it is a safe way to extend the capabilities of proof assistants in practice, as the core of the proof assistant is not modified or enriched in any way: the proof assistant still only trusts arguments it (re)checks. Second, the external tool can be swapped for another, provided the new one is instrumented to output traces that the proof assistant can still check. This is important for maintenance, where tools can be optimized or upgraded easily enough, with only an instrumentation effort. Third, it is much easier to check a series of computations done by an external algorithm A that to prove that A itself is correct.

However, some applications seem to require the latter, where algorithm A itself is coded, proved and run inside the proof assistant. This approach is called *deep reflection*, and was pioneered in [17,3]. In Coq, one first application is Boutin's Ring tactic [2] deciding equalities in the theory of rings, mixing shallow and deep reflection. One of the largest deep reflection endeavours is certainly the work by Verma *et al.* [16], where binary decision diagrams are integrated in Coq through total reflection. In the last two cases, total reflection was called for, as traces produced by external tools would have grown far too much to be usable in practice: this is the case for binary decision diagrams, as Harrison shows [10]. Total reflection can roughly be thought as "replacing proofs in the logic by computations", and will be described in more detail in Section 3.

3   A Short Tour of Coq

Coq is a proof assistant based on the Calculus of Inductive Constructions (CIC), a type theory that is powerful enough to formalize most of mathematics. It properly includes higher-order intuitionistic logic, augmented with definitional mechanisms for inductively defined types, sets, propositions and relations. CIC is also a typed λ-calculus, and can therefore also be used as a programming language. We describe here the main features of Coq that we shall need later.

Among the *sorts* of CIC are Prop, the sort of all propositions, and Set, the sort of all specifications, programs and data types. What it means for Prop to be the sort of propositions is that any object F : Prop (read: F of type Prop) denotes a proposition, i.e., a formula. In turn, any object π : F is a *proof* π of F. A formula is considered proved in Coq whenever we have succeeded to find a proof of it. Proofs are written, at least internally, as λ-terms, but we shall be content to know that we can produce them with the help of *tactics*, allowing one to write proofs by reducing the goal to subgoals, and eventually to immediate, basic inferences.

Similarly, any object t : Set denotes a data type, like the data type $\mathbb{N}$ of natural numbers, or the type $\mathbb{N} \to \mathbb{N}$ of all functions from naturals to naturals. Data types can, and will usually be, defined inductively: e.g., the standard definition of $\mathbb{N}$ in Coq is by giving its two constructors $0 : \mathbb{N}$ and $S : \mathbb{N} \to \mathbb{N}$; that is, as the smallest set containing $0 : \mathbb{N}$ and such that $S(n) : \mathbb{N}$ for any $n : \mathbb{N}$. In particular, every natural number must be of the form $S(\ldots S(0) \ldots)$, which is expressed by Peano's induction principle.

If t : Set, and $p : t$, we say that p is a *program* of type t. Programs in Coq are purely functional: the language of programs is based on a λ-calculus with variables, application pq of p to q, abstraction $[x : T]p$ (the function mapping each x of type T to p), case splits (e.g., Cases n of $0 \Rightarrow v \mid S(m) \Rightarrow fm$ end either returns v if $n = 0$, or fm if n is of the form $S(m)$), and functions defined by structural recursion on their last argument. For soundness reasons, Coq refuses to accept any non-terminating function. In fact, Coq refuses to acknowledge any definition of a recursive function that is not primitive recursive, even though its termination might be obvious.

In general, propositions and programs can be mixed. We shall exploit this in a very limited form: when π and π' are programs (a.k.a., descriptions of data), then $\pi = \pi'$ is a proposition, expressing that π and π' have the same value. Deep reflection can then be implemented as follows: given a property $P : T \to$ Prop, write a program $\pi : T \to$ bool deciding P (where bool is the inductive type of Booleans). Then prove the correctness lemma $\forall x : T \cdot \pi(x) = \text{true} \to P(x)$. To show $P(a)$, apply the correctness lemma: it remains to prove that $\pi(a) = \text{true}$. If this is indeed so, one call to the Reflexivity tactic will verify that the left-hand side indeed reduces to true, by *computing* with program π. At this point, the proof of $P(a)$ will be complete.

Not only data structures, but also predicates can be defined by induction. This corresponds to the mathematical practice of defining the smallest set or relation such that a number of conditions are satisfied. For instance, we may define the binary relation $\leq$ on natural numbers as having constructors le_n $: \forall n : \mathbb{N} \cdot n \leq n$ and le_S $: \forall n, m : \mathbb{N} \cdot n \leq m \to n \leq S(m)$. This defines it as the smallest binary relation such that $n \leq n$ for all $n \in \mathbb{N}$ (the le_n clause) and such that whenever $n \leq m$, then $n \leq m + 1$ (the le_S clause). Note that the constructors le_n and le_S play the role of clause names, whose types are Horn clauses. (In Prolog notation, they would be $n \leq n$ and $n \leq S(m) \leftarrow n \leq m$.) It is in fact useful to think of inductively defined predicates as sets of Horn clauses, a.k.a. pure Prolog programs.

4   Tree Automata

A *signature* Σ is a collection of so-called *function symbols* f, together with natural numbers n called *arities*. We shall always assume that Σ is finite. The set $T(\Sigma, X)$ of first-order *terms*, a.k.a. *trees*, over Σ with variables in X is defined inductively by: $x \in T(\Sigma, X)$ for every $x \in X$, and $f(t_1, \ldots, t_n)$ for every n-ary function symbol f and every $t_1, \ldots, t_n \in T(\Sigma, X)$. Elements of $T(\Sigma, \emptyset)$ are called *ground terms* over Σ. Note that there is a ground term over Σ if and only if Σ contains at least one constant, i.e., one 0-ary function symbol. In the sequel, we shall assume Σ fixed.

Tree automata are finite data structures that represent possibly infinite sets of terms, the so-called *regular tree languages*. (As in [7], we only consider languages of *finite* terms. For more information on regular infinite term languages, see [15].) Tree automata generalize ordinary (word) finite-state automata, where the word $a_1 a_2 \ldots a_n$ is represented as the linear term $a_1(a_2(\ldots(a_n(\epsilon))\ldots))$, where $a_1, a_2, \ldots, a_n$ are unary (arity 1) function symbols and ϵ is a distinguished end-of-word constant.

There are many ways in which tree automata, not to mention regular tree languages, can be described [7]. While they are all equivalent in theory, the precise choice of data structure weighs heavily on algorithms working on them. We define:

Definition 1 (Tree Automata). *A tree automaton $\mathcal{A}$ is a tuple (Q, F, Δ), where Q is a finite set of so-called states q, $F \subseteq Q$ is the subset of final states, and Δ is a finite set of transitions $f(q_1, \ldots, q_n) \to q$, where f is an n-ary function symbol, and $q_1, \ldots, q_n, q$ are states in Q.*

A ground term t is recognized at q in $\mathcal{A}$ if and only if the judgment $\mathrm{Rec}(q, t)$ is derivable in the system whose rules are:

$$\frac{\mathrm{Rec}(q_1, t_1) \quad \ldots \quad \mathrm{Rec}(q_n, t_n)}{\mathrm{Rec}(q, f(t_1, \ldots, t_n))} \text{ (Rec)}$$

where $f(q_1, \ldots, q_n) \to q$ ranges over Δ. The term t is recognized by $\mathcal{A}$ if and only if it is recognized at some final state (in F).

It might seem curious that tree automata do not have any *initial* states. Their roles are taken up by nullary transitions. Consider for example the automaton of Figure 1(a). The state q_{even} (resp. $q_{\mathrm{list_{e}ven}}$) recognizes even natural numbers (resp. lists of even natural numbers). Transitions are represented by arrows labeled by a constructor. Then the constant term 0 is recognized at q_{even} by following the nullary transition $0 \to q_{\mathrm{even}}$. Note also that we have transitions of arity more than 1: consider the transition $\mathrm{cons}(q_{\mathrm{even}}, q_{\mathrm{list\text{-}even}}) \to q_{\mathrm{list\text{-}even}}$ pictured around the $\mathrm{cons}(\_, \_)$ label in the upper right. The circled state $q_{\mathrm{list\text{-}even}}$ is the only final state.

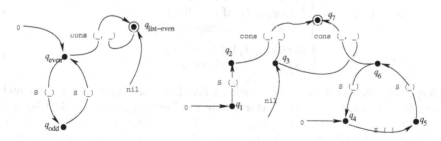

(a) Lists of Even Natural Numbers.

(b) One Element Lists Containing 1 or $3k + 2$, $k \in \mathbb{N}$.

Fig. 1. Tree Automata.

A classic alternate description of tree automata is through the use of rewrite systems [5]: tree automata are then rewrite systems consisting of rules of the form $f(q_1, \ldots, q_n)$

$\rightarrow q$, where the states $q_1, \ldots, q_n, q$ are constants outside the signature Σ. Then a ground term t over Σ is recognized by a tree automaton if and only if t rewrites to some $q \in F$. This representation of tree automata recognizes terms bottom-up. For example, the term $\mathtt{cons}(\mathtt{S}(\mathtt{S}(0)), \mathtt{nil})$ is recognized by the automaton of Figure 1(a) by the rewrite sequence $\mathtt{cons}(\mathtt{S}(\mathtt{S}(0)), \mathtt{nil}) \rightarrow \mathtt{cons}(\mathtt{S}(\mathtt{S}(q_{\mathrm{even}})), \mathtt{nil}) \rightarrow \mathtt{cons}(\mathtt{S}(q_{\mathrm{odd}}), \mathtt{nil}) \rightarrow \mathtt{cons}(q_{\mathrm{even}}, \mathtt{nil}) \rightarrow \mathtt{cons}(q_{\mathrm{even}}, q_{\mathrm{list\text{-}even}}) \rightarrow q_{\mathrm{list\text{-}even}}$. In general, we may decide to recognize terms bottom-up or top-down, and while this makes no difference in theory, this does make a difference when considering *deterministic* tree automata [7]. In the sequel, we shall only consider non-deterministic tree automata, allowing us to avoid the bottom-up/top-down dilemma.

Another, perhaps less well-known data structure for representing tree automata is as sets of first-order Horn clauses [6,4]. Each state q is translated to a unary predicate P_q—think of $P_q(t)$ meaning "t is recognized at state q"—while transitions $f(q_1, \ldots, q_n) \rightarrow q$ are translated to clauses of the form $P_q(f(x_1, \ldots, x_n)) \leftarrow P_{q_1}(x_1), \ldots, P_{q_n}(x_n)$, and recognizability of t means derivability of the empty clause from the goal that is the disjunction of all $P_q(t)$, $q \in F$. It turns out that this representation is particularly attractive in Coq, where sets of first-order Horn clauses can be thought as particular inductive predicates (see Section 3).

In proof assistants that include a programming language, typically a form of λ-calculus as in Coq or HOL, an alternate representation is as a recognizer *function*—rather than as an axiomatized predicate. That is, we may define $\mathrm{Rec}(q, t)$ by primitive recursion on t by $\mathrm{Rec}(q, f(t_1, \ldots, t_n)) \hat{=} \bigvee_{(f(q_1, \ldots, q_n) \rightarrow q) \in \Delta} \bigwedge_{i=1}^{n} \mathrm{Rec}(q_i, t_i)$. This will actually be our first choice in Section 5. The example of Figure 1(a), for instance, becomes:

$$\mathrm{Rec}(q_{\mathrm{list\text{-}even}}, t) \hat{=} \begin{cases} \mathtt{True} & \text{if } t = \mathtt{nil} \\ \mathrm{Rec}(q_{\mathrm{even}}, t_1) \wedge \mathrm{Rec}(q_{\mathrm{list\text{-}even}}, t_2) & \text{if } t = \mathtt{cons}(t_1, t_2) \\ \mathtt{False} & \text{otherwise} \end{cases} \quad (1)$$

$$\mathrm{Rec}(q_{\mathrm{even}}, t) \hat{=} \begin{cases} \mathtt{True} & \text{if } t = 0 \\ \mathrm{Rec}(q_{\mathrm{odd}}, t_1) & \text{if } t = \mathtt{S}(t_1) \\ \mathtt{False} & \text{otherwise} \end{cases} \quad (2)$$

$$\mathrm{Rec}(q_{\mathrm{odd}}, t) \hat{=} \begin{cases} \mathrm{Rec}(q_{\mathrm{even}}, t_1) & \text{if } t = \mathtt{S}(t_1) \\ \mathtt{False} & \text{otherwise} \end{cases} \quad (3)$$

Interpreting these equations as rewrite rules from left to right, we recognize $\mathtt{cons}(\mathtt{S}(\mathtt{S}(0)), \mathtt{nil})$ by the computation: $\mathrm{Rec}(q_{\mathrm{list\text{-}even}}, \mathtt{cons}(\mathtt{S}(\mathtt{S}(0)), \mathtt{nil})) = \mathrm{Rec}(q_{\mathrm{even}}, \mathtt{S}(\mathtt{S}(0))) \wedge \mathrm{Rec}(q_{\mathrm{list\text{-}even}}, \mathtt{nil}) = \mathrm{Rec}(q_{\mathrm{even}}, \mathtt{S}(\mathtt{S}(0))) \wedge \mathtt{True} = \mathrm{Rec}(q_{\mathrm{odd}}, \mathtt{S}(0)) \wedge \mathtt{True} = \mathrm{Rec}(q_{\mathrm{even}}, 0) \wedge \mathtt{True} = \mathtt{True} \wedge \mathtt{True}$, which is clearly provable. Note in passing that this recognizes terms top-down.

Many standard operations are computable on tree automata. Computing an automaton recognizing the intersection or the union of two languages given by automata can be done in polynomial (near-quadratic) time and space. Similarly, testing whether an automaton recognizes no term—the *emptiness* test—takes polynomial time. On the other hand, computing an automaton recognizing the complement of the language recognized by a given automaton $\mathcal{A}$ requires exponential time, as do testing whether $\mathcal{A}$ recognizes all terms—the *universality* test—, or whether all terms recognized by $\mathcal{A}$ are recognized by another automaton—the *inclusion* test. In implementations, the latter operations all require constructing a *deterministic* bottom-up automaton recognizing the same terms as $\mathcal{A}$, explicitly or implicitly, and this takes exponential time and space.

In this paper, we shall only be interested in polynomial time algorithms such as computing intersections and unions, and testing for emptiness. This allows us to only work with non-deterministic automata, therefore keeping our algorithms simple. More to the point, it turns out that this is essentially all we need in applications like [9], where non-deterministic top-down automata are used (we need to make these algorithms work on automata of up to 300 states). Note that, then, we may always assume that there is exactly one final state in F, which we call *the* final state.

We shall also consider polynomial-time optimizations that aim at reducing the size of automata while keeping the languages they recognize intact. Such optimizations are important in practice, since the complexity of operations on automata are primarily functions of their sizes. Particularly useful optimizations are:

- Removal of empty states: say that $q \in Q$ is *empty* in $\mathcal{A}$ if and only if no ground term is recognized at q. Such states, together with transitions incident with q, can be removed from $\mathcal{A}$ without changing the language it recognizes. Empty states are frequently created in computing intersections of automata, notably.
- Removal of non-coaccessible states: say that $q \in Q$ is *coaccessible* in $\mathcal{A}$ if and only if we can reach q by starting from a final state and following transitions backwards. Removing non-coaccessible states and transitions between them leaves the language recognized by the automaton unchanged.

There are many other possible optimizations, e.g., merging states recognizing the same languages, erasing transitions $f(q_1, \ldots, q_n) \to q$ in the presence of $f(q'_1, \ldots, q'_n) \to q$ where a polynomial-time sufficient inclusion test ensures that all terms recognized at q_i are recognized at q'_i, $1 \le i \le n$, and so on.

5   Shallow Reflection

We start with a shallow reflection embedding of tree automata in Coq, where automata are described by mutually recursive functions $\text{Rec}(q, \_)$. Such automata are not first-class citizens in Coq: the external tool that computes on tree automata has to output corresponding definitions of $\text{Rec}(q, \_)$ functions for Coq, as well as expected properties about them, and proofs of these properties. (Automata *will be* first-class citizens in the deep reflection approach of Section 6.) This is in contrast with [10,11,18], where objects residing in the proof assistant are exported to the external tool, the latter computes on them, then produces a proof back for the proof assistant to check. Here the objects of interest, namely tree automata, are generated by and reside in the external tool, which also computes on them and feeds the proof assistant corresponding definitions, statements of correctness lemmata, and proofs of these lemmata.

While this is not as general as one may wish, this is exactly what we would want to check computations done in a tool such as CPV [9]: while CPV generates automata during the course of its verification process, an instrumented version of CPV will output their definitions to Coq, as well as correctness lemmata and proof scripts. The final Coq file will then validate the whole series of computations done by CPV.

5.1   Instrumenting Automaton Subroutines

Let us consider an example. Assume CPV calls its automaton intersection subroutine on the automata of Figure 1(a) and Figure 1(b). These automata have been produced by earlier computations. Our first change to the subroutines is to have them name the automata they produce, and output corresponding Coq functions. In particular, before the intersection subroutine is called, the input automata have received names, say A and B, and corresponding recursive functions $\mathtt{rec}\_N\_q$ of type $\mathtt{term} \to \mathtt{Prop}$ are defined for every automaton name N and every state q of N: $\mathtt{rec}\_N\_q(t)$ returns $\mathtt{True}$ if and only if t is recognized at state q in N. For example, the Coq function corresponding to the automaton B of Figure 1(b) is:

$$\mathtt{rec\_B\_}q_7(t) \;\hat{=}\; \begin{cases} (\mathtt{rec\_B\_}q_2(t_1) \wedge \mathtt{rec\_B\_}q_3(t_2)) \vee \\ (\mathtt{rec\_B\_}q_6(t_1) \wedge \mathtt{rec\_B\_}q_3(t_2)) & \text{if } t = \mathtt{cons}(t_1, t_2) \\ \mathtt{False} & \text{otherwise} \end{cases}$$

$$\mathtt{rec\_B\_}q_2(t) \;\hat{=}\; \begin{cases} \mathtt{rec\_B\_}q_1(t_1) \text{ if } t = \mathtt{S}(t_1) \\ \mathtt{False} \qquad\quad \text{otherwise} \end{cases}$$
$$\cdots$$

where the ellipsis abbreviates five other equalities. The definition of $\mathtt{rec}\_A\_q$ follows easily from Equations (1)–(3). Note that this also requires the instrumented CPV tool to first output the definition of an inductive type $\mathtt{term}$ of all terms, with constructors $0 : \mathtt{term}, \mathtt{nil} : \mathtt{term}, \mathtt{S} : \mathtt{term} \to \mathtt{term}, \mathtt{cons} : \mathtt{term} \to \mathtt{term} \to \mathtt{term}$.

Intersection is usually computed by a product construction, where states in the intersection automaton are in one-to-one correspondence with pairs of states of A and B. (This is certainly so in CPV.) We now instrument the intersection subroutine so that it keeps track of this mapping. For example, assume that the intersection subroutine computes the automaton of Figure 2, claiming it to be the intersection of A and B. We have labeled each state in such a way that pairs of states are obvious, e.g., state $q_{\mathrm{even},6}$ is the state that recognizes exactly those terms that are recognized at state q_{even} in A and at state q_6 in B. Note that all pairs are not represented: the CPV library does not compute non-coaccessible states, and eliminates empty states like $q_{\mathrm{even},2}$.

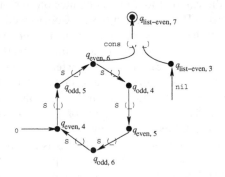

Fig. 2. Automaton Recognizing One-Element Lists of $6k + 2, k \in \mathbb{N}$.

Next, we instrument the intersection subroutine so that it generates the *correctness lemma*:

$$\forall t : \mathtt{term} \cdot \mathtt{rec\_C}\_q_{final}(t) \iff \mathtt{rec\_A}\_q_{final}(t) \land \mathtt{rec\_B}\_q_{final}(t) \qquad (4)$$

where q_{final} is the name of the final state in each automaton: $q_{\text{list-even},7}$ for C, $q_{\text{list-even}}$ for A, q_7 for B.

Finally, we let the intersection subroutine output a proof of the correctness lemma (4). It is interesting to examine how we might prove it in the case of the example C $=$ A $\cap$ B. This can only be proved by structural induction on the term t. However, we need to generalize the lemma first. Indeed, if $t = \mathtt{cons}(t_1, t_2)$, then the body of (4) simplifies (by reduction in the λ-calculus) to $(\mathtt{rec\_C}\_q_{\text{even},6}(t_1) \land \mathtt{rec\_C}\_q_{\text{list-even},3}(t_2)) \iff$ $(\mathtt{rec\_A}\_q_{\text{even}}(t_1) \quad \land \quad \mathtt{rec\_A}\_q_{\text{list-even}}(t_2)) \quad \land \quad ((\mathtt{rec\_B}\_q_2(t_1) \land \mathtt{rec\_B}\_q_3(t_2)) \lor (\mathtt{rec\_B}\_q_6(t_1) \land \mathtt{rec\_B}\_q_3(t_2)))$. This in turn obtains from the equivalences:

$$\mathtt{rec\_C}\_q_{\text{even},6}(t_1) \iff \mathtt{rec\_A}\_q_{\text{even}}(t_1) \land \mathtt{rec\_B}\_q_6(t_1)$$
$$\mathtt{rec\_C}\_q_{\text{list-even},3}(t_2) \iff \mathtt{rec\_A}\_q_{\text{list-even}}(t_2) \land \mathtt{rec\_B}\_q_3(t_2)$$
$$\mathtt{False} \iff \mathtt{rec\_A}\_q_{\text{even}}(t_1) \land \mathtt{rec\_B}\_q_2(t_1)$$

where the latter expresses that there is no term recognized both at state q_{even} in A and at state q_2 in B—note that there is no state $q_{\text{even},2}$ in C: it was empty, so was deleted. However, proving (4) by induction does not generate these equivalences, and we have to prove the conjunction of (4) and the above equivalences (at least) simultaneously.

In general it is necessary to generalize (4) to the conjunction of mn statements, where m is the number of states in A and n is the number of states in B: for each state q_i in A and each state q_j in B, either there is a corresponding state q_{ij} in C and we generate C_{ij}, the conjunct $\mathtt{rec\_C}\_q_{ij}(t) \iff \mathtt{rec\_A}\_q_i(t) \land \mathtt{rec\_B}\_q_j(t)$, or there is none and, if the intersection subroutine is correct, no term is recognized both at q_i and at q_j, so we generate C_{ij}, the conjunct $\mathtt{False} \iff \mathtt{rec\_A}\_q_i(t) \land \mathtt{rec\_B}\_q_j(t)$. We let the instrumented intersection subroutine generate the generalized correctness lemma $\forall t : \mathtt{term} \cdot \bigwedge_{i,j} C_{ij}$.

The proof script of the generalized correctness lemma is actually obvious, and is the same for all possible automata: do an induction on t; on all generated subgoals, compute, i.e., simplify as much as possible (use the Simpl tactic of Coq). All generated subgoals, if valid, are then provable using only rules of propositional logic (even intuitionistic): so use the Tauto tactic, which finds precisely such proofs. The proof of (4) is generated from the generalized correctness lemma using Tauto again.

Instrumenting the union subroutine is either similar (in tools that work on deterministic bottom-up automata, where union is computed by a similar product construction), or simpler. In the case of CPV, which works on non-deterministic top-down automata, this is definitely simpler: computing the union of two automata with disjoint sets of states amounts to generating a new final state q', and generating new transitions $f(q_1, \ldots, q_n) \to q'$ for each transition $f(q_1, \ldots, q_n) \to q$ in either input automaton such that q was final. It follows that the correctness lemma for unions only requires a case analysis, and no induction, and that it needs no prior generalization.

Instrumenting the emptiness test is also easy. Given an automaton C, either it is empty, and because CPV eliminates empty states, its corresponding function in Coq is the constant function False, so there is nothing to prove (in general, a polynomial-time emptiness test should be run in the automaton library to get this information); or it is not empty, and we instrument the code to output a witness t, i.e. a term t that is recognized by C. We then let the code output a non-emptiness lemma $\exists t : \mathtt{term} \cdot \mathtt{rec}\, \mathcal{L}\, q_{final}(t)$, and its proof: exhibit t, simplify, call $\mathtt{Tauto}$.

5.2 Experimental Evaluation

The approach of Section 5.1 has several nice features. It is easy to instrument almost any automaton library to get similar results; we may choose to change or upgrade the automaton library, and this only requires modifying the instrumentation code; finally, the generated Coq proofs are short and do not depend on the automata we compute on.

However, as is apparent from the discussion on instrumenting intersection in Section 5.1, this approach generates huge generalized correctness lemmata. It is therefore necessary to evaluate the approach on a few practical examples. To test it, we used the signature O, S, nil, cons as above; we generated automata $\mathcal{A}_n$ recognizing the lists of natural numbers whose elements are all congruent to $n - 1$ modulo n. $\mathcal{A}_n$ has $n + 1$ states and $n + 3$ transitions and contains only one cycle of length n. We then let Coq check proofs as generated by the method of Section 5.1, computing unions and intersections of automata $\mathcal{A}_n$. All tests were done on a Pentium Celeron 400Mhz notebook with 128 MO RAM running Linux 2.2.13.

As far as unions are concerned, we check unions of $\mathcal{A}_n$ and $\mathcal{A}_{n+1}$ for various values of n: this involves generating the automata, lemmata stating that all automata are not empty, the correctness lemma, and their proofs. The resulting automaton has $2n + 4$ states; we sum up the times taken by Coq to do the whole verification of one instance (parsing, type-checking, checking non-emptiness and correctness proofs), the times taken to check the correctness lemma alone, and memory usage:

n	10	20	30	40	50	60	70	80
# states	24	44	64	84	104	124	144	164
total check (s.)	4	9	19	33	59	84	126	181
correctness (s.)	1	2	3	4	5	7	8	9
memory (Mb.)	7.5	8	9	10	12	14	17	18

Notice that checking that unions are computed correctly takes negligible time compared to parsing plus checking non-emptiness. This is to be expected, as checking unions only involves a case analysis and no induction.

We conducted exactly the same test with intersection. The results, as the reader may see, are extremely disappointing. When $n = 1$, checking takes 6s. and 8Mb; 74s. and 24Mb when $n = 2$; 513s. and 96Mb when $n = 3$; we ran out of memory when $n = 4$. Both checking time and space increase quickly. This is due to the large size of generalized correctness lemmas: the size of the formula is $O(n^2)$; if Σ has k constructors, the induction proof will generate k subgoals of size $O(n^2)$ each. This has to be multiplied by the time taken by $\mathtt{Tauto}$, a relatively inefficient, exponential-time-and-space tactic. Prompted by this remark, we tried to replace $\mathtt{Tauto}$ by hand-crafted sequences of elimination and introduction tactics, to no significant avail.

As mentioned in Section 4, tree automata can also be represented as sets of Horn clauses of a particular format, and sets of Horn clauses are naturally encoded in Coq as inductive predicates. It was suggested by C. Paulin-Mohring and B. Werner that this format usually has distinctive advantages over recursive functions as in Section 5.1: the main one is that induction and case analysis proofs only consider cases that actually happen. For example, if a state has two incoming transitions, the corresponding inductive predicate will have two clauses, even though terms might be built on more constructors (4 in our examples). In the encoding using recursive functions, any switch on the shape of terms actually always compiles to a k-way switch, where k is the number of constructors.

However, this alternate implementation of tree automata also turned out to be disappointing, as experience with hand-generated examples demonstrated. Compared to the technique of Section 5.1, proof scripts are harder to generate. In principle, it is enough to use the Auto resolution tactic instead of Tauto; however the use of conjunctions $\wedge$ and disjunctions $\vee$ foils this strategy: in Coq, conjunctions and disjunctions are not primitive and need to be decomposed by some other mechanism. The crucial point however is that checking proofs, in particular for intersection, in this new scheme is only roughly twice as fast as with the scheme of Section 5.1, and uses as much memory.

6   Deep Reflection

As said in Section 3, deep reflection means implementing tree automata and operations on them in Coq's λ-calculus, and proving the correctness of the latter in Coq. However, tree automata may be represented in several different ways, so one first contribution here is the choice of a workable data structure for tree automata in Coq (Section 6.1). We shall opt for a compromise between efficiency of algorithms and simplicity of proofs, and describe the computation of unions, intersections, and removal of empty and non-coaccessible states in Sections 6.2, 6.3 and 6.4 respectively. This will be rather cursory, and we shall only stress salient features.

6.1   Data Structures

We have chosen to represent tree automata as top-down non-deterministic tree automata. Previous experience with CPV [9] indicates that this is probably one of the simplest possible implementations. Such automata are described as a table mapping each state q to the set of possible transitions reaching q. This set is itself organized as a table mapping each function symbol f labeling such a transition to the set of lists $[q_1, \ldots, q_n]$ of states such that $f(q_1, \ldots, q_n) \to q$ is a transition. Note that all lists in a given set have the same length n.

To represent tables, we use the map library of [8]. This provides a data type ad of *addresses*, a.k.a. *keys*, and a type constructor Map, such that Map(τ) is the type of *maps* over τ, i.e., tables mapping keys to objects of type τ. The implementation of maps over τ is an efficient binary trie representation, where addresses are essentially finite lists of bits, or alternatively natural numbers in binary. The map library provides functions such as MapGet to fetch the object associated with a given key—or return the constant NONE if there is none—, and MapPut to produce a new map obtained from a given map m by adding a binding from a given key a to a given object x, erasing any possible preexisting binding to a. We shall simply write $f(a)$ to denote $\mathtt{MapGet}(f, a)$ when it is *defined*, i.e., does not return $\mathtt{NONE}$.

This is used to define *pre-automata* as objects of type $\mathtt{Map(st)}$ mapping states q to elements of $\mathtt{st}$; the latter map function symbols of arity n to sets of lists of states of length n, as indicated above. Since maps only take addresses, i.e., elements of $\mathtt{ad}$ as indices, this requires us to encode states as addresses, as well as function symbols.

In particular, we define *terms*, of inductive type $\mathtt{term}$ with one constructor $\mathtt{app}$: $\mathtt{ad} \to \mathtt{term\ list} \to \mathtt{term\ list}$, where $\mathtt{term\ list}$ is defined simultaneously as the type of finite lists of terms. For example, $f(t_1, \ldots, t_n)$ is coded as $\mathtt{app}(f, [t_1, \ldots, t_n])$. Each function symbol $f : \mathtt{ad}$ has an arity; this is summed up in a *signature* Σ, i.e., a map from function symbols f to their arities, of type $\mathtt{Map}(\mathbb{N})$.

Returning to pre-automata, the only remaining difficulty is to represent sets of lists of states of length n. The standard way to represent finite sets with maps is to encode them as elements of $\mathtt{Map}(*)$, where $*$ is a one-element type. However, this only allows us to encode sets of addresses, and while states are addresses, lists of states are not. Since addresses are natural numbers, it is in principle feasible to encode lists of addresses as natural numbers, solving this conundrum. However, this solution is complex, not particularly efficient in practice, and hard to reason about formally. Instead, we create a new data structure to represent sets of lists of states of length n as binary trees whose nodes are labeled with states: each branch in the tree is taken to denote the list of all states labeling nodes to the left of which the branch goes, provided it is of length n. Formally, the type $\mathtt{prec\_list}$ of sets of lists of states is the inductive type with two constructors $\mathtt{prec\_cons} : \mathtt{ad} \to \mathtt{prec\_list} \to \mathtt{prec\_list} \to \mathtt{prec\_list}$ and $\mathtt{prec\_empty} : \mathtt{prec\_list}$. The formal semantics $[\![pl]\!]_n$ of $pl : \mathtt{prec\_list}$ as a set of lists of length n is defined by: $[\![\mathtt{prec\_empty}]\!]_0 \mathrel{\hat{=}} \{[]\}$; $[\![\mathtt{prec\_empty}]\!]_{n+1} \mathrel{\hat{=}} \emptyset$; $[\![\mathtt{prec\_cons}\ q\ \ell\ r]\!]_0 \mathrel{\hat{=}} \emptyset$; $[\![\mathtt{prec\_cons}\ q\ \ell\ r]\!]_{n+1} \mathrel{\hat{=}} \{q :: pl \mid pl \in [\![\ell]\!]_n\} \cup [\![r]\!]_{n+1}$, where $q :: l$ is the list obtained from l by adding q in front.

Recall that, then, $\mathtt{st} \mathrel{\hat{=}} \mathtt{Map(prec\_list)}$ and the type of pre-automata is $\mathtt{predta} \mathrel{\hat{=}} \mathtt{Map(st)}$. *Tree automata*, of type $\mathtt{dta}$, are pairs of a pre-automaton A and a state, taken to be the final state. They are *well-formed* w.r.t. a signature Σ provided the following conditions hold:

1. each state q is mapped to a map $A(q)$ from function symbols f to sets of lists *of length n*, where $n = \Sigma(f)$ is the arity of f;
2. for every state q, every function symbol f, every list $[q_1, \ldots, q_n] \in A(q)(f)$, q_i is in the domain of A for every i, $1 \leq i \leq n$ (no dangling pointers);
3. Similarly, the final state is in the domain of A.

Conditions 1–3 are necessary to establish the correctness of operations in the following. In particular, Condition 1 is crucial to be able to give a semantics to $\mathtt{prec\_list}$s.

The semantics of tree automata is defined by mutually inductive predicates $\mathtt{rec\_predta} : \mathtt{predta} \to \mathtt{ad} \to \mathtt{term} \to \mathtt{Prop}$ (recognizing a term at a given state), $\mathtt{rec\_st} : \mathtt{predta} \to \mathtt{st} \to \mathtt{term} \to \mathtt{Prop}$ (recognizing a term at a state given by its set of incoming transitions), $\mathtt{rec\_prec\_list} : \mathtt{predta} \to \mathtt{prec\_list} \to \mathtt{term\ list} \to \mathtt{Prop}$ (recognizing a list of terms at a list of states in some set of lists of states), where $\mathtt{rec\_predta}(A, q, t)$ provided $A(q)$ is defined and $\mathtt{rec\_st}(A, A(q), t)$; where $\mathtt{rec\_st}(A, tr, t)$ provided $t = \mathtt{app}(f, [t_1, \ldots, t_n])$, $tr(f)$ is defined and $\mathtt{rec\_prec\_list}(A, tr(f), [t_1, \ldots, t_n])$; finally, $\mathtt{rec\_prec\_list}(A, \mathtt{prec\_empty}, [])$, `rec_prec_list(A, prec_cons(q, ℓ, r), t :: tl)` provided either `rec_predta(A, q, t)` and `rec_prec_list(A, ℓ, tl)`, or `rec_prec_list(A, r, t :: tl)`.

6.2 Implementing Union

Computing unions is done by the algorithm used in CPV, described in Section 5.1: generate a new final state q', and generate new transitions $f(q_1, \ldots, q_n) \rightarrow q'$ for each transition $f(q_1, \ldots, q_n) \rightarrow q$ in any of the input automata $\mathcal{A}$ or $\mathcal{B}$ where q was final. However, this is only correct provided $\mathcal{A}$ and $\mathcal{B}$ have disjoint sets of states. In implementations like CPV, states are memory locations pointing to maps of type `st`, and disjointness is not required for correctness, as any state common to both automata points to the same sub-automaton. The latter condition is hard to ensure (we might have modeled a full store as in [16], but this looked like overkill), while the disjointness condition is simpler to implement in the representation of Section 6.1: therefore, in Coq, we first copy each input automaton by adding a 0 bit in front of any address in $\mathcal{A}$ (i.e., changing q into $2q$) and a 1 bit in front of any address in $\mathcal{B}$ (i.e., changing q into $2q + 1$), then add a new final state and all relevant incoming transitions.

We prove that this algorithm is correct: the term t is recognized by the union of two well-formed automata if and only if t is recognized by one or the other, by structural induction on t. That the input automata are well-formed (Conditions 1–3) is needed in the proof. Condition 1 is needed to give a meaning $[\![pl]\!]_n$ to `prec_lists` $A(q)(f)$, where n is the arity of f. Conditions 2 and 3 are needed to give meaning to the set of all transitions $f(q_1, \ldots, q_n) \rightarrow q$ where q is given. We also prove that the union of two well-formed automata is again well-formed, one condition at a time. Notice that we never had to impose any well-formedness condition on terms, only on automata.

6.3 Implementing Intersection

Intersection of two automata $\mathcal{A}$ and $\mathcal{B}$ is trickier. The standard product construction consists in generating new states $\langle q, q' \rangle$ that are in one-to-one correspondence with pairs of states q of $\mathcal{A}$ and q' of $\mathcal{B}$. There is a transition $f(\langle q_1, q_1' \rangle, \ldots, \langle q_n, q_n' \rangle) \rightarrow \langle q, q' \rangle$ in the computed intersection automaton $\mathcal{C}$ if and only if $f(q_1, \ldots, q_n) \rightarrow q$ is a transition in $\mathcal{A}$ and $f(q_1', \ldots, q_n') \rightarrow q'$ is a transition in $\mathcal{B}$, and the final state of $\mathcal{C}$ is $\langle q_{final}, q'_{final} \rangle$, where q_{final} is final in $\mathcal{A}$ and q'_{final} is final in $\mathcal{B}$. Our first problem here is that states $\langle q, q' \rangle$ should be of type `ad`, so we need a one-to-one mapping from pairs of addresses to addresses. There are several solutions to this. The one we choose is one of the simplest, and also of the most efficient to compute: looking at q and q' as sequences of bits, we interleave them to get $\langle q, q' \rangle$. For example, if q is 10010 in binary and q' is 01011, then $\langle q, q' \rangle$ is 1001001101.

Linking in such an explicit way the states $\langle q, q' \rangle$ to q and q', i.e., making sure that we can get back q and q' easily from $\langle q, q' \rangle$ without the help of any outside machinery is a great help in proofs of correctness. The construction of the intersection automaton $\mathcal{C}$ is then direct: generate all states $\langle q, q' \rangle$, and add transitions as specified above. This involves quite many nested structural inductions, though: we have to induct on the tries that encode the pre-automata $\mathcal{A}$ and $\mathcal{B}$, then on the tries that encode transitions with symbol function f, for each f in each of the two input automata, then induct on two prec_lists. It then turns out that the intersection construction applied to two automata indeed computes the intersection, provided Condition 1 is satisfied; this is proved by structural induction on the terms fed to each automaton. Finally, we prove that the intersection construction preserves well-formedness, as expected.

Nonetheless, this intersection construction is naive: it generates many empty or non-coaccessible states. To correct this, it is common practice to only generate states $\langle q, q' \rangle$ by need. Intuitively, generate $\langle q_{final}, q'_{final} \rangle$; then, for each f, for each pair of transitions $f(q_1, \ldots, q_n) \to q_{final}$ in $\mathcal{A}$ and $f(q'_1, \ldots, q'_n) \to q'_{final}$ in $\mathcal{B}$, generate the states $\langle q_1, q'_1 \rangle, \ldots, \langle q_n, q'_n \rangle$ (observe that they may fail to be new), and recurse. Note that this is not well-founded induction, and a loop-checking mechanism has to be implemented: when some state $\langle q, q' \rangle$ is required that has already been generated, stop recursing. Coding such an algorithm in Coq, and above all proving it, is daunting—recall that the naive algorithm already requires 6 nested inductions. Thus, we have refrained from doing so.

6.4   Removing Empty and Non-coaccessible States

Instead, we have implemented algorithms to delete empty and non-coaccessible states as separate functions. This is already rather involved, as this involves some form of loop-checking. First, we observe that, from the logical point of view, recursing with loop checks is just an implementation of a least fixpoint computation. For example, define the set $\mathcal{NV}$ of *non-void states* of $\mathcal{A}$ as the smallest such that for every transition $f(q_1, \ldots, q_n) \to q$ such that $q_1, \ldots, q_n \in \mathcal{NV}$, then $q \in \mathcal{NV}$. While this is naturally coded in Coq as an inductive predicate, such a predicate does not lend itself to computation. To compute $\mathcal{NV}$, we must instead compute the least fixpoint of the function NV mapping any set S of states to $NV(S) \hat{=} S \cup \{q \mid f(q_1, \ldots, q_n) \to q \text{ transition in } \mathcal{A}, q_1 \in S, \ldots, q_n \in S\}$. We then prove that both definitions are equivalent, by well-founded induction on the definition of the non-vacuity predicate in one direction, and by Tarskian fixpoint induction in the other direction.

This however requires that we develop a Tarskian theory of fixpoints of monotonic functions over complete lattices—at least over complete Boolean lattices of finite height. Indeed, subsets of a given set of states Q of cardinality n form a Boolean lattice of height n. In Coq, we represent subsets of Q as objects of type Map(bool), constrained to have Q as domain. We show in Coq that this can be given the structure of a complete Boolean lattice of cardinality 2^n and height n, taking as ordering $m \leq^* m'$ if and only if $m(q) \leq m'(q)$ for every $q \in Q$, where $\leq$ is the ordering false $\leq$ true in bool. Independently, we show in Coq that, for every complete lattice L of height n, with bottom element $\bot$, for every monotonic $f : L \to L$, $f^n(\bot)$ is the least fixpoint of f. This is especially convenient for computation, as $f^n(\bot)$ can be defined by structural recursion on n in Coq, while general fixpoints cannot be defined as recursive functions.

Summing up, we obtain a function that computes the set of non-void states of a given automaton, together with a proof of its correctness. Observing now that a state q is non-void if and only if it is non-empty, where a state q of $\mathcal{A}$ is *non-empty* if and only if there is a term t recognized at q in $\mathcal{A}$, we deduce that the automaton $\mathcal{B}$ obtained from $\mathcal{A}$ by only keeping non-void (a.k.a, non-empty) states has the same semantics as $\mathcal{A}$. Therefore, composing empty states removal with the naive intersection algorithm yields another correct intersection algorithm. (The empty state removal algorithm is actually slightly trickier, in that it also removes transitions $f(q_1, \ldots, q_n) \to q$ where at least one q_i, $1 \le i \le n$, is empty, even when q is non-empty; and also in that it does not remove the final state, even if it is empty. These considerations complicate the algorithm and the proofs, but are not essential to the present discussion.)

Removal of non-coaccessible states is coded, proved and applied to intersection in a similar way. In both the non-emptiness and non-coaccessibility cases, the precise correctness theorems proved rest on input automata being well-formed; we also show that these removal algorithms preserve well-formedness.

6.5 Experimental Evaluation

It is interesting to evaluate how deep reflection works in practice, and whether it yields any significant advantage over shallow reflection (Section 5.2). We report on times and memory consumed for operations of union, intersection, and removal of useless states. Noticing that useless state removal is slow, we also include measures of efficiency for removal by shallow reflection (see below). We also compare these results, obtained by running our algorithms inside Coq's λ-calculus, with results obtained by running the OCaml program that one gets by Coq's extraction feature. While efficiency depends on many parameters (number of states, number of transitions, maximal arity of function symbols), we have decided to focus first on evaluating the algorithms on the same examples as in Section 5.2 for the sake of comparison (this also tests how the algorithms fare in the presence of cycles), then on other examples featuring large transition tables. Tests were run on the same Pentium Celeron notebook with 128 Mb RAM.

Results on the cyclic examples A_n of Section 5.2 are as follows:

n	10	15	20	30	50	500	n_{max}
$A_n \cup A_{n+1}$	0.57(26)	0.75(26)	1.19(26)	1.71(27)	2.89(28)	51.8(48)	1500
$A_n \cap A_{n+1}$	2.09(27)	4.55(32)	10.6(36)	32.1(45)	–	–	70
$\emptyset$-removal	104.7(48)	438.9(95)	–	–	–	–	25
$\emptyset$-check	3.16/0.25	6.65/0.56	21.8/1.04(38)	44.0/2.34(49)	–	–	50

Results are in the form $t(m)$ where times t are in seconds, and memory sizes m are in megabytes. The last column reports the largest n for which computation ran in the available 128 Mb plus 200 Mb swap space, without a time limit. (But times are only reported for cases where swap usage is negligible.) The $\emptyset$-removal row measures the time to remove empty states from automata computed in the second row. The $\emptyset$-check row measures the efficiency of the following procedure: instead of computing the fixpoint $\mathcal{NV}$ in Coq, let an external tool written in OCaml do it and feed it to Coq; then Coq checks that $\mathcal{NV}$ indeed is a fixpoint, and removes all empty states. Reported measures are $t/t_{\mathcal{NV}}(m)$, where t is time to remove empty states given $\mathcal{NV}$, $t_{\mathcal{NV}}$ is the time to check that $\mathcal{NV}$ is a fixpoint, and m is the amount of memory used. Although the last two rows report on computations done on $A_n \cap A_{n+1}$, times do not include intersection computation times. Note that input automata and $A_n \cup A_{n+1}$ have $O(n)$ states and transitions, while all others have $O(n^2)$ states and transitions.

Clearly, intersections are costly, but empty state removal is even costlier. Here shallow reflection helps (last row). Also, results are much better than with a wholly shallow reflection approach (Section 5.2), but not quite usable: CPV [9] typically needs to handle automata of 200–300 states.

Comparatively, the extracted OCaml code computes unions up to $n = 150,000$, intersections up to $n = 400$. It is roughly at least 300 times faster and consumes about 100 times less memory, although it is hard to draw a comparison: there are too few values of n for which both Coq computations succeed and OCaml times are measurable at all. Note that the extracted OCaml code would in general be able to deal with automata of the size that CPV generates. We believe that this vindicates using compiled OCaml code as a reduction machine inside Coq, instead of the current λ-calculus interpreter.

In our second series of tests, we worked with automata $\mathcal{B}_n$ on a signature with one constant α and one binary function symbol β; $\mathcal{B}_n$ has $n+1$ states s_k^n, $0 \le k \le n$, which recognize trees with k occurrences of β, and the final state is s_n^n. $\mathcal{B}_n$ has $1 + n(n+1)/2$ transitions, and is therefore dense. Tests (see table below) are similar to the ones above, except we test intersections by computing $\mathcal{B}_n \cap \mathcal{B}_n$ on two disjoint copies of $\mathcal{B}_n$—testing $\mathcal{B}_n \cap \mathcal{B}_{n+1}$ would result in an empty automaton. Unions have $O(n)$ states and $O(n^2)$ transitions, while intersections have $O(n^2)$ states and $O(n^4)$ transitions.

n	5	10	15	25	50	100
$\mathcal{B}_n \cup \mathcal{B}_{n+1}$	0.45(26)	1.47(30)	2.54(32)	5.76(37)	23.9(50)	156(100)
$\mathcal{B}_n \cap \mathcal{B}_n$	2.79(31)	29.9(50)	196(87)	–	–	–
$\emptyset$-check	0.89/0.36(32)	18.4/3.14(46)	62.7/12.5(91)	–	–	–

Again, OCaml is 400–600 times faster, and uses negligible memory compared to Coq.

7   Conclusion

We have presented two ways to formally verify tree automata computations in a proof assistant like Coq. The surprising conclusion is that the most promising method, checking computations by shallow reflection, gives disastrous results. On the contrary, deep reflection works much better—with a zest of shallow reflection for useless state removal —, up to the point that an extracted OCaml version—hence a certified algorithm— tackles computation on tree automata of sizes comparable to those dealt in a realistic cryptographic protocol verification application. These sizes are modest, still, and more work remains to be done. In particular, computing states of intersection automata by need instead as eagerly, as we did, is required. However, this is definitely a lot of work— our naive, deep reflection implementation and proofs already take about $14,000$ lines of Coq—and doing so involves implementing unbounded recursion with loop checks, i.e., computing least fixpoints, which we have seen was inefficient in Coq. Replacing the λ-calculus interpreter of Coq by a machine that would compile λ-terms to OCaml and run the compiled code also appears as a good way to gain efficiency.

Acknowledgements

We wish to thank the LogiCal team, and the anonymous referees for their suggestions.

References

1. B. Barras, S. Boutin, C. Cornes, J. Courant, J.-C. Filliâtre, E. Giménez, H. Herbelin, G. Huet, C. Muñoz, C. Murthy, C. Parent, C. Paulin-Mohring, A. Saibi, and B. Werner. The Coq proof assistant reference manual: Version 6.3.1. Technical report, INRIA, France, 1999.
2. S. Boutin. Using reflection to build efficient and certified decision procedures. In M. Abadi and T. Ito, editors, *TACS'97*. Springer-Verlag LNCS 1281, 1997.
3. R. Boyer and J. S. Moore. Metafunctions: Proving them correct and using them efficiently as new proof procedures. In *The Correctness Problem in Computer Science*. Acad. Press, 1981.
4. W. Charatonik and A. Podelski. Set-based analysis of reactive infinite-state systems. In B. Steffen, editor, *TACAS'98*, pages 358–375. Springer Verlag LNCS 1384, 1998.
5. H. Comon, M. Dauchet, R. Gilleron, F. Jacquemard, D. Lugiez, T. Sophie, and M. Tommasi. Tree automata techniques and applications. Available at http://www.grappa.univ-lille3.fr/tata, 1997.
6. L. Fribourg and M. Veloso Peixoto. Automates concurrents à contraintes. *Technique et Science Informatique*, 13(6):837–866, 1994.
7. F. Gécseg and M. Steinby. Tree languages. In G. Rozenberg and A. Salomaa, editors, *Handbook of Formal Languages*, volume 3, pages 1–68. Springer Verlag, 1997.
8. J. Goubault-Larrecq. Satisfiability of inequality constraints and detection of cycles with negative weight in graphs. Part of the Coq contribs, available at http://pauillac.inria.fr/coq/contribs/graphs.html, 1998.
9. J. Goubault-Larrecq. A method for automatic cryptographic protocol verification. In *FMPPTA'2000*, pages 977–984. Springer Verlag LNCS 1800, 2000.
10. J. Harrison. Binary decision diagrams as a HOL derived rule. *The Computer Journal*, 38:162–170, 1995.
11. J. Harrison. Stålmarck's algorithm as a HOL derived rule. In J. von Wright, J. Grundy, and J. Harrison, editors, *TPHOL'96*, pages 221–234. Springer Verlag LNCS 1125, 1996.
12. J.-P. Jouannaud. Rewrite proofs and computations. In H. Schwichtenberg, editor, *Proof and Computation*, volume 139 of *NATO series F: Computer and Systems Sciences*, pages 173–218. Springer Verlag, 1995.
13. D. Monniaux. Abstracting cryptographic protocols with tree automata. In *SAS'99*, pages 149–163. Springer-Verlag LNCS 1694, 1999.
14. O. Müller. A verification environment for I/O automata based on formalized meta-theory. Master's thesis, Technische Universität München, 1998.
15. W. Thomas. Automata on infinite objects. In J. van Leeuwen, editor, *Handbook of Theoretical Computer Science*, chapter 4, pages 133–191. Elsevier Science Publishers B. V., 1990.
16. K. N. Verma, J. Goubault-Larrecq, S. Prasad, and S. Arun-Kumar. Reflecting BDDs in Coq. In *ASIAN'2000*, pages 162–181. Springer Verlag LNCS 1961, 2000.
17. R. W. Weyhrauch. Prolegomena to a theory of mechanized formal reasoning. *Artifical Intelligence*, 13(1, 2):133–170, 1980.
18. S. Yu and Z. Luo. Implementing a model checker for LEGO. In J. Fitzgerald, C. B. Jones, and P. Lucas, editors, *FME'97*, pages 442–458. Springer-Verlag LNCS 1313, 1997.

Mizar Light for HOL Light

Freek Wiedijk

Department of Computer Science
University of Nijmegen, The Netherlands
freek@cs.kun.nl

Abstract. There are two different approaches to formalizing proofs in a computer: the procedural approach (which is the one of the HOL system) and the declarative approach (which is the one of the Mizar system). Most provers are procedural. However declarative proofs are much closer in style to informal mathematical reasoning than procedural ones.

There have been attempts to put declarative interfaces on top of procedural proof assistants, like John Harrison's Mizar mode for HOL and Markus Wenzel's Isar mode for Isabelle. However in those cases the declarative assistant is a *layer* on top of the procedural basis, having a separate syntax and a different 'feel' from the underlying system.

This paper shows that the procedural and the declarative ways of proving are related and can be integrated seamlessly. It presents an implementation of the Mizar proof language on top of HOL that consists of only 41 lines of ML. This shows how close the procedural and declarative styles of proving really are.

1   Introduction

We describe a programming experiment with the HOL system. To be able to read this paper one has to have some familiarity with both the HOL [10] and Mizar [12,17] systems. The software described here is not meant to be used for serious work (and it certainly doesn't emulate the full Mizar language). Rather it's a kind of 'thought experiment' to clarify the relation between the procedural and declarative styles of proving.

This paper uses HOL for the procedural prover. However the way the paper integrates Mizar-style proofs with it also applies to other procedural systems like Coq [2] and Isabelle [14]. For each of these systems a set of 'Mizar tactics' could be written as described in this paper, giving them 'Mizar style' declarative proofs without a separate syntactic layer.

The plan of this paper is as follows. It first presents the procedural and declarative styles of proving and the HOL and Mizar systems. Then Section 6 presents the main idea of the paper which is implementing Mizar steps as HOL tactics. For each of these 'Mizar tactics' this section gives an ML type in the framework of the HOL system. After that the paper discusses various variations on this Mizar mode for HOL. The paper concludes with a bigger example and an outlook. The source code of the Mizar mode is an appendix.

R.J. Boulton and P.B. Jackson (Eds.): TPHOLs 2001, LNCS 2152, pp. 378–393, 2001.
© Springer-Verlag Berlin Heidelberg 2001

2   Procedural versus Declarative Proving

The idea of formalizing mathematical proofs in such a way that a computer can check the correctness is not new but only recently it has become practical and popular. Most of the proofs that are currently checked are proofs of the correctness of computer software or hardware but some people have also been formalizing other kinds of proofs (for instance of mathematical theorems [3,6]).

There are two main styles of proof checking programs (the so-called proof checkers or proof assistants): the *procedural* style and the *declarative* style.

The procedural proof checkers descend from a system from the seventies called LCF [8]. Such a system has a *proof state* which consists of a set of 'proof obligations'. This state is transformed by means of so-called *tactics* which take a proof obligation and reduce it to several simpler ones (possibly none). The proof process starts with the statement to be proved as the sole proof obligation; once no proof obligations remain, the proof is complete. Procedural proofs consisting of a sequence of tactics cannot be understood without interactively running them on a computer because they only contain the transitions between the proof states and not the proof states themselves.[1] Also since the initial proof obligation is the final statement to be proved, procedural proofs tend to run *backwards*, from the conclusion back to the assumptions.

The other two proof checkers from the seventies, Automath [13] and Mizar [12,17], both are of the declarative kind. (Another system that is declarative is the Ontic system by David McAllester [11].) In a declarative system, a proof doesn't consist of instructions to transform statements but of those statements themselves. Furthermore, the statements are present in deductive order: the assumptions are at the start and the conclusion is at the end.[2]

The procedural and declarative styles differ in several ways:

- Declarative proofs are closer to informal mathematical reasoning and therefore are more readable than procedural proofs because in a declarative proof the statements are present themselves and in the proper order.
- Most current proof assistants are procedural (perhaps because LCF style provers are programmable by their users, while declarative systems can generally only be extended by its developers).
- Declarative proofs can be written without the proof assistant running and then checked with a batch oriented system. Procedural proofs can only be developed interactively because the computer has to keep track of the proof obligations. Indeed, some declarative provers only have a batch mode while procedural provers always also have an interactive mode.

---

[1] Procedural proofs are therefore sometimes presented using *runs* of proof scripts (or, even better, proof trees) showing intermediate goals.

[2] The relation between backward and forward reasoning as related to procedural and declarative proofs is more subtle than is suggested here. Declarative proofs (and informal mathematical reasoning as well) also take backward steps. And many procedural provers also can do forward reasoning. However the particular tactic collections found in procedural provers tend to be biased towards backward reasoning.

– Since a declarative proof contains a chain of statements, it is fairly robust with respect to errors. If one step in the proof is erroneous, a declarative system can recover from the error and check the rest of the proof file reasonably well. In contrast, a procedural prover stops checking at the first error it encounters. So after the point in the file where an error occurs, a procedural system can't say much about correctness.

It seems natural to look for a way to integrate the procedural and declarative approaches to proving. Two attempts to put a declarative interface on a procedural prover are the Mizar mode for HOL by John Harrison [9] and the Isar mode for Isabelle by Markus Wenzel [16].

The Mizar mode for HOL by John Harrison is a true integration, in the sense that the Mizar commands behave like ordinary HOL tactics. However this doesn't become clear from the way this mode is presented. For instance, the Mizar sub-language has a separate parser from the (ML based) HOL proof language. Also once the Mizar mode is active, the normal parser of the HOL terms is no longer easily available. This seems to suggest that once the Mizar mode has been activated, the 'normal' style of procedural HOL proving is not meant to be used anymore.

The Mizar mode for HOL in this paper is a variation on the Mizar mode of John Harrison. Its main difference with Harrison's Mizar mode is that the Mizar primitives *are* HOL tactics (so are not just compiled to them) and therefore the integration is very tight. Also the implementation of our Mizar mode takes only 41 lines of ML, which is smaller than Harrison's implementation which consists of about 650 lines of ML.

The Isar mode for Isabelle differs from the Mizar mode for HOL in that it has outgrown the experimental stage and has been used for serious proofs [3,5,4]. However it really is a second layer on top of the Isabelle layer (although it is possible to 'embed' tactic scripts in Isar proofs), so in this case there is no mixture between the two approaches. In fact, both layers have their own proof state (called 'the static proof context' and 'the dynamic goal state') which are to be synchronized at certain checkpoints. This is presented as a benefit because it makes it possible to give a different order to the proof steps from the order imposed by the underlying procedural basis but it shows that there is no tight integration.

Two other declarative systems that integrate declarative proofs with higher order logic are the SPL system by Vincent Zammit [18] and the Declare system by Don Syme [15]. These two systems are not meant as a declarative interface to a procedural prover. Instead they are autonomous declarative systems. (The SPL system is *implemented* on top of the HOL system but it is not an interface to HOL.)

Procedural and declarative proof checkers both might or might not satisfy what Henk Barendregt calls *the de Bruijn principle* and *the Poincaré principle* [1]. This paper is about the relation between procedural and declarative proof styles. This is unrelated to the issue of whether a system should satisfy either of these principles or how to make it do so.

3 Example: The Drinker

As a running example in this paper, we will use the so-called *drinker's principle*. This says that in every group of people one can point to one person in the group such that if that person drinks then all the people in the group drink. This somewhat surprising statement becomes in first order predicate logic:

$$\exists x. (P(x) \rightarrow \forall y. P(y))$$

The HOL version of this is:

```
?x:A. P x ==> !y. P y
```

(so in HOL '?' is the existential quantifier and '!' is the universal quantifier) and the Mizar version is:

```
ex x st P x implies for y holds P y
```

Here is an informal proof of the drinker's principle (we will see below how this textual version compares both to the proofs of this statement in the HOL and Mizar systems):

Suppose that $P(x)$ is false for some x. Then for that x the implication holds because from a false proposition one may deduce anything. That means that in this case the proposition follows.

Now suppose that $P(x)$ is false for no x. Then $P(x)$ is true for all x. But that statement is the conclusion of the implication and so the proposition again follows.

Almost all example proofs in this paper are proofs of this simple statement. In Section 8 we will present a bigger example.

4 HOL

The HOL system [7] by Mike Gordon is a descendant from LCF that implements Church's *Higher Order Logic* (hence the acronym 'HOL'), which is a classical higher order logic encoded by simply typed lambda calculus with ML style polymorphism. The system guarantees the correctness of its proofs by reducing everything in LCF style to a 'proof kernel', which because of its small size (nine pages of ML code, about half of which is comment) can be thoroughly checked for correctness by inspection.

The HOL system has had several implementations: HOL88, HOL90, HOL98, ProofPower (a commercial version) and HOL Light. The HOL Light system [10] which is the HOL re-implementation by John Harrison, is the version of the system that we have used for this paper (but all versions are similar). It has been written in CAML Light and consists of slightly under two megabytes of ML source, which implement a mathematical framework containing a formalization of the real numbers, analysis and transcendental functions and several decision procedures for both logical and arithmetical problems. It has been both used for computer science applications and for formalizing pure mathematics (like the fundamental theorem of algebra).

The drinker's principle can be proved in HOL in the following way:

```
let DRINKER = prove
  ('?x:A. P x ==> !y. P y',
   ASM_CASES_TAC '?x:A. ~P x' THEN
   RULE_ASSUM_TAC (REWRITE_RULE[NOT_EXISTS_THM]) THENL
   [POP_ASSUM CHOOSE_TAC; ALL_TAC] THEN
   EXISTS_TAC 'x:A' THEN
   ASM_REWRITE_TAC[]);;
```

There are various ways to prove this statement, but this tactic sequence is a fairly normal way to prove something like this in HOL.

5   Mizar

The Mizar system [12,17] by Andrzej Trybulec and his group in Bialystok, Poland, is a declarative prover that goes back to the seventies. It implements classical first order logic with ZFC-style set theory. The current version, called PC Mizar, dates from 1989. It consists of a suite of Pascal programs which are distributed compiled for Intel processors (both Windows and Linux). These programs are accompanied by a huge library of all kinds of mathematics, in the form of a series of 686 so-called 'articles' which together are about 1.3 million lines of Mizar.

In Mizar a proof of the drinker's principle looks like:

```
ex x st P x implies for y holds P y
proof
  per cases;
  suppose A0: ex x st not P x;
    consider a such that A1: not P a by A0;
    take a;
    assume A2: P a;
    A3: contradiction by A1,A2;
    thus A4: for y holds P y by A3;
  suppose A5: for x holds P x;
    consider a such that A6: not contradiction;
    take a;
    thus A7: P a implies for y holds P y by A5;
  end;
```

Note that this is readable and similar to the informal proof in Section 3.

The Mizar system has many interesting ideas. For instance it has a complicated type system with polymorphic types, overloading, subtyping and type

modifiers called 'adjectives', together with powerful type inference rules. Also it
has a mathematical looking operator syntax with not only prefix and infix operators but also 'aroundfix' operators, which behave like brackets. However in this
paper we will restrict ourselves to the proof language of Mizar. That means that
from now on we will only have HOL types and HOL term syntax and we will
not mix those with Mizar types and Mizar term syntax. The same restriction
to just the proof fragment of Mizar was chosen for the Mizar mode for HOL by
John Harrison.

The reasoning part of Mizar turns out to be simple. In its basic form it is
given by the following context free grammar:

proposition = [*label* :] *formula*

statement = *proposition justification*

justification =
   empty
| **by** *label* { , *label* }
| **proof** { *step* } [*cases*] **end**

step =
   statement ;
| **assume** *proposition* ;
| **consider** *variable* { , *variable* }
         such that *proposition* { **and** *proposition* } *justification* ;
| **let** *variable* { , *variable* } ;
| **take** *term* { , *term* } ;
| **thus** *statement* ;

cases = **per cases** *justification* ; { **suppose** *proposition* ; { *step* } }

empty =

The main Mizar proof feature that is missing from this language fragment is the
use of '.=' for equational reasoning.

Note that this grammar has only seven kinds of proof elements: a statement
without keyword, **assume**, **consider**, **let**, **per cases**, **take** and **thus**. (Compare
this with the hundreds of different tactics, tacticals, conversions and conversion-
als that appear all over the HOL proofs.)

6   Mizar as HOL Tactics

We will compare the way the Mizar and HOL systems implement natural deduction. That will lead to a natural ML type (in the framework of HOL) for each
of the Mizar steps. The table that lists these types is the essence of our Mizar
implementation on top of HOL. (The appendix will show how to implement the
Mizar steps according to these types.)

There are two kinds of Mizar steps:

- *skeleton* steps: the natural deduction way of reasoning
- *forward* steps: statements that get added to the context after having been justified with the 'by' justification

The natural deduction rules correspond to Mizar steps according to following table (rules for which a '–' appears in this table are implemented as forward steps and don't have a Mizar step of their own):

natural deduction	*Mizar*
$\rightarrow$ introduction	assume
$\rightarrow$ elimination	–
$\wedge$ introduction	thus
$\wedge$ elimination	–
$\vee$ introduction	–
$\vee$ elimination	per cases
$\forall$ introduction	let
$\forall$ elimination	–
$\exists$ introduction	take
$\exists$ elimination	consider

The HOL language has natural deduction as well. The main difference is that the Mizar steps make the propositions explicit that the HOL steps leave implicit.

Compare the two ways to do $\rightarrow$ introduction. Suppose we want to reduce the goal:

$$A, B \vdash (C \rightarrow D) \rightarrow E$$

to:

$$A, B, (C \rightarrow D) \vdash E$$

(this is the *introduction* rule because a goal oriented prover reasons backwards). The Mizar step doing this is:

assume A2: C implies D;

(here 'A2' is the label of the assumption). The same is accomplished in HOL by:

DISCH_TAC

or if we write out the proof state transformation explicitly:

```
it : goalstack = 1 subgoal (1 total)

 0 ['A']
 1 ['B']

'(C ==> D) ==> E'

#e DISCH_TAC;;
it : goalstack = 1 subgoal (1 total)
```

```
0 ['A']
1 ['B']
2 ['C ==> D']

'E'
```

The Mizar statement gives the 'redundant' information what the discharged statement is and where it ends up in the context. We can imitate this in HOL by defining a tactic ASSUME_A such that the HOL tactic becomes:

$$\texttt{ASSUME\_A(2,'C ==> D')}$$

or explicitly:

```
it : goalstack = 1 subgoal (1 total)

 0 ['A']
 1 ['B']

'(C ==> D) ==> E'

#e (ASSUME_A(2,'C ==> D'));;
it : goalstack = 1 subgoal (1 total)

 0 ['A']
 1 ['B']
 2 ['C ==> D']

'E'
```

All that the ASSUME_A tactic does is check that the number and statement fit and then apply DISCH_TAC.

The ASSUME_A tactic has the type:

$$\texttt{int} \times \texttt{term} \to \texttt{tactic}$$

If we continue along this line of thought, it turns out that every Mizar construction has a 'natural' HOL type. The table that gives these types is the essence of our Mizar mode for HOL:

A	int × term → tactic → tactic
ASSUME_A	int × term → tactic
BY	int list → thm list → tactic
CONSIDER	term list → (int × term) list → tactic → tactic
LET	term list → tactic
PER_CASES	tactic → ((int × term) × tactic) list → tactic
TAKE	term list → tactic
THUS_A	int × term → tactic → tactic

Note that this table corresponds to the Mizar proof grammar from Section 5. Implementing these eight tactics is trivial, as shown in the appendix. The first of these tactics, the A tactic, corresponds to a Mizar step without a keyword: a forward reasoning step. The BY tactic is used to justify steps. It takes two lists of arguments. The first list is a list of integers referring to the assumption list of the current goal, the second list is a list of thms.

Now we can write down the proof of the drinker's principle as a normal HOL proof (so with prove and a chain of tactics put together with THEN), this time using the 'Mizar tactics':

```
let DRINKER = prove
  ('?x:A. P x ==> !y. P y',
   PER_CASES (BY [] [])
   [(0,'?x:A. ~P x'),
    (CONSIDER ['a:A'] [(1,'~(P:A->bool) a')] (BY [0] []) THEN
     TAKE ['a:A'] THEN
     ASSUME_A(2,'(P:A->bool) a') THEN
     A(3,'F') (BY [1;2] []) THEN
     THUS_A(4,'!y:A. P y') (BY [3] []))
   ;(0,'!x:A. P x'),
    (CONSIDER ['a:A'] [] (BY [] []) THEN
     TAKE ['a:A'] THEN
     THUS_A(1,'P a ==> !y:A. P y') (BY [0] []))]);;
```

Note that this is similar to the Mizar version of this proof from Section 5. The main difference is that type annotations are needed ('(P:A->bool) a' instead of 'P a'). This problem of having to put type annotations in terms is standard in HOL. A possible approach to this problem will be presented in Section 7.5.

7   Enhancements

The Mizar tactics that we presented in the previous section are very basic. They can be enhanced in various ways. Because we lack the space we don't give all the details. Curious readers are referred to the HOL Light source file miz.ml at the URL http://www.cs.kun.nl/~freek/mizar/miz.ml.

7.1   The BECAUSE Tactic

The common way to justify a Mizar step in our Mizar mode is with a justification that looks like:

$$(\text{BY } [local\ statement\ list] \, [global\ statement\ list])$$

This has the prover 'hardwired in' (in the implementation from the appendix, this prover first tries REWRITE_TAC and if that fails tries MESON_TAC). However the BY tactic is built on top of a tactic called 'BECAUSE' which has the type:

$$(\text{thm list} \to \text{tactic}) \to \text{int list} \to \text{thm list} \to \text{tactic}$$

This means that one can use it with any tactic that has the type `thm list` → `tactic` like `REWRITE_TAC`, `SIMP_TAC`, `MESON_TAC` and so on. (One also could use it with tactics like `ASM_REWRITE_TAC` but that would be silly, because the assumptions already are accessible through the 'local statements' argument.) For instance one could justify a step by:

(BECAUSE ONCE_SIMP_TAC [*local statement list*] [*global statement list*])

This would prove the statement being justified using the `ONCE_SIMP_TAC` tactic with the relevant `thm`s.

The `BECAUSE` tactic gives control over the exact behavior of the prover if that is needed, making a refined version of `BY` unnecessary.

7.2   A More Powerful ASSUME_A Tactic

The `ASSUME_A` tactic is the declarative version of the procedural `DISCH_TAC` tactic. The implementation from the appendix mirrors `DISCH_TAC` exactly. However since the `ASSUME_A` tactic contains the statement that is discharged, it can be more general. It becomes more powerful if we implement it as:

```
let ASSUME_A (n,tm) =
  DISJ_CASES_THEN2
    (fun th -> REWRITE_TAC[th] THEN N_ASSUME_TAC n th)
    (fun th -> REWRITE_TAC[REWRITE_RULE[] th] THEN
      MIZ_ERROR_TAC "ASSUME_A" [n])
    (SPEC tm EXCLUDED_MIDDLE);;
```

For instance in that case one can use it to reason by contradiction:

```
it : goalstack = 1 subgoal (1 total)

'A'

#e (ASSUME_A(0,'~A'));;
it : goalstack = 1 subgoal (1 total)

 0 ['~A']

'F'
```

This is also how the `assume` step of the real Mizar system behaves.

7.3   An Interactive Version of the PER_CASES Tactic

The `PER_CASES` tactic has the type:

PER_CASES : tactic → ((int × term) × tactic) list → tactic

In order to debug a proof interactively a version that has type:

PER_CASES : tactic → (int × term) list → tactic

and that leaves the cases as subgoals is more practical. Using this variant makes the proof look less like Mizar because the list of the statements of the cases has been separated from the list of proofs of the cases.

A hybrid is also possible that has the type of the original PER_CASES but doesn't require all the cases to be completely proved after the tactic finishes.

7.4 Tactics versus Proofs

Some of the `tactic` arguments of the Mizar tactics not only have to *reduce* the proof obligations but they have to prove the goal altogether. So those arguments are more 'proofs' than 'tactics'. One might try to reflect this in the typing of the Mizar tactics by at certain places changing `tactic` (which is defined as `goal` → `goalstate`) to `goal` → `thm`. The second type is in a way a special case ('subtype') of the first. Then functions:

$$\text{PROOF : tactic} \to \text{goal} \to \text{thm}$$
$$\text{PER : (goal} \to \text{thm)} \to \text{tactic}$$

map these two types to each other and:

$$\text{prove' : term} \times \text{(goal} \to \text{thm)} \to \text{thm}$$

runs a proof. Using this approach, the Mizar mode tactics will get the following type assignments:

A	int × term → (goal → thm) → tactic
ASSUME_A	int × term → tactic
BY	int list → thm list → goal → thm
CASES	(goal → thm) → ((int × term) × (goal → thm)) list → goal → thm
CONSIDER	term list → (int × term) list → (goal → thm) → tactic
LET	term list → tactic
TAKE	term list → tactic
THUS_A	int × term → (goal → thm) → tactic

(Note that we have separated the PER_CASES tactic into a combination of PER and CASES.) The example proof becomes, using these tactics:

```
let DRINKER = prove'
  ('?x:A. P x ==> !y. P y',
   PROOF
   (PER (CASES (BY [] [])
     [(0,'?x:A. ~P x'),
      PROOF
      (CONSIDER ['a:A'] [(1,'~(P:A->bool) a')] (BY [0] []) THEN
       TAKE ['a:A'] THEN
       ASSUME_A(2,'(P:A->bool) a') THEN
       A(3,'F') (BY [1;2] []) THEN
```

```
    THUS_A(4,'!y:A. P y') (BY [3][]))
;(0,'!x:A. P x'),
 PROOF
 (CONSIDER ['a:A'] [] (BY [][]) THEN
  TAKE ['a:A'] THEN
  THUS_A(1,'P a ==> !y:A. P y') (BY [0][]))])));;
```

7.5 Terms in Context

The HOL system parses a `term` in an empty context because the HOL implementation is functional. So if we write an expression of type `term` it doesn't
have access to the goal state. This means that '`n`' will always be read as a
polymorphic variable, whatever is in the current goal. If a goal talks about a
natural number '`n`' of type '`:num`', then to instantiate an existential quantifier
with this '`n`' one has to write `EXISTS_TAC` '`n:num`' instead of `EXISTS_TAC` '`n`'.
Generally this doesn't get too bad but it is irritating.

In our Mizar mode this problem is worse because there are more statements
in the tactics. So we might try to modify things for this. The idea is to change
the type `term` to `goal → term` everywhere. This means that the 'term parsing
function' `X` will have to get the type `string → goal → term`. Again a variant
function `prove''` of type `(goal → term) × tactic → thm` is needed.

If we follow this approach then most type annotations will be gone, except
in the statement of the theorem to be proved and in the arguments of `LET` and
`CONSIDER` (where they also are required in the 'real' Mizar).

Because in that case the terms are parsed in the context of a goal, we can give
a special meaning to the variables '`antecedent`' and '`thesis`'. See Section 8
for an example of this.

The main disadvantage of this modification to our Mizar mode is that the
original HOL proof scripts will not work anymore because the `X` function has
been changed. That is a big disadvantage if one wants true integration between
the 'pure' HOL and the Mizar mode.

7.6 Out of Sequence Labels and Negative Labels

Another thing that can be changed is to be less restrictive which numbers are
allowed for the labels. Until now they had to be the exact position that the
statement would end up in the assumption list of the goal. However there is no
reason not to allow any number and put the statement at that position, padding
the assumption list with '`T`' thms if necessary. That way we can make the labels
in the example match the labels in the original Mizar version. If we do this in
the example proof, then the second `CONSIDER` will see a goal like:

```
it : goalstack = 1 subgoal (1 total)

 0 ['T']
 1 ['T']
```

```
2 ['T']
3 ['T']
4 ['T']
5 ['!x. P x']

'?x. P x ==> (!y. P y)'
```

Related to this is an enhancement that implements Mizar's **then**. In Mizar a step can refer to the step directly before it with the **then** prefix. A way to imitate this in our Mizar mode is to allow negative numbers in the labels, counting back from the top of the assumption stack. The label -1 will then refer to the top of the stack (which contains the statement from the previous step). Therefore use of -1 will behave like **then**.

7.7 Symbolic Labels

Instead of numeric labels we also can have symbolic labels. HOL Light supports symbolic labels already. It is straight-forward to change the set of Mizar tactics to work with these symbolic labels instead of with the numeric positions in the list of assumptions.

In the rest of this paper we have presented our Mizar mode with numeric labels. We had two reasons for this:

- In HOL the symbolic labels are almost never used, so proof states that contain them are un-HOL-like.
- In Mizar the 'symbolic' labels generally just are A1, A2, A3, ... That means that the Mizar labels really are used as numbers, most of the time. Therefore we didn't consider numeric labels un-Mizar-like.

7.8 Error Recovery

A declarative proof contains explicit statements for all reasoning steps. Because of this a declarative system like Mizar can recover from errors and continue checking proofs after the first error.[3] This behavior can be added to our Mizar mode for HOL by catching the exception if there is an error, and then continue with the appropriate statement added to the context as an axiom. This was implemented by using a justification function that just throws an exception.

Having this enhancement of course only gives error recovery for 'reasoning errors' and will not help with other errors like syntax errors or ML type errors.

One of the referees of this paper liked the idea of error recovery for the Mizar tactics, and suggested a stack on which the goalstates of the erroneous steps could be stored for later proof debugging. We implemented this idea, but we think that the standard HOL practice of running a proof one tactic at a time is more convenient (for which the 'Mizar tactics with error recovery' are unusable).

---

[3] The Mizar mode by John Harrison does not have this feature. Isar satisfies the principle that sub-proofs can be checked independently, but the present implementation simply stops at the first error it encounters.

8 Bigger Example

In this section we show a larger example of our Mizar mode (it uses the variant
from Section 7.5, so terms are parsed in the context of the proof):

```
let FIXPOINT = prove''
 ('!f. (!x:A y. x <= y /\ y <= x ==> (x = y)) /\
       (!x y z. x <= y /\ y <= z ==> x <= z) /\
       (!x y. x <= y ==> f x <= f y) /\
       (!X. ?s. (!x. x IN X ==> s <= x) /\
                (!s'. (!x. x IN X ==> s' <= x) ==> s' <= s))
       ==> ?x. f x = x',
  LET ['f:A->A'] THEN
  ASSUME_A(0,'antecedent') THEN
  A(1,'!x y. x <= y /\ y <= x ==> (x = y)') (BY [0][]) THEN
  A(2,'!x y z. x <= y /\ y <= z ==> x <= z') (BY [0][]) THEN
  A(3,'!x y. x <= y ==> f x <= f y')(BY [0][]) THEN
  A(4,'!X. ?s. (!x. x IN X ==> s <= x) /\
              (!s'. (!x. x IN X ==> s' <= x) ==> s' <= s)')
   (BY [0][]) THEN
  CONSIDER ['Y:A->bool'] [(5,'Y = {b | f b <= b}')] (BY [][]) THEN
  A(6,'!b. b IN Y = f b <= b') (BY [5][IN_ELIM_THM;BETA_THM]) THEN
  CONSIDER ['a:A'] [(7,'!x. x IN Y ==> a <= x');
   (8,'!a'. (!x. x IN Y ==> a' <= x) ==> a' <= a')] (BY [4][]) THEN
  TAKE ['a'] THEN
  A(9,'!b. b IN Y ==> f a <= b')
   (LET ['b:A'] THEN
    ASSUME_A(9,'b IN Y') THEN
    A(10,'f b <= b') (BY [6;9][]) THEN
    A(11,'a <= b') (BY [7;9][]) THEN
    A(12,'f a <= f b') (BY [3;11][]) THEN
    THUS_A(13,'f a <= b') (BY [2;10;12][])) THEN
  A(10,'f(a) <= a') (BY [8;9][]) THEN
  A(11,'f(f(a)) <= f(a)') (BY [3;10][]) THEN
  A(12,'f(a) IN Y') (BY [6;11][]) THEN
  A(13,'a <= f(a)') (BY [7;12][]) THEN
  THUS_A(14,'thesis') (BY [1;10;13][]));;
```

This is a translation to our framework of an example proof from John Harrison's
Mizar mode which proves the Knaster-Tarski fixpoint theorem.

9 Conclusion

The tactics that are presented here might be the basis of a realistic system that
offers the best of both the procedural and declarative provers. One hopes this
to be possible: to build a prover that has the readable proofs of the declarative
provers and the programmability of the procedural ones. The Mizar mode for
HOL by John Harrison and the Isar mode for Isabelle might claim to be just

that, but in those systems it feels like one has to learn *two* provers if one wants to be able to use both styles of proving.

The Mizar mode of this paper makes clear that that both kinds of prover are very similar. Although the proofs using our Mizar tactics look awkward and fragile compared with their Mizar counterparts, we have shown that it is possible to bridge the gap between the procedural and declarative proof styles in a more intimate way than had been accomplished thus far.

Acknowledgements

Thanks to Dan Synek, Jan Zwanenburg and the anonymous referees for valuable comments. Due to space limits we have not been able to incorporate all of them.

References

1. Henk Barendregt. The impact of the lambda calculus. *Bulletin of Symbolic Logic*, 3(2), 1997.
2. Bruno Barras, e.a. *The Coq Proof Assistant Reference Manual*, 2000. `ftp://ftp.inria.fr/INRIA/coq/V6.3.1/doc/Reference-Manual-all.ps.gz`.
3. Gertrud Bauer. Lesbare formale Beweise in Isabelle/Isar — der Satz von Hahn-Banach. Master's thesis, TU München, November 1999. `http://www.in.tum.de/~bauerg/HahnBanach-DA.pdf`.
4. Gertrud Bauer. The Hahn-Banach Theorem for real vector spaces. Part of the Isabelle99-2 distribution, `http://isabelle.in.tum.de/library/HOL/HOL-Real/library/HOL/HOL-Real/HahnBanach/document.pdf`, February 2001.
5. Gertrud Bauer and Markus Wenzel. Computer-assisted mathematics at work — the Hahn-Banach theorem in Isabelle/Isar. In Thierry Coquand, Peter Dybjer, Bengt Nordström, and Jan Smith, editors, *Types for Proofs and Programs: TYPES'99*, volume 1956 of *LNCS*, 2000.
6. Jan Cederquist, Thierry Coquand, and Sara Negri. The Hahn-Banach Theorem in Type Theory. In G. Sambin and J. Smith, editors, *Twenty-Five years of Constructive Type Theory*, Oxford, 1998. Oxford University Press.
7. M.J.C. Gordon and T.F. Melham, editors. *Introduction to HOL*. Cambridge University Press, Cambridge, 1993.
8. M.J.C. Gordon, R. Milner, and C.P. Wadsworth. *Edinburgh LCF: A Mechanised Logic of Computation*, volume 78 of *LNCS*. Springer Verlag, Berlin, Heidelberg, New York, 1979.
9. John Harrison. A Mizar Mode for HOL. In *Proceedings of the 9th International Conference on Theorem Proving in Higher Order Logics, TPHOLs '96*, volume 1125 of *LNCS*, pages 203–220. Springer, 1996.
10. John Harrison. *The HOL Light manual (1.1)*, 2000. `http://www.cl.cam.ac.uk/users/jrh/hol-light/manual-1.1.ps.gz`.
11. David A. McAllester. *Ontic: A Knowledge Representation System for Mathematics*. The MIT Press Series in Artificial Intelligence. MIT Press, 1989.
12. M. Muzalewski. *An Outline of PC Mizar*. Fondation Philippe le Hodey, Brussels, 1993. `http://www.cs.kun.nl/~freek/mizar/mizarmanual.ps.gz`.
13. R.P. Nederpelt, J.H. Geuvers, and R.C. de Vrijer. *Selected Papers on Automath*, volume 133 of *Studies in Logic and the Foundations of Mathematics*. Elsevier Science, Amsterdam, 1994.

14. L.C. Paulson. *The Isabelle Reference Manual*, 2000. http://www.cl.cam.ac.uk Research/HVG/Isabelle/dist/Isabelle99-1/doc/ref.pdf.
15. Don Syme. Three Tactic Theorem Proving. In *Theorem Proving in Higher Order Logics, TPHOLs '99*, volume 1690 of *LNCS*, pages 203–220. Springer, 1999.
16. M. Wenzel. *The Isabelle/Isar Reference Manual*. TU München, München, 1999. http://isabelle.in.tum.de/doc/isar-ref.pdf.
17. F. Wiedijk. Mizar: An impression. http://www.cs.kun.nl/~freek/mizar/mizarintro.ps.gz, 1999.
18. Vincent Zammit. On the Implementation of an Extensible Declarative Proof Language. In *Theorem Proving in Higher Order Logics, TPHOLs '99*, volume 1690 of *LNCS*, pages 185–202. Springer, 1999.

A   Implementation

Here is the full listing of the Mizar implementation as described in Section 6.

```
 1   let miz_error msg nl =
 2     failwith (rev_itlist (fun s t -> t^" "^s) (map string_of_int nl) msg);;

 3   let MIZ_ERROR_TAC msg nl = fun g -> miz_error msg nl;;

 4   let N_ASSUME_TAC n th (asl,_ as g) =
 5     if length asl = n then ASSUME_TAC th g else miz_error "N_ASSUME_TAC" [n];;

 6   let A (n,tm) tac =
 7     SUBGOAL_THEN tm (N_ASSUME_TAC n) THENL
 8     [tac THEN MIZ_ERROR_TAC "A" [n]; ALL_TAC];;

 9   let ASSUME_A (n,tm) =
10     DISCH_THEN (fun th -> if concl th = tm then N_ASSUME_TAC n th
11       else miz_error "ASSUME_A" [n]);;

12   let (BECAUSE:(thm list -> tactic) -> int list -> thm list -> tactic) =
13     fun tac nl thl (asl,_ as g) ->
14       try tac ((map (fun n -> snd (el (length asl - n - 1) asl)) nl) @ thl) g
15       with _ -> ALL_TAC g;;

16   let BY = BECAUSE (fun thl -> REWRITE_TAC thl THEN MESON_TAC thl);;

17   let CONSIDER =
18     let T = 'T' in
19     fun vl ntml tac ->
20       let ex = itlist (curry mk_exists) vl
21         (itlist (curry mk_conj) (map snd ntml) T) in
22       SUBGOAL_THEN ex
23         ((EVERY_TCL (map X_CHOOSE_THEN vl) THEN_TCL EVERY_TCL (map
24           (fun (n,_) tcl cj ->
25             let th,cj' = CONJ_PAIR cj in N_ASSUME_TAC n th THEN tcl cj')
26           ntml)) (K ALL_TAC)) THENL
27         [tac THEN MIZ_ERROR_TAC "CONSIDER" (map fst ntml); ALL_TAC];;

28   let LET = MAP_EVERY X_GEN_TAC;;

29   let PER_CASES =
30     let F = 'F' in
31     fun tac cases ->
32       let dj = itlist (curry mk_disj) (map (snd o fst) cases) F in
33       SUBGOAL_THEN dj
34         (EVERY_TCL (map (fun case -> let n,_ = fst case in
35           (DISJ_CASES_THEN2 (N_ASSUME_TAC n))) cases) CONTR_TAC) THENL
36         ([tac] @ map snd cases) THEN MIZ_ERROR_TAC "PER_CASES" [];;

37   let TAKE = MAP_EVERY EXISTS_TAC;;

38   let THUS_A (n,tm) tac =
39     SUBGOAL_THEN tm ASSUME_TAC THENL
40     [tac THEN MIZ_ERROR_TAC "THUS_A" [n]
41     ;POP_ASSUM (fun th -> N_ASSUME_TAC n th THEN REWRITE_TAC[EQT_INTRO th])];;
```

Author Index

Lecture Notes in Computer Science

For information about Vols. 1–2048
please contact your bookseller or Springer-Verlag